Truth and Interpretation

Truth and Interpretation

PERSPECTIVES ON THE PHILOSOPHY OF DONALD DAVIDSON

Edited by
Ernest LePore

Basil Blackwell

© Basil Blackwell Ltd., 1986
Chapter 11, D. Reidel Publishing Co.
Chapters 16, 17, 24, Donald Davidson

First published 1986
First published in paperback 1989

Basil Blackwell Ltd
108 Cowley Road, Oxford OX4 1JF, UK

Basil Blackwell Inc.
432 Park Avenue South, Suite 1503
New York, NY 10016, USA

British Library Cataloguing in Publication Data

Truth and interpretation: perspectives on the philosophy of Donald
    Davidson.
    1. Davidson, Donald, 1917- —Linguistics
    2. Languages—Philosophy
    I. LePore, Ernest
    409′.2′4   P85.D3

ISBN 0−631−14811−6
ISBN 0−631−16948−2 Pbk

Library of Congress Cataloging in Publication Data

Truth and interpretation.
    Includes index.
    1. Davidson, Donald, 1917-00—Addresses, essays, lectures.
I. LePore, Ernest, 1950-
B945.D384T78   1986   191   85-18720

ISBN 0−631−14811−6
ISBN 0−631−16948−2 (pbk.)

Typeset by Photo Graphics, Honiton, Devon.
Printed in Great Britain by T. J. Press Ltd, Padstow

To my dear friends: Steve Herman, who first taught me philosophy, and Loretta Mazlen Mandel, whose calm efficiency and constant encouragement were invaluable during the preparation of this volume.

Contents

Part IV   Radical Interpretations

Part V   Language and Reality

Part VI   Limits of the Literal

Preface

How often one has sent a typescript or an offprint to a friend or potential critic with the hopeful words 'I will be most grateful for any comments.' And how meager, to the point of invisibility, the response in general is, at least at the time. This should not surprise us. Our friends and critics cannot be expected to interrupt their own work to attend to our latest productions; and serious responses are usually slow in forming.

In any case I can no longer complain at the lack of comments. Thanks to Ernie LePore, I was treated to an avalanche of friendly criticism, suggestion and comment at the conference responsible for this volume (and for its companion volume on actions and events).

One is grateful for such an avalanche; but it also can be overwhelming. Here was a vast international educational effort with the apparent aim of relieving me of error and confusion. I confess that for the moment I thought I finally understood the concept of the *tabula rasa* – a mind from which everything has been erased. Even so conceived, the generosity and scope of the enterprise deserved my endless thanks; but of course clearing *my* mind was not its sole purpose or most important outcome. What mattered was the ideas and problems themselves, and everyone involved in the conference gained from the scrutiny to which they were subjected.

The material in these two books has been invaluable to me: it has shown up weaknesses and errors in my work of which I was barely, if at all, aware; it has in many cases indicated better solutions than mine to problems I had tried to solve; and it has provided me with an overview of my thinking which I could not have achieved in any other way. Above all, it has given me a sense of having a place in a proud and admirable intellectual tradition, a tradition whose ideals are clarity and an openness to criticism. No doubt I have often failed to embody these ideals; but the present volume is evidence of their lasting strength and value.

Donald Davidson

Preface

About four years ago, I set out to organize a conference on the philosophy of Donald Davidson. My plans were for a small group of philosophers who had written on Davidson's philosophy to gather for a day to discuss his work. Within a few months, the project mushroomed, exceeding anything I had intended or anticipated. By April 28, 1984, when the conference convened, some 500 academics from a wide range of disciplines gathered at Rutgers University (New Brunswick, New Jersey), representing 26 countries, participating in some 70 sessions, squeezed into four short days. With this present volume, the second published by Basil Blackwell,[1] I have completed everything I set out to do when I first thought a conference on Davidson's philosophy was a reasonable project to undertake. I'm glad I did it.

Almost every essay in this volume was presented at the Davidson Conference, and it is intended to be a companion to Davidson's *Inquiries into Truth and Interpretation*. The volume divides into five sections, corresponding to the sections of *Inquiries into Truth and Interpretation*: Truth and Meaning, Applications, Radical Interpretation, Language and Reality, and Limits of the Literal. Before making some introductory comments about Davidson's and the contributors' views on these topics, I would like to thank the many people and institutions who supported the Conference, and thus, contributed to this volume. The following members of Rutgers University deserve special thanks: Brian P. McLaughlin, of the Philosophy Department, Peter Klein, Chairperson of the Philosophy Department, Phyllis Cohen, Director of the Voorhees Assembly Board, Renee' Weber, Director of the Council for Integrated and Cross-Disciplinary Studies; Mary Hartman, Dean of Douglass College; John Yolton, Dean of Rutgers College, David Mechanic, Dean of the Faculty of Arts and Sciences; Kenneth Wolfson, Dean of the Graduate School; Kenneth Wheeler, Provost. I am most grateful to Elizabeth Woodward and David Cayer of Research and Sponsored Programs, and to the President of Rutgers University, Edward Bloustein.

Individuals in the philosophical community from outside Rutgers University who deserve special thanks are: Francesca Bertelli, Gilbert Harman, Barry Loewer, and David Rosenthal. Of course, an enormous debt is owed to Donald Davidson for his help throughout.

I wish also to thank Carol Busia, the desk editor, and Kim Pickin, the philosophy editor, of Basil Blackwell. They have been extremely patient and helpful in putting this volume together.

---

[1] The first is *Actions and Events: Perspectives on the Philosophy of Donald Davidson*, 1985, edited by myself and Brian P. McLaughlin.

This project was generously supported by the National Endowment for the Humanities; the National Science Foundation; the Exxon Educational Foundation; the New Jersey Committee for the Humanities; Rutgers University Research and Sponsored Programs; the Dean's offices of Douglass and Rutgers Colleges, Rutgers' Faculty of Arts and Sciences, the Graduate School of Rutgers University, Rutgers University Cost Sharing Fund and the Douglass College Fellows.

Ernest LePore
Rutgers University

Part I
Introduction

1

Truth in Meaning

ERNEST LEPORE

The corpus of Donald Davidson's work is broad and resists terse summarization. I do not intend to offer an exhaustive overview here. Nothing substitutes for a careful reading of his papers on truth, meaning, interpretation, and their connections. In summarizing important aspects of his views, I hope only to give the reader a frame of reference for the essays that follow. My purpose in discussing these disparate contributions is to show how they link to major motifs in Davidson's work that are, in turn, elements of a coherent philosophic vision of significant breadth and scope.[1] Although I will, where appropriate, discuss briefly the ideas expressed in the following essays, I intend to offer neither synopses nor evaluations of these contributions.

The semantic project

In the early 1960s, the philosophy of language was radically altered when Davidson redefined both what form a semantic theory for a natural language

---

[1] Much of what I say here is drawn from published and unpublished manuscripts of mine (and Barry Loewer). Cf. Ernest LePore, 'In Defense of Davidson,' *Linguistics and Philosophy*, 5, 1984:277–294; 'Truth and Inference,' *Erkenntnis*, 18, 1982:379–395; 'What Model Theoretic Semantics Cannot Do,' *Synthese*, 54, 1983:167–187; 'The Concept of Meaning and its Role in Understanding Language,' *Dialectica*, 37, 1983:133–139; 'Interpretation, Belief and Behavior,' *Philosphia*, 1983:323–336; 'Animal Thought and Action,' unpublished manuscript; Ernest LePore and Barry Loewer, 'Translational Semantics,' *Synthese*, 48, 1981:121–133; 'Three Trivial Truth Theories,' *Canadian Journal of Philosophy*, 13, 1983:433–447; 'Solipsistic Semantics,' *Midwest Studies in Philosophy*, 1985:587–606, 'Dual Aspect Semantics,' unpublished manuscript; 'Absolute Truth Theories for Modal Languages as Theories of Interpretation,' unpublished manuscript. For help with the present introduction, I thank Francesca Bertelli, Akeel Bilgrami, Marcia Cavell, Richard Foley, Jody Heaps, Gail Herman, Steve Herman, Peter Klein, Carol Rovane, and John Tienson. My debt to John Wallace and Michael Root is different. They first awakened my interest in semantics. Donald Davidson sustained this interest first through his writings, and later, through numerous wonderful discussions. Indeed, he opened paths for discussion that would have been difficult, if not impossible, to travel without him. Barry Loewer deserves special thanks. Much of this introduction is borrowed from our co-authored manuscripts. All bracketed abbreviations and pagination are to Davidson's papers in *Inquiries into Truth and Interpretation*.

can take, and what conditions of adequacy, both empirical and formal, such theories should meet. Along with Quine, he discouraged philosophers from analyzing such individual concepts as meaning. Instead, he framed questions about semantics in the context of understanding language.

What distinguishes someone who understands a language from someone who does not? The former person possesses a set of very complicated capacities to both articulate and recognize sounds, words, sentences and other linguistic forms, from his language in various ways. Which capacities? Not just *any* employment or recognition of sounds, words, and sentences, constitutes understanding. Learning to recite English sentences is not understanding English. What if someone learned to recognize and produce questions, answers, commands, requests, ironies, metaphors, complaints, excuses, promises, paraphrases, inferences, and a large range of other sophisticated speech acts? Does the sum of understanding amount to any more than possessing capacities to perform these sorts of acts? Yes! These acts are linguistic – mere sounds, words, and sentences. Someone might acquire the capacity to recognize, produce, and respond, to questions in English, for example, without understanding it. He may have acquired this capacity by acquiring simpler capacities for recognizing key expressions, structures, intonation patterns, and so on, indicative of question (and answer) formation. Understanding is not a game we play with words and sentences alone. Still, something is right about characterizing understanding in virtue of what speakers can *do* that non-speakers cannot do. Although linguistic behavior is *a* mark, it is not *the* mark. Understanding a language sensitizes us in special ways to specific sounds and shapes in our non-linguistic environment. The problem is to explain what this involves.

Suppose Arabella understands English, and Barbarella does not, and in the presence of both, Cinderella utters, 'If you raise your hand, I will give you anything you want'. Both Arabella and Barbarella trust Cinderella and have no reason to believe she is insincere. Arabella's understanding and Barbarella's non-understanding manifest themselves in Arabella's raising her hand, and Barbarella's remaining still. Or, suppose Cinderella utters in their presence, 'Only when it's midnight can you leave,' and also, 'It will be midnight ten minutes hence.' Arabella manifests her understanding and Barbarella her non-understanding when Arabella retires ten minutes hence and Barbarella, again, remains still.

This approach to characterizing understanding is behavioristic in spirit inasmuch as each illustration refers to a particular act a speaker is more likely to perform upon hearing certain sounds from her language than a non-speaker. That it only refers to such acts guarantees its inadequacy. Someone might respond to our words appropriately without understanding our language. Someone might raise her hand upon hearing 'Raise your hand' and yet not understand English. Sheer quantity of appropriate linguistic/non-linguistic responses may cause us to wonder whether such deception is possible in principle. But it is not quantity which should instill doubt; what is doubtful is that someone could respond appropriately to various linguistic behavior including that of countless novel sorts, without having the appropriate kinds of beliefs and other mental attitudes about the world and minds of others? This mentalistic feature and not any linguistic or non-linguistic behavioral fact is for Davidson the mark of understanding.[2]

Empirical adequacy conditions

Cinderella runs. Some belief and attitude brought about her action. She runs because she believes that she must be somewhere by midnight, and she is deathly afraid that she won't be there by midnight unless she runs. To the extent we think that this belief, together with her fear, can issue in her act, we think her running reasonable. Her belief and fear provide a reason (and an explanation) for her action.[3] But suppose Cinderella runs because she believes Arabella yelled to her 'It's midnight!' Cinderella's act might still be reasonable, especially if Cinderella understood Arabella's words (and also thought her sincere and reliable). If these conditions obtain, in normal circumstances, Cinderella would be warranted in believing it is midnight. But why? Cinderella's understanding English would not warrant her belief that it is midnight regardless of which English sentence Arabella might utter. What is it about this piece of behavior, Arabella's utterance, which warrants Cinderella's belief in this instance?[4]

This point is sharpened once we recognize that Arabella's uttering to Cinderella, 'Your carriage has just turned into a pumpkin,' 'Your clothes are rags,' or any of indefinitely many other English sentences justifies various other appropriate beliefs on Cinderella's part. Distinguishing speakers from non-speakers in virtue of linguistic and non-linguistic behavioral capacities alone obscures these justifications. And it is hard to determine the roots of such justification if not from knowledge, belief, or other propositional attitudes about language itself. What about understanding language justifies, for example, the belief that it is midnight, when this understanding combines with other attitudes, for example, the belief that Arabella uttered 'It's midnight'? It is hard to see how else we could justify such a belief without ascribing additional beliefs, knowledge, or other propositional attitudes the speaker might have but the non-speaker lack.

---

[2] 'I despair of behaviorism, and accept frankly intensional attitudes ... '

[3] Cf. Davidson's 'Actions, Reasons, and Causes,' in his *Essays on Actions and Events*, Oxford, 1980:3–21, for further discussion of rationalizing explanations. Cf. also Ernest LePore and Brian P. McLaughlin, 'Actions, Reasons, Causes, and Intentions,' in *Actions and Events: Perspectives on the Philosophy of Donald Davidson*, Basil Blackwell, 1985:3–13.

[4] This question is put somewhat misleadingly. There may be no intrinsic feature of this linguistic behavior in virtue of which it has the (semantic) import it does. Derrida, Dummett, Quine, and Davidson argue, though not obviously in the same sense, for the view that semantic properties must somehow be understood in terms of a relation to utterances. What words mean is derived from how people use them. In his contribution, Samuel Wheeler, elucidating Derrida's position, puts the point this way: 'Linguistic signs are arbitrary, so they have no intrinsic properties to tie them to any particular referent or use. Linguistic signs, being arbitrary, require interpretation to supply their meaning. Since they are not self-interpreting' [480]. Davidson concurs. Cf. also the exchange among Davidson, Dummett, and Hacking, in their contributions, for further discussion about the relationship between use and understanding and the role of interpretation in understanding.

Meaning and truth

The 'argument' from the preceding section moved fast and requires much more careful development. But I am attempting only to highlight what I perceive to be Davidson's major train of thought. However, conventional wisdom about understanding bears out Davidson's view. Sentences have meanings and knowledge of these meanings warrants, in part, certain beliefs upon hearing these sentences uttered in various sorts of circumstances. This wisdom, inherited from Plato, Descartes, Locke,, Hume, Frege, Russell, Chomsky, and others who share fraternal dissatisfaction with behavioristic accounts of linguistic understanding, encourages us to elucidate Cinderella's justification by specifying the meanings for Arabella's words. One way to understand Davidson's project, first characterized in [TM:17–36], is to see him asking for specifications which would provide the needed connections.

Suppose we knew that:

(1) The words 'It's midnight' means that it is midnight.

Assuming Arabella to be sincere and reliable, we can infer and add to (1) knowledge that:

(2) 'It's midnight' is true.

Our challenge now is how to combine meaning in (1) with truth in (2). An intuitive principle which provides the needed connection is:

(3) If a sentence S is true, and if S means that p, then p.

Knowledge that (1)–(3) justifies the belief that it's midnight. It is not important whether the belief *is* acquired upon hearing the asserted utterance by a reliable speaker. What is acquired will vary according to the information the listener already possesses and also according to how the outside world impinges on him.

Nothing said thus far establishes that speakers in fact know meanings or that it is this knowledge they employ in understanding [RI:126]. Knowledge of meanings suffices in the present case to account for the justificatory element, but perhaps such knowledge is not *necessary*. Indeed in the above account, meanings seem to do little work. Knowing conditions under which Arabella's utterance is true licenses the move from heard utterance to the belief that it is midnight. So we could replace (1) and (3) with (1'):

(1') The words 'It's midnight' are true in English (when uttered to me) iff it is midnight at the time of utterance.

Without appeal to meanings, knowledge that (1')–(2) suffices to warrant the belief that it is midnight.

If X can be explained by appealing to concepts a, b, and c, but also by appealing only to b and c, then a is superfluous and not really part of the justification. Although we can account for understanding by appealing both to truth *and* meaning, we apparently do equally well with truth alone. Davidson concurs and settles for the answer that knowledge of the truth conditions of sentences for a language, assigned as in (1'), suffices for linguistic understanding.

This might seem surprising; in stating the original puzzle, we were led to the view that an adequate characterization of knowledge sufficient for understanding include meanings. The present line of investigation, though, suggests that meanings and therefore knowledge of the meanings of expressions is not obviously *needed* to justify these beliefs.[5] However, all we really have established so far is that it is not needed in one case. If Davidson's position is to be bolstered, meanings would have to be shown always superfluous. At least one contributor, Jerry Katz, argues that meanings are not always superfluous, since sometimes knowledge of truth conditions, as Davidson construes them, is insufficient to characterize linguistic understanding.

Intensionalism

Katz is an intensionalist. He holds that thought is fundamentally non-linguistic and that public, conventional language acquires its meaning from non-linguistic thought, including some cases in which sentence components – words and phrases – are associated with thought components – senses. Thus, Katz holds that thinking, believing, inferring, and so forth involve entertaining propositions, or as Frege said, apprehending thoughts.

Most intensionalists conclude that synonyms are interchangeable *salva veritate*. Synonyms are, for the intensionalist, words and phrases that express the same sense. If you replace one linguistic item by another that expresses the same sense, the result will express the same thought or proposition and hence will have the same truth value. But many philosophers have argued that synonyms are not interchangeable in all contexts *salva veritate*: they are not interchangeable in propositional attitude contexts. This has become known as 'Mates' Problem'.[6] Katz believes that Davidson was so convinced by Mates' Problem that it became the basis for his case for an extensionalist form of linguistic analysis. According to Katz, Davidson uses Mates' Problem to justify replacing the intensionalist 'means that' paradigm of linguistic analysis with the extensionalist 'S is true iff p' paradigm. To justify the replacement, Davidson says that he knows of no other way to 'account for even as much as the truth conditions of [belief sentences and others containing opaque contexts than] on the basis of what we know of the meanings in them' [TM:21]. The central point

---

[5] 'What I call a theory of meaning has after all turned out to make no use of meanings ... [but it] supplies all we have asked so far of a theory of meaning' [TM:24].

[6] Cf. B. Matese, 'Synonymity,' Leonard Linsky (ed), *Semantics and the Philosophy of Language*, University of Illinois Press, Urbana, 1952:111–138.

in Katz's paper is that inference from intensionalism to substitutivity is invalid.[7] He suggests a version of intensionalism on which substitutivity fails. By providing such an alternative, he concludes that he has preempted the need to give up intensionalism in favor of any brand of extensionalism, including Davidson's.

To further support the case against Davidson and what they regard as his dogmatic allegiance to extensionalism, Katz and others advance an argument to show that Davidson's theory entails various untoward consequences. If the sole adequacy condition for an account of understanding is that it contain a sentence of the same form as (1') for every sentence of English, then (4) would be indistinguishable from (5):

(4) 'Snow is white' is true iff snow is white.
(5) 'Snow is white' is true iff grass is green.

Since both biconditionals are true, and since they argue that Davidson only requires materially equivalent truth conditions, he has no ground to distinguish (4) from (5).[8]

Davidson might respond to this criticism by pointing out that an adequate account must issue in consequences such that the sentence used on the right hand side can be used correctly to interpret the sentence named on the left hand side of the biconditional i.e. additional constraints need to be imposed on a truth theory to qualify it as a theory of meaning. (5) violates this *empirical* condition because it cannot be employed in justifications of beliefs and behavior – a fundamental feature of Davidson's project. Another reply Davidson could make is that since he treats 'theories of truth as empirical, the axioms and theorems [must] be viewed as laws... taken not merely as true, but as capable of supporting counterfactual claims' [XIV]. (4) but not (5) can be so viewed. Cf. [RF: 171–9]. Here is not the place to adjudicate between the 'intensionalists' and the 'extensionalists.' My concern now is not with this formidable task. Rather, I hope to connect the view that it is knowledge of truth conditions which justifies our beliefs based on testimony with Tarski-like truth theories for natural languages.

---

[7] For a criticism of intensionalism, cf. Burge's contribution to the present volume. He holds that intensionalists have done little to connect meaning with understanding, particularly of non-sentential expressions, or to connect thought with conceptual abilities. He also is dissatisfied with the intensionalists' differential treatment of related notions like necessity, knowledge, and belief, on the one hand, and the notion of truth, on the other. All these notions have apparently similar grammatical features, but in intensional logics they are treated differently, truth as a predicate, the others as operators. Cf. G. Harman, 'Logical Form,' ibid. These differences do not seem, to either Burge or Harman, to have been given a satisfactory motivation.

[8] Cf. J. Katz, 'Logic and Language: an Examination of Recent Criticisms of Intensionalism,' Keith Gunderson, ed., *Language, Mind, and Knowledge*, Minnesota Press, 1975; H. Putnam, 'The Meaning of "Meaning",' ibid., B. Loar, 'Two Theories of Meaning,' J. McDowell and G. Evans, eds, *Truth and Meaning*, 1976:138–161; J. Foster, 'Meaning and Truth Theory,' ibid., 1–32; John Wallace, 'Logical Form, Meaning, and Translation,' M. Guenthener-Reutter, and F. Guenther, eds, *The Theory of Translation: Linguistic and Philosophical Approaches*, London, 1978. Also cf. Burge's contribution for a discussion about Davidson's ontological views about abstract entities.

Theory

Davidson proposes an account of an adequate interpretation for a language, and also, a measure for when this task has been accomplished: an adequate semantics for a language L should provide a statement T such that if a person knows that T, he would, partially, understand L [TM:25; DCT:71; BBM:141; RI:126; TT:157; SNL:62]. It is well known that Davidson's solution for T is a Tarski-like truth theory for L. Why, though, does Davidson think we must resort to theory at all?

As Chomsky and others argue, speakers of a natural language have the potential to understand indefinitely many sentences. This fecundity prevents a general description of Cinderella's linguistic competence comprised solely of a list of truth conditions for each sentence she potentially understands:

> 'Snow is white' is true iff snow is white.
> 'Grass is green' is true iff grass is green.
> 'Water is clear' is true iff water is clear.
> 'Snow is white and grass is green' is true iff snow is white and grass is green.
> 'Dark green snow is white' is true iff dark green snow is white.

We could never complete this list. Pressure to describe exhaustively a speaker's knowledge has suggested to some the following strategy: construct a theory which has as consequences infinitely many sentences using the words 'is true if and only if' as a link between a description of a sentence and a sentence. We can utilize this theory to provide a finite, yet discernible, description of knowledge sufficient for understanding.[9] We can describe a speaker's knowledge as consisting of what is expressed by a specifiable subset of the consequences of the theory, in particular, those consequences which provide a statement of the truth conditions for each sentence of the language [BBM:153]. Such a theory enables us to characterize an infinite competence by finite means. Davidson holds that 'empirically well founded' Tarski-like truth theories do this job. With this brief characterization of Davidson's program behind us, we turn to some details and some criticisms.

Compositionality

Davidson subscribes to the Fregean principle that the semantic properties of a complex expression is always a function of semantic properties of its component expressions.[10] This principle is not, however, presupposed by Tarski-type truth

---

[9] Cf. my 'In Defense of Davidson,' ibid., 280–283 for an elaboration of this point.

[10] Its meaning may also depend on context. Davidson's endorsement of this principle is evident in almost every essay in *Inquiries into Truth and Interpretation*. Cf., also, John Wallace's 'Only in the Context of a Sentence Do Words Have Any Meaning,' *Midwest Studies in Philosophy*, 2, 1977:144–164.

theories. Neither Tarski nor Davidson came armed with a picture of how language is fragmented and, therefore, how the solution for T is to go. Davidson has a picture of how to account for linguistic understanding. His own solution involves utilizing a theory which includes recursion clauses, but this is a convenience, not a requirement. If he could find a way of stating T which made no use of a recursion, he would not object. 'Convention T…makes no mention of extensionality, and truth functionality, or first-order languages. It invites us to use whatever devices we can contrive appropriately to bridge the gap between sentence mentioned and sentence used' [DCT:68]. 'The suggested conditions of adequacy for a theory of truth do not (obviously, anyway) entail that even the true sentences of the object language have the form some standard logical system' [SNL:58]. (Cf. also [RWR:217].) Nevertheless, Davidson agrees with Frege that it is difficult to imagine how to construct a non-compositional semantic theory for a natural language [TMLL:2–16; TM:17–36; SNL:55–64].[11]

The question whether a semantics for a natural language must be compositional has become entwined with questions about how a language can be learned. In [TMLL:1–15], Davidson argues that is a necessary feature of a learnable language that 'it must be possible to give a constructive account of the meaning of the sentences in the language,' [3]; that 'a learnable language has a finite number of semantical primitives' [9]. Several philosophers argue Davidson's learnability proposal is too strong.[12] I have responded to Davidson's critics.[13] Although Robert Matthews also replies to these critics he disputes my defense. He agrees with the critics that Davidson's learnability condition is too strong but argues that there is 'no reason to believe that recursive enumerability is a relevant feature of learnable languages, even if it does turn out to be relevant to the semantic productivity characteristic of natural languages [49].

Truth theories, logical form, and inference

Understanding a language involves not only a competence to interpret sentences, but also knowledge of the logical geography of this language: someone who understands a language L knows that certain inferential relationships obtain among the sentences of L. Davidson agrees, and he claims that:

---

[11] However, nothing is sacrosanct in semantics. Compositionality has undergone heavy attack recently. Cf. in particular Stephen Schiffer, *The Case Against Meaning*, forthcoming; J. Hintikka's 'A Counter-example to Tarski-type Truth Definitions as Applied to Natural Languages,' *Philosophia* 5, 1975:207–212; and his 'Theories of Truth and Learnable Languages,' S. Kanger and S. Ohman, eds, *Philosophy and Grammar*, Reidel Dordrecht, 1980:37–57. Cf. also Hacking's contribution for a discussion of whether recursion is required in semantics. Hacking interprets Davidson to require that semantics be recursive. N. Tennant, 'Truth, Meaning, and Decidability,' *Mind*, 1977, also thinks Davidson is committed to a recursive semantics.

[12] Charles Chihara, 'Davidson's Extensional Theory of Meaning,' *Philosophical Studies*, 28, 1985; R. Haack, 'Davidson on Learnable Languages,' *Mind*, 1978; I. Hacking, *What Does Language Matter to Philosophy?*, 1975; G. Harman, 'Meaning and Semantics,' M. Munitz and P. Unger, 1974; A. Reeves, 'On Truth and Meaning,' *Nous*, 8, 1974; S. Stich, 'Davidson's Semantic Program,' *Canadian Journal of Philosophy*, 1976.

[13] 'In Defense of Davidson,' ibid.

(A) Theories of absolute truth necessarily provide an analysis of structure relevant to truth and inference. Such theories yield a non-trivial answer to the question what is to count as the logical form of a sentence [DCT:71].

(B) There is no giving the truth conditions of all sentences without showing that some sentences are logical consequences of others [SNL:61].

These claims should seem surprising [cf. also BBM:141–154; RI:135–140, ST:93–108]. The sole aim in constructing a truth theory for a language L is that this theory has as a logical consequence, for each sentence of L, an instance of the schema:

Con T: X is true iff p,

where 'X' is replaced by a structural description of a sentence of L, and 'p' is replaced by a translation of that sentence in the language of the theory. Nothing is said about how a truth theory is to go except that we need a method for describing sentences on the left hand side of Con T and also we must have a method for constructing sentences used on the right hand side of Con T. How these are put together or what resources we need bring in to satisfy Con T is not specified. Why, then, does Davidson commit himself in (A) to the view that no matter how you may try to describe sentences of a natural language L, in constructing a finite truth theory for L, our description must 'show' logically relevant structure? Several authors have explored and evaluated routes Davidson might take in defending his claim (A).[14]

Higgonbotham deepens and continues this exploration. He aims to show how Davidson is on track in his effort to discover a combinatorial basis for semantics. His contribution is primarily concerned with the project of describing and understanding the semantic principles of English, and to that extent, with the logical forms of sentences and other expressions of English. He advocates a particular view toward English syntax and towards the structure of the clauses of a semantic theory that assigns semantic values to syntactic elements. Higgonbotham distinguishes three questions, questions Davidson himself has been careful not to conflate: What sorts of objects should be taken as the values of interpretable constructions? What is the proper syntax on the basis of which semantic values are assigned? And, given one's assumptions about values, and relevant syntactic combinations, how do values get assigned to these linguistic constructions? Davidson's answer to the first question is that the only values that both need to be posited and that useful work in combinatorial semantics are those included in what Quine has called 'a theory of reference': denotation, satisfaction, and truth. Higgonbotham argues for a particular syntactic theory, a phrase structure grammar, which he takes to diverge from

---

[14] Cf. Gareth Evans, 'Semantic Structure and Logical Form,' J. McDowell and G. Evans, eds., *Truth and Meaning*, Oxford, 1977:199–222; Gilbert Harman, 'Logical Form,' D. Davidson and G. Harman, eds, *The Logic of Grammar*, Dickenson, 1975:289–307, and his 'Meaning and Semantics,' M. Munitz and P. Unger, eds, *Semantics & Philosophy*, NYU Press, 1974:1–16; Ernest LePore, 'Truth and Inference,' *Erkenntnis* 18, 1982:379–395. Cf. also section (IV) of Burge's contribution for a discussion about Davidson and logical form.

Davidson's approach [SNL:55–64]. However, Higginbotham does not think this divergence poses a serious threat to Davidson's overall semantic program.[15]

Harman, at one time, thought that the clauses for logical constants in a Davidsonian truth theory told us more about their meanings than do the clauses for nonlogical predicates.[16] He no longer holds this view. In his contribution, he argues that logically equivalent connectives – a notion he defines in his paper – can have different meanings. But if connectives are logically equivalent, Harman holds that they make the *same* contributions to truth conditions and are subject to exactly the same rules of logical implication, even though they do not have the same meaning. If this is right, then Davidson cannot be correct in holding that a truth theory for a natural language will fix the logical form for the sentences of this language.

Suppose, though, that the structure assigned to sentences by an adequate truth theory is invariably logically revealing, for example, this structure is invariably identical to the structure assigned by standard predicate logic symbolizations. Why does Davidson commit himself in (B) to the view that this structure can be employed *within* the truth theory for L to determine which sentences L are logical consequences of others? This raises the question just how much logic is needed in a truth theory for L in order to satisfy Con T. Richard Grandy previously explored this question, and returns to it in his contribution.[17]

Higginbotham's, Grandy's, Harman's and Burge's contributions bring out how complicated the relationship is between a truth theory and theories of logical form and consequence. We should distinguish between the (logical) grammar and the logic of the metalanguage. We must isolate those resources of the metalanguage which describe the object language from those resources from which instances of Con T are provable within the truth theory.

Absolute truth theories for 'intensional' languages

Donald Davidson, Gilbert Harman, Jerry Katz, John Wallace, and others, have identified difficulties in constructing absolute truth theories for languages

---

[15] Some authors see Davidson dogmatically opting only for Tarski-like truth theories which have first-order quantification as their logics. This imposition would constrain semanticists to specify truth conditions entirely within a first-order language. As the quote from [DCT:65–76] in the last section bears out, this is a misreading of Davidson. For further support, see [XV] and his *Essays on Actions and Events*, ibid., 1980:137–146. Higginbotham in his contribution, considers arguments that English is a higher order language. Cf. Lauri Carlson, 'Plural Quantification,' ms., MIT, 1980; George Boolos, 'To be is to be a Variable (or Some Values of Some Variables),' ms., MIT, 1983; Edwin Williams, 'Semantic vs Syntactic Categories,' *Linguistics and Philosophy*, 6, 1983:423–446; Gennaro Chierchia, *Topics in the Syntax and Semantics of Infinitives*, University of Massachusetts Dissertation, 1984. Higginbotham concludes, with some reservation, that these various arguments for a move towards higher order treatments of English can be answered within a first order framework.

[16] Cf. his 'Meaning and Semantics,' ibid., and also, his 'Three Levels of Meaning,' *Semantics*, D. Steinberg and I. Jakobovits, (eds) Cambridge University Press, 1971.

[17] R. Grandy, 'A Definition of Truth for Theories with Intensional Definite Description Operators,' *Journal of Philosophical Logic* 1, 1972:137–155, and 'Some Remarks about Logical Form', *Nous*, 8, 1974: 157–63. Cf. also my 'Truth and Inference', ibid. In my paper, I limit discussion to the logics of truth theories for propositional object languages. Grandy extends the discussion to quantifier object languages as well.

containing intensional operators.[18] Davidson argues that the standard recursion clause for negation, (1), has no analogue for 'belief' and a range of other apparently intensional operators. (2), for example, is false:

(1) 'It is not the case that *p*' is true iff it is not the case that '*p*' is true.
(2) 'Galileo believed that *p*' is true iff Galileo believed that '*p*' is true.

'Galileo believed that the earth moves' can be true, even though Galileo had no beliefs about 'The earth moves'. He may have known no English.

Faced with a variety of arguments of this sort, Davidson argues it is incorrect to view such operators as functioning as genuine semantic operators on sentences, intensional or extensional. Instead, he argues that it is best to view them as extensionally predicative. On his *paratactic* account, sentence modifiers like 'said' are parsed as two place predicates satisfied by a person and an utterance [ST:93–108; MP:109–122].[19] First, sentences like (3) are regimented into sentences like (4):

(3) Galileo said that the earth moves.
(4) Galileo said *that*. The earth moves.

The first sentence in (4) refers to the second, by the demonstrative 'that' and predicates of it a certain semantic relationship between me, who wrote the sentence and Galileo, namely, that we are samesayers. Galileo said something in virtue of which my uttering (4) makes us samesayers. This notion of samesayers is an 'unanalysed part' of the 'content' or 'said' [ST:104]. Contrary to what Davidson's critics have thought, as Burge notes, there is nothing illegitimate in invoking this notion to explicate the predicate 'said'. It does nothing to complicate the predicate's logical form, the uncovering of which is Davidson's primary aim in [ST:93–108].

On Davidson's account, the target sentence for (3) is not (5):

(5) 'Galileo said that the earth moves' is true iff Galileo said that the earth moves.

The sentence 'The earth moves' is not a semantic component of (3), and therefore, does not have its ordinary semantic role. Those substitutions ordinarily required for deriving an instance of Con T for (3) do not preserve truth. The truth condition for (3) is not the same as that for (6):

(6) Galileo said that the earth does not have zero velocity.

---

[18] [ST:83–108; MTM:119–214; DCT:65–76]; Cf. also John Wallace, 'On the Frame of Reference,' *Semantics of Natural Language*, D. Davidson and G. Harman, Reidel, 1972:219–252; 'Non-standard Theories of Truth,' *The Logic of Grammar*, D. Davidson and G. Harman, eds, Dickenson, 1975:50–59; Gilbert Harman, 'Logical Form,' ibid., 289–307.

[19] Burge, in his contribution, argues that 'said,' under Davidson's analysis, must be a three place predicate, with an argument place for a person, the sayer, and an argument place for an utterance event.

(3) demonstrates 'The earth moves,' and therefore, substitutions leading to (6) are unlicensed.

The truth of a sentence like 'Galileo said *that*,' with the 'that' taken as a demonstrative whose reference is fixed by pointing, as it were, in the direction of a certain item could not entail the assertion of a different sentence with the same truth conditions yet with the reference of this other demonstrative fixed by pointing, as it were, at a different item.

The arguments against Davidson's treatment are many, various, highly contested, and by now familiar. I shall not rehearse them all here, but only mention a few. Some argue that, under Davidson's account, his analyzans are not always logically equivalent to the original analysed sentence, that anaphoric cross references between the that-clause and the main clause break down, that there are difficulties with so-called *de re* readings of subordinate that-clauses, in particular, that Davidson's analysis precludes *de re* readings, and that there are scope problems. The upshot of these various complaints is that, under Davidson's analysis, we shouldn't need to look inside the displayed subordinate that-clause to see if words there interact with the wider environment of the sentence. The critics argue that we have such a need.[20]

Higginbotham, in his contribution, raises different problems with Davidson's account, and offers a variant. He holds that sentences of indirect discourse and propositional attitudes really do occur embedded as the objects of their verbs. As a result, there is no 'concealed demonstrative construction' [TM:35]. Higginbotham argues that Davidson's suggestion that these sorts of sentences do harbor hidden demonstratives is both 'local and inessential' [39].

Burge's contribution also explicates and evaluates Davidson's recommendation for a treatment of logical form for indirect quotation. Though Burge finds Davidson's view important and provocative, he argues that it is implausible. He presents three specific problems for Davidson's account, one he thinks he can solve, but the others he thinks have no satisfactory solutions consistent with Davidson's point of view. The first concerns shifts in reference for propositional attitude or indirect quotation ascriptions with embedded demonstratives. For

---

[20] Cf. for some criticism and rejoinders, R. J. Haack, 'On Davidson's Paratactic Theory of Oblique Contexts,' *Nous*, 5, 1971; Ian McFetridge, 'Propositions and Davidson's Account of Indirect Discourse,' *Proceedings of the Aristotelian Society*, 75, 1975–6; Jennifer Hornsby, 'Saying of,' *Analysis*, 37, 1976–7; Simon Blackburn, 'The Identity of Propositions,' in Simon Blackburn, ed., *Meaning, Reference, and Necessity*, Cambridge University Press, 1975; Peter Smith, 'Blackburn on Saying That,' *Analysis*, 33, 1972–3; Stephen Schiffer, 'Compositional Semantics and Parataxis: Davidson on Meaning and Belief,' unpublished manuscript; J. Hintikka's 'Saying What: an Examination of Davidson's Treatment of Subordinate That-Clauses,' B. Vermazen and M. Hintikka, eds, *Essays on Inquiries into Truth and Interpretation*, forthcoming; John Wallace's 'On Davidson's Analysis of Indirect Discourse, ibid.; William Lycan, 'On Saying That,' *Analysis*, 33, 1973; Mark Platts, *Ways of Meaning*, RKP, 1979:109–132; S. Boer and W. Lycan, 'A Performadox in Truth-Conditional Semantics,' *Linguistics and Philosophy*, 1980:93; William Lycan, *Logical Form in Natural Language*, MIT Press, 1984: 194–152, 275–294; W. V. O. Quine's 'Reply to Davidson,' D. Davidson and J. Hintikka, eds, *Words and Objections: Essays on the Work of W. V. Quine*, D. Reidel, Dordrecht, 1980:33–335; J. McDowell, 'Quotation and Saying That,' Mark Platts, ed., *Reference, Truth and Reality*, RKP, 1980:206–237; Susan Haack, *Philosophy of Logics*, Cambridge University Press, 1978:123–127; Stephen Stich, *From Folk Psychology to Cognitive Science*, Bradford/MIT Press, 1983:83–84.

example, Frank said that George said that the earth moves. On Davidson's account, *according to Burge*, the logical form of this sentence is:

Frank said that. George said that. The earth moves.

The problem is that the second 'that,' does not have its intuitive referent.[21] This problem Burge thinks is resoluble within what he sees as Davidson's framework. His second criticism is a variant on the Church–Langford argument against Carnap's analysis of propositional attitudes. We may say that Galileo said something, in the indirect discourse sense of 'said,' without there being any utterance of ours that samesays Galileo's utterance. Similar problems arise for mentalistic discourse. As Burge notes, 'there are surely beliefs and other attitudes that are never expressed or characterized by any actual utterances produced by the reporter, the subject, or anyone else'. He proffers a solution to this problem, but does so by giving up what he takes to be Davidson's 'nominalism'. He interprets Davidson as restricting analyses so that they appeal only to concrete entities as truth bearers. In its place, he recommends we regard 'natural discourse as quantifying over abstract objects'.[22] His final criticism of the paratactic account concerns validity and logical form. According to Burge, *formally valid* arguments forms are not so rendered under Davidson's account.

Indexicals

What about the truth theory for a language containing sentences like (3) above? Since, under Davidson's proposal, this language contains indexicals, his recommendation that we modify Tarski's theory such that the truth predicate is characterized not as a one place predicate of sentences, but as a three-place predicate of sentences, speakers, and times, recommends itself: S is true, as potentially uttered by P at time t [TM:34–35; MTM:213].[23] With this modification, standard equivalences are derivable:

(7) 'Galileo said that' is true in English for a speaker at a time iff the demonstrated object by the speaker at this time is something in virtue of which Galileo and the speaker are samesayers.

---

21 However, cf. Davidson's [RF:176–178].

22 It is true that Davidson's account of indirect discourse is presented in a way that makes reference to entities located in time and space, but why Burge thinks Davidson is, in principle, opposed to abstract entities, he does not say. Indeed, in many of Davidson's papers, he seems quite unperturbed about countenancing abstract entities. Cf. in particular, [DCT:68; TM:21; ST:108].

23 Cf. also Ernest LePore and Barry Loewer, 'Dual Aspect Semantics,' forthcoming; Scott Weinstein, 'Truth and Demonstratives,' D. Davidson and G. Harman, *The Logic of Grammar*, Dickenson, 1974:60–63; Tyler Burge, 'Demonstrative Constructions, Reference and Truth,' *The Journal of Philosophy*, 71, 1974:203–223; and Barry Taylor, 'Truth Theory for Indexical Languages,' Mark Platts, ed., *Reference, Truth, and Reality*, RKP, 1980:182–198, for elaboration of absolute truth theoretic accounts for indexicals.

The theory is apparently formally feasible: it seems to meet Con T, and structural constraints seem to be adequately respected. However, Barry Richards raises doubts about Davidson's suggestion for a semantics for languages with tenses. He offers his own account in which semantic innocence is denied, a view Davidson endorses. (Both Frege's account of the sense of expressions in opaque contexts [TM: 17–36] and Quine's account of quotation [Q: 79–92] violates this view). Richards, based on some consequences of his proposal for a semantic treatment of tense, rejects the view that sentences which occur in subordinate position have the same semantic role which they have in main clauses.[24]

Reference

Putnam distinguishes two questions: Is it possible to give some kind of definitional reduction of reference to notions such as information, counterfactuals, and causation? What would the metaphysical significance of such a reduction be were it to be successfully carried out? His central claim is that neither counterfactuals nor causation will serve to naturalize reference in a way acceptable to a physicalist, because these notions do not really take us outside the circle of intentional notions. His reason for this claim is, roughly, that the truth conditions of counterfactual and causal statements essentially involve pragmatic factors – relating to similarity and salience – which cannot properly be explained independently of the knowing subject. Accordingly, we have not shown, by means of such definitions, that reference can be explicated non-intentionally. Davidson in various places also has argued against a definitional reduction of reference to physicalist notions [IR:215–242], though his reasons for such scepticism are quite different from Putnam's. In [RWR:215–226], Davidson responds to critics who say that a proper theory of meaning must include a theory of reference.

Methodological solipsism

Lycan raises a question about the relationship between semantics and methodological solipsism.[25] If Putnam's Twin-Earth arguments are sound, then the speaker's believing the sentence has a truth condition is not (entirely) a function of what's in the speaker's head.[26] But, then, beliefs about truth conditions cannot produce behavior, as assumed it could above.[27]

---

[24] For further discussion of tense and truth theories, cf. Gareth Evans, 'Does Tense Logic Rest Upon a Mistake?,' forthcoming; Michael Woods, 'Existence and Tense,' G. Evans and J. McDowell, eds, *Truth and Meaning*, Oxford University Press, 1977:248–262.

[25] Cf. also J. Fodor, 'Methodological Solipsism Considered as a Research Strategy in Cognitive Psychology,' *Behavioral and Brain Sciences*, 3, 1980; S. Stich, *From Folk Psychology to Cognitive Science*, Bradford Press/MIT Press, 1983; William Lycan, *Logical Form in Natural Language*, ibid., 1984: 235–48.

[26] H. Putnam, 'The Meaning of "Meaning." *Mind, Language, and Reality: Philosophical Papers*, vol. 2, Cambridge University Press, 1975:215–271.

[27] Cf., McGinn, 'The Structure of Content,' A. Woodfield, ed., *Thought and Object*, Oxford University Press, 1982:215–271.

Imagine two planets, Earth and Twin-Earth, and two of their residents, say, Arabella and twin-Arabella. Twin-Earth is almost a physical replica of Earth. The only difference is that on Twin-Earth the clear liquid the twin-people drink, that fills their oceans, and that they call 'water,' is composed not of H_2O molecules, but of XYZ molecules. According to Putnam, the expression 'water' on Earth refers to the stuff composed of H_2O, and not composed of XYZ. It is exactly the reverse on Twin-Earth. This is so even if no speaker of English and twin-English knows the molecular structures of water and twin-water, or can distinguish between them. Thus, Arabella's belief that 'Water is wet' is true iff H_2O is wet, and twin-Arabella's belief that 'Water is wet' is true iff XYZ is wet, are indistinguishable in causal role; the difference in propositional content between their beliefs about truth conditions is irrelevant to their matching behavior, and so plays no direct role in explaining it. But, if, as we have been assuming, semantics can play some role in explaining behavior, then there must be a notion of semantic content, contra Davidson, distinct from truth conditions. Various authors have attempted to construct a non-truth conditional notion of content sufficient for the cognitivist's goals.[28]

Lycan argues that methodological solipsism yields a theory of belief and hence, understanding, that does not allow one to understand the truth conditions of one's beliefs. He is led to an alternative semantic theory, conceptual role semantics, which gives meaning to beliefs that can be grasped. Conceptual role semantics assigns the same content (individuated by conceptual role) to thoughts with very different truth conditions. Lycan grants that for certain sorts of psychological explanations of behavior, conceptual role semantics is adequate. However, he claims that there are *linguistic* phenomena which show the need for truth in linguistics (or semantics).

A unified theory of linguistic and non-linguistic interpretation

Davidson aims to account for linguistic phenomena in an intensional idiom: intentional action, desires, beliefs, fears, wishes, hopes, and so on.[29] He begins with an analogy between the interpreter and the Bayesian decision theorist.

Bayesian decision theory, as developed by Frank Ramsey, deals with two fundamental elements: belief and desire.[30] Choice of one course of action over another, or preference that one state of affairs obtain rather than another, is the product of these two considerations: the value we set on its possible consequences, and the liklihood of those consequences occuring if we perform the

---

[28] For a detailed discussion and evaluation of these attempts, cf., Ernest LePore and Barry Loewer's 'Dual Aspect Semantics,' forthcoming, and 'Solipsistic Semantics,' *Midwest Studies in Philosophy*, 1985: 587–606. In these papers, we argue, first, that an adequate truth conditional account can be given which avoids the Twin-Earth, and related, criticisms of truth conditional semantics, and, secondly, that the prospects of devising a solipsistic account of content are quite dim.

[29] Davidson discusses this project in various places. In addition to [RI:125–140; TT:170], cf. also, his 'A New Basis for Decision Theory,' *Theory and Decision*, 17, 1985; 'Toward a Unified Theory of Meaning and Action,' *Grazer Philosophische Studien*, 1981:1–12; and his 'Expressing Evaluations,' Lindley Lecture, University of Kansas Press, 1982.

[30] F. P. Ramsey, 'Truth and Probability,' in his *Foundations of Mathematics*, NY, 1950.

action. To the extent we are rational, we *maximize expected utility*. What Ramsey's theory seeks to explain is relatively open to observation: preferences or choices among options. The explanatory mechanism – degrees of beliefs and utilities is not observable. Ramsey solved the problem of showing how in principle under idealized conditions to find the unknowns – belief and desire – on the basis of looking at preferences for outcomes alone [BBM:145–148].

A theory of verbal interpretation assigns truth conditions to each of the potential infinity of utterances in the speakers' repertoire, and so a theory is called for that derives the truth conditions of an utterance from the semantic properties of its parts. Davidson takes the basic evidence for a theory of verbal interpretation to be the manifestation of assent to, or holding true, sentences in the act of assertion (just as preference manifests itself in choice). Thus, he bases his theory of interpretation on assent to sentences events in the world cause. A problem arises because, just as choosing a course of action is the result of belief and desire, so holding a sentence true is the result of meaning (truth conditions) and belief. How are we to distinguish the roles of each in the determination of sentences held true? We cannot hope to discover interpretation first, and then read off beliefs and *vice versa*, so Davidson has argued [BBM:147–148].

What we need for an adequate theory of belief and meaning (truth conditions) is not merely knowledge of what causes a speaker to hold a sentence true, but knowledge of the degree of belief in its truth. We would then be able to detect degrees of evidential support by noting how changes in degree of belief placed on one sentence were accompanied by changes in degree of belief placed on another. But this is not something open to observation – the analogue to Bayesian decision theory. Starting with preferences or choices over options, we get beliefs and desires. Starting with sentences held true (under certain circumstances), we get meaning and belief. However, there is more than analogy here; there is a marriage.

According to Davidson, the Bayesian decision theorist presupposes that he can identify the propositions to which attitudes like belief and desire (or preference) are directed. This capacity, though, is inseparable from understanding what the subject says. We find out exactly what someone wants, prefers, or believes, generally, by interpreting his speech [TT:127, 143f]. Thus, Davidson saw the need for a theory of verbal interpretation to elicit attitudes and beliefs which explain preferences and choices and the need for a theory of degree of belief to make serious use of relations of evidential support. We have need for two theories which cannot be developed independently of each other. This need forced Davidson to seek a unified theory that would yield degree of belief on a rationality scale, utilities on an interval scale, *and* interpretation of speech without assuming any of them.

In this unified theory, the following attitude is basic: the agent prefers one sentence to be true rather than another. All the interpreter has to go on is information about what events in the world cause a subject to prefer that one rather than another sentence be true. Clearly, the interpreter can know this without knowing what the sentences mean, what state of affairs the subject values, or what he believes. The structure which Davidson thinks sufficient to channel this evidence into a unified theory of interpretation and action is a

Tarski-like truth theory, modified in various ways to apply to natural language, and combined with structural assumptions, on the side of belief and desire. For example, the beliefs and desires of the subject incorporate a pattern that is in essential respects like the pattern of our own beliefs. Many of these constraints are discussed in the section on conceptual relativism below.

Indeterminacy, evidence, and form

Quine and Davidson both subscribe to the indeterminacy of translation (interpretation), but their reasons differ. Quine's argument for indeterminacy rests essentially on his observational/theoretical distinction. It is the theoretical sentences of our languge for which we must construct analytical hypotheses in translation. And it is these hypotheses which are indeterminate with respect to all the possible data. Davidson rejects this distinction [CS:183–198], and so, must base his argument for indeterminacy on something else. For Davidson, indeterminacy is a natural consequence of the way we interpret others. Since there will be many ways to maximize agreement between us and whoever we interpret, indeterminacy invades. In their contributions, Wallace and Wheeler distinguish between Quine's and Davidson's brands of indeterminacy. Quine's indeterminacy of translation depends on a dualism between observation and theory, what Davidson dubbed 'the third dogma of empiricism' [CS:189; 193–4].[31] Quine must hold that there is a level of semantic content, the observation sentence, which is invulnerable to theoretical change.

Wallace criticizes both Quine's and Davidson's views about what the correct *form* a semantic theory, interpretation, or translation, should take, what the evidential base for such theories should be, and how these evidential bases should be marshalled in confirming or disconfirming specific models chosen. Wallace's argument rests largely on his effort to exploit what he sees as an analogy between translation (interpretation) and Ventris' decipherment of Linear B.[32] He argues that careful examination of the form Chadwick's decipherment took, the kind of evidence on which he based his decipherment, and the ways in which he channelled this evidence in confirming his decipherment, has critical ramifications for evaluating Quine's and Davidson's views on translation and interpretation. Vermazen, elucidates and evaluates Wallace's claims. He concludes that Wallace has not made a convincing case against Quine and Davidson. He argues Wallace has provided little reason to entertain seriously his analogy.

Conceptual relativism

Davidson rejects the idea that there can be radically different conceptual schemes. His rejection involves subtle connections among the concepts of

---

[31] Cf. Quine's reply 'On The Very Idea of a Third Dogma', *Theories and Things*, Cambridge, Harvard University Press, 1981: 38–42.

interpretation, translation, truth, reference, and observationality. He associates having a language with having a conceptual schema; a conceptual schema might be viewed as a set of intertranslatable languages [CS:191]. Different conceptual schemes would correspond to languages among which translation is not possible. But, so Davidson argues, it is hard to make sense of a total failure of translatability between languages [CS:185]. In summary he argues: we could not be in a position to judge that others had concepts or beliefs radically different from our own [CS:197].

In part, Davidson holds this view because he argues that strong pressures arise from the very nature of belief (and interpretation, in general), pressures which limit what we can and cannot attribute to another. For example, one thing that strikes us about the attribution of belief is that the field of beliefs has a holistic character. It does not make sense to ascribe a single belief to a person, except against the background of a very large number of other beliefs. Beliefs are not like little atoms we can pick out one at a time. We cannot suppose, for example, that somebody thinks a tiger is before him, unless we suppose he believes tigers are entities of a certain sort, e.g., he thinks they are physical objects, that they have mass, take up space, are not toys, and perhaps, have stripes and cannot fly. It is hard to say where to stop. How many beliefs must a person have before we can ascribe a single belief to him? Holism, Davidson has argued imposes constraints upon interpretation.[33]

Holism is not the sole source of pressure. When we ascribe beliefs to people, certain conditions must be met. Beliefs must cohere. We cannot intelligibly ascribe beliefs to a person that are wildly erroneous on logical grounds without undermining the intelligibility of a particular attribution. If I say Arabella believes it is raining in Kansas now and she also believes it is not raining in Kansas now, it may be possible to make sense of this, but it is difficult, because one of the best reasons for supposing someone does *not* believe it is raining is that she does believe it is not raining. It is hard to think up a better reason. But just because of the evidential relation between these two beliefs, it is difficult to comprehend that she has two flatly contradictory beliefs.

Quine has emphasized logical contradiction, which is just one source of incoherence. Suppose Cinderella chooses a pear over an apple, the apple over an orange, and the orange over the pear. How are we to interpret this? One way is to say she has incoherent preferences. Another is to say she has changed her mind. Or, perhaps she thinks that when a pear is paired with an apple it is different than when paired with an orange. There may be no one correct way to view this, but the pressure is there not to ascribe intransitive sets of preferences. If we decide the evidence points to her preferring a pear to an apple, and the apple to an orange, then that is some of the best evidence we can have that she prefers the pear to the orange.

Another question we must bear in mind when we ascribe beliefs to a person is whether what that person believes is true. It is Davidson's view that the more

---

[32] Cf. John Chadwick, *The Decipherment of Linear B*, and also, Michael Ventris and John Chadwick, *Documents in Mycenaean Greek*, 2nd ed., Cambridge University Press, 1973.

[33] Besides [CS], cf. [TT:155–170] and his 'Psychology as Philosophy,' *Essays on Actions and Events*, Oxford, 1980:229:39.

false beliefs we ascribe to a person, the less sense we can make of any of our ascriptions to that person.[34] We ascribe beliefs to another to make him agree with us as much as possible [BBM:153; TT:159f]. Since we believe our own beliefs are true, Davidson believes wer are under pressure to limit the number of 'false' beliefs (and similarly for desires) we ascribe to him. This is Davidson's Principle of Charity. For example, I ascribe to another, perhaps on the basis of testimony, a belief that Ronald Reagan died within the last few years. I am surprised my acquaintance is so ill-informed, but I know there are islands of ignorance in every pool of knowledge. Next, perhaps on the basis of additional testimony, I ascribe to him a belief that Ronald Reagan's wife's name is 'Muriel'. Finally, I ascribe to him the belief that Reagan is from Minnesota. No one of these ascriptions strains credulity, but each, when added to the others, makes us wonder whether this fellow is pulling my leg, or whether I have understood him correctly. A person who believes little about Reagan may be entirely mistaken, but how can a person who has many beliefs about Reagan have gotten all of it wrong [TT: 168]?

Some authors interpret such Davidsonian argumentation to mean that it is the *number* of false beliefs that puts the strain on the attributions. This is not right. For example, suppose I think I hear you utter 'Ruth is a witch,' and on this basis, I ascribe to you the belief that Ruth is a witch, a belief I hold false. Holistic pressures force me to ascribe a great deal more to you, e.g., that Ruth has supernatural powers. Later, I discover you do not believe Ruth can cause sickness or death, disappear at will, enter into pacts with the Devil, and so on. Each of these I also believe false of Ruth, but true of witches. As this list increases, I make less and less clear sense about what I suppose you think when I suppose you think Ruth is a witch, for my best reason for thinking you do *not* think Ruth a witch is that you *do* think she lacks supernatural powers. To preserve coherence, either I must say that what you mean by 'witch' differs from what I mean by it, or I must ascribe another false belief to you, namely, that witches do not have supernatural powers. If I say the former, I had better find a better way to describe what it is I think you believe. If I say the latter, I lose my grip on what I thought I ascribed to you when I initially thought you believed Ruth a witch. The moral, Davidson's moral, is that not all false beliefs are equal [BBM: 13]. Once I ascribe to you the false belief that Ruth is a witch, it makes more sense to ascribe to you the false beliefs that she can cause sickness and death, disappear at will, and so on – in other words, it makes more sense to ascribe to you a whole raft of false beliefs – than to ascribe to you a single false belief that witches lack supernatural powers.

None of this means that we cannot ascribe all sorts of silly beliefs and all kinds of errors. In the first example, I may discover that you have all those silly beliefs about Reagan because you think his name is 'Hubert Humphrey'. Certainly we can make sense of other people having different ways of working things out, and organizing them. And in many contexts we expect others to be

---

[34] This is an early view of his [TM:27]. However, it emphasized more in his [CS:183–198; BBM:141–154; TT:168–9]. And, it is used to support some major metaphysical and epistemological views more recently in his [TIM:199–214; TT:127, 143f], and two of his contributions to this volume, 'A Coherence Theory of Truth and Knowledge,' and 'Empirical Content'.

wrong. We expect people to be wrong about how things are when we see them badly placed for observation, or when we can see exactly why someone is apt to be wrong about it. Everything that goes into epistemology (and much cognitive psychology) about the role of evidential support has to enter this process. We know humans are constructed in such a way that we cannot see through skin and trees. Thus, *prima facie*, we do not expect someone to be right about what is happening on the other side of a building he is standing in front of, or about whether any internal injury was suffered when a friend fell. If we discover that this individual had sighted a dog running towards the other side of the building a moment ago, or that that strange object in his hand is an instrument for diagnosing internal injury, initial doubt about his judgement may fade. Within the context of determining the conditions under which belief-attributions are justified, we are asked to take *less* than usual for granted, but we still are allowed to draw upon a major body of beliefs about the world [BBM: 152]. But there is a limit to how much logical foolishness we can ascribe to someone. Beyond a certain point, we lose our grip on the intelligibility of these attributions.

Austin writes if you really want seriously to disagree with somebody, you have to find a large platform of agreement. Take away those countless presuppositions and the question whether two people seriously disagree loses its clarity. Davidson's point is that the platform, small or large, has only to have key planks. Take away the presupposition that witches have strange powers, and the question whether you and I disagree about Ruth begins to lose its clarity.

Many authors have objected to Davidson's attack on conceptual relativism.[35] Robert Kraut defends Davidson against some of these attacks, and then constructs his own attack, based to some extent on insights of other writers.[36] Kraut argues that, the evidential base in radical interpretation, as Davidson envisages it, involves attitudes persons have toward sentences, and also an intimate relationship between the expressive resources of a discourse and the *referential* apparatus plausibly defined over the discourse. Kraut believes that Davidson ignores this connection, and as a consequence has been blocked from seeing the intelligibility of the idea that there might be different conceptual schemes.[37]

Carol Rovane investigates the connection between theories of meaning and metaphysics. Unlike Davidson, she does not place much emphasis on the Principle of Charity (which she argues has a very limited significance for metaphysics), but proposes, rather, that separate metaphysical categories, such

---

[35] Nicholas Rescher, 'Conceptual Schemes,' in French, Uehling, and Wettstein, eds, *Midwest Studies in Philosophy*, 5, Minnesota Press, 1980:323–345; Chris Swoyer 'True For', M. Krauz and J. Meiland (eds), *Relativism*, University of Notre Dame Press, 1982.

[36] Kraut cites Quine, Dummett, and Haugeland.

[37] Hilary Putnam, *Meaning and the Moral Sciences*, RKP, 1978; Colin McGinn, 'Charity, Interpretation and Belief', *Journal of Philosophy*, 74, 1977: 521–35 argue for a similar view. They argue we can 'separate the possession of concepts appropriate to some object. From having beliefs about the object. Once we make this separation, there is no difficulty in imputing preponderantly false beliefs to others; reference to autonomous with respect to truth. However, cf. Davidson's [RWR:215–226; RI:127–137] for a critical discussion about the utility of any appeal to the referential apparatus in determining the expressive resources of a discourse.

as person, object, event, and even cause, are from the outset built into Davidson's interpretive conception of metaphysics.[38]

Michael Root shows how Davidson's views on interpretation oppose the idea of a radical other, i.e., oppose conceptual relativism. He shows what bearing this has on the social sciences. He surveys the place and importance of the conceptual relativism in sociology and anthropology, presents Davidson's theory of interpretation, and focuses on one consequence of this theory, viz., that there is a limit to how different another can be from us. Finally, he offers a Kantian interpretation of Davidson's theory, which, he argues reveals the tension between Davidson's theory of interpretation and his realism. Can Davidson defend the view that there are minds?

Coherentism, foundationalism, and skepticism

Two of Davidson's previously published papers are included in this volume: 'Empirical Content' and 'A Coherence Theory of Truth and Knowledge.' In *Inquiries into Truth and Interpretation*, Davidson says:

> ...it cannot be assumed that speakers never have false beliefs. Error is what gives belief its point. We can, however, take it as given that *most* beliefs are correct [TT: 168].

In 'A Coherence Theory of Truth and Knowledge' Davidson explains what he takes to be the consequences for epistemology of the account of radical interpretation. He says[39]:

> What stands in the way of global skepticism of the senses is, in my view, the fact that we must, in the plainest and methodologically most basic cases, take the objects of belief to be the causes of that belief. And what we, as interpreters, must take them to be is what they in fact are [CTTK:317–18].

More specifically, Davidson employs the account of radical interpretation to argue that:

(1) The foundationalist epistemologist cannot provide an answer to 'skepticism in one of its traditional garbs' [CTTK:309] without supposing that there is some way of 'confronting certain of his beliefs with the deliverances of the senses one by one, or perhaps confronting the totality of his beliefs with the tribunal of experience' [CTTK:312].

---

[38] For one interpretation about the relationship between semantics and ontological commitment in Davidson's philosophy, cf., Ernest LePore's 'The Semantics for Action, Event, and Causal Sentences,' *The Philosophy of Donald Davidson*, eds, Ernest LePore and Brian P. McLaughlin, Basil Blackwell, 1985.

[39] It is important to point out that Davidson adds in a footnote that his causal theory of meaning has little in common with the causal theories of reference of Kripke and Putnam. Those theories look to causal relations between names and objects of which the speakers may well be ignorant. The chance of systematic error is thus increased. My causal theory does the reverse by connecting the cause of a belief with its object. [CTTK:318]

(2) Such a confrontation is not possible [CTTK:307].
(3) On the other hand, a coherentist account of justification – an account which holds the claim that 'nothing can count as a reason for holding a belief except another belief' [CTTK:310] – coupled with the account of radical interpretation can provide the skeptic with a reason for supposing that coherent beliefs are true in general [CTTK:307].

Klein argues that Davidson's account of radical interpretation does not provide a secure refuge from skepticism. He contends that when the argument used to show that we have a reason to believe our beliefs are true in the main is examined, we see that one of its premises presupposes the very knowledge of the causal order of things which the skeptic believes beyond our ken.

McGinn argues that if Davidson's charitable account of interpretation did have the consequence that massive error in our system of beliefs is impossible, then, for that very reason, the account seems to stand in need of revision. McGinn also advances other reasons for giving us pause about the account. One of its consequences is the extreme failure of the mental to supervene on the cerebral. McGinn argues that the content of some beliefs – those involving observational concepts – need not depend upon extrinsic relations. Thus, skepticism once again becomes possible.

Rorty endorses Davidson's account of the project of radical interpretation agreeing that a 'regulative principle' of the hermeneutical project is that most of the as yet uninterpreted assertions are true. But, he argues, that principle and the account of belief which follows from it do not provide an 'answer' to the skeptic's questions, as Davidson says. Rather it provides the basis for rejecting the picture of the relationship of belief to its objects which makes both the skeptical question and its various answers (e.g., idealism, physicalism, analytical pragmaticism), possible.

Sosa agrees with Davidson that confrontational foundationalism is absurd. Nevertheless, Sosa argues that Davidson's attack on foundationalism is inconclusive, because foundationalism, as he understands this notion, need not suppose that confrontation is necessary for providing the justification of foundational beliefs.[40] The supervenience of the 'epistemically evaluative' on what is not epistemically evaluative could provide such a basis without requiring confrontation. Sosa also raises several questions about Davidson's defense of coherentism: Why, for example, does Davidson's causal theory of the meaning uphold the importance of a coherentism? Why couldn't a set of largely independent beliefs share the presumption of truth? Couldn't beliefs be independent and cohere?

Whatever one thinks of the merits of the various positions developed by Davidson and the other contributors, one thing is clear: Far from being dead, epistemology is well and flourishing!

Limits of the literal

Davidson, in 'A Nice Derangement of Epitaphs,' concludes that 'there is no such thing as a language, not if a language is anything like what many

---

[40] But cf.

philosophers and linguists have supposed. There is therefore no such thing to be learned, mastered, or born with' [446]. Davidson's present view is that speakers bring no such thing as a language, a prior or standard theory, to their conversations. What makes conversation possible is a theory that steadily evolves in the course of the conversation.[41] Hacking argues that this present view is incompatible with Davidson's views about understanding and interpretation in most of the essays in his *Inquiries into Truth and Interpretation*, in particular, cf. [RI:125; IR:240; SNL:60; RF:172–173].

Although Dummett also believes Davidson is recanting formerly held positions, he thinks that Hacking misunderstands Davidson's use of the expressions 'prior theory' and 'passing theory'. Prior theory is a theory about how, in general, to understand a speaker when he addresses you. This theory may change, contingent upon what the speaker says during the particular conversation. The hearer's passing theory is what he uses to understand particular utterances the speaker makes during the specific conversation. He may posit that the speaker is using a word in an unusual way, but not be prepared to infer that the speaker always uses the word in this way. According to Dummett, Hacking goes astray because he assumes that 'prior theory' to whatever theory a hearer brings with him to the conversation, and 'passing theory' to whatever theory evolves in the course of the conversation. A hearer uses his prior theory throughout the conversation. He does not give it up and adopt the passing theory.

Instead, Dummett agrees with Hacking that Davidson is recanting earlier views, that Davidson's use of 'interpretation' in discussing the semanticist's project is quite extended, and Davidson has not made the distinction between these two sorts of theories precise. Dummett's strongest complaint is that Davidson has not sufficiently argued for his claim that 'there is no such thing as language'.

Akeel Bilgrami explores the relationship between the truth conditional conception of meaning and the dictum that meaning is use. On the basis of his analysis, he criticizes both Dummett's attack against Davidson and McDowell's attack against Dummett.[42] Against Dummett, he argues that the dictum can only be exploited for verificationist purposes if one fails to appreciate the merits of a holistic conception of meaning, as he argues Dummett does. This, Dummett does, Bilgrami argues, because Dummett has a very inflated conception of the meaning as use dictum. All Davidson means by the dictum, as a constraint on a theory of meaning, is that whatever meaning is, it be public. In McDowell's views on the connection between understanding and meaning, he sees a threat to the theoretical nature of meaning, which is so central to Davidson.

Davidson's views on metaphor are a consequence of his theory that the meaning of a sentence is given by its truth conditions. While most theorists of metaphor ascribe two meanings to a metaphorical sentence, Davidson argues

---

[41] Cf. also, [CC:265–280].

[42] Bilgrami's discussion of McDowell is based on two papers by McDowell 'In Defense of Modesty,' *Festschrift for Dummett*, Barry Taylor, ed., Oxford University Press, forthcoming, and 'Anti-Realism and the Epistemology of Understanding,' J. Bouvresse and H. Parrett, eds., *Meaning and Understanding*, Berlin, 1981.

that a metaphorical sentence means nothing beyond what it literally says. Metaphor is a particular use of language, and not a particular kind of meaning. This is not to deny that metaphor changes our view of things, but rather, it is to insist that, as Davidson says, 'words are the wrong currency to exchange for a picture' [WMM:263]. While metaphor is propositional in character, the 'seeing as' response it prompts is not.

Marcia Cavell uses Davidson's own metaphor of metaphor as 'the dream-work of language' [WMM:245] to explain Freud's notion of dream work as hallucinatory wish fulfillment. On her analysis, hallucinatory wish fulfillment is another kind of envisioning that escapes articulation in propositional form. At the same time it plays an important role in some irrational thoughts and actions. Other resemblances as well between metaphor and dream work facilitate the latter; though metaphor, *per se*, has nothing to do with irrationality, and, on the contrary, can throw light on a particular structure of beliefs and desires that reworks its irrationality.

Conclusion

Donald Davidson argues that language, mind, and action are inseparable and that the traditional effort to understand them in isolation was bound to fail. Beginning with the question, What is it for words to mean what they do?, he argues that a theory of meaning can only be satisfactory if it discovers a finite basic vocabulary in the verbal phenomena to be interpreted. Then, arguing that a Tarski-like truth theory, suitably modified for natural language, would suffice for interpretation, he insists that an adequate exploration of verbal behavior results in symmetric accounts of belief and meaning.

Davidson confronts the philosophical consequences. On the basis of his semantic views, Davidson is led to abandon as unintelligible claims that different languages or conceptual schemes 'divide up' or 'cope with' reality in different ways. It follows that when we settle on a truth conditional semantics for our own language, what we take there to be is pretty much what there is. Theories frequently yield insight into problems that they were not specifically designed to solve. However, a careful reading of Davidson's writings bears out, not only how broad in scope his philosophical interests are, but, more importantly, how well this breadth coheres. The essays which follow are a testimony both to this breadth and, perhaps, more impressively, to its coherence.

Part II
Truth and Meaning

2
Linguistic Theory and Davidson's Program in Semantics*

JAMES HIGGINBOTHAM

In his essay, 'Truth and Meaning' and in a number of other publications, Donald Davidson urged us to investigate the semantic structure of given natural languages. He mentioned several motivations for this type of inquiry, among them that of achieving a clear grasp of a fundamental aspect of language mastery, namely its semantic productivity. In speech and understanding we employ a storehouse of particular facts about words, and a humanly controllable set of combinatorial devices to arrive at conditions on truth and reference without which the ordinary use of language would be impossible. Davidson's program is to discover the combinatorial basis of semantics.

Davidson's enterprise is conceptually distinct from that of perspicuously introducing a language form for this or that philosophical or scientific purpose. As Davidson says, commenting on this difference between himself and Tarski on natural language, 'the task of a theory of meaning as I conceive it is not to change, improve, or reform a language, but to describe and understand it.' And again, 'Much of what is called for is just to mechanize as far as possible what we now do by art when we put ordinary English into one or another canonical notation. The point is not that canonical notation is better than the original idiom, but rather that if we know what idiom the canonical notation is canonical *for* we have as good a theory for the idiom as for its kept companion.'[1]

This note is concerned with the project of 'describing and understanding' the semantic principles of English, and to that extent with the logical forms of sentences and other expressions of English. In it, I shall advocate a particular point of view toward the syntax of English, and the structure of the clauses of semantic theory that assign semantic values to syntactic elements: in other words, I shall offer hypotheses about the idiom that canonical notation is canonical for. The syntax of the idiom is theoretical: it cannot simply be read off the expressions themselves. As I proceed, I shall consider some of Davidson's

* This article originated as a paper delivered at the Rutgers Conference on the philosophy of Donald Davidson, in April 1984. I am grateful to Richard Cartwright for discussion and comment on an earlier draft, and to F. J. Pelletier for his comments at the Conference, as reported below.
[1] Davidson (1984), p. 21. References by title to Davidson's essays are to this volume.

more specific suggestions, especially as regards action sentences and certain types of opaque contexts. Only a small amount of the territory can be scrutinized, and I will have to dwell on a few examples requiring an unfortunately lengthy setting-out. Still, it seems to me that certain apparent difficulties for Davidson can be overcome if my conjectures on the English idiom are on the right track.

I should like to distinguish three sorts of questions that typically arise when one is in the middle of a more or less specific inquiry into the semantic nature of constructions in natural language. The first of these questions concerns the nature of semantic values: the sorts of objects that should be taken as the values of these constructions, or of parts of them. The second is the proper form of syntax: what categories do elements belong to, and according to what principles do they combine to form complex expressions? The third question, which I would think of as that of semantics proper, is: how, given one's assumptions about values, and given also an account of the modes of syntactic combination of words and phrases, do values get assigned to those words and phrases?

A simple application of these distinctions is provided by interpreted quantificational languages. Here the values (relative to an assignment to variables) are sets of satisfiers for expressions of the category formula or sentence, and objects for expressions of the category of terms; the syntax is fixed by an inductive definition of termhood and sentencehood (equivalently, by a context-free grammar); and the semantic problem is to project values, taken as given for the basic clauses of the syntax, from simpler to more complex expressions. This problem is the simplest one solved by Tarski's work.

When we turn to natural languages, we can hardly take for granted what the values of expressions are. (Historically, in fact, Tarski could not take values for granted in mathematical systems in use, to which his theory was intended first of all to apply; in particular, that the values of formulas with free variables are sets of satisfiers is a crucial step in the construction as a whole.) Equally, we can hardly take for granted what the syntax is, since we did not make it up.

It may be said that for many of the semantic problems that most exercise the field, deeper syntactic investigation is unlikely to point the way to a correct choice among existing solutions, or to guide us to a solution where none presents itself. Of course, the point is correct: but I am inclined to think that it should carry much less weight than seems often to be supposed. My reason is that, in many cases, a close attention to the irregularities and bumps of syntax has proved to be a significant clue to how the language is working.

I have spoken of semantics as a technical enterprise pursued against a background of assumptions both metaphysical and syntactic in nature. On the metaphysical side, it has been Davidson's view that the only values that both need to be posited and do useful work in combinatorial semantics are those of a referential character: denotation, satisfaction, and truth. Adopting this view, I proceed to the side of syntax.

The syntactic objects under investigation I shall call *phrase markers*. The term is taken from Chomsky (1955), although the conception that I shall use is somewhat different from the one he suggested. Phrase markers are abstract objects, consisting at a minimum of the following three components:

(i) an underlying finite set *P* of points;

(ii) a partial ordering $<$ of *P* (read 'dominates'), such that $(P,<)$ is a tree in the usual mathematical sense, and has a unique root;

(iii) A function *L* called the *syntactic labelling*, which assigns to each *p* in *P* its label $L(p)$.

A phrase marker, then, is minimally a structure $A = (P,<,L)$.

A *sub-phrase marker B* of a phrase marker $A = (P,<,L)$ is a subset *Q* of *P* that is a phrase marker when $<$ and *L* are restricted to points in *Q*. If $(P,<,L)$ is a phrase marker, and *p* is a point in *P*, then the set $D(p)$ consisting of those points in *P* dominated by *p*, together with the restrictions of $<$ and *L* to $D(p)$, is always a sub-phrase marker $(D(p),<|D(p),L|D(p))$ of $(P,<,L)$. In concrete examples, we can refer to phrase markers and their sub-phrase markers by the labels of their roots; thus the sentence 'Theaetetus flies', under the phrase marker (1), is an S whose VP is a sub-phrase marker of it:

(1)

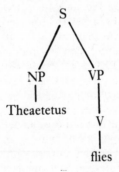

In standard formalized languages, the semantic account proves true statements of the form exhibited in (2):

(2)   *x* is a value of the expression *E* on the assignment $f \longleftrightarrow F(x,E,f)$

Natural languages do not, as it happens, have the property that from the spelling of an expression its grammatical structure is uniquely recoverable; in consequence, reference to expressions should be replaced with reference to grammatical structures – phrase markers, on the view that I am advocating. The semantics of first-order languages could be expressed in terms of phrase markers too, namely those that are given by the standard context-free grammars for those languages. If this were done, and devices for grouping were dropped from the languages themselves, then their surface appearances would partake of the familiar structural ambiguities of English.

In natural languages, then, the phrase markers are the fundamental objects for which we aim to provide a theory of semantic values; their spelling provides an often contextually reliable, but in principle imperfect, guide to their identity.

The view that I have just expressed about grammatical structure seems to diverge from that in at least some of Davidson's writings. In 'Semantics for Natural Languages', he considers Chomsky's (1965) diagnosis of the differences between (3) and (4):

(3)   I expected John to leave.
(4)   I persuaded John to leave.

Davidson thinks that 'the contrast between [them] emerges dramatically the moment we start thinking in terms of constructing a theory of truth.' The reason, of course, is that the NP 'John' of (4), but not of (3), is in a referentially transparent position. But Davidson is doubtful whether Chomsky has shown any relevant difference of structure between them.

However, a structural difference may be proposed between (3) and (4), from which the referential transparency of the position of 'John' in (4) follows as a matter of course. Expressed in the vocabulary I will assume, (3) has a phrase marker whose VP consists of a verb, 'expected', in construction with an infinitival sentence, 'John to leave'; but in the VP of (4) the verb 'persuade' is in construction with *two* arguments, namely 'John', and a subjectless infinitival clause 'PRO to leave', where PRO is an 'empty category' necessarily anaphoric to 'John'. Thus 'persuade' is a three-place predicate, as you would expect just on the basis of being able to say 'I persuaded somebody of something', whereas 'expect' is a two-place predicate like 'believe', as again you would expect from the impossibility of 'I expected somebody of something.' But now the basis for the referential transparency of the position of 'John' in (4) follows: this word in fact occurs only as a matrix argument, and not within the infinitival clause at all. Hence, the native speaker's different judgements about (3) and (4) cease to be problematic; and of course the desiderata of a theory of truth are met as well.

Individual examples are individual examples, and morals cannot be drawn across the board on their basis. However, I think that the intertwining of syntactic and semantic assumptions, and in particular the capacity of syntactic theory to reduce the burden on semantics, has been underestimated, by Davidson in this case.

I return now to phrase markers and to the types of statements about values that I envisage as growing out of Davidson's program. The schema (2) depicted values as accruing to expressions relative only to assignments f. For natural languages, we must add a contextual parameter C, insofar as contexts are sufficiently clear objects to enter the theory; I will have nothing to say about this here. Moreover, I have urged, values should be thought of as attaching to phrase markers first, and to expressions only insofar as they are given by the phrase markers. But now I would like to suggest a further parameterization, namely that values attach to phrase markers B only as sub-phrase markers of phrase markers A, the possibility not being excluded that $A = B$. Thus I will introduce the five-place predicate

$$V(x,B,A,C,f)$$

to be read

> x is a value of the sub-phrase marker B of the phrase marker A in context C under assignment f

so that the statements about values are to be as shown in (5):

(5) $V(x,B,A,C,f) \longleftrightarrow F(x,B,A,C,f)$

where the right-hand side of (5) is to be free of semantic, but not necessarily of syntactic, terms.

The formalism suggested has an extra power, owing to its double use of phrase markers in the most basic clauses. I shall give two examples of constructions that seem to me to argue for this move. One of them occurs in simple, extensional (or nearly enough extensional) language, and the other in the contentious domain of the propositional attitudes.

In standard formalized languages, the value of a constituent does not depend upon what it is embedded in. For languages like this, the statement (6) holds which might be called an *indifference principle*:

(6) $V(x,B,A) \longleftrightarrow V(x,B,B)$

for all phrase markers A and B, such that B is a sub-phrase marker of A (and for all contexts, and assignments of values to variables). It seems to me that this principle does not hold for natural language. If so, then we shall require a basic predicate at least of the complexity that I have suggested.

My first example concerns the behavior of the subordinating conjunctions (as they were called in traditional grammar) 'if' and 'unless'. Elementary inferences involving these proceed very well when they are understood as truth-functional connectives, the material conditional and the non-exclusive 'or' respectively. Notoriously, the actual distribution of these words in English is a more complicated story than would be expressed by their basic syntax and truth-functional interpretation. The literature on their proper interpretation, most of it on the word 'if', is legion. But the puzzle that I wish to discuss is independent of the issues of most prominent concern in that literature, and it will be just as well to state it initially with the understanding that these classical terms of logical theory are truth-functional. The puzzle is this: the words 'if' and 'unless' seem to have different interpretations, depending on the quantificational context in which they are embedded. Consider 'unless', for example. Given (7):

(7)   John will succeed unless he goofs off.

where the role of 'unless' is pretty well represented by non-exclusive disjunction, we should expect that (8):

(8)   Every student will succeed unless he goofs off.

predicates of every student what (7) predicates of John. This expectation is fulfilled. But consider (9):

(9)   No student will succeed unless he goofs off.

(9) does not say that there is no student having the property alleged of John in (7); on the contrary, (9) for every student *x* ties the prospects for *x*'s success to *x*'s goofing off, where (7) on the other hand ties John's prospects for success to his not goofing off.

The subordinating conjunction 'unless' assimilates to 'or' as well in (7) as it does anywhere. So let us represent (7) by (10):

(10)   (John will succeed) $\lor$ (John goofs off).

(8) and (9), with quantification and anaphoric connections explicitly rendered, come out as (11) and (12), respectively:

(11)   [Every *x*: student(*x*)] [(*x* succeeds) unless (*x* goofs off)]
(12)   [No *x*: student(*x*)] [(*x* succeeds) unless (*x* goofs off)]

The truth-functional '$\lor$' can replace 'unless' in (11) as well as it can in (7); but the same replacement in (12) yields a sentence manifestly different in significance from (9). In fact, (9) seems to say that no student both succeeds and fails to goof off. So, still keeping within the truth-functional paradigm, we would paraphrase (11) by (13), but (12) by (14):

(13)   [Every *x*: student(*x*)] [(*x* succeeds) $\lor$ (*x* goofs off)]
(14)   [No *x*: student(*x*)] [(*x* succeeds) & $-$(*x* goofs off)]

The puzzle now is: why this odd behavior of 'unless'? And what characteristics of its linguistic environment trigger it?

The data just presented for 'unless' repeat themselves, *mutatis mutandis*, for the subordinating conjunction 'if', as follows. The conditional (15):

(15)   John will succeed if he works hard.

and the universal predication (16):

(16)   Every student will succeed if he works hard.

are alike in that (16) says of every student what (15) says of John. With 'if' as the material conditional '$\rightarrow$', (15) goes over into (17), and (16) into (18):

(17)   (John works hard) $\rightarrow$ (John will succeed)
(18)   [Every *x*: student(*x*)] [(*x* works hard) $\rightarrow$ (*x* will succeed)]

But for (19), this maneuver leads to the wrong result:

(19)   No student will succeed if he works hard.

The proper interpretation, on the contrary, is that there is no student x such that x's working hard is compatible with x's success. This interpretation, the proper one within the limits of a strictly truth-functional representation, is given in (20):

(20)   [No x: student(x)] [(x succeeds) & (x works hard)]

The pattern for conditionals, then, is the same as for 'unless', and the same puzzle arises.

For uniformity of notation, let us write conditionals with the subordinate clause, the antecedent, in its usual position to the right of the main clause. Letting '$q \leftarrow p$' be interchangeable with '$p \rightarrow q$', we can put (17) in the form (21), and replace (18) with (22):

(21)   (John will succeed) $\leftarrow$ (John works hard)
(22)   [Every x: student(x)] [(x will succeed) $\leftarrow$ (x works hard)]

The subordinating conjunction 'if' then alternates between '$\leftarrow$' and '&', and 'unless' alternates in the same environments between '$\lor$' and the hybrid '& –'. Such is the outline of the puzzle.

The solution to the puzzle, briefly, lies in the semantic difference between the determiners (quantifiers) 'every' and 'no'. Specifically, in the domain of 'every', and the other monotone-increasing quantifiers in the sense of Barwise and Cooper (1981), 'if' behaves like '$\leftarrow$' and 'unless' like '$\lor$'; but in the domain of monotone-decreasing quantifiers such as 'no', 'if' behaves like a conjunction, and 'unless' is interpreted by the hybrid shown in (14). The contrasts shown in (23) and (24) exemplify the generalization:

(23) (a)   Most students in this program succeed if they work hard.
    (b)   Few students in this program succeed if they goof off.
(24) (a)   At least three students in this program will fail unless they work hard.
    (b)   Few students in this program will fail unless they goof off.

It should be noted that the correlation is not perfect, as, e.g. 'at most three' counts, properly, as a monotone-decreasing quantifier licensing negative polarity items, but does not yield the hybrid 'unless' in a context like (18)(b); possibly, 'unless' is really sensitive to some further 'negative' feature of a quantifier, possessed only by a subset of the monotone-decreasing class. This circumstance does not alter the point to be made here, in my opinion, and I shall continue to speak throughout this discussion as though it were merely a matter of whether the quantifier is monotone-decreasing.

An adequate, if unilluminating, description of the facts can be had by simply positing an ambiguity: 'if' would be ambiguous between the material conditional and conjunction, and 'unless' between disjunction and the truth-functional connective with the truth-table for sentences 'p' and 'q' of 'p & $-q$'. The description, however, would simply label what we would like to explain. Now it turns out that the behavior of 'if' and 'unless' can be rationalized in such a way that these words may be said to have a core significance that is independent of their context.

The words 'if' and 'unless' can be said to be different ways of *hedging* a predicate; i.e., of producing one that, for an object a, has an a priori better chance of being true of a than does the original. Their hedges are different: the use of 'if' produces a predicate that is not false of a if the condition following it is false of a; the use of 'unless' produces a predicate that is not false of a if the condition following it is true of a. Their use in closed sentences follows along as a special case.

The truth-functional interpretations of 'if' and 'unless' both satisfy the general description just given: the predicate (25):

(25) $Q(x)$ '$\leftarrow$' $P(x)$

is not only false, but even true of a, when '$P(x)$' is false of a; and (26):

(26) $Q(x) \lor P(x)$

is likewise true of a when '$P(x)$' is true of a.

Not let the predicates (25) and (26) be within the scope of a monotone-increasing quantifier Z. Since Z is monotone-increasing, '$(Zx)\ F(x)$' is true whenever '$(Zx)\ G(x)$' is true and all Gs are Fs. Since '$Q(x)$' implies (25), (27) implies (28):

(27) $(Zx)\ Q(x)$
(28) $(Zx)\ [\ Q(x) \leftarrow P(x)\ ]$

Then in the context represented by Z, 'if' continues to serve its hedging function as interpreted by '$\leftarrow$'. Likewise, since the extension of (26) is at least as large as that of '$Q(x)$', (27) implies (29):

(29) $(Zx)\ [\ Q(x) \lor P(x)\ ]$

so that the function of 'unless' is properly served as well.

But if Z is monotone-decreasing, the situation alters. Hedging the predicate '$Q(x)$' within the scope of such a Z cannot mean producing a predicate that has a larger extension than '$Q(x)$'; on the contrary, since entailments now go in a direction opposite to the case last discussed, it may be expected that hedging will produce a predicate with a smaller extension than the original. And that is just what happens in the examples that we gave above. When Z is monotone-decreasing, then (27) implies, not (28) and (29) indeed, but (30) and (31):

(30) $(Zx)\ [\ Q(x)\ \&\ P(x)\ ]$
(31) $(Zx)\ [\ Q(x)\ \&\ -P(x)\ ]$

Our hypothesis is that the words 'if' and 'unless', chameleon-like, alter their logical behavior so as to satisfy the general condition that they create something that has a better chance of being true than the original.

The above account may be said to have shown how 'if' and 'unless' satisfy the demand that each have a core interpretation, whose sensitivity to the surrounding environment produces the phenomena given. I cannot, of course, claim to have shown that these words *must* behave in just the way described: for anything I have said, for instance, they could have switched places, so that 'if' within the scope of a monotone-decreasing quantifier behaved like 'unless', and 'unless' like 'if'. But the system as a whole is suggestive, and perhaps conceals a further pattern that is waiting to be discovered.[2]

The properties of 'if' and 'unless' illustrate how the indifference principle can be false: for their interpretation is not fixed within the clauses themselves, but depends upon phrasal features that are not found in their local environments. In his comments to this article as originally given at the Rutgers Conference, Professor Jeffrey Pelletier drew attention to the potential costs of abandoning the indifference principle, which he identified with a version of compositionality. With this judgement I think one must concur, insofar as the indifference principle ruled out a number of possibilities for the interaction of syntactic structure and conditions on interpretation, and therefore implied a more restrictive theory of the nature of human languages. Inversely, since the principle does appear to hold for a great variety of constructions, a good overall theory would be expected to set limits on the nature and scope of violations of it, a task I do not attempt to carry out here. I turn now to another and more complex application of semantics without the indifference principle.[3]

In treating the classical opaque constructions from the point of view toward syntactic objects that is taken here, we can implement a suggestion of Gilbert Harman's from several years back, that the objects of the attitudes, when singled out by 'that'-clauses, are, or are objects similar to, interpreted logical forms. In this respect, I think we can take advantage of the doubly relative predicate V in a useful way. Consider a simple example, such as 'John believes that Bill saw Mary', with the phrase marker (32):

---

[2] The area to be mapped here is not small. Richard Cartwright pointed out to me extensions to expressions like 'even if', which do not appear to contradict what is reported here. The analysis can also be extended to a non-truth-functional setting, such as that in Lewis (1973).

[3] Professor Pelletier at the Conference also offered an account of the data on subordinate conjunctions, that attempted to preserve the indifference principle. It appears to me that his alternative is not sufficiently general to cover non-standard generalized quantifiers, like 'few'; in any case, the discussion is too long and detailed to be set forth in this space.

(32)

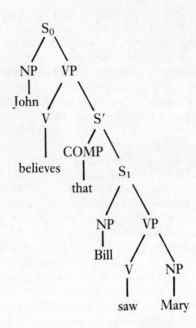

Suppose that the sub-phrase markers of S', including the phrase marker B with root S_1, have as sub-phrase markers of S' just the values that they would have were S_1 considered in isolation. The value of the subject NP 'Bill' is Bill in S_1, that of 'Mary' is Mary, that of 'saw' is each ordered pair $<z,w>$ such that z saw w, and, finally, the value of B is truth if Bill saw Mary, falsehood otherwise (where this last statement follows from general principles governing predicational sentences S = NP–VP). Suppressing as redundant reference to context and to assignments, and using '$<>$' for truth, we may express all this succinctly by (33):

(33) $V(y,S',S') \longleftrightarrow y = <>$ & Bill saw Mary

Now, S' is also the direct object of 'believe', a transitive verb. Its values, the values of the point V in (32), comprise those $<x,y>$ such that x believes y. The VP will therefore have as values those objects x such that x believes y for some y a value of S', where S' is now considered as a sub-phrase marker of S_0. Suppose (34):

(34) $V(y,S',S_0) \longleftrightarrow y$ is similar to B

Since the indifference principle has been abandoned, there is no conflict between (33) and (34). What has been said about the values of VPs, and of elementary predications, then suffices for (35):

(35) $V(<>,S_0,S_0) \longleftrightarrow (Ey)$ (y is similar to B & John believes y)

The last clause exhibits an implementation of Harman's suggestion: the objects of the attitudes, at least when indicated by clauses, are objects similar to the interpreted structures of the clauses themselves.[4] It is not difficult to 'quantify into' these contexts; I shall touch on this briefly below.

The type of view that I have just sketched borrows from Davidson's 'On Saying That' the notion 'similar to' a term of art that I use in imitation of Davidson's 'samesaying' relation. It differs, however, in supposing that the sentences of indirect discourse and the attitudes (to which I assume Davidson intends his view to apply) really do occur embedded as the objects of their verbs, as shown in (32). Davidson's 'paratactic' analysis is different. He suggested that the word 'that' be taken in its demonstrative role, its reference being supplied by the subsequent utterance. Indirect discourse and the attitudes make use of a 'concealed demonstrative construction', to quote the terms that he used in 'Truth and Meaning'.

One difficulty with Davidson's view, I think, is local and inessential, namely the idea that the 'that' of indirect discourse is a demonstrative. It was Jespersen who called sentence-introducers 'complementizers', among which must be reckoned the infinitival marker 'for ... to', the gerundive ' 's ... ing' of 'I regret John's leaving', and likely also the 'whether' and 'if' of so-called 'indirect questions'. These items cannot with any plausibility be called demonstratives. A more serious problem, however, is that, if it were true that indirect discourse and the like involved a concealed demonstrative construction, we should expect it to behave like an overt demonstrative construction, and this is conspicuously not the case. As Stephen Stich remarks, an attractive feature of Davidson's idea is that it makes the reporting of saying or belief by means of 'that'-clauses analogous to reporting them by the indicating of inscriptions. But just this feature also makes it dubious, since indications of inscriptions are sealed off from any interaction with linguistic elements in main clauses. Suppose I write on the blackboard (36), and, pointing to it, say (37):

(36)   He is a nice fellow.
(37)   Every boy believes that.

In my judgement, it is quite impossible to get this activity to convey that every boy has a good opinion of himself; but just this is one of the things I can surely convey by saying (38):

(38)   Every boy believes that he is a nice fellow.

There are innumerable similar examples, not all of them involving pronouns. For instance, if I say, 'I said yesterday that John was unhappy', I can be right on one interpretation, if what I said yesterday was 'John was unhappy' (past tense),

---

[4] I find 'arguments from translation' against this type of view indecisive, in view of the discussion in Burge (1978).

and on another if all I said was, 'John is unhappy' (present tense). But suppose I write (39):

(39)   John was unhappy.

and, pointing to it, say (40):

(40)   I said that yesterday.

Now, I think, I must have said 'John was unhappy' (past tense) if my present utterance is to count as true.

None of these judgements proves Davidson's view to be incorrect. It would be possible to maintain that concealed demonstrative constructions show one array of data, overt demonstratives another (even this would have to be reconciled with Davidson's view that quotation itself is a demonstrative construction). But they do, I think, make it doubtful.

Up to now, I have spoken of phrase markers in such a way that they might be taken as disambiguation devices, grouping constituents in a way that reflects their internal structure. I now wish to suggest a more radical departure, one that pays off, I believe, in the realm of quantification.

As Davidson has remarked, Frege's insights into the functioning of expressions of generality was a discovery of how a piece of our language worked, that stands as an exemplar for investigations into other areas. It has taken some time to see clearly that the quantifiers of natural language are best considered as one and all restricted; i.e., as building sentences from two expressions at a time. With this modest correction, however, Frege's original idea survives intact in most modern studies.

Some years back a number of investigators, especially those that grouped themselves around what was called 'generative semantics', proposed that generality was represented at an abstract level of structure, the interpretation of which was trivial as far as the role of quantifiers went, but which was distant in form from the surface constituent structure. This type of position was adopted by David Lewis in (1972). It has subsequently fallen from favor, and a number of persons are more inclined to favor more or less complex interpretive principles, applying to surface-like structures, over the abstract syntactic method. My view is that the early idea of the generative semanticists was correct, though not quite in the form that they assumed.

In brief outline, the proposal is as follows. Scope-bearing elements, including quantificational NPs, are one and all to be adjoined to appropriate syntactic positions; the products of scope-assignment are new phrase markers, and the linguistic level at which they are found is dubbed, following Chomsky (1976) 'LF', (read 'Logical Form'). Ordinary ambiguities of scope, on this conception, become a special case of sentential homonymy, like the ambiguity of 'Flying planes can be dangerous.' The sentence 'Some person saw Mary' has (41) for its phrase marker at this level:

(41)

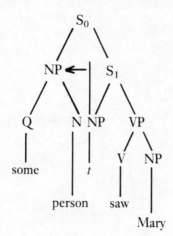

where *t* is an empty position, or 'trace', left behind by the adjunction, and the arrow indicates that it is anaphorically related to the quantifier 'some person'. Semantically, the trace functions as a variable (so an assignment for S_1 will assign a value to *t*). The relation → is taken to be part of the phrase marker, so that these are now structures $(P, <, L, \rightarrow)$, with → a relation on the points of P, interpreted as antecedence by the semantics.

It is possible to formulate general principles of interpretation that will prove the equivalence of the truth of (41) to 'Some person is such that that person saw Mary,' or (42) in the canonical idiom:

(42) [Some *x*: person(*x*)] saw(*x*, Mary)

(42) contains three occurrences of variables, whereas (41) need not be seen as containing any (the role of the trace *t* is recoverable from the relation →). The variables are formatives of the extension of English used in (42). I doubt that English itself contains any such things. Quine (1951) pointed out that the notation of bound variables could be dispensed with, in favor of other devices that would show which quantifiers linked up with which positions. The relation is an example of such a device.

If nominal quantifiers are to undergo assignment of scope, then so must other elements for which ambiguities of scope can be constructed. Adverbs of quantification, words like 'rarely' or 'never', for instance, will fit in here as quantifying over events. Assuming Davidson's view on action sentences, we will regard (43):

(43) John rarely walks.

as asserting the rarity of walks by John, against some contextual background, such as John's travels to work.

Quantification into the clausal arguments of verbs of propositional attitude yields a 'relational' construal of those verbs. The phrase marker of 'Ralph believes some person to be a spy' for which the expression 'some person' has wide scope is (44):

(44)

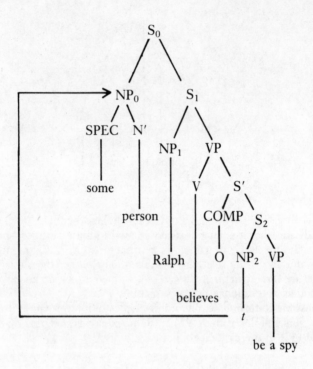

and if f is an assignment, then the value of the clausal argument is (45):

(45)

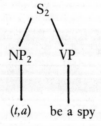

where $a = f(t)$.

The identity of (45) depends only on what f assigns to t; that is, only on a. So if (45)*(a) is the value of the clausal argument for each object a, we will be able to show (46):

(46)   (44) is true $\longleftrightarrow$ [some z: person(z)] (Ew) (w is similar to (45)*(z) & believes (Ralph,w))

There is much that needs elaboration, and filtering through the complexities of the language, if the view sketched here is to be defended in detail. But I do not see any insuperable difficulties at present. If the view is correct, then we can express the 'relationality' of belief without having to augment the adicity of that verb, a step that Stich is concerned about in (1983), and others have commented upon. The notion of similarity remains unexplicated, of course, but that does not seem to me an objection.

Davidson's preference, amounting to a 'bias for first-order extensional languages', as he calls it in his 'Reply to Foster', is well known. The departures that I have suggested so far do not seem to fall far outside that realm (though I have taken the step of using generalized quantifiers). Now, the most popular frameworks for semantics in linguistics in recent years have been higher-order, and non-extensional. I will raise some points about the former question, though not about extensionality.

The view that English is a higher-order language, perhaps involving a whole hierarchy of types, is an attractive one that has been argued for and also used in semantic analyses for some time. Certain plural sentences, and especially sentences with anaphoric properties such as those noticed by Lauri Carlson (1980) and George Boolos (1983) seem to show that, if English is not higher-order, then there is at any rate a rudimentary amount of something like set theory embedded in the most ordinary speech. But sets or pluralities, the denotations of phrases like 'the philosophers', will be other objects, references to which are made in the usual quantifiable places, so that decisive considerations seem unlikely to come from this direction. Of more significance are examples that seem to call for predicate variables; but even here, I think, the evidence must be assessed with caution.

In natural languages, it is overwhelmingly the case that quantifiers occur with nouns, so that quantificational expressions are NPs, which of course go where names go. Apart from WH-expressions, such as the 'how' of 'How good a lawyer is he?' we do not find quantifiers in construction with verbals or adjectivals. The possibility is open, then, that second-order schemata such as '(EF) $F(a)$' do not have instances in natural languages. The possibility is no insult to second-order logic; but if it does obtain, it would mean that second-order languages are launched from a conception that is not exemplified in the most basic parts of language.

A number of arguments in support of the second-order conception have to be answered. There is, first of all, the case of predicate nominals, as in 'Socrates was something that Plato was not.' Still more significant, in my view, is the observation, due to Edwin Williams (1982), that the restrictions on quantification in predicate-nominal position are sensitive to whether quantification is over ordinary NP positions, or over verbal or adjectival positions. Thus I cannot say (47):

(47)   John is every lawyer in Pittsburgh.

even if, in fact, John is the only lawyer in Pittsburgh. But one can perfectly well say (48):

(48)   John is everything we wanted him to be.

where the quantification (note: still through NPs) is over a position occupiable by adjectives. Perhaps an account of quantification over something like properties is wanted for these cases.

As a final example, I will consider an argument due to Chierchia (1984), which he brings against Bealer's (1982) suggestions in favor of a first-order account of quantification, but with properties in the domain. As will be seen, I think that Chierchia can be answered on the basis of Davidson's analysis of action sentences. Chierchia considers the argument (49):

(49)   John does anything that Bill does.
        Bill jogs.
        ―――――――――――――――――――――
        John jogs.

He takes this argument to be a valid one, and points out that if the quantification in the first premise is taken in a second-order way, then it can be construed as an instance of a valid second-order argument schema, namely (50):

(50) $(AP) \ P(b) \rightarrow P(j)$
        $J(b)$
        ――――――――
        $J(j)$

But Chierchia remarks, Bealer's system would at least require a premise connecting the having of the property of jogging with jogging, perhaps using the latter's special predicate Δ for 'has' or 'instantiates'. The argument might then be rendered as in (51):

(51) $(Ax) \ b \ \Delta \ x \ \rightarrow j \ \Delta \ x$
        $J(b)$
        $(Ax) \ J(x) \longleftrightarrow x \ \Delta$ [the property of jogging] (unstated)
        ―――
        $J(j)$

Furthermore, Chierchia raises questions about how Bealer's type of account could be integrated with VP-deletion, as in 'John jogs, but Bill doesn't.'

These issues do not seem to me of consequence, since the verb 'do' of the last example is the auxiliary 'do' (as is shown by the impossibility of 'John jogs, but Bill doesn't do'). However, the verbs 'do' of the first premise of (49) are both main verbs, as is shown by the possibility of any and all options in (52):

(52)   John does (do) anything Bill does(n't) do.

There remains, however, the necessarily enthymematic nature of the argument (49), according to first-order accounts.

I think that Chierchia's considerations are answerable if we take a leaf from Davidson's views on action sentences. The logical form of the second premise of (49), on that view, would be (53):

(53)   (*Ex*) jog(*b*,*x*)

roughly 'There is a jogging by Bill.' In some of the later papers in the collection (1980), although not in the original 1966 paper, Davidson takes the natural step of decomposing predications like 'jog(*b*,*x*)' into two parts, one of which indicates the type of event, while the other expresses the relation of the object mentioned to that event – agency, in this case. Thus (53) might be decomposed as (54):

(54)   (*Ex*) jog'(*x*) & Agent(*b*,*x*)

Suppose now that the main verb 'do' simply expresses agency. The sense of the first premise of (49) would not of course be adequately rendered by (55):

(55)   (*Ax*) do(*b*,*x*) → do(*j*,*x*)

In fact, (55) is going to be false; John was not the agent of Bill's jogging. Still, I think that we are on the right track. Why is it to be supposed that (49) is in fact valid? We do not infer from the first premise, together with 'Bill scratched his arm', that John scratched Bill's arm. In fact, what the first premise asserts is that, for everything that Bill did, John did something *like that*. So that premise becomes, in effect, (56):

(56)   (*Ax*) do(*b*,*x*) → (*Ey*) (*y* is similar to *x* & do(*j*,*y*))

Now if Bill jogged, then there was an event, namely his jogging, of which he was the agent; i.e., which he did. So, by (56), there was a similar event done by John; and insofar as only joggings are similar to joggings, (57) follows:

(57)   (*Ex*) jog'(*x*) & Agent(*j*,*x*)

But (57) is just the logical form of the conclusion of (49).

If my response to Chierchia is correct, then we do not need second-order schemata, or even first-order quantification over properties, to get the facts to follow. Naturally, a host of issues remains; Chierchia, for example, raises many other interesting problems.

In summary, I have presented a view about the organization of syntax and semantics that is rather spare in its conception of semantic values, but pretty complicated syntactically. I am all too aware of many of the points that have not been considered here at all. In concluding, I should like to return to my theme, that syntactic and metaphysical conceptions have a joint role to play in the articulation of semantic theory.

Certain of the writings of Quine give a picture of syntax, or the enterprise of 'the grammarian', as Quine calls him, as entirely disinterpreted, except insofar as its recursive demarcation of well-formed strings is tested against the behavior of the persons whose syntax is in question.[5] This view doesn't fit linguistic practice well, and also fails to reflect the links between syntax and semantics that we see even in self-consciously constructed languages, where the syntax is chosen in such a way that the semantics can run in tandem with its inductive definition. One point to which I would call attention with respect to natural languages is that it would be a definite mistake to confine the domain of objects receiving interpretation to those that are well formed according to the syntax. I am not speaking of ellipses, such as an utterance of 'John' meaning, 'It is John that I expect to succeed where others have failed', or of other cases that arise in connected discourse, but rather of expressions that have definite interpretations, or ranges of definite interpretations, although they are of doubtful grammatical status, or even ungrammatical. Davidson himself gave an example of such a sentence, namely (58):

(58)   The child seems sleeping.

remarking that the usual biconditional disquotational statement of its truth-conditions goes through despite its doubtful status as an English sentence. I think that this observation should be extended. (58) is understood by me, and by others, in the same way as 'The child seems to be sleeping'; grammar somehow prevents the gerund 'sleeping' from being used as the adjective is in the well-formed sentence, 'The child seems sleepy.' It follows that any account of my language that fails to give (58) the same interpretation as 'The child seems as though it is sleeping' would be wrong. There are many similar examples. As David Dowty (1979) has pointed out in connection with questions of the interpretation of words, there are a number of semi-productive morphological processes that endow non-words with interpretations grasped at once by the native speaker: 'uglify', for example. The same lesson applies in the more productive realm of syntax. But if this is so, then the proper relation between syntax and semantics cannot be that semantics comes in to figure out the interpretation of just those strings in the class of well-formed ones according to the grammarian. For the same reason also, we should not rest content with grammars for parts of English, that give no hint as to how they are to be extended to expressions that fall just outside the perfectly well-formed class.

It seems often to have been assumed that the relation between syntax and semantics is: syntax tells you what the sentences of a language *are*, and semantics only then comes along to tell you what these sentences *mean*. This view cannot be entirely right, inasmuch as there are expressions that have sentential interpretations, as determined by the rules of grammar, but are not well-formed sentences. However, I am inclined to think that it is more seriously wrong than that: simple ambiguities show that principles of form and principles

---

[5] See Quine (1969) and (1970).

of interpretation are to be articulated together, and not in theoretical isolation; and explanations of semantic facts obviously require both syntactic and semantic premises. Davidson's program, as I understand it, stresses this intertwining of considerations on form and meaning.

In this note, I have indicated some points where I believe that Davidson's program, of clarifying our grasp of language by uncovering the combinatorial principles that govern conditions on truth and reference, can be advanced within a linguistic theory that takes phrase markers at one or more linguistic levels as its fundamental objects, or logical forms. The relativization of the values of these objects to their larger environments, in other words the abandonment of what I called the indifference principle, seems to me a useful step in bringing a number of contexts under control. Furthermore, I think that the positing of an abstract syntactic level of logical form is a benefit.

Semantic accounts such as Davidson's, that do not multiply values, must be long on analysis; the rather abstract syntax that I have sketched here is a case in point. However, in several places in this essay, I have argued that Davidson's views gather strength from a close attention to the role of theoretical syntax in elaboration of the semantic theory, and I have offered some examples in support of this thesis. Whatever be the fate of these suggestions, I, like so many others, am indebted to Davidson for showing where there is concrete work to be done.

References

Barwise, Jon, and Robin Cooper (1981): 'Generalized Quantifiers and Natural Language'. *Linguistics and Philosophy*, 4 (2), 159–219.

Bealer, George (1982): *Quality and Concept*. New York: Oxford University Press.

Boolos, George (1983): 'To be is to be a Value of a Variable (or to be Some Values of Some Variables)'. MS, Massachusetts Institute of Technology.

Burge, Tyler (1978): 'Self-Reference and Translation'. In F. Guenthner and Geunthner-Ratner (eds), *Meaning and Translation*, New York: NYU Press, 137–53.

Carlson, Lauri (1980): Plural Quantification. MS, MIT.

Chierchia, Gennaro (1984): Topics in the Syntax and Semantics of Infinitives and Gerunds. Ph.D. Dissertation, University of Massachusetts.

Chomsky, Noam (1955): *The Logical Structure of Linguistic Theory*. Reprinted with emendations and an introduction, 1975. New York: Plenum Press.

(1965): *Aspects of the Theory of Syntax*. Cambridge, Massachusetts: MIT Press.

(1976): 'Conditions on Rules of Grammar'. *Linguistic Analysis*, 2 (4), 303–51.

Davidson, Donald (1980): *Essays on Actions and Events*. New York: Oxford University Press.

(1984): *Inquiries into Truth and Interpretation*. New York: Oxford University Press.

Dowty, David (1979): *Word Meaning and Montague Grammar*. Dordrecht, Holland: D. Reidel.

Harman, Gilbert (1972): 'Deep Structure as Logical Form'. In D. Davidson and G. Harman (eds), *Semantics of Natural Language*, Dordrecht, Holland: D. Reidel, 25–47.

Lewis, David (1972): 'General Semantics'. In D. Davidson and G. Harman (eds), *Semantics of Natural Language*, Dordrecht, Holland: D. Reidel, 169–218.

(1973): *Counterfactuals*. Cambridge, Massachusetts: Harvard University Press.

May, Robert (1977): *The Grammar of Quantification*. Unpublished doctoral dissertation, MIT.

Quine, W. V. (1951): *Mathematical Logic*. Revised edition. New York: Harper Torchbooks.

    (1969): 'Reply to Geach'. In D. Davidson and J. Hintikka (eds), *Words and Objections: Essays on the Work of W. V. Quine*, Dordrecht, Holland: D. Reidel, 328–32.

    (1970): *Philosophy of Logic*. Englewood Cliffs, New Jersey: Prentice-Hall.

Stich, Stephen P. (1983): *From Folk Psychology to Cognitive Science: The Case Against Belief*. Cambridge, Massachusetts: Bradford Books, MIT Press.

Williams, Edwin (1982): 'Semantic vs Syntactic Categories'. *Linguistics and Philosophy*, 6 (3), 423–46.

3

Learnability of Semantic Theory

ROBERT J. MATTHEWS

1 *Introduction*

It is of no small significance for a theory of natural language that natural languages are learned, since any such theory will be adequate only if it explains (or is at least consistent with) this fact. Not surprisingly, many philosophers have made claims concerning the properties that a language must have if it is to be, even in principle, learnable. Davidson's own learnability proposal is to be found in his paper 'Theories of Meaning and Learnable Languages' (1965), where he argues that it is a necessary feature of a learnable language that 'it must be possible to give a constructive account of the meaning of the sentences in the language' (p. 3),[1] that 'a learnable language has a finite number of semantical primitives' (p. 9). Davidson takes it to be a virtue of the truth-conditional semantics that he advocates that natural languages would possess this feature. Charles Chihara (1975), Robin Haack (1978), and others have criticized Davidson's learnability condition as being too strong. It is, they argue, an empirical fact that languages that fail to meet his condition are learned and are therefore learnable. In a recent paper, LePore (1982) has attempted to turn these criticisms by denying that Davidson is in fact concerned with learnability considerations; he argues that Davidson's 'learnability condition' is justified on what in effect are independent epistemological grounds; thus, these criticisms are beside the point.

Davidson's attempt to levy learnability conditions on semantic theory is well motivated; there is good reason to require that the semantics of a natural language be learnable. Yet the particular condition that Davidson endorses is not defensible, though not for the sorts of reasons that Haack, Chihara, and others adduce. The problem in a nutshell is that there is no reason to believe that recursive enumerability is a relevant feature of learnable languages, even if it does turn out to be relevant to the semantic productivity characteristic of natural languages. The structure of my remarks is this: I shall begin with a brief exposition of Davidson's learnability claims and the criticisms that have been raised against them. I then turn to the reason for requiring that the semantics of a natural language be learnable. Finally, I consider whether any specific

---

[1] References are to the version of this paper reprinted in Davidson's *Inquiries into Truth and Interpretation* (Clarendon Press, Oxford, 1984).

constraints of the sort that Davidson has in mind follow from this learnability requirement on the semantics of natural language.

2 *Davidson on learnable languages*

In his 'Theories of Meaning and Learnable Languages' (1965) Davidson expresses serious doubt that a priori considerations can suffice to determine the features of the *mechanisms*, or the stages, of language learning. But he nevertheless believes that we can say something about the properties a *language* must have if it is to be, even in principle, learnable:

> In contrast to shaky hunches about how we learn language, I propose what seems to me clearly to be a necessary feature of a learnable language: it must be possible to give a constructive account of the meaning of the sentences in the language. Such an account I call a theory of meaning for a language, and I suggest that a theory of meaning that conflicts with this condition, whether put forward by philosopher, linguist, or psychologist, that conflicts with this condition cannot be a theory of language. (1965, p. 3)

Davidson, it should be noted, draws a sharp distinction between speculations concerning the mechanism and sequence of language acquisition, on the one hand, and conditions on the languages acquired, on the other. Only the latter, he believes, are the legitimate subject for a priori consideration. Again, Davidson:

> It is not appropriate to expect logical considerations to dictate the route or mechanism of language acquisition, but we are entitled to consider in advance of empirical study what we shall count as knowing a language, how we shall describe the skill or ability of a person who has learned to speak a language. ... we must be able to specify, in a way that depends effectively and solely on formal considerations, what every sentence means. ...
>   These matters appear to be connected in the following, informal way with the possibility of learning a language. When we can regard the meaning of each sentence as a function of a finite number of features of the sentence, we have an insight not only into what there is to be learned; we also understand how an infinite aptitude can be encompassed by finite accomplishments. Suppose on the other hand the language lacks this feature; then no matter how many sentences a would-be speaker learns to produce and understand, there will remain others whose meanings are not given by the rules already mastered. It is natural to say such a language is *unlearnable*. (1965, pp. 7–8)

The idea here is clear: a language is *learnable* only if there is some finite piece of knowledge the acquisition of which would enable a speaker of that language to assign the appropriate meanings (truth-conditions) to the infinite number of sentences that constitute that language. Davidson contends that many recent theories of meaning are not, even in principle, applicable to natural languages, since the languages to which they apply are not learnable in the sense described above. These theories attribute to language a non-finite number of semantical primitives, and this, Davidson argues, is incompatible with the assumption of finitary knowledge.

3 *Criticisms of Davidson's learnability condition*

Chihara and Haack have separately criticized Davidson's assumption that a learnable language must have a (partially) recursive semantics. In both cases the criticism rests on the claim that non-recursive systems are in fact learned and hence are learnable. Chihara asks, 'how could one justify the claim that only finitely axiomatizable systems are learnable? Neither Peano arithmetic nor Zermelo-Frankel set theory is finitely axiomatizable; yet humans are able to learn these systems' (1975, p. 4). Haack argues that 'there is no necessary connection between finiteness and recursion on the one hand and learnability on the other, because there are many mathematical theories which are not finitely axiomatizable but which are learnable' (1978, p. 237). Against Davidson's more specific claim that a learnable language can have only a finite number of semantical primitives, Haack points out that

> it is an empirical fact that methods of truth utilizing (1) are learnable, and that such methods
> (1)   a sequence s of objects satisfies $F^n(t_k,...,t_n)$ iff the interpretation assigns $s_k,..., s_n$ to F.
> apply whether or not there is a denumerable set of predicates, and, assuming a distinct meaning to a distinct predicate, a denumerable set of meanings in the language, so that Davidson's contention that an infinite set of words meanings would impugn the learnability of language is mistaken. (1978, p. 236)

LePore's response to these criticisms is to deny that the justification of Davidson's 'learnability condition' rests on learnability considerations at all. For LePore the justification is epistemological: he argues that Davidson's requirement that a semantic theory be finitely axiomatizable is motivated by the requirement that one be able to specify explicitly the semantic knowledge that enables a speaker to understand the sentences that constitute his language. LePore further denies that Davidson holds that an adequate semantics for a natural language must be recursive. He concedes that Davidson's account of what a speaker knows utilizes a theory which in fact includes recursion clauses, but this, LePore argues, is a convenience and not a requirement: 'If he could find a way of stating [this knowledge] which for some reason did not make use of a recursive theory, that would be perfectly acceptable' (1982, p. 283).

Perhaps Davidson's learnability condition can be justified on other grounds; however, the fact remains that such grounds are not Davidson's, at least not in the paper that Chihara and Haack criticize. In that paper Davidson *is* concerned with the constraints imposed by learnability considerations on a semantic theory for natural language. LePore is correct in his claim that Davidson is not concerned with the psychological question of *how* semantic knowledge is acquired, used, stored, or represented, but this is fully compatible with a concern with constraints on *what* must be known if a language is to be learnable.

LePore, to my mind, goes to unnecessary lengths to defend Davidson from Chihara's and Haack's criticisms. It is certainly true that many systems that are not finitely axiomatizable are nonetheless learned. But this hardly tells against Davidson's claim, since there is little reason to suppose that these systems are learnable under conditions of access to data relevantly similar to those under which natural languages are learned. The point here is this: learnability constraints of the sort that Davidson proposes are intended as necessary features of languages that are learnable *under the given conditions of access to data*; they are not intended to preclude the possibility that languages failing to satisfy these constraints might be learnable, or indeed learned, under different conditions of access to data. Davidson surely intends his learnability condition to be understood in just this way, for in the lengthy passage quoted above, he suggests that our 'infinite aptitude' for assigning meanings to sentences in our language is based on our understanding of the meaning of a finite number of sentences. The suggestion is that we learn the semantics of a language by inducing a semantic theory for that language from this finite number of sentences which constitutes the data for the learning task. Certainly this is *not* the way that we learn Zermelo-Frankel set theory or Peano arithmetic; rather we are taught these systems explicitly.

4 *Learnability and compositionality*

In a recent paper, 'Theories of Truth and Learnable Languages' (1980), Jaako Hintikka offers a different criticism of Davidson's learnability condition, which he construes as requiring that learnable languages satisfy a Fregean principle of compositionality, namely, that the meaning (truth-conditions) of a complex expression is a function of the meanings (truth-conditions) of the expression's constituent parts. Hintikka argues that learnability alone does not entail compositionality, and moreover that compositionality fails in natural languages in a wide variety of ways.

It may well be true that learnability alone does not entail compositionality; however, there is little evidence that Davidson thinks it does. Davidson, it will be recalled, argues that it must be possible to give a constructive account of the meaning of sentences in a learnable language: the meaning of each sentence, he argues, must be a function of a finite number of features of the sentence, features which Davidson calls the semantical primitives. But a language could possess this property yet nonetheless fail to satisfy the principle of compositionality inasmuch as nothing requires that the semantical primitives be constituents (parts) of the sentence in any well-defined formal sense of that term. That is to say, nothing in Davidson's argument presumes what Hintikka dubs the *parallelism thesis*, namely, that 'to each syntactical rule of formation, telling us how a complex expression E is constructed from simpler ones ... there corresponds ... a semantical rule which tells how the meaning of E depends on the meanings of those of simple input expressions' (1980, pp. 40–1). Davidson does require that the meaning of each sentence can be established on formal grounds alone, but this does not, as Hintikka suggests (p. 42), constitute a commitment to parallelism. Nor does Davidson's argument seem committed to yet a second assumption that Hintikka takes to be entailed by the principle of compositionality, namely, the assumption that Hintikka dubs the *invariance thesis*, which states that when E is formed from certain simpler expressions [...], these very expressions will become *parts* (constituent express-ions) of E.

Although Davidson has not provided a learnability argument for composi-tionality, nor does it seem that he intended to do so, it is clear that a semantic theory that entailed compositionality, as Davidson's presumably does, would satisfy the learnability condition that Davidson defends. Davidson is explicit on this point: 'I do not mean to argue here that it is necessary that we be able to extract a [Tarski-style] truth definition from an adequate theory ... but a theory certainly meets the condition I have in mind if we can extract a truth definition' (1965; p.8).

So to summarize our progress thus far, it appears as if Davidson's learnability condition survives the criticisms of Chihara, Haack and Hintikka, even in the absence of the epistemologizing defense offered by LePore. Before developing my own criticism of Davidson's condition, I would like to explain why it is appropriate to impose a learnability constraint on a semantic theory for natural language, even if one's interest in semantic theory is purely epistemological.

5 *Why require that a natural language be learnable?*

The principal task of a theory of language is to state the knowledge that speakers have in virtue of which they are able to understand their language. Following Davidson (cf. 1974, p. 309; 1973, p. 313), we might put the matter more precisely as follows: for any language L, an adequate linguistic theory of L will provide us with a statement T such that a person understands L just in case he knows that T. So construed it is not sufficient simply that the theory provide us with some T such that if a speaker were to know that T then he would understand L. The requirement is rather that the theory provide a specification of what a speaker of L *actually* knows. Such a specification requires that T be learnable (more specifically, learnable by normal speakers under normal conditions of access to data), for otherwise one could hardly claim that T is what a speaker of L actually knows.

It should be clear that the rationale for imposing a learnability constraint on linguistic theory stems not from any particular interest in empirical psychology but from the presumption that an adequate theory will provide a specification of a speaker's linguistic knowledge: if T purports to be what a speaker knows, then to the extent that what a speaker knows is learned, T should be learnable. Of course, the presumption that an adequate theory will provide a specification of what a speaker actually knows effectively 'empiricizes' what might otherwise be an a priori theory, for specific proposals will be shaped by empirical assump-tions about what normal speakers can learn under the normal conditions of access to data, and these assumptions will in turn be shaped by further empirical assumptions about how speakers learn what they learn. Davidson is clear on this point: he speaks of the argument for his learnability condition as depending on a number of empirical assumptions.

Given this dependence on empirical assumptions, it is, to be sure, an open question whether an adequate theory can be approximated in the absence of a developed empirical psycholinguistics. Davidson, like Chomsky, presumes that it can, at least it can if we levy some plausible learnability constraints on the theory. The presumption, in other words, is that plausible learnability constraints on T, in conjunction with the usual constraints of descriptive adequacy, will so constrain the theory as to insure that a theory meeting such constraints will be a good approximation to the correct theory. This may seem a very thin straw upon which to float a philosophical program of the magnitude of Davidson's, but what is the alternative? One can hardly abandon the underlying presumption that an adequate theory will specify a speaker's knowledge of his language and still preserve the epistemological import of the theory. For suppose that one required only that the theory specify some statement T such that if the speaker were to know that T then he would understand L. Such a theory would be of little epistemological interest, for one would have effectively abandoned the project so central to Davidson's program of specifying the *linguistic* knowledge that enables us justifiably to acquire certain beliefs upon hearing certain utterances in our language. More specifically, we would have abandoned the project of specifying for any sentence of a speaker's language what it is that speaker knows about that particular sentence which justifies the speaker in believing what is asserted by someone uttering the sentence. One would in effect have abandoned any pretense to draw a principled distinction between knowledge of language and knowledge of the world.

6 *Learnability constraints on semantic theory*

If, as I have argued, there is good reason to require that the linguistic knowledge imputed to speakers be learnable, then for any language L the theory should provide us with a statement T such that a person understands L just in case he knows that T, where T can be learned (acquired) by a normal learner on the basis of the normal conditions of access to data. We can formulate this rather vague requirement more precisely as follows: assume, as seems reasonable, that the acquired knowledge of a language L_i and the data on the basis of which this knowledge is acquired can be characterized formally in terms of a knowledge-sentence T_j and data sequence D_k, respectively. Assume further that the notion of a normal learner can be explicated in terms of a class of functions F that the normal learner can compute. Then the learnability requirement (LR) on a theory of language can be stated precisely as follows:

(LR) the theory associates with every natural language L_i a knowledge-sentence T_j such that for every T_j and every D_k such that T_j can in fact be acquired on the basis of D_k, there must be a function f on the natural numbers, from indices of data sets to indices of knowledge-sentences, such that $f \in F$ and $j \in f(k)$.

If we wanted (LR) to reflect the presumed fact that speakers of L_i need not share precisely the same knowledge-sentence in order to count as speakers of that language, then we could modify (LR) to require only that the learning function $f \in F$ map the indices of data sets into sets of indices of knowledge-sentences that bear the appropriate relation to one another. But let us forgo this nicety here and focus instead on general features of the proposed reformulation of the learnability requirement.

(LR), it should be noted, makes no assumptions about the relation between a natural language L_i and the knowledge-sentence T_j that the linguistic theory associates with L_i; in particular, it is not assumed that T_j is a finite axiomatization of L_i, even though such an assumption would be consistent with (LR). Nor does (LR) assume that T_j is induced from the data sequence D_k drawn from L_i, though again such an assumption would be consistent with (LR). Neutrality with respect to these assumptions leaves open the relation of the knowledge-sentence T_j to both acquisition data sequence D_k and to the acquired language L_i. This is as it should be. It is presumably an open empirical question just how T_j relates to both D_k and L_i. How these relate presumably depends on the nature of the learning process. Neutrality with respect to these two assumptions insures that (LR) is compatible with both inductive and so-called triggering models of language acquisition; it also insures compatibility with the possibility, argued by Chomsky in recent papers, that the notion of a language is not theoretically well defined.[2]

(LR)'s neutrality with respect to the first assumption bears special emphasis. In 'Theories of Meaning and Learnable Languages' Davidson suggests that it is a requirement on *learnable* languages that speakers be able to pair arbitrary sentences of their language with their meanings (or truth-conditions). This ability, Davidson assumes, requires that T_j provide a finite axiomatization of L_i. It may well be correct that the ability to pair arbitrary sentences of their language with their meanings can be explained only on the assumption that T_j provides a finite axiomatization of L_i; however, it is not obvious that this is a *learnability* requirement on T_j, as can be seen from the fact that the presumed ability of speakers to pair arbitrary sentences with their meanings would be no less necessary to an account of language understanding if natural languages were innate rather than learned.

In point of fact, (LR) does not entail any specific constraints of the sort that Davidson proposes; in particular, it does not entail that the knowledge-sentence T_j which the semantic theory associates with L_i provides a finite axiomatization of L_i. Consider, for example, a learnability model that captures the widely held assumption that language learning is a matter of hypothesis-testing, where the learner makes a conjecture about the identity of the language to be acquired and then tests that conjecture against an ever-growing sample drawn from that language. On this model, a natural language is construed as a set of ordered pairs $<s_i,\ m_j>$ consisting of sentences paired with their meanings (or truth-conditions) represented in some suitably formal fashion. The data on the basis of which a natural language is learned is taken to consist of a sequence of pairs drawn arbitrarily from the language to be acquired. The learning process is modelled as follows: time is divided into discrete trials. At each trial t, a new datum is added to the learner's sample, and the learner then conjectures a name for the language from which resulting sample is drawn. A class of languages is

---

[2] Chomsky (1981, ch. 1); Chomsky (forthcoming, ch. 2). Also Lightfoot (1984, ch. 2).

considered learnable (in the limit) with respect to a specified type of data if there is an algorithm that the learner could use to make a guess at every trial *t* as to the language of the class from which the sample is drawn, where the algorithm has the following property: given any language of the class, there is some finite time after which the guesses will all be the same and will furthermore be correct. Put another way, the algorithm must after some finite time converge on a name for the language from which the sample is drawn.

On this model, the formal properties of which were first investigated by Gold (1957), a class of languages will be learnable only if there is an effective procedure for determining that a conjectured name fails to name the language from which the sample is drawn, either because the conjectured language fails to include at least one sentence which is a member of the language from which the sample is drawn, or because it includes at least one sentence which is not a member of that language. This obviously requires that the languages that are learnable on this model be decidable, and hence that they be finitely axiomatizable. But nothing requires that what the learner acquires in acquiring a language, viz., a name of the language, is a finite axiomatization of the language named. Consider, for example, the class of languages consisting of two finite-cardinality languages, 'L_α' and '$L_{\sim\alpha}$', that differ only in that one contains α, while the other does not. On the learnability model under consideration, the learnability of this class does not require that the names 'L_α' and '$L_{\sim\alpha}$' be finite axiomatizations of the respective languages that they name, even though L_α and $L_{\sim\alpha}$ must be, and obviously are, finitely axiomatizable. This example brings out an important point overlooked by Davidson's critics, namely, that his learnability condition requires not simply that learnable languages be finitely axiomatizable, but also that what is acquired in acquiring a language, what I have been calling a knowledge-sentence, be a finite axiomatization of the acquired language. The point is important because it shows that even if learnability considerations were to require that natural languages be finitely axiomatizable, it does not follow that such considerations therefore require that a speaker's linguistic knowledge provide a finite axiomatization of his language. The presumption that it will stems rather from the very reasonable requirement that if language acquisition is to be construed as a matter of acquiring certain knowledge, then the knowledge acquired must in some clear sense of the expression be *knowledge of the language acquired*. The presumption that the knowledge acquired is a finite axiomatization of the language acquired satisfies this requirement in a very transparent fashion. Mere knowledge of a name for the language would surely not do, for such knowledge would not qualify as knowledge of a language. I know the names of many languages, but have nothing even remotely approximating a knowledge of those languages; I can perform none of the linguistic feats that those who know these languages perform with ease.

The point, then, that I wish to make here about the presumption that the knowledge acquired is a finite axiomatization of the language acquired is this: it is a particularly transparent way of satisfying the requirement that what is acquired is knowledge *of a language*. But it is not obviously the only way of satisfying the requirement; and more importantly, the requirement that it satisfies is not a learnability requirement at all, but rather a requirement that we have a robust notion of linguistic knowledge. That this is not a learnability requirement can be seen once again in the fact that this requirement on characterizations of linguistic knowledge would be no less appropriate in the event that all natural languages were innate.

The foregoing argument is open to the following objection: it may be true that there exists an effective procedure by which a learner could learn (or acquire) a name of a language without that name's providing a finite axiomatization of that language. It may also be true that Davidson's learnability condition is motivated by non-learnability considerations, viz., by the need to be able to explain in what sense the acquisition of this name constitutes the acquisition of linguistic knowledge. But these two points, taken separately or together, do not establish that the learnability of *natural* language does not require the acquisition of a finite axiomatization of the language acquired. Perhaps as a matter of empirical fact the learnability of natural language does require such an acquisition, even if knowledge of a finite axiomatization of a speaker's language is required on independent grounds of the sort that you adduce.

The objection is well taken: I have not shown that what is acquired in acquiring a natural language need not as a matter of empirical fact be a finite axiomatization of that language; at best I have shown that Davidson has provided no learnability considerations for thinking that it does. But the point that I would wish to emphasize here is this: given what we know about language acquisition (and admittedly this is very little), there is no reason to suppose that learnability considerations require as a matter of empirical fact that what is acquired is a finite axiomatization of the language acquired. Current linguistic theory provides no grounds for supposing that empirical accounts of natural language acquisition must assume that what is acquired in acquiring a natural language is a finite axiomatization of the language acquired. Chomsky's Revised Extended Standard Theory, for example, assumes that language acquisition is a matter of *parameter-fixing*. The idea is this: the grammars for natural languages can vary only in finitely many ways with respect to finitely many parameters (i.e., there are only a finite number of parameters, and each parameter can take only a finite number of values). To specify values for each of these parameters is to specify a grammar for a natural language. Learners are presumed to know innately this fact about natural languages; in particular, they are presumed to come to the learning task with something like an innate grammar-schema whose parameter values will be fixed in the course of the learning process. Parameter-fixing is assumed to be a matter of triggering rather than inductive inference. That is to say, learners do not induce the parameter values from primary data; rather these data simply trigger a particular value for each parameter. (The point here, I take it, is that learning is a causal process, somewhat like imprinting, that cannot be reconstrued as a form of inductive inference.) The grammar that is determined by this parameter-fixing is not held to provide a finite axiomatization of the language acquired; indeed, the notion of a language, construed as a set of ordered pairs of sound and meaning, is said not to be theoretically well defined, inasmuch as this pairing is a function not just of the grammar for that language but also of various features of the speaker's non-linguistic conceptual system. So that far from the grammar's providing a finite axiomatization of the language acquired, there is not even assumed to be a function from grammars onto languages. Whether there is any truth to all of this is irrelevant, the point is simply that current linguistic theory provides no support for a learnability condition of the sort that Davidson proposes.

7 *Conclusion*

The conclusion that I draw from the foregoing is this: Given how little we know about the acquisition of semantics, both about the data on the basis of which the semantics is acquired as well as about what is acquired, it would be *very surprising* if we were able to justify a learnability condition of the sort that Davidson proposes. For if the condition does not follow directly from (LR), which it does not, then it must follow from (LR) in conjunction with certain empirical facts about the acquisition of semantics for natural language. But what is presently known about these matters does not suffice to justify a learnability condition of the sort that Davidson proposes. The simple fact is that we are not now in a position to say whether learnability conditions on natural language dictate that what one acquires in acquiring a language is a finite axiomatization of that language. Whether learnability considerations levy such a requirement is a matter for empirical research.

References

Chihara, C. (1975): 'Davidson's Extensional Theory of Meaning'. *Philosophical Studies*, 28, 1–15.

Chomsky, N. (1981): *Lectures on Government and Binding*. Dordrecht, Holland: Foris.
   (forthcoming): *Knowledge of Language: Its Nature, Origins, and Use*. New York: Basic Books.

Davidson, D. (1965): 'Theories of Meaning and Learnable Languages'. In Y. Bar-Hillel (ed.), *Logic, Methodology, and the Philosophy of Science*, Amsterdam: North Holland, reprinted in Davidson (1984).
   (1973): 'Radical Interpretation'. *Dialectica*, 27, 313–28.
   (1974): 'Belief and the Basis of Meaning'. *Synthese*, 27, 309–23.
   (1984): *Inquiries into Truth and Interpretation*. Oxford: Clarendon Press.

Gold, E. (1957): 'Language Identification in the Limit'. *Information and Control*, 10, 447–74.

Haack, R. J. (1978): 'Davidson on Learnable Languages'. *Mind*, 87, 230–49.

Hintikka, J. (1980): 'Theories of Truth and Learnable Languages'. In S. Kanger & S. Ohman (eds), *Philosophy and Grammar*, Dordrecht, Holland: D. Reidel, 37–57.

LePore, E. (1982): 'In Defense of Davidson'. *Linguistics and Philosophy*, 5, 277–94.

Lightfoot, D. (1984): *The Language Lottery*. Cambridge, Massachusetts: MIT Press.

4

Why Intensionalists Ought Not Be Fregeans

JERROLD J. KATZ

I

Frege's semantics is generally thought to be the very model of an intensionalist semantics. Frege's conceptions of sense and compositionality are typically treated as the jumping off point for all future intensionalist theorizing. His justifications for positing senses are regarded, by intensionalists and extensionalists alike, as *the* justifications. Intensionalists take them as what must be successfully defended, while extensionalists take them as what must be successfully attacked to block the introduction of senses into the study of logical structure of natural language.

In the present paper, I challenge this view of Fregean semantics. My principal thesis will be that Frege's conceptions of sense and compositionality are deeply flawed and that these flawed conceptions are responsible for the problems that have beset his justifications for positing senses. Thus, by following Frege as closely as they have, intensionalists have allowed their side in the controversy to rest on unnecessarily vulnerable arguments. The result has been an unnecessary disaster for intensionalism and an undeserved windfall for extensionalism.

Frege had two justifications for senses. Senses are needed to give us the best principle for inference by substitution into opaque contexts: by taking the reference of expressions in such contexts to be 'what is customarily their sense', we maintain substitutivity of coreferentials in spite of the fact that truth is not preserved on substitution of expressions with the same direct reference.[1] And senses are needed to explain why true identities of the form a = b are

I wish to thank Hans Herzberger, Paul Horwich, Arnold Koslow, Richard Mendelsohn and D. T. Langendoen for helpful comments on an earlier draft of section II. I also wish to thank Murray Kiteley, Tom Tymoczko, Jay Garfield, Steve Weisler and Meredith Michaels of the Five College Group on Propositional Attitudes for useful discussions of the same section. Thanks go as well to the students in my philosophy of language seminars at the Graduate Center and to the Philosophy Department of the University of Toronto to whom a version of the paper was read.

[1] G. Frege, 'On Sense and Reference' in *Translations from the Philosophical Writings of Gottlob Frege* (Basil Blackwell, Oxford, 1952), p. 66.

informative, whereas ones of the form a = a are not. In the next section, I shall try to show that the one serious problem facing the first of these justifications, Mates's problem, disappears once Frege's conceptions of sense and compositionality are replaced. I shall explain the conceptions that replace them, indicating thereby how intensionalist semantics can be done on a non-Fregean model. In the third section, I try to show that the problems that brought about the demise of the description theory as well as Kripke's puzzle – which they pave the way for – disappear once we make this replacement. In the final section, I show that the conceptions of sense and compositionality with which I replace Frege's provide a far broader range of justifications for senses than Frege's.

II

Much discussion in the philosophy of language, logic and mind over the past thirty years has centered on the problem that Mates raised for Fregean criteria for inferences by substitution into opaque contexts.[2] He pointed out that Frege's criterion of synonymy and Carnap's criterion of intensional isomorphism imply that, from the fact that nobody doubts that whoever believes D believes D, it follows that nobody doubts that whoever believes D believes D', where 'D' and 'D'' are synonymous or intensionally isomorphic sentences. Mates claimed that Frege's and Carnap's criteria fail if anybody does doubt that someone who believes D believes D'.[3]

The attention that Mates's problem has received is due to its being thought that the controversy between intensionalism and extensionalism turns on the solution to the problem. Extensionalists have tried to exploit Mates-type cases to undermine the Fregean posit of senses, while intensionalists, also accepting the relevance of Mates's problem to the controversy, have challenged the extensionalists' treatment of these cases. Extensionalists have argued that Frege and Carnap are wrong on the grounds that it seems beyond question that someone somewhere at some time for some reason has doubted a proposition of the form *whoever believes D believes D'*. Some extensionalists are so confident that Mates-type cases provide a knock-down argument against intensionalism that they have based their entire case for extensionalism on them. To choose the most prominent example, Davidson uses Mates's problem to justify his replacement of the intensionalist *s means that p* paradigm of analysis with the extensionalist *s is T iff p* paradigm.[4] By way of justifying the replacement, Davidson says that he knows of no way other than shifting to the extensionalist paradigm to deal with the difficulty that 'we cannot account for even as much as the truth conditions of [belief sentences and others containing opaque contexts]

[2] B. Mates, 'Synonymity', in *Semantics and the Philosophy of Language*, ed. L. Linsky (University of Illinois Press, Urbana, 1952), pp. 111–38.

[3] Ibid., p. 125.

[4] D. Davidson, 'Truth and Meaning', *Synthese*, 17 (1967), pp. 304–23; reprinted in *Readings in the Philosophy of Language*, eds J. F. Rosenberg and C. Travis (Prentice-Hall, Englewood Cliffs, 1971) pp. 450–71.

on the basis of what we know of the meanings in them.'[5] Mates's problem is supposed to prove that it is impossible for intensionalists to give a coherent account of compositional meaning in natural language. The problem is supposed to show that virtually any non-semantic, grammatical difference between an expression and a synonymous one substituting for it can lead to cases where truth is not preserved.

Church and Carnap have replied to such uses of Mates's problem, arguing that anyone who doubts a proposition of the form *whoever believes D believes D'* must, given the fact that 'D' and 'D''' are synonymous, be confused about the meaning of 'D' and 'D'''. For anyone who is clear about their synonymy has to realize that 'it is after all not possible to doubt [whoever believes D believes D'] without also doubting [whoever believes D believes D]'.[6] Thus, intensionalists can make the plausible point that the only doubts that can arise are not germane: the possible doubts stem from a confusion about what propositions 'D' and 'D''' express, and hence, the doubts are not relevant to the cases on which Frege's and Carnap's criteria must be judged. The criteria concern only cases where 'D' and 'D''' express the same proposition or are intensionally isomorphic.

The burden of this section will be to show that both sides in this controversy are mistaken in supposing that Mates's problem has any relevance to the choice between intensionalism and extensionalism. The reason that the problem is irrelevant is that *intensionalism per se is compatible with any decision one makes about whether substitutional inferences go through in any or all Mates-type cases.* This is, of course, not to say that any intensionalism is compatible with any such decisions. In particular, Frege's intensionalism is incompatible with some such decisions. The assumption that Frege's semantics is the archetype for all intensionalist semantics confuses both the intensionalist–extensionalist controversy and Mates's problem by connecting them so directly. The assumption leads to assimilating of non-Fregean versions of intensionalism to Fregean intensionalism, and this conceals the possibility that an intensionalist might decide Mates-type cases on other than doctrinal grounds. The assimilation has

---

[5] *Readings in the Philosophy of Language*, pp. 453–54. I am construing Davidson's reference to the 'difficulty' which makes him choose the 'simple and radical' move of replacing the intensional paradigm with the Tarskian paradigm as the difficulty that he refers to earlier as 'the standard semantic problem' (p. 453) but arising in the attempt to explain the 'apparently non-extensional "means that"'. As he puts it, 'we will encounter problems [in our attempts to explain this idiom] as hard as, or perhaps identical with, the problems our theory is out to solve' (p. 455). It is worth pointing out that there is no disagreement with Davidson's criticisms of Fregean answers to questions about the meanings of sentences as 'bogus' (p. 453). See J. J. Katz, 'Logic and Language' in *Language, Mind, and Knowledge, Minnesota Studies in the Philosophy of Science*, Vol. VII, ed. K. Gunderson (University of Minnesota Press, Minneapolis, 1975), pp. 64–6. This essay argues that these criticisms apply to Fregean answers precisely because the answers are based on a conception of sense and compositionality with the defects I am describing in the present paper.

[6] A. Church, 'Intensional Isomorphism and the Identity of Belief', *Philosophical Studies*, 5 (1954), pp. 65–73, and R. Carnap, 'On Belief Sentences', in *Philosophy and Analysis*, ed. M. MacDonald, *Philosophical Library* (New York, 1954), pp. 128–31; also J. J. Katz, *Semantic Theory* (Harper & Row, New York, 1972), pp. 265–80.

not only kept both sides in the controversy occupied with irrelevant issues but has kept philosophers from seeing the real nature of Mates's problem.

The first step in showing the irrelevance of Mates's problem is to separate Frege's intensionalism from intensionalism *per se*. To do this, I begin by setting out the principal differences between the intensionalist and extensionalist positions. Then I will explain, with respect to each of the distinguishing features of intensionalism, just how a non-Fregean version of intensionalism would differ from a Fregean version. Finally, on the basis of the non-Fregean intensionalism thus specified, I will show why extensionalist construals of Mates-type cases challenge Fregean intensionalism without challenging some non-Fregean intensionalisms.

The fundamental thesis of intensionalism is that sentences of natural languages have a sense structure over and above their phonetic, syntactic and referential structure, and that their sense structure must be taken into account for an adequate understanding of their logical behavior. Intensionalists thus hold the following theses: (I) Sentences in natural language have a sense; (II) Such senses or meanings are compositional, that is, the senses of sentences are a function of the senses of their syntactic constituents and the syntactic relations between these constituents; (III) The sense or meaning of a sentence determines its logical structure, that is, the grammatical features of the sentence on which its logical relations to other sentences turn; (IV) Sense or meaning is essential to reference. Extensionalists reject (I), and hence, reject (II)–(IV).

Different intensionalisms hold different versions of (I)–(IV). In order to exhibit a non-Fregean intensionalism, I will now describe the differences in how Frege's intensionalism and my intensionalism hold (I)–(IV). Frege adopts (I), of course, but he does so in a very special form. Frege adopts (I) under a characterization of sense as the mode of presentation of the referent.[7] This defines sense indirectly *via* reference. Senses, for Frege, are like humble servants who announce important personages under one or another of their titles. In contrast, my intensionalism characterizes sense directly as the aspect of sentence structure on which such grammatical properties and relations as meaningfulness, ambiguity, synonymy, antonymy, redundancy, etc. depend.[8] To appreciate the importance of this difference, it suffices to note that one consequence of the difference is that Frege's characterization of sense commits him to claiming that proper nouns have sense while mine has no such commitment. Proper nouns, being associated with particular modes of present-

---

[7] G. Frege, 'On Sense and Reference', p. 57. On Frege's other notion of sense i.e. *conceptual content* in the *Begriffsschrift*, and in 'The Thought' (*Mind*, LXV, 1956, pp. 289–311), there are good reasons not to discuss it here. Frege's remarks about conceptual content as what is the same in an active and its corresponding passive illustrate but do not explain. Moreover, the effectiveness of the illustration is undercut when one considers more complex active/passive sentences and whether such sentences are synonymous (see Katz, J. J. 'Chomsky on Meaning', *Language*, 56, 1980, pp. 25–29). Further, Frege's other remarks are not coherent. He characterizes sameness of conceptual content in terms of sameness of consequent set and of logical form (in the sense that sentences with the same logical form are not distinguished in the conceptual notation). However, these characteristics diverge for non-identical but equivalent logical and mathematical truths (see Rosado Haddock, G. E. 'On Frege's Two Notions of Sense', *History and Philosophy of Logic*, to appear). Finally, it is sense as mode of presentation that is the notion that has played the major role in the philosophical issues with which I am concerned.

[8] J. J. Katz, *Semantic Theory* (Harper & Row, New York, 1972), pp. 1–10.

ing their referents, are naturally taken to have sense, and Frege gives us other reasons to think that he has a description theory of the sense of proper nouns.[9] My characterization of sense commits us to nothing more than that their having sense or not having sense is a matter of which hypothesis best accounts for the facts about their semantic properties and relations.[10]

Frege strongly endorses (II), even anticipating the role of compositionality in what Chomsky has called 'the creative use of language'. But, as in the case of sense, Frege's conception is highly specialized. It is based on his 'building block' metaphor. This metaphor turns out to contain very misleading elements, particularly, the suggestion that the sense of each constituent in a sentence sits there in the sense of the sentence as an intact component of it, like a building block in a physical construction. Thus, Frege speaks eloquently about sense-compositionality:

> The achievements of language are wonderful. By means of a few sounds and connections of sounds it is capable of expressing a vast number of thoughts, including even such as have never before been grasped or expressed by anyone. How are these achievements possible? It is in virtue of the fact that thoughts are built up out of thought-building-blocks. The building blocks correspond to groups of sounds from which the sentence is constructed, so that the construction of the sentence from sentence-components corresponds to the construction of thoughts from thought-components. One can call the thought-components the sense of the corresponding sentence-components, just as one conceives the thought as the sense of the sentence.[11]

But not only do these eloquent words express a flawed conception, Frege kept himself from having the opportunity of recognizing and perhaps removing the flaws by his failure to match these words with deeds. He failed to examine the actual workings of sense-compositionality because, perhaps under the influence of his characterization of sense, he concentrated exclusively on the study of how the reference of complex expressions is built up from the reference of their constituents. In the discussion below, I shall show that this masonary conception of compositional structure is one of the factors making Frege's intensionalism vulnerable to Mates-type cases. I show also how my intensionalism, assuming nothing more about sense-compositionality than is explicitly stated in (II), can do justice to the construction of the senses of syntactically complex expressions from the senses of their parts without opening itself up to the possibility of Mates-type objections.

No doubt, Frege accepted some version of (III), but this is a complex question which cannot be fully taken up here. Although it is perhaps too strong to say that Frege only concerned himself with sense when appeal to sense could

---

[9] G. Frege, 'On Sense and Reference', p. 57; also, G. Frege, *Posthumous Writings* (Basil Blackwell, Oxford, 1979), pp. 191–2.

[10] Thus, counter-examples like Wittgenstein's Moses case and Kripke's Schmidt case do not cause any problem of my intensionalism. See S. Kripke, 'Naming and Necessity', in eds D. Davidson and G. Harman, (D. Reidel, Dordrecht-Holland, 1972), pp. 284–308. But, of course, my intensionalism faces, as does Kripke's position but not Frege's, the question of why true identity statements with different proper names are informative whereas ones with the same proper name are not. This is the crux of Kripke's puzzle.

[11] I am indebted to Hidé Ishiguro for bringing this passage (*Nachlass* 243) to my attention.

get his account of reference out of a problem, it is perfectly correct to say he never undertakes a systematic examination of the contribution of senses generally to the logical structure of sentences. However, one of Frege's excursions into the domain of sense and logical structure had unfortunate consequences in connection with Mates's problem. Frege undertook to explicate Kant's notion of analyticity. But Kant had a Janus-headed notion: on one side, definitional, on the other, logical.[12] Frege made a composite head, both logical and definitional. For Frege, analytic sentences are consequences of laws of logic plus definitions.[13] We shall see below that, because Fregean senses include logically as well as definitionally entailed properties, Fregean intensionalism, as it stands, cannot develop an adequate principle for substitutional inference into opaque contexts. In contrast, my intensionalism, explicating analytic sentences as ones where the sense of one term contains the full predicate and all the terms, can develop an adequate principle for such inference.

Finally, Frege adopts (IV), but in the strongest possible form, both much stronger than necessary and much stronger than desirable.[14] My intensionalism adopts a significantly weaker form of (IV). Frege adopts the stronger form because he does not distinguish the reference of linguistic entities from the reference of speakers. I distinguish between the reference of linguistic types (in the language) from the reference of their tokens (in speech). I then use this distinction to restrict the statement of (IV) to the claim that sense determines *type-reference*. This claim is weaker than Frege's because it concedes that sense does not determine *token-reference*. Because Frege makes no such distinction, his statement of (IV) has been taken to assert the strong claim that sense determines token-reference as well. This strong statement of (IV) has been disastrous for modern intensionalism because, in making sense responsible for everything upon which a speaker's reference depends, it has allowed philosophers like Donnellan and Putnam to criticize necessity in language on the basis of contingency in the speech context.[15]

Having distinguished Fregean intensionalism from at least one other form of intensionalism, we can now tackle the question of whether Mates's problem plays any role in the issue between intensionalism and extensionalism. The natural way to approach this question is to consider whether the non-Fregean intensionalist has reason to be unhappy with Frege's principle of substitution. Thus, let us put the intensionalist-extensionalist controversy aside for a moment, and look at the adequacy of Frege's principle from a purely intensionalist perspective. When one does this, it emerges, surprisingly, that

   [12] I. Kant, *Prolegomena to Any Future Metaphysic* (The Liberal Arts Press, New York, 1951), pp. 14–15.
   [13] G. Frege, *The Foundations of Arithmetic*, ed. J. L. Austin (Basil Blackwell, Oxford, 1953), pp. 3–4, and pp. 99–104. For recent discussions of my notion of analyticity, see J. J. Katz, *Cogitations* (Oxford University Press, New York, 1986), and G. E. Smith and J. J. Katz, *Intensionally Admissible Models* (forthcoming).
   [14] J. J. Katz, 'A Proper Theory of Names', *Philosophical Studies*, 31 (1977), pp. 1–80; also, 'The Neoclassical Theory of Reference', in *Contemporary Perspectives in the Philosophy of Language*, eds P. A. French, T. E. Uehling, Jr. and H. K. Wettstein (University of Minnesota Press, Minneapolis, 1977), pp. 10–124.
   [15] H. Putnam, 'It Ain't Necessarily So', *The Journal of Philosophy*, 59 (1962), pp. 658–71; 'Is Semantics Possible?', *Metaphilosophy*, 1 (1970), pp. 189–201.

Frege's principle is not adequate. The fact that no notice is taken of the problems which beset it from within the intensionalist viewpoint shows, I think, how strong the influence of the Fregean model of semantics has been even among intensionalists.

The Fregean principle amounts to (FP).

> (FP) One can substitute into an opaque context on the condition that the expression substituted is synonymous (intensionally isomorphic) with the expression substituted for.

The glaring fault with this principle for intensionalists is that it is too narrow: there are intensionally acceptable inferences that (FP) does not account for. Although it captures substitutional inferences like that from (1) to (2):

(1) Hansel believes that he has a sister
(2) Hansel believes that he has a female sibling

The principle does not capture equally legitimate inferences like that from (1) to (3):

(3) Hansel believes that he has a sibling

where the substituted expression is not synonymous with the expression for which it substitutes. Frege's clever move of making the sense of an expression its referent in an opaque context preserves sameness of reference as the condition for such substitutional inference. The move thus has the quite considerable virtue of providing a single general principle for the entire class of substitutional inferences. But the principle breaks down in the case of inferences like (1) to (3) because the sense of 'a sister' is *not* the same intensional object as the sense of 'a sibling'. Thus, Frege would preclude such inferences on the grounds that the indirect reference of these expressions differs, but an intensionalist ought to allow them as valid.[16]

---

[16] In the discussion following the presentation of this paper at the Davidson Conference, Igal Kwart and Paul Benacerraf asked whether the fact that the person referred to by the subject of sentences like (1) and (3) might not know the word 'sibling' does not undermine the claim that (3) follows from (1). In the present context, the answer is straightforward. At this point in the text, I am assuming a 'purely intensionalist perspective' in order to raise an internal problem for Frege's approach. Thus, we are assuming that the object of a propositional attitude like belief is a sense, not an expression. Accordingly, Church (A. Church, 'Intensional Isomorphism and Identity of Belief', *Philosophical Studies*, 5 (1954), p. 69) says that the persons referred to in Mates-type cases 'are supposed ... to have had a sufficient knowledge of the English language so that the doubt was not, for example, about the meaning of the word'. This means that, for all intents and purposes, such persons may be assumed to be ideal speakers in Chomsky's sense. Hence, in the present context where I am arguing against fellow intensionalists who adopt some such construction as Church's, Kwart's and Benacerraf's question does not arise. Now, outside the present context, as a question that an extensionalist might raise in response to an argument of an intensionalist, the question is trickier. If the intensionalist is using the inference as a way of justifying the posit of senses, then their question is to the point and unanswerable. But if the intensionalist is merely explaining how an inference like that from (1) to (3) can be dealt with, the question, though still to the point, is answerable. Intensionalists can reply that, on their view, the person need not know the word 'sibling' in order to *have* the belief expressed by the complement of (3), but only to express the belief in certain ways. Having the belief, on this view, is *inter alia* having the belief expressed by the complement of (1).

As soon as one notices this difficulty, the thought comes to mind that the difficulty might be overcome by replacing the operative condition in (FP) with one employing the weaker relation of sense inclusion. But Frege's definition of analyticity puts this weaker relation of sense containment beyond his reach. Frege's definition gives him the fully fledged logical notion of containment and hence a condition for substitution into opaque contexts that allows the inference when the conclusion is a logical consequence of the premise. This, of course, has the infamous result that we believe all the logical consequences of a proposition we believe. Does Hobart know he has a sister? – well, then, he knows all the truths of logic.

It is true that principles of substitution based on logical inclusion can be restricted in various *ad hoc* ways to mitigate the full force of the result that logical consequences of beliefs are necessarily also beliefs. But no such restrictions can eliminate such counter-intuitive results entirely. It is possible, for example, to introduce clauses to reduce the cases where someone who believes A is unacquainted with its logical consequent B or where someone who believes A is ignorant or confused about the logical steps to B, but nothing can be done to reduce the cases of illogical belief. These are cases where someone believes A, knows B, knows also that B follows logically from A, but does not believe B. Paul claimed that his faith was 'to the Greeks foolishness', Tertullian claimed that such faith is 'impossible', and Luther that it contradicts reason. Most of us have encountered highly compassionate Christians who believe God's creation to contain unnecessary and undeserved suffering and who see this as entailing that God cannot be both all good and all powerful but who still believe God to be both. There is no getting around the fact of illogical belief.

The move we have been considering is quite a curious one for intensionalists, and especially Fregeans, to entertain. Frege's original intention in formulating (FP) was to demonstrate the advantage of positing senses by showing that the posit plugs a gap in extensional treatments of inference. The gap exists because the extensionalist condition for substitutional inference, i.e., sameness of reference or inclusion of extension, would enable us to go from truths to falsehoods in some substitutional contexts. (FP) takes care of these contexts. But, on the replacement of (FP) we have been considering, the condition for substitution in all contexts is that the conclusion be a logical consequence of the premise. Well, this replacement would seem to put Frege back where he started, namely, with the original problem of trying to formulate a general condition for all substitutional inference on a purely extensional basis in the face of a range of contexts in which such a condition fails. If logic could have provided an adequate principle for substitution, there would have been no problem about opaque contexts in the first place, and hence, no initial reason to invoke senses. Invoking them was a genuine step forward in plugging the gap in our account of inference, but reconstructing the promising construct in terms of notions already seen to be inadequate for the job is a giant step backwards.

But giving Frege his intensionalist due does not go very far toward saving him from the present difficulty. The closest that Frege comes even to setting up apparatus for a sense relation that is appropriately weaker than logical containment is his notion of *marks of a concept*. But, even if this notion were to be used to restrict the power of the relation of logical containment that gives rise to the absurd consequences about belief, it would not help. The notion of marks of a concept is too limited. Frege's discussion of the notion makes it clear that marks correspond only to syntactic constituents of linguistic constructions.[17] Thus, Frege's notion might handle an inference like that from 'Hobart is thinking of an even number' to 'Hobart is thinking of a number', but it certainly cannot handle an inference like that from 'Hobart is thinking of one of his sisters' to 'Hobart is thinking of one of his siblings'. An inference of the latter kind requires a definition of analyticity involving syntactically free analysis of word meanings. Only such a definition, that is, one based on apparatus for decompositional analysis, can formulate a substitution condition which is able to refer to parts of complex meanings with no syntactic representation, as in expressions like 'sister' and 'sibling'.

But the failure to consider a decompositional theory of sense is not the only fundamental problem with Frege's approach. Even if his approach had formulated a condition based on the weaker relation of sense inclusion, it would not be adequate. In a sense, such a condition would hurt as much as it would help. Replacing the sameness of sense (or intensional isomorphism) condition in (FP) with one based on sense inclusion, we obtain the principle (FP').

(FP') One can substitute into an opaque context on the condition that the sense of the expression substituted is included in the sense of the expression substituted for.

This principle captures valid inferences like that from (1) to (3), but it also counts *in*valid inferences like that from (4) to (5):

(4) Gretel doubts that there are bachelors in the gingerbread house
(5) Gretel doubts that there are males in the gingerbread house

as valid. The Fregean approach to inference in opaque contexts is like a bad tire whose bulge cannot be flattened without causing a new one.

The new bulge appears at another weak point in Frege's approach. This weak point is due to his failure to attend to the internal workings of compositionality. Had he attended to them, he would surely have seen that sense-altering operations take place in the compositional construction of sentence meanings and that a substitution principle must be sensitive to the effects of such operations. But, not seeing these things, his desire for a single substitution condition for both transparent and opaque contexts lead directly to a principle in which the substitution condition is imposed on the expression substituted for and the expression substituting for it. Such a principle cannot take account of sense-altering operations which, like the negative function of 'doubts' in (4), takes place at a point higher in the compositional process than the point at which the substitution condition is imposed.

Consider (4). When the sense of 'doubts' combines with the sense of its complement clause to form a meaning for the full verb phrase, the negative

---

[17] G. Frege, 'On Concept and Object', pp. 51–2.

element in the sense of 'doubts' operates on the sense of 'there are bachelors in the gingerbread house'. The operation puts the concepts in the complex sense of 'bachelor' such as 'male' beyond the scope of the propositional attitude. The case of (4) is thus different from that of (1) as normally understood, since in the latter case these concepts are in the scope of the attitude of belief. One way in which this might occur is if the negative element in the sense of 'doubts' were to operate DeMorganwise to form a disjunction of the negations of the component concepts and the disjunction were to be presented with the original complex sense as the alternatives between which Gretel's belief (concerning who is present in the gingerbread house) is suspended.

Details are of no importance here. The point that matters is that an operation of some kind takes place at the level of the verb phrase in the sentence (4) that restructures the sense of 'bachelor' so that the sense of 'male' in (5) cannot enter into an inclusion relation of the proper kind, i.e. in the way that it does in an inference like that from 'Gretel believes there are bachelors in the gingerbread house' to 'Gretel believes there are males in the gingerbread house'. Because the sense of the verb phrase, which results from this semantic operation, is what specifies the propositional attitude of the whole sentence, a principle of substitutional inference must apply *above* the level at which (FP′) applies in order to take account of the semantic operations that explain why (5) does not follow from (4).

'Doubts' is not the only verb that causes this difficulty.[18] 'Deny' and other negative verbs, of course, behave the same way. But there also seem to be other kinds of verbs that cause the difficulty. Chomsky once suggested that the verb 'realize' raises Mates's problem. He wrote:

> ... consider such sentences as Everyone agrees that *if John realizes that p then he realizes that* ..., where the space is filled either by p itself or by an expression q distinct from but synonymous with p. No doubt the truth value may change, as q replaces p, indicating that any difference of form of an embedded sentence can, in certain cases at least, play a role in the statement of truth conditions, hence, presumably, the determination of meaning.[19]

Let us suppose that Chomsky is completely right about the verb 'realize': the verb is sensitive to 'any difference in the form of the embedded sentence' (i.e. the complement clause). On this supposition 'realize' creates a context for the senses of its complement clauses in which these senses undergo semantic operations that form the object of the propositional attitude.

It is not completely clear how we ought to state the operation in the meaning of 'realize' to express exactly what Chomsky has in mind about the way in which this verb makes reference to the form of the complement clause, but this doesn't matter. Something like the following seems to be what Chomsky wants to say about 'realize'-sentences:

---

[18] It should be noted that the problem already arises in non-opaque cases. For example, the sentence 'There are no bachelors' does not entail the sentence 'There are no males'.

[19] N. Chomsky, *Studies on Semantics in Generative Grammar* (Mouton, The Hague, 1972), p. 88.

(P) A sentence of the form 'X realizes that p' means that X sees that 'p' depicts what is the case

On the construal (P), 'realize' expresses a relation between a person, a particular sentence and a state of affairs. The construal explains, in the desired way, how someone can realize that *p* but not that *q* even though the two sentences are strictly synonymous. Accordingly, a sentence like (6) does not imply one like (7).

(6) Gretel realizes that she is an adult human female who never married
(7) Gretel realizes that she is a spinster

(6) asserts that Gretel comes to see that the expression 'adult human female who never married' applies to her whereas (7) asserts that Gretel comes to see that the expression 'spinster' applies to her. The operation in the sense of 'realize' incorporates reference to the particular form of words in its complement clause, thereby transforming the sense of the embedded sentence in constructing the object of the propositional attitude.[20]

In general, the object of the propositional attitude expressed in a full sentence $NP + V + that + S$ is a function of the meaning of V and the meaning of its complement clause $that + S$. But, as we have seen, the function may involve an operation on the sense of the complement clause in the process of forming the sense of the larger verb phrase from the sense of the verb and the sense of its complement clause. Let us call an opaque verb and the context it creates 'hyperopaque' when, and only when, the sense of the verb operates to change the sense of the complement clause in the process of determining the sense of the higher verb phrase.[21] If a hyperopaque verb is a verb of propositional attitude, then, as a consequence of its hyperopacity, the object of the propositional attitude expressed by the full sentence $NP + V + that + S$ will be different from the sense of S by itself.

It is clearly possible that there are hyperopaque verbs beyond those we have considered thus far, and it is even possible that such further cases may exemplify new forms of hyperopacity. But, for us, the philosophically more interesting possibility is that every opaque verbal construction that the language can contain, including 'believes', is hyperopaque. This, of course, is the worst possible case from the viewpoint of Fregean intensionalists like Church and Carnap. But, in fact, all that would happen in such a case is that every inference from a sentence of the form $NP + V + that + S$ to one of the form $NP + V + that + S'$, where V is opaque and S' differs from S in some aspect of syntactic or phonological form, would be invalid. So what? Such cross-the-boards invalidity would be nothing more than what we have already seen in

---

[20] I take no stand on whether the reference to the complement sentence involves an explicit representation of the sentence within the meaning of the higher verb phrase or simply a reference to the sentence specified indexically as the complement clause of the verb in question.

[21] See J. J. Katz, *Semantic Theory* (Harper & Row, New York, 1972), pp. 274–80. Note, however, that this discussion employs the less apt term 'translucent' to refer to the verbs and contexts here referred to as 'hyperopaque'.

inferences like that from (4) to (5) or (6) to (7). Intensionalisms that concern themselves with the workings of compositionality can explain all such invalid inferences along the same lines sketched above in connection with inferences like that from (4) to (5) or (6) to (7).

The explanation of such invalid inferences would be based on the operations taking place at the compositional step where the sense of the verb phrase is formed. There may well be all sorts of unusual operations that take place at this step. No matter. They pose problems only for descriptive semantics. As long as we may suppose that, synchronically, a hyperopaque verb, like any other word in the language, has a grammatically fixed sense and makes a grammatically fixed contribution to the sense of constructions in which it is a constituent, we can, in principle, separate invalid inferences from valid ones. We can succeed in this even if absolutely all inferences involving opaque verbs turn out invalid.

The significance of the possibility that all opaque verbs turn out hyperopaque is, therefore, the opposite of what intensionalists and extensionalists alike have supposed. Rather than intensionalism itself being refuted, only one form of intensionalism, Frege's, is. That form requires that no opaque verb be hyperopaque. If one or more are hyperopaque, then separation of valid from invalid inferences requires a form of intensionalism sensitive to the workings of compositionality. There is, therefore, no threat to compositionality or to intensionalism *per se*. The threat is only to intensionalisms that ignore the workings of compositionality or restrict the ability of their semantic theory to explain it.

No intensionalism has to ignore these workings or restrict its semantic theory. One that concerns itself with these workings is in a position to allow the possibility that every inference by substitution into an opaque context turns out to be invalid, while one that does not restrict its semantic theory is in a position to capture those inferences by substitution into opaque contexts which turn out to be valid. This shows that it is not intensionalism itself that is threatened by Mates-type objections. The question in a Mates-type case is not a philosophical question but merely a descriptive one: Is the particular verb in the language just opaque or hyperopaque? For instance, the question in the cases of whether 'Everyone who believes D believes D''' is implied by 'Everyone who believes D believes D' is no more than the question whether 'believes' is hyperopaque. Extensionalists like Davidson who claim that such implications fail and intensionalists like Church who claim that they hold both wrongly think that the issue is theoretical and concerns the doctrinal matters that divide them. Since the issue pertains to no more than whether the English word 'believes' is hyperopaque and since nothing requires an intensionalist to hold that the verb in a Mates-type case is non-hyperopaque, it hardly matters which way the descriptive lexicographer resolves the issue. True enough, many intensionalists have held that 'believe', 'know', and other opaque verbs are non-hyperopaque, and this lexicographical position is by no means outlandish, but nothing in intensionalist doctrine requires an intensionalist *qua* intensionalist to take such a lexicographical position. No intensionalist has to accept the parts of Frege's approach that commit him to taking it.

Frege took no interest in the nuts and bolts of sense compositionality, and as a consequence, failed to see the possibility of hyperopaque contexts. Frege's desire to obtain a single principle for substitutional inference in both transparent and opaque contexts led him to preserve the principle of substitutivity of coreferentials by taking the reference of expressions in opaque contexts to be their (customary) sense. This had the effect of saddling him with a principle that must apply below the point in the compositional process at which the sense of a verb interacts with the sense of its complement clause. Since, in the case of hyperopaque verbs, the propositional attitude of the sentence is determined by such interaction, Frege's desire for a single principle and his neglect of sense compositionality leads him, in effect, to claim that there are no hyperopaque verbs.

Could Frege save his position by biting the bullet and denying, as a matter of policy, that there are hyperopaque verbs in the language? The option is open to Fregeans, of course, but it is highly unattractive for a number of reasons. For one thing, taking it is adopting a powerful thesis about natural languages on an a priori basis for no apparent reason but to save a shortsighted approach at the eleventh hour. There has been no comprehensive examination of natural languages to determine whether their verbs express opaque, non-hyperopaque contexts, and there is no appropriate explanatory principle about natural languages from which the total absence of such verbs follows. For another thing, although it may be possible to defend this thesis with respect to the verbs that are presently found in English, the thesis can be shown to be false with respect to the senses that English can express. Indeed, it is quite clear that the grammar of English enables us to construct, and hence, allows as possible forms in the language, both verbal forms that introduce hyperopaque contexts and verbal forms that introduce opaque but non-hyperopaque contexts. An example of the former is the sense of 'realize' given in (P), and an example of the latter is the sense of 'qelieves' (which behaves syntactically the same way as 'believes') given in (Q):

(Q) 'Qelieving that p' means *believing 'p' with full understanding of all the synonymy relations into which 'p' enters in the language, i.e., a qeliever of 'p' understands the proposition 'q' expresses to be the proposition 'p' expresses, for all 'q' synonymous with 'p'.*

Then, inferences like that from (6) to (7) provide cases of invalid inference by substitution into a hyperopaque context and inferences like that from (8) to (9) provide cases of valid inferences by such substitution.

(8) Hansel qelieves that he has a sister
(9) Hansel qelieves that he has a sibling

These reflections on the semantics of compositionality and the semantics of propositional attitudes take us beyond Frege's view that sentences in natural languages involving such attitudes can be understood simply as expressing a relation between a person and a proposition. Intensionalism commits us to claiming that the representation of propositional attitudes requires reference to a proposition as well as reference to a person, but it does not commit us to claiming there is no further reference necessary. Frege's limitation of the terms of the relation to these two was a consequence of his taking the sense of propositional attitude verbs to be opaque but non-hyperopaque. If such verbs can be taken in this way, the object of the attitude can be specified in terms of the sense of the complement clause. This is because only the things that enter into the substitution condition can be terms of the relation and the only things that enter for Frege are the sense of the complement clause and the sense of the expression substituting for it. But since intensionalism is not bound by the assumptions of Frege's intensionalism, it can allow more complex relations in connection with propositional attitudes, as for instance, in the case of (P) and (Q) where the relation is between a person, a proposition (sense of a sentence), a sentence and a state of affairs. Such flexibility is a feature of intensionalism that can construct the semantics of propositional attitude verbs on the basis of a case-by-case examination of these verbs, without a priori constraints on the complexity of the relations these verbs express.

Such an intensionalism can go further and replace Frege's account of analyticity and analytic entailment with a purely definitional one. This would make it possible to formulate the condition for substitution into opaque contexts in terms of no stronger relation than sense inclusion. In particular, the stronger relation that Frege introduces by combining definition with laws of logic plays no role in the formulation of the condition for substitution. The condition is simply that the result of the substitution be a sentence that is analytically entailed by the sentence into which the substitution is made, where the relation of analytic entailment is, roughly, (AE).[22]

> (AE) A sentence s_1 analytically entails a sentence s_2 (on a sense of s_1 and s_2) just in case the sense of s_1 has the form of a predicate P_1 with terms $T_1, ..., T_n$ occupying its argument places and the sense of s_2 has the form of a predicate P_2 with terms $T'_1, ..., T'_m$, ($m \geqslant n$), and (i) P_2 is included in P_1 and (ii) each T'_i is included in its corresponding T_i.

Let us now take stock to be sure that (AE) succeeds where (FP) and (FP') failed. First, it is clear that (AE) straightforwardly captures both inferences like that from (1) to (2) and inferences like that from (1) to (3). Second, (AE) does not license us to infer that someone who has a belief A also has a belief B if B is a logical consequence of A. (AE) licenses no ascription of belief beyond A itself or one of the propositions out of which A is compositionally constructed. Not only does none of the common counter-intuitive consequences about our belief systems follow from (AE), but (AE) even handles the case of impossible belief. Recall the tottering Christian who recognizes that the existence of unnecessary and undeserved suffering logically implies that God cannot be both all good and all powerful but nonetheless continues to believe God to be both. (AE) does not falsely predict that the Christian believes God to be either not all good or not all powerful. (AE) does not take being a logical consequence of a set of beliefs to be sufficient for being a belief. (AE) does, however, take being an analytic entailment of a belief to be sufficient for being a belief. The difference

---

[22] See J. J. Katz, *Semantic Theory*, pp. 171–97. For a full treatment of analytic entailment in which sense inclusion is expressed as a formal relation over representations of senses, see Smith, G. E. and Katz, J. J. *Intensionally Admissible Models*, Harvard University Press, forthcoming.

between the tottering Christian case and the case of John who believes he has a sister but who (because he thinks 'sibling' means 'spouse') might say such things as 'I ain't got no sibling' is that nothing in the former case requires the existence of the anti-Christian belief, even though not having it would be illogical, while something in the latter case does require the existence of a belief of John's that he has a sibling. *Ex hypothesi* John believes he has a sister, *ex hypothesi* 'believes' is non-hyperopaque, and *ex hypothesi* 'sister' means 'female sibling' in English, so, therefore, the belief that he has a sibling is one of the beliefs he has in believing he has a sister.

Third, since (AE) applies to *full* sentences, it applies after every step in the compositional construction of the meaning of a sentence takes place, and hence, it guarantees that no step is missed. Assuming that the semantic representations of sentences to which (AE) applies mark the effects of operations on the sense of expressions within hyperopaque contexts, then, unlike (FP'), (AE) has available to it everything required to distinguish the valid inferences by substitution from the invalid ones. If, for example, 'believes' is not hyperopaque while 'doubt' and 'realize' are, properly constructed semantic representations of sentences containing these verbs will enable (AE) to mark both the inference from (1) to (2) and the inference from (1) to (3) as valid and both the inference from (4) to (5) and the inference from (6) to (7) as invalid.

Let us recap. It was supposed that if Mates's problem is resolved as Davidson and other extensionalists hoped, intensionalism must be abandoned, whereas if it is resolved as Church and Carnap hoped, extensionalism must be abandoned. Mates-type cases were seen as test cases. For both sides the critical question was: can one always substitute coreferential expressions preserving truth (reference being customary sense in opaque contexts)? Can one always substitute a synonymous (intensionally isomorphic) expression in an opaque context? Both sides adopted the equation: the addition of semantic equals always gives semantic equals. Both sides accepted the reasoning: synonymy (intensional isomorphism) guarantees semantic equals, so the replacement of one component by one equal to it should leave the compositional edifice unchanged. 'It does!', say the intensionalists. 'It does not!', say the extensionalists, and they add, 'It doesn't even leave the truth conditions unchanged!' But, as we have seen, the reasoning on which both sides draw their conclusion is deeply flawed: intensionalism does not have to claim that sense composition works like building blocks.

Therefore, Mates-type cases pose no problem for compositionality or intensionalism. This fact undermines arguments like Davidson's which use them to try to eliminate an intensionalist paradigm of semantic analysis in favor of an extensionalist one. As will be recalled, Davidson's grounds in 'Truth and Meaning' for replacing the *'s' means that p* form of analysis with the Tarskian *'s' is true if, and only if, p* form were that replacement is the only way to deal with the difficulty that 'we cannot account for even as much as the truth conditions of [belief sentences and others containing opaque contexts] on the basis of what we know of the meaning of the words in them'.[23] The argument must now be seen as no longer having force, since the difficulty in question is properly dealt with by *more* meaning analysis rather than less.

---

[23] *Readings in the Philosophy of Language*, pp. 353–4.

III

In this section, I want to show that the mistake of thinking of intensionalism exclusively in Fregean terms that made Mates's problem seem a stumbling block to intensionalism is also responsible for what many philosophers now consider the most serious objections to intensionalism and what Kripke considers the most serious problem in the study of belief. In particular, I want to show that the same shortcomings of Fregean semantics that caused the difficulties in connection with Mates-type cases now stand in the way of vindicating intensionalism against Putnam's objections and in the way of solving Kripke's puzzle about belief. I shall argue that the same alternative intensionalism that was successful in removing Mates's type objections is also successful in removing Putnam's objections and solving Kripke's puzzle.

The historical path that leads to Kripke's puzzle begins with the other of Frege's two justifications for senses, their alleged value in explaining why true identity statements of the form a = b are informative. It leads from there through various stages of philosophical criticism of the Fregean position erected to explain such informativeness to a point at which almost all intensionalism has been thrown out with the Fregean bathwater. At this point, Kripke's puzzle arises, because, I shall argue, in the course of this critical exchange our semantic hold on the propositional attitudes has been undermined. Let us re-examine this history.

Frege claimed that we can explain the difference in 'cognitive value' between (10) and (11):

(10) Hesperus is Phosphorus
(11) Hesperus is Hesperus

if we take proper names like 'Hesperus' and 'Phosphorus' to have a sense over and above their reference. If so, (10) and (11) express different propositions, even though 'Hesperus' and 'Phosphorus' present the same object as their referent. Since 'Hesperus' presents the planet as the evening star and 'Phosphorus' presents it as the morning star, (10) expresses the informative proposition that the evening star is the morning star while (11) expresses the uninformative proposition that the evening star is the evening star.[24]

Frege's explanation has considerable plausibility. Hence, in the absence of an alternative explanation on the extensionalist's side, Frege's justification of senses has considerable force. Thus, intensionalists felt they could rest secure in the knowledge that few would be willing to exchange Frege's explanation for what seems, on the extensionalist's account, an utter mystery. The first sign that all was not well came when Wittgenstein criticized the conception of proper names on which Frege rested this explanation. Wittgenstein trenchantly argued

---

[24] G. Frege, 'On Sense and Reference', p. 56.

that proper names cannot be taken to have a sense expressed in a description because such putative defining descriptions can be false of the referent of the name without propositions using the name being rendered false. He writes:

So my definition of 'N' would perhaps be 'the man of whom all this is true'. – But if some point now proves false? Shall I be prepared to declare the proposition 'N is dead' false – even if it is only something which strikes me as incidental that has turned out false? But where are the bounds of the incidental? – If I had given a definition of the name in such a case, I should now be ready to alter it.[25]

Searle tried to salvage something of Frege's conception of proper names by developing the suggestion of Wittgenstein's that the use of proper names is only 'loosely' connected with descriptions.[26] Searle proposed that the reference of a proper noun is given by a sufficient number of the descriptions speakers associate with the noun. But Kripke was able to successfully press Wittgenstein's line of criticism against Searle's proposal by choosing a case where there is only one description that speakers associate with the name.[27] Kripke argued that the only description speakers generally associate with the name 'Gödel' is 'discoverer of the incompleteness of arithmetic', but it is perfectly possible for Gödel to have stolen the discovery from another mathematician, Schmidt, so that, in this case, Schmidt is the discoverer of the incompleteness of arithmetic but, none the less, 'Gödel' denotes Gödel.

Philosophers are as reluctant as scientists to relinquish an explanation in the face of contrary evidence so long as no alternative explanation is available, preferring to look for a construal of the evidence or of the explanation on which there is no conflict between them. Thus, Kripke's Schmidt case, and similar contrary evidence, would not have caused philosophers to abandon Frege's theory of proper names and its explanation of why sentences like (10) and (11) have different cognitive values were it not for the fact that Kripke also provided an alternative theory explaining how proper names can refer without having a sense that presents their referent.[28]

Kripke suggests that proper names refer in virtue of the speaker's and listener's knowledge of a designation relation that was instituted in a baptismal ceremony. There is no need to say more now about Kripke's explanation of how proper nouns can refer without having a sense beyond making the observation that the attempt to use this explanation of the reference of proper nouns in an alternative explanations of why sentences like (10) and (11) have different cognitive value is puzzling from the start. Why should (10) be more informative than (11)? Aren't we now back in essentially the pre-Fregean situation?

But we are getting ahead of our story. Just before Kripke's criticism of Searle's proposal about proper nouns, a parallel attack was launched against a parallel description theory of the sense of common nouns by Donnellan,

---

[25] L. Wittgenstein, *Philosophical Investigations* (Basil Blackwell, Oxford, 1953), pp. 36e–38e.

[26] J. R. Searle, 'Proper Names', *Mind*, LXVII (1958), pp. 166–73.

[27] S. Kripke, 'Naming and Necessity', pp. 285–308.

[28] Ibid., p. 302.

Putnam and others.[29] They argued that if common nouns have a sense expressible in a description, then the sentence formed by taking the common noun as subject and the description as predicate would be analytic. If 'feline animal' is the description expressing the sense of 'cat', then 'cats are feline animals' is analytic. But, their argument continues, the sentence cannot be analytic because it can be false: the referents of 'cat' can be non-animals.

This criticism of the notion that common nouns refer on the basis of their sense merged with the Wittgensteinian–Kripkean criticism of the notion that proper nouns refer on the basis of their sense to make a formidable case against the Fregean thesis that sense is the basis of reference. The case was, of course, strengthened significantly by the fact that Kripke's account of how proper nouns can refer without having a meaning could be easily transferred to provide an account of how common nouns can refer without having a sense. The upshot of the merger was a robust anti-Fregeanism free from Quine's dubious assumptions about linguistic methodology, his anti-mentalist bent, and his commitment to Skinnerian psychology. Such a position, championed by such articulate spokesmen as Putnam and Kripke, has proved irresistible to many philosophers who, unlike these spokesman themselves, have been willing, and often eager, to present it as a triumph of extensionalism.

It is in the context of such an attack on traditional intensionalism that Kripke's puzzle about belief assumes its special significance. This formidable attack on Fregean intensionalism together with the identification of intensionalism with Fregean intensionalism has caused many philosophers to give up on intensionalism and to see the study of reference as reduced to one approach, an extensionalism in which the account of references proceeds on the basis of something like Kripke's causal theory. The significance of Kripke's puzzle is that it raises a fundamental problem with what seems to be the only approach to the study of reference left. The puzzle threatens to leave the study of reference with nothing.

Kripke's puzzle is the following.[30] There is a bilingual Frenchman, Pierre, who assents to (12):

(12) Londres est jolie

on the basis of favorable descriptions of London that he has heard and read while growing up in France. Pierre then goes to London, taking up residence in a particularly ugly part of the city. On the basis of acquaintance, Pierre now assents to (13).

(13) London is not pretty

We are to assume that assent on the part of sincere, reflective speakers implies their belief in the propositions expressed by the sentence to which their assent

---

[29] See note 13; also, e.g., G. Harman, *Thought* (Princeton University Press, Princeton, 1973), pp. 84–111.

[30] S. Kripke, 'A Puzzle about Belief', *Meaning and Use*, ed. A. Margalit (D. Reidel, Dordrecht, 1979), pp. 239–83.

is given. We are also to assume that a sentence in one language and its translation in another language express the same proposition, and hence, have the same truth value. Now, on the one approach to reference left, the semantic value of a name is just the object to which it refers (as a consequence of the relevant baptismal ceremony). Thus, we can infer that Pierre believes that London is pretty and that he believes that it is not pretty. This is paradoxical because Pierre cannot be faulted for anything that would account for his ending up with contradictory beliefs. We seem, therefore, to be in the bad position of having to say that Pierre both should and should not be ascribed contradictory beliefs.

This completes our brief historical sketch. I now want to go back over the philosophical controversies chronicled to show that my intensionalism does not end up the way Frege's did. There are three principal questions: the Wittgenstein–Kripke attack on the Fregean view that proper nouns refer on the basis of their sense, the Donnellan–Putnam attack on the Fregean view that common nouns do likewise, and Kripke's puzzle about belief. I shall take them in turn.

My intensionalism is not subject to the Wittgenstein–Kripke attack for the simple reason that it agrees with Wittgenstein and Kripke in their criticism of Frege. On Frege's intensionalism, names have a sense, but, on my intensionalism, it is, theoretically, an open question whether they do. This difference is a function of the difference between my notion of sense and Frege's. My notion, as explained in section I, treats senses as that part of the grammatical structure of expressions which determines whether the expressions have semantic properties and relations like meaningfulness, ambiguity, synonymy, analyticity etc. Thus, there is no theoretical commitment to the claim that proper nouns have sense. Whether proper nouns have sense becomes an independent question about the nature of the relevant semantic facts in natural language. If the facts are that proper nouns have semantic properties and relations like those just mentioned, then we will have to say that proper nouns have a sense, since positing that they have a sense will be required to explain their having these properties and relations. On the other hand, if proper nouns turn out to have none of these properties and relations, then we have to say they have no sense, since this will be the simplest and most natural way of explaining their lack of such properties and relations.

As it turns out, the evidence from English seems to show that proper nouns do not have semantic properties and relations, and hence, do not have sense. One form of such evidence is suggested by Mill's famous example 'Dartmouth'. Mill's discussion does not directly fit our criterion for deciding whether an expression has a sense because his discussion is, as it were, in the material mode. But we can easily transpose it. We note that 'Dartmouth' and other proper names do not enter semantic relations like antonymy. They have no antonym the way that a common noun like 'bachelor' does (i.e. 'spinster') or an adjective like 'happy' (i.e. 'sad'). If 'Dartmouth' had an antonym, it would be 'town lying somewhere other than at the mouth of the river Dart', but there is no incompatibility in the sentence 'Dartmouth lies somewhere other than at the mouth of the river Dart', as there is in 'Bachelors are spinsters'. To take another kind of evidence, 'Dartmouth' is not two ways ambiguous in virtue of referring both to the English town and to the American city; similarly, 'John Smith' is not thousands of ways ambiguous. To take one more kind, a noun phrase like 'The Gödel who proved the incompleteness of arithmetic' is not redundant, but one like 'The king who is a monarch' is. The relative clause in the former cannot duplicate the meaning of noun which is its head because this noun being proper, has none.[31]

This evidence contrasts the absence of semantic properties and relations in the case of proper nouns with their presence in the case of common nouns. Consequently, such evidence, on my notion of sense, also shows that common nouns have sense. This position on proper and common nouns contrasts with both the Fregean conception and Kripke's historical conception of reference. The Fregean conception claims that both proper and common nouns have sense, and that they both refer on the basis of their sense. Kripke's conception says that neither proper nouns nor common nouns have a sense,[32] and that both kinds of nouns refer on the basis of historical knowledge of the bare designation relation created in a baptismal ceremony. My conception disagrees with both Frege's and Kripke's conception, agreeing with Mill that common nouns have a sense while proper nouns do not.

But if there is agreement with Frege in the case of common nouns, the question arises whether my intensionalism succumbs to Putnam's argument against common nouns having sense. Putnam's argument is the following. Intensionalists hold that common nouns have a sense which is explicated in the predicate of analytic sentences with these nouns as subject. 'Cats are animals' would be an example of one of the analytic sentences explicating the sense of 'cat'. Thus, intensionalists are committed to asserting (P′).

(P′) 'Cat' expresses a concept that analytically, and hence, necessarily, includes the concept of being an animal.

Since sense determines reference, the intensionalist is also committed to claiming that (P′) entails (Q′), and hence, to claiming (Q′).

(Q′) The referents of 'cat' in statements could not be non-animals.

---

[31] Further evidence is presented in 'The Neoclassical Theory of Reference', pp. 112–13. See also J. S. Mill, *System of Logic*, I, ch. 2, and the much neglected work A. Gardiner, *The Theory of Proper Names* (Oxford University Press, London, 1954).

[32] I have corresponded with Kripke about whether he himself takes the view that no common noun has a sense. He denies taking this extreme position and provides examples of sentences he would consider analytic, e.g. 'Sages are wise'. Although these days analyticity can use every friend it has, particularly a philosopher of Kripke's stature, it is in a way puzzling that he should be willing to accept any cases of analyticity. The kind of argument that he uses in 'Naming and Necessity' in connection with natural kind common nouns to show that they do not have a sense are of exactly the same form as the arguments used by Putnam, Harman and others to show that no common noun has a sense. (See the reconstruction of this kind of argument in the text below.) If this kind of argument goes through in the case of 'gold', why does it not also go through in the case of 'sage'? If blue gold and robot cats suffice to refute analyticity in the range of natural kind nouns, why do stupid sages, such as Chance in Kosinski's *Being There*, not refute analyticity outside this range?

But (Q') is false, since, for contingent reasons, the objects to which 'Cat' has referred can be non-animals. It is entirely possible, for example, for such objects to turn out to be robot spy devices cleverly designed to make us think they are animals. Hence, by *modus tollens*, (P') is false.

Clearly, this argument works *only if* the intensionalism against which it is directed is committed to the claim that (P') entails (Q'). Thus, although the argument works against Fregean intensionalism, it does not work against an intensionalism like mine which does not make sense responsible for everything on which reference depends but assigns sense a weaker role in reference. For if an intensionalism does not claim that sense determines reference, Putnam cannot argue from the falsehood of (Q') to the falsehood of (P'). Rather than showing that there are no analytic connections, the argument shows nothing more than that it was mistaken of Frege to make sense responsible for everything on which reference depends. The science fiction possibilities that Putnam imagines can be taken to show that the referents of 'cat' are reference to robot spy devices under the widespread, but *ex hypothesi* false, belief that animal-looking things are actually animals.[33] Thus, nothing compels us to take these possibilities to show that the sense of 'animal' is not analytically included in the sense of 'cat'.

One thing that might encourage some philosophers to think that such analytic connection *is* challenged is the tendency to read Fregeanism into any intensionalism. Such philosophers would argue as follows. Frege introduced senses to fix reference. This was their sole function. Thus, if, as Putnam has shown, senses do not perform the function they were introduced to perform,

---

[33] In H. Putnam, 'The Meaning of "Meaning"', *Language, Mind, and Knowledge*, Vol. VII, *Minnesota Studies in the Philosophy of Science*, ed. K. Gunderson (University of Minnesota Press, Minneapolis, 1975), pp. 131–93, Putnam extends this type of argument in the case of synonymy. The result is the now famous twin-earth argument. Putnam puts the argument forth as a refutation of the 'traditional concept of meaning'. This, however, is, as we have seen in the text, mistaken. At best, the argument refutes the Fregean assumption that sense determines reference. Putnam explicitly rests that the argument on the assumption that 'the meaning of a term (in the sense of intension) determines its extension (in the sense that sameness of intension entails sameness of extension)' (pp. 135–6). Since Putnam's argument rests on this assumption, it is not good against intensionalism but only against intensionalisms that share Frege's strong form of (IV). Thus, to suppose that the argument refutes the 'traditional concept of meaning' involves supposing that the traditional concept *must* be reconstructed in a Fregean intensionalism, with the strong form of (IV). The fact that this latter supposition is false suffices to show that the twin-earth argument does not work against the traditional concept *per se*.

To be fair to Putnam, it should be noted that the only philosophers he refers to as espousing the traditional concept of meaning are Frege and Carnap, so possibly it is only their concept of meaning he has in mind. This interpretation is put into question, however, by the fact that the line of argument in 'The Meaning of "Meaning"' is of a piece with Putnam's earlier criticism of other reconstructions of the traditional concept of meaning. This suggests that he has his sights set on intensionalist semantics. (See the articles referred to in note 15).

If one wants an absolutely clear case of the view that the twin-earth argument refutes the concept of meaning no matter what the reconstruction, see Jerry Fodor's discussion in J. A. Fodor, 'Methodological Solipsism Considered as a Research Strategy in Cognitive Psychology', *The Behavioral and Brain Sciences*, 3 (1980), pp. 63–109; J. A. Fodor, 'Cognitive Science and the Twin Earth Problem', *Notre Dame Journal of Formal Logic*, 23 (1982), pp. 98–118. See my discussion of the first of these papers, J. J. Katz, 'Fodor's Guide to Cognitive Psychology', *The Behavioral and Brain Sciences*, 3 (1980), pp. 85–9.

they are idle. So, talk about sense inclusion is pointless if there is no direct pay-off in fixing an extensional inclusion.

This supposition is correct in the case of Frege's intensionalism, but not in the case of mine. On my view, the posit of senses is not based on their function of fixing reference. Rather, the posit is based on their function of explaining purely grammatical properties and relations in terms of a level of grammatical structure. The posit of senses is thus on a par with the posit of deep syntactic structure to explain why 'John is easy to please' and 'John is eager to please' do not have the same subject and direct object. Senses are introduced as the locus of the grammatical structure responsible for properties and relations of sentences like meaningfulness, ambiguity, synonymy, antonymy, redundancy and analyticity.

On my intensionalism, then, senses are not idle even if we leave reference out of the picture: the point of positing senses is to identify the locus of the grammatical structures underlying these properties and relations, and on this basis, to explain them in terms of their underlying grammatical structure. It is, therefore, an independent question how sense, so posited, is related to reference. As noted in section I, my intensionalism approaches this question by first making a distinction Frege's intensionalism fails to make, namely, the distinction between the reference of linguistic tokens in speech and the reference of their grammatical types in the language. As noted also, my intensionalism rejects Frege's strong thesis that sense determines both type and token reference, adopting the weaker thesis that senses determines only the reference of types. It, of course, assigns sense a role in token reference: sense is the common starting point for speakers of the same language in working out the reference of linguistic tokens in speech and writing, but many other factors, such as beliefs, intentions, perceptual information, pragmatic strategies, etc. play a major role. Such extra-semantic factors often cause the reference of a token to depart from the reference of its type. One might think of sense as determining token reference in the highly idealized case where no other factor enters to complicate the situation.[34]

---

[34] A few words are needed here to explain how senses and type references of expressions are determined, since, clearly, given the discussion in the text, they cannot be determined by inferences based on observations of uses of language and token referents. Such inferences might contribute indirectly to determining what the sense, and hence, the type reference, of an expression is, but it cannot be the basis for such determinations. That would make the account in the text incoherent, since, in this case, there would be no way to distinguish, as the account requires, between linguistic and extra-linguistic aspects of reference.

This issue about distinguishing then is, of course, at the heart of the controversy provoked by Putnam's critique of intensional semantics. The critique, it will be recalled, began with just this issue. The target of the papers that began it, Donnellan's 'Necessity and Criteria' and Putnam's 'It Ain't Necessarily So', was C. I. Lewis's account of analyticity in terms of inclusion of criteria of application. In Lewis's account, criteria are Fregean modes of presentation for referents cast in the role of a test for the applicability of a word. The point of the Donnellan and Putnam criticism, which was completely correct, was that the account provided no way of distinguishing linguistic tests from non-linguistic tests. Without a distinction between semantic criteria and empirical criteria, the Frege–Lewis position does not really distinguish analytic from contingent truth.

On my intensionalism, in contrast, there is a way of distinguishing sense and type reference that proceeds independently of the empirical conditions of language use. The claim that the sense of

Thus, the term 'referents' in (Q') is ambiguous: on the one hand, it can mean 'type referents' and on the other, it can mean 'token referents'. On the former interpretation, we have a claim to which my intensionalism subscribes, but the claim is one to which Putnam's counter-examples are irrelevant, while, on the latter interpretation, we have a claim to which Putnam's counter-examples are relevant, but the claim is not one to which my intensionalism subscribes.

Kripke's puzzle about belief and Kripke's claims about it have to be seen in the context of the widely held view that Putnam's (and Kripke's) arguments wipe away any possibility of using sense to explain the reference of nouns in identity statements. Kripke claims that his puzzle is a difficulty on a par with the Liar Paradox.[35] He says the puzzle is a problem for any theory of belief and naming just as the Liar Paradox is a problem for any theory of truth. Initially, I want to question this claim about the scope of the puzzle about belief. That the puzzle does not have the theory independence that Kripke claims for it seems clear from the fact that there is no puzzle on Frege's theory: (12) and (13) would express different propositions just as (10) and (11) do. What makes the puzzle seem to have such general scope is that Frege's theory has been put out of the running and this has made philosophers think that there is no form of intensionalism available to appeal to. If this were the case, then, in virtue of the fact that the only approaches to the study of reference left would be extensionalist ones employing something like Kripke's explanation of naming, the puzzle would be a difficulty for any approach.

None the less, the seriousness of the puzzle cannot be minimized: Frege's approach is out of the running, and the only alternative that has been formulated, namely, the one I have sketched above, agrees with Kripke that proper nouns do not have sense. Thus, it is not clear how, in practice, the situation that results from the introduction of my intensionalism differs from the situation Kripke has in mind in stressing the generality of his puzzle about belief. But I shall try to show that it is. I shall argue that my intensionalism's ability to bring to bear both a theory of sense developed within linguistic theory and a theory of reference (elsewhere called the 'neoclassical theory')[36] developed independently of Frege's theory of reference makes it possible to avoid ascribing contradictory beliefs to Pierre. The upshot of my argument will be that Kripke's puzzle about belief is only a difficulty for extensionalist conceptions of language, exhibiting a limitation of them in the very area – naming – generally regarded as their stronghold.[37]

'cat' involves an analytic connection to the concept of animality, like other claims about meaning, is evaluated on the basis of intuitions concerning the grammatical structure of expressions and sentences. As such, these claims are fully on a par with claims about syntactic form, e.g. whether a sentence is interrogative or clausally compound. Nothing about the extra-linguistic features of use enters the picture. In general, claims about semantic structure are acceptable in case their acceptance is necessary to achieve the simplest explanation of the available facts about ambiguity, redundancy, synonymy etc. of the expressions and sentences in question. Extra-linguistic considerations that plague the Frege–Lewis account fall out here in virtue of the fact that they complicate the explanation.

[35] 'A Puzzle about Belief', p. 267.

[36] 'The Neoclassical Theory of Reference', pp. 103–124.

[37] The solution proposed in R. B. Marcus, 'A Proposed Solution to a Puzzle about Belief', that appeared in *Midwest Studies in Philosophy*, Vol. VI, *The Foundations of Analytic Philosophy*, eds. P. A.

As with Mates's problem, so with Kripke's puzzle, the solution lies in looking more closely at the inner workings of compositionality. When this is done, we can construct a solution of the kind that Frege would give, i.e., (12) and (13) express different propositions, but on a semantic basis that Kripke can accept. Such a solution is never considered because it is supposed that, if proper nouns have no sense, then, insofar as (12) and (13) are the same except for the proper nouns, there can be no way for the meanings of (12) and (13) to be different, i.e. no way for the component meanings of (12) and (13) to differ at at least one point.

In order for (12) and (13) to express different propositions even though the proper nouns in them have no meaning, it must be possible for the process by which the meaning of a sentence is formed from the meanings of its parts to confer a derived meaning on words that have no meaning in themselves. Does such a thing happen in natural language? It certainly happens in the case of certain pronouns. 'It' and 'something' are semantically empty, but typically they acquire a derived meaning from other words with which they are grammatically related in a sentence. For example, in the sentence 'The dog drank it (something)', the pronoun 'it' ('something') acquires the meaning 'a liquid'. If

---

French, E. E. Uehling, Jr and H. K. Wettstein (University of Minnesota Press, Minneapolis, 1981), pp. 501–10, is inadequate for three reasons. First, on Marcus's view, we asked to drop the plausible epistemological principle that one cannot explicitly believe what one explicitly believes to be impossible and replace it with the principle that one cannot explicitly believe the impossible. But the principle we are asked to accept as a replacement would enable Hilbert and those who believed his program to develop a provably complete and consistent formalized mathematics to respond to Gödel by saying '[we never] *had* those beliefs to begin with' (p. 505). Moreover, Frege could have said more to Russell than 'I never concealed from [myself the] lack of self-evidence [of Basic Law V]' (see G. Frege, *The Basic Laws of Arithmetic*, trans. and ed. M. Furth (University of California Press, Berkeley, 1967), p. 127); he could have said he never even believed Basic Law V, despite the fact that he published it as a basic law, and Russell could not accuse him of any moral fault. Surely, Marcus's principle allows the mathematicians to get away with too much. Further, it is clear that Marcus's justification does not support the full strength of the principle she is proposing, since the intuition she gives as a basis for it is only relevant in the case of 'blatant impossibility' (p. 505), whereas the full principle most needs justification in cases like the above where no trace of blatancy exists.

Second, Marcus's solution requires us to take the objects of belief to be states of affairs, possible worlds, but this move, like taking propositions to be Montaguean intensions, has the disastrous consequence of collapsing all mathematical truths into one proposition, thus, for example, making the simple belief that $2 + 2 = 4$ the same belief as the belief that the equation $a^n + b^n = c^n$ is not solvable in integers for any $n > 2$. For a critique, see F. Katz and J. J. Katz, 'Is Necessity the Mother of Intension?', *The Philosophical Review*, LXXXVI (1977), pp. 70–96.

Third, Marcus's solution focuses on the disquotation principle, but this principle is, in fact, dispensable. Many of the things she says about the principle are, I think, important and true, and well worth philosophical consideration in connection with philosophical programs that place too much emphasis on the behavioral side of belief. But Kripke's puzzle about belief can be formulated without the step from assent to belief. The step from assent to belief is required because we view the situation from the outside, from our perspective on Pierre. Hence, we require some behavioral basis for inferring Pierre's internal epistemic states. But the puzzle might also be put in terms of Pierre's perspective, or from the first person perspective we would have were we in Pierre's position. From a first person, introspective perspective, a person in Pierre's position would know he believed the proposition expressed by (12) on the basis of descriptions available in France and know he believed the proposition expressed by (13) on the basis of acquaintance with his locale in London. The question of making an inference from a speech act of assent does not arise. Pierre, or we ourselves in his position, might then pose Kripke's puzzle to ourselves, or we might, if we could read Pierre's mind, pose the puzzle about him. In any of these cases, the puzzle is the same.

this is not intuitively clear, note that 'The dog drank it' is non-redundant in contrast to the redundant sentence 'The dog drank a liquid'. To the latter, a New Yorker would respond, 'So, what else could it drink?'. But even a New Yorker would not respond to 'The dog drank it' with 'So, what else could it drink?'. Hence, *the meaning of a word (in the language)* and *the meaning of a word in a sentence* are not the same thing.[38]

Proper nouns can acquire a derived meaning in a sentence in the same way as semantically empty pronouns like 'it' and 'something'. This is shown by the fact that 'Budweiser' also acquires the meaning 'a liquid' in the sentential context 'The dog drank—'. Therefore, it is a mistake for philosophers who quite rightly have been convinced by Mill's, Wittgenstein's or Kripke's arguments about proper nouns to jump to the conclusion that, because a proper noun has no meaning, it does not refer on the basis of meaning. After all, the reference of words normally takes place in a situation in which they are part of sentences, since sentences are the basic unit of language use. There is, then, a gap in the usual line of argument on the part of philosophers who invoke some version of the causal theory of reference immediately upon the successful use of Millian, Wittgensteinian or Kripkean examples to try to show that proper nouns do not refer on the basis of sense. It is thus too quick to go from such arguments to a doctrine of direct reference, as Kaplan and others have done.[39] There is the

---

[38] 'The Neoclassical Theory of Reference', pp. 118–19. There is a possible objection to this distinction on the part of philosophers who take it that Frege's 'fundamental principle', 'never ... ask for the meaning of a word in isolation, but only in the context of a proposition', (*Foundations of Arithmetic*, p. x) challenges the legitimacy of the notion of the meaning of a word in the language (see, for example, J. Wallace, 'On the Frame of Reference', in *Semantics of Natural Language*, pp. 219–52). This, however, is not the only way to construe Frege's none too transparent slogan. On what is perhaps the most natural construal of the slogan by itself, it constitutes an endorsement of compositionality that might serve as the epigraph of this essay. But the construal on which the slogan challenges the legitimacy of the notion of the meaning of a word outside a broader grammatical context seems clearly truer to Frege's intent as seen in the way he justifies his 'fundamental principle'. Frege says that, if one fails to observe the principle, then '... one is almost forced to take as the meanings of words mental pictures or acts of the individual mind, and so to offend against the distinction between the psychological and the logical, the subjective and the objective' (*Foundations of Arithmetic*, p. x). There are three objections to Frege's principle under this construal. I give them as support for my distinction between the meaning of a word in the language and the meaning of a word in a sentence in the language. First, Frege's principle is contradicted by plain examples. We make obviously correct statements about the meaning of words in a language without relativization to particular sentential or propositional contexts. For example, we say that 'perhaps' and 'maybe' are synonyms in English, that 'happy' and 'sad' are antonyms, that 'bank' is ambiguous. Indeed, we explain the unambiguousness of an occurrence of 'bank' in a particular sentential context in terms of the way the context disambiguates. Second, Frege's principle is inconsistent with compositionality. If the notion of the meaning of a word in the language is illegitimate, then there could be no account of the meaning of sentences as a function of the meanings of the words in them. The words in them would not come with meanings. Third, Frege's principle does not, in fact, receive support from the threat of psychologism and subjectivism, as Frege claims. Frege had a psychological and subjectivistic conception of natural languages, but one can take languages and their words and meanings to be logical and objective in the way Frege conceived of logic and propositions. See J. J. Katz, *Language and Other Abstract Objects* (Rowman & Littlefield, Totowa, 1982), for a Platonist conception of language.

[39] D. Kaplan, *Demonstratives* (preprint, UCLA Department of Philosophy, second draft). The supposition that Fregean propositions are the very model of propositions for intensionalists has misled those philosophers who have embraced the notion of direct reference and tried to build the objects referred to into propositions.

possibility, *via*, derived meaning, of explaining the reference of proper nouns on the basis of meaning, even though these nouns themselves have no meaning in the language.

In order to take advantage of this possibility, it is necessary to show that the assignment of derived meanings to proper nouns in the compositional process can operate beyond the range of transitive verbs (e.g. 'drink'). For note that the cases we are interested in are copula sentences like (10)–(13). Hence, if the way in which 'it', 'something', 'Budweiser' and other nominals obtain a derived meaning generally depends on semantic features of a transitive main verb, which is not present in copula sentences, then there will be no way to assign the proper nouns in (10)–(13) and similar sentences a derived meaning under which reference can take place. The copula is not like main verbs in the critical respect: it does not have rich enough intrinsic semantic structure to be the source of a derived meaning for proper nouns. If Pierre is to be absolved of the charge of believing irrationally, we must exhibit the existence of a parallel mechanism for assigning derived meanings in the case of copula sentences.

The stark simplicity of examples like (10)–(13) makes such a search seem hopeless. Indeed, if sentence structure were nothing more than what is heard or seen on the page when we observe sentences like (10)–(13), we would be stymied. But transformational grammar has taught us that there is a deeper structure to sentences underlying what we hear or see. Dramatic examples like 'John is easy to please' and 'John is eager to please' have shown that significant grammatical structure lurks beneath the surface. Taking account of transformational theory, we find that there is a possible source for the derived meaning of proper nouns in copula sentences and others lacking a semantically rich verb.

According to transformational theory, the level of deep syntactic structure contains, in addition to the sequence of morphemes from which the surface words of a sentence derive, an abstract system of categories or features that provide the syntactic classification of the morphemes. This system includes categories like noun, verb, count-noun, etc. Furthermore, the linguistics literature provides examples of such abstract syntactic categories that determine aspects of the meaning of the words assigned to them.[40] For instance, the syntactic distinction between singular and plural determines the semantic distinction between one and more than one, and the syntactic distinction between first, second and third person determines the semantic distinction between addressor, addressee and neither.[41] Such cases of the syntactic governing of a semantic distinction is accounted for on the basis of a semantic rule that operates in the compositional process at the point where the

---

[40] For a general discussion, see N. Chomsky, *Aspects of the Theory of Syntax* (MIT Press, Cambridge, 1965), pp. 75–106 and pp. 153–84. See also *Semantic Theory*, pp. 363–84, and J. J. Katz, *Propositional Structure and Illocutionary Force* (Harvard University Press, Cambridge, 1980), pp. 69–77.

[41] There are cases like 'scissors' and 'pants' which are called plural in many treatments of English grammar but which specify one item rather than more than one. These are not, however, cases where there is a singular/plural distinction, since no singulars exist. In fact, the 's' form is part of the morphological structure of the word, rather than a suffixed ending. When there is a singular/plural distinction in these cases, i.e. 'a pair of scissors (pants)' and 'two pairs of scissors (pants)', there is a semantic one/more than one contrast.

assignment of compositionally formed meanings reaches the governing syntactic category or feature. The rule would then assign the noun in question the conceptual interpretation (e.g. 'more than one' or 'addressor') specified by the governing syntactic category or feature (e.g. plurality or first person).

There is a syntactic distinction between proper nouns and common nouns. The categorization of nouns as 'proper' and 'common' controls their occurrence in contexts like the genitive construction 'the man's—'. Common nouns like 'doctor' occur in this context, but proper nouns like 'Benjamin Spock' do not. Just as the syntactic categorizations of singular and plural are the compositional source of certain number meanings, so the syntactic categorization of 'proper' is the compositional source of meaning of proper nouns in sentences. As a first approximation, we say that the occurrence of a proper noun *n* categorized as a proper noun receives the meaning 'bearer of "n"' in virtue of this categorization, while an occurrence of a noun categorized as a common noun does not receive such a meaning. One piece of evidence for this relationship is the fact that (14) is redundant in the manner of the sentence 'The dog drank the liquid'.

(14) Benjamin Spock who bears the name 'Benjamin Spock' ...

Just as we can respond in the case of 'The dog drank the liquid', 'So, big surprise – a liquid', we can respond in the case of (14), 'So, big surprise – the name "Benjamin Spock"'. Note, in contrast, the inapplicability of such a response to (15):

(15) The doctor who bears the name 'the doctor' ...

in which a common noun appears instead of a proper noun. Here, the response would be, 'Wow, some doctor!'

According to the neoclassical theory, the relationship exhibited in such evidence is handled by writing a semantic rule that specifies such a derived name meaning for proper nouns.[42] The rule must operate at the point in the compositional process where the syntactic structure of the sentence assigns a noun *n* to the category 'proper'. The rule, triggered by the syntactic symbol(s) expressing the category 'proper', will specify a derived name meaning *M* at this point.[43] Some care is required in formulating *M*. The neoclassical theory suggests (M).

---

[42] 'The Neoclassical Theory of Reference', p. 120.

[43] This point about the place of the operation is more important than it might seem at first glance. The reasons for having the rule operate where the syntactic structure of the sentence assigns the noun to the category '*Proper*' explains why the concept of being the bearer of 'n' is not to be taken as a sense of 'n' in isolation, and hence, why I can continue to maintain that proper nouns have no sense in isolation. There are two alternatives to such a rule each of which would be a way of saying that proper nouns have such a sense in isolation. The rationale for preferring such a rule to these alternatives is, then, the grounds for claiming that proper nouns do not even have this limited sense in isolation. The first alternative would be simply to write a representation of the concept 'the thing that is a bearer of 'n' as part of the dictionary entry for the noun "n". A single rule of the kind we are proposing is preferable to writing separate representations in the case of each proper noun

(M) the thing that is a bearer of 'n'

One aspect of (M) to note is that this concept contains both an element of
definiteness and an element of indefiniteness. It is widely observed that proper
nouns are definite whether or not they contain an occurrence of the definite
article; for example, compare 'God' with 'the Lord' or 'Satan' with 'the Devil'.
But the *in*definiteness of the relation of names in a language to their bearers in
the world causes some to question this element of definiteness. How can the
proper noun 'London' be definite if it names more than one London? (M) has
been formulated to show that the indefiniteness and definiteness in the concept
of a name appear in *different* aspects of the concept.

Indefiniteness, as (M) shows, is a matter of the existence of (typically)
multiple, contextually independent, correlations of a proper noun with bearers.
In the case of 'London', there is a correlation with London, England, a
correlation with London, Ontario, and a correlation with London, Ohio. Each
correlation is prior to and independent of the contexts where tokens of
'London' are used. Definiteness, as (M) shows, is a matter of contextually
dependent referential uses of a proper noun. This definiteness can be
understood as, roughly, the contextually fixed unique reference of a speaker's
use. The speaker chooses one correlation and uses the proper noun with the
intention that its bearer in that correlation be the contextually unique referent
of that use. If we take the correlations to be established by baptismal
ceremonies in the Kripkean sense and take such contextually unique reference
to encompass rigidity, we obtain a form of Kripke's doctrine that names are
rigid designators.[44]

---

both because it is far more economical and because it expresses the syntactic/semantic correspondence, whereas writing separate representations loses this generalization (i.e. there is no principle for
new cases). The second alternative would be to have a rule for assigning (M) but make it apply to an
occurrence of the feature proper in the syntactic specification of the noun within a dictionary entry.
This alternative would be both less economical and inadequate as an account of the productiveness
of naming in natural language. There is a general feature of English (presumably other natural
languages, too) of turning anything into a name. A string of words like:

> Thy cheeks are comely with rows of jewels, thy neck with chain of gold persuaded Jones to
> buy the car

is ill formed when its initial portion up to 'persuaded' is taken to belong to the category '*Common*'
but well formed when this portion is taken to belong to the category '*Proper*'. Such quotes from the
Bible are in fact used as names in parts of the South. Further, there is no restriction on what can be
so used in English. I can name my dog 'nothing nothings' or 'the meaning of a sentence is its
method of verification', or even 'Barkeley'. The full productiveness of natural languages in this
respect precludes the expressions in the class of potential names appearing in the dictionary with a
syntactic specification containing an occurrence of the feature [+ proper]. The simplest and most
adequate approach is, then, to impose no such syntactic requirement.

[44] Although there is no space here for a full discussion of the claim that the theory underlying our
treatment of proper names provides a reconstruction of the thesis that names are rigid designators,
the claim cannot be left without a few remarks. First, on our theory, the claim is not a claim about
proper nouns *per se* but a claim about their use. The ability of proper nouns to designate rigidly is not a
grammatical matter or a matter of the correlations between name and bearers, which may change in
all sorts of ways, but a matter of the use speakers make of a name based on a prior selection of one

Given this account of the meaning of proper nouns in sentences, the solution to Kripke's puzzle is straightforward. Since the semantic rule which assigns (M) interprets the occurrence of 'Londres' in (12) and the occurrence of 'London' in (13), the compositional meaning of (12) is that the bearer of 'Londres' is pretty and the compositional meaning of (13) is that the bearer of 'London' is not pretty. These propositions are, of course, logically compatible. Thus, we can say that Pierre proceeded faultlessly in arriving at his beliefs, and there is no temptation to say that he replaced an earlier belief with a later one. Pierre believes both that (12) and that (13), but having these beliefs, as our analysis shows, is not believing the contradiction that one and the same city is pretty and not pretty.

Kripke points out that his puzzle can be generated even within a single language:

> Peter (as we may as well say now) may learn the name 'Paderewski' with an identification of the person named as a famous pianist. Naturally, having learned this, Peter will assent to 'Paderewski had musical talent' and *we* can infer – using 'Paderewski,' as we usually do, to name the Polish musician and statesman:

(8) Peter believes that Paderewski had musical talent.

---

correlation. This selection specifies a bearer of the name, from that particular correlation, and the definite element in (M) functions in the use of the name to insure uniqueness of the referent in any context where the use is the same.

Second, given this reconstruction, there are direct rejoinders to the criticisms of the thesis that names are rigid designators in P. Ziff, 'About Proper Names', *Mind*, LXXXVI (1977), pp. 319–33. Some alleged counter-examples to the thesis involve the use of forms like 'a Nixon', e.g. 'Nixon might not have been (a) Nixon had someone given him adequate moral instruction in his youth'. Ziff calls these forms *count* nouns, but they are also common nouns. They are common nouns that have been formed from proper nouns on the basis of the attribute for which the bearer of the proper noun has become famous or infamous, e.g. the meaning of 'a Hitler' is derived from Hitler's tyrannical nature. (A name of someone who is not famous or infamous for anything – including being not known for anything – cannot be converted to a common noun.) But if such count nouns are also common nouns, the alleged counter-examples fail. Another set of alleged counter-examples which Ziff presents use what he calls 'names' of books, for example, 'The Brothers Karamazov'. But Ziff is wrong to call them 'names'. They are titles. Titles, unlike proper names do have meaning. Dostoyevsky might have titled his novel 'The Brothers Katkov' but not 'The Sisters Karamazov'. Because titles have meaning, a book which offers guidance in selecting a title will say that the meaning of the expression to be used as a title ought to reflect what the book is about. No such reference to literal meaning is involved in the case of names. A book which offers guidance in selecting a name for the baby deals only with associations that various names have.

Third, there is the question of whether our reconstruction does express Kripke's intent. It might be objected that it is true that Nixon might not have been a bearer of the name 'Nixon', but it is false, as Kripke says, that Nixon might not have been Nixon. This, I think, is wrong. When one says it is possible that the bearer of 'Nixon might not have been a bearer of "Nixon"', the statement expresses the claim that Nixon has a certain modal property, in virtue of the verb phrase of the sentence functioning as an attributive. To put Kripke's example in terms of my analysis requires an identity like 'The contextually definite man who is a bearer of "Nixon" might not have been the self-same man who is a bearer of "Nixon"'. This has the same truth value as Kripke's 'Nixon might not have been Nixon'. The proper application of (M) to cases in which there are two or more occurrences of the same proper noun in a sentence proceeds under the usual anaphora constraint (e.g. in 'Ronald Reagan can do whatever Ronald Reagan likes'). Hence, two or more occurrences of the same proper noun in a sentence are treated in terms of the same name/bearer correlation.

Only the disquotational principle is necessary for our inference; no translation is required. Later, in a different circle, Peter learns of someone called 'Paderewski' who was a Polish nationalist leader and Prime Minister. Peter is skeptical of the musical abilities of politicians. He concludes that probably two people, approximate contemporaries no doubt, were both named 'Paderewski.' Using 'Paderewski' as a name for the *statesman*, Peter assents to, 'Paderewski had no musical talent.' Should we infer, by the disquotational principle,

(9) Peter believes that Paderewski had no musical talent

or should we not?[45]

In earlier discussions of the semantics of proper nouns,[46] I observed that the bearer relation that occurs in (M) does not specify the kind of name that the value of 'n' can be. Another way of putting this is to say that the relation in (M) abstracts away from the specific information that differentiates Christian names, codenames, pen-names, stage names, nicknames, pet-names, and so on.[47] But, although the referential indicator in (M) is bare of identifying attributions, it has to have some sort of place-holder for such attributions. We have already seen a case where such a place-holder receives semantic content in the earlier example of how the proper noun 'Budweiser' receives the compositionally derived meaning of 'a liquid' (from the verb in the sentence 'The dog drank the Budweiser'). Another example is found in the meaning of noun phrases like 'Einstein the musicologist' where the modifier functions to distinguish the Einstein in question from *the* Einstein. A technical rendering of (M) will have to represent the place-holder in such a way that the attributions that are put there compositionally function as constraints on the object(s) that can be the bearer of 'n'.[48]

As Kripke says, Peter learns the name 'Paderewski' 'with an identification of the person named as a famous pianist'. Thus, when we express what Peter believes in this connection, our expression of it will be (16).

---

[45] 'A Puzzle about Belief', p. 265.

[46] 'A Proper Theory of Names', pp. 57–61.

[47] It should be clear from the lack of specificity of the bearer relation in (M) that the present theory is not another description theory of the sort that Kripke criticizes in 'Naming and Necessity' (pp. 283–84). Kripke is right to criticize Kneale's claim that 'Socrates' means 'the man called "Socrates"'. The telling point is that people might not be called by their names. Kneale's claim is, on the theory I am proposing, a contingent claim, having implications for the class of past acts in which reference was made to Socrates, while my claim, that Socrates is a bearer of the name "Socrates", has no such implications (e.g. it would be true even if the reference under 'Socrates' were brought off in virtue of a newly concocted convention on the part of speaker and audience, so that that use of 'Socrates' were the initial such naming use; see 'The Neoclassical Theory of Reference', p. 120, and 'A Proper Theory of Names', pp. 61–3). Note also that there is no violation of the noncircularity condition, such as Kripke accuses Kneale of. The bearer relation may, as I suggested in the papers just referred to, have referential conditions that are exactly as Kripke suggests in his baptismal account of naming.

[48] In the formalism that (M) informally represents, the element corresponding to 'thing' would be a categorized variable, to be replaced by a semantic representation of the concept of a sentient creature. See the discussion of (6.60) in *Semantic Theory*, pp. 259–60, for a similar use of categorized variables.

(16) Peter believes that Paderewski the famous pianist had musical talent.

The sense of 'the famous pianist' incorporates into the sense of the name in (16) in the same fashion that the concept 'a liquid' incorporates into the sense of the name 'Budweiser' in 'The dog drank Budweiser'. As Kripke also says, Peter, who does not think that a politician can have musical talent, learns that some Paderewski was a famous Polish politician. Thus, when we express what Peter believes in this connection, our expression of it will be (17).

(17) Peter believes that Paderewski the famous politician had no musical talent.

Similarly, the sense of 'the famous politician' incorporates into the sense of the name in (17). Peter believes that Paderewski the famous pianist and Paderewski the famous politician were different people, but, in fact, they are one and the same. Hence, to Kripke's question whether we should infer from what we have said about Peter's beliefs the principle (18):

(18) Peter believes that Paderewski had no musical talent.

the answer is clearly no. From a proposition of the form 'X believes A is P' and a proposition of the form 'X believes B is not-P', we cannot infer a proposition of the form 'X believes that C is not-P'.

Does Peter believe of the actual pianist–politician Paderewski, that he had no musical talent? This depends, I think, on how Peter acquires his information and the nature of the information. We might say that Peter has no beliefs about the actual pianist–politician Paderewski, except perhaps for thinking no such person exists. Peter has *de dicto* beliefs about a pianist Paderewski who is not a politician and *de dicto* beliefs about a Polish politician who is not a pianist, but no *de re* beliefs about any actual person. This would be reasonable to say if Peter had acquired his information by hearsay, from unauthenticated channels, and pieced together from various sources, with perhaps interpolation on Peter's part as well. On the other hand, if Peter's information comes from acquaintance with Paderewski, the situation is otherwise. Lois Lane believes *de re* that Clark Kent is a wimp (since his deception is successful) and she believes *de re* that superman is a fearless crusader for truth and justice. She has a mistaken and a correct belief about one and the same immigrant from the planet Krypton.[49]

---

[49] A number of further questions arise in connection with my account of compositionality and its application to proper names and Kripke's puzzle. I will briefly discuss what I think is the most important of the questions: *what form do translations of foreign sentences containing proper names take?* Well, if we are translating a French sentence that begins 'Pierre Elliott Trudeau ...' or 'François Mitterand ...' we preserve the French names; we do not render them 'Peter Elliott Trudeau ...' and 'Francis Mitterrand ...'. So my answer is that the technically correct translations preserve the foreign names. This is not to say that there are never overriding reasons to use a local form of the foreign names. Thus, we sometimes prefer the anglicized name 'Confucius' to the name 'K'ung Fu-tzu' for reasons such as ease of pronunciation, familiarity, not wishing to appear to be showing off, etc. Also, translation of sentences and translation of utterances are not the same thing. An English person translating the sentence 'Londres est jolie' would give 'London is pretty', but a translation of Pierre's sentence in the present circumstances is better given as 'Londres is pretty'

To recap, Kripke's puzzle arises because of a fallacy in the reasoning used to reach the paradoxical conclusion that Pierre seems to believe the impossible, even though he has proceeded in an epistemically faultless way. The fallacy occurs, on my analysis, at the step from the (true) premise that 'Londres' and 'London' have the same semantic value, namely London, to the (false) conclusion that (12) and (13) express inconsistent propositions. This step is taken because it is mistakenly thought that there cannot be a difference between the proposition expressed by (12) and the proposition expressed by (13) except for the negation. This thought is based on the observation that, apart from the negation, the sentences (12) and (13) have exactly the same syntactic structure and corresponding words in them have the same sense when they have sense and the same semantic value when they do not have sense. But this observation alone is not enough to yield the conclusion that there can be no difference between the proposition. The conclusion also requires an assumption about the nature of compositionality. I submit that those who have had this thought in taking the fallacious step have assumed that word meanings combine in the manner of Frege's 'building stone' metaphor, so that, when two words in corresponding positions in otherwise identical sentences have no meaning, there are two identical windows.

Therefore, the mistake in the case of Kripke's puzzle is the same as the mistake in the case of Mates's problem. Both depend on the false assumption that sameness of meaning for expressions of the language must correspond to sameness of meaning for those expressions in sentences of the language. Both of them lose their power to bewilder when we fully appreciate the power of compositionality.[50]

IV

In this paper, I have sought to exonerate intensionalism and to put the blame that it has received where it rightly belongs, on Frege's intensionalism and the supposition that his intensionalism is the last word on intensionalism. This section adds a coda.

---

even though this would sound strange in the mouth of an English speaker (since here 'London' can claim privilege). For Pierre did not say, as he might have, 'London est jolie', in the way that we might say, being deferential to the Chinese, 'K'ung Fu-tzu is a philosopher', but rather 'Londres est jolie'. Had Pierre said the former, we would have to suppose either that he sees his mistake on arrival in London or has used 'London' as Peter used 'Paderewski', with some distinguishing description corresponding to 'the pianist' that he got from his informants in Paris. Since it is in the nature of the case that he sees no mistake, and since, as we have seen from the discussion of the Peter case in the text, our solution works even when the names are the same, one might as well, for purposes of clarity, translate Pierre's Paris utterance as 'Londres is pretty'.

[50] Murray Kiteley (personal communication) points out that the present account of the sense of sentences with proper names explains the fact that there are *de re/de dicto* readings of sentences such as 'Oedipus thought Jocasta a good match'. Since *de re/de dicto* readings seem to be scope phenomena, where the scope of the propositional attitude verb or modal interacts with that of a quantified noun phrase including descriptions, how would the explanation go if names are not somehow to be interpreted descriptively in the senses of sentences?

There is one more mistake resulting from the assimilation of intensionalism to Fregean intensionalism. This assimilation gives the impression that the range of justificatory arguments available to the intensionalist is quite narrow, being restricted to the two that Frege gave. This mistaken impression both makes the intensionalist position seem less robust than it is and makes the task of extensionalists seem easier than it is.

The source of this restriction on the range of justificatory arguments is found, I believe, in Frege's indirect way of characterizing sense. Thinking of sense as merely a mode of presenting reference directs our attention to reference when we turn to the task of trying to justify sense. Indeed, Frege's two justificatory arguments, which turn on the explanation of the difference in cognitive value between identity sentences like (10) and (11) and on stating the conditions for inference by substitution into opaque contexts, seem to arise from a direct concern with the theory of reference. Be this as it may, when senses are introduced as I have introduced them, as the grammatical structure in sentences on which their ambiguity, synonymy relations, redundancy or non-redundancy etc. depend, our attention is directed to the full range of justificatory arguments. For there is an argument for positing senses wherever there is such a semantic property or relation whose explanation requires reference to senses.

One way to appreciate the scope of the full range of justificatory arguments available to intensionalism once we have emancipated intensionalism is to note that the justificatory arguments Frege gave are special cases in the new approach. The Fregean attempt to justify senses as playing an essential role in explaining why certain inferences by substitution into opaque contexts go through is the special case of justifying senses on the basis of explaining analytic entailment. The Fregean attempt to justify senses as playing an essential role in explaining the informativeness of sentences like (19) in contrast to the uninformativeness of sentences like (20)

(19) Mark Twain is Samuel Clemens
(20) Mark Twain is Mark Twain

is the special case of justifying senses on the basis of explaining the non-synonymy of (19) and (20) and on the basis of explaining the syntheticity of (19) and the analyticity of (20) (i.e. (19) expresses the synthetic proposition that the bearer of the name 'Mark Twain' is the bearer of the name 'Samuel Clemens' and (20) expresses the analytic proposition that the bearer of the name 'Mark Twain' is the bearer of the name 'Mark Twain').

But not only are analytic entailment, synonymy and analyticity just three of the semantic properties and relations with respect to which justificatory arguments can be formulated – there is also meaningfulness, ambiguity, redundancy, antonymy etc. – the cases of analytic entailment, synonymy and analyticity considered are simply an arbitrary few from among the wealth of cases in natural language. There is, then, an enormously wider range of options available to intensionalists for justifying their posit of senses than is ever considered in the discussions of the intensionalist/extensionalist issue.

5

How to Turn the *Tractatus* Wittgenstein into (Almost) Donald Davidson

J. J. C. SMART

Some years ago, when I was lecturing to third-year undergraduates at the University of Adelaide on Wittgenstein's *Tractatus*, which after all attempts to show how there could be a certain sort of truth theory for a language, I thought that it would be fun to introduce the students to the ideas of Donald Davidson by comparing the *Tractatus* with some of Davidson's earlier writings. My hope is that, especially towards the end of a conference containing so many deep and demanding papers, some of my audience today may be in the mood for a little light relief and may be disposed to find my comparisons fun too. I shall refer particularly to Davidson's papers 'True to the Facts', 'Theories of Meaning and Learnable Languages', and 'Truth and Meaning'.[1] I am not saying that Wittgenstein necessarily had in the forefront of his mind the Davidsonian concerns that I shall attribute to him. I am merely wanting to say that with hindsight we can see the *Tractatus* as interesting, in a way in which we would not find the *Investigations* interesting, because we can see the *Tractatus* in a Davidsonian light. Of course the *Investigations* is interesting in other ways, and perhaps is even the greater work of the two, but nevertheless its main concerns are not really incompatible with what I shall suggest is most interesting about the *Tractatus*, and perhaps the later Wittgenstein was unkind to his earlier self when he held that one purpose of his later philosophy was to show how wrong he had been in the *Tractatus*. In the *Investigations* Wittgenstein is concerned to see language in terms of its *use*, its relation to intellectual, social, or practical contexts (forms of life), or as Davidson put it in a letter to me in 1971, with what speakers mean, not with what words mean. The latter is the theme of the *Tractatus*, and the two interests are quite consistent with one another. In the context of radical interpretation the two interests presumably come together.[2]

---

[1] Reprinted in Donald Davidson, *Inquiries into Truth and Interpretation* (Clarendon Press, Oxford, 1984).

[2] See 'True to the Facts', especially *Inquiries into Truth and Interpretation*, p. 45. I think that the difficult question of the relation between word meaning and speaker meaning is further illuminated by Davidson's recent paper, 'A Nice Derangement of Epitaphs' [cf. This volume: 433–46]. The notion of word meaning is compatible with the fact of speakers having idiosyncratic idiolects.

There is also much of interest in the later writings of Wittgenstein in the discussion of 'following a rule', and of such matters as 'family resemblance' and what Friedrich Waismann developed into the idea of the 'open texture' of concepts. Much of this of course has to do only with the learning of particular predicates (e.g. '... is a game') and is supplementary to truth theoretical semantics, and quite consistent with it.

Of course to defend the view that the things I find most interesting in the *Tractatus* (i.e. the almost Davidsonian concerns) were Wittgenstein's own real or main concerns (in his earlier phase) I would need a much greater familiarity than I possess with the vast corpus of Wittgenstein's writings and correspondence. I have no patience with the idea (characteristic, I am told, of the hermeneutic school of philosophy in Europe) that biographical evidence (even if used with caution) has no importance for interpreting a writer's words. As Davidson has argued in many of his various writings, in radical interpretation we need to guess simultaneously at beliefs, desires and meanings.[3] In trying to understand a philosopher our interpretation is not radical, and if biographical evidence enables us to get at beliefs and desires independently, then this evidence should surely be important for getting at meanings. But I shall not attempt to consider such evidence here, and so this paper should not be seen as a contribution to Wittgensteinian scholarship.

A language, such as English, contains a finite number of words and other symbols. On the other hand a person understands an indefinitely large number of sentences. (Idealizing a bit, we could say that a person understands a potential infinity of sentences, but of course this *is* idealization, because of the finiteness of the human memory store, the finiteness of the length of possible neural computations, and so on. Compare the way in which the notion of a Turing machine provides a useful idealization of that of a real computer, or the way in which in electrical theory it can be mathematically easier to study infinite lines, with results that make a useful approximation to what happens in long lines.) In his early paper, already mentioned, on 'Theories of Meaning and Learnable Languages', Davidson contended that this makes plausible the contention that the meanings of the infinite class of sentences of the language are somehow recursively definable in terms of the meanings of the individual words and symbols. It is hard indeed to see how language learning would be possible without some underlying recursive mechanism (of which of course we are not consciously aware).[4] Semantics should be part of the totality of natural science,[5] and so should be pursued in close association with psycho-linguistics. Psycho-linguistic plausibility should strengthen the plausibility of a semantic theory.

---

[3] See also David Lewis, 'Radical Interpretation', *Synthese*, 27 (1974), pp. 332–4.

[4] Of course *some* of our linguistic abilities may depend on the capacity to perceive vague analogies and other informal features. But to give a general explanation of our linguistic abilities recursiveness must surely play a central role in the story.

[5] I am not sure how far Davidson agrees here. Semantics is bound up with the notion of interpretation and hence with the psychology of the propositional attitudes, and Davidson has contended that this can not be made fully scientific, as (for example) neurophysiological theories in psychology can be fully scientific. See Donald Davidson, 'Psychology as Philosophy', in his *Essays on Actions and Events* (Clarendon Press, Oxford, 1980).

Davidson showed that this demand for recursiveness explodes some influential theses. Consider, for example, his criticism of the view that phrases with inverted commas round them (so as to mention the interior phrases) are unanalyzable names. We would have to learn indefinitely many such primitive names, whereas clearly we have a way of understanding such an inverted comma expression even if we have never come across it before. The demand for recursiveness also gives rise to problems, such as with indirect speech and assertions of propositional attitudes (beliefs, desires, etc.). Davidson grappled with these latter problems in his 'On Saying That'.[6] A different way of giving a recursive semantics for the propositional attitudes has recently been proposed by Howard Burdick.[7]

In his 'Truth and Meaning', Davidson contended that even though the notion of meaning is useless it is nevertheless the case that to understand the meaning of a sentence is at least to understand its truth conditions. Understanding the truth conditions of a sentence is of course not to be confused with knowing how to tell whether a sentence is true. Davidson therefore proposed to replace the intuitive notion of the meaning of a sentence by that of the sentence's truth conditions as shown by the way in which the corresponding T-sentence (of the form 'S is true if and only if p') can be deduced from a suitable 'truth theory' for the language. Tarski showed how the truth-conditions for all sentences of a language that can be formalized in the notation of quantification theory (first-order predicate logic) can be defined in terms of a finite set of axioms giving the truth (or rather satisfaction) conditions for a finite number of entities, namely the primitive predicates, the truth functional connectives and the quantifiers.[8] Davidson's research programme is based on the assumption that the underlying structure of a language is that of quantification theory. The success or otherwise of the research programme will of course decide the goodness or otherwise of his assumption. If some other structure proved necessary, it would still be plausible that it also admitted a recursive characterization of truth. In this paper I shall not question Davidson's research programme, and will assume that (at least with unimportant exceptions) all sentences of colloquial languages can indeed be bent into a quantificational form.

Certainly Davidson has already gone a long way in this direction. He has shown how Tarski's method can be extended to deal with tenses and other indexical and context-dependent expressions. As already noted, there is trouble with sentences about propositional attitudes. Putatively intensional sentences have to be shown to have an underlying extensional form. Again adverbs and modifying adjectives give trouble. 'Bill is a good burglar' is not equivalent to 'Bill is good and is a burglar.' Davidson's heroic programme is to exhibit these

---

[6] In *Inquiries into Truth and Interpretation*.

[7] Howard Burdick, 'A Logical Form for the Propositional Attitudes', *Synthese*, 52 (1982), pp. 185–230.

[8] See Tarski's great paper 'The Concept of Truth in Formalized Languages', in A. Tarski, *Logic, Semantics, Metamathematics* (Clarendon Press, Oxford, 1956). The most readable exposition of Tarski's theory that I know can be found in W. V. Quine, *Philosophy of Logic*, (Prentice-Hall, Englewood Cliffs, NJ, 1970), and the account is completely general, whereas Tarski illustrates his method by reference to a special sort of case.

apparently non-quantificational structures as quantificational after all. Thus Davidson exhibits the deducibility of '*x* walks' from '*x* walks rapidly', which at first sight seems to be beyond the resources of quantification theory, by supposing that the first sentence has the underlying structure of '(∃*y*)(*y* is a walking of *x*)' and that the second sentence has the underlying structure of '(∃*y*)(*y* is a walking of *x* and *y* is rapid).' Davidson's strategy is therefore to try to exhibit the logical forms (as opposed to the surface grammatical forms) of apparently non-quantificational sentences so that their non-quantificational appearance is seen to be illusory. Then one can explain (as in the last example) certain facts about deducibility, and if one can show that there is a mechanical way of getting from surface grammatical form to logical form the recursiveness of a Tarski-type truth theory will go *some* way towards explaining how our finite brains can understand an arbitrarily large class of arbitrarily complex sentences.

Now to Wittgenstein. It seems likely that when he wrote the *Tractatus*, Wittgenstein's motivation was considerably different from Davidson's. However, like Davidson, he tried to demonstrate that language is at bottom extensional and that the truth conditions for all sentences can be given in a recursive manner. Indeed Wittgenstein held not only that language is quantificational but that it is truth functional. Complex sentences are truth functions of atomic ones. Atomic sentences, such as '*aRb*' for example, where '*a*' and '*b*' are names and 'R' a predicate, picture atomic facts. For my purposes, all that I need to say about Wittgenstein's notion of picturing is that the base clauses of a *Tractatus*-style truth theory would include such clauses as ' "*aRb*" is true if and only if *aRb*'.[9] Wittgenstein does make use of universal and existential quantification, but he interprets universally quantified and existentially quantified sentences as possibly infinite conjunctions and disjunctions respectively. It is clear from this that for Wittgenstein the quantifiers have a deviant sense. They are not defined in terms of satisfaction (by objects in the world) of predicates or open sentences, as occurs in Tarski's theory. Wittgenstein's quantifiers are not 'objectual' as are Tarski's but are 'substitutional'. Thus when Wittgenstein says that '(∃*x*)F*x*' should be interpreted as 'F*a* ∨ F*b* ∨ F*c* ∨ ...' where '*a*', '*b*', '*c*', are the names in the language, he is cheating a bit, as the dots indicate. He is pretending to write out what he can not write out. (*A fortiori* should there be infinitely many names, though this in itself raises problems about learnability, except in such cases as that of arithmetic, where there is a way of constructing infinitely many numerals, '0', '0′', '0″' ... and correlating them with numbers. But of course in the *Tractatus*, Wittgenstein did not regard arithmetical sentences as expressing propositions, and did not regard numerals as names of entities. He seems to have had a rather narrow conception of arithmetic anyway.)

In some of his earlier papers F. P. Ramsey adopted Wittgenstein's notion of existential and universal quantification as possibly infinite disjunction and conjunction. However in a later paper he pointed out that this was no good because such expressions could never be written out. He said 'What we can't

---

[9] Wittgenstein has more than this to say about picturing, of course. Isomorphism is important for him. On atomic sentences as pictures see G. E. M. Anscombe, *Introduction to Wittgenstein's Tractatus*, 4th ed., (Hutchinson, London, 1971), p. 100, and Wilfrid Sellars, *Science and Metaphysics* (Routledge and Kegan Paul, London, 1968), chapter 4, paragraph 45 (p. 108).

say we can't say, and we can't whistle it either.'[10] Nevertheless there is a way of 'whistling it'. This is to give an account of quantification as substitutional. Or, at least there would be if substitutional quantification were always an acceptable notion. Substitutional quantification can be all right if merely in certain ways *supplementary* to objectual quantification. Thus if someone were to write '(*p*) it is true that *p* if and only if *p*' we would have to interpret the '(*p*)' as substitutional. The sentence does not give a finitely axiomatized truth theory or insight into the logical forms of sentences of the language as a Tarski-type theory does. It is semantically useless because it lacks the property of recursively defining truth conditions in terms of a finite set of axiomatic truth conditions. Nevertheless '(*p*) it is true that *p* if and only if *p*' does at least *make sense* if the quantifier is substitutionally interpreted. The quantifier can not be an objectual one, because '*p*' is a dummy for a sentence: it is not a variable (not in name position, not referential as a variable is). Moreover what can be said with this sort of substitutional quantification can be said more perspicuously without it, by going up to the meta-language. It should be noted that since '*p*' is not in name position, this substitutional quantification is introduced without any ontological commitment. Since sentences assert but do not denote there is no question of anything being denoted by the substitutionally quantified variable '*p*'. This is even more obvious in the case of Leśniewski's remark (in conversation with Quine in 1933)[11] that we could quantify substitutionally over a left-hand parenthesis. We could write, say,

$$[(\exists x) \, [xa + b)^2 = a^2 + 2ab + b^2].$$

(The outer brackets are written as square for visual clarity only.)

In discussing the *Tractatus* we need not consider such rather pathological uses of substitutional quantification because it is clear that if Wittgenstein's theory of the quantifiers as possibly infinite disjunctions and conjunctions is interpreted as a substitutional one, as I have suggested that it should be, then the substitution class for the quantifiers consists only of names, and in the *Tractatus* every name is the name of some entity. Clearly 'Mr Pickwick' can not be one of the substitution class, since there is no Mr Pickwick in the universe and 'Mr Pickwick' can not be a *Tractatus*-style name. We should understand assertions ostensibly about Mr Pickwick as they occur in *Pickwick Papers* as follows. We should take Dickens to be pretending (in some weak sense of 'pretend') to talk about Mr Pickwick, i.e. to be pretending to refer to a real person, not actually talking about a pretence (or fictional) person, because there are no pretence persons, and *a fortiori* no pretence persons to be referred to or named.[12] According to this view, Dickens was pretending (or half-pretending)

---

[10] In his paper 'General Propositions and Causality'. See F. P. Ramsey, *Foundations*, ed. D. H. Mellor, and *Introductions* by D. H. Mellor, L. Mirsky, T. J. Smiley and Richard Stone (Routledge and Kegan Paul, London, 1978), p. 134. Ramsey here considers the suggestion that '(x)Fx' represents a conjunction.

[11] See W. V. Quine, *Ontological Relativity and Other Essays* (Columbia University Press, New York), p. 106.

[12] On the 'pretence' theory of fiction see Gilbert Ryle, 'Imaginary Objects', *Aristotelian Society*, supp. vol. 12 (1933), 18–43, reprinted in Ryle's *Collected Papers* (Hutchinson, London, 1971). See

to operate an objectual and extensional semantics, not actually operating an intensional one or a non-classical one.

Someone might object to my remark that in the *Tractatus* there is always an object referred to by any name on the grounds that Wittgenstein says in *Tractatus* 1.1 that 'The world is the totality of facts, not of things.' However it is likely that what Wittgenstein is doing in 1.1 is to make the point (perhaps in a rather obscure way) that only in the context of a sentence does a word have a sense, and that science could not be a mere recital of names. Most of us, of course, would want to say the opposite to what Wittgenstein says in 1.1, if this proposition is construed literally. The world surely consists of things not of facts. There is great difficulty in believing that the world even *contains* facts. Indeed in 'True to the Facts', Davidson plausibly argues that if there are facts then there is only one fact: the Great Fact. (There is a slight puzzle here. Davidson's argument to the Great Fact uses what Wittgenstein would count as molecular sentences. This may show that 'is the same fact as' is an equivalence relation, but it cannot be used *directly* to show that 'is the same *atomic* fact as' is an equivalence relation. However, if atomic facts are facts, and there is only one fact, it would follow that there is only one atomic fact!) If we do not think of facts as objects in the world there is a problem about even stating a correspondence theory of truth. What are these facts to which a sentence could or could not correspond? According to Wittgenstein, sentences and pictures are themselves facts and not things. Ordinarily of course, we would say that sentences and pictures are things (sequences of symbols, photographic films, or whatever) not facts. The elements in the picture must correspond to elements in the fact. The sentence is a picture in the sense that it is a fact that names stand in a certain relation to one another. (See 3.1432.) This strongly suggests that corresponding to the names there must be named objects as the other terms of the correspondence. (No doubt Wittgenstein would object that I am here talking of what can be shown but not said, but I shall here ignore this obscure side of his thought.)

We may take it then that the '*a*', '*b*', '*c*', ... in the *Tractatus* are names that refer to things outside themselves, and hence that if quantification is defined substitutionally the substitution class in question does consist of expressions that refer to extra-linguistic objects, and the language does carry ontological commitment to named objects.[13]

What seems to be a decisive objection to holding that quantification is everywhere substitutional is that we have names for relatively few of the objects in the world.[14] For how many kangaroos, puddles, or stones have I got names or

also Michael Devitt, *Designation* (Columbia University Press, New York, 1981), pp. 170–1. The theory has been opposed by my colleague Richard Routley, in his *Exploring Meinong's Jungle and Beyond* (Department of Philosophy, Research School of Social Sciences, Australian National University, Canberra, 1980), pp. 598–605.

[13] For good remarks on the absurdity of supposing that the possibility of substitutional interpretation must necessarily deprive a language of ontological commitment, see Saul Kripke, 'Substitutional Quantification', in Gareth Evans and John McDowell (eds), *Truth and Meaning* (Clarendon Press, Oxford, 1976). See especially pp. 413–4.

[14] See W. V. Quine, *The Roots of Reference* (Open Court, La Salle, Illinois, 1973), p. 103, and Saul Kripke, 'Substitutional Quantification', pp. 380–1. If one *already* believes in objectual

has anyone got names? 'All kangaroos hop' can hardly be interpreted by 'For any x if x is the name of a kangaroo then if x is substituted for "y" in "y hops" the result is a true sentence'. This last sentence could be true even if some unnamed kangaroos failed to hop. (Notice also the use of what seems to be objectual quantification in this meta-linguistic sentence.)

As Davidson pointed out to me in the letter of 1971 to which I have already referred, substitutional quantification and the picture theory go together. Atomic sentences and atomic facts are supposed to correspond, and quantification comes from substitution in atomic sentences so as to form conjunctions or disjunctions of them. On the other hand, as Davidson argues in 'True to the Facts', with objectual quantification the fundamental relation between language and the world is not one of sentences picturing facts but of predicates being satisfied by things (or sequences of things). Thus Davidson's theory is not a correspondence theory, though it is within the *spirit* of the correspondence theory of truth. Truth is elucidated in terms of a relation between language and something in the world,[15] though the relation is not correspondence but satisfaction.[16] We should say that the world consists of things, not of facts, that pictures are things not facts, and that sentences are not pictures.

---

quantification, one will be disposed to say that substitutional quantification can not be adequate for mathematics. A language could not have more than denumerably many names, but there are indenumerably many real numbers. However, Cantor's proof of the indenumerability of the class of real numbers (or of the class of classes of natural numbers) will be interpreted by the advocate of substitutional quantification as merely showing the unspecifiability of the naming relation. So the argument against substitutional quantification from the indenumerability of the reals would be a circular one. See Quine, ibid. pp. 113–14 (if I have not misunderstood the argument, which is quite possible). Quine gives other objections from set theory against substitutional quantification. Against Wittgenstein unnamed kangaroos provide a good enough argument. In the *Tractatus* there does not seem to be provision for set theory anyway. Wittgenstein seems to reduce even arithmetic to the trivially computable, which suggests a very serious weakness in his system. Indeed even among the trivially computable there are semantic problems for the *Tractatus*. This is because Wittgenstein says that arithmetic consists of equations (6.2) and these are not sentences or pictures, and numerals are not names. So it is not quite clear how the *Tractatus* allows even such a sentence as '$(\exists x)\ (x < 7)$', though of course a slight modification could easily fix this up, by allowing molecular composition of equations no less than of sentences and substitutional quantification not on names but on symbols for exponents of operations (6.02, 6.021).

[15] See Davidson, 'True to the Facts', p. 48.

[16] Semantics, to be harmonized with total science, surely does need to show how language hooks onto the world. An extensional theory such as Davidson's or Wittgenstein's in the *Tractatus* does attempt to meet this requirement. One problem I have with Richard Routley's very interesting and ingenious post-Meinongian semantics (in Routley's *Exploring Meinong's Jungle and Beyond*) is that his 'aboutness' relation is a non-classical one (he gives the word 'reference' to his opponents, and so I follow him in using 'about'). One can talk about the King of France without being committed to the existence of the King of France. From the point of view of classical semantics the context 'N is about ...' is an intensional one, but from within Routley's theory that would not be quite the right way of putting it. This of course has its advantages – one can talk about sets or unicorns or ideal mass points or whatever one likes without actually believing in them. I hanker after a real relation to hook language onto the world. Classically the supposed relation of 'Pegasus' to Pegasus is not a real relation, because one term of the relation does not exist to be related to the other term – at least this is obvious if one allows a relation to be a set of ordered pairs. In an ordered pair, both elements of the pair exist. In reply to me (see *Exploring Meinong's Jungle and Beyond*, pp. 613–17) Routley points out that a classical reference relation is easily defined by means of his non-classical one. Nevertheless I still have a strong desire to say that the *fundamental* semantic relation should be

This is all to the good because (as was noted above and as Davidson argued) facts are suspect entities anyway. We may hold that Davidson has made the right choice here, and that Wittgenstein, writing at an earlier time (and before Tarski), understandably made the wrong one. Nevertheless we can say that in the *Tractatus*, Wittgenstein was far in advance of his time in his awareness of the main semantic issues. We do see some sort of anticipation of Davidson's programme. Wittgenstein does try to give a recursive account of the infinity of sentences of our language. Moreover he does puzzle (though less fruitfully than Davidson) about some at least of the apparent exceptions to the quantificational structure of language. For example *Tractatus* 5.542 shows Wittgenstein's desire to avoid saying that '*A* believes that ...', '*A* has the thought that ...' and '*A* says that ...' are non-truth-functional (intensional) operators. Wittgenstein's solution that '*A* says *p*' is of the form '"*p*" says *p*' does not seem to be satisfactory.[17] But it does at least show a desire to grapple with the problem that Davidson confronted in his 'On Saying That', and Burdick confronted in his aforementioned paper.

To sum up. In his paper 'True to the Facts' Davidson revives the *spirit* of the correspondence theory of truth. However, because of objectual quantification his theory is based on a relation between predicates and things (or sequences of things), not between sentences and facts (Wittgenstein's 'picturing'). This is all to the good because facts are questionable entities anyway, and questionable also is the substitutional quantification that goes with the picture theory. Davidson has made the right decision here and Wittgenstein the wrong one, but we may allow that Wittgenstein was in advance of his time in his awareness of the main semantic issues. Later on, in the *Investigations* and other writings he seems to have lost sight of them, and to have concerned himself mainly with the pragmatics of language use and language learning. His interest had largely shifted from the use of words in sentences (how words function semantically) to questions of the way we use sentences, how language functions within a form of life. In so far as there is a semantics implicit in the *Investigations*, the approach is behaviouristic and it can give the impression that learning language is rather like the conditioning of pigeons. Recursiveness has dropped out of sight. We

---

classical (and indeed that if it is not so it is not really a relation). But in a mere footnote I can not do justice to the originality, ingenuity and philosophical virtuosity displayed in Routley's book, and so what I say here should be taken more as indicative of a point of view than as a proper philosophical argument against Routley.

[17] Irving M. Copi, in his paper, ' "Tractatus" 5.542', *Analysis*, 18 (1958), 102–4, reprinted in Irving M. Copi and Robert W. Beard, *Essays on Wittgenstein's Tractatus* (Routledge and Kegan Paul, London, 1966), interprets '"*p*" says *p*' as asserting a correlation between the elements of a sentence '*p*' (or possibly a sentence-like structure in the mind) with the elements of the fact that *p*. But here, in consonance with Wittgenstein's thought, structures have to be taken as facts not things. To deal with false assertions and false beliefs, the correlations of elements in the mental or linguistic facts have to be with how things are related in the world, and in the case of false assertions and beliefs the correlations will be with things related to one another as in fact they are not related. But there are no things related as they are not related in the actual world. (At least if there are no merely possible but not actual worlds.) Moreover even if Copi's account worked it would do so only for Wittgensteinian atomic propositions, with rigid names. The troubles over assertion and belief typically arise out of referential opacity, and this presupposes definite descriptions and hence molecular, not atomic, propositions.

must not forget the indefinite extent of our ability to understand ever more complex sentences, which implies that after all – at least at a deep level – language must have more of the characteristics of a calculus than the later Wittgenstein allows it to have. Anyway, I have tried to explain why one can (almost) turn the Wittgenstein of the *Tractatus* period into Davidson (change picturing into satisfaction and substitutional quantification into objectual), and that is one reason why in a way I have come to like the *Tractatus* better than the *Investigations*.[18]

---

[18] As indicated in the text I have been much aided by correspondence with Davidson, but of course he should not be saddled with any errors which occur in this paper! I am also grateful to William Demopoulos for so ably acting as commentator on my paper at the conference. Since completing this paper I have seen that Saul Kripke has pointed out similarities between the *Tractatus* and Davidson's theory of semantics for natural languages. See Saul A. Kripke, *Wittgenstein on Following a Rule and Private Language* (Basil Blackwell, Oxford, 1982), pp. 71–2, footnote.

6

Meaning, Holism and Use

Akeel Bilgrami

I

There is the thesis, to paint it in broad stroke, that the meaning of a sentence is its truth-condition. There is the proposal that the study of meaning is best approached via theories of meaning. There is the doctrine of the holistic character of theories of meaning. And there is the dictum: 'meaning is use.' In a series of papers, now gathered in his *Inquiries into Truth and Interpretation*, Donald Davidson has constructed an important and highly influential conception of linguistic meaning upon the first three of this congeries of views.[1] He has remained altogether silent on the fourth. This essay investigates the relation between the idea that meaning is use and these interconnected tenets of Davidson's conception.

The ideas and ideologies summarized in the dictum are notoriously various and vague.[2] Michael Dummett, however, has a quite precise understanding of the slogan and exploits it towards a quite specific end. Of the three central Davidsonian ideas, he accepts the proposal that theories of meaning will illuminate the subject of linguistic meaning but argues that the force of the idea that meaning is use, when constraining this proposal, is to undermine the thesis that the meaning of a sentence is given by its truth-condition, an argument he fortifies by a rejection of the doctrine of semantic holism. Even such a brief statement of his dialectic suggests that it would be very natural to study the relations between the dictum and the three articles of the Davidsonian conception by scrutinizing his argument.[3] That is the somewhat oblique approach I shall adopt.

---

[1] The volume was published by Oxford University Press (1982). In this essay I shall assume a basic familiarity with Davidson's conception of meaning.

[2] It has meant many things to many people and I make no effort to sort these out here. In the last section there are hints of how one may exploit the dictum, in a way that Wittgenstein himself tended to do, towards a scepticism about the proposal.

[3] In my exposition of Dummett I shall rely most on his 'What is a Theory of Meaning II' in G. Evans and J. McDowell (eds), *Truth and Meaning* (Clarendon Press, Oxford, 1976), citing other texts where necessary.

II

To begin with: the proposal, the thesis and the dictum. The proposal yields the following general question: what semantic knowledge suffices for the mastery of a given language? And theories of meaning are intended to specify that knowledge. The thesis adapts a well-known Fregean idea to this non-Fregean question about natural languages and offers the answer that the knowledge is the knowledge of the truth-conditions of the sentences of the language; and, as is also well-known, Davidson's particular answer adopts a Tarski-style specification of the truth-conditions. The dictum, as I said, enters because Dummett thinks that embracing it pre-empts endorsing this answer.[4]

Why does he think so?

It is a fair thing to ask of any answer to the meaning-theoretic question (whether a truth-conditional answer or some other) for some statement of the sort of behaviour that will count as reflecting the requisite knowledge. Fair, that is, if we follow Wittgenstein in thinking that meaning is something public and open to view, and not purely 'inner' as it were.[5] In other words, the question about knowledge must be asked with the constraint that there is a discoverable difference between someone who is said to have that knowledge and someone who is said to lack it. Dummett explicitly imposes this desideratum, and we might think of it as satisfying Frege's anti-psychologistic intuitions[6] but in a way that is peculiarly Wittgenstein's, i.e., with no platonist commitments whatever since the stress is on behaviour rather than on meanings. I will abbreviate this constraint as (M).

(M) when applied to the thesis under attack raises the question: How does the master of a language manifest his knowledge of the truth-conditions of the sentences of his language? At this point Dummett makes a negative claim. It will not do, he says, to answer this question by saying that if a master of a language can *state* the truth-conditions of all the sentences of the language then he has manifested his knowledge of them. To say this would be to attribute what he calls merely *explicit* knowledge. But what is needed is *implicit* knowledge, for otherwise the account would be regressive (where the language in which the truth-conditions are stated is other than the language in question) or circular (where it is the same). The capacity to state the truth-conditions must be anchored in something else, if the constraint (M) is to be met in a satisfying way.

Dummett, then, offers the suggestion that the only satisfactory way in which knowledge of truth-conditions may be manifested is by the exercise of a capacity to recognize them as obtaining if and when they obtain. In general, to have such a capacity we would have to have a disposition such that, if and when

---

[4] For the most part Dummett attacks Davidson's Tarski-style theory of truth but he is also clear that he has a more general target in mind.

[5] In this paper I do not question the necessity for this constraint.

[6] One should qualify the remark about anti-psychologism since there are ways of being psychologistic that, strictly speaking, meet the publicness requirement as in many recent versions of functionalism.

it is required of us, we can engage in some finite activity that culminates in some routine behavioural manifestation of the recognition of the obtaining (or non-obtaining) of the truth-conditions. This suggestion of Dummett's is the substance, for him, of the dictum 'meaning is use.' I will abbreviate it as (R).

Armed with (R), he raises for the thesis the following difficulty. There are many sentences in our language for which we cannot be said to have such a recognitional capacity, sentences whose truth-conditions we cannot recognize as obtaining, if and when they obtain. The finite process mentioned in the last paragraph is just not to be had. Among such problem sentences, he counts sentences quantifying over infinite and non-surveyable domains, sentences about other persons' sentient and other mental states, sentences about the remote past and the future, and the highly theoretical sentences of our scientific theories.[7]

The difficulty (R) poses for these sentences is that we cannot be said genuinely to know their truth-conditions. Yet we do know the *meaning* of these sentences, i.e. Dummett is not saying that because we cannot be said to know their truth-conditions, we cannot be said to understand them. Rather he is saying that what we know in virtue of which we understand them cannot be their truth-conditions, as the thesis suggests.

He is now in a position to put forward an alternative thesis, an alternative that is not vulnerable to the foregoing critique: to know the meaning of a sentence is to know the conditions that warrant the sentence's assertion (or denial).[8] Given the general thrust of the critique, these emerge as the natural replacement of truth-conditions. For the sentences that raise no difficulty, Dummett thinks that the two sorts of condition are indistinguishable; but for those which do, his contention is that it is much better to explain what we know when we know their meaning, not by grasp of some recognition-transcendent conditions of truth but rather the conditions which we are able to recognize as obtaining when they obtain – for they are after all the conditions which justify and often motivate our assertion of these sentences in the first place.

Dummett has not yet developed a way of applying this alternative thesis to the proposal of devising theories of meaning – no specification of the details of the form of these theories or of the story of their construction and testing comparable to Davidson's has been offered. Nevertheless, an urgent foundational question seems to have been raised against the truth-conditional thesis for Dummett is not merely interested in adding to or filling out the truth-theoretic conception of meaning by a *further* theory specifying the canonical evidence for the truth of the sentences of a language. Rather, he claims to have given an argument based upon considerations about meaning (in particular considerations involving the dictum 'meaning is use' as interpreted in (R)) to show that the truth-theoretic conception is wrong and needs replacement.

---

[7] Dummett discusses the possibility of meeting this difficulty by invoking a point of view that is an extension of our recognitional powers in infinite ways, such as God's, and argues that this cannot be of any help in giving a theory of meaning for human beings' mastery of language.

[8] Dummett sometimes makes the point in terms of an alternative notion of truth tied to what we are capable of recognizing. The difference is in the word.

III

There is a dogmatic quality to (R) and it invites a dogmatic and naive response.

Take the traditional scientific realist,[9] committed, irrespective of where and however lightly the line between theory and observation is drawn,[10] to the truth-value bearing nature of theoretical sentences; and committed, in the context of the present discussion, to saying that we know the meaning of these sentences in virtue of knowing their truth-conditions, where this transcends the strictures placed by (R). Someone who takes this position might point out that in Dummett's own line of argument (M) precedes (R). And (M) raises a question for this position for which there is a perfectly adequate reply. The question is: How does one manifest one's knowledge of the truth-conditions of a theoretical sentence of a scientific theory? And the answer is: by using the sentence in successful explanations. Having answered to his own satisfaction the question raised by (M), he would decline the invitation to address a quite different question raised by (R): Can we *recognize* that these truth-conditions obtain if and when they do? He would refuse to answer this on the grounds that it is rendered irrelevant by the adequacy of the reply to the question posed by (M). There is a point to this since in Dummett's argument (R) is introduced as an elaboration of what is supposed to be implied by (M), given that merely being able to state the truth-conditions will not meet the demands of (M). But the reply just given is not as bleak as the 'stating' response (because unlike it, there is here an assumption of holism, on which more below) and yet falls well short of the manifestation required by (R). We need, then, to know why the answer will not do before we even entertain (R).

Essentially the same response can be made with examples other than theoretical sentences, i.e., for all the kinds of sentence that Dummett finds problematic. Naive as the response is, it needs addressing if Dummett's argument is to go through.

It is very natural, at this point, to think that here is where one of Dummett's formulations of anti-holism should be introduced. For it would seem that one way in which this naive response to his argument can be repudiated (and his commitment to (R) made less dogmatic) is to point to the assumption of holism in the naive response and find the assumption untenable. Yet natural as the move is, I think it is misleading to think that the anti-holism can prop up the commitment to (R) in this way.

To see the point – and perhaps the initial motive – for one version[11] of Dummett's anti-holism it is better to start with another response to his

---

[9] The position, for instance, taken by Hilary Putnam in his paper 'What Theories are Not' reprinted in his *Philosophical Papers* vol. 2 (Cambridge University Press, Cambridge, 1977). I have used the term 'realism' here as an innocuous label. I have decided to drop the use of 'realism' or 'anti-realism' in this entire discussion of Dummett because they are distracting terms and the points I wish to raise can be raised without their use. I have also ignored Dummett's discussions of the principle of bivalence as a criterion for realism. That, too, is not essential for my purposes.

[10] Dummett discusses scientific realism in his 'Common Sense and Science' in G. MacDonald (ed.) *Perception and Identity* (Oxford University Press, Oxford, 1979). Here he recognizes the problem of drawing a clear line between observation and theory and raises a question only about 'highly' theoretical statements.

[11] There are other formulations of anti-holism. See section VII.

argument than the one just given, a response which is every bit as naive but a good bit more facile. The challenge, as above, is to meet the demands of (M) without falling into the 'stating' response and so avoid having to meet the demands of (R). The facile response does this by offering to the question raised by (M): 'How does one manifest one's knowledge of the recognition-transcendent truth-conditions of a given sentence?' the following answer: we manifest it in our common belief (reflected in our logic) that the sentence, like any sentence, is determinately either true or false. In short, the use or practice which manifests the relevant knowledge is simply our bivalent logical practice.

It is, I suspect, in order to block a response of this kind that Dummett first formulates his anti-holistic doctrine of 'molecularism.'[12] This is the doctrine that the meaning of a sentence does not depend on the meaning of any sentence whose logical complexity is greater than it. This means that an atomic or simple sentence's meaning must be given without appeal to any other sentence but only to its component expressions. He explains the point in terms of the idea of a conservative extension. Suppose we have a theory which consists only of atomic sentences and we append to it the logical constants so as to get a theory that consists of atomic and complex sentences, then the latter is a conservative extension of the former if and only if no unprovable sentence of the former is a provable sentence of the latter. One can see easily the relation between molecularism as a doctrine about meaning and the intuitionist disallowance of the Law of Excluded Middle. To allow the use of the law in deductions in order to prove some concluding sentence is to allow that the sentence's meaning is such that it may be proven by a deduction which has as a premise a sentence of greater logical complexity than its own. Molecularism rules this out, insisting always on a 'normal' deduction of the sentence, where the premises do not contain any sentence of greater logical complexity. Thus in this view, a non-conservative extension goes hand in hand with a revision of the meaning of the sentence of the initial theory by the addition of logical constants.

It should be plain how molecularism rules out the facile response against Dummett's argument. But is it of any force against our original, naive response?

What is the holistic assumption of this latter response? Since the manifestation suggested by it involves the use of theoretical sentences in explanations, it cannot be that the (recognition-transcendent) truth-conditions of these sentences, knowledge of which is so manifested, are known singly. The sort of manifestation appealed to forces a semantic holism because explanations are made by sentences interlocking in a theory and not one by one.[13]

It is central to the doctrine of molecularism as defined above that there be a ground-floor of simple or atomic sentences and in the doctrine as it applies to the facile response, there is a straightforward criterion for simplicity or atomicity of sentencehood. It would be enough to define a simple sentence with that target in mind, in terms of the absence of the logical connectives. Against the original response, however, a richer semantic criterion is required since the issue there is not about logical operators but the interdependence of the

---

[12] See his 'Justification of Deduction' in his *Truth and Other Enigmas* (Duckworth, London, 1978). Also his *Elements of Intuitionism* (Oxford University Press, Oxford, 1978). I should add that the rest of this paragraph is compatible with Dummett's allowing that some logical laws under certain conditions, be self-justifying.

[13] None of this rules out a Tarski-style specification of the truth-conditions.

non-logical terms, the predicates. But as the early pages of Wittgenstein's
Philosophical Investigations make so gripping, the idea of this broader simplicity
of sentencehood is desperately hard to make clear. One cannot of course
assume that a definition of simplicity in terms of the absence of logical operators
can suffice for the revised target, the original response. Take Dummett's own
favored assertibilist semantic criterion. For example, many colour-blind people
find themselves unable to assert with justification that a particular patch of
colour is green and unable also to assert that it is brown. Yet they feel warranted
in asserting that it is *either* green *or* brown; thereby making a sentence complex
by the first criterion and simple by the second. There is no non-question
begging way of treating such cases as special and, besides, other less gorgeous
examples can be multiplied.[14]

Now, of course, none of this means that Dummett cannot devise or does not
have in mind some broader criterion for simplicity. In a critical discussion of
Quine's holism of 'Two Dogmas of Empiricism', he ponders – with what seems
like approval – an interpretation of Quine's view that the 'sense of a sentence
could only be explained by reference to its being a constituent in a total theory,'
nevertheless,

> we should derive the significance of the total theory only from the sentences of
> which it was composed. This would mean that we would determine whether or
> not experience was recalcitrant to a given total theory and what overall revisions
> were possible in response to it, from the senses of the constituent sentences of the
> theory. These senses would therefore have to consist in a direct relation between a
> sentence and an experience and in the interconnections between sentences ... [15]

This is a perfectly fair method for sketching a molecularist account. It delivers a
molecularism in which the atomic sentences are defined in terms of our direct
perceptual experience.

However, it has, in the context of the dialectic I have set up, an absolutely
disastrous consequence. It has the consequence of *identifying* Dummett's
anti-holism with his opposition to the truth-conditional thesis via (R), for (R)
after all appeals to precisely the same perceptual or recognitional foundations
for meaning. In my dialectic I had said that it would be natural to think that his
anti-holism could prop up his commitment to (R). But if it is identical with that
commitment it could hardly prop it up.

It is misleading, therefore, to think of the anti-holism, at least in this
formulation, as something established independently of the critique of the
truth-theoretic conception of meaning. Either Dummett would have to justify
them as an integrated doctrine or characterize and argue against holism in a way
that is genuinely independent of the critique of the truth-theoretic conception
of meaning and then exploit that anti-holism in support of that critique.[16]

---

[14] I owe this example to the colour-blind but philosophically insightful Josh Guttman.

[15] *Frege: Philosophy of Language* (Duckworth, London, 1973), p. 595.

[16] See section VII for a second version of anti-holism that is independent in this way. See also
footnote 35.

IV

Is the integrated position which has emerged in sections II and III defensible? At this point I will raise a difficulty for the position, and argue against one way of overcoming it. In the next two sections I will argue against two other ways of overcoming it.

In the integrated position there is, as became clear in the last section, a commitment to a ground floor of sentences immune to Dummett's critique of section II. Natural language is to be seen as a conservative extension of some fragment of itself which consists only of these unproblematic sentences. How is one to understand the distinction between the problematic and unproblematic sentences? Or, in other words, when is it that truth-conditions outrun assertibility conditions and when is it that they coincide?

Dummett, sometimes, makes the distinction in terms of another: that between conclusive and non-conclusive or defeasible verification. The problematic sentences cannot be conclusively verified and there, or so the argument is supposed to show, we must give up the truth-conditional view and attribute to speakers knowledge only of assertibility conditions. However, this way of making the distinction would prevent him from making his argument for all the sentences deemed problematic in a uniform way since a mathematical sentence whose proof, presumably, establishes it conclusively, would turn out to be non-problematic, even if it were a sentence which quantified over an infinite and non-surveyable domain. Yet he is very clear that such sentences are problematic and that there is, for them, a vital distinction to be made between knowing their truth-conditions and knowing or being capable of recognizing a proof of them. It is, perhaps, difficulties of this kind that prompt him, at other times, to make the distinction in terms of yet another: not conclusive and defeasible but direct and indirect verification. Here he seems to rely on a common idea of a canonical mode of direct verification which covers both mathematical and empirical sentences. Just as direct verification for empirical sentences might paradigmatically require perceptual encounters, so direct verification for a sentence, say, of the form, 'Every number has a certain property F' would paradigmatically require going through all the cases and not merely to recognize a proof. The difference in the paradigms, of course, reveals a difference between empirical and mathematical sentences that is to be expected but one can now contrast all the problematic sentences (whether empirical or mathematical) with the non-problematic ones in terms of the ascribability of knowledge of truth-conditions only for the latter, i.e. where direct verification is possible.

The difficulty I want to raise for Dummett can be raised by concentrating on a very narrow range of sentences, which he finds non-problematic: sentences about the large, observable features of the world around us. The question in an initial form is obvious: Why are such sentences better off than, for example, sentences about another person's mental states? The point is not that the latter are directly verifiable – though that is something one may want to say, not simply by raising this initial question, but eventually after an elaborate argument against the distinction between direct and indirect verification – but rather that (accepting, for now, the distinction) one might wonder why one should assume that one can directly verify 'There is a table in front of me' any more than one can directly verify 'Margaret is in pain.' Even granting that perceptual encounters are the canonical mode of verification for empirical sentences, one might wonder why *both* are not indirectly verified in terms of perceptual experiences, arguing with traditional empiricism that sentences capturing these experiences alone meet the direct verification requirement.[17]

This line of questioning raises a difficulty that can be avoided by one of three responses, none of which can have much plausibility or attractiveness for Dummett.

The first is to succumb to the empiricist pressure that forces one to a base of unproblematic sentences describing directly verified inner experiences, whose truth and assertibility conditions coincide. This position has, in fact, been attributed to Dummett by some recent commentators.[18] Many of them have been motivated by a goal that Dummett has not adopted or even written much about – that of giving an account of propositional attitudes along what are called 'methodological solipsist' lines.[19] The idea is to promote a notion of propositional attitude content that leaves out their individuation in terms of truth-conditions, so as to explain an agent's behaviour wholly in terms of what is available inside the Cartesian boundaries of his head and his skin. One natural way to do it would be by exploiting the obvious relation between such contents and the meanings of our words, and to seek out a conception of meaning that precisely relies upon a Cartesian base of inner experiences. The concept of truth does not enter in this picture of meaning and propositional attitude content.[20]

It should not, of course, come as a surprise to anyone that such a programme for the concept of content would seek support in a theory of meaning in which truth-conditions that were outside the direct experiential ken of speakers played no role whatsoever, given that the empiricist claim that we do not directly verify statements about public objects in the shared world around us holds; 'methodological solipsism' about content is bound to sit comfortably with a radical verificationism about meaning (even if it is not the only view of meaning that lends it support).[21]

---

[17] One could, of course, claim that not even these meet the requirement, i.e. that all sentences are indirectly verified. But that is tantamount to accepting holism and giving up on the integrated position. So Dummett cannot meet this difficulty by simply saying that his critique applies across the board to all sentences.

[18] This interpretation was first suggested by Putnam in his discussion of Dummett in *Meaning and the Moral Sciences* (Routledge and Kegan Paul, London, 1978). It is most explicitly made by Colin McGinn in his 'Realism and Content Ascription' in *Synthese* (1982) and endorsed by W. Lycan in his discussion of Dummett in *The Logical Form of Natural Language* (MIT Press, Massachusetts, 1984).

[19] The term is due to Putnam and has been taken up by Fodor and others as a label for this view of the content of propositional attitudes.

[20] It enters *later* to explain the reliability of our beliefs and our success in our dealings with the environment, etc.

[21] There are other ways of specifying the content of attitudes along methodological solipsist lines, ways which don't invoke verification or assertibility conditions at all. See Stephen White's 'Partial Character and the Language of Thought' in *Pacific Philosophical Quarterly* (1982) which

The inherent plausibility or implausibility of such a retreat to the interior of these Cartesian boundaries in the study of mind and meaning is beyond the province of this paper.[22] But there is a serious worry about whether those who have read or exploited Dummett in this way have not made a gross blunder in interpretation; for how can this brand of Cartesianism be set alongside the constraint (M), which, one would have thought, in its original Wittgensteinian setting had been formulated precisely with a view to blocking such a retreat.[23]

It will not do to say on behalf of this interpretation of Dummett that Dummett and Wittgenstein had different targets in mind and so no tension exists between the Cartesianism and the commitment to (R) *in Dummett*. To say this would be to say that since Dummett's target is the truth-conditional theory and not any Cartesian view of meaning, his idea of 'use' summarized in (R) can be elaborated quite independently of, and not as a gloss on, the constraint (M); and it is (R) not (M) that is essential to hitting that target. But it does not seem to me possible to complete the argument Dummett does actually give – and which I have sketched in section II – without connecting the use he makes of (R) against the truth-conditional view with the more general constraint (M). The connection is this: the truth-conditional theorist must according to Dummett give some non-trivial account of what our knowledge of the recognition-transcendent truth-conditions of a sentence is reflected in. Since, *ex hypothesi*, the exercise of our recognitional abilities will not reflect them and our ability to state them will reflect them only trivially, the truth-conditional theorist must lapse into some purely *inner* conception of this knowledge – becoming, thereby, identical with Wittgenstein's target. So, to repeat, it will not do to have Dummett abandon (M) in order to get out of the inconsistency on pain of leaving the argument he gives quite unfinished. Without it, it will always be open for the truth-conditional theorist to claim that he is no worse off than the Dummett of this interpretation in aspiring to an inner, Cartesian conception of meaning and mind. The fact is that neither view in any way aspires to this conception.

---

invokes Kaplan's notion of character. It is a nice question, whether these other specifications will not be too parasitic on truth-conditional content to fulfil methodological ambitions.

[22] It is probably, in the end, quite implausible but one should not easily assume that it is so because it smacks of phenomenalism. The Cartesian position may reject phenomenalism and use the vocabulary for items in the external world in its specifications of content, for instance with an 'It appears to me that ...' operator. This is far harder to argue against. In the end, it fails because there isn't any way of accounting for the indispensability of this vocabulary without giving up on the Cartesianism. But that is a point which needs much greater elaboration than I can give here.

[23] It is not really possible for a Cartesian position along the traditional empiricist lines mentioned on p. 108 to satisfy (M). Only two positions satisfy (M). First, one which repudiates methodological solipsism altogether and insists on relational descriptions of what manifests mentality, where the relations are to the environment. Clearly the Cartesian position cannot take this view of the manifestations since the whole point of Cartesianism is that the same content is in play whether there is something in the environment or not, as in cases of illusion or hallucination. Second, one which takes manifestations to be non-relationally described but all the same *bodily* motions. This is akin to behaviourism. It is incompatible with a Cartesian position along *traditional* empiricist lines. It is compatible with a naturalistic empiricism which appeals to peripheral stimuli and not experiences. Hence it is not the position we are pushing Dummett towards. However, see section VI.

V

A more promising response on Dummett's behalf, and one that he most likely intends, is to resist the empiricist pressure forcing an inward retreat. Since any characterization of the fragment of sentences that forms an unproblematic basis must keep faith with the Wittgensteinian spirit of (M), it would be far better to count the sentences about shared, public objects as unproblematic. And so far as I know, he has nowhere written of them as raising the problem that the others raise. If I am right in representing Dummett's argument, one must conclude that for him these sentences must be counted as directly verified. The claim on the one hand that for the unproblematic sentences knowledge of truth and assertibility conditions coincide and, on the other, that knowledge of truth-conditions is only ascribable where direct verification is possible, makes this conclusion inevitable.[24]

Yet curiously enough Dummett has written as if a 'naive realism' of this kind for these sentences is one that a *truth-conditionalist* must embrace.[25] His reason for thinking so is that without embracing it the truth-conditionalist cannot give anything but a trivial answer (as in the stating response) to the question of what a speaker's knowledge of the meaning of these sentences consists in. To avoid giving a trivial answer he thinks that a speaker who is said to know the meaning of the sentence must be attributed a faculty of *unmediated* recognition, if we insist that he knows the truth-conditions. As he says, 'that which renders the sentence true is the very thing of which we are directly aware when we recognize it as being true.' Now, if what I said in the discussion of the naive response (I hope it is obvious that 'naive' here has nothing to do with naive realism) in sections III and IV is plausible, it should be clear that the choice between a trivial answer and the *direct* verification answer to the question of how a speaker manifests his knowledge of meaning of such sentences is by no means exhaustive. To point to the speaker's use of any one of these sentences in appropriate circumstances is a perfectly adequate answer to this question, if we can presuppose that he can use other sentences with which that sentence is related in obvious ways. If this assumption of holism is denied to the truth-conditionalist, then of course he may have no way out of a trivial response but to adopt naive realism, but we haven't yet been given a non-question-begging reason for not helping ourselves to the holistic assumption.

So if Dummett is to avoid the Cartesian retreat[26] it is he – and not the truth-conditionalist, as he thinks – who must adopt a naive realism for these sentences. But in the same discussion he finds that the 'naive realist's notion of immediate awareness, consisting in a direct contact between the knowing

---

[24] It should be clear that the problem I have raised for Dummett in the last section and continue to discuss in this section and the next can just as easily be raised if we replace his talk of direct and indirect verification with conclusive and non-conclusive verification. The point is that it is hard to justify the claim that sentences about the world of public objects are directly *or* conclusively verified.

[25] See his paper 'Realism' in *Synthese* (1982), pp. 105–11.

[26] Of course, keeping in mind that he won't accept holism either.

subject and the object of his knowledge is probably in all cases incoherent....'[27] His chief criticism is that the doctrine has no account of how we can ever be mistaken in making an assertion using one of this class of sentences. This is, of course, an old and serious difficulty and so far as I can see, one that is impossible to overcome. Dummett, in this discussion, points out that Locke's discussion of secondary qualities is confused in thinking on the one hand that, for example, colour, is a dispositional property of bodies external to us and, on the other, in naively realistic fashion, thinking that the concept of colour is solely explainable in terms of the appearance of a surface, 'under normal conditions' and not a dispositional property 'in the object' at all. He points out that 'a disposition of any kind is not a quality of which we can be directly aware' in the sense of a naive realist. As he says, 'a disposition is something that is manifested on some occasions and not on the others and may be variously manifested in differing circumstances.' All this seems on the mark and of a piece with the difficulty that if we take seriously the idea that truth-conditions and assertibility-conditions of such sentences are indistinguishable in the sense that we directly verify these sentences, then we will find it impossible to allow for the possibility of error in the judgements we make with these sentences. But if so, we had better find a way of making the naive realist doctrine less naive, i.e. make it so that it avoids Dummett's criticisms; for some version of it, alone, will in general account for why these sentences may be counted as non-problematic. As we have seen, counting them as problematic, while opposing holism, can only lead to the Cartesian retreat, which in turn, leads to a contradiction of Dummett's argument.[28]

One way in which this might be done is by giving up the thought that, for a sentence of this kind, truth and assertibility conditions are indistinguishable, and replacing it with the thought that, given a careful and detailed enough analysis of the relations between the truth-conditions and the assertibility-conditions, the latter determine the former. Like the naive realist position, this would have the advantage over the Cartesian retreat of seeing the role of truth-conditions as absolutely crucial as well as the advantage over the truth-conditionalist of seeing the crucial role of assertibility-conditions, which allows for these sentences to comprise the fragment to be conservatively extended.

How does it go beyond naive realism? First, if it is viable, this position would not fall into the difficulty that Dummett finds in Locke, of having to give up the idea of causally operative powers in the world external to an experiencing subject, because of the naive realist idea of direct verification. The move from 'indistinguishable from' to 'determined by', in describing the relations between

---

[27] Note that naive realism so characterized is quite different from the view that the content of our perceptual beliefs is fixed by looking to their external causes (i.e. the public objects). The latter view is perfectly compatible with holism, whereas the former view which is about the relationship between *evidence* and truth rather than content and truth, has foundationalist and anti-holist implications.

[28] It is possible that Dummett thinks that though *one* can be wrong in the making of perceptual judgements in the face of the best evidence, *everyone* cannot be. It is not clear that this is any more plausible than the case of one but in any case Dummett nowhere writes as if he thinks so. What he does say in the course of the discussion is that *one* cannot be mistaken in *all* one's beliefs.

truth-conditions and assertibility-conditions, is made precisely so as to have the causally operative powers in their place external to agents. And second, the experiences of the agent though independent, in this way, of the features of the world outside should – if the analysis is correct – reach out, as it were without remainder, to those features. The possibility of error is indeed excluded but the details of the analysis of the relationship between the two sorts of conditions are intended to remove the intuitive difficulty in accepting such an exclusion.

Christopher Peacocke in an interesting recent work has argued for a position roughly like the one I have been describing for certain classes of sentence, including the class I have been discussing.[29] Peacocke comes to the relationship between assertibility – (or as he calls it 'acceptance') and truth-conditions via a schematic specification of what he says a person making a contentful assertion using a sentence of this class *is committed to*. Like Dummett he thinks of certain sorts of conditions (commitments) as canonical, i.e. in my exposition those given in the paradigmatic perceptual encounters. As a first approximation of an analysis he offers the following:

> The spectrum of canonical commitments of one who judges a content at t 'That block is cubic' is that: for any position from which he were to perceive the block at t in normal external conditions when his perceptual mechanisms are minimally functioning, he would experience the block from that relative position as cubic, or as a cubic object would be perceived from that relative position.

This initial analysis by which the assertibility-conditions of such a sentence determine the truth-conditions will not exclude the possibility of error, and that is all to the good, for intuitively we feel that, given what has gone into the analysis so far, error ought to be possible. That was Dummett's complaint against the naive realist. Peacocke, too, asks: 'is it a necessary condition of a subject's being a minimally functioning perceiver that if his experience represents his environment as being in a certain way, it is so?' He adds 'This is a coherent speculation' and gives the example of how even in normal light one may be caused to see a square by an arrangement of different, irregular trapezoids. So he introduces into the analysis the idea of 'projection class'. Objects in the vicinity of an agent are, under a certain description, in the projection class of a particular pattern of stimulation in the agent just in case they could figure, given normal lighting, in the causal explanation of the pattern's occurrence. He then adds one more crucial element into the analysis, that of *all* the successive patterns of retinal stimulation so as to reduce down the set of what goes into the projection class. This of course brings in a viewing of the object from all relative positions. The initial approximate analysis has undergone a rather big transformation. Peacocke says

> The point is not that whenever, for instance, a minimally functioning subject has an experience as of something cubic in normal external circumstances, his experience will be caused by the perceived object's being cubic: we have already

---

[29] Christopher Peacocke, 'A Theory of Content' (unpublished MS). Though Peacocke often writes with sympathy for aspects of Dummett's view on meaning, it is not at all clear that he would accept the use I make of his analysis on behalf of Dummett.

seen that to be false. What *is* true is that the only property of the presented object which would explain its appearing (or as a cubic object would) from all relative positions is its being cubic.[30]

This fuller analysis of the relation between an agent's visual experiences (which comprise the canonical assertibility-conditions for sentences about saliences of the world external to him) and the properties in the world external to him which cause those experiences (which constitute the sentences' truth-conditions) does make it possible to say that the assertibility-conditions determine the truth-conditions. Those interested in the analysis itself might worry about an element of circularity; and there may be other worries yet. But the concern here is to see whether the fact that this is made possible gives Dummett a way of marking out these sentences as unproblematic so as to resist being forced into a Cartesian retreat and whether it does so in a way that avoids the incoherences of the more naive realism. The analysis does indeed do this, it does provide a way of showing why exactly naive realism seemed too strong in ruling out the possibility of error (too strong because based on an incomplete analysis of the relations between experience and external cause) and showing how a fuller analysis may exclude error without seeming implausible. It also, therefore, keeps *distinct* (what we intuitively want to distinguish and what direct verificationism collapses) the visual experiences and the causal operative powers in the objects external to experiencers.

Yet none of this can be of any help to Dummett's overall project because the assertibility-conditions that by this analysis are supposed to determine the truth-conditions make an appeal to an agent experiencing some object from *all* relative positions. If a theory of meaning is supposed to yield the canonical assertibility-conditions for each sentence of the language, then this consequence of the analysis would make such a theory unspecifiable and if the theories are supposed to capture what goes into the understanding of a language, this would amount to admitting that the language is unlearnable – for there are an infinite number of positions from which one may visually experience an object. Part of the point of introducing the idea of a canonical mode of verification was to reduce the bewildering variety of assertibility-conditions for a sentence, but the analysis just given reintroduces exactly the same problem in a far worse form by making for an infinite number of canonical assertibility-conditions for each sentence at the very base from which other kinds of sentence are built up. In a word, Peacocke's analysis is of no help to Dummett, if for no other reason that that it runs foul of Dummett's own strictures against sentences quantifying over infinite and non-surveyable domains. A spectrum of commitments that an agent undertakes upon an assertion of a sentence of this kind cannot be unbounded in this way and yet be manifested by that agent in the way Dummett requires.[31]

---

[30] He restricts this feature to primary qualities but that does not matter for our purposes.

[31] This is not a criticism of Peacocke's analysis but of someone who thinks Dummett may use the analysis to meet the difficulty raised in the last section. There is a point worth adding here. One may allow that these commitments can be manifested if there is an analogue (for such universally quantified sentences) of the manifestation invoked by the naive response in section III for theoretical sentences in science. However, that response presupposes holism and so this move is not open to Dummett.

To summarise the last two sections: I have raised a difficulty for Dummett's integrated anti-truth-conditionalist, anti-holist position, a difficulty about whether he can without going holist, maintain that the meaning of a sentence of a particular sort is given by its assertibility and not its truth-conditions. I, then, suggested two ways in which he may get out of this difficulty: first by adopting a Cartesian view of meaning and mind that some commentators have, in any case, thought to be the main point in his argument. Or second, by adopting a view which, modifying the naive realism he himself criticizes, elaborates an intimate enough relation between the assertibility-conditions and truth-conditions of such sentences so as to avoid the threat of holism and Cartesianism. Both ways out, I have argued, are unpromising. The first runs afoul of (M) which is an essential feature of his argument and the second runs afoul of (R) in its application to sentences quantifying over non-surveyable and infinite domains and has the effect of making the languages we know and understand, unlearnable.

VI

If the second move is unacceptable, then there cannot be an intimate enough relation between truth and assertibility conditions of these sentences for there to be any resistance to the pressures from (R) which force a Cartesian retreat. And, the retreat, in turn, is intolerable to Dummett because of the demands of (M). So we are left once again with the challenge of meeting the demands of (M) and (R) at once, without invoking holism.

There *is* a possibility of meeting the demands of (R) in this way which has no Cartesian consequences and that is to treat the concept of recognition in a way that makes no appeal to an agent's experiences at all. Rather one may think of the idea of recognition in a strictly naturalistic way. The decision procedure essential to the explication of (R) in my summary of Dummett's argument in section II was described as culminating in a standard behavioural manifestation of the recognition of the obtaining of a state of affairs. This is of course a kin of the assent-behaviour familiar from Quine's writings on radical translation. Quine himself at different times has thought of assent in different ways. At times he has talked of it as a propositional attitude and at other times as a more purely behaviouristic item, which he has called 'surface-assent';[32] but it is clearly the latter one must rely on to meet the challenge posed at the end of the last paragraph. Thus with a Quinean naturalistic and behaviouristic conception of how to satisfy the constraint (R), one would have to give up experiences and assent for (presumably) peripheral stimuli and surface-assent respectively. Now, one could satisfy that constraint while also keeping faith with (M) since both peripheral stimuli and surface-assent are perfectly open to public view. If a question is raised as to whether appeal to peripheral stimuli is really keeping faith with the non-naturalistic spirit with which (M) was first formulated by Wittgenstein, the answer will presumably be that it is a fetish to retain every

---

[32] See his 'Mind and Verbal Behaviour' in S. Guttenplan (ed.), *Mind and Language* (Oxford University Press, Oxford, 1976).

aspect of Wittgenstein's view and so long as one is true to the spirit of what is *essential* to his arguments against the inner Cartesian conception of meaning and mind, there is no need to follow him in every detail of the anti-Cartesian picture he favours.

Such an interpretation of Dummett has been proposed by John McDowell in two recent papers.[33] McDowell finds this a natural way to read Dummett's arguments. I am much less certain that Dummett intends anything like a behaviourist conception of a theory of meaning and in this paper I suggest the view here only as a last ditch effort to get him out of the difficulty we have been struggling with over the last two sections.

This interpretation sees him as committed to promoting a conception of theories of meaning that make no appeal, in their descriptions of agents' manifestations, to the intentional or contentful idiom, on the grounds that to do so would be to be satisfied with too modest an achievement in the study of meaning. This, of course, does not suggest that the theory or theorist may not employ language – that would be too extreme, indeed incoherent. But there is an intermediate position between the modest and the extreme ones. In terms of (M), it may be spelt out as follows. Dummett has demanded that a speaker's knowledge of meaning must be manifested in his use or practice and in particular he has asked it of the knowledge of truth-conditions of any sentence. A modest theory simply says that knowledge of the truth-conditions of a sentence like 'It's raining' is manifested, for instance, in a speaker's *assertion that* it's raining. The intermediate position finds this too unambitious because the descriptions of the manifestations are, as McDowell puts it, 'inside of' the idiom of content, i.e. an idiom employing the ' -that' clause. One may only, according to his position, appeal to descriptions that are much more spare, for instance descriptions of discriminating bodily motions; behaviour in the strict behaviourist's sense. However the *meaning-theorist* may then go on to see these as reflecting the speaker's grasp of some contents or concepts. Hence, these descriptions, because spare in this way, will take us further than the modest theorist's position, and because descriptions at all will stop us short of the incoherent position.

In this sketch of Dummett as intermediate theorist of meaning there is no inclination to emphasize the special role of recognition as (R) did. Recognition cannot now be recognition-that or even recognition as sheer experience with no intentionality. If anything, it is sheer behaviour and assimilated into the overall behaviourism of the position's view of language.[34] This fact alone assures us that the difficulties of the last two sections may now be said to recede since the threat of Cartesianism is brutally repudiated by the adoption of behaviourism.

Hardly anybody will deny today that this last ditch effort to get Dummett out of those difficulties does not have utterly crippling difficulties of its own. Indeed

---

[33] 'Anti-Realism and the Epistemology of Understanding' in J. Bouvreese and H. Parrett (eds), *Meaning and Understanding* (Berlin, 1981) and 'In Defense of Modesty' to be published in a Festschrift for Dummett edited by Barry Taylor.

[34] The reason why I think this position cannot be what Dummett intends – even if it is the only way for him to avoid the Cartesian retreat – is that if one treats 'recognition' in these terms, one has no explanation for why Dummett finds some sentences problematic and others not.

even to raise them would be to rehearse points which are, by now, fairly deep within our philosophical sensibilities. Yet it would be well worth sparing a word to mention one of McDowell's own objections to this position, not only because it is a subtle and interesting objection, but because it will be of use in a point I wish to develop in the last section.

McDowell asks whether the knowledge being attributed to a speaker about some concept, say the concept square, can be said to be manifested in behaviour described in the spare non-intentional idiom. And he says 'It may seem that nothing could be simpler: the manifestation would be someone's treating a square thing in whatever way is in question. But any such performance would be an equally good manifestation of any of an indefinite number of different pieces of such implicit knowledge.' And he asks us to consider as just one among these alternatives 'knowledge to the effect that that is the way to treat things that are either square or ...', pointing out that though we will, if we know English, refuse to take such alternatives seriously, the intermediate position, if correct, would not explain why we may so refuse. For the spare descriptions of behaviour that the intermediate position restricts itself to cannot make manifest that a speaker is a speaker of a language which makes all such alternatives non-serious; at any rate cannot be said to make it manifest without begging the question at stake. There isn't any way of ruling out these alternatives without trading the intermediate position for the modest one, that is, by allowing the richer descriptions of the manifestations.

This objection seems to me utterly devastating of the project of a theory of meaning along these intermediate lines since it puts into doubt whether there will be any more or less stable and coherent set of axioms, knowledge of which may be attributed to a speaker; put into doubt, that is, the very idea of a theory of meaning. I will return to this point briefly again.

VII

If this last ditch effort fails the difficulty raised in section IV is still in place and appears to be invincible for the integrated position which combines (indeed identifies) the critique of truth-conditional conceptions of meaning with the anti-holist formulation of section III. Moreover, only a version of anti-holism that does not collapse into the critique can remove the dogmatic nature of (R) and rebut the naive response of section III. Not that such a version, even if it were forthcoming in a convincing way, would make the *integrated* position plausible. But it might encourage one to spell out an assertibility semantics which made no appeal to the first version of anti-holism.

I will raise in this section one other version of anti-holism and argue against it, so as to pre-empt being encouraged in this way.

This anti-holism is motivated by considerations of language-learning.[35] Language learning proceeds by stages of learning one fragment and then

---

[35] See his chapter 'Original Sinn' in his *Frege: Philosophy of Language*. There are other formulations of holism yet, which Dummett opposes but they are not really distinct from the holism

another, and so on. But if mastering a part of language requires learning other remote parts of it, as holism demands, then it is difficult to be accurate to the facts of language-learning, in fact, difficult to say how languages may be learned. Thus one cannot omit, in giving an account of what is learned (i.e. of what it is to be the master of a language), keeping in mind the facts about how it is learned. These facts force one to give a non-holistic account of what is learned. Since the truth-conditional account of what is learned assumes holism, it must be replaced by an account which uses as its central notion one that applies isolably to each sentential part of a language. The concept of assertibility-conditions, justifying each such part one by one, is the candidate Dummett favours.[36]

This motivation is not very compelling. The holist need not deny that there is a more or less routine way in which language is learnt (and perhaps even in the way theories are devised and tested). She needn't deny that we in fact acquire language, mastering some one fragment and then some other and so on, nor even which fragment we are more likely to begin with ('tables' and 'chairs' before 'mass' and 'unconscious'). She cannot deny this because these are manifestly facts. So obviously, a holist must look for how she can accommodate it in her philosophical doctrine. An obvious move would be to say that these facts are not relevant to the tasks of a theory of meaning,[37] which is only concerned with specifying what knowledge suffices for someone to be the master of a language; and that this specification need not mirror the process by which one came to be a master. The facts, therefore, have no philosophical significance. The holist only needs to say that though one, of course, learns a language by learning one fragment and then another, in learning an initial fragment one has not *fully* mastered it, and one will only learn it fully if one learns others. In learning the others one may not only add to but even revise one's understanding of the initial fragment. This last point is important in that it brings out clearly why holism is a natural philosophical ally of a *truth*-conditional view of meaning. Though there may be no harm in talk of assertibility-conditions at the starting point while the subject is the subject of language-acquisition, an acknowledgement (as one acquires more) of the possibility of revision at the starting point makes clear that when the subject is that of understanding or meaning, that acknowledgement forces us to graduate to talk of *truth*-conditions which outrun assertibility even at the starting point. The idea that truth in some strong sense of correspondence is not really forced by such an acknowledgement of the revisability of items in the starting points, since mere coherence would account for that, has been much in the air in recent years. This seems to me, as it does to many others, to presuppose a notion of correspondence that is dubiously coherent. At any rate there is

---

mentioned in section II. For instance, sometimes holism can be characterized in terms of the inextricability of meaning and belief or theory. But this collapses with the holism of section II because the chief point of the inextricability idea is to deny that there is a coherent sense to a sentence having a fund of meaning all of its own.

[36] It is tempting to relax this one by one requirement, saying that a meaning of sentences depends at most on a fragment of a language, but not as the holists think on the whole language. However, it is not obvious that Dummett can do so since a fragment of a language *can* be thought of as self-standing. And in any case the extreme holism is not essential to the truth-conditionalist view.

[37] This is a response Davidson has made in conversation.

certainly a notion of correspondence that is compatible with coherentist views of the nature of the truth of our beliefs. There is no need to adjudicate here on the question of which notion of truth as correspondence is the genuine article. The point of importance is that even the weaker notion stands opposed to the conclusions of Dummett's critique.[38]

Something stronger can be said in favour of the holistic, truth-conditional picture than that facts about language-learning are irrelevant to it. It is arguable that, in fact, it gives an account that *better* captures our intuitions about the nature of language, than the anti-holist assertibilist picture. Take, for example, the term 'mass'. The term as we might apply it to tables or tomatoes is learnt in the context of such things as picking up and holding or placing on a weighing-scale. But the assertibility-conditions for the same concept when it applies to planets and stars are quite different, for they are learned in the context of the most complicated calculations. The holist wants to say that anyone familiar with only a small fragment of a language covering the former contexts has not got a full understanding of the term 'mass' and will do so only upon learning its full theoretical role, which he never may, if he doesn't master some remote fragments. This idea of an incomplete understanding of initial fragments allows us to say what is surely intuitively right: that it is a single concept of 'mass' we have here. The anti-holist picture which expects language to be fully learnt in different stages does not allow for this but instead for the much less intuitively plausible view that a concept like 'mass' is ambiguous when applied to tomatoes and to stellar objects. Unintuitive, because mass, we want to say is, mass – not one thing in one context of acquisition and another in some other context. Holism, alone, captures this intuition.

VIII

I have tried, in sections III and VII, to counter Dummett's negative argument against the truth-theoretic conception of meaning. In the middle sections (IV, V and VI) I have tried to show that his positive assertibilist alternative to that conception runs up against a difficulty that cannot be overcome without giving up some vital part of his general view. Anti-holism, in one version or another, has played an important role in both his anti-truth-theoretic argument and his assertibilist alternative and it has been the focus or target of much of my criticism. This may encourage the thought that perhaps one could repudiate the truth-theoretic view and adopt the assertibilist alternative without rejecting holism and thereby avoid the focus of these criticisms. Though that raises a large subject, the brief remarks about revisability at the starting point made in the last section should form the basis of an argument against that possibility – an argument that I cannot develop here. But on the assumption that such an argument is forthcoming, there should at the end of all this be cause for real

---

[38] The stronger notion will emerge only if one thinks that all one's beliefs are, *en bloc*, revisable. This is one of the targets of Davidson's arguments in his 'On the Very Idea of a Conceptual Scheme'. Admitting to revisability at the starting point does not entail any such comprehensive revisability.

scepticism against Dummett's strategy of exploiting the dictum connecting meaning and use in a general argument against the truth-theoretic conception.

So a final question remains about how a truth-theoretic conception might look upon the connection. Davidson, as I said, has not written anything explicitly about this. It is absolutely clear that he cannot and doesn't view it in the form of (R). But it is also very clear from his approach to the theory of meaning – the approach of radical interpretation – that (M) is a constraint he has embraced pretty much from his earliest essays, even when the approach was never fully worked out in detail.[39]

If the motive and point behind the naive response is properly appreciated (and the shell of assumptions about holism as they emerged in section III – and indeed assumptions about the irreducibility of meaning as they emerged in section VI – have shown the response to be less naive than in its initial formulation), then, with all those assumptions in place, it becomes evident that (M) is a self-standing constraint with no need of elaboration in terms of (R) or any other terms whatever. This should have the effect of deflating the idea that meaning is use to a minimal Wittgensteinian anti-Cartesian reading. That deflationary reading has absolutely no destructive implications for the truth-theoretic conception; if anything, it promotes it. Yet, to say this is to raise an issue that has to be handled rather delicately.

The point of saying that the connection between meaning and use (as seen by the truth-theoretic conception), is merely to adopt (M) as a constraint on theories of meaning, amounts to saying that a speaker's knowledge of meaning must be manifested in his use of language, i.e. in the use of sentences to effect speech-acts (this last rules out the strictly behaviourist notion of use discussed in VI). But none of this should mislead one into denying the theoretical character of linguistic meaning (i.e. of Fregean sense). There is a real danger that talk of meaning being plain and manifest in 'use', so interpreted, may make it appear that meaning is *not* a genuine abstraction from use. It is a danger that many sympathizers of Wittgenstein have failed to perceive and have, thus, fallen into sympathy with a further, more idle, aspect of Wittgenstein's views on language, viz. a scepticism about the theoretical tractability of meaning. One can only resist the danger by seeing clearly that though meaning is manifest in use, it is all the same at some theoretical distance from it.

One may fail to resist the danger by taking the view that understanding the meaning of someone's words may be very much like a form of perception, as McDowell does.[40] If this amounts to saying that (despite the fact that meaning is at a theoretical distance from use) understanding is a non-inferential matter, the view may be harmless – though it is a view worth scrutinizing for all its phenomenological intuitiveness. It is harmless because of what it concedes in the parenthesis. But I suspect those who hold the view, including McDowell, have in mind to contest precisely what is in parenthesis.

Here is a way of bringing out the point about theoretical distance. McDowell says: 'The basis of the truth-conditional conception of meaning, as I see it, is

---

[39] It is most explicitly formulated in the opening paragraph of his paper 'Toward a 'Unified Theory of Meaning and Action' in *Grazer Philosophische Studien* (1980).

[40] See section 7 of his 'Anti-Realism and the Epistemology of Understanding'.

the following thought: to specify what would be asserted, in the assertoric utterance of a sentence apt for such use, is to specify a condition under which the sentence (as thus uttered) would be true.'[41] Now the minimal connection between meaning and use to be found in the commitment to (M) does not yield anything like this basis for the truth-conditional conception of meaning. That connection, to repeat, only demands manifestation in use. It makes no demand that the specifications of truth-conditions are specifications of what would be asserted by an assertoric use of the sentence. The reason is simply that one may make virtually any assertion with the assertoric use of a given sentence, given a special enough context. And it is a failure to keep in mind the distance between truth-conditions (meaning, on the view under discussion) and use, that encourages one to fall into this stronger notion of the connection which we find in the quotation from McDowell. (M) falls far short of this. Thus talk of directly perceiving the meaning of someone's words in his utterances is misleading if it implies this stronger notion.

It is important to stress this not only in order to keep straight what the most plausible part of the dictum 'meaning is use' is, but also because to see a closer connection between meaning and use may promote a scepticism about the proposal that the study of meaning is best approached via theories of meaning. Take, for instance, the behaviourist conception of 'use' which is supposed to manifest a speaker's knowledge of meaning that was discussed in section VI. McDowell's conclusion that one cannot give a theoretical account of meaning if we take 'use' in this way follows compellingly from his criticism of any effort to produce a theoretical account along these lines. The criticism invoked essentially rule-following considerations as can be seen in the example of the alternative axiom about the concept 'square'. The example has essentially the same relation to our ordinary understanding of square as the examples of non-standard rules of adding in Wittgenstein's discussion of rule-following scepticism have to adding. The criticism is so effective because it implies that if one restricts 'use' to behaviour in the spare and strict sense, then the enterprise is subject to rule-following scepticism; and since the analogue for rules in the context of a theory of meaning are the axioms of the theory, the scepticism is about the very possibility of a theory of meaning.

This can only be avoided by thinking of 'use' in far richer terms, thinking of it as the speech-acts that speakers produce by their utterances of sentences. Once we enrich the descriptions of the manifestations in this way we can repudiate the lunatic alternatives. But having said that, one should not go away with the impression that there is no more to the study of meaning than a specification of the assertions (or other speech-acts) that different sentences can be used to effect. If we were under this impression, the simple fact that a sentence can be used to effect any number of assertions in different contexts is a fact that would threaten the possibility of theorizing systematically about meaning. My knowledge of the truth-conditions of the sentence 'Man is a wolf' can be manifested in my use of that sentence to effect the assertion that the human race is inherently competitive. And that is one among an almost indefinite number of

---

[41] Section II, 'In Defense of Modesty'. One might think that adding 'what would be asserted *literally or standardly*' would take care of the objection to McDowell in the next paragraphs — wrong, for it is precisely the literal that 'truth-conditions' are called upon to serve.

assertions I could effect by uttering the sentence. If one took seriously the idea that the truth-conditional conception of meaning has its basis in the thought that 'to specify what would be asserted, in the assertoric utterance of a sentence apt for such use, is to specify a condition under which the sentence is true,' then the study of meaning would become a detailed description of the use of sentences case by case. And this is the very antithesis of the proposal mentioned at the outset of the paper. In meeting the sceptical threat to theories of meaning via rule-following scepticism, we have arrived at a quite different scepticism about it.

The proposal presupposes that linguistic meaning is a *theoretical* core that is indispensable in the explanation of our use of language – and so, unsurprisingly, manifest in it. Davidson's own method for making a stab at specifying this theoretical core cannot, thus, accept McDowell's view of the truth-conditional conception's connection with 'use'. The point of the method of radical interpretation is to distil or abstract out of the assent behaviour of an agent (via a combination of observation of the world around the agent and an application of the constraint of charity) this theoretical core. The method's decision to begin with evidence in terms of assent or 'holds-true'[42] is vitally different from the decision to restrict oneself to sparely described behaviour since 'holds-true' is a propositional attitude.[43] On the other hand, the point of starting with something less than an assumption of an understanding of what is being asserted by the agent is to come to a genuinely informative and non-question-begging specification of the theoretical core that we call meaning or sense.

Thus any criticism of the behaviourist position must not go on to suggest a remedy of the situation such that the possibility of this specification is ruled out. McDowell's conception of meaning as truth-conditions, if I am right, does rule it out. The method of radical interpretation does not. The behaviourist position, if McDowell is right, yielded a threat to the possibility of theorizing about meaning because of the threat of something akin to rule-following scepticism. An interesting point to note is that if one relaxes on the behaviourism and adopts Davidson's method which employs 'holds-true' (a propositional attitude with a certain methodological interest), one gets something far less destructive of theories of meaning than rule-following scepticism – one gets indeterminacy of translation or interpretation. It is less destructive because if one starts with something richer than strict behaviourism we have enough already to place genuine constraints upon (constraints such as the principle of charity) so that we are not in the situation of saying what can be said in the case of rule-following scepticism, viz. no matter how a person goes on, some rule or other will capture it. And so genuine limits exist for the different ways in which we can make sense of an agent. Because starting with assent has the methodological interest of not presupposing on the part of the interpreter, knowledge of the speech acts being effected by the agent, *some* freedom of

---

[42] Dummett's talk of manifestations emerges more naturally in the context of radical interpretation, as talk of evidence. Behaviourism results if one restricts either the manifestations or (in Davidson's context) the evidence in the requisite way.

[43] McDowell certainly sees this point. But I am less certain that the point made by my next sentence is compatible with his view of the truth-conditional conception of meaning.

choice in explanation of his linguistic behaviour will have to be admitted. The important point is that unlike rule-following scepticism there will still be enough in common among these explanations to allow us to argue that the alternatives capture in different ways something invariant in the agent. The behaviourist position does not give us enough to place the constraints that Davidson's method does and that is why the alternative explanations in McDowell's example about the concept square are so unlike the case of indeterminacy.

So there are two points I am making. First, that the project of radical interpretation because it starts with something richer than the behaviourist has to deal with is a far more tractable problem than the one the behaviourist has to deal with in McDowell's criticism: indeterminacy rather than rule-following scepticism. But second, radical interpretation, because it starts with something which (even if richer than the behaviourist) is not so rich as to assume an understanding of an agent's speech-acts, provides a way of abstracting from those speech-acts a core of theory that is a necessary component in the explanation of those speech-acts.[44]

The second point shows that for Davidson, what radical interpretation delivers, i.e. truth-conditions, is quite far removed from the use of language in its full sense. It is removed in the sense that a theory is removed from the phenomena it explains. This does not mean that use, the *explanandum*, is not shot through with theory. It is. What we need is a distinction from the inside of theoretical descriptions between truth-conditions (a further theoretical core) and the use of language which manifests our knowledge of these truth-conditions. The mature Wittgenstein's great contribution to our thinking about language was to place the whole question of linguistic meaning within the context of use. But there are also strands in Wittgenstein's writing in which he does not discriminate a special enough place for meaning. It is in this respect that Davidson's conception of a *theory* of meaning represents a genuine advance on Wittgenstein's conception of meaning as use.[45]

---

[44] McDowell's version of truth-conditional conception of meaning, as I have said, is closely linked to his view of understanding as a kind of perception. Both, in turn, are allied to his hostility to any claim that language masters have a tacit knowledge of theoretical specifications. In opposing him, one would have to address that question also. I must acknowledge, therefore, that my criticism here remains only a small part of a longer and fairer treatment of his views and themes.

[45] My thanks to Steve White, Chris Peacocke, Carol Rovane and John McDowell for their helpful comments on this paper.

Part III
Applications

7

The Meanings of Logical Constants

GILBERT HARMAN

It seems to illuminate the meanings of logical constants to say how they contribute to the truth conditions of propositions containing them, as in the account of certain sentential connectives such as truth functions, the Frege-Tarski analysis of quantification, Kripke's semantics for modal operators in a quantified modal logic, and Davidson's treatment of certain sorts of adverbial modification in his paper about the logical form of action sentences.[1] In all these instances, an account of contribution to truth conditions seems to tell us significant things about the meanings of the logical constants involved.

It is not clear why this should be so. Compare the following examples:

(1) the predicate 'horse' is true of something if and only if it is a horse.

(2) a construction of the form *P and Q* is true if and only if *P* is true and *Q* is true.

There is something trivial about these clauses since you can know they are true simply by knowing that 'horse' is an extensional (one-place) predicate and that 'and' is a (two-place) truth functional connective. You do not even have to know what these expressions mean. Compare:

(3) the predicate 'borogrove' is true of something if and only if it is a borogrove.

(4) a construction of the form *P zop Q* is true if and only if *P* is true zop *Q* is true.

If you know that 'borogrove' is a one-place predicate and 'zop' is a two-place truth functional sentential connective, then you know that (3) and (4) hold even

---

[1] Alfred Tarski, 'The Concept of Truth in Formalized Languages', in *Logic, Semantics, Metamathematics* (Oxford University Press, Oxford, 1956); Saul A. Kripke, 'Semantical Considerations on Modal Logic', *Acta Philosophica Fennica*, 16 (1963); Donald Davidson, 'The Logical Form of Action Sentences', in *The Logic of Decision and Action*, ed. Nicholas Rescher (University of Pittsburgh Press, Pittsburgh, 1967).

though you do not know what 'borogrove' and 'zop' mean, as long as you know what 'true' and the other words in these sentences mean.

Yet there seems to be an important difference between predicates and logical constants. A theory of truth of the sort Tarski describes,[2] containing clauses like (1) and (2), is often thought of as giving the meanings of sentential connectives corresponding to 'and', 'or' and 'not' and quantifiers corresponding to 'everything' and 'something'. The theory is not normally thought of as giving the meaning of predicates like 'horse'. People may refer to Tarski's account of the meanings of certain quantifiers, but not to his account of the meaning of the predicate 'horse'.

(Well, the predicate 'horse' does not appear in the example Tarski actually develops. The only non-logical predicate is the relation of set inclusion. So I should really say here that people do not refer to Tarski's account of the meaning of the predicate 'is included in'.)[3]

At one time, I thought that the clauses for logical constants in the relevant sort of theory of truth say more about their meanings than do the clauses for non-logical predicates for the following reason. The meanings of logical constants are determined by the role these constants play in reasoning, whereas the meanings of non-logical predicates are not to the same extent determined by the role such predicates play in reasoning. Furthermore, the roles logical constants play in reasoning are determined by the logical implications that depend on those logical constants, where these implications are determined by the contribution logical constants make to truth conditions. In other words, I saw the following dependencies, each determining the next:

> contribution to truth conditions
> relevant logical implications
> role in reasoning
> meaning.

I no longer believe this. I still think the meanings of logical constants arise from their roles in reasoning, but these roles are not determined by relevant logical implications. The trouble is that logically equivalent connectives can have different meanings. For example, consider the two connectives that combine propositions P and Q to get the following results, respectively:

> P and Q
> not $((\text{not } P) \text{ or } (\text{not } Q))$

Since these results are logically equivalent, the two connectives make exactly the same contributions to truth conditions and are subject to exactly the same rules of logical implication, even though they do not have the same meaning.

Still, I feel that something might be salvageable from the attempt to see a particular sort of connection between principles of conceptual role and truth clauses. One might attempt to characterize the meanings of logical constants in

---

[2] Tarski, 'The Concept of Truth'.
[3] Ibid, New York University Press, 1974.

terms of principles of natural deduction that resemble or parallel the truth clauses for such logical constants. I will discuss this idea in the next section of the paper. To be sure, this does not yet avoid the problem that logically equivalent constants are assigned the same meaning. But I will suggest that we might avoid this problem by thinking of the relevant rules as rules of *immediate* implication, and perhaps also rules of immediate exclusion, not just rules of implication, although this loses the parallel with the truth clauses.

Natural deduction

The idea that the meanings of logical constants are determined by certain characteristic implications has been elaborated in theories of 'natural deduction'.[4] In this view, each logical constant is associated with 'introduction rules' and 'elimination rules' which fix its meaning. For example, logical conjunction, i.e. 'and', is defined as that sentential connective C such that, for any propositions, P and Q,

> P, Q logically imply $C(P,Q)$
> $C(P,Q)$ logically implies P
> $C(P,Q)$ logically implies Q.

The first of these clauses gives an *introduction rule* for logical conjunction in the sense that it permits the introduction of a conjunctive statement into a proof. The second and third give *elimination rules* for conjunction in the sense that they allow a consequence not containing conjunction to be derived from a conjunctive statement.

Now, to say one proposition logically implies another is to say the first cannot be true without the second being true. So, the introduction rule for conjunction is just another way of saying that, necessarily.

> $C(P,Q)$ is true if P is true and Q is true.

Similarly, the elimination rule is just another way of saying that, necessarily,

> $C(P,Q)$ is true only if P is true and Q is true.

Putting these together yields the clause for conjunction in a theory of truth, supposing that theory is supposed to be necessary in the relevant sense (saying what holds necessarily, given what the relevant terms mean). So far, then, there is a close connection between the idea that the meanings of logical constants are determined by their truth conditions and the idea that these meanings are determined by characteristic logical implications.

But things are less simple for logical disjunction ('or') and logical negation ('not'). Consider logical disjunction. The introduction rule is easy:

---

[4] See Dag Prawitz, *Natural Deduction* (Almqvist and Wiksell, Stockholm, 1965) and references therein.

P implies $D(P,Q)$
Q implies $D(P,Q)$.

And this is just another way of expressing the 'if' half of the truth conditions for logical disjunction:

$D(P,Q)$ is true if P is true or Q is true.

The trouble comes with the elimination rule. Notice, first of all, that the disjunction $D(P,Q)$ by itself does not logically imply either of its disjuncts, P or Q, although it does imply one of its disjuncts (e.g. P) given also the negation of the other disjunct ($N(P)$). This may seem to suggest taking the following as an elimination rule:

$D(P,Q)$, $N(P)$ logically imply Q
$D(P,Q)$, $N(Q)$ logically imply P.

But this has the disadvantage of appealing to one logical constant (negation) while defining another (disjunction). It leaves it unclear whether disjunction is being defined, or negation, or both simultaneously. The definition also lacks generality, since it would not work for a language containing disjunction but lacking negation.

So it is customary in systems of natural deduction to adopt a more complex rule:

IF P and certain other assumptions logically imply C
AND Q and those other assumptions also logically imply C
THEN $D(P,Q)$ and those other assumptions logically imply C.

However, this yields an elimination rule that is not just another way of expressing part of the truth conditions for disjunction.

Multiple conclusion logic

This difference between conjunction and disjunction can be avoided by giving up appeal to rules of natural deduction in favor of rules of a 'sequent calculus'. A sequent calculus is a 'multiple conclusion logic', whose multiple conclusions are in a certain sense understood disjunctively. Where an ordinary argument is valid if and only if the premises cannot all be true unless its single conclusion is also true, a multiple conclusion argument is valid if and only if its premises cannot all be true without *at least one* of its possibly many conclusions being true. Instead of saying that the premises in a valid multiple conclusion argument logically imply its conclusions, we can say that they logically *involve* its conclusions.

In a multiple conclusion logic, the following might be used as an elimination rule for disjunction:

$D(P,Q)$ logically involves P,Q^5

And this rule does express exactly what is expressed in the clause giving the 'only if' part of the truth conditions of disjunction.

$D(P,Q)$ is true only if P is true or Q is true.

However, it must be confessed that appeal to the notion of involvement seems a trifle *ad hoc* in this connection.

Negation

Now, consider how negation might be defined in terms of introduction and elimination rules. First, the elimination rule for negation can be taken to be this:

If $N(P)$ and certain other assumptions logically imply P, then those other assumptions by themselves logically imply P.

Alternatively, we can use this:

P, $N(P)$ logically imply anything.

The following introduction rule corresponds to the latter elimination rule:

If P and certain other premises logically imply everything, then those other premises logically imply $N(P)$

It might seem this would not be useful in a system of natural deduction, in which one is interested in using such rules in proofs, since it might seem one would first have to prove infinitely many things to order to show that P and the other premises logically imply everything before being able to conclude $N(P)$. But, given the second elimination rule, it is enough to show that P and the other premises logically imply $N(P)$, for in that case they imply anything. So, the introduction rule could also be stated like this:

If P and certain other assumptions logically imply $N(P)$, then those other assumptions by themselves logically imply $N(P)$.

So, we can state introduction and elimination rules of natural deduction for negation, but clearly these rules are not simply restatements of the truth conditions of negated propositions. Nor does it help to state introduction and elimination rules in a sequent calculus or multiple conclusion logic for negation. It turns out that we still need basically the same rules.

---

[5] D. J. Shoesmith and T. J. Smiley, *Multiple Conclusion Logic* (Cambridge University Press, Cambridge, 1978).

Negative conclusion logic

Now, in the case of disjunction, we can get introduction and elimination rules that express truth conditions by appealing to a multiple conclusion or disjunctive conclusion logic. We could do the analogous thing for negation by introducing a negative conclusion logic.[6] Let us say that a negative 'conclusion argument is valid if and only if the premises cannot all be true unless the conclusion is not true. We can say that the premises of a valid negative conclusion argument logically *exclude* its conclusion. Then it is easy to give simple, straightforward introduction and elimination rules for negation:

> P logically excludes $N(P)$
> $N(P)$ logically excludes P.

These rules express the truth conditions for negative propositions in exactly the way in which the rules for disjunction in a multiple conclusion logic express the truth conditions of disjunctive propositions.

In short, we can equate the usual sorts of clauses in a truth theory for logical connectives with rules of natural deduction only if we extend the notion of implication in various seemingly *ad hoc* ways. More straightforward rules of natural deduction in terms of logical implication do not coincide with clauses giving truth conditions except in the case of conjunction.

Improved rules: immediate implication

We have, then, two rather different ideas about the meaning of logical constants. One is that the meaning of a logical constant is determined by the contribution that the constant makes to truth conditions. The other is that the meaning of a logical constant is determined by certain principles of logical implication involving that constant.

Even though these ideas do not coincide, I have remarked already that they are both subject to the objection that they assign logically equivalent connectives the same meaning. To repeat my earlier example, consider the two connectives that combine propositions P and Q to get the following results, respectively:

> P and Q
> not ((not P) or (not Q))

Since these results are logically equivalent, the two connectives make exactly the same contributions to truth conditions and are subject to exactly the same rules of logical implication, even though they do not have the same meaning.

I believe the difference in meaning in this case has to do with how *immediate* certain implications are. In particular, the simple conjunction, 'P and Q',

---

[6] My own invention, as far as I know.

immediately implies '*P*' in a way that the more complicated proposition, 'not ((not *P*) or (not *Q*))', does not.

Immediate implication is a psychological notion. An immediate implication is one that is immediately obvious, one that can be immediately recognized. I try to say more about this elsewhere.[7] For present purposes let us simply take this notion as primitive. Then we can ask whether we can reformulate rules of natural deduction as rules of immediate implication and use these reformulated rules to define logical constants.

So, we might define conjunction as that sentential connective *C* such that

> *C(P,Q)* immediately implies *P*
> *C(P,Q)* immediately implies *Q*
> *P, Q* immediately imply *C(P,Q)*.

By this criterion, 'not ((not *P*) or (not *Q*))' fails to be the conjunction *C(P,Q)*, for example, because it does not immediately imply *P*, etc.

Notice that, although there is a certain similarity between this definition and the clause giving the contribution to truth conditions of 'and', the present definition is by no means equivalent to that clause. Even if *logical implication* is solely a matter of truth conditions, *immediate implication* is not.

Logical disjunction might be defined as that connective *D* that satisfies the following conditions:

> *P* immediately implies *D(P,Q)*
> *Q* immediately implies *D(P,Q)*
> '*P*, θ imply *C*' and '*Q*, θ imply *C*' immediately imply '*D(P,Q)*, θ imply *C*'.

These conditions parallel the usual natural deduction rules but are not at all similar to the truth conditions for disjunction. Nor does the last condition seem correct as a principle about *immediate* implication.

What principles should be adopted for logical negation? Certain principles, paralleling natural deduction rules, seem clearly incorrect, for example:

> *P*, *N(P)* immediately imply anything.

This implication seems to be mediated by several steps. Similarly for

> '*P*, θ imply everything' immediately implies 'θ imply *N(p)*'.

The following are not so clearly inadequate:

> '*N(P)*, θ imply *P*' immediately implies 'θ imply *P*'.
> '*P*, θ imply *N(P)*' immediately implies 'θ imply *N(P)*'.

They do not suffice to establish all the relevant principles involving negation, for example that a contradiction implies everything. However, these related principles of *reductio ad absurdum* proof will do the trick:

---

[7] Gilbert Harman, *Change in View*, MIT Press; Cambridge, Mass.: 1986.

'*N(Q)*, θ imply *P*' and '*N(Q)*, θ imply *N(P)*' immediately imply 'θ imply *Q*'.
'*Q* and θ imply *P*' and '*Q* and θ imply *N(P)*' immediately imply 'θ imply *N(Q)*'.

Still, it is far from clear that these principles are correct as principles of *immediate* implication.

Immediate inconsistency

It is not clear that *reductio ad absurdum* proof is immediately perspicuous for everyone who grasps negation. A better idea might be to borrow the notion of *exclusion* from the imaginary negative conclusion logic I have mentioned. More precisely, the idea would be to appeal to a notion of *immediate exclusion* or *immediate inconsistency*. Things are immediately inconsistent for someone if he or she can immediately see that they are incompatible, if they are obviously inconsistent. Using this notion, we can then define negation as that (one-place) sentential connective *N* such that

> *N(P)* is immediately inconsistent with *P* and is immediately implied by any set of propositions immediately inconsistent with *P*; furthermore, any set of propositions immediately inconsistent with *N(P)* immediately imply *P*.

Given this, it is possible to derive a principle of *reductio ad absurdum* proof. (To show this we appeal to the principle that, if *P* and *A* are immediately inconsistent, so are *P*, θ and '*P*, θ imply *A*'. Then, by the definition of negation, θ and '*P*, θ imply *A*' imply *N(P)*.)

Using immediate inconsistency in addition to immediate implication allows a more plausible elimination rule for disjunction:

> *D(P,Q)* plus any set of propositions immediately inconsistent with *P* immediately imply *Q*.
> *D(P,Q)* plus any set of propositions immediately inconsistent with *Q* immediately imply *P*.

This would allow us to avoid the somewhat implausible claim about immediate implication in the previous rules based on the usual natural deduction rules.

One might instead try to account for disjunction by appeal to the principle of 'immediate involvement' in a multiple conclusion logic. However, the notion of immediate involvement is not a natural notion like immediate implication and immediate inconsistency. Propositions do not immediatley involve one another in the way they immediately imply or exclude one another.

Quantifiers

Rules for quantifiers might be adapted from the introduction and elimination rules in some system of natural deduction, for example:

A universal quantification *(x)P(x)* immediately implies any instance *P(a)*.

'θ implies *P(a)*' and '*a* does not occur in θ' immediately imply 'θ implies *(x)P(x)*.

A singular proposition *P(a)* immediately implies any existential generalization *(Σx)P(x)*.

'θ, *P(a)* imply *C*' and '*a* does not occur in any other relevant place, i.e. in θ, *C*, or *(Σx)P(x)*' immediately imply 'θ, *(Σx)*P(x) imply *C*'.

However, these rules do not fully characterize ordinary 'objectual' quantification, since they do not distinguish 'objectual' from 'substitutional' quantification. (A universal substitutional quantification is true if and only if all its substitution instances are true, whereas a universal objectual quantification is true if and only if all things in the range of the quantifier satisfy the predicate or open sentence to which the quantifier is attached.) Furthermore, the rules of universal quantifier introduction and existential quantifier elimination do not seem true as principles of immediate implication.

To meet the first complaint, what is needed are rules like the following:

'For every referring name or pronoun or variable *a*, no matter what it is taken to refer to, θ implies *P(a)*' immediately implies 'θ implies *(x)P(x)*'.

'For every *a*, no matter what it is taken to refer to, θ, *P(a)* imply *C*' immediately implies 'θ, *(Σx)*P(x) imply *C*'.

These would yield ordinary objectual quantification and not just substitutional quantification. The first seems to me true as a claim about immediate implication. I am not sure about the second, but maybe it is true too.

A caveat about ordinary language

This kind of account of logical concepts is not intended as analysis of ordinary language. If definitions of this sort are correct, they say what it is for a concept to be the concept of classical negation, classical disjunction, or whatever. The definitions do not imply that such concepts occur in ordinary language or are actually used by anyone. If these logical concepts are used at all, it may well be in some special calculus that has been devised for some special purpose. Such a 'calculus' would be used in the first instance for a certain sort of 'calculation' rather than for communication. Furthermore, it may be that we never actually use it for calculation but merely reflect on certain aspects of what it would be like to use it in that way. So, to talk of immediate implication and exclusion in this connection is to talk about what would be immediately obvious to users of such a calculus.

Final remarks

Even if the meanings of logical constants are determined by their roles in inference, it is imprecise to say that these roles are determined by characteristic implications. It is important which implications (and perhaps also which exclusions) are *immediate*. And this is not just a matter of the contribution a construction makes to truth conditions. So there is no argument here for thinking that truth conditions are more relevant to the meanings of logical constants than to the meanings of non-logical predicates.[8]

---

[8] I am indebted to Sarah Stebbins's comments on an earlier version of this paper. I have not been able to respond to all her worries. To mention one point, she argued forcefully that the meanings of the logical constants might be determined holistically in the sense that, for example, the meaning of disjunction might be affected by whether classical negation was present. In that case, the concept of classical disjunction would not be captured just by the rules for disjunction.

8

Tenses, Temporal Quantifiers and Semantic Innocence

BARRY RICHARDS

Introduction

How does temporal reference relate to the semantics of tense and temporal quantification? Broadly speaking, there are two perspectives one can adopt, a Russellian one and a Priorean one. The Russellian view is that temporal reference is an essential feature of the meaning of both tenses and temporal quantifiers. They involve explicit reference to time and this is crucial to understanding their semantic import. In contrast, the Priorean view is that temporal reference is irrelevant to the semantics of tenses and temporal quantifiers. While their meaning can be defined over time segments, they invoke no explicit reference to them.

While it is natural to wonder which view does more justice to the facts of language, one may suspect that neither can be uniformly satisfactory. The Russellian account seems more appropriate to tenses while the Priorean account appears better suited to temporal quantifiers. Tensed sentences are typically sensitive to the time of utterance in that they may be true on one occasion and false on another. This shift in truth value can be plausibly traced to a shift in time reference. As the Russellian view would have it, utterances of a tensed sentence involve reference to the time of speech, and thus what is past, present or future is determined relative to that time. Since different utterances invoke different speech times, the truth value of a sentence may vary from time to time. But when sentences are modified by temporal quantifiers, e.g. *always*, *twice* or *never*, there seems to be a certain independence from the time of speech. What is always, twice or never the case can be judged only from a perspective which surveys the whole of time rather than being located in it. In

For many valuable discussions, suggestions and criticisms I should like to thank the members of the Tense and Discourse Workshop in Edinburgh, in particular Ewan Klein, David McCarty, Marc Moens, Jon Oberlander, Mark Steedman, Lesley Stirling, Jan de Vuyst and Henk Zeevat. I should also like to thank Kit Fine and Dana Scott for a number of useful suggestions. I am particularly grateful to Marc Moens for his generous efforts in helping to improve the final draft. Needless to say, no one but myself is responsible for the remaining deficiencies.

the circumstance a Priorean formulation is perhaps more natural, although not inevitable.

Despite the convenience of eclecticism, there is a disposition to hope that one of the approaches may emerge as uniformly satisfactory. The form in which this might arise, i.e. the nature of a generally adequate theory, has been the subject of considerable speculation, but the results to date have been less than conclusive. No comprehensively suitable proposal has yet been identified and hence, it seems not inappropriate to consider another alternative. We propose to sketch a theory which, though innovative in some technical and philosophical respects, is essentially Russellian in spirit. Basically, we take temporal reference to be the key to a general explanation of the semantics of both tenses and temporal quantifiers.

Among the more fundamental aspects of the theory is the distinction between tensed and untensed sentences. When one utters a tensed sentence, one is understood to refer deictically to the time of utterance and thus to say something about that time. In contrast, an utterance of an untensed sentence is taken to have no special connection with the time of speech. No reference to speech time occurs when one utters an untensed sentence, unless the sentence contains some appropriate adverb, and thus an untensed utterance does not generally say anything about the occasion of utterance.

Russell is not the only one to regard tensed utterances to be about the time of speech. Reichenbach has a similar view, although he envisages a somewhat more elaborate system of reference. He suggests that tensed assertions involve reference not only to speech time but also to what he calls event time and reference time. It has been noted that his tripartite system of temporal reference may make it difficult, if not impossible, to treat tenses as sentential operators.[1] Since we intend to treat tenses in just this way, i.e. as sentential operators, it is worth noting that nowhere do we resort to Reichenbach's notions of event time and reference time. Although we invoke reference to time, we never appeal to his special concepts of reference time and event time.

While speech time plays an essential role in the analysis of tense, we take it to be irrelevant to the treatment of temporal quantifiers, i.e. of such expressions as *always*, *sometimes* and *never*. This is not to say, however, that reference to time is generally irrelevant. Temporal quantifiers are understood to invoke temporal reference just as tenses do, but reference is not always or even typically to speech time. The interval denoted may be any one at all, and its role is to restrict the range of quantification. In effect, temporal quantifiers range over an interval fixed referentially at the time of utterance. This referential aspect of temporal quantifiers figures significantly in their interaction with temporal connectives, in particular with *when*, *before* and *after*.

Although we confine our attention to intrasentential phenomena, there is an emerging view that the real test of a temporal theory lies in discourse.[2] Any truly satisfactory theory must generalize to cover temporal relations among sentences in a discourse. What these relations might be, and how they should be characterized, is not easy to decipher, but it is reasonable to suppose that

---

[1] See Dowty (1979).
[2] See Kamp and Rohrer (1983).

temporal connectives must be among the more pertinent phenomena. Any approach which is suitable for the treatment of temporal connection might be expected to suggest how discourse itself is to be handled. We would hope that our theory might indicate some of the 'ingredients' of a theory of discourse, although we shall not attempt to elaborate any of them here.

Among our more philosophical concerns will be certain issues revolving around two familiar Davidsonian themes, viz. logical form and semantic innocence. The logical form of tensed sentences has been difficult to characterize, especially in relation to other temporal devices such as adverbs, quantifiers and connectives. We shall argue that if tenses are characterized in a Russellian way, i.e. in the manner we suggest, a fully comprehensive account of temporal phenomena can be constructed. One of the more surprising consequences of the proposal is that semantic innocence may be a misdirected semantic aspiration. Sentences which occur in subordinate position do not generally have the same semantic role which they have as main clauses. This is an important fact of language which can be explained if the role of tenses is appropriately specified.

Untensed sentences

Let us start by considering untensed sentences. Linguists may debate whether there are any such sentences, but it cannot be denied that English contains a range of putative candidates, particularly in subordinate position. One might note, for example, the following instances.

(1) It was important that Max exercise regularly.
(2) The doctor recommended that Max run daily.

Prima facie one seems justified in supposing that the two sentences in subordinate position, viz.

(3) Max exercise regularly
(4) Max run daily

are both untensed. For one thing there is no apparent syntactic marking for tense, and for another this fact seems to be semantically important. Note the following variant of (1) where the subordinate sentence is tensed as past.

(5) It was important that Max exercised regularly.

Clearly (5) implies that Max did exercise regularly, but no similar implication attaches to (1) which is consistent with the assertion,

(6) But he never did.

The difference between (1) and (5) is naturally attributed to tense, although it may equally be associated with mood. The subordinate sentence in (5) is in the indicative mood while the subordinate sentence in (1) is in the subjunctive mood. It is interesting to note that the subjunctive mood in English seems to coincide with the absence of tense. In the case of (2) the subordinate sentence can only be read 'subjunctively', and significantly it can never be tensed, as one can see by replacing *run* with *ran*.

(7)   *The doctor recommended that Kim ran.

There is, in effect, no factive reading of *recommended* as there is of *was important*. In the circumstance, one is tempted to conjecture that subordinate sentences can be read factively only if they are tensed; when they are untensed, they must be read counterfactually.

It may be suggested that English is perhaps not a sure guide to universal syntax. When (1) and (2) are translated into other languages, the subordinate sentences are typically marked for tense, even though their status is counterfactual. There is a sense, nevertheless, in which such counterfactual sentences are 'semantically' untensed. Later we shall indicate just what sense this is, at which point it may emerge that English is not entirely misleading to drop tense.

Since we shall use untensed sentences as a basis for analysing tensed sentences, we must address the difficult problem of how they are to be semantically characterized, a problem which has worried many philosophers and logicians. It does not seem appropriate to regard untensed sentences as having a truth value, since there is no occasion on which it would be correct to say that they are true or false. Utterances of sentences such as (3) and (4) are not assertions about what is purportedly true and hence, they cannot be rightly seen as bearing truth value. In this respect their status can only be seen as independent of truth. From the perspective of formal semantics this is awkward, for it suggests that the concept of truth cannot be invoked to analyse sentences like (3) and (4). Although truth may yield a natural account of sentences that can bear truth value, there is genuine doubt that it can be applied to other kinds of sentences.

Despite such scepticism, it is arguable that truth can still be invoked to characterize the semantic content of untensed sentences. It is helpful to recall the 'speech act' view of declarative and non-declarative sentences. According to this theory, both types of sentence express propositions, the only difference being that declaratives assert them and non-declaratives do not. For example, these two sentences are said to express the same proposition.

(8)   Max exercises regularly.
(9)   Max, exercise regularly!

Significantly, the proposition is taken to be the one expressed by the untensed sentence,

(3)   Max exercise regularly.

While (8) is understood to assert this proposition (with respect to the present), (9) is held to command it (with reference to the future).

Bearing in mind the status of (3), viz., that it never bears a truth value relative to an utterance, one might legitimately use truth values to characterize the proposition expressed by (3), provided there is no implication that (3) ever has a truth value simpliciter. Let us suppose, then, that propositions take the form of functions from moments of time to truth values; that is, let us assume that propositions are distinguished by functions which identify those moments in which the proposition is true. In the case of (3) the proposition expressed picks out those moments of time at which Max has the property of exercising regularly. This is not to say that an utterance of (3) is tantamount to asserting, or even implying, that the given proposition is true at the moment of utterance. Although the proposition may well be true at this particular time, the utterance neither says nor implicates that it is. In effect (3) does not take on truth values relative to utterances. While it expresses a proposition, it does so in what might be called a value-free way; that is, it is of the essence of (3) that it carries no indication (contextual or otherwise) about where, i.e., at which moment, the proposition is to be evaluated, whether at the moment of utterance or somewhere else. This is characteristic of all untensed sentences, which never invoke any moment as a moment of evaluation. Although the propositions expressed are represented as functions from moments to truth values, no moment can have the status of being the intended moment of evaluation.

Evaluation is invoked through the medium of tense, e.g., the present tense, as in (8). To utter (8) is to invoke the time of speech as the intended interval of evaluation; it is tantamount to asserting that the proposition expressed by (3) is true for this particular interval. As a result, (8) is appropriately regarded as bearing a truth value relative to the time of speech. One might say that it is, as it were, value-specific for that interval. This is in marked contrast to (3), no utterance of which identifies any interval as the intended interval of evaluation. What the truth value of (3) is relative to a particular interval is not something which an utterance of (3) can raise by itself. Only through tense does this emerge.

If (3) is seen to result from (8) by 'factoring' present tense, it is natural to view the mood of (8) as associated with its tense. Since introducing present tense into (3) must then be sufficient to realize (8), the mood of (8), viz., the indicative mood, seems a parasitic phenomenon; it requires no characterization independent of tense. In effect there is no component of (8), other than the present tense, which corresponds to what has been called the speech act device, here the device associated with assertion. Tense is what makes (8) assertible. Significantly, (8) is not taken to express the same proposition as (3). While (8) always asserts something about the time of utterance, viz. that (3) is true there, (3) itself never expresses this proposition. The proposition expressed by (3) is, as it were, value-free while the one expressed by (8) is value-specific.

The contrast between value-specific and value-free propositions will play a central role both in the characterization of tense and in the analysis of sentential subordination. Sentences which occur in subordinate position typically express value-free propositions, as can be seen in the following example.

(10) It is my wish that God save the Queen.

For me to utter (10) is of course to express a wish relative to the time of utterance, viz., that God save the Queen. However, it is not a wish merely about the present moment, for I plainly intend to invoke God's good offices for some indefinite period in the future. In fact there is a sense in which my wish might be seen to be omnitemporal; it is a wish that the proposition expressed by the subordinate sentence

(11)   God save the Queen

evaluate to true for any moment of time, at least for all future moments. So understood, the proposition expressed by (11) must be regarded as value-free, i.e. as not involving any moment in particular. How this interpretation can be technically realized will subsequently become clear.

Let us now turn to the task of characterizing the content of sentences that are assumed to be both moodless and tenseless. As we have indicated, albeit obliquely, we propose to treat propositions in general as functions from intervals of time to truth values. Intervals may be of any length as long as they are continuous, with points of time being just minimal intervals. The need for intervals, as well as points, is sometimes justified on metaphysical grounds. It is arguable that some things are true for intervals but not for all points in those intervals, like taking a run which is punctuated with periods of rest. Such considerations, however, do not figure among our reasons for regarding intervals as the fundamental notion. Since tenses and other temporal devices typically involve reference to intervals, it seems appropriate to have them in the theory from the beginning. To be sure, there are other reasons for admitting them but these will become evident in due course.

Much has recently been made of Vendler's classification of verbs according to whether they express activities, accomplishments, achievements or states.[3] Doubtless there are important semantic differences, of which some may be relevant to formal semantics. One thinks of the adverb *in an hour* which occurs with verbs expressing achievements and accomplishments but not normally with those expressing activities or states.[4] We shall not, however, be concerned with such matters in this paper and thus need not seek to characterize the relevant factors. Moreover, we shall not attempt to account for certain semantic anomalies, e.g. the incommensurability between achievement verbs and durational adverbs.

(12)   *Sandy arrived for ten minutes.

Some would be disposed to require that a fully adequate semantic theory should explain why (12) is anomalous and the following is not.

(13)   Sandy walked for ten minutes.

We shall set such problems aside and treat all verbs as having a common semantic structure. Although this may seem linguistically shortsighted, our

---

[3] See Vendler (1967).
[4] See Dowty (1979), p. 54.

general concern is with semantic structure that abstracts from 'lexical' differences.

The envisaged semantic theory will be defined over a quasi-logical language supplemented with certain propositional operators. The syntax of this language is based on a categorial analysis of a fragment of English and is extended to include certain resources from quantified modal logic. The resulting compromise between formality and informality is intended to allow for ease of comprehension while maintaining a certain rigour.

Although we shall focus on those aspects of semantics relating to temporal structures, it will also be necessary to invoke possible worlds. With this in mind we let a model for a our quasi-logical language be a quintuple $(D, W, I, <, f)$ such that

(14) (i) D, W and I are non-empty disjoint sets to be understood respectively as the set of possible objects, possible worlds and intervals of moments of time;

(ii) The relation $<$ is the partial ordering of I induced by the 'earlier than' relation defined over moments of time; that is, for intervals i and j, $i<j$ iff all the moments in i are earlier than all the moments in j;

(iii) and f is a function that assigns a suitable intension to each non-logical constant of the language.

Since we do not propose to pin down any particular logic, there is no need here to restrict the definition of a model to any specific temporal structure. Our strategy is to investigate certain issues relating to logical form which do not immediately require a general definition of logical consequence. Once these issues are clarified we can then seek to identify an appropriate model structure. This task we shall leave to another time.

We must, however, specify the range of admissible intensions, for which we invoke two special conditions. The possible extensions of constants will be as usual: the extension of a name will be an individual in D unless the name is a temporal one, in which case its extension will be an interval in I; and the extension of an n-ary relation will be a subset of n-tuples from D^n. The intension denoted by a constant will then be a function with domain $(W \times I)$, the cartesian product of W and I, which satisfies the following conditions.

(14) (iv) If b is a name and $f(b)(w,i)$ is an entity d of D, then for all subintervals j of i $f(b)(w,j)$ is also d.

(v)   If r is an n-ary relation, $f(r)(w,i)$ is a subset d of D^n only if for all subintervals j of i $f(r)(w,j)$ includes $f(r)(w,i)$.

The point of (iv) and (v) is basically to ensure that if an atomic sentence is true at a world for an interval it will be true at that world for all subintervals of the given interval.

It will be noted that (iv) and (v) admit the possibility of defining intensions which are partial functions, since there is no requirement that intensions be defined for all intervals. This possibility emerges independently of whether intensions are defined for all moments of time, i.e. for the smallest intervals.

With a view to speculating about the general nature of temporal quantification, we shall allow f to assign partial functions; but we shall assume that all such functions are still defined for each moment of time. That is, we shall adopt the following condition on the definition of f:

(14) (vi) If c is a non-logical constant and i a moment of time in I, f(c)(w,i) must be defined.

Apart from (iv)–(vi) f is free to assign any appropriate intension to a non-logical constant.

Given the admissibility of partial functions, we must specify their import for the intensions of sentences. Suppose that a sentence (relative to a world) is not true for every subinterval of a given interval. Is it to be taken as false or undefined for that interval? Although it would be convenient (and possible) to adopt the former view, an interesting distinction emerges if the latter is chosen. It will arise from our formalization that the intension of an untensed sentence is usually a partial function but the intension of a tensed sentence (and other types of sentence involving temporal quantification) is always a total function.[5] There is thus a clear semantic difference between tensed and untensed sentences, one that will become more precise below.

The definition of truth will be seen to yield the following homogeneity property for untensed sentences.

(15) An untensed sentence will be true at an index (w,i) only if for all subintervals j of i the sentence is true at (w,j).

It should be stressed that homogeneity is not intended as a restriction on the truth definition; rather it is a property which characteristically (though not always) emerges from it. With this clarification, we specify the initial clauses in the following way, taking A and B to be any sentences of the language, and M any model.

(16) (i)   An atomic sentence consisting of an n-ary relation R_n and n terms $a_1, ..., a_n$ is true in M at (w,i) if the sequence $f(a_1)(w,i), ..., f(a_n)(w,i)$ belongs to $f(R_n)(w,i)$; it is false at (w,i) if the given sequence does not so belong; and otherwise it is undefined.

      (ii) (A *and* B) is true in M at (w,i) if both A and B are true in M at (w,i); it is false at (w,i) if either A or B is false at (w,i); and otherwise it is undefined.

      (iii) (A *or* B) is true in M at (w,i) if either A or B is true in M at (w,i); it is false at (w,i) if both A and B are false at (w,i); and otherwise it is undefined.

      (iv) *Not* (A) is true in M at (w,i) if A is false in M at (w,i); it is false at (w,i) if A is true at (w,i); and otherwise it is undefined.

---

[5] The semantic theory suggests that tenses and temporal quantifiers should be grouped into one class and time adverbials into another class.

Before giving the clauses for the quantifiers, we should note that there is a choice in how to specify the range of quantification. Consider a sentence of the form,

(17) *Every x* (A).

Given a model, (17) may be treated in at least two different ways. Relative to an index (w,i) it can be interpreted as asserting that every object in the domain of the model has the property A at (w,i). Here the quantifier is understood to range over the whole of the domain. Alternatively, the quantifier can be interpreted as ranging only over those objects in the domain which exist at the index (w,i). In this case (17) will be read as saying that each of the entities in this set has the distinguished property at (w,i). From the point of view of natural language the 'restricted' reading of the quantifier may seem more suitable. Typical quantifier phrases, such as *every swimmer*, seem paradigm instances of restricted quantification. It is arguable, nevertheless, that *every* itself should be treated as an unrestricted quantifier, i.e. as an example of a generalized quantifier. This in effect is how we propose to define it.

Let A(b/x) be the sentence which results from A by replacing all the free occurrences of x by a name b which does not already occur in A. Let M^b be a model which is like M except possibly for what the function f assigns to b. The standard quantifiers *every* and *some* are then defined as follows.

(16) (v) *Every x* (A) is true in M at (w,i) if A(b/x) is true at (w,i) for every M^b; it is false at (w,i) if A(b/x) is false at (w,i) for some M^b; and otherwise it is undefined.

(vi) *Some* (A) is true in M at (w,i) if A(b/x) is true at (w,i) for some M^b; it is false at (w,i) if A(b/x) is false at (w,i) for every M^b; and otherwise it is undefined.

It should be noted that quantified sentences may be undefined at an index because they contain a predicate or a name that is undefined at that index.

We can now illustrate how the given semantics may be appropriate for untensed moodless sentences like

(18) Hilary swim.

Relative to a model, (18) will express a proposition represented by a possibly partial function. This proposition will be determined by the intensions of *Hilary* and *swim* and will be indifferent as to the intended interval of evaluation. Not only does (18) not contain devices for explicit reference to intervals, but its analysis at the level of logical form does not presuppose any such reference. In effect, the proposition is characterized in a value-free way: there is not, nor can there be, an intended interval of evaluation. This is just what distinguishes an untensed moodless sentence.

Tensed sentences

From the beginning we have supposed that tensed sentences are in a certain sense context-sensitive; that is, they express a determinate proposition only relative to an occasion of utterance. Thus the present-tense sentence,

(19)   Hilary swims

does not in itself express any particular proposition; only relative to an utterance does it say anything definite. For such an occasion it says essentially that the proposition expressed by (18) is true at the designated time. On this interpretation the proposition expressed by (18) must be different from the proposition expressed by an utterance of (19). The latter will be about a specific interval of time while the former will not be so.

The source of difference lies in the deictic nature of tense. Tenses involve deictic reference to speech time, and it is this semantic fact which explains why (18) and (19) diverge in the propositions they can express. Since (19) is tensed, an utterance of it involves reference to the time of utterance and thus says something about it: it says, as we have noted, that the proposition expressed by (18) is true at that interval. Since (18) is not tensed, no utterance of it can invoke reference to the interval of utterance, and for that reason it can only express a proposition different from (19).[6]

To reflect the referential aspect of tense we shall give the tense operators a complex syntactic structure. The present tense, for example, will be represented as $PRES_{(v,t)}$ with v and t read as deictic parameters ranging over worlds and intervals. These parameters are to be seen as acquiring their values relative to the context of utterance. A certain latitude will be allowed in the possible assignments to t in that they need not be strictly confined to the intervals of utterance. While the value of t must always have a final segment representing the interval of utterance, it may extend back into the past, indeed indefinitely far back. Such an assignment, i.e. where the value of t extends beyond the interval of utterance, is sometimes called the 'extended now'.

While reference to time seems a natural ingredient of tense, one may wonder about invoking reference to possible worlds. It is not clear that possible worlds

---

[6] Some have argued that (18) and (19) are not to be seen as differing in this way. The propositions they express do not diverge at the point of utterance, since they always express the same proposition. Where (18) and (19) differ is in respect of a certain conversational convention. There is a general convention that when one utters a tensed sentence, one offers the proposition expressed as being true for the interval of utterance. Thus when one utters (19), one commits onself by convention to the claim that the proposition expressed by (19) (and also by (18)) is true at the time of speech. One does not actually assert this to be so, either by referring to the given time or in any other way. If one did, the proposition expressed by (19) would then be different from the proposition expressed by (18), which it is said not to be. Hence one can only be taken to implicate the intended state of affairs in some indirect sort of way. By eschewing reference to speech time such a view coincides with the Priorean perspective. While it may seem appropriate here to venture a counterargument, we prefer to let the counterargument emerge as a 'by-product' of developing our Russellian alternative. If the theory is seen to explain a wide variety of complex phenomena, no further argument may be necessary.

have any special relation to tense, that is, one which they do not have to other parts of language. It is arguable, nevertheless, that the value-specific character of tensed utterances involves more than just time. When one utters a tensed sentence, it is not only speech time that is deictically fixed but also the intended 'location', normally the actual world. When one utters (19), for example, one usually intends to say something that is true at the time of speech in the actual world. While reference to the actual world does not obviously arise from tense, it also does not obviously arise from any other device. In the circumstance it is not unreasonable to regard tense as involving deictic reference to worlds. This at least allows a certain economy of analysis and may even lead to an unexpected insight, a matter we shall subsequently consider.

As for the syntactic role of $PRES_{(v,t)}$, we propose to treat it as a sentential operator but, for reasons that will emerge below, do not allow it to iterate without restriction. We let $PRES_{(v,t)}$ apply only to those sentences which later will be defined as context-free. Roughly speaking, a context-free sentence will be one that does not contain any occurrences of the deictic parameters, i.e. those ranging over worlds and intervals. On the assumption that A is a context-free sentence, we can specify the semantic content of the present-tense operator by extending the truth definition appropriately. Let g_c be a (possibly partial) function which assigns values to the 'deictic' parameters v and t relative to a context c.

(20) $PRES_{(v,t)}$ A is true in a model M at a world-interval index (w,i) if $w=g_c(v)$ and $i=g_c(t)$ and A is true in M at (w,i); it is false in M if either $w \neq g_c(v)$ or $i \neq g_c(t)$ or A is false in M at (w,i); and otherwise it is undefined.

It should be noted that (20) is actually a definition schema in that it gives rise to different intensions for different assignments to v and t.

By way of example let us consider the logical form of (19). Since (18) is a paradigm instance of a context-free sentence, (19) can be analysed as follows.

(21) $PRES_{(v,t)}$ (Hilary swim).

Relative to an utterance, v and t will acquire specific values, which for convenience may be referred to as V and T. With respect to V and T (19) is construed basically as expressing the proposition that the proposition expressed by (18) is true at (V,T). When formally characterized in terms of (21), this proposition is the intension which takes at most one world-interval pair to true, vis. (V,T). From the definition given in (20), it can be immediately seen that this intension will be true at (V,T) only if the intension denoted by (18) is true at (V,T); otherwise it will be either false or undefined. Since the intension denoted by (21) is, as it were, value specific for (V,T), it captures the special character of an utterance of a tensed sentence.

Some would argue, however, that (20) leads to counterintuitive consequences. Suppose that the two context-free sentences.

(18) Hilary swim
(22) Kim walk

are both true in a model at (V,T). Then (20) would imply that

(23)   PRES$_{(V,T)}$ (Hilary swim)
(24)   PRES$_{(V,T)}$ (Kim walk)

denote the same intension in that model. This may be seen to be awkward since it suggests that cotemporal utterances of

(19)   Hilary swims
(25)   Kim walks

will express the same proposition and hence convey the same information.

Although it is true that the intensions will be the same, there is a clear sense in which the utterances will still convey different information. For an occasion (V,T) (19) will convey the information that the proposition expressed by

(18)   Hilary swim

is true at (V,T), while for the same occasion (25) will intimate that the proposition expressed by

(22)   Kim walk

in true at (V,T). Since the intensions denoted by (18) and (22) will typically differ in a given model, the information content of (19) and (25) will not usually be the same for the utterance at (V,T). The difference becomes relevant in statements of propositional attitude. How this difference is to be accommodated technically will be considered in some detail below. For the moment let it suffice to emphasize the main point. Although (19) and (25) may denote the same intension relative to (V,T), they will do so with respect to different intensions, viz. the ones expressed by (18) and (22). These intensions account for the difference in information content between utterances of (19) and (25) and have special relevance in contexts of propositional attitude.

Let us now formalize the notion of a context-free sentence. We first define the concept of a context-sensitive sentence. All tense operators are assumed to have a common form which can be represented as $Q_{(v,t)}$, with Q having PRES, PAST and FUT as substitution instances. Where A and B are sentences,

(26)   A is said to be context-sensitive if it has the form $Q_{(v,t)}B$ where v and t are parameters or contains a subformula of this form.[7]

We take B to be a subformula of A if it is one of its main clauses, for example if A is of the form B *or* C, but not if it is a subordinate clause of A, such as *Sandy*

---

[7] It is important to appreciate that the context-sensitive parameters, viz. v and t, serve to identify the intended index of evaluation. Their role is actually fixed in the definitions of the tense operators, which follow immediately. While v and t receive their assignments from context, they are not the only parameters that do so. They are, however, the only parameters to be styled as context-sensitive, i.e. according to (26).

said that B. Given the definition of a context-sensitive sentence, we shall say that

(27)   A is context-free if each occurrence of a tense operator in a subformula is of the form $Q_{(v',t')}$ where v' and t' are variables.

As we have indicated above, (27) will be invoked to restrict the iteration of tenses.

The need to restrict iteration becomes apparent once we define the past and future tenses. Though they have a certain familiar form, the definitions are not entirely standard, mainly because of the role of the deictic parameters. Let A be any context-free sentence; then,

(28) $PAST_{(v,t)}A$ is true in a model M at (w,i) if $w = g_c(v)$, $i = g_c(t)$ and there is an interval $j < i$ such that A is true in M at (w,j); it is false at (w,i) if either $w \neq g_c(v)$ or $i \neq g_c(t)$ or there is no $j < i$ such that A is true at (w,j); (and otherwise it is undefined).

(29) $FUT_{(v,t)}A$ is true in M at (w,i) if $w = g_c(v)$, $i = g_c(t)$ and there is an interval j such that $i < j$ and A is true in M at (w,j); it is false at (w,i) if either $w \neq g_c(v)$ or $i \neq g_c(t)$ or there is no j such that $i < j$ and A is true at (w,j); (and otherwise it is undefined).[8]

Since tense operators are intended to apply only to context-free sentences, the following formula is not syntactically well formed.

(30) $PAST_{(v,t)} [PAST_{(v,t)} A]$

That (30) is also not semantically coherent can be readily appreciated. According to definition (28), (30) would be true in a model at (w,i) if $w = g_c(v)$, $i = g_c(t)$ and there is a $j < i$ such that $PAST_{(v,t)} A$ is true at (w,j); and this obtains only if $j = g_c(t)$ and there is a $k < j$ such that A is true at (w,k). But obviously no j can satisfy these conditions since it cannot satisfy both $j = g_c(t)$ and $j < g_c(t)$.

Since the parameters v and t obviously occupy referential positions, it is natural to envisage the possibility of binding into these positions. It will be immediately clear that such binding must give rise to context-free sentences. If all the occurrences of v and t give way to bound variables, the resulting sentence will by definition be context-free, for it will contain no instances of the given parameters. It will, accordingly, be an open formula. With a view to creating a particular kind of context-free sentence we introduce a new operator whose role will be to bind only into those positions where v and t can occur. To this end let v' and t' be variables ranging over worlds and intervals respectively. Where A is any sentence, either context-free or context-sensitive,

---

[8] It should be noted that for fixed values of v and t, (28) and (29) always give rise to intensions which are total functions, hence the reason for the parentheses. This suggests that tenses, and perhaps other devices of temporal quantification, may characteristically determine total functions. In the event it may be possible to distinguish a class of 'temporal' propositions.

(31)   Gv′[A] and Gt′[A] are also sentences.

In the first sentence G binds all the free occurrences of v′ in A, and in the second it binds all the free occurrences of t′. For sentences of the form Gv′[Gt′[A]] it is convenient to adopt the abbreviation Gv′t′[A], which will be used to define the semantics of G. To minimize the complexity of the definition we supplement our quasi-logical language with the following convention: given a world-interval index (w,i) let w* be a name of w and i* a name of i, and let A[w*/v′,i*/t′] be the formula which results from A by replacing all free occurrences of v′ by w* and all free occurrences of t′ by i*. Now for any context-free sentence A, we say that

(32)   Gv′t′[A] is true in a model M at (w,i) if A[w*/v′,i*/t′] is true in M at (w,i); it is false at (w,i) if A[w*/v′,i*/t′] is false at (w,i); and otherwise it is undefined.

It should be noted here that the intension of Gv′t′[A] will typically be a partial function when A does not contain any tense operators.

Let us illustrate the role of G by considering the following instance of tense iteration, where A is assumed to be context-free.

(33) $PAST_{(v,t)}Gv′t′[PAST_{(v′,t′)}A]$

Unlike (30), (33) has a coherent interpretation, since it will express a definite proposition in every model. To be precise, (33) will be true in a model at (w,i) if $w = g_c(v)$, $i = g_c(t)$ and there is a j<i such that Gv′t′[$PAST_{(v′,t′)}A$] is true at (w,j); and this formula will be true at (w,j) if $PAST_{(w*,j*)}A$ is true at (w,j) which obtains if there is a k < j such that A is true at (w,k). If (33) is to be true in a model, there must be distinct intervals i, j and k which satisfy the indicated conditions, one of them being that k < j < i. Plainly there are possible models in which these conditions are met. As for the import of (33), it is tempting to think that it may represent the pluperfect, which is sometimes taken to be a tense. Although it may be possible to characterize the pluperfect as a compound of two past tenses, i.e. as given in (33), it can also be analysed as a compound of past tense and perfective aspect. Below we offer an account of perfective aspect and illustrate the analysis.

To exemplify our approach to tense iteration let us characterize the difference between these two sentences.[9]

(34)   A prince was invested who would be king.
(35)   A prince was invested who will be king.

Clearly (34) and (35) do not mean the same thing, and this can be traced to the different roles of the future tense in the subordinate clauses. In (35) the future tense is to be evaluated relative to the time of utterance: (35) will be true relative

---

[9] For an alternative treatment see Kamp (1971).

to an occasion of utterance only if there is some future time at which a prince invested in the past will be king. In contrast, the future tense of (34) is to be evaluated relative to the past tense in the main clause: (34) will be true relative to an utterance only if there is some time in the past at which a prince was invested such that relative to it there is some future time at which he is king.

To capture the difference in truth conditions we invoke the operator G and render the logical form of (34) as follows.

(36) *Some* x [PAST$_{(v,t)}$ [[Prince (x) *and* x be invested] *and* Gv′t′[FUT$_{(v′,t′)}$(x be king)]]]

It can be easily seen that (36) renders the intended sense of (34). Relative to a model and an index (w,i), (36) will be true if there is some b in the model such that

(37) PAST$_{(v,t)}$ [[Prince (b) *and* b be invested] *and* Gv′t′[FUT$_{(v′,t′)}$(b be king)]]

is true at (w,i). This will obtain only if $w = g_c(v)$, $i = g_c(t)$ and there is some $j < i$ such that

(38) [[Prince (b) *and* b be invested] *and* Gv′t′ [FUT$_{(v′,t′)}$ (b be king)]]

is true at (w,j). Obviously this will hold just in case both the conjuncts hold at (w,j), i.e. if and only if these two formulas are true at (w,j).

(39) [Prince (b) *and* b be invested]
(40) Gv′t′[FUT$_{(v′,t′)}$ (b be king)]

Since (40) will be true at (w,j) only if

(41) FUT$_{[w*,j*)}$ (b be king)

is true at (w,j), it is plain that the future tense operator is evaluated relative to (w,j). In effect (41) will be true at (w,j) if there is some k such that $j < k$ and

(42) b be king

is true at (w,k). At this point it should be evident that (36) is an appropriate characterization of the logical form of (34), at least as far as the tenses are concerned.

It is easy to see, moreover, how (36) can be adjusted to capture the intended meaning of (35) where both tenses are to be interpreted relative to speech time. Since neither tense has scope over the other, (35) should be analysed as follows.

(43) *Some* x [PAST$_{(v,t)}$(Prince (x) *and* x be invested) *and* FUT$_{(v,t)}$(x be king)]

Now (43) will be true in a model at an index (w,i) only if there is some b such that

(44) $PAST_{(v,t)}$ (Prince(b) *and* b be invested) *and* $FUT_{(v,t)}$ (b be king)

is true at (w,i). Since both occurrences of v and t in (44) will be instantiated to the same world and interval, viz. to $g_c(v)$ and $g_c(t)$ respectively, the past and future operators will be evaluated relative to the same world-interval pair. In effect, (44) will be true only if there is some interval j earlier than the time of speech such that

(45)   Prince(b) *and* b be invested

is true at (w,j), and also some interval k later than speech time such that

(46)   b be king

is true at (w,k). Plainly these are the truth-conditions of the desired reading of (35).

Tenses and temporal reference

Tenses are not the only devices which involve reference to time; other examples are adverbials such as *at 9.0*, *before 1493*, *on 1st April '84*, and *yesterday*. We shall treat these adverbials like tenses, i.e., as sentential operators. It has been argued, however, that they function rather differently, finding their proper role only in the context of tense. In effect, time adverbs occupy an argument position created by tense and their role is to specify the time of the event.[10] This would suggest that where there is no tense there can be no time adverbs, a situation which is plainly counterfactual. Note the subordinate clause in the sentence

(47)   The secretary requests that Sandy phone at 9.0.

Clearly *at 9.0* is not to be taken as specifying the time of the secretary's requesting. It is rather associated with the untensed verb *phone*, or as we see it, with the untensed sentence *Sandy phone*. How it is so associated remains to be specified.

At 9.0 might be read intuitively as referring to the time at which the proposition expressed by *Sandy phone* is to be considered; it invites one to consider this proposition with respect to the interval 9.0. This idea can be rendered technically by introducing a sentential operator corresponding to *at 9.0* and defining it as follows. Where A is a context-free sentence,

(48)   AT 9.0 (A) is true in a model M at (w,i) if i = 9.0 and A is true in M at (w,i); it is false at (w,i) if i ≠ 9.0 or A is false at (w,i); and otherwise it is undefined.

---

[10] See Tichy (1980).

It will be observed that if *9.0* is read 'specifically', i.e. as referring to a definite interval on a definite day, the proposition denoted will be value-specific in respect of time. That is, it can evaluate to true at only one interval, viz. the one referred to by *9.0*. This is not to imply that the proposition will also be value-specific with respect to a particular world. There may be many worlds for which the intension evaluates to true.

By way of example let us consider the logical form of the subordinate clause in sentence (47), viz.

(49)   Sandy phone at 9.0.

Its logical structure will be represented by this quasi-logical formula:

(50)   AT 9.0 (Sandy phone).

The proposition expressed by (50), i.e. the intension it denotes, will be taken as the object of the relation *requests*, at least on one natural analysis. It is significant, therefore, that this intension does not necessarily coincide with the one denoted by the formula,

(51)   AT 9.0 (Sandy arrive).

Although both intensions will be value-specific with respect to 9.0, they will not generally be true at the same possible worlds. Hence, the propositions expressed by (47) and

(52)   The secretary suggests that Sandy arrive at 9.0

will be appropriately distinct.[11]

In this connection we should note that (49) and its present-tense 'derivative',

(53)   Sandy phones at 9.0

will be characterized as expressing different propositions.[12] Since the latter involves tense, it will be value-specific for both world and time. This would lead one to ask whether the difference between (49) and (53) will be reflected in a difference between (47) and,

(54)   The secretary requests that Sandy phones at 9.0.

We shall consider the matter below.

There is a certain 'efficiency' in definition (48) in that it allows for an ambiguity in the use of *9.0*. It might be used, as we have noted, to refer to a

---

[11] Here we see the reason for introducing possible worlds into the model theory.

[12] There is a natural disposition to read (53) either as saying something about the future, viz. about what Sandy will do at 9.0, or as saying something about Sandy's current habits, i.e. his habit of phoning at 9.0. But (53) may also be read as identifying a current event, although perhaps less naturally.

definite time on a definite day; and it might also be used to indicate a definite time simpliciter, i.e. without regard to any particular day. The latter usage will not by itself engender a value-specific proposition; that is, the intension denoted by

(55)   AT 9.0 (A)

may be true at a number of intervals, provided each one has the property of being a '9.0 o'clock' interval. The interpretation of (48) will of course depend upon how *9.0* is used in the definiens, whether with respect to a particular day or not.

Adverbs of temporal reference will generally be treated in a manner similar to *at 9.0*, i.e. in regard to their logical form. For example, the clauses defining *before 1493* and *on 1st April '84* will be as follows, with A understood as a context-free sentence.

(56)   BEFORE 1493 (A) is true in a model M at (w,i) if i is earlier than 1493 and A is true in M at (w,i); it is false at (w,i) if i is not earlier than 1493 or A is false at (w,i); and otherwise it is undefined.

(57)   ON 1st April '84 (A) is true in M at (w,i) if i is a subinterval of 1st April '84 and A is true in M at (w,i); it is false at (w,i) if either i is not a subinterval of 1st April '84 or A is false at (w,i); and otherwise it is undefined.

It may be helpful to illustrate (56) with respect to a tensed sentence, e.g.

(58)   Columbus crossed the Atlantic before 1493.

The logical form of (58) must be represented as in (59) since *before 1493* can apply only to a context-free sentence.

(59)   PAST$_{(v,t)}$ [BEFORE 1493 (Columbus cross the Atlantic)]

On the given definitions (59) will be true at (w,i) if w = $g_c(v)$, i = $g_c(t)$ and there is a j < i such that

(60)   BEFORE 1493 (Columbus cross the Atlantic)

is true at (w,j); (60) will be true at (w,j) if j is earlier than 1493 and

(61)   Columbus cross the Atlantic

is true at (w,j).

We take this analysis of (58) to reveal in a paradigmatic way the connection between tense and adverbs of temporal reference. Note, in particular, that the analysis invokes no reference to any specific value of j at which (61) is given to be true. The role of *before 1493* is to indicate that the verifying value of j, whatever it may be, falls before 1493. No further specification is given. Those who would approach (58) from a Reichenbachian perspective would, in contrast, be disposed to look for a precise reference, viz. to the time of the event type distinguished by (61). What they would assume is that (58) invokes a reference to some interval before 1493. This assumption, however, is not immediately obvious. Not only does (58) not contain a suitable referring phrase, it is not easy to add one without anomaly, which can be seen from this sentence.

(62)   *Columbus crossed the Atlantic before 1493 in 1492.

Plainly one of the two adverbs must go, in this case the so-called locating adverb *in 1492*. It seems to have no proper role to play in the analysis of (58). Since our theory implies as much, it seems not to make use of the Reichenbachian notion of reference time.

It also appears not to invoke the Reichenbachian concept of event time, as can be seen from the treatment of negative sentences like

(63)   Columbus did not cross the Atlantic before 1492.

Intuitively there is no event which is being referred to here, nor any particular time at which (as opposed to during which) it is alleged not to have occurred. Our theory respects this intuition by rendering the logical form of (63) as follows.

(64)   *Not* [PAST$_{(v,t)}$ [BEFORE 1492 (Columbus cross the Atlantic)]

This formula will be true at (w,i) if

(65)   PAST$_{(v,t)}$ [BEFORE 1492 (Columbus cross the Atlantic)]

is false at (w,i). On the assumption that $w = g_c(v)$ and $i = g_c(t)$, (65) is false at (w,i) only if there is no $j < i$ such that

(66)   BEFORE 1492 (Columbus cross the Atlantic)

is true at (w,j). This holds (given the analogue of definition (56)) only if there is no such j earlier than 1492 for which

(61)   Columbus cross the Atlantic

is true, i.e. at (w,j). The import of the analysis can be summarized by the paraphrase,

(67)   Columbus never crossed the Atlantic before 1492.

Some may find this somewhat odd since *not* does not generally mean *never*. Still there seems no denying that (63) and (67) coincide in import.

Let us consider another example, one that happens to invoke the non-specific use of *9.0*.

(68)   Mandy did not phone before 9.0 on 1st April '84.

The logical structure of (68) will be represented in the following way.

(69)   *Not* [PAST$_{(v,t)}$ [ON 1st April '84 [BEFORE 9.0 (Mandy phone)]]]

Now (69) will be true at (w,i) if

(70)   PAST$_{(v,t)}$ [ON 1st April '84 [BEFORE 9.0 (Mandy phone)]]

is false at (w,i). On the assumption that w = g_c(v) and i = g_c(t), (70) is false at (w,i) if there is no j < i such that

(71)   ON 1st April '84 [BEFORE 9.0 (Mandy phone)]

is true at (w,j), which itself holds if for no j < i is j a subinterval of 1st April '84 and

(72)   BEFORE 9.0 (Mandy phone)

true at (w,j); and finally this obtains if there is no such j falling before 9.0 such that

(73)   Mandy phone

is true at (w,l). In effect (68) emerges as equivalent to the paraphrase

(74)   Mandy never phoned before 9.0 on 1st April '84.

Though (74) may be linguistically awkward, it does seem to capture the truth conditions of (68). What Mandy never did before a certain date she did not do before that time, and vice versa.

But there are, it must be said, certain problematic cases, in particular negative sentences which contain no time adverbials, as in the following.

(75)   Mandy did not phone.

On the assumption that (75) is similar in structure to (68), its logical form will be

(76)   *Not* [PAST$_{(v,t)}$ (Mandy phone)]

and it will thus be equivalent to the paraphrase

(77)   Mandy never phoned.

But (77) is not an obvious paraphrase of (75); at least it is not obvious that (77) and (75) coincide on truth conditions. When one utters (75), one typically intends to say something about some specific time in the past, viz. that Mandy did not phone *then*. No similar specificity seems to be involved in an utterance of (77); one does not purport to assert anything about Mandy's phoning at any particular time in the past. Since there is no explicit reference to past time in (76), it seems insufficient as an analysis of (75), although it may be suitable for (77). To make it adequate for (75) it seems necessary to include some sort of referential parameter.

One natural idea is to interpret such a parameter as identifying a past time at which the event, viz., Mandy's phoning, is purported not to have occurred. This suggestion, which seems similar to Reichenbach's proposal, is not only plausible but predicts that any utterance of (75) 'requires' a certain completion, either by context or explicitly. To express something definite there must be an indication of when the event is claimed to have happened. This could be given by context and thus be implicit in the utterance; it could be understood that the envisaged past time is, say, 9.0 on 1st April '84. On the other hand it could be specified explicitly by continuing the utterance with the phrase *at 9.0 on 1st April '84*. Though somewhat pedantic, the following sentence is complete in the intended sense.

(78)   Mandy did not phone at 9.0 on 1st April '84.

One might be led to conjecture, therefore, that the logical form of (75) is perhaps similar to that of (78), with the 'underlying' structure being something like this.

(79)   *Not* [PAST$_{(v,t)}$ [AT u (Mandy phone)]]

Here u is to be taken as an interval parameter which receives its values from context. From an intuitive point of view (79) may be seen to offer an adequate analysis of (75). It may also be seen to 'underlie' (78) whose analysis is arguably as follows.

(80)   *Not* [PAST$_{(v,t)}$ [AT 9.0 [ON 1st April '84 (Mandy phone)]]]

Intuition notwithstanding, there are grounds for supposing that (79) cannot constitute the correct analysis of (75), even though the import of uttering (75) may occasionally suggest as much.

Note that (75) can be made explicitly complete (in the intended sense) in ways other than exemplified in (78).

(81)   Mandy did not phone after March '84.
(82)   Mandy did not phone before Easter '84.
(83)   Mandy did not phone during 1984.

Insofar as the intended past interval is concerned, these sentences are entirely explicit and independent of contextual factors. Indeed, if one attempts to add any further specification, e.g. *at 9.0 on 1st April '84*, the effect will be uniformly anomalous. This suggests that (79) cannot generally be the analysis of (75); if it were, it would have to figure in the analyses of (81)–(83) in the way exemplified in the putative analysis of (78), i.e. as in (80). The incompleteness of (75) does not in general arise from a need to specify a particular past time at which Mandy's phoning is supposed not to have happened; it rather arises from the need to indicate an interval during which it supposedly happened. Once this is understood, one might reasonably claim that (81)–(83) are equivalent in truth conditions to (84)–(86) respectively.

(84)   Mandy never phoned after March '84.
(85)   Mandy never phoned before Easter '84.
(86)   Mandy never phoned during 1984.

But what then is the logical form of (75) and how is it related to the logical forms of (81)–(83)?

At this point we would question the 'intuitive' assumption about (75), viz. that it is semantically incomplete. It has been supposed that if (75) is to express a definite proposition it must be supplemented by a reference to some past interval. This can be achieved implicitly at the time of utterance or it can be realized explicitly by adding a suitable referring phrase. But is there always a need for such referential supplementation? Consider the following sentence which is very similar to (75).

(87)   Wittgenstein did not die in Vienna.

What proposition (87) expresses does not depend upon any reference to a past time, either implicit or explicit; there is no need to indicate any specific time in the past in order to fix the proposition expressed by (87). In fact any attempt to add such a reference will give rise to a proposition different from the one expressed by (87) simpliciter. For example no utterance of (87) will be equivalent in import to an utterance of

(88)   Wittgenstein did not die in Vienna at 9.0 on 1st April '49.

To assert that Wittgenstein did not die in Vienna is not to say anything about any specific time in the past. It is rather to say something about the whole of the past, viz. that nowhere in it did Wittgenstein die in Vienna. In effect the truth conditions of (87) coincide with those of

(89)   Wittgenstein never died in Vienna.

Hence the logical form (87) should be represented as follows.

(90)   *Not* [PAST$_{(v,t)}$ (Wittgenstein die in Vienna)]

As far as time reference is concerned, there is no further structure to be uncovered.

Since (75) is similar in surface form to (87), it should presumably be represented as having a similar logical form. That is, the logical structure of

(75)   Mandy did not phone

should be the following.

(91)   *Not* [PAST$_{(v,t)}$ (Mandy phone)]

But as we have noted, this would imply that (75) means

(77)   Mandy never phoned.

Although there may be occasions on which (75) does mean (77), this is not generally or even typically the case. Usually there is a specific time in the past which is at issue, one that is implicitly determined by context. It is thus natural to look for a term in the analysis of (75) whose referent would be fixed contextually. But this is not the only option, nor one that is easy to sustain in the light of (87). We would conjecture that utterances of (75) are actually elliptical when they do not coincide in meaning with (77). This is not to say that (75) is syntactically elliptical; it cannot be because it sometimes means (77). But when an utterance of (75) is not equivalent to (77), the utterance is strictly speaking incomplete or, as we would say, elliptical; it is in need of some further specification which could be given by a deictic expression. For example an utterance of (75) might be equivalent to,

(92)   Mandy did not phone then

where the deictic *then* is interpreted as referring to a specific past interval. We might say that this utterance of (75) is 'contextually' elliptical for (92). The relevant analysis is thus the logical form of (92) which is the following.

(93)   *Not* [PAST$_{(v,t)}$ (Mandy phone then)]

Below we shall indicate how temporal adverbs like *then* are to be treated but in the meantime it is enough to say that the analysis will entail that (92) is equivalent in truth conditions to

(94)   Mandy never phoned then.

While (94) may be stylistically strange, it nevertheless expresses a coherent proposition.

   Having resorted to paraphrases where *not* and *never* seem to have the same import, we should emphasize that they will not in general be characterized as meaning the same thing. Before turning to define *never* and other temporal quantifiers, let us first consider temporal adverbs like *yesterday* and *then*. Both of these are paradigmatically contextual in that their interpretations are given relative to the occasion of utterance. It should be noted, nevertheless, that they acquire these interpretations under somewhat different constraints. In the case of *then* the interpretation may depend partly upon the intentions of the speaker;

which time he is talking about is to some degree a matter of which time he intends to talk about. No similar choice is possible with respect to *yesterday*. If a speaker utters a sentence containing *yesterday* on Wednesday, then he must be talking about Tuesday, whatever his intentions at the time of utterance.

There is another difference between *then* and *yesterday* which becomes apparent in the interpretations of these two sentences.

(95) Sammy arrived then.
(96) Sammy arrived yesterday.

The proposition expressed by (95) is that Sammy arrived at a particular time, viz. then; it was at that time that his arriving is claimed to have occurred. In contrast, the proposition expressed by (96) is that Sammy arrived sometime during a certain day, viz. yesterday; his arriving is said to have occurred, not at that time, but somewhere in it. To reflect this difference between *then* and *yesterday* at the level of logical form, we shall invoke an ambiguity which is exemplified in the way we indicated the contrast: *then* and *yesterday* can not only be temporal adverbs but also nouns, i.e. referring expressions. From a logical point of view the adverb *then* can be analysed in terms of the prepositional phrase *at then*, where *then* is the object of the preposition *at*. The adverb *yesterday* may be similarly analysed, although the choice of preposition is perhaps not uniquely determined. It could be *during* or *within* or *on*. In view of the definition of *on*, which we formulated above, it seems reasonable to render the content of the adverb *yesterday* in terms of the prepositional phrase *on yesterday* where *yesterday* is a noun. Although the chosen analysans is in neither case a linguistic equivalent to its analysandum, i.e. not strictly intersubstitutable *salve congruitate*, it does nevertheless give a fair rendering of semantic content. As a result we shall represent the logical status of *then* and *yesterday* in terms of their 'prepositional' analyses which will be treated as sentential operators. Let A be any context-free sentence.

(97) AT then (A) is true in a model M at (w,i) if i = then and A is true at (w,i); it is false at (w,i) if i $\neq$ then or A is false at (w,i); and otherwise it is undefined.

(98) ON yesterday (A) is true in a model M at (w,i) if i is a subinterval of yesterday and A is true in M at (w,i); it is false at (w,i) if i is not a subinterval of yesterday or A is false at (w,i); and otherwise it is undefined.

It should be noted that (97) and (98) are both definition schemas since the occurrences of the nouns *then* and *yesterday* in the definiens admit of alternative interpretations.

With these definitions in hand, we can now consider the logical forms of (95) and (96), which will be represented as follows.

(99) $PAST_{(v,t)}$ [AT then (Sammy arrive)]
(100) $PAST_{(v,t)}$ [ON yesterday (Sammy arrive)]

For the sake of illustration it will be enough to unpack (100). This formula will be true at (w,i) if $w = g_c(v)$, $i = g_c(t)$ and there is a $j < i$ such that

(101)   ON yesterday (Sammy arrive)

is true at (w,j); this will obtain if j is a subinterval of yesterday and

(102)   Sammy arrive

is true at (w,j). The analysis here is tantamount to taking (95) to be true if Sammy arrived sometime yesterday, i.e. sometime within yesterday.

It should be noted that the definitions of the time adverbs differ in one important respect from the definitions of the tenses: while the latter all involve quantification over intervals, the former do not. It is significant, therefore, that the definitions of the time adverbs allow for partial intensions but those of the tenses do not; they will always be total functions. This suggests a characteristic semantic difference. It is relevant here that perfective aspect also requires a quantificational analysis not unlike tense. Although the interval of quantification is not fixed by speech time, as it is for tense, the nature of the quantification is similar. It is natural to expect then that the definition will admit only total functions.

Before defining perfective aspect, however, we must first distinguish it from tense. Note that perfective sentences can apparently be unmarked for tense. Consider the complement sentence in this example.

(103)   It is important that Ben have finished by the time Hilary comes back.

Here the verb phrase *have finished* cannot properly be construed as involving past tense. If any tense is involved, it must surely be the present tense since the import of (103) can arguably be paraphrased by replacing *have finished* with *finishes*. It is interesting to note, however, that in this position *finishes* does not invoke any reference to speech time, unlike the main verb *is*. Since reference to speech time is taken to be an essential feature of tense, it is reasonable to suspect that the morphology of *finishes* is not a sure guide to its semantic role in complement position. In the circumstance it seems appropriate to envisage a 'tenseless' analysis of *have finished*. We suggest that *have* in conjunction with the morpheme *ed* be understood as marking perfective aspect and be treated as a sentential operator. In our quasi-logical language it will be convenient to represent this operator as HAVE.

Before we define it, it may be helpful to note that perfective aspect is normally taken to have something to do with perspective. It is widely thought that perfective aspect invokes reference to a time from which a certain event is to be viewed. This interval, i.e. the interval of perspective, can be regarded as constituting a time within which the event is supposed to have occurred. When understood in this way, the interval is sometimes called the 'extended-now', which suggests that perfective aspect is essentially related to speech time, viz. in the form of *now*. Although we do not see perfective aspect as having any special relation to speech time and hence to tense, we nevertheless interpret the interval of perspective as comprehending the supposed event.

To render the idea of perspective we introduce the concept of an anchored interval. Where i and j are intervals, we say that

(104)   i is anchored to j if j is a final segment of i.

Intuitively i constitutes a perspective relative to j and is thus a relative notion. Whether this is as it should be will hopefully become clear in the discussion below. Let us now define the operator HAVE for any context-free sentence A.

(105)   HAVE (A) is true in a model M at (w,i) if there is an interval j which is anchored to i such that for some subinterval k of j A is true in M at (w,k); it is false at (w,i) if there is no j anchored to i such that for some subinterval k of j A is true at (w,k); (and otherwise it is undefined).

Since (105) makes no provision for speech time, it effectively distinguishes perfective aspect from tense. To illustrate the definition, it will be useful to consider aspect together with tense, say in the form of the pluperfect.

(106)   Ben had finished before 9.0.

The logical structure of (106) is to be analysed as follows.

(107) $PAST_{(v,t)}$ [BEFORE 9.0 [HAVE (Ben finished)]]

Working through the definitions again, (107) will be true at (w,i), provided $w = g_c(v)$ and $i = g_c(t)$, if there is a $j < i$ such that

(108)   BEFORE 9.0 [HAVE (Ben finish)]

is true at (w,j); (108) will be true at (w,j) if j is earlier than 9.0 and

(109)   HAVE (Ben finish)

is true at (w,j). Now this obtains if there is a k anchored to j such that for some subinterval l of k

(110)   Ben finish

is true at (w,l). What is interesting here is that no unique perspective is identified from which to view the proposition expressed by (110). Only the range of admissible values of k and j is restricted, viz. to those intervals which precede 9.0. Thus the perspective fixed by k and j will be a variable one.[13]

Where the perspective is less variable is in the present perfect, as in this sentence.

---

[13] Below we shall consider the interaction of perfective aspect and temporal quantifiers like *exactly twice*. Tichy (1985) has argued that an interval approach to the semantics of temporal expressions, such as we propose, may not yield a satisfactory characterization.

(111)   Ben has finished.

The logical rendering of (111) is,

(112)   PRES$_{(v,t)}$ [HAVE (Ben finished)]

which will be true at (w,i), given that w = g$_c$(v) and i = g$_c$(t), if

(109)   HAVE (Ben finish)

is true at (w,i). And this holds if there is a j anchored to i such that for some subinterval k of j

(110)   Ben finish

is true at (w,k). Since j is anchored to i, which here is speech time, the interval of perspective, viz. j, has one of its ends fixed. The other end, however, is variable, which reflects a certain indefiniteness in the perspective. This, we would venture, is just as it should be, i.e. as intuition would have it.

Temporal quantifiers and connectives

Temporal quantifiers, such as *always*, *never* and *exactly twice*, will be treated in conformity with the 'standard' structure of temporal modifiers; that is, they will be characterized as sentential operators applying only to context-free sentences. With a view to motivating the envisaged analysis, which is similar to that of the tense operators, let us examine the following sentence.

(113)   Scott always dined at home.

It is clear (113) cannot naturally be interpreted as an unrestricted assertion, i.e. as saying that for the whole of time Scott had the property of dining at home. It must rather be understood as a statement restricted to some intended interval; only of this period is it asserted that he had the property.[14] Depending upon context, the intended period might be the one in which Scott lived in Edinburgh, or the one in which he lived at Abbotsford, or perhaps some entirely different interval. Which interval is intended on a given occasion of utterance is a pragmatic matter. However, the role it plays in determining the proposition expressed is a semantic matter, i.e. of the semantic structure of (113). Here there is a question. Is the intended interval to be seen as the referent of some deictic expression revealed at the level of logical form? Or is it to be seen as identified in some non-referential way, say by a 'suppressed' *when* clause?

Let us consider a situation which evokes both possibilities. Suppose that one wanted to make an assertion about Scott's dining habits during the period when he lived at Abbotsford. If the context is sufficient to identify this as the intended

---

[14] Plainly it is a dispositional property that is relevant here.

interval, one might utter (113) with the intention of asserting that Scott always dined at home during that time. If, on the other hand, the relevant interval is not clear from context, one might opt to be more explicit by uttering this sentence.

(114)   When he lived at Abbotsford, Scott always dined at home.

There may be some uncertainty as to whether (114) expresses the same proposition as (113), but there is no doubt that the propositions are closely related, close enough to make them on occasion 'pragmatically' equivalent. What their exact semantic relation is, however, is not uninteresting.

Indeed, since (113) occurs as the main clause of (114), they can only be analysed together. Thus if (113) is represented as containing a deictic expression at the level of logical form, (114) must be similarly represented. Such an analysis seems very plausible in the case of (113) but it raises an awkward question with respect to (114). The *when* clause in (114) is typically regarded as specifying the interval over which *always* quantifies. If the deictic in the main clause also serves to identify the intended interval, one of them must be semantically redundant. Given that the deictic is part of the logical form of (113), it seems that the *when* clause may be expendable. While such clauses might be useful for emphasis or clarification, they would have no essential semantic role, which seems a rather curious result.

An alternative approach is to start with the analysis of (114) which intuitively requires no deictic reference to specify the interval over which *always* quantifies. The *when* clause seems sufficient for this purpose and hence can be seen to have an essential semantic role, given that there is no deictic with the same role. But this would imply that there is then no deictic in the analysis of (113). As a result there would arise a need to explain how the intended interval is identified in an utterance of (113). It may be ventured that an utterance of (113) is perhaps elliptical for some more explicit utterance, e.g. (114). Although this idea might be worth exploring, it seems a less plausible proposal than the suggestion that (113) involves deictic reference. It is moreover unnecessary to opt for the more heroic alternative, since the 'deictic' account can be developed in a way which reveals that the *when* clause in (114) is not in fact redundant.

Since (113) is taken to involve deictic reference to an interval over which the quantifier *always* ranges, it is natural to locate it as being part of the quantifier itself. Hence *always* will be represented as a complex sentential operator of the form $ALWAYS_r$, where r is a parameter whose values are intervals assigned from context. Since this operator, like all temporal operators, is taken to apply only to context-free sentences, the logical form of (113) is analysed by the following formula.[15]

---

[15] It should be noted that the occurrence of the parameter r in

(i) $ALWAYS_r$ (Scott dine at home)

does not make (i) context-sensitive in the technical sense, i.e. according to definition (26).

(115) PAST$_{(v,t)}$ [ALWAYS$_r$ (Scott dine at home)]

Before we proceed to define ALWAYS$_r$, let us also consider the logical form of (114). As we said above, there is an inclination to feel that the *when* clause serves to fix the interval over which *always* quantifies. Although the intuition is not without substance, it is somewhat misleading since it tends to obscure the fact that the *when* clause has another independent semantic role.

To specify this role it is necessary to 'factor' tense from the sentences conjoined by *when*. In sentences like (114) the tenses of the conjoined sentences are not independent of each other; they are related by what is sometimes called sequence of tense, which is to say that the sentences must be in the same tense. Since the sentences must also be evaluated conjointly, i.e. relative to the same speech time, they are in a sense semantically bound.[16] We can capture this relationship by 'factoring' past tense from the two constituents and representing it as an operator over the resulting compound. To indicate that *when* is a conjunction, the compound will be given in this form.

(116) Scott dine at home *when* he live at Abbotsford.

The logical form of (114) may now be analysed in at least two different ways.

(117) PAST$_{(v,t)}$ [ALWAYS$_r$ (Scott dine at home *when* he live at Abbotsford)]
(118) PAST$_{(v,t)}$ [ALWAYS$_r$ (Scott dine at home) *when* he live at Abbotsford]

These might naturally be thought to correspond to two different interpretations of (114).

Suppose that Scott had several different periods of residence at Abbotsford but that one wished to say something about just one of these periods. One could utter (114) with the intention of making an assertion about that particular period, in which case it would be asserted that for every subinterval of that period Scott had the property of dining at home. Clearly it is the dispositional property one would have in mind here, since this can be true of Scott even at times when he is not actually in the process of dining at home.[17] The intended reading of (114) may be taken to be characterized by (118), since it would seem natural to interpret *always* as occurring within the scope of *when*.

The other reading of (114) would interpret the scope relation in reverse; in effect it would take (114) to be equivalent to the following paraphrase.

(119) Whenever Scott lived at Abbotsford, he dined at home.

---

16 The following sentence is not really a counterexample.

(i)   When he leaves, Max will be happy.

From a semantic point of view the *when* clause is plainly about the future which agrees with the future tense in the main clause. This would be reflected at the level of logical form.

17 Dispositional properties are typically involved in sentences like (114). In fact the attribution of non-dispositional properties seems to be the special case.

Usually one would utter (119) with the intention of attributing to Scott the property of dining at home through each of the intervals during which he was resident at Abbotsford. One might also utter (114) with the same intention and thereby express the same proposition. Here the appropriate analysis seems to be (117), since *always* must be taken to have wider scope relative to *when*. Although (117) and (118) seem appropriate analyses of (114) for the given situations, there is a question as to whether they reflect genuinely distinct interpretations of (114). In fact it remains to be seen whether they really capture any reading of (114). Before we can explore these matters we shall of course have to define $ALWAYS_r$ and *when*.

To this end we invoke the concept of a cover for an interval. The underlying strategy is to partition an interval into its subintervals so as to consider whether some proposition is true in each of them. Each subinterval of such a partition is to be read as determining a potential instance or case of the proposition's being true. With this in mind we define the concept of a cover for an interval as follows.[18]

(120)   A set of intervals P is a cover for an interval i if the elements of P are mutually distinct (non-overlapping) subintervals of i whose 'sum' is identical to i.

The special significance of a cover will not emerge until we consider the treatment of *when*. In the meantime it may be said that *always* is naturally interpreted as quantifying over intervals and hence it is not inappropriate to invoke the concept of a cover. It is with a view to *when*, however, that we define $ALWAYS_r$ in the following way. As usual we assume A to be any context-free sentence.

(121) $ALWAYS_r(A)$ is true in a model M at (w,i) if $i = g_c(r)$ and there is a cover P of $g_c(r)$ such that for each p in P, A is true in M at (w,p); it is false at (w,i) if $i \neq g_c(r)$ or there is no such cover; (and otherwise it is undefined).

We can illustrate (121) by unpacking (115), which is the analysis of (113).

(115) $PAST_{(v,t)}$ [$ALWAYS_r$ (Scott dine at home)].

This formula will be true at (w,i) provided $w = g_c(v)$ and $i = g_c(t)$, if there is a $j < i$ such that

(122) $ALWAYS_r$ (Scott dine at home)

---

[18] Intuitively the 'sum' of P is given by the idea that if all the elements of P are matched with their place in i, the result is exactly i.

It should be noted that a cover may consist of both closed and open intervals; this will be the case for any cover of a real interval.

is true at (w,j), which holds if $j = g_c(r)$ and there is a cover P of $g_c(r)$ such that for each p in P

(123)   Scott dine at home

is true at (w,p). Note that if there is a cover for $g_c(r)$ which verifies (123), then (123) will be true for all the points in r (and vice versa). If (123) is true at (w,p), it will (by the homogeneity condition) be true for every subinterval of p, including the singleton points.

As for the connective *when*, there may be a temptation to think that it just means cotemporal with, but it is easy to see that this is not in general the case. Consider these two sentences.

(124)   When Jocelyn received a letter, she wrote a reply.
(125)   When Jocelyn went on holiday, she notified the police.

Clearly (124) will be true if Jocelyn wrote a reply to each letter she received, even though the reply was written sometime after the time of receipt. Since one typically replies only to those letters one has received (although not always so), the event in the *when* clause is ordinarily taken to precede the event in the main clause. In the case of (125), however, there seems to be a perfectly acceptable interpretation where the event in the *when* clause is taken to come after the event in the main clause. If Jocelyn notified the police before she went on holiday, say to protect her house from burglary, (125) is true.

To accommodate these readings, as well as the preferred interpretation of (114), we shall distinguish two senses of *when*, the case sense and the cotemporal sense. The former is intended to account for both (124) and (125) while the latter is invoked to explain (114). The case sense of *when* is formulated in the following definition, where A and B are any context-free sentences.

(126)   (A *when* B) is true in a model M at (w,i) if there is a unique subinterval j of i such that B is true at (w,j) and at least one subinterval k of i such that A is true at (w,k); it is false at (w,i) if there are no j and k of i which satisfy the indicated conditions; (and otherwise it is undefined).

The requirement that an interval uniquely satisfy certain conditions is a relative notion which we define roughly in this way. Assuming an account of what it is for an interval to satisfy a set of conditions S, we say that

(127)   An interval j uniquely satisfies S with respect to i if j is a subinterval of i which satisfies S, and for any subinterval k of i if k satisfies S, k is a subinterval of j.

There are at least two features of the case account of *when*, i.e. as defined in (126), that should be stressed. First, the temporal order of subintervals j and k is undetermined; it does not matter what the order of precedence is, nor indeed whether they overlap. Second, (A *when* B) is not equivalent to (B *when* A). To see this it is enough to assume for some interval i that j uniquely satisfies B with respect to i and that there are two subintervals k of i which satisfy A. By (126) (A *when* B) is true at i, but (B *when* A) is not.

The case sense of *when* is actually the more basic one since the cotemporal sense can be derived from it by adding the requirement that the subinterval j be a subinterval of k or, as we shall say, that k subsume j. One may wonder why k should subsume j and not be identical to it, given that the point is to capture cotemporality. If the relation between j and k were one of identity, then (A *when* B) would imply (B *when* A), and this seems almost as counterintuitive on the cotemporal reading as it is on the case reading. The stipulation that k subsume j blocks this entailment. For the sake of completeness we give the full definition below.

(128)   (A *when* B) is true in a model M at (w,i) if there is a unique subinterval j of i such that B is true at (w,j) and a subinterval k of i such that k subsumes j and A is true at (w,k); it is false in M at (w,i) if there are no j and k which satisfy the indicated conditions; (and otherwise it is undefined).

It is this definition we shall use in considering the two interpretations of (114), i.e. the readings associated with (117) and (118). To begin with, it may be helpful to examine (114) without the quantifier *always*, that is, to consider this sentence first.

(129)   When he lived at Abbotsford, Scott dined at home.

The logical form of (129) is as follows.

(130) $PAST_{(v,t)}$ (Scott dine at home *when* he live at Abbotsford)

Now (130) will be true at (w,i) if $w = g_c(v)$, $i = g_c(t)$ and there is a $j < i$ such that

(116)   Scott dine at home *when* he live at Abbotsford

is true at (w,j). This will hold if there is a unique subinterval k of j such that

(131)   He live at Abbotsford

is true at (w,k), and a subinterval l of j such that l subsumes k and

(123)   Scott dine at home

is true at (w,l). It should be noted that while the value of k may be the whole of the period during which Scott lived at Abbotsford, it need not be so. What matters is that there is some part of that period during which Scott dined at home. If there is such a part, it is (modulo j) an appropriate value of k, and of course also of l.

It should perhaps be mentioned that the definitions of *when*, i.e. both (126) and (128), are best not construed in terms of events, at least not in general. Although there may be a map from intervals to events, the subintervals distinguished in (126) and (128) will typically map to parts of events; and this may lead to some confusion. Since there is no reference to events in the definitions, there is no need to consider parts of events, nor any overlap relations that may be involved.

Let us now turn back to (114), in particular to the reading putatively represented by (118).

(118) PAST$_{(v,t)}$ [ALWAYS$_r$ (Scott dine at home) *when* he live at Abbotsford]

On the familiar pattern, (118) will be true at (w,i) if $w = g_c(v)$, $i = g_c(t)$ and there is a $j < i$ such that

(132) ALWAYS$_r$ (Scott dine at home) *when* he live at Abbotsford

is true at (w,j). Since ALWAYS$_r$ falls within the scope of *when*, (132) will be true at (w,j) if there is a unique subinterval k of j such that

(131) He live at Abbotsford

is true at (w,k) and there is a subinterval l of j such that l subsumes k and

(122) ALWAYS$_r$ (Scott dine at home)

is true at (w,l). Here the contextually determined referent of r becomes significant; (122) will be true at (w,l) if $l = g_c(r)$ and there is a cover P of $g_c(r)$ such that for each p in P

(123) Scott dine at home

is true at (w,p). This is just to say that (123) must be true throughout $g_c(r)$ since there will be an appropriate cover if and only if this is true.

The role of $g_c(r)$ is semantically pivotal since it picks out the interval of temporal quantification. The *when* clause, in contrast, has no semantic status in determining the past interval referred to; this is fixed solely by the reference of r. Nevertheless, the *when* clause helps to identify the object of reference, since (118) will be true only if $g_c(r)$ is an interval for which Scott lived at Abbotsford. If one intends to tell the truth in uttering (118), one must intend to refer to a past interval satisfying this condition. But of course one may not want to tell the truth or may unintentionally say something false.

There is, however, a 'wrinkle' in (118) which deserves comment. Suppose that $g_c(r)$ is only part of some period in which Scott lived at Abbotsford.

Suppose that during that subinterval Scott always dined at home but that for some other subinterval of the period he did not do so. Now if one utters (114) intending to refer to the former subinterval, one would be represented by (118) as saying something true. But can (114) be uttered felicitously in such a situation, (118) notwithstanding?

We would say that it can if the context is right. Imagine a situation in which one is in a discussion about Scott's daily habits, say, during the period in which he was writing *Waverley*. Suppose that one wishes to say of some part of that period that he had the habit of dining at home. If that subinterval is contained as a part of an interval during which Scott resided at Abbotsford, one might locate the intended subinterval for one's audience by uttering (114): the combination of the *when* clause and the context might well serve to identify the relevant subinterval. One's assertion would be restricted, as intended, to just this part of the time during which Scott lived at Abbotsford.

Although it seems possible to use (114) in this way, one will more typically utter it with the intention of referring to the whole of an interval for which Scott lived at Abbotsford. Nevertheless, there is no semantic requirement that one do so. One may refer to just a part of such an interval and may also refer to a more comprehensive interval. Here we turn to the second interpretation of (114), i.e. the one associated with (117).

(117) $PAST_{(v,t)}$ [ALWAYS (Scott dine at home *when* he live at Abbotsford)]

As usual (117) will be true at (w,i) if $w = g_c(v)$, $i = g_c(t)$ and there is some $j < i$ such that

(133) $ALWAYS_r$(Scott dine at home *when* he live at Abbotsford)

is true at (w,j). In contrast to (132), $ALWAYS_r$ has scope over *when* in (133). Thus (133) will be true at (w,j) if $j = g_c(r)$ and there is a cover P of $g_c(r)$ such that for each p in P

(116) Scott dine at home *when* he live at Abbotsford

is true at (w,p). Here the contextual assignment to r will normally be some significant stretch of past time in which there may be several distinct periods of residence at Abbotsford. Given a cover P, (116) will be true at each (w,p) if there is a unique subinterval k of p such that

(131) He live at Abbotsford

is true at (w,k) and a subinterval l of p subsuming k such that

(123) Scott dine at home

is true at (w,l). What this means is that for each interval p of the cover there must be a unique instance of Scott's living at Abbotsford throughout which he had the habit of dining at home. If there is a cover of $g_c(r)$ meeting these conditions, then (117) is true.

It is important to stress that $g_c(r)$ does not necessarily embrace all the relevant intervals during which Scott was resident at Abbotsford. One might utter (114), or alternatively,

(119)   Whenever he lived at Abbotsford, Scott dined at home

without intending to make an assertion about all the periods in which Scott lived at Abbotsford. One might wish to invoke only some particular subset of these periods. In the event one's assertion would be restricted to this interval.[19] The restriction here is similar to that noted above in connection with (118).

We have still to resolve whether (114) really has two distinctive interpretations, one identified by (117) and the other by (118). The issue might be seen to hinge on the intended value of r, viz. on $g_c(r)$. If one intends to refer to an interval throughout which Scott lived at Abbotsford, then (118) seems to give the appropriate reading. On the other hand, if one intends to refer to an interval which comprehends several distinct instances of Scott's living at Abbotsford, then (117) seems to be the right rendering. The fact is, however, that for any particular $g_c(r)$ (118) entails (117). Although the converse does not hold, it may be argued that (117) uniquely represents the logical form of (114). No matter what the intended assignment to r, (117) is sufficient to capture the truth conditions. Moreover, it may be ventured that there is something curious about distinguishing two senses of (114) simply on the basis of different kinds of assignment to r. We shall not pursue the issue further, except to say that the conclusion remains undecided.

Before we leave the semantics of *when*, it might be useful to examine a sentence where the case reading is appropriate, particularly one that involves *always*.

(134)   When she went away, Jocelyn always phoned the police.

For the purpose of illustration let us restrict our attention to the reading whose logical form is represented in this way.

(135)   PAST$_{(v,t)}$ [ALWAYS$_r$ (Jocelyn phone the police *when* she go away)]

The case interpretation of *when* allows for any ordering between the intervals of Jocelyn's going away and her phoning the police: the former might precede the latter, or succeed it, or overlap it to some degree. With *when* so read, (134)

---

[19] A more compelling example is perhaps the following.

(i) When he travelled by bus, Franky always took a flask of gin.

Plainly *always* is not naturally read as quantifying over all the cases of Franky's travelling by bus. What he did as a child is irrelevant. But what he did during some interval of his adult life may well be topical, depending upon the context and the intentions of the speaker.

expresses the proposition that for some designated past interval there is at least one case of Jocelyn's phoning the police for each case of her going away. This emerges clearly from the truth conditions of (134), which is true at (w,i) only if there is some $j < i$ such that

(136)   ALWAYS$_r$ (Jocelyn phone the police *when* she go away)

is true at (w,j). And (136) is true at (w,j) if $j = g_c(r)$ and there is a cover P of $g_c(r)$ such that for each p in P

(137)   Jocelyn phone the police *when* she go away

is true at (w,p). Here we invoke the case definitioin of *when*, viz. the one given in (126). According to (126), (137) will be true at (w,p) if there is a unique subinterval k of p such that

(138)   She go away

is true at (w,k) and at least one subinterval l of p such that

(139)   Jocelyn phone the police

is true at (w,l).

   Jocelyn might well have had the habit of phoning the police more than once for each occasion of her going away. Perhaps she was never confident whether the initial call was noted and always phoned a second time to be sure. Let us suppose that the following was the case.

(140)   When she went away, Jocelyn always phoned the police exactly twice.

The quantifier *exactly twice* will be treated very similar to *always*; it will be represented as involving a deictic parameter and as quantifying over a cover. The definition goes as follows, with *exactly twice* represented as TWICE!$_r$.

(141)   TWICE!$_r$ (A) is true in a model M at (w,i) if $i = g_c(r)$ and there is a cover P of $g_c(r)$ such that for exactly two elements p_1 and p_2 in P A is true at (w,p_1) and (w,p_2) and for any other cover Q of $g_c(r)$ and element q of Q if A is true at (w,q) then q is a subinterval of either p_1 or p_2; it is false at (w,i) if $i \neq g_c(r)$ or there is no cover P satisfying the indicated conditions; (and otherwise it is undefined).

To characterize the logical form (140) one must bear in mind that each of the temporal quantifiers has its own deictic parameter. It is clear, moreover, that the parameters are not to be given the same assignment since there is a significant scope relation; that is, *exactly twice* must be read as occurring within the scope of *always*. In effect the deictic parameter of *exactly twice* must be interpreted relative to the elements over which *always* quantifies.

We have seen an analogous situation with regard to the scoping of tenses, i.e. in respect of tense iteration. To represent such iteration on our approach it is necessary to invoke the quantifier G, and this is just what is required here. The logical form of (140) is thus given by the following formula.[20]

(142) $\text{PAST}_{(v,t)}$ [ALWAYS$_r$[Gr′[TWICE!$_r$ (Jocelyn phone the police) *when* she go away]]]

As usual (142) will be true at (w,i) only if there is a j < i such that

(143) ALWAYS$_r$[Gr′ [TWICE!$_{r′}$ (Jocelyn phone the police) *when* she go away]]

is true at (w,j). This will obtain if $j = g_c(r)$ and there is a cover P of $g_c(r)$ such that for each p in P

(144) Gr′[TWICE!$_{r′}$ (Jocelyn phone the police) *when* she go away]

is true at (w,p). Since G has widest scope here, (144) will be true at (w,p) if

(145) TWICE!$_{p*}$ (Jocelyn phone the police) *when* she go away

is true at (w,p), which will hold if there is a unique subinterval k of p such that

(138) She go away

is true at (w,k), and at least one subinterval l of p such that l = p and there is a cover Q of p for which there are exactly two subintervals m and n of p where

(139) Jocelyn phone the police

is true at (w,m) and (w,n). What all this amounts to can be summarized as follows: (142) is true at i (modulo w) if there is some past interval j where each case of Jocelyn's going away is matched with exactly two cases of her phoning the police. Clearly this is just what (140) means on one of its interpretations.[21]

Finally we turn to the quantifier *never*. It was noted earlier that sentences involving the connective *not* can sometimes be paraphrased using *never*. In fact there is an inclination to conjecture that they may actually be so close in

---

[20] Note that r′ is a variable rather than a parameter.

[21] Tichy (1985) has suggested that an interval semantics will find it difficult, if not impossible, to provide an adequate analysis of temporal quantifiers like *exactly twice* while at the same time giving an appropriate rendering of both perfective aspect and adverbials like *yesterday*. It is worth noting, therefore, that the following two sentences seem to be adequately characterized within the present framework.

(i) Jocelyn has visited London exactly twice.
(ii) Jocelyn went to London exactly twice yesterday.

meaning as to make the difference semantically uninteresting. With a view to pursuing this, let us define *never*. Where A is any context-free sentence,

(146) NEVER$_r$(A) is true in a model M at (w,i) if i = g$_c$(r) and there is no cover P of g$_c$(r) such that for some p in P A is true in M at (w,p); it is false at (w,i) if i ≠ g$_c$(r) or there is a cover P of g$_c$(r) such that for some p in P A is true at (w,p); (and otherwise it is undefined).

By way of illustration consider the sentence,

(147) Sally never stayed at the Savoy when she went to London

whose logical form is represented in the following way.

(148) PAST$_{(v,t)}$ [NEVER$_r$ (Sally stay at the Savoy *when* she go to London)]

This formula will be true at (w,i) only if there is a j < i such that

(149) NEVER$_r$ (Sally stay at the Savoy *when* she go to London)

is true at (w,j), which will hold if j = g$_c$(r) and there is no cover P of g$_c$(r) such that for some p in P

(150) Sally stay at the Savoy *when* she go to London

is true at (w,p). On the case reading of *when* this obtains if there is no unique subinterval k of p such that

(151) She go to London

is true at (w,k), or any subinterval 1 of p such that

(152) Sally stay at the Savoy

is true at (w,l). In effect (148) will be true only if there are no cases in g$_c$(r) where Sally went to London and stayed at the Savoy.

Although there is undoubtedly a difference between *never* and *not*, it is interesting to examine the sentence which results from (147) by replacing *never* by *not*.

The logical forms of (i) and (ii) are given respectively by these formulas.

(iii) PRES$_{(v,t)}$ [HAVE [TWICE!$_r$ (Jocelyn visit London)]]
(iv) PAST$_{(v,t)}$ [TWICE!$_r$ (ON yesterday (Jocelyn go to London)]]

To see that (iii) and (iv) result in the intended truth conditions it is essential to appreciate that the value of the parameter is determined contextually in both cases. Its value is g$_c$(r) and is fixed, as it were, from the beginning, i.e. before the operators are 'peeled off'. Since the verification is straightforward, we shall leave the exercise to the reader.

(153)   Sally did not stay at the Savoy *when* she went to London.

Significantly (153) can be used in either of two ways. It can be uttered with the intention of making an assertion about Sally's habit when she went to London, in which case its logical form would be rendered in this way.

(154)   *Not* [PAST$_{(v,t)}$ (Sally stay at the Savoy *when* she go to London)]

The import of (154) is equivalent to (148) if the assignment to r is the whole of past relative to the time of speech. On the other hand, (153) can also be used with the intention of making an assertion about some particular occasion on which Sally went to London. To render the resulting proposition in terms of *not* it is necessary to invoke a 'suppressed' time reference, which (as above) is represented by the time adverbial *at then*. The desired formula is the following.

(155)   PAST$_{(v,t)}$ [*Not* [AT then (Sally stay at the Savoy)] *when* she go to London)]

In (155) *when* has wider scope relative to both *not* and AT *then*.
    An alternative way of characterizing the same proposition can be formulated in terms of NEVER$_r$, viz. in this way.

(156)   PAST$_{(v,t)}$ [NEVER$_r$ (Sally stay at the Savoy) *when* she go to London]

Here *when* has scope over NEVER$_r$. Given that $g_c(r)$ coincides with some period in which Sally went to London, (156) says that Sally never stayed at the Savoy during that period. This is just what (155) says if the referent of *then* meets the conditions on $g_c(r)$. In fact when the referent of *then* is identical to $g_c(r)$, (155) and (156) are equivalent.
    This is not to say of course that one can always substitute *never* for *not* salve congruitate. It does suggest, however, that where propositions are represented in terms of both negation and time reference they can always be recharacterized in terms of NEVER$_r$. This may not be linguistically significant, but it is of some semantic importance.
    Although we have only examined one temporal connective, viz. *when*, it should be clear how we would proceed to treat other cases, in particular *before* and *after*. The definition of *after* will be straightforward since it seems to have just one meaning which is strictly temporal in character. In the case of *before*, however, the situation is rather different. While it has a temporal sense which can be defined in the manner of *after*, it seems also to have a modal sense which emerges in this sentence.

(157)   Max stopped the car before he hit the tree.

Since (157) implies that Max did not hit the tree, it is clear that *before* does not have the same existential import that *after* does. That is, the sentence

(158)   Max stopped the car after he hit the tree

can only be interpreted as implying that Max hit the tree. The question then is how to formulate the modal sense of *before*. It is not inconveivable that *before* may only have a modal sense. For those 'special' cases where it has existential import, the reasons may be non-logical: it may be due to lexical features, or contextual factors, or perhaps something entirely different. In any case there is an issue here which we must leave for another time.

Oblique contexts and the subjunctive

Davidson has suggested that the logical form of sentences of indirect discourse, e.g.

(159)   Galileo said that the earth moves

should be understood in terms of two sentences which are related paratactically, in this case the sentences

(160)   Galileo said that

and

(161)   The earth moves.

The expression *that* in (160) has the status of a demonstrative pronoun which in utterances of (159) is used to refer to the utterances of (161). Since (161) occurs as part of (159) it is not itself asserted. What is asserted is (160), with the utterance of (161) serving to identify what Galileo said. One who utters (161) as part of (159) represents himself as being a samesayer with Galileo. That is, Galileo is given to have uttered some sentence in his language, Italian or Latin, whose purport is the same as one's own utterance of (161).

Let us suppose that sameness of purport consists in expressing the same proposition.[22] The question then is what proposition does (160) attribute to Galileo. On our Russellian theory an utterance of (161), when it stands as an independent sentence, expresses a value-specific proposition, i.e. one which is true at most of the time of utterance. Since the past tense in this context engenders reference to speech time, the utterance amounts to an assertion about that time and must be true of it if it is to be true at all. When (161) stands as part of (159), however, its utterance will have a rather different relation to the time of speech. Plainly there can be no reference to the present speech time if the utterance is to express the same proposition which was expressed by Galileo. Since Galileo will have referred to his speech time, one can be a samesayer with him only if one refers to that time. If one does so refer in uttering (161), it may seem that one would express the same proposition as he did. This must of course be a value-specific proposition, at least according to our theory.

---

[22] Although Davidson eschews reference to propositions, it is useful here to set this aside.

But can such a proposition be a suitable relatum for the relation of saying? To be more precise, can the occurrence of *said* in the utterance of

(160)   Galileo said that

be interpreted as a relation between Galileo and some value-specific proposition? To see that it cannot be one need only consider another contingent sentence, say

(162)   The moon has craters

and suppose that it happens to be uttered with respect to the same speech time as (161). Given that both utterances are true of this time, they will express the same value-specific proposition (modulo a common reference to possible world). In fact there are just two propositions possible here, one that evaluates to true only for the interval of utterance and the other that evaluates to false for all intervals. If one takes all the utterances uttered simultaneously with Galileo's utterance (regardless of who may have done the uttering), all the true utterances will express one value-specific proposition and all the false ones the other. Hence any relation Galileo sustains to one true utterance he also sustains to the others, and similarly for any false utterance. Clearly, value-specific propositions are not appropriate relata for saying, since they cannot discriminate among the different things that may be said. The same is obviously true in the case of all propositional attitudes.

From the viewpoint of our theory it is significant that oblique contexts, such as the one formed by *Galileo said that*, do not allow contained sentences to be asserted. No utterance of (159) can give rise to an assertion of (161). Davidson's analysis of (159) does not explain why this is so. Since he represents (161) as having the status of an independent sentence which is related paratactically to (160), he portrays it as having an occurrence suitable for assertion. The fact that the occurrence is plainly otherwise is a fact that stands against his analysis. If one amends the analysis by supposing that (160) and (161) are connected more than paratactically, it seems possible to explain why (161) is not assertible. On the assumption that (161) occurs as a genuine contained formula in (159), one can say that in such contexts there can be no appropriate reference, i.e. of the sort that occurs when (161) is uttered as a main clause. Assertion requires reference to the actual world and to speech time and thus, it is natural to trace the unassertability of (161) to the impossibility of appropriate reference. Where there can be no reference to the actual world time of utterance, there can be no assertion. The point to note is that if there were such reference in uttering (161), it would express a value-specific proposition, which is something we have just seen to be unacceptable in the context.

How then is (161) to be represented when it occurs as part of (159)? The answer is foreshadowed in the treatment of the tense operators. As such operators can apply only to context-free formulas, so (161) will require a context-free rendering when it occurs in an oblique position. Given that the subordinate verb *moves* falls within the scope of the main verb *said*, (161) must be characterized as follows.

(163)   Gv', t' [PRES$_{(v,t)}$ (the earth move)]

Recall that (163) expresses a value-free proposition which may be true at indices other than the index of utterance. Note moreover that the 'context-free' rendering of (162), viz.

(164)   Gv',t' [PRES$_{(v',t')}$ (the moon have craters)]

expresses a different value-free proposition. Even if (163) and (164) both happen to be true at the time of utterance, they will not always be true together and hence do not express the same proposition. Since this is the sort of propositional discrimination required for oblique contexts, it is natural to think that value-free propositions are proper objects for the attitudes.

At this point it seems not unreasonable to abandon Davidson's approach to (159). Indeed it now seems right to analyse (159) in the obvious way, with (161) taken as a genuine subordinate clause. While we agree that *said*, or rather *say*, is to be interpreted as a relation, we take *that* to be a propositional operator which creates a name; the result of applying *that* to a formula is a name which refers to the proposition expressed by that formula. Thus the logical form of (159) is represented as follows.

(165)   PAST$_{(v,t)}$ [Galileo say that [Gv',t' [PRES$_{(v,t')}$ (the earth move)]]]

Here *that* applies to the subformula (163) to name the value-free proposition expressed by (163). It should be noted that both occurrences of the tense operators apply to context-free formulas, i.e. to formulas which contain no occurrences of the parameters v and t.[23]

On this approach to indirect discourse it emerges that sentences are not semantically innocent, even though their subcomponents may be. An utterance of the sentence,

(161)   The earth moves

will express a different kind of proposition depending upon the linguistic context in which the sentence occurs. It will express a value-specific proposition if the sentence stands as a main clause, but when it is embedded in an oblique context, as in (159), it will express a value-free proposition. This would suggest a rather paradoxical situation: it may appear impossible to report what someone said through indirect discourse. The 'feeling' of paradox seems most tangible in this sentence.

(166)   The moon has craters and I said that the moon has craters.

Anyone who utters (166) would seem not to be a samesayer with himself, since his two utterances of

(162)   The moon has craters

---

[23] See definitions (26) and (27).

will express different propositions.

The paradox, however, is more apparent than real. There is an inclination to suppose that the proposition one expresses in uttering (162) must be what one says. After all, there is a long philosophical tradition which would hold just that. Nevertheless, it is still possible to draw a distinction between what one says and the proposition expressed. Since the concept of a proposition is a technical term, it can be defined as one chooses. We choose to define it in a way which implies that it cannot always be identified with what is said. On our analysis one who utters (162) expresses a value-specific proposition whose status is closely related to the truth value of the utterance. If the utterance is true for the index of utterance, it expresses one of the two possible value-specific propositions for that index, viz., the one which is true for that index alone. If the utterance is false, it expresses the universally false value-specific proposition, i.e. the proposition which is false for all indices. The content of one's utterance is plainly not given by either of these propositions.

We take its content to be given by the value-free proposition expressed by the following formula.

(164) Gv',t' [$PRES_{(v',t')}$ (the moon have craters)]

What one says in uttering (162) is distinguished, not by its truth value, but by its content, and this is discriminated by (164). Hence if one wishes to report what one says in such an utterance, one must invoke the value-free proposition expressed by (164). If one wishes to report more, e.g. that what one says is true, one must refer to the index of utterance. This requires an explicit reference, which is not found in (159).

Certain tense phenomena lend support to the view that oblique contexts are not semantically innocent. The 'relational' import of tenses in oblique contexts is not always the same as their import in main clauses. Take this sentence.

(167)   Someone will say that Bush was a great President.

If one were to utter (167) today (17 May 1985), one would naturally intend the complement sentence,

(168)   Bush was a great President

to be understood as saying something about the future relative to some later time in the future. One would at least not wish to be taken as saying something about the past relative to the present time, not unless there were some misapprehension. Note that the future time relative to which (168) is to be interpreted is indeterminate; it is just some time in the future. If one wishes to make the time definite, say 17 May 2000, one could modify (167) as follows.

(169)   Someone will say on 17 May 2000 that Bush was a great President.

It is important to appreciate that the indicated future time cannot be fixed from within the subordinate position itself, i.e. in this way.

(170)   Someone will say that Bush was a great President on 17 May 2000.

In fact there is no way of modifying the contained occurrence of (168) to refer to the time relative to which it is to be considered. When (168) stands as a main clause, however, there is no avoiding such a reference since it must be the time of speech. This strongly suggests that (168) does not occur innocently in (167).

In this connection it may be mentioned that the tenses in (167) should not be seen as iterated. Since the future tense occurs in the main clause and the past tense in the complement claue, the two cannot be rendered at the level of logical form as a 'prenex' prefix to any formula. The relation between the tenses is not really a matter of logical scope but of the linguistic contexts within which the tenses occur. The tense of the subordinate sentence is a significant constituent of the relatum of the main verb and thus, its relation to the tense of the main verb is not strictly a relation of iteration.

We are now able to speculate about what is semantically characteristic of subjunctive sentences, e.g., of occurrences like (168) in (167). Subjunctive sentences may be typically marked for tense (though perhaps not always so), but they are not sensitive to the time of speech, as indicative sentences are. In this respect they may be said to be semantically untensed. Accordingly the logical form of a subjunctive sentence will never have occurrences of the context parameters v and t and hence will always be represented as expressing a value-free proposition.

References

Davidson, Donald (1975): 'On Saying That'. *Synthese*, 19, 130–46.

Dowty, David (1979): *Word, Meaning and Montague Grammar*. Dordrecht, Holland: D. Reidel.

Heny, F. (1982): 'Tense, Aspect and Time Adverbials II'. *Linguistics and Philosophy* 5, 109–54.

Kamp, J. A. W. (1971): 'Formal Properties of "Now"'. *Theoria*, 37, 227–73.

Kamp, Hans and Christian Rohrer (1983): 'Tense in Texts'. In Baeuerle, Schwarze and von Stechow (eds), *Meaning, Use and Interpretation of Language*, Berlin: Walter de Gruyter, 250–69.

Lewis, David (1975): 'Adverbs of Quantification'. In E. L. Keenan (ed.), *Formal Semantics of Natural Language*, Cambridge: Cambridge University Press, 3–15.

Prior, A. N. (1967): *Past, Present and Future*. Oxford: Clarendon Press.

Reichenbachn, Hans (1947): *Elements of Symbolic Logic*. New York: The Free Press, reprint 1966.

Richards, Barry (1982): 'Tense, Aspect and Time Adverbials I'. *Linguistics and Philosophy*, 5, 59–107.

Russell, Bertrand (1903): *The Principles of Mathematics*. Cambridge: Cambridge University Press.

Taylor, Barry (1977): 'Tense and Continuity'. *Linguistics and Philosophy*, 1, 199–220.

Tichy, Pavel (1980): 'The Logic of Temporal Discourse'. *Linguistics and Philosophy*, 3, 343–69.

(1985): 'Do We Need Interval Semantics?', *Linguistics and Philosophy*, 8, 263–282.

Vendler, Zeno. (1967): 'Verbs and Times'. In Z. Vendler, *Linguistics in Philosophy*, New York: Cornell University Press, 97–121.

9

What a Truth Theory Need Not Tell Us

RICHARD E. GRANDY

Many claims have been made on behalf of the philosophical value of truth theories. Among them are the claim that a truth theory reveals the logical form of a sentence,[1] and that a theory of truth can, and should, serve as a theory of meaning. These claims have been much debated for over twenty years now, but I believe that some light can still be shed on these areas. In this paper I will try to illuminate some of the claims about logical form a little.

A classification of truth theories

I must begin by distinguishing several kinds of truth theories, in order to indicate the focus of my attention which will be what are often called 'homophonic truth theories'.[2] These are theories for a language L in a metalanguage ML which exceeds L only to the minimum extent necessary for a definition of truth in L (E.g., it might include apparatus to refer to the syntactic structures of L and a satisfaction relation.) Tarski's original definitions of truth for type theory and any standard definition in first-order languages would be familiar examples. In such cases the target biconditionals have the form:

$$T'\phi' \longleftrightarrow \phi$$

or if we imagine a truth theory carried out for English in a minimally augmented metalanguage we would have the familiar examples such as

'Snow is black' is true iff snow is black.

---

[1] Davidson (1968, p. 131; 1970, p. 144; 1971, p. 461; 1975, p. 22–3).
[2] I will continue to use this terminology since it is fairly standard. It is not entirely apt, however, for the relationship between the languages requires not only sameness of phonology but identity of syntax and meaning as well. The importance of this point will emerge near the end of this paper.

Heterophonic truth theories are truth theories for a language L in a distinct L'; heterophonicity clearly comes in degrees but an extreme case would be a theory of truth for English in (suitably augmented) German or Sanskrit. No full theory of this kind has ever been given for any language, although fragments of or allusions to such theories abound in the literature. In such cases the target biconditionals are quite different for quite different sentences appear on the two sides of the biconditional:

'Schnee ist weiss' is true iff snow is white.

There is a vast difference between the two types of target sentences – the first type are obvious and trivial, the latter very informative. One major debate about truth theories seems to me to revolve around whether the heterophonic truth theories are informative in themselves or whether they are only informative because they generate the informative target sentences. I shall not enter in detail this debate over where the action is in such truth theories for I mention the heterophonic case mainly to distinguish it from the homophonic and heteromorphic. An argument could be given, however, that the heterophonic truth theory could be generated by putting together an inter-linguistic set of biconditionals of the form

'Schnee ist weiss' is true iff 'snow is white' is true

and a homophonic truth theory for English. This suggests that the informativeness comes less from the truth theory than from the inter-linguistic mapping.

Both the homophonic and heterophonic truth definitions attempt to preserve a considerable similarity of form. One cannot always preserve word for word structure, as when 'snow' must be mapped onto 'la neige' but similarity of structure is a constant major goal. By contrast, in heteromorphic truth theories the goal is not to preserve the superficial form of the L sentence but to reveal its true underlying logical form. Two examples of target sentences would be

'The King of France is fat' is true iff there is at least one King of France, there is at most one King of France and all Kings of France are fat

and

'Shaun kicked Shem' is true iff there is an event that is a kicking and that is by Shaun and is of Shem.

Both sentences display more structure on the metalinguistic side of the biconditional, but there is a sense in which the first is reductive while the second is ontologically inflationary. In its usual setting, Russell's analysis of definite descriptions provides a means to define truth for a first-order language with definite description operators in a metalanguage without definite descriptions. Similar but less significant examples would be a definition of truth for a language with both quantifiers in a language with only one and the case where the object language has a biconditional and the metalanguage does not.

Proponents of the eventful treatment of the kicking sentence would almost certainly object to my characterization of the theory as inflationary. Surely, they would argue, the truth definition only reveals structure that is really lurking beneath the surface of the English sentence and thus the analysis, if correct, only shows that our ontology was already richer than we realized. I will return to the problems of assessing this claim later – for now it suffices if I have made sufficiently clear the distinction between types of truth theory so that one can scrutinize a truth theory and separate those that are ontologically inflationary (or revealing) from those that smoothly pass the syntactic and semantic structure across the biconditional with minimal alteration, and also from those that juggle logical structure while leaving ontology alone.

Minimalist truth theories

Let us concentrate our attention on homophonic homomorphic truth theories, ones which I shall call *conservative* for brevity; I concentrate on them not because I think they are the most informative, but because they are the least informative. Whatever we learn from such truth theories we can be sure that we learn from the truth theory itself and not from smuggled-in translations or independent ontological analysis. For specificity and familiarity, I will focus on first-order quantificational languages in this section.

It has been claimed that in such cases we learn about the logical forms of sentences by giving a truth theory for the language. (I should say that I will sometimes speak of a truth theory for a sentence – this is sloppiness or laziness – I believe that properly one should speak only of truth theories for a language including the sentence.) It certainly appears that in these cases we learn from the truth theory more than the biconditionals – for example we can easily derive within standard truth theories that any specific instance of excluded middle is true; indeed we can derive that they are all true. Surely this is information about logical form.

But how much of it comes from the truth theory? We can divide the derivation of the sentence T ('Av–A') into two parts, the first consisting of a derivation of a biconditional with that on the left and Av–A on the right, the second consisting of a derivation of Av–A followed by the result desired. The truth theory enters only into the first portion. To put the point more strongly, one can give a perfectly adequate truth definition for a classical language using a intuitionistic metalanguage, and in that case the result about excluded middle is clearly not forthcoming.[3] Thus at least in the sense I have in mind, the truth theory itself does not tell us that excluded middle is valid. And what concerns me in this paper is *what the truth theory itself tells us*.

One way of posing the question, or at least part of it, is to ask whether some logic more minimal than intuitionistic will suffice to give us the biconditionals

---

[3] I made this point in my (1972).

from the standard clauses, for although intuitionistic logic does not yield the conclusion that excluded middle is valid, it does yield comparable conclusions about other forms, such as non-contradiction. We can make a beginning of an answer to the question by focusing on the sentential connectives. (It is important to emphasize that we require that the metalanguage be a minimal extension of the object language. As Professor McCarty noted in commenting on an earlier version, adding a naming function[4] makes the development of a truth theory very simple.) That is, let us assume we are given the biconditionals for atomic sentences and consider how we turn those into biconditionals for molecular sentences. For each connective $ there is a clause:

$$T \text{ `A\$B'} \longleftrightarrow T \text{ `A'} \, \$ \, T \text{ `B'}$$

which, together with the biconditionals for atomic sentences and substitutivity of equivalents gives the desired result. Thus the only logical principle of inference required is substitution of equivalents.

This suggests the intriguing possibility of a[5] minimalist truth theory – one that had clauses for each type of connective but whose logical apparatus consisted entirely of substitution of equivalents, effectively isolating the *truth* component from the logical component.[6] Of course it becomes apparent that this possibility is only an apparent possibility when we turn to quantification theory. Although the principal connective of the right-hand side recurs on the right, it does not do so in the simple fashion that the sentential connectives do.

Shuffling the sequences

The problem is not primarily due to the introduction of sequences, the treatment of sentential connectives is still very straightforward as in

s satisfies 'A\$B' $\longleftrightarrow$ s satisfies 'A' \$ s satisfies 'B'.

Rather the problems arise in the tricks that must be done with sequences in the quantifier clauses. You will recall that a typical quantifier clause is

s satisfies '(x)A' $\longleftrightarrow$ (s') [V('x',s,s') $\rightarrow$ s' satisfies 'A']

(where V is the relation of being variants with regard to the variable mentioned) shifting the quantifier from the objects of the domain to sequences (although, of course, that is an indirect way of getting at the objects in the domain). The most glaring difference from the sentential cases, though, is the intrusion of the V

---

[4] The naming function required is one that for any object in the range of object language variables forms a name of that object.

[5] The choice of the indefinite article here is deliberate – I see no reason to think that there will be a unique minimal truth theory for a given language.

[6] Grandy (1972) exploited the fact that most of what one needs is transitivity of biconditionals. LePore (1982) considered the question under discussion for an object language without quantifiers.

relation. This is an indication of the second, underemphasized element, in a quantifier phrase; the first element, the upside down and backwards A or E, indicates the kind of quantification the operation is; the second element, the variable, in effect, indicates the location. Yet another disparity is the occurrence of the conditional on the right-hand side.

The typical presentation of a truth theory disguises somewhat the pervasiveness of sequences and the satisfaction relation; truth is *defined* as satisfaction by all sequences. Perhaps a clearer way of putting the point is that a truth theory typically generates a multitude of biconditionals like the last two mentioned and only a few of the biconditionals that get generated are target biconditionals in the sense used at the beginning of the paper. But perhaps we have been conceiving the target too narrowly – why should we not demand of a truth theory that in addition to the truth biconditionals it provide biconditionals for the significant substructures of sentences? Of course there will be no uncontroversial pretheoretic list of such significant substructures but the theory itself must provide such a list and if two theories disagree on this it might provide additional possible grounds for choosing between them.

One awkwardness of the suggestion is that the resulting sentences are hardly as obvious as the standard target biconditionals. Examples (paraphrased into English) would be:

A sequence satisfies 'x_{17} is red' iff the object assigned to the 17–th place in the sequence is red.

One cause of this awkwardness is that we are constructing sentential clauses to flank the central biconditional, parallel to the truth biconditionals. However *open* sentences are more naturally associated not with truth values but with sequences, or with sets of sequences. We can connect this last point with the earlier observation that truth itself is typically defined in terms of a relation to sequences, in fact to the set of all sequences.

Thus I suggest that we can shift our semantic focus and see every formula as associated with a set of sequences, those that satisfy it in the usual definition. And we can think of this associated set as itself the semantic value of the formula. Thus if we make shift to a Fregean perspective and think of the formula as denoting its semantic value, we can replace the biconditionals with identity signs in the cases of the so-called sentential connectives.

S'A$B' = S'A' $ S'B'

where S 'A' replaces T 'A' and means something like 'is an A satisfier'. (A reader of an earlier version was puzzled by the apparent ambiguity of '$', an instance of which for English might be 'and' on the left but would look like intersection on the right – my point is that on this view conjunction *is* intersection.)

Of course this doesn't help yet with the quantifiers, so let us consider them again. It is not so much the quantifiers themselves that cause the problems as the use of variables to locate the operating point of the quantifier. It is not difficult to define an operation on a set of sequences that gives the set of sequences appropriately related to the first by existential quantification of a specified argument. The operation forms the new set by including any variants of the appropriate place formed from sequences in the first set (using objects from a specified domain). This operation is known as 'cylindrification' because it is the semantic analogue of the geometric process by which one generates a cylinder from a circle.[7]

Thus we could, instead of quantifiers–with–variables, have cylindrification operators C_j where the index indicates the location of the quantification. One slight problem that intrudes at this point is that, as the indices indicate, we have infinitely many operations. If we continue with infinite sequences, as we have implicitly done since we started from the standard semantic approach, this is a major difficulty. But if we note that most of an infinite sequence is irrelevant and that only a finite subset is semantically significant, then we can switch to finite sequences. This is helpful because the effect of the infinite array of cylindrification operations can be achieved by a single cylindrification operation which operates on the first place of sequences plus an infinite array of permutation operations that serve to move the desired argument place to the front to be cylindrified and then move it back where it came from. This would be no gain at all, except that the infinite array of permutations can be defined from three: one of which moves the first element of a sequence to the end, the second of which reverses that process, and the third of which permutes the first and second elements. We will need to also add an identity predicate that will do the work of identifying argument places as desired,[8] and thus we must let satisfaction denote a set of sequences of various lengths without finite bound.

However, if we wish to use finite sequences and reflect the fact that only finitely many argument places actually matter to any particular formula, then we should use not cylindrification, which leaves the argument place intact, but a closely related operation that deletes the relevant argument place. Since we have seen that we can, and indeed want to, restrict ourselves to a single operation applied to the first argument place, we can describe the operation thus:

EX = the set of sequences such that some sequence obtained by prefixing an element of D to the sequence is a member of X.

The E operation applies to a set of sequences and produces a set of shorter sequences; we also need an operation that lengthens each element of a set of sequences by prefixing objects from the domain. Thus $\#X$ is the set of all sequences which can be obtained by prefixing an element of the domain to a sequence in X.

Finally, we can return to the satisfaction relation. Standardly, it is a relation between a formula and a sequence, but the point of the previous several paragraphs has been to rethink semantic values so that all formulas denote sets

---

[7] The classic text is Henkin, Monk & Tarski (1971).

[8] The original work is in Quine (1966); for a survey and comparison of systems see Grandy (1979, chs XIII and XIV).

of sequences. We could let satisfaction denote the set of pairs whose first element is a formula and whose second is a sequence that satisfies it. But the sequence which the formula on the right of an identity denotes would be buried in the second argument place of the satisfaction relation on the left. So instead we will let satisfaction denote a set of sequences whose first element is a formula and whose remainder is a sequence that satisfies the first element. This introduces yet another new wrinkle, of course, in that we cannot fix the length of the sequence that satisfies a formula (i.e., there is no upper bound on the required length).

This in turn induces another complication. We will need formulas with essentially one argument which will pick out various syntactic objects, e.g., the conjunction of some specified pair of formulas. But if that formula is associated with a set of one-element sequences and satisfaction with longer ones of variable length, then their conjunction (intersection) will be null. In an earlier work[9] on this topic I overpowered this problem by adding to the language an operator that takes a set of sequences and produces all finite continuations of sequences in the set (using objects from the specified domain). This was stronger than necessary, however, for it will suffice to let the set of sequences associated with atomic formulas be the set of all sequences that are finite continuations of the assigned interpretation. Thus if 'F' is assigned the set of red objects, i.e., all the one-element sequences whose objects are red, then the semantic value of 'F' will be the set of all finite sequences formed from the domain beginning with a red object. The property of having all finite continuations will be preserved under all the operations in the language except negation. The stronger language I used earlier had the disadvantage of not being recursively axiomatizable; the current system is almost certainly axiomatizable, though I do not yet have a detailed proof. It is not essentially different from the interpretation of quantification theory in which infinite sequences are assigned to formulas – most of the sequence doesn't matter.

We have now revised the syntactico-semantic basis of the language sufficiently that the target sentences are identities of the form

$$S\ \text{`A\$B'} = S\ \text{`A'}\ \$\ S\ \text{`B'}$$

for binary connectives and

$$S\ \text{`\$A'} = \$S\text{`A'}$$

for singulary connectives. This still does not mean that the truth theory can consist entirely of substitutions of identicals, however, for the infinite list of target sentences must be derived from a finite basis, and this means that we will need some version of universal instantiation.

Unless we make some further changes in the treatment of the object language syntax, we will also need detachment of conditionals, for the recursion clauses in the definition are typically conditional on the form of the particular

---

[9] Grandy (1979), ch. XIV.

construction involved. That is, they would be the predicate functor analogues of axioms such as

$$(x,y,z,w) \ (Cxyz \rightarrow \{ \ Sat(w,x) \longleftrightarrow Sat(w,y) \ \& \ Sat(w,z)\})$$

where Cxyz is interpreted as 'x is the conjunction of y and z'.

An alternative is to use functional notation for the syntax, i.e., instead of a three-place predicate Cxyz to have a two-place function c(x,y), whence the axiom would have the simpler form:

$$(x,y,w) \ [Sat(w,c(x,y)) \longleftrightarrow [Sat(w,x) \ \& \ Sat(w,y) \ ] \ ]$$

If the conjunction function is to be total we must make some decision as to what value it is to assign when the arguments are not formulas – probably the simplest answer is to let it denote the first argument. In this way if a string is not well formed neither it nor its negation will be satisfied by any sequence.

A more complex problem is exactly how one ought best integrate singular terms into a predicate functor language. In any of the formulations I have thus far considered, some permutation operations must intrude on the purity of the recursion clauses, although this may not be inevitable.

Nonetheless, we have greatly reduced the amount of logic that the truth theory appears to read into the object language. I had anticipated being able to give an exact statement of the minimum required, but at this point there appear to be two options; both require transitivity and substitution of identicals and instantiation, the first additionally requires *modus ponens* while the second additionally requires some properties of the permutation operators.

Summarizing this section, a minimal truth theory mainly does two things: it specifies a class of semantically significant syntactic operations and relates the object language expressions to their metalanguage counterparts. It does this by setting out equivalences (or identities) between various metalinguistic expressions (most of) which mention object language formulas.

When substitution fails

In the last section I restricted my attention to a language essentially like standard quantification theory, one in which the substitution of coextensive terms is unproblematic and well understood. However, if we are to extend truth definitions beyond that well-regulated territory, we must consider the problems that arise when coextensive terms are not substitutable.

From the point of view of model theory, some apparently recalcitrant contexts can be treated if one discerns extra structure. Modal contexts, temporal or tensed contexts, sentences like 'Shem kicken Shaun' have all been considered to contain disguised argument places or indices. Bringing in explicit treatment of the possible worlds, times or events makes it clear that the apparently coextensive formulas contain hidden parameters. It may appear that one has one place predicates F and G, and that (x) (Fx $\longleftrightarrow$ Gx) when in fact both contain a second parameter z and substitutability requires the much stronger (x)(z) ['Fxz $\longleftrightarrow$ Gxz]. One might wonder whether such extra parameters can always be found. If we restrict ourselves to the substitutions required for a truth theory and do not inquire too closely into what the phrase 'such extra parameters' requires, the answer is a fairly simple 'yes'. Consider a language for which for some apparently coextensive formulas in some contexts substitution fails to preserve truth (or semantic value). Such formulas can be partitioned into equivalence classes such that substitutions within a given equivalence class does preserve substitutability. (The classes exist since a formula is everywhere substitutable for itself *salva veritate*.) Let each atomic formula be expanded to include an additional, specially designated, argument place and take the equivalence classes themselves to be the range of that variable.

This in itself is a rather cheap formal trick.[10] But it underlines the fact that what makes a particular appeal to additional arguments or indices plausible is the ability to identify the objects that fill those places with some antecedently plausible candidates for entityhood. I should also emphasize here the difference between the introduction of such arguments or indices in truth theories as opposed to model theories. In the latter we seek to characterize validity and consequence by virtue of characterizing truth in an arbitrary structure. In the formulation of a truth theory we need only ensure that the appropriate biconditionals (or identities) are derivable. Thus we can rest content in the latter case with a strong sufficient condition for substitution and need not be concerned with whether weaker conditions suffice as well.

It might be helpful at this point to consider an objection that has been raised against this method of treating modalities in the truth theoretic context (Wallace, 1972). The argument is that the requisite intermediate biconditionals are unacceptable as part of a truth theory because false.

> 'Necessarily snow is snow' is true iff necessarily 'Snow is snow' is true

is thought to be false because while the left-hand side is presumably true the right is not – English might have been different and 'is' might have meant 'is not' or 'loves'. Consider the parallel

> 'Snow will be green' is true iff 'Snow is green' will be true

which could be argued to be false because the left side is false while the right-hand side could become true if English changes appropriately. In both cases, it seems to me, we can fix an appropriate sense of 'True' which is tied rigidly to the current character of English. What is intended in the last biconditional is that 'Snow is green' will be true in the current sense of 'true'. In each case we are evaluating the semantic properties of a sentence within the

---

[10] To avert potential misunderstanding, in the preceding construction I am not claiming to be able to determine when one expression is substitutable for another *salva veritate* – the argument begins with some such determination being given.

given framework of the current language, and are not contemplating the possible alternative past or future developments leading to or from that framework.

A similar point can be raised with regard to LePore's argument (1982) against the adequacy of relevance logic as the logic of a metalanguage for a truth theory. He argues that the base clauses for sentences such as 'Snow is white' is true $\longleftrightarrow$ snow is white are problematic for a relevance based metalanguage. The argument is that reading $\longleftrightarrow$ as a material conditional is too weak to permit the inferences required, and read as a relevance conditional it is false because relevance biconditionals are stronger than strict implication. He does not explain why he thinks them false but I take it he believes the biconditional is not necessarily true for reasons like those discussed above. However, if we stipulate (as we did in the first section) that the metalanguage be the object language itself with minimal augmentation then any change in one will be paralleled by a change in the other.

Conclusion

I have argued for three main points:

(A)   If we want to know what truth theories in themselves provide by way of information or insight with regard to a language, it is useful to focus on the homophonic homomorphic theories. This isolates what is unarguably contributed by the truth theory.
(B)   If we take care in constructing our truth theory, we can reduce the imputation of logical validity to the object language to a minimum. In such minimalist truth theories we, as much as possible, reduce the theory to stating substitution principles that relate objected language syntactic constructions to metalinguistic semantic operations. This also, at least implicitly, identifies a class of semantically significant syntactic structures.
(C)   In cases of apparent failure of substitutability, the truth theory can put at least minimum constraints on what substitutions are needed. Substitution can always be regained by introducing additional argument places or indices, but there will be, in each case, a question whether the alleged entities filling those places are *ad hoc* constructions or legitimate entities that were merely lurking below the syntactic surface. Or, to paraphrase Davidson (1963, p. 349), the question is whether the extensional gain is worth the ontological candle.

There is also a fourth point that I have not specifically argued, but which is of at least equal importance, a point that Davidson has stressed in a number of his writings. The main value of the truth theory is not in the target biconditionals, it is in the analytic means that we use to generate them. The account of the semantically significant structures and of substitution classes provides a theoretical background that contributes to our understanding of the overall semantic structure of the language. The target biconditionals are like scientific observation – a novel theory is not valuable because it allows us to deduce the known observations, its value lies in what it tells us about the underlying structures, in its *explanation* of the observable. We tend to trust such explanations to the extent that they do enable us to deduce the observable facts, and, just so, we trust a truth theory on the basis of its generation of the target biconditionals.*

References

Davidson, Donald (1963): 'The Method of Extension and Intension'. In P. A. Schilpp (ed.), *The Philosophy of Rudolph Carnap*. LaSalle, Illinois: Open Court, 311–49.
  (1968): 'On Saying That'. *Synthese*, 19, 130–46.
  (1970): 'Action and Reaction'. *Inquiry*, 13, 140–8.
  (1971): 'Truth and Meaning'. In Jay F. Rosenberg and Charles Travis (eds), *Readings in the Philosophy of Language*, Englewood Cliffs, New Jersey: Prentice-Hall.
  (1975): 'Semantics for Natural Languages'. In Donald Davidson and Gilbert Harman (eds), *The Logic of Grammar*, Encino, California: Dickenson.
Grandy (1972): 'A Definition of Truth for Theories with Intensional Definite Description Operators'. *JPL*, 1, 137–55.
  (1974): 'Some Remarks about Logical Form'. *Nous*, 8, 157–64.
  (1979): *Advanced Logic for Applications*, rev. ed. Dordrecht, Holland: D. Reidel.
Henkin, Monk and Tarski (1971): *Cylindric Algebras*, Amsterdam: North-Holland.
LePore, Ernest (1982): 'Truth and Inference'. *Erkenntnis*, 18, 379–95.
Quine, W. V. (1966): 'Variables Explained Away'. In *Selected Logic Papers*. New York: Random House.
Wallace (1972): 'On the Frame of Reference'. In G. Harman and D. Davidson (eds), *Semantics for Natural Language*, Dordrecht, Holland: D. Reidel.

---

*David McCarty and Stephen Hess made critical comments on an earlier draft that reduced the number of inaccuracies.

10

On Davidson's "Saying That"

TYLER BURGE

Natural discourse sentences in which surface substitution of coextensional expressions may not preserve truth–value – 'non-extensional contexts – form the chief watershed for theories of logical form and content. On one side are the various intensional logics, deriving from Carnap and C. I. Lewis. These logics, where applied, represent such contexts as flouting the principle that extensionally equivalent, or co-denotational, expressions are inter-substitutable *salva veritate*. On the other side of the divide are the various strategies, deriving from Frege and Russell, that preserve this principle at the level of logical analysis by denying that apparent counterexamples involve genuine substitutions of extensionally equivalent expressions. 'Non-extensional context' is deemed a solecism, justified by convenience only. These latter strategies take one of two forms. Either they argue, as Russell did, that surface syntax of the relevant contexts is misleading in suggesting that the purported counterexamples utilize exchanges of expressions of the same logical type to yield variations in truth value of the relevant sentence. Or they argue, as did Frege, that it is mistaken to count the relevant expressions as having the same semantical values in the relevant contexts. Versions of the two strategies can be combined.

It may be that the intensional-logic and Frege-Russell approaches will come to seem more similar than they have in the past. But as of now, they offer the first momentous choice for a theory of the formal-semantical workings of natural language.

In his account of indirect discourse in 'On Saying That', Professor Davidson stands on the Frege-Russell side of the divide.[1] I stand there too. The various intensional logics have made profound contributions to the understanding of modality – and lesser, but significant, contributions to understanding tense, deontology, and so on. But their handling of propositional-attitude discourse has been inelegant or unilluminating. They have done little to connect meaning with understanding – particularly of non-sentential expressions – and thought

---

[1] Donald Davidson, 'On Saying That', *Synthese*, 19 (1968–9), pp. 130–46. Citations of page numbers will occur in the text.

with conceptual abilities. And in my view, they have failed to come to grips with detailed use of language that leads to paradoxes for 'intensional notions'.

There are more general considerations for favoring the traditional Frege-Russell line. First among them is a worry about how intensional logics treat the relation between notions like necessity, knowledge and belief, on one hand, and the notion of truth on the other. All of these notions have apparently similar grammatical features; but truth is treated as a predicate, whereas the others are treated as operators. There is a corresponding difference, on the standard treatments within intensional logic, between the logic and semantics of the truth-theoretic metalanguage and those of the intensional object language. These differences do not seem to me to have been given a satisfyingly deep motivation.

Davidson's strategy for maintaining the substitutivity of extensionally equivalent expressions is more similar to Russell's than to Frege's. The appearance of counterexample is attributed at least partly to misleading grammar, rather than purely to mistaken assignment of semantical values. Davidson's account differs from Russell's in where it lays the blame. The problem is said to be in the sentence divisions of superficial grammar, not (with an exception to be noted in section IV) in the characterization of the grammatical types of expressions. Davidson locates the expressions that appear to resist substitutivity in a different sentence from the one that attributes the indirect discourse. Since substitutivity principles in logic apply to sentences taken one at a time, the counterexamples are disarmed. This purely technical innovation is, of course, ingenious. But what is striking about it is that Davidson manages to embed it in an account that goes some way toward working.

Like Russell's very different view, Davidson's has long seemed to me important and provocative, but implausible. I think that our grip on the syntax of the relevant discourse is too fundamental and firm for us to be persuaded that we have been misled regarding how to categorize the singular terms or how to divide among the sentences. At any rate, I think that our grip on sentence division is much firmer than our grip on the semantics of 'intensional' contexts.

My purpose here is to discuss three more specific problems for Davidson's account. I think that I can solve one of these. One of the other two is widely known; but I do not see solutions to either. I doubt that they have satisfactory solutions from Davidson's point of view. All three seem to me to raise interesting general issues for theories of the logical form of 'non-extensional' contexts. After discussing these problems, I shall conclude with some brief remarks on the relative merits of the Frege and Russell approaches to indirect discourse and the propositional attitudes.

I Davidson's account

Davidson proposes to give an account of the logical form and formal semantics of indirect discourse sentences like 'Galileo said that the earth moves.' I shall sketch only the outlines of the account.

The main idea is that the logical form of the illustrative sentence is that of

Galileo said that. The earth moves.

The word 'that' is held to be a demonstrative used to refer to the utterance of the sentence 'the earth moves.'[2] Expressions that are coextensive with 'the earth' (or with 'moves') may be freely exchanged without altering the truth value of the containing sentence 'the earth moves.' Such exchanges are irrelevant to logical substitutions in 'Galileo said that' (indicating the relevant utterance) since they occur in a different sentence. 'Said' is a predicate with an argument place for a person, the sayer, and an argument place for an utterance event, picked out by a demonstrative.

Davidson holds that that is all there is to the account of the logical form of indirect discourse (p. 142). There is in addition an account of the use or meaning of indirect discourse 'said'. 'Galileo said that' is held to be a 'definitional abbreviation' (p. 142) of a longer expression:

(A) $(\exists x)$(Galileo's utterance x and that utterance of mine make us same-sayers)

where we ignore tense, and where 'that utterance of mine' refers to the utterance of 'the earth moves' that follows the utterance of 'that'.

The remark about definitional abbreviation is uncongenial with the remark(p. 142) that 'sentences in indirect discourse ... wear their logical form on their sleeves [except for the period, in our example, between "that and "the earth moves"]' and with the statement that 'said' is a two-place predicate (p. 142). For if 'Galileo said that' really abbreviates the above-cited expression, it does not wear its logical form on its sleeve. The ordinary expression hides a quantification over Galileo's utterance; and although the logical form of (A) is not explicit, it clearly makes reference to me, the reporter (both in 'my' and in 'us'), and thus appears to require an argument place not only for Galileo and my utterance, but for 'me', the reporter. One could either make 'said' two-place and revise (A) to $(\exists x)$(Galileeo's utterance x, and *that* utterance (indicating an utterance) samesays with x).' Or one could retain reference to the reporter and provide an extra argument place in 'said'. There are further options. To provide a full account, one would have to settle this issue. But settling it will not be necessary for our purposes.

The notion of samesaying deserves comment. Davidson's idea is that the notion is an 'unanalyzed part' (p. 140) of the 'content' of 'said'. It is invoked, I think quite legitimately, to explicate the use of the predicate; and its complexity (saying the same thing) is not seen as complicating the predicate's logical form. To use indirect discourse, one must master the practice of samesaying. One must be able to use utterances that are relevantly synonymous with the utterances of the original speaker. The utterance to which 'that' is held to refer is a performance whose point is to mimic the content (not necessarily the mode) of the original speaker's utterance.

It might be noted that the account that Davidson's theory provides of the conditions under which the truth value of 'Galileo says that' might change exactly parallels the accounts of more traditional theories. If one were to

---

[2] Davidson characterizes the utterance as an act. I suppose, though Davidson is not ideally explicit, that this act is to be distinguished not only from the sentence type 'The earth moves' but also from the sentence token. The issue will not be relevant to our purposes as long as the referent of 'that' is not the sentence type. On that point Davidson is quite definite; ibid., p. 142.

substitute for our utterance of 'the earth moves' another utterance that did not samesay that utterance, then 'Galileo said that' (where 'that' is taken to refer to the substituted utterance) might differ in truth value from the original token of 'Galileo said that' (where 'that' refers to our original utterance). In agreement with Frege's view, Davidson's holds that exactly those changes that preserve 'samesaying' in the expressions following 'that' are bound to preserve the truth value of the sentence in which the attribution is made. Davidson's theory differs primarily in its account of sentence division and in its assignment of semantical values.

Except for its peculiar claim about syntax, the theory has an appealing simplicity. It invokes a relatively simple logical form, a straightforward logic, an ordinary ontology, and a familiar and inevitable notion of synonymy that need be no more precise than the standards governing reports in indirect discourse.

II A problem about samesaying

The first of our problems concerns the relation between the hypothesized demonstrative 'that' and the relation of samesaying. The problem emerges by comparing ordinary reports that contain demonstratives in the sentence following 'that' with embedded reports of indirect discourse.

First, consider 'Galileo said that that moves' (where our second 'that' refers to the moon). Davidson's theory parses the sentence as

(B) Galileo said that. That moves.

For the report to be true, there must have been an utterance by Galileo that samesays my utterance of 'That moves.' What does samesaying consist in here? Clearly, Galileo would have to have uttered something in which he referred to the moon (perhaps demonstratively) and predicated something synonymous with 'moves' of the moon. In other words, in order to samesay with Galileo by using a demonstrative like 'that' in our content clause, we must preserve Galileo's reference in the subject of his sentence token and preserve Galileo's meaning in the predicate of his sentence token. I think that this point is intuitively obvious. It does not depend on interpreting 'reference' and 'meaning' in any technical or very precise way. So far so good.

Now, consider 'Galileo said that Copernicus said that the earth moves.' Davidson's theory parses the sentence

(C) Galileo said that. Copernicus said that. The earth moves.

The first occurrence of 'that' must refer either to the act of uttering 'Copernicus said that' or to the act of uttering 'Copernicus said that. The earth moves.' It will not matter which for our purposes. The second occurrence of 'that', the one in 'Copernicus said that', must refer to the act of uttering 'The earth move'.

We need some terminology here. Let the sentence token(s) produced by the utterance referred to by the first occurrence of 'that' in (C) be called 'Alpha'. Let the sentence token produced by the utterance referred to by the second occurrence of 'that' in (C) be termed 'Beta'. So Alpha is the relevant token of

'Copernicus said that. The earth moves' (or of 'Copernicus said that'); Beta is the relevant token of 'The earth moves.'

To report Galileo correctly, our token Alpha must samesay with some token of his (or must bear a relation for sentence tokens that is analogous to the samesaying relation between utterances). What does samesaying consist in here? Clearly our token Beta must samesay some token that Galileo produced in the course of attributing a statement to Copernicus. And our tokens 'Copernicus' and 'said' must attempt some match (presumably in meaning or, for the name, at least in reference) with tokens that Galileo produced. But what of the second 'that' in (C)? Clearly we cannot expect it to preserve the reference of any demonstrative or other expression that Galileo used. For our second 'that' refers to an utterance of Beta, and clearly Galileo made no reference to that utterance.

The problem then is this. There is a need to specify a notion of samesaying that constrains us to preserve the reference of the second 'that' in (B) and allows us not to preserve any reference in our use of the second 'that' in (C).

Substantially the same problem may be stated differently. There is a need to give an account of samesaying that enables one to treat the second 'that' in (C) as a demonstrative referring to an utterance, even though its use does not preserve reference under samesaying. On the hypothesis that the second 'that' in (C) refers to an utterance (or utterance token), it clearly differs in function from the second 'that' in (B). The second 'that' in (B) illustrates the most common function of demonstratives in that-clauses: They pick out the same objects that the original speaker (or thinker) made reference to. Their use *preserves reference* under samesaying. Can one articulate a coherent notion of samesaying that explains a different function for the second 'that' in (C), one that fails to preserve reference?

The threat here should be apparent. If some such explanation is not forthcoming, then a natural conclusion would be that *if* 'that' is a demonstrative in 'says that', it must refer to something (in unembedded as well as embedded contexts) that will be preserved under samesaying. This something cannot plausibly be an utterance or token of any kind. It must literally be something that might be said by different people in common. Some sort of abstraction lies at the end of this reasoning. The resulting theory would be different in philosophically significant ways from Davidson's.

Can this problem be solved? I think so. We need to find a non-*ad-hoc* notion of samesaying that will generate failures to preserve the references of expressions, here demonstratives. I think that we need look no farther than the ordinary notion of translation. Although it is normal for literal translation to preserve, as far as possible, the referents of expressions being translated, there are certain contexts in which it systematically avoids doing so. These contexts exhibit various varieties of or approximations to self-reference.

Clearly, if e_1 is a term in sentence s_1 and e_1 refers to s_1 (or to e_1), then a truth-value-preserving translation of s_1 into a sentence s_2, and e_1 into a term e_2 contained in s_2 (where $s_1 \neq s_2$ and $e_1 \neq e_2$), will make e_2 refer to s_2 (or itself) if and only if e_2 does not refer to what e_1 refers to. Briefly, non-homophonic translation preserves self-reference if and only if it does not preserve reference.

Where self-reference is more important to the point of a discourse than what is referred to, self-reference is preserved at the expense of reference. Sometimes self-reference is more important. The point can be established by a wide range of cases independent of indirect discourse. For example, translations of expositions of diagonal arguments in metamathematics often preserve self-reference instead of reference.[3] One can get a taste of the phenomenon by reflecting on a translation of '(3) is not a theorem,' where '(3)' refers to the sentence that contains it. One should imagine (3) embedded in a diagonal argument. A translation into Polish would provide a sentence that referred to itself, not to our sentence (3). Otherwise the validity of the surrounding self-referential argument would not be preserved without adding special premises.

The example from metamathematics is meant to forestall a claim that self-reference-preserving translation is non-literal. Standard translations of metamathematical treatises can hardly be dismissed as literary indulgences. Self-referential translations are sometimes superior to reference-preserving translations at preserving 'information value' or 'cognitive content', in intuitive, non-theoretical uses of those phrases. Coherence of the surrounding discourse and soundness of argument are also better preserved. A reference-preserving translation would be less intelligible to a native Pole, inasmuch as it would describe the self-reference without illustrating it. But the primary purpose of translation is to make foreign discourse intelligible to one who does not already understand that discourse.

A variety of other examples of self-reference-preserving translation could be adduced. But perhaps the point is already sufficiently clear for us to apply it to the case at hand. Our problem was that although the demonstrative 'that' must preserve reference under samesaying in (B), it must not in (C). If the second occurrence of 'that' in (C) could be associated with some phenomenon like self-reference and if this phenomenon could be seen as part of the point of the discourse – more important to its point than actual reference – then a natural notion of samesaying would generate and explain the difference in referential behavior between the 'thats' in (B) and (C).

Once this sketch of a solution is drawn, it becomes evident how to begin filling it in. The point, on Davidson's view, of uttering a sentence that gives the content of the original utterance is to reproduce in the language or context of the reporter's report a sentence that says the same as a sentence produced by the original speaker. We need but tie the reference to the utterance of the sentence following 'that' in 'says that' together with a reference to the language (or context, or utterance) of the introducing sentence to elicit the relevant sort of self-reference.

Thus 'Galileo said that the earth moves' could be represented

(A') $(\exists x)$(Galileo's utterance x and that (next) utterance of mine, taken in the context of this very utterance, make us samesayers). The earth moves.

---

[3] The general point of these pages is developed in greater detail and with greater precision (without special reference to Davidson's theory) in my 'Self-Reference and Translation' in *Meaning and Translation*, (eds) Guenthner and Guenthner-Reutter, (Duckworth, London, 1978). Examples of non-reference-preserving translation from various fields are cited.

The embedded sentence, 'Galileo said that Copernicus said that the earth moves' goes:

(C') (∃x)(Galileo's utterance x and that (next) utterance of mine, taken in the context of this very utterance, make us samesayers). (∃x) (Copernicus' utterance x and that next utterance of mine, taken in the context of this very utterance, make us samesayers). The earth moves.

Note that sameness of interpretative context (see section IV) is insured by the transitivity of identity as one proceeds to deeper embeddings. It is critical to the explanation that the languages or contexts-of-lexical-interpretation of the introducing and introduced utterances be connected, even identified. Otherwise, the element of self-reference in the introducing predicate would have no effect on interpreting the referent of 'that' in 'says that'. Lacking this effect, we have no suitably general explanation as to why 'that' fails to preserve its referent, in embedded occurrences, under samesaying.[4]

The point of indirect discourse might be fairly taken to be to introduce and produce an utterance that gives the content of the original speaker's utterance, *in the interpretative-grammatical context of the introducing utterance*. Self-reference within the introducing utterance to its own context is thus very much in the spirit of Davidson's proposal. Perhaps it is not crucial to explaining why samesaying does not preserve reference that one include an element of self-reference in the very logical form of indirect-discourse sentences. One might take the self-reference to be embedded in a general convention presupposed in the use of indirect discourse. The failure to preserve reference, however, does demand explanation. And I know of no other than that of making explicit the element of self-reference in the exemplar approach that Davidson proposes.

The need to explain failures of reference-preservation under translation or samesaying is not peculiar to Davidson's account. It arises for nearly every theory of intensional contexts that postulates context-bound or language-bound exemplars (whether concrete or abstract) – rather than propositions that are language and context invariant.

The problem that we raised for Davidson's account is a variant of the Church-Langford translation argument.[5] This argument has been commonly

---

[4] It seems to me that this connection between the contexts, or languages, of introducing and introduced utterances might help Davidson explain why it is *ungrammatical* to follow 'that' in 'says that' with non-English words. As the analysis stands, it is unclear why this should be so: If the introducing and introduced sentences were really separate, then no grammatical rules and nothing in Davidson's original analysis beyond pragmatic considerations of convenience would prohibit switching languages after 'that' in indirect discourse. But the prohibition is on a par in its normative status with other grammatical rules. By construing indirect-discourse 'says' in the manner of (A') and (C'), and by construing 'context' in such a way as to require introduced utterances to maintain the grammatical and semantical norms suggested by the introducing utterance, we have some account in Davidson's terms, of the grammatical rule. Since I do not think that there are separate sentences in ordinary indirect discourse, I shall not pursue the details of this matter.

[5] The tradition of appealing to exemplars, which Davidson's account continues, derives from Carnap, Scheffler and Quine. Scheffler's theory is an exception to the rule I am stating, but it fails to provide a satisfactory account, partly for reasons Davidson gives (p. 139). Further discussion occurs in my 'Self-Reference and Translation', and 'The Content of Propositional Attitudes' *Nous* 14 (1980), pp. 53-8.

rejected for bad or confusedly stated reasons. It seems to raise a quite legitimate question for exemplar approaches about reference preservation. Why should reference not be preserved under translation? I think, however, that the question can always be answered by appeals to self-referential elements that are important for the intensional discourse being represented. The details of the answer will, of course, vary with the approach. But all exemplar approaches interpret intensional discourse in such a way as to make the appeal natural.[6]

The invocation of self-reference-preserving translation does more than check a threat from more traditional theories of intensional contexts. It illustrates one of the ways in which traditional approaches over-idealize translation practice. What one preserves under good translation is far harder to characterize than traditional appeals to meaning invariance or proposition invariance would suggest.

III A problem about what is said

Our second problem is widely appreciated. I raise it less because I want to develop it in detail than because it provides a useful foil for the third problem. The difficulty is that the entities that Davidson appeals to as the referents of 'that' in 'says that' do not seem appropriate for certain quantifications on indirect discourse or relevantly analogous discourse.

Seemingly, we may say that Galileo said something at 6 p.m. 3/15/1638 in the indirect-discourse sense of 'said', without being committed to there being an actual utterance token of ours that samesays Galileo's utterance. Even though we reporters may have the resources to report Galileo's utterance, we may never actually utter anything that samesays his sentence token.

The problems raised by mentalistic discourse are more varied and complex.[7] Occurrent thoughts yield a problem analogous to the one just adumbrated. But

---

[6] Davidson uses the Church-Langford argument against Carnap's analysis of propositional attitude sentences, arguing that the analysis 'Galileo spoke a sentence in his language that means what "the earth moves" means in English,' would not preserve reference under translation (p. 135). Davidson revises this analysis to 'Galileo spoke a sentence in his language that means what "the earth moves" means in this language.' Davidson argues against this revision also. He says that in a translation into French, the demonstrative reference (of 'this language') will shift 'automatically' from English to French; but he says that the quotational singular term that denotes the English sentence will be translated in such a way that its reference will remain unchanged. The result would be false (since 'the earth moves' means nothing in French), though the original sentence in English is true. This argument against the revision involves two mistakes. The reference of a demonstrative does not automatically shift under translation; it takes some special condition to motivate its doing so. Moreover, since translation should preserve truth value, a translation that preserved the reference of the quotation but shifted the reference of the demonstrative would simply be a bad one. A sympathetic development of Carnap's basic idea would motivate self-referential translation – in which, roughly, both the demonstrative and the quotation would shift reference. There are examples of translation within quotation marks in ordinary translation practice that are motivated by self-reference. (Cf. note 3.) Carnap does not himself develop his idea in this way. But appeal to self-reference and its effect on translation seems to be needed by, and natural for, both Davidson's approach and Carnap's.

[7] A lesser difficulty is that the samesaying relation needs replacing by some relation more appropriate to mental states and events. The subject need not produce utterances for each attitude for us to 'samesay' with. I think that it can be argued that propositional-attitude discourse in natural

mental states force a further difficulty. When we quantify over what people believe, we seem to be saying that there *are* certain truths or falsehoods that they are committed to and that have logical structure and semantical attributes (e.g., truth, falsity). But there are surely beliefs and other attitudes that are never expressed or characterized by any actual utterances produced by the reporter, the subject, or anyone else.

There is a further problem along these lines for quantification on that-clause position in semantical and modal discourse. 'It is true that $2 + 3 = 5$' and 'It is necessary that $2 + 3 = 5$' are clearly syntactically analogous to indirect discourse. The truth and necessity predicates seem to have at least one fewer argument place than indirect-discourse 'said'. But sentences that contain them seem to demand an account of logical form that otherwise parallels the account for indirect discourse. It seems that there are truths of, say, arithmetic, that will never be uttered, written down, or otherwise instantiated. There are plausibly even truths that will never be believed, or otherwise associated with any propositional attitude. There need be no 'concrete' state of a person that is associated with such truths. Similar remarks apply to necessities, probabilities and so forth.

All of these problems of quantification arise because Davidson's account of what is said is nominalistic. It appeals only to concrete entities as truth bearers – entities that are localized in time (probably in space as well). In the general case, there do not appear to be concrete entities of the right sort (or perhaps even number) to account for quantifications onto that-clauses.

There are, of course, various ways of coming to grips with these difficulties. One might interpret the quantifications in a special way – for example by reference to one's *ability* to substitute names (or demonstratives) for the quantified variable, or by reference to possible concrete sentence tokens. These issues are, of course, complicated and in some respects rather technical. I shall not develop them here.

I believe, however, that neither interpretation in terms of possibility (or ability) is particularly plausible as an exclusive account of natural discourse. Quantification onto that-clauses does not seem markedly different from ordinary objectual quantification in non-intensional contexts. Moreover, pressing the notions of ability and possibility yields familiar difficulties: ability to substitute given what? – what one already knows or understands? Further, I believe that neither interpretation in terms of possibility has been shown to be capable of avoiding all commitment to non-concrete entities. In any case, any attempt to make these interpretations nominalistic would be more plausible as a *reduction* of the commitments of natural discourse than as an account of its actual prima facie commitments.

I doubt that Davidson's account can be extended in a natural and conservative way to deal with these difficulties. I think that the most plausible response to the problem is simply to regard natural discourse as quantifying over abstract objects in the relevant cases.

---

language does not make reference to inner sentence-like entities produced by the subject even in the case of mental events, much less in the case of mental states. But perhaps Davidson need only hold that some utterance of the reporter 'gives-the-content-of' the subject's mental state or event.

The pressure toward abstraction derives from the need to interpret quantification in discourse that yields knowledge. We are committed to objects needed to interpret such discourse. Perhaps the commitments to abstractions can be shown to be reducible. I am doubtful, but I shall not consider this question here. I do want to emphasize, however, that such reductions must fall out of reductions of the discourse that we have been considering to other discourse adequate to the same cognitive purposes. Metaphysical or epistemic preconceptions about ontology, for all their philosophical interest, have in themselves little cognitive payoff to back their prescriptions or proscriptions. Ontological positions should derive from, not dominate, the interpretation of cognitively successful discourse.[8] Grand metaphysical or epistemic schemes (such as nominalism or global causal theories of knowledge) have not established themselves as cognitively successful discourse.

Davidson raises two objections to approaches to indirect discourse that would postulate abstract expression types as the denotations of content clauses in indirect discourse (pp. 134–7). Davidson calls these 'quotational approaches'. One concerns preservation of reference under translation. It can be passed over here, since it can be answered using the sort of considerations needed to sustain Davidson's own approach in the light of the problem discussed in the previous section. (Cf. note 6.)

Davidson's other objection concerns the need to fix an interpretation of the sentence type that is postulated by such approaches. Since words (word forms) may be understood in infinitely many different ways, we need to fix the relevant understanding or interpretation of the word forms. As means of fixing an interpretation, Davidson considers only specifying a language, say, English. And he marshalls Quine's objections in *Word and Object* to languages or, equivalently, propositions: the individuation conditions of propositions and languages are obscure; such questions of individuation are unconnected to indirect discourse; and postulating languages or propositions as entities is shown to be mistaken by the indeterminacy of translation (p. 138).

I think that these objections are not sound. But even taken as acceptable, the objections tell not against abstraction *per se* but against a particular means of fixing an interpretation.[9]

---

[8] The position derives from Frege's methodology in *The Foundations of Arithmetic* and Quine's pragmatism in 'Two Dogmas of Empiricism' and *Word and Object*. Quine sometimes deviates from the method, it seems to me, in his preoccupation with physicalism. Davidson has expressed sympathy with such pragmatism in numerous places. I am therefore puzzled by the nominalistic aspect of his account of indirect discourse. The problems that we have discussed in this section are known to apply not just to his view but to previous nominalistic approaches. Yet I know of nothing in his writings that mitigates their seriousness.

[9] I do not intend this last sentence as a criticism of Davidson since he does not claim or clearly presuppose the contrary. On the other hand, he does not consider other options for fixing an interpretation. It should be noted that on Quine's conception of indeterminacy the logical form as well as the interpretation is comprehensively indeterminate. I shall be ignoring this complication. Even relativity to a choice about interpreting form, however, is compatible with abstraction. One may see the logical form of a sentence as roughly analogous to the way Quine sees the number associated with a numeral. Any of several forms will do within a certain system of interpretation. I am sceptical of Quine's position here; but I cannot develop either the scepticism or the position's ramifications in this sketch.

It is important to distinguish the issue over whether the entities denoted by the noun-phrases following propositional-attitude verbs are abstract from issues over the nature of interpretation. The two overlap but are not the same. There are two primary disputed issues regarding the specification of an interpretation. One concerns the cognitive status or type of objectivity of linguistic interpretation: Quine's indeterminacy thesis bears on this issue. The other concerns the type of idealizations about language- and context-independence that are most fruitful in studying language. What is the relation between the use of language (human activity) and truth bearers? How far can one reasonably idealize beyond momentary contexts of use in giving an interpretation?

But abstraction is compatible with non-objectivist positions on the first issue and with nearly any reasonable position on the second. Thus to return to the 'quotational' approach Davidson criticizes: One need not say that Galileo said (indirect discourse) some S, taken as a sentence of English. One might, for example, say instead that Galileo said some S, taken as it would be if I (the reporter) were to use it now. Compatibly with taking S to be abstract, one might regard interpreting Galileo (or indeed oneself) as relative to some non-cognitive decision about analytical hypotheses, and one might interpret my would-be use in as context-dependent a manner as one pleases.

The counterfactual in this specification of the interpretation of S is no more obscure than what is required to know how to apply 'samesays'. We have to master some procedures for interpreting utterances beyond those actually at hand, in order to make use of the notion of samesaying. As in the case of Davidson's analysis, the specification of how the abstraction is to be interpreted might be regarded as implicit in the use of indirect discourse 'said' or the propositional attitude predicate. Alternatively, and I think preferably, it might be seen as part of a convention presupposed in the use of such predicates in such a way as not to affect their logical form. (See Davidson, note 3.)

This is not the place to discuss the issues regarding interpretation that I mentioned two and three paragraphs back. The main point is that the issues over the cognitive status of interpretation, and the appropriate level of idealization in specifying it, are separable from the issue of abstraction. Commitment to abstraction *per se* is not impugned by the sort of arguments that Davidson and Quine urge in favor of indeterminist, non-intensionalist, and relatively contextualist (or in Quine's case, individualist) positions on issues of interpretation and intentionality. Postulating abstractions does not in itself do much to advance (or retard) our understanding of linguistic interpretation. But it improves and simplifies semantical theory.

IV A problem about validity

The original and primary purpose of a theory of logical form is systematically to identify those formal structures in a language or discourse that mirror the deductive arguments that are formally valid. Such a theory will inevitably serve not only an account of validity, but also an account of truth conditions, whose interest and importance Davidson has done much to make manifest. Giving a semantical theory of truth will sometimes lead to the identification of formal structures that do not necessarily mirror deductive relations but that enter into non-deductive reasoning. But a minimum requirement on a theory of logical form is that it assign structures to sentences by reference to which valid arguments that intuitively depend on form can be systematically explained.

What it is to be a *formally* valid argument becomes a difficult and subtle question when pressed. But the answer is traditionally bounded by two contrasts. In the first place, formally valid arguments contrast with valid arguments that depend essentially on the meaning of lexical items that are 'non-logical'. In recent times, what counts as a logical term has sometimes been regarded as almost purely a matter of what the logician decides to give a logic of (what to hold constant under model-theoretic reinterpretations). But traditionally, logical terms are those that are relevant to all subject matters. This characterization is vague (because of 'relevant' and 'subject matter') and leaves room for philosophical dispute over cases (e.g. truth, number, necessity). But it will serve our purposes.

In the second place, formally valid arguments contrast with arguments whose validity depends essentially on a context of application. Thus 'That is a man; so that is a man or a woman' – or 'I am tired and hungry; so I am hungry – are valid – but only in a 'context' (context of application) in which the two occurrences of 'that' pick out the same object (or the two occurrences of 'I' and present tense pick out the same person and time). These cases could perhaps be assimilated to cases in which validity depends on the 'meaning' of the non-logical term 'that' ('I', 'am') – but only at the prohibitive cost of assimilating contextual reference to lexical meaning.

There are trivializations of this second boundary condition on formal validity. For example, since all formally valid arguments, construed as sequences of sentences, depend for their validity on some context – say, a broad linguistic context – in which at least some of their expressions receive their 'intended' interpretations, it might be held that there are no formally valid arguments, or that there is no genuine contrast between formal and context-dependent validity.

The attempted trivialization depends on running together two notions of context. There is what one might call the *context of interpretation*, the environment that one investigates in order to determine the grammar and lexical meaning of the expressions of a language. No expressions have meaning apart from a context in which they are related to various entities that they represent, to action, and to various other expressions. By varying the context of interpretation one may, trivially, vary the meaning of expressions. So any argument can be trivially rendered invalid if the context of interpretation is allowed to vary between premises and conclusion. Saying that the context of interpretation is to be held fixed may be seen as a way of enforcing the requirement that one avoid the fallacy of equivocation.

Even after a context of interpretation is fixed, thereby fixing the lexical interpretations of linguistic expressions, one has not yet fixed what one might call the *context of application*. Such contexts are more or less local and short-lived circumstances in which an expression is actually uttered or otherwise used. Even given a fixed lexical interpretation (or set of interpretations for ambiguous expressions), the references of indexical expressions vary with contexts of application. And lacking a specific context of application, indexical expressions lack reference, though they do not lack lexical meaning. Arriving at a precise theoretical meaning for 'context of application' is a delicate matter that we need not pursue. Our purposes are served by the obvious point that the form and lexical meaning or interpretation of both indexicals and demonstratives do not suffice to fix their referents. Hence they do not suffice to explicate intuitions regarding the validity of arguments involving such expressions.

The notions of context interpretation and context of application must each be distinguished from the notion of a *context of evaluation*. These are possibly counterfactual circumstances (or circumstance-descriptions) by reference to which necessity or validity may be evaluated. Arguments are evaluated for validity by varying the context of evaluation. Formally valid arguments do not depend for their validity on fixing a context of application, though arguments involving 'context-dependent' devices do. Argument itself depends on fixing a context of interpretation, on avoiding equivocation.

Serious questions do indeed attend attempts to explicate in depth the contrast between the notions of context of interpretation and context of application. In particular, there are issues about the levels of idealization from contexts of application that are appropriate in arriving at a lexical and grammatical interpretation of linguistic expressions: What aspects of an individual and his environment enter into fixing an interpretation? How do these aspects relate to actual momentary uses?

For all the difficulty of these questions there remains an important distinction between formal validity and validity that depends on a particular context of application. The project of formal logic and that of providing logical forms for informal discourse are based on distinguishing form from immediate context as well as from non-logical meaning or interpretation. These projects table the large philosophical questions about the relation between interpretation and application, and isolate forms for their purposes that they presume are invariant across at least some particular, immediate contexts of application. This presumption has been vindicated many times over by the success and fruitfulness of logic, pure and applied.

To do and apply formal logic, then, we have to isolate forms that we can presume remain the *same* through the duration of an argument. Or on a nominalistic logical theory, we have to give proof-theoretic and semantic principles that hold for all 'replicas' of given tokens through the duration of arguments. Such forms are given constant meanings or interpretations. We can ignore *how* 'context-free' these meanings or interpretations of constants are – presuming only that variation of interpretation and form with contexts of application is not the norm. Forms are *individuated* partly with an eye to providing for stability of interpretation.

Demonstratives and indexicals are expressions whose interpretations do normally vary with particular, momentary contexts. A logic that operates on discourse that contains such expressions cannot be purely formal. It must relativize its principles to contexts of application.

All of this is background for our third problem for Davidson's theory. The problem is that the theory fails to capture the obvious formal validity of various arguments. I will raise the problem in two stages: the theory fails to capture the formal character of certain validities; it also fails to capture the validity of certain validities.

To begin with, take the argument by repetition: 'Galileo said that the earth moves; so Galileo said that the earth moves.' It is, I think, obvious that this argument, and infinitely more arguments in indirect discourse like it, are valid. Moreover, they are formally valid if any arguments at all are.

Davidson's representation of the argument is

(D) Galileo said that. The earth moves.
     So Galileo said that. The earth moves.

Each occurrence of 'that' picks out a different utterance: the utterance that follows it. I shall assume that the sentence tokens produced by the utterances are replicas of one another and that there is no equivocation in interpretation between them. Both utterances make the reporter and Galileo, samesayers.

On Davidson's account, the argument does not come out formally valid. This point holds even if one explicates the notion of formal validity within a generally nominalistic account of truth bearers. To give the semantics of Davidson's representation, we must explain what the two occurrences of 'that' refer to in their respective contexts of application. For insofar as 'that' is a demonstrative, its referents *ipso facto* depend on the particular contexts of its application, not purely on its form and lexical interpretation. So in explicating the argument, there must be a further story relating the different utterances of premise and conclusion – over and above the story that insures that they have the same form and that their lexical interpretation has not shifted. To explain the validity one would have to enter further premises about the relation between the two occurrences of the supposed demonstrative 'that', or an extra premise about its referents. In sum, the argument can never, on Davidson's theory, be treated as an instance of 'p; so p'. This is a problem because there is no intuitive basis for thinking that such a further story need be told.

The same problem can be developed from another perspective. Let us lay aside for the moment complexities introduced by indexicals or demonstratives within sentential clauses following 'says that'. So we concentrate on sentences, like, 'Galileo said (tense ignored) that $2 \times 2 = 4$'. As long as the lexical interpretation of the sentence following 'that' remains unchanged (as long as utterances of the sentence samesay one another), one can shift utterances and tokens of that sentence *ad libitum* without discernibly affecting the truth conditions, logical potential, or meaning of the indirect discourse. So claiming that the noun phrases following 'says' refer to particular tokens, in these cases, does no work. And it undermines, or at least pointlessly complicates, an account of the form and validity of relevant arguments containing indirect discourse sentences.

This reasoning suggests two conclusions: first, the specification of the referents of noun phrases following indirect discourse verbs does not depend on a context of application but only on a context of interpretation. So those referents are not picked out by a demonstrative. Moreover, since the referents of such noun phrases do not normally vary with contexts of application, either they are constant, concrete paradigms or (more plausibly, I think) they are abstract. The referents of such noun phrases can be specified formally – by fixing the form (and lexical interpretation) of the sentence following 'that' – and independently of the particular context of utterance. Since we *can* specify the referents formally, we should. For if we do not, we cannot explain arguments by repetition in indirect discourse by appeal to their logical form. Since such arguments' validity is clearly formal (by the reasoning of the preceding paragraph) we should explain it by formal means.[10]

Davidson's theory is subject to a further, more powerful and more simply stated objection. The theory not only fails to represent the formal character of valid arguments in indirect direct discourse. It fails to account for their validity.

To see this, note that the utterances referred to in the premise and conclusion of argument (D) are different events. Call the first event 'Alpha' and the second, 'Beta'. The truth of premise and conclusion is explained in terms of the referents or extensions of their parts. Suppose now that the premise of (D), explained according to Davidson's theory, is true. The conclusion we suppose is also true. But can we conceive of a possible circumstance (a context of evaluation) in which the premise is true and the conclusion is simultaneously not true? Clearly we can. We need only conceive, counterfactually, Alpha to exist while Beta does not. Since Alpha and Beta are, on Davidson's theory, individual concrete events, there is no necessity that they co-occur. In such a case the premise of (D) would be true, while the conclusion would be either false or without truth value. Thus the argument on Davidson's interpretation is not valid. But the English argument to be interpreted is valid.

As indicated earlier, the counterexample is compatible with assuming that Alpha and Beta samesay one another (or make their utterers samesayers). Depending on the metaphysics of utterances, there may be further counterexamples. For example, if it is not *necessary* that where they both exist, Alpha and Beta samesay one another, then there will be countermodels for (D) even where Alpha and Beta both exist. The countermodel of the preceding paragraph does not, however, depend on metaphysical delicacies. There is simply no ground for thinking that the two individual, dated, concrete utterances logically (or even 'metaphysically') must co-occur.[11]

---

[10] In the previous paragraph we laid aside cases where indexicals or demonstratives occur in sentences following 'says that'. When they do occur, the particular utterance of the reporter does, or at least may, matter to an account of truth conditions or logical form. Does this fact help Davidson's account? I do not think so. The semantic behavior of demonstratives in that-clauses is recognizably different from that of other expressions. They do not motivate the linguistic problems that make non-extensional contexts difficult and interesting. On any account their role in non-extensional discourse must be treated differently from that of expressions that resist surface substitutivity. Proper treatment of this matter would require a positive theory. The main features of such a theory are explained in my 'Belief De Re', *The Journal of Philosophy*, 74 (1977), pp. 338–62; and 'Russell's Problem and Intentional Identity', in *Agent, Language, and the Structure of the World*, ed. Tomberlin (Hackett Publishing Co., Indianapolis, 1983).

[11] In conversation David Kaplan pointed out that on certain views about the necessity of origin, it is necessary that a given father exist if his son does. But, as Kaplan also noted, almost no one would hold that the son must exist if the father does. An analogous claim that Alpha and Beta must both exist if Alpha does would be even more outlandish because there *need be no causal relations between utterances among which valid implications hold*. This latter point tells against revisions of Davidson's theory which would take the second 'that' in arguments by repetition to refer anaphorically back to the first.

Thus Davidson's theory fails to account for the validity of arguments by repetition in indirect discourse. Clearly, if the validity of such arguments cannot be accounted for, the theory can represent as valid no valid arguments that essentially involve more than one occurrence of a that-clause. I think that this consequence is unacceptable.

I have ignored the option of denying that arguments by repetition in indirect discourse are valid. This is the sort of move that someone with primarily ontological motivations might make. I take it that the deductive implication is intuitively obvious, and that ontological theory should serve such cognitive practices as intuitively valid inferences, rather than vice-versa. Denying the argument's validity would be reminiscent of earlier attempts to obscure structure to save ontological doctrine – for example, the orthographic accident theory of the structure of belief sentences, which Davidson has ably criticized.

The argument in this section has rested on claims about what a theory of logical form for natural discourse should capture, and how. I am aware that there are those, for example in the Wittgensteinean diaspora, who have maintained that such a theory is pointless or impossible: formal studies of language are said to be worthless; only radically 'context-dependent' explications of semantical intuitions are supposed viable; or only global theories of what meaning, interpretation, or understanding 'consists in' are of interest. I shall not discuss this recrudescence in detail here. The view seems to me to depend on ignorance of linguistics and its use of work on logical form. Still, some very general remarks are perhaps apropos.

Radical anti-formalist positions, to the effect that judgments about validity and other semantical features can never be adequately captured by appeal to formal structures, often stem from reaction against the traditional tendency among logicians to underestimate the prevalence of such context-dependent or 'messy' phenomena as indexicality, vagueness, presupposition, implicature, metaphor, irony, malapropism, differences of idiolect or dialect, and so on. There is, however, a gulf between recognizing the complexities that these phenomena force upon theories of language and embracing the anti-formalist position. Numerous validity judgments that are widely shared generalize across arguments (and argument tokens). Many such generalizations parallel the recursive aspects of language mastery. To try to account for such phenomena 'contextually' or piecemeal (or to ignore them) would be to lose the strongest theoretical grip we now have on the semantical – and indeed, the pragmatic – aspects of language use. Worse, it flies in the face of well-established facts about grammar and its relation to logical consequence.

Theories of logical form depend on assuming some conception of form that generalizes, or idealizes, beyond particular momentary contexts of application. But as I suggested earlier in this section, they are compatible with numerous options regarding how the resulting structures depend on, and how they are to be attached to, contexts of application.

Often anti-formalist positions arise out of preoccupation with philosophical problems about semantical content or about what exactly theories of logical form are doing. The problems are genuine. Again, however, there is a gulf between recognizing them, or even being sceptical about their solvability, and the anti-formalist view.

Theories of logical form are compatible with a variety of philosophical views about what goes into interpreting a person's sentences, about the relation between a person's understanding and the forms of his or her sentences, and about what goes into interpreting those sentences. Considerable agreement on appropriate forms is compatible with unclarity or disagreement about the relationship between those forms and minds or behavior.

Here as elsewhere, success in a cognitive practice does not presuppose success in answering philosophical questions about it. Sometimes the philosophical issues persist; sometimes they dissolve or lose interest; sometimes some semblance of agreement is attained regarding them. Though often inseminated by philosophical questions, cognitive practices usually mature without depending on answers to them. Anti-formalist views are in the unenviable position of comprehensively denying, on 'philosophical' grounds, the viability of a cognitive practice, pursued by linguists, logicians and philosophers, that has already taken root.

V Fregean vs. Russellian approaches to 'intensional' contexts

We began by contrasting Fregean and Russellian strategies for explicating 'intensional' contexts. The Russellian strategy denies natural assumptions about grammar. The Fregean strategy denies common assumptions about the semantical values of sentential parts. Davidson offers one consideration against the general Fregean strategy. (I pass over specific arguments against specific versions of the strategy.) It is a consideration that has deflected many. Davidson writes:

> Since Frege, philosophers have become hardened to the idea that content-sentences in talk about propositional attitudes may strangely refer to such entities as intensions, propositions, sentences, utterances, and inscriptions. What is strange is not the entities, which are all right in their place (if they have one), but the notion that ordinary words for planets, people, tables and hippopotami in indirect discourse may give up these pedestrian references for the exotica. If we could recover our pre-Fregean semantic innocence, I think it would seem to us plainly incredible that the words 'The earth moves', uttered after the words 'Galileo said that,' mean anything different, or refer to anything else, than is their wont when they come in other environments. No doubt their role in *oratio obliqua* is in some sense special; but that is another story. Language is the instrument it is because the same expression, with semantic features (meaning) unchanged, can serve countless purposes. (pp. 144–5)

Despite the wisdom expressed in its last sentence, I think that this passage encourages a common misconstrual of Frege's view based on too narrow a reading of his text. The reading is partly fostered in English speaking philosophy by too unqualified a translation of 'Bedeutung' as 'reference', and by the common (mis)construal of 'Sinn' as linguistic meaning.[12]

---

[12] Cf. my 'Frege on Extensions of Concepts, from 1884 to 1903', *The Philosophical Review*, 93 (1984), pp. 3–34, sections I and VI; 'Frege on Truth', in *Frege Synthesized*, Hintikka and Taiminea (eds) forthcoming.

Frege's strategy assigns semantical values to expressions in 'non-extensional' contexts that differ from their semantical values in other contexts. But there is no special need to think of the semantical values of terms in non-extensional contexts as their 'referents'. Nor can they be identified with meaning in the ordinary, intuitive sense of the word. There is a function from the semantical values of expressions in non-extensional contexts to their semantical values in ordinary contexts. These latter are plausibly identified with the expressions' referents. So, in Frege's theory, semantical values in non-extensional contexts uniquely fix referents. There is no reason why the Fregean strategy cannot grant, to anyone who insists on it, the intuition that terms in non-extensional occurrences retain their customary referents. What it must hold is that in such occurrences such referents do not enter into the computation of the truth values of the larger sentences. I think it unreasonable for anyone to have or rely on strong intuitions regarding this latter claim. It is a theoretical claim whose relation to intuition is quite indirect.

Bedeutungen of expressions other than independent sentences in Frege's theory are semantical values that are assigned in accord with the principle that a sentence's truth value is a function of the values of its parts. The *Bedeutungen* of singular terms in extensional contexts are referents. But it has been unfruitful in interpreting Frege to think of the *Bedeutungen* of sentences, expressions in non-extensional contexts, and even functional expressions, as 'referents'. The point of this remark is not to suggest that such *Bedeutungen* are ontologically neutral. The notion of *Bedeutung*, like that of semantical value, is a theoretical extension of the notion of reference. The point is rather that these notions are more theoretical than that of reference. There are solid theoretical reasons to think that the semantical values of terms in non-extensional contexts differ from those in extensional contexts. I think that intuitions about the reference of terms are of severely limited import to this issue.

This claim is associated with a methodological view about the status of various intuitive judgments in a theory of logical form. The basic evidence for such a theory (and for a theory of truth) derives from reflective judgments regarding the truth or falsity of sentences (or propositions) and the validity of arguments; from judgments about the reference of certain singular terms in certain unproblematic, extensional contexts; and from reflective judgments about the logically relevant grammatical structures of sentences. Perhaps needless to say, all evidence from these sources is defeasible and subject to theoretical reflection. But these sources yield agreement. Both our intuitive judgments on these matters and our theoretical understanding regarding the logically relevant grammar of sentences are more reliable and more definite than our intuitive judgments or theoretical understanding concerning the semantical values of sentential parts, with the exception of demonstratives and certain other singular terms in unproblematic extensional contexts. I think that this point is borne out by comparing the amount of agreement and knowledge there is regarding syntactical categories (in logic and linguistics) with that regarding the semantical values of non-sentential expressions (other than certain acknowledged singular terms, prototypically names and demonstratives). The point favors Frege's strategy for dealing with non-extensional contexts, though not necessarily his particular hypotheses, over Russell's. Frege's strategy builds from intuitive and theoretical strength.

The value of Davidson's theory, in my view, lies not merely in its challenges to the unpersuaded. It also lies in its shift of perspective. The theory takes over from Quine, and extends much further, the perspective on propositional attitudes that emphasizes interpretation. While I believe that this perspective has its pitfalls, it is several steps beyond traditional discussions that glibly appealed to metaphors of grasping propositions that are expressed by sentences. It has facilitated identification of philosophical problems about understanding and expression that underlie semantical theories of non-extensional contexts.

Part IV
Radical Interpretations

11

Translation Theories and the Decipherment of Linear B

JOHN WALLACE

> Signs are small measurable things, but interpretations are illimitable.
> *George Eliot*

In this paper I approach theories of radical translation from two directions. First, I formulate two questions which are more general than those to which theories of radical translation are explicitly addressed, but which can be seen as motivating the theories. Second, I test theories of radical translation against the decipherment of Linear B.

I *Motivation and theories*

The two leading questions in the drama of ideas I am sketching concern a Distinction and a Danger. First, the distinction. There is a persistent vision, shared by philosophers, psychologists, and ordinary mortals, of our conceptual scheme as divided into two interlocking parts. One part is basic and covers everything; everything can be described in its terms; it is the physical part of our conceptual scheme, our system of physical concepts. The other part of our conceptual scheme is our system of semantic, psychological, moral, aesthetic, and social concepts. For brevity, let us call it the mental system. The mental system sits on top of, is supervenient on, the physical system. Some but not all things which can be described in the physical system can be described again, redescribed, in the mental system.[1]

The question to which this picture gives rise has two parts: (1) how may the boundary between the two systems be clearly and explicitly drawn? and (2) how are the two systems related to each other?

---

[1] Bernard Williams has dubbed this picture of the place of the mind in nature 'attributive (as opposed to substantial) dualism'. See his *Descartes: The Project of Pure Enquiry* (Penguin, New York, 1978), p. 293.

Next, the danger. As students of and actors on the human scene, we have an interest in understanding, describing, and appraising other persons, their experiences, actions, institutions, works of art, and cultures. This interest meets obstacles, one of the most perplexing of which is the danger of projecting onto others our own patterns of thought and action, our own wishes, interests, and plans, our own standards, criteria, ideals, categories, concepts, and forms of life. In concrete cases the error of illegitimate projection is no doubt more often alleged than proved, but it is proved often enough to make us certain that our present sense of others is wrong at many as yet unsuspected points. The history of historical scholarship and of anthropology provides many examples of error due to projection. I will give just one example, from a different area. The following is taken from a recent book on aphasia:

> Historical case material is invaluable for extending one's frame of reference in regard to aphasia. It is, however, necessary to view reported judgments with considerable skepticism. For example, the report, 'He understood everything that was said', occurred again and again in the protocols. Somehow or other, this is something people always say about aphasic patients, particularly when they have no speech. It is said, again and again, about patients who cannot follow directions as simple as 'Put the spoon in the cup'. Perhaps the patient picked up the spoon and looked questioningly at the examiner, not knowing what to do next; perhaps he picked up the cup; perhaps he touched a pencil and a key, uncertainly.
>
> Patients with little or no speech are usually highly motivated to communicate and to perform well. They frequently respond appropriately by making maximal use of visual cues, situational cues, and occasional words they grasp. They observe the social amenities, smile, and appear responsive when spoken to. Since they have little or no speech, they tend not to give themselves away when they misunderstand, as hard-of-hearing individuals frequently do. Sometimes when the patient makes an obvious error, the speaking person ascribes it to his own difficulty communicating with the aphasic patient. This is a very curious phenomenon.[2]

The question to which examples of this kind give rise is simply: how can we guard against and overcome the danger of projection?

With the distinction between the mental and the physical, and the problem of projection, on stage, enter radical translation. The philosophy of radical translation in effect identifies the problem of projection with the problem of distinguishing and connecting the mental and physical systems, or as one might say, it plays one problem off against the other and offers a simultaneous solution to both. The basic strategy might be called the ethnographical method. We are to imagine ourselves anthropologists arriving to study an isolated and hitherto unstudied culture with a hitherto untranslated language. At home, of course, we are linguistic and conceptual adults, fully competent in the application of all parts of the home conceptual scheme. But when we disembark on the foreign shore, we are in *some* respects babes in the woods. In the new situation part of our already acquired conceptual scheme is immediately applicable without fear

---

[2] James J. Jenkins, Edward Jiménez-Pabón, Robert E. Shaw, and Joyce Williams Sefer, *Schuell's Aphasia in Adults* (Harper and Row, New York, 1975).

of falsification or distortion: the physical part. Application of the other part, the mental system, is not immediate, but has to be worked out. In working out the application of mental concepts what we have to go on are descriptions in physical terms of the environment and of the behavior of the inhabitants. The connection between the two systems is that of data to theory, and the problem of articulating the connection between the systems becomes one of spelling out how, in this case, data supports theory. Notice what has become of the problem of projection. We have marked off – at least, the strategy is to mark off – an area of description of human beings which (i) is immune to the danger of projection and (ii) provides an evidential basis for application of descriptions from our remaining, projection-prone, stock. The pressure and temptations, whatever they may be, which lead us to project are now concentrated – forced to express themselves – in the move from evidencing descriptions to theoretical descriptions. If the move from evidence to theory is opened to inspection and analysis in the right way, our worries about projection will be laid to rest.

To sum up, the ethnographical method suggests and makes plausible the following identifications;

> physical descriptions = descriptions immune to projection
> mental descriptions = descriptions which are projection-prone

And it suggests and makes plausible also the idea that the common solution to the problem of how the mental is related to the physical and to the problem of removing the danger of projection will be a spelling out of how mental descriptions, as theory, rest on physical descriptions, as data.

Starting with the ethnographical outlook, we have arrived at a certain project of articulating how theory fits data. Other starting points can lead to the same place. An ethnological viewpoint, for example, might lead one to seek light on human behavior by comparing human behavior with that of other animal species. One would then need a system of description that suits both human and non-human behavior, and does not anthropomorphize the behavior of the non-humans. Tinbergen has in fact taken up a position like this. He writes:

By far the most serious obstacle in behaviour comparison is the fact that we describe and interpret our own behaviour in terms quite different from those we use to describe animal behaviour. We describe human behaviour really in three kinds of terms:

(1) We may really describe what movements a man makes. This is what we do (though in a superficial way) when we say, e.g. 'He ran as fast as he could'; 'She smiled at him'.
(2) We often describe, not movements, but a subjective experience: 'He became very angry'; 'He fell in love'.
(3) We also describe behaviour in terms of effects of movements: 'He ran for cover'; 'His overriding aim was to silence opposition'. As a rule we even mix these types of descriptions ('She irritated him by smiling indulgently'), and one of our difficult tasks is to extract from such statements the objective, descriptive part which refers to observed movements and distinguish them from interpretation of function or subjective phenomena.

Now when we describe animal behaviour, we try to use exclusively the first method, that of describing actually observed movements. This is because whatever subjective experiences animals have (and even though most of us *believe* they must have them) we have no scientific means of deciding whether or not they experience them. Nor do we know to what extent the future effect of an animal's behaviour really controls at any given moment what it is going to do.

If we want to compare human and animal behaviour, the first thing we have to agree on is the use of a common language. But, as I said, we are used to describing human behaviour in a mixture of terms, some objectively descriptive, some relating to subjective experiences, others again relating to the 'aim', the effects of our behaviour. This discrepancy of method, the use of entirely different languages in descriptions of human and of animal behaviour, is really at the root of our lack of comparative knowledge.[3]

The 'common language' which would fulfil Tinbergen's requirements will presumably be close to, if not identical to the system of physical descriptions at which we have already arrived by another route.

To take up yet another starting point, consider Miss Anscombe's idea of some facts being 'brute' relative to others. Her examples are:

The facts that (i) I asked you for a quarter of potatoes, (ii) you delivered them, and (iii) you sent me a bill are brute relative to: I owe you so much for the potatoes.

The facts that (i) you carted a quarter of potatoes to my house and (ii) left them there are brute relative to: you supplied me with a quarter of potatoes.

The fact that X owes Y money is brute relative to: X is solvent.[4] Now one might look for a level of brutest facts, facts relative to which no facts are brute, and then ask how all other facts rest on this foundation of brutest facts. Miss Anscombe does not herself take this step indeed, it is pretty clear that she would think the project hopeless. Nevertheless, it is a project which is suggested by the 'brute-relative-to' relation, and it seems likely that it would be close to the project to which we have been led by the ethnographical and ethnological outlooks.

Our system of mental concepts and mental descriptions, as we have so far roughly marked it off, is very extensive. The following, for example, are all mental descriptions.

Greta is angry.
Daniel is proud.
William believes that pigs can be trained to jog.
Gwendolen voted for Nixon.
'red' denotes the class of red things.
Millet's 'Gleaners' is sentimental.

---

[3] Niko Tinbergen, 'The Search for Animal Roots of Human Behaviour,' in *The Animal in Its World* (Harvard University Press, Cambridge, Mass., 1972), p. 164.

[4] G. E. M. Anscombe, 'On Brute Facts', *Analysis*, 19 (1958–9), pp. 69–72.

Less than half of those eligible to vote voted in the last election.
'snow is white' means in English that snow is white.
'Der Schnee ist weiss' translates from German to English as 'snow is white'.

The system is so large and various that one hardly knows where to begin in sorting out how it is based on the physical data. Here again the ethnographical method makes an important contribution, for it makes it plausible that the central concepts in the mental scheme, the ones to be fitted first to the physical data, are ones that equate foreign sentences in meaning with our sentences: concepts of sentence meaning and translation.

An important and relatively clear case is the way in which the notion of sentence meaning bridges the gap between so-called (and relatively physical) sentential attitudes – e.g. Hans believes-true 'der Schnee ist weiss' – and the (definitely mental) propositional attitudes – e.g., Hans believes that snow is white. The paradigm here is the relation between direct discourse and indirect discourse spelled out in the formula:

Smith said that p if and only if (i) Smith said 'S' and (ii) 'S' means in Smith's language that p.

Exactly parallel formulas, with clause (ii), in which the notion of meaning figures, remaining constant, connect propositional attitudes with the corresponding sentential attitudes. Note that this formula requires adjustment when S contains indicator words and tense.

Descriptions of people's emotions, dispositions, traits of character, and intentional actions, and descriptions of their works of art and cultural institutions are not tied to the meanings of their sentences in such a neat way as the propositional attitudes. But if we imagine what it would be like to be in the shoes of the freshly disembarked anthropologist, it is plausible enough that the interpretation of speech and the ascription of propositional attitudes are a natural entering wedge, and a necessary foundation for application of the rest of the mental scheme.

It should be noted that translation and sentence-meaning are different ideas. Between

'Der Schnee ist weiss' translates from German to English as 'snow is white'

and

'Der Schnee ist weiss' means in German that snow is white

there is, on the right side, a one step difference in use-mention level. For certain issues and purposes this difference is crucial. But for present purposes the similarity between the concepts, that they both, as we may roughly say, correlate sentences of two languages which are alike in meaning, is all that matters. I will be discussing simultaneously Davidson's theory of radical interpretation, which has sentence meaning as its central notion, and Quine's theory of radical translation. For simplicity I will follow Quine and speak of translation.

Thus translation emerges as a key concept connecting the physical and mental systems. It is a mental concept on which the anthropologist in the field may focus in making the transition from application of just the physical system to the environment and the behavior of the human beings we find, to application of both systems. What we want then is an account, a theory, of radical translation. The theories advanced by Quine and Davidson are divided into three parts, which answer three basic questions:

(1) What is the evidence on which translation is based?
(2) How is the evidence marshalled? That is, what are the principles for sifting and sorting the evidence so that it speaks for or against competing schemes of translation?
(3) What is the evidence marshalled for? That is, in what form are translations stated?

Let us quickly review the answers Quine and Davidson give to these questions, taking them up in the order (3), (1), (2).[5]

About the answer to the third question there is essential agreement: translation takes the form of a translation manual, a recursively established correlation between the sentences of foreign language and the sentences of the ethnographer's language. Thus a particular output of the manual for German would be:

> 'Der Schnee ist weiss' translates from German to English as 'snow is white'

Actually, the output of a recursive scheme of correlation would most likely be, not the displayed sentence, but one of the same general form which uses structural-descriptive names, not quotation mark names, of the sentences.

Turning to question (1), Quine and Davidson give us the hang of what is included in the physical scheme, that is, of the evidence the radical translator has to go on, more by example than by precept. The basic idea seems to be that if a description of the inhabitants of their environment does not state, or imply, or presuppose anything about how the inhabitants think of or conceptualize their environment, then it is a physical description; otherwise it falls in the mental system. The physical are the descriptions we could confidently apply immediately on arriving at the site, or are somehow directly based on such immediately accessible descriptions. As paradigm cases, descriptions of the colors and shapes of naturally occurring objects, and descriptions of the electrical activities in human nervous systems, are physical. Descriptions of

---

[5] The main sources for the summaries I am about to give are: W. V. Quine, *Word and Object* (MIT Press, Cambridge, Mass., 1960), chapter two; Donald Davidson, 'Radical Interpretation', *Dialectica*, 27 (1973), pp. 313–28, and 'Belief and the Basis of Meaning,' *Synthese*, 27 (1974), pp. 309–23, and 'Psychology as Philosophy', in S. C. Brown, ed., *Philosophy of Psychology* (Barnes and Noble, New York, 1974), pp. 41–52.

what sentences mean or of how they are to be translated, descriptions in indirect discourse of what someone has said, and descriptions of persons' propositional attitudes (e.g. believing and wanting) are in the other camp. Important kinds of descriptions with respect to whose status the criterion is ambiguous or indecisive, but on which Quine and Davidson take an explicit stand are: (a) causal descriptions in the indicative mood, where the events are alleged to be causally connected are physically described, are physical; (b) descriptions ascribing dispositions to respond in certain physical ways to certain physical inputs are physical; (c) the predicate 'x is a sentence' (in a more refined exposition this might turn into 'x is a sentence in the language of speaker y') is physical; (d) direct discourse descriptions of what a person says, e.g., 'person z uttered sentence x', 'person z assented to sentence x', and sentential attitudes, i.e., direct discourse reflections of propositional attitudes, e.g., 'sentence x expresses a belief of person z in z's language', are physical; for Quine, but not for Davidson, the predicate 'person y and person z speak the same language' is physical.

In order to give ourselves a first-hand sense of how this distinction works, let us consider one of Wittgenstein's descriptions of a language game. Wittgenstein's description, with inessential modifications, runs as follows:

> A man goes shopping and takes a slip marked 'five red apples' to the shopkeeper, who opens the drawer marked 'apples', then he looks up the word 'red' in a table and finds a color sample opposite it; then he says the series of cardinal numbers – I assume he knows them by heart – up to the word 'five' and for each number he takes an apple of the same color as the sample out of the drawer.[6]

Observing this scene as radical translators, there is much that Wittgenstein puts into his description that we could not see. Some of Wittgenstein's words – 'goes shopping', 'shopkeeper' – imply or presuppose a form of economic organization which is familiar to us but which may not be shared by, and which we therefore cannot immediately identify in, the foreign culture. A marked slip of paper, a table correlating words and colors, and even a drawer, are artifacts which are what they are only as parts of a network of purposes and practices which we cannot take for granted and cannot immediately observe. To identify a series of words as the first five numerals is, of course, tantamount to translating them. With these points in mind we might put together a cleaned-up description of the scene along the following lines:

> A man walks along with a piece of paper bearing the inscription 'zipplety dipplety den'. He meets another man inside a building which contains a lot of commodities. The first man holds out the piece of paper and the second man takes it. The second man then pulls out an open-topped wooden box bearing the inscription 'den'. He surveys a piece of paper on which there is a column of colored patches beside a column of inscriptions. He focuses his attention on the patch next to the inscription 'dipplety'. Next he utters the series of sounds, 'ace', 'mia', 'hen', 'dio', 'zipplety'. For each of these utterances he takes out of the open-topped box an apple of the same color as the patch on which he had focused his attention.

---

6 Ludwig Wittgenstein, *Philosophical Investigations* (Macmillan, New York, 1953), pp. 2–3.

Even this is almost certainly over-rich. It exceeds the boundaries of the physical, perhaps in several ways, but at least in describing the second man as focusing his attention on a certain colored patch. Still, I hope it serves to give a sense of the kind of degradation or washing-out of the mental that purely physical description involves. If the washing-out does not, in this example, go far enough, at least it goes in the right direction. Notice that is easier to go from Wittgenstein's description to the more nearly physical description, than it is to reverse the process.

Let us now turn to the remaining question which a theory of radical translation answers: how is the evidence marshalled?

Davidson's rule for using the evidence is simple: translate so as to maximize the foreigners' agreement with us. As an illustration of how this works, suppose the evidence is that 'blip' and 'blap' are sentences of the foreign language and that a certain foreigner, say Anderson, is such that

> A believes 'blip'
> A does not believe 'blap'.

Then Davidson's principle of charity tells us that, so far, a translation manual which establishes the correlations

> blip → grass is green
> blap → grass is black

is to be preferred to one which establishes the correlations

> blip → snow is black
> blap → grass is green.

Quine's rules for using the evidence are more elaborate and can only be sketched here. Quine is especially concerned with a certain province of physical descriptions, those which describe a speaker's dispositions to respond to an environment containing language. The situation treated as paradigm in Quine's exposition of his theory is one in which a speaker responds by assenting or dissenting to heard language while viewing a scene. He thinks he can reconstruct in the physical terms he allows himself the concept of an observation sentence: a sentence assent or dissent to which on the part of any speaker of the language depends only on past learning of the language and on present stimulation and on no other learning. The physicalistic reconstruction: all speakers of the language are prompted to assent to and to dissent from the sentence by the same patterns of stimulation. He requires that an adequate translation correlate with an observation sentence of the foreign language an observation sentence of the ethnographer's language which is keyed to the same range of stimulation. Quine also believes he can reconstruct meaning relations between sentences, e.g., that between 'Henry is a bachelor' and 'Henry is a male'; it is a matter solely of learning the language that if a speaker assents to the first he assents to the second. The physicalistic reconstruction of his relationship would be: every speaker of the language who assents to the first assents to the second. Quine's other main principle for using evidence is that meaning relationships of this sort be preserved by translation.

It is worth pointing out that while these two theories of translation are similar in motivation and in the broad outlines of their development, the differences between them which my rough summary brings out are not trivial, but imply diverging answers to an important traditional question: can any two languages be translated? Davidson's answer is yes, for we can always find a translation that maximizes agreement. Quine's answer is no; we have no guarantee that the observation sentences of one language will be keyed to the same ranges of stimulation as those in another. That is, the observation sentences of two languages may not match.

It is also illuminating to ask what, on the two accounts, could force us to revise a translation manual. On Quine's account revision could be forced only by a discovery (i) that an observation sentence was being translated by a non-observation sentence, or by an observation sentence keyed to a different range of stimulation or (ii) that one of the various meaning relationships was not being preserved by translation. Because observation sentences are few, these constraints are weak; if all the observation sentences of a language can be translated into those of another, and vice versa, it is likely that the two languages can be translated into each other in many different ways: this is Quine's thesis that translation is indeterminate. On Davidson's account, revision of an on-going translation scheme could be forced only by discovery of another scheme which placed translator and translatee in greater agreement. Here also indeterminacy is a serious possibility; if two investigators working independently come up with different translation manuals, it is possible that neither will be able to convince the other that his produces the greater overall agreement.

The problem of projection suffers curious fates at the hands of these theories. The problem, as traditionally described, is that we may misdescribe others through failure to appreciate the existence, or the implications, of ways in which their lives differ from ours. To this problem Quine brings a distinction, between observation sentences and behaviorally based meaning relations, aspects of language with respect to which there is, within the linguistic community, the requisite sort of uniformity of response to linguistic and extra-linguistic stimuli, and other sentences and aspects of language with reespect to which there is diversity. With respect to the one side of the division, no difference between ourselves and those whose language we translate into ours, beyond a purely notational difference of symbols used, is tolerable or intelligible; with respect to the other side of the division, any difference is tolerable. Thus, on this view, if a difference makes a difference, i.e., if it falls on the side where behavioral uniformity is required, it makes translation impossible.

The traditional way of thinking of projection, that grasping a fundamental difference between others and ourselves may be the key to understanding them, seems to go against the spirit of Davidson's theory. For it would seem that on that theory, one's first response to the appearance of a fundamental difference should be to go back to the drawing board, reinterpret the physical data so that the difference disappears. From Davidson's point of view, the problem of projection must be a matter of where to locate disagreement; it is compatible with the view that an interpretation that left a fundamental area of difference could nevertheless be overall the most economical, as compared with other interpretations, in positing disagreement. It can happen, that is, that a big difference, in a concentrated area, is the least difference overall; noticing that this is so could, in a particular case, be the key to constructing an adequate interpretation.

II *Linear B: a test case*

When Arthur Evans began to dig at Knossos in March, 1900, he was looking for writing, because he thought he would there be sifting the remains of a civilization contemporary with and related to that which Schliemann had uncovered at Mycenae and because he thought that a civilization so complex and highly developed could not function without written records: in a complex economy someone has to keep the books. He found what he was looking for in the form of inscribed clay tablets which were baked, and so preserved, in the fire that destroyed the palace in whose ruins they were found. The tablets are of two types, distinguished as Linear A and Linear B. We shall be concerned here only with Linear B. Other tablets of this type subsequently were found in similar circumstances at Knossos, Pylos, Mycenae, and Thebes, so that the total number of B tablets now recovered is of the order of 4,300.

The B tablets are written in a script which, at the time of their discovery, was unknown; i.e., the phonetic values of the signs were not known. It was unknown, also, what language the script was being used to write. These problems were solved in 1952 when Michael Ventris, building on results of and carrying further a strategy initiated by Alice Kober, deciphered the script as Greek.

It will be instructive for us to compare the philosophical theories of radical translation with some of the actual steps leading up to the decipherment. I describe these steps in terms and in a way that the decipherers use in their own accounts.

The tablets are inventories, accounts, or receipts. They record commodities, persons, or other items by means of ideograms, which are introduced by names, words, and sentences written phonetically, and followed by numerals or numerals together with signs from the system of weights and measures. Thus the basic entry on the tablets has the form: sequence of phonetic signs, space, ideogram, space, numeral (or numeral plus signs for weights and measures). The ideograms and the numerals were a crucial entering wedge in the interpretation of the documents. And at first blush the way in which they were used seems to lend support to both Quine's theory and Davidson's. Thus some of the ideograms are naturalistic and self-explanatory pictures; it is immediately obvious what they picture. It is taken for granted that the preceding word, phrase, or sentence names or describes an object or objects of the kind pictured. This evidently semantic information about the tablets is obtained prior to and independently of decipherment and puts important constraints on any decipherment that may be proposed. The source of this information is, at first sight at least, an almost perfect instance of Quine's view of how evidence works: the piece of language is keyed to something visual, the naturalistic ideogram.

What seems to be Davidson's principle of charity seems to enter in a transparent way in the interpretation of the numerical signs, which also preceded decipherment. The case is concisely and convincingly described by Miss Kober:

> Numerals are based on a decimal system. Units are represented by short vertical strokes, tens by short horizontal strokes, and hundreds by circles. A good many tablets contain a list of items, each followed by a number, and end with a sum. Several of these additions are complete, and confirm what has been said about the numerical system. ('The Minoan Scripts: Fact and Theory', *American Journal of Archaeology*, 52 (1948), p. 90.)

The conclusion that the system is decimal is supported by a further observation. As Evans put it, 'That we have to deal with a decimal system is clearly shown by the fact that the units are never more than nine in number, the same rule applying to the tens and hundreds' (*The Palace of Minos*, Volume IV: Part II (Macmillan, London, 1935), p. 691.) Actually, Evans' 'fact' is not a fact, but the exceptions are few and easily enough explained, so his observation stands as support for the conclusion that the system is decimal. Here the basic argument is: if we take the system to be anything but decimal, (almost) all their additions will be incorrect; if we take the system to be decimal, (almost) all their additions are correct; therefore, the system is decimal. Seemingly a perfect application of Davidson's principle of charity.

On further reflection, our initial impression that these two early steps in the decipherment, the role of the naturalistic ideograms and the interpretation of the numerals, support Quine's and Davidson's theories of translation evaporates. In the first place, though neither of them discusses pictures, it seems clear that for both of them a picture is as much a symbol as one of the phonetic signs. The possibility that any symbol should have a self-evident interpretation is ruled out by their theories. The scholars are here taking as evidence, immediately accessible evidence, what for the philosophers has to be theory, a semantical piece of the mental framework. This is a point to which we will return.

Nor was the way in which the numerals were interpreted really an instance of Davidson's principle of charity. The reason is this: if all we knew was that the inscriptions on the tablets were asserted by those who wrote them, or that the inscriptions expressed beliefs of the writers, then we would have no reason to think that the signs on the right end of the inscriptions are numerals. If they are merely asserted or believed, then they may be narratives in which numerals would not normally occur, they may be religious documents in which the recurrent circles, bars, and slashes represent ritual chants; they may be countless other things, we simply do not know.

Our evidence is coming to us in a kind of direct speech construction – so far the theories are right. But the construction is not '*x* assents to *S*' or '*x* asserts *S*' or '*S*' expresses a belief of *x*'. It is rather something like:

> it is recorded in the administrative records of the palace, either as part of an inventory or an account or a receipt INSCRIPTION.

And because of the placement in the inscription of ideograms, some of which have self-evident interpretations, this is immediately refined to:

> it is recorded in the administrative records of the palace, either as part of an inventory or an account or a receipt, that persons, animals, or commodities named or described INSCRIPTION and pictured IDEO-GRAM are present or were received or expended in INSCRIPTION amount or number.

I think it will be obvious that evidence cast in this form is incomparably more powerful as a basis for interpretation than evidence, if there ever is any, cast in the forms Quine and Davidson offer us. It allows us to use what we know about palaces and other central administrations; it allows us to use our sense of what it is going to be worthwhile to keep records of. It allows us to use archaeological evidence – about the size of the palace and the population, the range of the palace's control, the geography and the produce or likely produce of the surrounding territory– in ways we never could if the linguistic data presented itself in the washed-out form suggested by Quine and Davidson.

The point here is underlined by following up a bit on the interpretation of the numerals. Several tablets were found which evidently were lists and on which the entries take the form either of a single word followed by the ideogram for man and the numeral 1, or two words followed by the ideogram for man and the numeral 2. In every entry of the second type the second word ends a certain button-shaped or 'currant-bun' sign.[7] Given what we already know about ideograms and numerals, we see immediately that (a) these tablets are lists of men's names and (b) that the button sign is used with the meaning of an enclitic 'and'. Again, we are able to advance confidently in this way because lists are something we are not surprised to find in an archive of administrative records. If the tablets were a narrative we would be surprised. If they merely recorded someone's beliefs, we would not know what to think.

It is worth observing that though the evidence on which the interpretation of Linear B was based is commonly richer than the philosophical theories would lead us to expect, it is sometimes poorer. The theories assume, for example, that the distinction between noise and speech, or between writing and doodling is given as part of the evidence. But in at least one instance, it was an open question whether an inscription was writing or not. Chadwick gives this account:

> One of the superficially most promising attempts at reading a Minoan text as Greek was made in 1930 by the Swedish archaeologist Professor Axel Persson. Four years earlier an expedition under his direction had found in a late Mycenaean tomb at Asine, near Nauplia in the north-east of the Peloponnese, a

---

[7] One tablet of this general sort (not a perfect example, as the discussion in *Documents* brings out) is Au 102, discussed as tablet 46 in Michael Ventris and John Chadwick, *Documents in Mycenaean Greek*, 2nd ed. (Cambridge University Press, Cambridge, 1973). This tablet is discussed also in Michael Ventris, 'A Note on Decipherment Methods', *Antiquity*, 27 (1953), pp. 200–6, and in Leonard R. Palmer, *Mycenaeans and Minoans*, 2nd ed. (Faber and Faber, London, 1965), pp. 68–70. A photograph of this tablet appears as the frontispiece in *Documents*.

jar with what appears to be an inscription on the rim. He compared these signs with those of the classical Cypriot syllabary, and on this basis transcribed a few words. With one exception these looked little like Greek; but *po-se-i-ta-wo-no-se* was a plausible form, assuming the Cypriot spelling rules, for the Greek *Poseidāwōnos*, genitive of the name of the god Poseidon. Unfortunately, those expert in the Minoan scripts have been unable to share Persson's confidence in his identifications. The signs on the jar are quite unlike Linear B or any other known Bronze Age script, and it requires a good deal of imagination to see the resemblance to the classical Cypriot syllabary. In fact Ventris after a careful examination of the original came to the conclusion that the marks are not writing at all; they may be a kind of doodling, or possibly an attempt by an illiterate person to reproduce the appearance of writing. The lack of regularity and clear breaks between the signs is obvious, and at one end it tails off into a series of curves, which look more like a decorative pattern. It is interesting to observe that the form of the name read by Persson is now known to be wrong for the Mycenaean dialect.[8]

It is fair to conclude, I think, that the evidence in the Linear B case is not naturally taken to be of the sort our philosophical theories say it should be.

Since the evidence is not what the theories say it should be the ways in which the evidence is marshalled can hardly be what they say it should be, either. If we try to mimic Quine's account of observation sentences using instead of his notion of assent the direct speech construction that seems actually to be used in the Linear B case, we get nonsense. It seems to make sense to say that assent to some sentences is keyed directly to current stimulation. It does not make sense to say that readiness to make such-and-such a numeral a matter of palace record is keyed directly to present stimulation: it does not make sense, because it is obvious that considerable specialized training had to be given the clerks and administrators, and that their readiness to make an inscription depends on this training as much as on current stimulation. It does not help to try to cash 'directly keyed' in terms of unanimity in response among all speakers of the language; there is no reason to think that all speakers were trained to function as palace clerks or administrators. Among the clerks and administrators there *may* have been (it is extremely unlikely that there was) the sort of unanimity in dispositions to make palace records required by Quine's account of observation sentence – we are talking now about sentences which are observational *for* those clerks *relative* to the task of making palace records. But if there was such unanimity, it is nothing to us and gives us nothing that translation should preserve, for we are not trained as Mycenaean clerks or administrators. There may seem to be more hope for the idea of charity, understood as charity with respect to what is worth recording in a Bronze Age palace in Crete, etc., and not as charity with respect to what is believed. There are two points to be made about this. The first is that with the shift in frame from '*a* believes-true *S*' to '*a* makes an administrative record of *S*' there is an important shift in the meaning of charity. With 'believes-true' the injunction to maximize agreement has a clear sense; if *a* believes-true *S* and I believe-true the translation of *S*, or *a* does not believe-true *S* and I do not believe-true the translation of *S*, the translation

---

[8] John Chadwick, *The Decipherment of Linear B*, p. 30.

manual makes us agree at this point; otherwise it makes us disagree. But with 'makes an administrative record of', even if I happen to keep some administrative records, it is hardly a plus for a translation manual that it makes it out that the Mycenaean scribe and I keep essentially the same records. Rather, the relevant test is that the manual make it out that the Mycenaean scribe record what I *would* record if I were in his place; this is quite a different sense of agreement. In order to maximize agreement in this sense, I must first grasp what 'his place' is like; it is very doubtful that 'his place' can be given to me in purely physicalistic terms. The second point is that as one surveys a range of examples, and I will turn to more examples in a moment, what strikes one is the diversity of the insights and interpretive moves that cumulatively make it possible to read the tablets with understanding. The principle of charity is trying to make it out that all the successful interpretative moves are basically alike. Well, of course, in a sense they are all alike: each is a successful interpretive move, one of a large number which taken together render the tablets intelligible. But I doubt that the idea of charity is something we grasp or can apply in a way that is prior to or independent of this trivial common element.

I come now to the third and last question: in what form is the translation given? It may seem that the answer Quine and Davidson give, that translation is a recursive correlation of expressions with expressions, and ultimately of sentences with sentences, is obviously correct, even tautological. There may be a sense of 'translation' in which their answer is tautological and true. But if we mean by the form of the translation the form in which the meanings of the tablets is explained to us, their answer is wrong. The real explanations have the form of a translation in the Quine–Davidson sense plus a gloss. For example, the Mycenaeans measured their land by the amount of wheat that would be needed to sow it if it were planted in wheat (whether it actually was or not). As part of the treatment of tablets concerned with land ownership and land use we have this gloss:

> The relation between the amounts of grain recorded and the land held needs to be explained. The practice of measuring land by the quantity of seed needed to sow it is widespread, from ancient Babylonia down to modern Mediterranean countries. In the Aegean islands, it is still possible to hear of a vineyard described as 'two *pinakia*,' where the *pinaki* is a measure of volume. But the practical reason for the system has not yet been grasped. There is no absolute equivalent possible between seed-measurement and acreage, because the ratio of seed to superficial area will vary widely according to the kind of land. A steep, stony hillside will clearly grow less wheat acre for acre, than a rich, level plain. But if both are measured in terms of productivity, it is possible to equate holdings of different types. Presumably the average yield would be known, and the quantity of seed would be a fixed proportion of this. The system has the same advantages as the Persian measurement of distance by the *parasang*, or the modern Greek practice of specifying a journey as so many hours rather than kilometres, which can easily be meaningless in a very mountainous country. (*Documents*, pp. 445–6.)

This is a gloss on a tablet whose inscribed words mean, for example, Lugros, servant of the commander, holds a lease from the plot of Mologuros the shepherd: 12 liters wheat. (This is Ea782 from Pylos tablet *109* in *Documens*, p. 240). The scholars in this business never give the meaning of a tablet simply by a word for word translation; there is always a gloss. And when you think of it, in ordinary life there is almost always a gloss when we say what someone meant or said or thought.

It appears that on the most natural description of some steps in the decipherment of Linear B – the description the scholars involved in the decipherment would themselves give – we get answers to the questions: what is the evidence? How is the evidence marshalled? What is the outcome? that are radically different from those given by Quine's and Davidson's theories of translation. The evidence appears to be often richer, and sometimes poorer, the ways of marshalling the evidence appear to be more diverse, and the outcome appears to be more complex than the theories say they should be. Let us check these impressions by examining in more detail some of the steps in the decipherment.

It is important to emphasize here that a great deal was learned about the interpretation of the tablets before Ventris's assignment of phonetic values showed their language to be Greek. This early progress provided an important and, indeed, essential check on the Greek meanings that emerged with the assignment of phonetic values. These early stages, which most nearly approximate the situation of radical translation, are the source of most of the examples (all but the last) we now take up.

The words for 'boy' and 'girl'

A. E. Cowley noticed on a large tablet listing personnel thirty-seven entries of the form

> sequence of phonetic signs–WOMAN ideogram–Number–XY–Number

or

> sequence of phonetic signs–WOMAN ideogram–Number–XZ–Number

or

> sequence of phonetic signs–WOMAN ideogram–Number–XY–Number–XZ–Number

The particular meanings of the sequences of phonetic signs were not known, but were taken to indicate either village or occupation or destination of the personnel. The WOMAN ideogram is one of the self-evident ones. The numerical system had already been cracked. What about 'XY' and 'XZ'? Cowley inferred that they must mean 'boy' and 'girl'. In his words: 'I suggest that "X" is the ideogram for "child", and "Y" means "male", and "Z" means "female". But they may have syllabic values, as if κουροδ and κουρη.'[9] Notice that Cowley comes to a conclusion about the meanings of 'XY' and 'XZ' without settling the question whether they are words, or compound ideograms.

---

[9] A. E. Cowley, 'A Note on Minoan Writing,' in *Essays in Aegean Archaeology Presented to Sir Arthur Evans* (Oxford, 1927), pp. 5–7.

Also, though Cowley's conclusion that the two signs mean 'boy' and 'girl' is correct and seems well founded, this further guess about which means which, based on the similarity between the syllabic sign I am representing by 'Z' and the WOMAN ideogram, was wrong. It is worth noticing also that the form in which the data presents itself in this case, is more specific – 'it is a matter of palace record that such-and-such personnel ...' – and more highly articulated – two or three slots for numbers with intervening ideograms or descriptions – than the standard form for data I set out earlier. This is typical, especially in that, as interpretation proceeds, the contexts and purposes of the tablets become more specific. It will not escape philosophers that Cowley's reasoning, while plausible, is not deductively valid. Its plausibility seems to depend on the presupposition that if women workers are regularly recorded as accompanied by other persons, these are likely to be their children. This would perhaps not be compelling for a society of sponges or intelligent magnetic fields, but what we know about human beings gives it a certain plausibility.

Personal names

Early on, Ventris classified the sequences of phonetic signs appearing on the Pylos tablets into four groups: (a) personal names of men and women; (b) names of departments, institutions, or places; (c) names of trades and titles applied to men and women; (d) general vocabulary, including adjectives, verbs, etc. As for the evidence for the classification, it was done, as Ventris and Chadwick put it, 'purely on the basis of an exhaustive comparison' of the contexts in which the sequences of signs occur. For example, in the case of personal names, an important criterion was that the sequence of signs occur along with other such sequences on lists in which each sequence of phonetic signs is followed by the man or woman ideogram, which is in turn followed by the number *one*.[10] The possibility of this as a criterion for picking out personal names obviously depends on the prior interpretation of numerals and of the man and woman ideograms; its plausibility depends on the context: these are administrative records of some sort of centrally organized economic activity. If we had had the prior interpretations of numerals and ideograms, but only a weak context such as 'this is believed ...' we might have come up either with no interpretation, or with quite a different one e.g., that the sequences of phonetic signs are uniquely individuating descriptions, 'the first man born at sea', etc.

Inflection

Perhaps the most important step in the pre-decipherment stage of work on the tablets was the identification of inflection – important because it simultaneously placed deep and systematic constraints on phonetics and semantics. The

---

[10] See Michael Ventris and John Chadwick, *Documents in Mycenaean Greek*, 2nd ed., (Cambridge University Press, Cambridge, 1973), p. 18 and also their initial paper, 'Evidence for Greek Dialect in the Mycenaean Archives', *Journal of Hellenic Studies*, 73 (1953), pp. 84–103, esp. p. 93. See also Alice E. Kober, 'Inflection in Linear Class B,' *American Journal of Archaeology*, 50 (1946), pp. 268–76, esp. pp. 268–9.

approach to this problem, worked out by Alice E. Kober, involves an extremely ingenious and sophisticated use of the evidence. Kober's description of the basic idea runs as follows:

> Since a study of the kind here contemplated is almost unprecedented, it is necessary to set down the rules governing what will be considered admissible as evidence. Any facts mentioned which do not conform strictly to these rules must be considered supplementary, and under no circumstances as evidence on which further theorizing can be based.
>
> The rules are simple. It is obvious that, in any language written in an alphabet or syllabary, a certain number of words can be found that have many signs in common and still are not related – e.g., in English, the pairs 'heavy' and 'heaven'; 'berry' and 'merry' each have four signs in common. Yet they are not related, although a careless alien might conclude that they showed suffixal and prefixal inflection respectively. The words chosen must come from statements dealing with the same subject matter; then the presumption that similar types of words are used is valid; if identical words or phrases appear in the different statements, the assumption is strengthened. If, in statements connected with one another by an identity of subject matter and a certain amount of identity in the words used, similar words appear, differing only slightly in spelling, the deduction that such changes are due to inflection is certainly permissible. Once the fundamental likelihood that a change of a certain type represents inflection is established, the findings may be supplemented by similar examples from extraneous material.[11]

Ventris and Chadwick add this useful remark about Kober's methods:

> From a number of published tablets she gathered a series of words which significantly appear in three alternative forms (that the basic word is really the same in each case is proved by the fact that they recur in lists together, or in identical positions on the same class of tablets).[12]

It is clear that the scholars here met a very serious problem, that of accidental similarity between words, Kober's 'heavy' – 'heaven' problem, which they overcame by paying careful attention to contextual clues, including those provided by the ideograms and by the fact that they were dealing with a certain type of administrative record. It also seems clear that without such definite information about the contexts of the tablets, for example, if the most we could say is that the tablets are a list, possibly random, of someone's beliefs, the 'heavy' – 'heaven' problem would be insoluble.

Sexing the ideograms

Livestock ideograms occur in variant forms, the two most common variations being (i) to add two horizontal bars, like an equal sign, to the main vertical stroke or axis of the sign and (ii) to divide the vertical stroke into a fork. What do these variations mean? Chadwick writes:

---

[11] Alice E. Kober, 'Evidence of Inflection in the 'Chariot' Tablets from Knossos', *American Journal of Archaeology*, 49 (1945), pp. 143–51, esp. pp. 144–5.

[12] *Documents*, pp. 15–16.

Evans correctly guessed that these signified male and female animals, but Sundwall reversed the sexes. Miss Kober finally settled the question by showing that the ideograms for men and male animals share one form of the word for 'total', while women and female animals have another form; the distinction of men and women was of course clear [because the ideograms for them are self-explanatory pictorial signs].[13]

Kober gives careful consideration to the possibility that the inflection in the word for 'total' is for case, and not for gender. In a key passage she writes as follows:

> It is, however, far more likely that the difference [in the form of the word] is due to gender. Each word is used in connection with several ideograms. No ideogram used with one is ever used with the other in any extant Linear Class B inscription.[14]

Here again the force of the reasoning depends on rather specific knowledge of the purpose of the tablets; e.g., the difference between male and female animals is of economic importance.

Sheep. The tablets from Knossos include a large archive (over 800 tablets) dealing with sheep (about 100,000 sheep are listed). There are related tablets dealing with wool and with sheep and wool. The history of the interpretation of these tablets provides an interesting case in which an initially plausible interpretation had to be fundamentally revised. The general form of an important class of these tablets is described by Ventris and Chadwick as follows:

> They begin with a man's name, presumably that of the shepherd as in the parallel tablets at Pylos, written in tall characters; then the tablet is usually divided by a horizontal line, the top line containing the name of the 'collector' in the nominative or genitive, and the number of rams and/or ewes; the lower line usually gives the place name and any minor entry, such as the deficit. These positions, however, are not invariable. Unlike the Pylos tablets, there is a separate tablet for each entry. The numbers are as a rule round hundreds, or in a series of lesser number adding up to a round total. In these cases the sum is never shown on the tablet.[15]

Leaving out the names of shepherd, 'collector', and place typical entries look like this, where 'RAMS' stands for the ram ideogram and 'EWES' for the ewe ideogram:

RAMS	70	EWES	29	def. RAMS	1
RAMS	264	EWES	22	def. RAMS	14.

---

[13] John Chadwick, *The Decipherment of Linear B*, 2nd ed. (Cambridge University Press, Cambridge, 1970), pp. 45–6.

[14] E. Kober, ' 'Total' in Minoan (Linear Class B)', *Archiv Orientalni*, 17 (1949), pp. 386–98, esp. 398.

[15] *Documents*, 2nd ed., p. 201. The text of the second edition at this point is the same as that of the first edition (though the pagination is slightly different). New ideas and material added to the second editions appears in a section of Additional Commentary, the last part of the above volume.

Two things are puzzling about these data: (i) the round sums and (ii) the great preponderance of rams over ewes. In the first edition of *Documents* Ventris and Chadwick interpreted these tablets as a record of tribute imposed on his subjects by the overlord of Crete. They argued as follows:

> It is on this fact [the roundness of the sums] that any theory of the transaction recorded must be based. They cannot be a simple census of flocks of sheep and other cattle, since a natural distribution would not show these round numbers, nor would this explain the deficits. Real flocks too would hardly show the disproportion of rams to ewes which is evident. It follows then that these are allocations or contributions, and that performance in many cases falls short of the amount due. The high numbers of rams would not occur if these were allocations by the palace; but they would naturally occur if the owners were obliged to supply so many sheep annually. They would of course pick out the least useful members for the regeneration of the flock. We may therefore feel sure that those are right who have seen in these tablets a record of tribute imposed on his subjects by the overlord. Sundwall, regarding the cattle as oxen, suggested that these were 'hecatombs' of sacrificial animals. Although this explanation cannot be ruled out, the numbers seem far too large for this purpose. Several of the Knossos tablets which apparently give totals have figures in excess of 2000; one fragment contains the numeral 19,000. This would have been piety indeed. Even if the figures are regarded as tribute, they are large for an annual contribution. Evans was certainly right in setting down cattle-raising as one of the principal sources of wealth. It might be tempting to regard these sheep not as real animals, but merely as a token of exchange, as oxen as used as a standard of measurement in Homer; but imaginary sheep cannot be divided into rams and ewes, apart from the other subdivisions. Nor is there any evidence in the tablets of anything approaching currency. Every commodity is listed separately, and there is never any sign of equivalence between one unit and another.[16]

Against this tribute theory J. T. Killen raised several objections. One, to the observation that a preponderance of rams would naturally occur if the owners were obliged to supply so many sheep annually, since they would of course pick out the least useful members for the regeneration of the flock, Killen responds that, 'it is not enough to ask whether the subject found it convenient to supply a large number of rams, without explaining why the palace specifically required rams, or at least was not averse to receiving them'.[17] Second, 'if the sheep population of Mycenaean Crete was anything like the latest modern figure of 529,910, ... it is extremely difficult to imagine that tribute of anything like 100,000 animals a year could have been extracted by the palace.'[18] Third, Killen has an important but intricate objection based on some features of some tablets that record both sheep and wool; I will not summarize the objection. The alternative interpretation which Killen proposed, and which is now generally accepted, involves two changes in the Ventris and Chadwick interpretation. (1) The RAM ideogram can in some contexts stand for wethers

---

[16] *Documents*, pp. 197–8.

[17] J. T. Killen, 'The Wool Industry of Crete in the Late Bronze Age', *Annual of the British School at Athens*, 59 (1964), pp. 1–15, esp. p. 3.

[18] *Ibid., p. 5, note 23.*

(castrated male sheep) as well as for rams proper; and in some contexts it can even stand also for ewes. (2) The function of the tablets was to record a kind of centralized management of wool producing flocks. The kind of management normally involves making each shepherd responsible for a round number of animals. Similar management, generating similar records, was used in medieval England. Much of Killen's paper is given over to developing analogies between the two sets of records.

Two points here are especially interesting for us. We see that, at least in this instance, when one interpretation is dismantled and another is put in its place, a principle of least action prevails. We do not call off all bets, and go back to first principles and basic data in some philosophically preferred sense. The interpretation of the ram ideogram is revised – to mean ram or wether or even (sometimes) ewe – but there is no tinkering with the species it indicates. Nor is there tinkering with the interpretation of other ideograms, except that in appropriate contexts what used to be MALE ANIMAL may now be MALE OR CASTRATED OR EVEN FEMALE ANIMAL. Similarly, the general function of the tablets as administrative records of economic activity remains in place, but the more detailed picture of the economic activity being recorded is revised.

The second point that seems especially interesting is this. In order to get on with their task, the interpreters every now and then have to put aside the puzzling inscriptions, and go off and study up on some aspect of the real world. How many sheep are there in Crete? What is the point of keeping wethers? How many rams are needed in breeding flocks? Do ewes and wethers produce the same amounts of wool? What about resistance to disease? These are some of the questions Killen finds it necessary to take up in the course of his article. The interpreter knows what aspect of the real world is relevant, because he has a good idea of the scheme of activity into which the records fit – contextual frame again. If all the interpreter knew was that the inscriptions record someone's beliefs, he would not know what to study. To put it better, he would not have any motivation to study anything. But it is surely a deep thing that when we undertake to interpret a foreign language we become, in a deep sense, the foreigners' students.

Conclusions

We have seen that the models of interpretation provided by theories of radical translation fail to fit what actually happened in interpreting the Linear B tablets in three basic respects:

(1) The evidence which supports the various parts of the interpretation is in some instances poorer, in many instances richer, and overall more heterogeneous than the models lead us to expect.
(2) The marshalling of the evidence is more complicated and less uniform than the theories lead us to expect.
(3) The form in which the meanings of sentences are given is not a simple correlation of sentences to sentences, but this plus a gloss.

We have now to ask: so what? What are we to make of this divergence between theoretical models and actual practice?

I do not think this question has a simple answer. It is natural to feel, I think, that the facts we have reviewed place the theory in some jeopardy. But do they? How exactly?

In the first place, any satisfying assessment here must take into account that the theories were not intended to be descriptive of the practice of translators. They were intended rather as analytical or idealized models which have bearing on all communication, including translators' practice. But what bearing.

A defender of the theories might reply along the following lines. Every time language is used to communicate, every time a piece of language is understood, radical translation is going on. In everyday uses of our own natural language we translate according to a scheme which has become habitual and which is the outcome of a sifting of evidence long forgotten; we apply all mental concepts according to a scheme entrenched in habit; almost the whole apparatus and the whole process are below the level of consciousness. From time to time, to be sure, there are breakdowns in communication and understanding which remind us that a process of interpretation is going on behind the scenes. When these breakdowns occur we make small, piecemeal adjustments in our ongoing scheme; we never explicitly and consciously stand back and examine the whole scheme in the light of all the evidence. In everyday life, that is to say, radical translation is an implicit, unconscious process. The decipherment of Linear B presents basically the same situation as everyday life. A little more of the interpretive process is exposed to view, but only a little, and it is only a matter of degree. The great mass of our habitual scheme is still in place and still hidden from view: this, indeed, is what is really shown by the facts which Wallace interprets by saying that 'the evidence is richer than the theories would lead us to expect'. Radical translation is present in the Linear B case, as it always is when language is understood, but it is tacit, just as it is in ordinary life.

Immersion in the Linear B case makes this line ring pretty hollow. Unlike most everyday uses of language, it is a case of linguistic interpretation in which the questions, 'What is the evidence?', 'How is the evidence marshalled?', 'What is the upshot?' have real application. By anybody's standards the evidence is thin, impoverished, the steps from evidence to interpretation tortuous and difficult. We can see that at many points further impoverishment of the evidence would simply leave us in the lurch. The distance between evidence and interpretation is stretched, it seems almost to the breaking point. Yet we are told that this distance is nothing compared to that which is always being bridged implicitly. But do we understand this at all? Do we have a grasp of ideas of evidence and of procedures for using evidence for situations so far removed from anything that ever occurs in conscious experience? Do we know what we are supposed to imagine going on unconsciously, implicitly, tacitly? I think not.

Quine's and Davidson's theories must be distinguished here. The intelligibility of the processes posited by Quine's theory depends on a physicalistic reconstruction of the notion of observation sentence. But the Linear B case suggests that, in real, tractable evidential situations, the contextual frames in which uninterpreted expressions are embedded are much more specific and much more variable than in Quine's model. So much so, that Quine's unanimity tests will be working always, or too frequently, on a population of one. No two speakers will be comparable, the reconstructed notion of observation sentence becomes vacuous. The intelligibility of Davidson's theory turns on the intelligibility of his holistic principle of charity: interpret so as to maximize overall agreement in belief. Here again the specificity of contextual frames gets in the way. These specific frames are the ones we know how to use, and the way we use them is frequently naturally described as being charitable to, making sense of, the other fellow. But this charity differs from that on which Davidson's theory rests in two ways: (1) the specificity of the frames gives us a grip on what it would be like to be in the other fellow's shoes, so that being charitable to or making sense of comes to be a matter not of having the other fellow think or do or say what I do think or do or say, but a matter of having the other fellow think or do or say what I would, or might plausibly, think or do or say *if* I were in his shoes; (2) the specificity of the frames makes application of the relevant kind of charity a local, not a holistic, enterprise. The locality may be large, for the activities, linguistic and otherwise, that must be made sense of overlap. But it is not a matter of imposing the whole apparatus to mental concepts in one fell swoop, then judging the result, as a whole, on the basis of how charitable it is overall. I do not think we have the faintest idea what it would be like to do this. It is not just that our computational powers might be swamped by the sheer bulk of the data to be handled; it is rather, I think, that we do not know what we are supposed to do with the data.

Is there anything that the theories get right? Yes, two points they make are solid and basic. The theories say, first, that evidence for the interpretation of language comes in a form in which as yet uninterpreted linguistic signs are embedded, or framed, in a description of behavior. That is, the evidence describes the language users as operating with or somehow related to the uninterpreted signs. This is so, but the frames are more various, and richer in content, than the theories allow. Second, the theories lead us to picture linguistic interpretation as a completing of a story set out, as it were schematically, in the description of behavior containing the framed, uninterpreted linguistic expressions. Giving the meaning of the expressions brings them to life, and completes the story. And this is a correct picture, but the theories do not recognize how much flexibility there can be in giving the meanings. In particular, giving the meaning of a foreign expression is usually a matter of correlating it with a home expression, and giving a gloss; it is rarely a matter of correlation alone.

How far these considerations go toward discrediting the models of radical interpretation the reader must be left to judge for himself. I would like to point out in conclusion that these models are of interest not only for their own sake, as clarifying or purporting to clarify the connection between the mental and the physical, but as premises or assumptions to be argued from, to throw light on other philosophical issues. Thus Quine has argued on the basis of his model of interpretation that translation, and application of associated mental concepts, is indeterminate relative to physicalistic data. Davidson has argued on the basis of his model that the kind of incommensurability between the conceptual schemes of people in different cultures or scientists at different stages of scientific development envisaged by some writers on conceptual change is impossible.[19] The weak spots we have exposed in the models show why these conclusions are shaky. In our actual practices of interpreting and learning about other people, both the evidence and the evidenced make, to borrow Wittgenstein's language, a medley, mixing physical concepts and mental concepts up together in a single report. (See *Philosophical Investigations*, I, Section 421.) Our study of the Linear B case suggests, then, that the proper response to the question: How is application of mental concepts constrained by application of physical concepts? is: The question presupposes a process – application of mental concepts on the basis of physical concepts – which does not exist. As for Davidson's argument, the Linear B case suggests that in the data on which interpretation is based uninterpreted linguistic expressions are embedded in specific and variable contextual frames. It is easy to see how a large amount of such data could defy interpretation as some writers on conceptual change have suggested: an interpretation which makes sense of an expression in some of its frames may make nonsense of it in others, and an interpretation which simultaneously makes sense of all its occurrences in all the frames may elude our ingenuity, and may even be impossible. Why not? Davidson's idea is that in such cases we can always move back to less committal and more uniform data and to processes of inference which are required only to maximize some global quality of agreement. I see nothing in the Linear B case to suggest that this is so.

The present paper is not the first time the decipherment of Linear B has been discussed in the literature on radical translation. N. L. Wilson has alluded to it in a way that is worth examining. Wilson first seems to claim that in the situation of radical translation, a speaker's intentions are inaccessible. He writes:

> Suppose I am crossing the Kalahari Desert. An African comes up to me and says (utters), 'Hut sut rawson ona rillaraw'. How do I find out what he means? I do *not* inquire into his intentions. Once I have deciphered what he means, then I may be able to hazard a guess as to what his intentions were in regard to me. What I do is follow him back to his village, whip out my trusty tape-recorder and make motions like a field-worker in linguistics.[20]

Wilson's picture seems to be that the field worker collects a corpus of utterances without any indication of the intentions behind the utterances. He goes on to illustrate his point:

> An illustration. The second sentence of III.50 of Thucydides is 'Mutilenaiòn teichè katheilon'. How do I find out what it means? I do not have a Greek–English lexicon and I know only that the text is about the Peloponnesian War. What I do is rent a computer, stuff it with all we know about the Peloponnesian War and then feed into it as a corpus of utterances the Greek text of Thucydides. If computers

---

[19] See D. Davidson, 'The Very Idea of a Conceptual Scheme', *Proceedings and Addresses of the American Philosophical Association*, 47 (1973–4), pp. 5–20.

[20] N. L. Wilson, 'Grice on Meaning: The Ultimate Counter-example', *Nous*, 4 (1970), pp. 295–302; esp. pp. 299–300.

are half as good as they are supposed to be then this one ought to be able to decipher the text before you can say 'Zeus', come up with a Greek–English dictionary, a translation of the text, and, in particular, tell us that the sentence in question means that they razed the walls of the Mytilenaeans. Of course any corpus of utterances can be given an arbitrary interpretation – any number of interpretations, for that matter. But not every corpus has a single *right* interpretation, right in the sense of being that interpretation under which the largest possible number of sentences of the corpus will be true. ... The computer seeks an interpretation which, in the light of what it knows of the facts, will maximize truth among the sentences of the corpus. In effect, it plays a very large number of games of twenty questions with the corpus and plays them simultaneously.

The point is that it is no good asking the computer to decipher a single sentence. It cannot work with anything less than a fairly large corpus. Ask Ventris.[21]

Wilson then refers to Chadwick's account of the decipherment in *The Decipherment of Linear B*. Now he is certainly right that the decipherment would have been impossible if the corpus had consisted of a single tablet or a single sentence. With such a small corpus the constraints on translation simply cannot get a foothold and translation is strongly indeterminate. As the corpus grows the range of acceptable interpretations narrows – in favorable circumstances, perhaps, to one. Why is this so? It seems to me that on Wilson's own view this question is very hard to answer. To put the reason abstractly, sheer number of sentences, in the absence of grammar, does not make constraints on translation more binding. I use grammar here in the broadest sense, to include what we have been calling the contextual frame as well as grammar in the traditional sense of parts of speech, methods of constructing sentences, etc. Much turns, then, on what Wilson means by 'the facts'. If the contextual frames we have to work with are simply

Thucydides believed-true INSCRIPTION
The scribes believed-true INSCRIPTION,

and that these are what we have to work with is compatible with and even suggested by what Wilson says, then it is clear that we can translate both Thucydides and the Linear B tablets as portions – you choose which ones – of the multiplication table. All their utterances will come out true; the translation of one sentence will be no more constrained, no more determinate, than the translation of one billion. The philosophical question then arises: what is the minimal system of description of uninterpreted utterances, the minimal grammar, which will permit intelligible, workable constraints on interpretation to get a foothold, so that in favorable cases, as the corpus widens, the range of acceptable interpretations shrinks? This question already presupposes too much – that there is a unique minimal grammar. I think we get a glimpse of what one minimal grammar is like in the Linear B case.

---

[21] Ibid., p. 300.

12

Testing Theories of Interpretation

Bruce Vermazen

In chapter 2 of *Word and Object*, W. V. Quine imagines a process he calls 'radical translation', as a first step in an attempt to show that the notion of linguistic meaning is not a scientifically useful one and that there is a great deal of 'scope ... for empirically unconditioned variation in one's conceptual scheme' (1960, p. 26), that is, that there is no reason to expect that inhabitants of a common world will tend to end up armed with common concepts for dealing with that world. Radical translation is 'The recovery of a man's current language from his currently observed responses' to his environment by a 'linguist who, unaided by an interpreter, is out to penetrate and translate a language hitherto unknown' (p. 28). The linguist will begin by collecting a stock of uninterpreted utterances of his subject, somehow devising a way to turn these utterances into queries (of his own), and then noting his subject's positive and negative responses to queries under various environing conditions. In this way he will build up a catalogue correlating some of the subject's sentences with sensory stimulations caused by things going on around him: a pairing, to use Quine's terminology, of occasion sentences with stimulus meanings. Translation begins when and if the linguist finds sentences in his own language with the same (or very nearly the same) stimulus meanings. The method of query and assent can also be used to translate any truth-functional sentential connectives that the subject's language may contain, once the linguist has some sentences to connect. Finally (in theory, though concurrently in practice), the linguist will segment the subject's sentences into words and correlate them with words or longer expressions in his own language in such a way as to preserve, for the most part, the sentence-to-sentence translations he has already settled on, as well as two other correlations: some of the subject's sentences may have been found to be 'stimulus-analytic', i.e., such that the subject assents to them under every stimulation, and these will be correlated with stimulus-analytic sentences from the linguist's own tongue; and some pairs of the subject's sentences may be 'stimulus-synonymous', i.e. such that the same stimulations prompt assent to

I am grateful to Brian Chellas and W. V. Quine for their responses to this paper at the Rutgers Conference.

both. The interlinguistic correlations between words and expressions (possibly with instructions for peculiarities of context) are set forth in 'analytical hypotheses', as is whatever is required 'to explain syntactical constructions' (p. 70). The linguist thus compiles a 'translation manual' which enables him to understand the subject's language, that is, his 'complex of present dispositions to verbal behavior' (p. 27). The manual will be expressible as a function that takes the subject's sentences as arguments and yields as values sentences in the linguist's language.

Donald Davidson agrees with Quine on the philosophical interest of the kind of thought-experiment embodied in radical translation, but takes exception to the details (see 1974a and b). Instead of the quasi-behaviorist notion of stimulus-meaning, Davidson uses the mentalistic (but, he thinks, not so mentalistic as to be inapplicable by an alien linguist) notion of holding an uninterpreted sentence true to generate the primary data for a scheme of translation. His idea is that the linguist will be able to tell in lots of cases which of his subject's utterances the subject holds true. Further, he thinks that their being held true is at least prima facie evidence for their truth, so that the linguist's task is primarily to figure out what features of the subject's situation (if any) constitute the reason why he holds that sentence true at that moment. This method will obviously work smoothly only for those sentences whose truth value changes in different situations, e.g. 'It's raining.' In fact, the class of sentences for which it works will be just the same as that for which Quine's method of query and assent is supposed to work. What the linguist gets from his initial round of conjecture will be, not exactly a correlation of the subject's sentences with sentences of his own, but a set of sentences of the form 'S is true in N's language at t if and only if ...', where the ellipsis is replaced by a statement concerning the salient features of the subject's situation. For example, '"Ich bin hungrig" is true in N's language at t if and only if N is hungry at t' would be such a datum sentence for a typical speaker of German. But, as the example shows, not every salient feature of the subject's situation is available to the linguist without his making some guesses as to the subject's mental economy; in fact, no such feature is available without some such guesses, since to attribute a holding-true to a speaker is to attribute a certain mental state to him; and the linguist's guesses concerning what the speaker holds true depend essentially on how the linguist thinks the speaker perceives his situation. So part of the task of 'radical interpretation', to use Davidson's label for his version of the thought-experiment, is to attribute enough beliefs and desires to the subject to make his utterances sensible, given the linguist's conjectures as to their truth-conditions and the subject's actual behavior. Davidson thinks that this attribution is to be accomplished according to a Principle of Charity (or of Rational Accommodation, as he relabelled it in his Carus Lectures, unpublished at this time), which involves attributing to the subject all one's own beliefs and desires at the outset and then making deletions and substitutions for cases where the overall pattern of the subject's acts and utterances would be more nearly rational if the linguist supposed the subject's mental economy to differ from his own. Then the linguist goes back to the statements of truth-conditions for individual utterances and tries to find a finitely stated consistent theory that will entail those statements. Davidson thinks that in order to do this we must find the structure of the first-order predicate calculus in the subject's utterances, and that we would probably do best to model the theory on Alfred Tarski's definitions of truth for artificial languages.

Neither Quine nor Davidson imagines that he is giving us a method for translation in the field, but both, I think, aim to give us a model of the way in which we understand one another's speech, even in cases where we are both speaking the same language. Davidson is quite explicit on this point at the beginning of the Carus Lectures; radical interpretation, he says, is the usual situation. It is only because the two processes purport to be models of understanding that Quine and Davidson can base far-reaching philosophical conclusions on them, e.g. (in Quine's case) that there are distinct conceptual schemes that different individuals or cultures operate with, or (in Davidson's) that there are not.

John Wallace has argued (1979) that both views of translation or interpretation are so remote from actual practice that any philosophical claims stemming from them are ill founded. To demonstrate this remoteness, he examines the details of Michael Ventris's and John Chadwick's decipherment of the Linear B script and shows that in three important respects Ventris's practice diverged radically from the practice of both Quine's and Davidson's imaginary linguists: the sort of evidence employed was different; the marshalling of the evidence was both 'more complicated and less uniform than the theories lead us to expect' (p. 134); and 'the form in which the meanings of sentences are given is not a simple correlation of sentences to sentences, but this plus a gloss' (p. 134).

The very statement of Wallace's objection raises a serious doubt about its cogency. How can a theory about translation or interpretation be tested by bringing to it a case of successful decipherment? There is a strong prima facie difference between translating a text and deciphering a text. Decipherment is a matter of figuring out what are the alphabetic, syllabic, or ideographic values of the characters in a text. Translation figures in the strongest sort of confirmation of a decipherment, since a decipherer wants ultimately to obtain a meaningful text. But a text could be deciphered and the meaning of the words obtained remain partly or wholly unknown, except of course in the ideographic case, where decipherment is tantamount to translation; but even in the ideographic case, decipherment amounts to translation of words only, not of stretches of discourse longer than words. Translation is a matter of figuring out what the text means; it is separable from decipherment in thought even if it is intertwined with it in practice. So why would Wallace think the *decipherment* of Linear B provided a test for theories of radical *translation* (or interpretation)?

It is hard to answer this question from Wallace's text. He points out that the language of the Linear B tablets was unknown, so perhaps his reason was this: both decipherment and translation were going on, and Wallace just used 'decipherment' as a label for the compound process, though his interest was focused on the translation part of the process. But that still wouldn't give him a test case, since the great bulk of the translation was accomplished after the decipherment had convinced Ventris and Chadwick that the language they were dealing with was Greek, and then it wasn't *radical* translation at all, but translation using an established Greek–English translation scheme (with a few exceptions). The analogue in the imaginary linguist's case would be translation using an interpreter who knew English and knew another language closely related to the subject's.

Late in the paper, he says, 'These early stages [of investigation or decipherment-cum-translation], which most nearly approximate the situation of radical translation, are the source of most of the examples (all but the last) we now take up' (p. 128). This is a bit more forthright than his introductory remarks: the *early* stages of the decipherment *approximated* radical translation. So it's not a test case in any straightforward way. It's interesting to see how little was accomplished during these early stages that could be called translation. Nothing was successfully conjectured that could be cast as the kind of sentence–sentence correlation that a translation manual would provide, nor were truth-conditions stated for any sentences. The closest approach to translation was a fairly small list of tentative word–word or morpheme–morpheme correlations. One accomplishment was the interpretation of some of the ideograms on the tablets: man, woman, chariot, horse, and a few others. The analogue in speech interpretation would be to assign the meaning 'rooster' to a cock's crow or 'pig' to a grunt. This won't get you very far with a natural language for a couple of reasons. One is that some sound–thing associations would have to be arbitrary enough that recovery of the thing from the sound would not be easy in the way it is for crows and grunts. The other is that such associations will give you at most word–word equivalences, and hence won't contribute to your understanding of the syntax of the language and the semantic facts that are associated with syntax: what is the verb in this sentence, and what are the subject and object? Both problems were present in analogous forms in the written case: many ideograms were uninterpretable (e.g., the ones for different kinds of grain and for different items of armor), and no syntactical conclusions were drawn in the pre-decipherment stage, except the conclusion that most of the texts were probably strings of nouns.

Another 'accomplishment', but of an attenuated sort, was the translation of *ko-wo* as 'girl' and *ko-wa* as 'boy' by A. E. Cowley (in 1927). Of course, Cowley didn't know that those signs corresponded to those sounds. And it also turns out that *ko-wo* means 'boy' and *ko-wa* 'girl'. So the translation is imperfect; but he did guess that these were words for different varieties of children. Wallace perhaps overstates Cowley's certainty. Cowley uses the word 'suggest', but Wallace uses 'infer' and 'conclude' (1979, p. 128).

A third accomplishment was the translation of the enclitic 'and', on the strength of the conjecture that the texts were lists and that some words, tentatively identified as names, had different terminations depending on their positions in the lists.

Fourth, words were classified into four groups on the basis of context, again on the strength of the conjecture that all the tablets were records of some kind: personal names, local or institutional names, titles or occupational expressions, and the rest of language. This is less than a morpheme–morpheme correlation, but it has a certain amount of semantic content.

Fifth, gender markers on livestock ideograms were identified, though, as in the boy–girl case, no one was sure which gender marker corresponded to which gender.

Sixth, the word 'total' was identified on the basis of its position at the bottom of sums.

Seventh, the number system was 'cracked'.

And that's really about all. The question is whether this provides a test case for theories of radical translation. I think that it falls far short of doing so, just because the amount of translating done doesn't amount to translating one language into another; it doesn't even amount to translating a small fragment of one language into another, since there are not resources here to go from a single *sentence* of Mycenaean Greek to one of English. In fact, aside from ideograms, the translatable vocabulary included only the number words, the word 'total' and the word 'and'.

A reader of Wallace's paper may think I have ignored one of Wallace's resources. When he draws specious parallels between the decipherment case and Quine's views early in the paper, he says 'it is immediately obvious what they [the ideograms] picture. It is taken for granted [by the decipherers] that the preceding word, phrase, or sentence names or describes an object or objects of the kind pictured' (p. 122). If this claim were true, then perhaps a certain undeciphered sequence of characters could be identified as meaning 'sheep' if it came right before the sheep ideogram. But it isn't true. Ventris and Chadwick didn't find that like-meaning words and ideograms were associated until after the decipherment. Indeed, the redundancy involved makes it prima facie unlikely that the words and ideograms would occur together, a point made by some critics of the decipherment (Chadwick, 1970, p. 94).

It might be thought that these few accomplishments show that Ventris and Chadwick were on the right track, so that if they hadn't discovered they were dealing with Greek, they could have gone on and radically translated whatever it was without deciphering. That seems to me very doubtful, but more important, that was never their plan. The aim was always first to decipher, then (if possible) to translate by finding some known language with enough similarities to the deciphered one to allow guesses at word–word, and so, ultimately, sentence–sentence equivalences. Since Ventris favored Etruscan as the related tongue (Chadwick, 1970, pp. 34, 48, 50), the success of the strategy would have had to wait upon an understanding, still unachieved, of that language; others had suggested or tried Basque, Anatolian, and Hittite. To use the speech-translation analogy again, the idea was to find a sort of interpreter who knew the unknown language or a closely related one and who knew English also. Translation, but not radical translation.

The actual decipherment went roughly as follows: 'Evans and the more cautious of his followers had observed that with few apparent exceptions all the documents were lists or accounts (1970, p. 26). Segmentation into words was no problem, since the character-strings were spaced. And the characters were grouped into a 'signary', so that variants of a sign were counted as occurrences of a single sign (like 'a' and 'A'), by Emmett Bennett. Alice Kober had identified differences in gender. It was decided that since there were about eighty-nine signs, the writing system (the part not obviously ideographic) must be syllabic, for there were not enough signs for a totally ideographic system and too many for an alphabet. Evans and Bennett respectively had figured out the numeral system and the notations for weights and measures (though not, of course, their amounts). After many of the obvious pictograms had been assigned tentative values, the decipherers had some clue to the subject matter of the associated syllabic texts, for example that they were lists of names or occupations, or that they repeated the word for the value of the pictogram, or that they classified types within the reference or extension of the pictogram. The word 'total' could be identified by its position on the tablets. Then there were the conjectures about 'boy' and 'girl' and 'and'. That was it, semantically speaking. But cryptographically speaking, there was that and more. Certain signs predominated at the beginnings of words and so were identified as vowels, since in an open-syllable syllabary, i.e., a syllabary whose syllables all end with vowel sounds, there would be no use for vowels elsewhere: they would always occur after consonants and so would not be separately represented. Erasures and corrections could be seen on the tablets, and these were used as evidence for similarity of sound between the erased character and the substituted one. Certain groups of characters were thought to represent noun declensions because they were suffixed to the same words at different points in the text, and these declensions suggested links between syllables that shared initial consonants, but differed in their vowel sounds. To use the gender identifications, it was conjectured that all masculine forms would terminate in one vowel and all feminine forms in another, so that once words had been sorted into genders, their terminal syllables could be supposed to share a single vowel (or a small number of them).

All this information was put in a syllabic grid, with a five-vowel horizontal axis and a fifteen-consonant vertical axis, and then Ventris set about finding values for the characters. At first he tried working by similarity between the Linear B signs and signs in known syllabaries: the Cypriot and the Etruscan. It turned out later that he had got a lot of these right, but the breakthrough came from these conjectures in conjunction with a different procedure.

The parallel-sign procedure had given him a- and ni- as probable (or maybe one should say possible) values for two characters. He had decided that a certain group of words, distinguished from others by their frequency and the order of their recurrence, were place names. So he started looking for place names that had survived into classical times. Amnisos was a possibility, and among the place names was one whose first and third syllables were the conjectured a- and ni-. This gave him the whole row of m- and s- syllables to work with, and via other tentative identifications, he found Knossos (*ko-no-so*) and Tulissos (*tu-li-so*); these confirmed and filled in yet other rows and columns. But the breakthrough to Greek came when he then decoded the endings already suspected of being declensions and found that they were Greek declensions (on 'boys', 'girls', 'total'). From then on he rapidly found more Greek words and filled in more values in the grid until the syllabary was complete. To sum up, *very* little translating was done before the decipherment was well under way.

So Wallace is wrong about the decipherment of Linear B being a test case for theories of radical translation. That doesn't mean, however, that his objections to the procedures of Quine and Davidson are wrong, just that they are ill founded. What are the objections that he makes, and how much attention should we pay to them?

The first objection is directed against what he thinks Quine and Davidson would say about the Linear B case, namely, that what is going on on the surface of the Linear B example is not radical translation, but that that *must* be going on implicitly, since it goes on whenever we interpret someone else's discourse; and further, that the distance between evidence and interpretation in the Linear B case 'is nothing compared to that which is always being bridged implicitly' (1979, p. 135). Wallace suggests that we don't understand this claim, that we don't 'have a grasp of ideas of evidence and of procedures for using evidence for situations so far removed from anything that ever occurs in conscious experience' (p. 135). But instead of pressing his claim that we can't understand the views of Quine and Davidson, he goes on to urge that their translation/ interpretation procedures are unworkable.

The unworkableness of Quine's procedure comes from an alleged vacuity of the notion of synonymy between occasion sentences: Wallace thinks that no two speakers will share stimulus-meanings for *any* sentence, so there will be stimulus-meanings only for single speakers, none for a whole community, and none to match the translator's. This is, I think, a viable criticism if sameness of stimulus-meaning is taken very strictly, but less viable as we loosen the notion and settle (as Quine says he will) for *approximate* stimulus-synonymy. But it's not clear how this criticism is motivated by the suggestion 'that, in real, tractable evidential situations, the contextual frames in which uninterpreted expressions are embedded are much more specific and much more various than in Quine's model' (p. 135). A better point to make against Quine, and one on which much of Davidson's work rests, is that though translation (or interpretation) can get going on fairly slim evidence, at some point we need to attribute a rich set of beliefs and desires to people in order to get very *far* with their language, for what they utter is a result not just of what they mean and assent to, but of what they believe and desire. We need to know, or guess at, what they think is the case and what they hope to be doing in or by their utterances and attendant acts. Belief and desire yield the varied contextual frames that Wallace seeks. That is, they tell us what the speakers see themselves as doing in their acts (including speech acts): making lists of sheep and slaves, dispatching soldiers to Korinthos, and so on.

But he criticizes Davidson for another failing: the Principle of Charity is unintelligible in the sense that we don't know how to apply it. Wallace cites it thus: 'interpret so as to maximize overall agreement in belief' (p. 135). I don't find this a felicitous summary of Davidson's remarks on the Principle. In 'Belief and the Basis of Meaning' (1974), Davidson describes its application as follows:

> The general policy ... is to choose truth conditions that do as well as possible in making speakers hold sentences true when (according to the theory and the theory builder's view of the facts) those sentences are true. That is the general policy, to be modified in a host of obvious ways. Speakers can be allowed to differ more often and more radically with respect to some sentences than others, and there is no reason not to take into account the observed or inferred individual differences that may be thought to have caused anomalies (as seen by the theory). (p. 320)

This is not mere maximization of agreement. In fact, Davidson shifted from talking of maximization to talk of optimization in a later paper (1975, p. 21), on the grounds that a subject will have an infinite number of beliefs, and it does not make sense to seek to maximize agreement between two infinite totalities.

Perhaps Wallace could have made this shift the basis of a separate objection, since the indications given as to what counts toward goodness of agreement yield an idea of optimization even more obscure than that of counting beliefs.

I think what Davidson is after is this: we start by attributing *all* our beliefs (and desires) to the informant. Then when we see him doing things that are irrational given those beliefs and desires, we change a few of them to account for the aberrant actions (including speech). But we make the fewest alterations we can (by some not entirely clear method of counting). It makes sense to call this 'maximizing', I think, though what we can count (if anything) is not the beliefs we share, but those we don't. Two problems complicate the picture: one is that some beliefs are more important than others (I develop this theme at greater length in (1982)), so disagreement on them counts for more than disagreement on less important ones – how much more, we don't know. The other problem is that there may be ties: two total attributions that impute the same amount of disagreement. And Davidson doesn't supply a tie-breaking procedure. I suppose he would say that the two solutions were equally defensible; and perhaps he would say there is no fact of the matter beyond what the rival systems impute. (I offer support for this claim in (1983). This, I suppose, would grate on Wallace, Ventris, and Chadwick, but perhaps Davidson would say that they all share the presupposition that there are fixed Greek–English equivalences that are more than merely customary, that are grounded in some way other than their playing some role in generating the right truth-conditions as output of a truth-theory for Greek in English. But Davidson thinks that is a mistake. So I am suggesting that Wallace is wrong. We *do* know more or less how to apply the Principle of Charity.

It is difficult to make much of Wallace's complaint that 'giving the meaning of a foreign expression is usually a matter of correlating it with a home expression, and giving a gloss; it is rarely a matter of correlation alone' (1979, p. 136). His support for and elucidation of this claim is only anecdotal. To convince us that Quine and Davidson are deficient in this respect, he would have to show that neither a Quinean translation manual nor a Davidsonian truth-theory could yield the same information regarding the sentences to be translated that is usually yielded by the correlation-plus-gloss he considers customary. It is hard to predict what success he would have in Quine's case, but I think he would fail in Davidson's. For Davidson's truth-theory is required to yield for each foreign sentence a statement of the conditions under which that sentence is true: far from being a mere correlation of a foreign expression with a home expression, such a statement may amount to just the kind of gloss that Wallace is after, especially in cases where some object or practice or condition referred to in the foreign sentence is one for which there is no word in the language used to state the conditions of truth.

His final comments on Quine and Davidson are two: for Quine, he says that the case study suggests that Quine's question, how the application of mental concepts (here, meaning something by an utterance) is constrained by application of physical concepts (here, the concepts of behavior and stimulus), presupposes a process 'which does not exist' (p. 137), for we don't apply mental concepts on the basis of physical concepts. A shorter and *ad hominem* route to this same conclusion is afforded by the observation that assent is already a mental concept. And it's hard to see how the Linear B case suggests the non-existence of *any* process that would be used in translating the speech of an informant whose time didn't matter and whose environment we could manipulate. For it is the latter sort of informant that Quine imagines, not the sort who makes marks on a clay tablet in unknown circumstances and dies 3,500 years before the linguist arrives to interpret his utterances.

For Davidson, he says that there is 'nothing in the Linear B case to suggest that "in cases where making sense of all an expression's occurrences" may elude our ingenuity ... we can always move back to less committal and more uniform data and to processes of inference which are required only to maximize some global quality of agreement' (p. 137). But how could the Linear B case suggest such a move? The evidence there is fixed, and it isn't evidence for translation of speech but for decipherment of a syllabary. Would the situation be the same if we had a Mycenaean scribe next to us, with a lot of time to listen to his utterances and figure out which of them he holds true, etc.? There's so little resemblance between the givens of Davidson's thought experiment and the situation that faced Ventris and Chadwick that it isn't surprising that the latter gives no suggestive support to Davidson's method of radical interpretation. But lack of support for a method doesn't amount to an objection to the method.

If there were to be a real test case for the views of Quine and Davidson, it would be the kind of translation or interpretation that everyone manages in everyday speech transactions. Since Davidson has already pointed out fatal weaknesses in Quine's view – most notably his failure to find a completely non-mentalistic basis of data – the view awaiting a test is Davidson's. But it is crucially important to be clear about just what empirical claim he is making, and that is therefore to be put to the test. The account of radical interpretation is supposed to be a sketch of a theory that rationalizes a certain practice we engage in: the interpretation of another's speech. But the rationalization does not, as I see it, go by way of setting up a *method* for interpretation. It's wrong to suppose that Davidson claims that there is some mistake in taking short-cuts in interpretation, for example, by consulting a Greek–English dictionary. The description of radical interpretation is only a way of presenting the real rationalization, which consists in stating *goals* for the interpreter, such that only an assignment of mental states and truth conditions that reaches those goals counts as an interpretation. The interpreter must find statements of truth-conditions for the sentences (at least the indicative ones) under interpretation, and must know that these are statements that issue from a theory that gets all its testable consequences right. (This idea becomes explicit in Davidson, 1975.) If the interpreter fails at this, or at making the speaker largely rational or largely in agreement with him on the facts (save those for which there is a rational route to error), he has not succeeded in interpreting the speaker's utterances.

Thus a counterexample would be a situation in which we were satisfied that some interpreter had succeeded in understanding the utterances of a subject without accomplishing those goals. Such a case would have the consequences for Davidson that Wallace wants the decipherment of Linear B to have, but the decipherment itself is remote from such a case. We do, in fact, suppose that the scribes were rational, in that, for example, their lists are not self-inconsistent.

But there is no room to deploy the requirement that we interpreters find the scribes largely agreeing with us in belief, except for background beliefs, perhaps, such as that no object is both a girl and a boy or both a sheep and an ox. For we don't know what the environing situation was at the time. Were there in fact forty amphorae in the ship's hold? But our ignorance doesn't matter, since decipherment is not interpretation in any case. In a clear sense, we are not in a position to interpret the utterances of the Mycenaean scribes, since we have no very clear idea of just what they were up to in marking their tablets. Ventris and Chadwick found the marks to be Greek, so they could advance a certain distance in radical interpretation, to revert for a moment to the misleading picture of radical interpretation as a method. They could attribute to the scribe a belief that he was writing Greek and the desires to present an account and to sum rows of figures; they could suppose that some, at any rate, of the Greek sentences on the tablets were held true by the scribes. But how much farther could they get? Was the scribe telling the truth, or was he embezzling the odd sheep or jug of oil? Did he round off the count of oxen upward to flatter his master, or downward, in anticipation of an audit? We need to answer such questions to satisfy ourselves that we have understood the scribe's utterances, that is, that we have succeeded in radical interpretation. Any advance beyond the very early stage reached by the decipherment of Linear B waits – and waits forever – upon further information about the scribe.

References

Chadwick, John (1970): *The Decipherment of Linear B*, 2nd ed. Cambridge.

Cowley, A. E. (1927): 'A Note on Minoan Writing'. In *Essays in Aegean Archaeology Presented to Sir Arthur Evans*, Oxford, 5–7.

Davidson, Donald (1973): 'Radical Interpretation'. *Dialectica*, 27, 313–28.

   (1974a): 'Belief and the Basis of Meaning'. *Synthèse*, 27, 309–23.

   (1974b): 'Psychology as Philosophy'. In S. C. Brown (ed.), *Philosophy of Psychology*, New York, 41–52.

   (1975): 'Thought and Talk'. In Samuel Guttenplan (ed.), *Mind and Language*, 7–23.

   (1976): 'Reply to Foster'. In Gareth Evans and John McDowell (eds), *Truth and Meaning*, Oxford, 33–41.

Quine, W. V. (1960): *Word and Object*. Cambridge, Massachusetts.

Vermazen, Bruce (1982): 'General Beliefs and the Principle of Charity'. *Philosophical Studies*, 42, 111–18.

   (1983): 'The Intelligibility of Massive Error'. *The Philosophical Quarterly*, 33, 69–74.

Wallace, John (1979): 'Translation Theories and the Decipherment of Linear B'. *Theory and Decision*, 11, 111–40.

13

Semantics and Methodological Solipsism*

WILLIAM G. LYCAN

> To know the semantic concept of truth for a language is to know what it is for a sentence–any sentence–to be true, and this amounts, in one good sense we can give to the phrase, to understanding the language. ('Truth and Meaning,' p. 456)

Donald Davidson has done more than anyone else to promote the view that knowledge of one's language is knowledge of the truth-conditions of its sentences; at any rate, he has argued forcefully and eloquently that knowledge of truth-conditions *suffices* for knowledge of meanings.[1] Other philosophers, influenced by Davidson and Richard Montague, have straightway identified sentence-meanings with trans-world truth-conditions, from which identity Davidson's thesis follows directly.[2] The defence of the thesis is enormously plausible, in my opinion; yet it has not convinced everyone, and the thesis has come under sharp attack from each of several quarters.[3] In this paper I shall

---

*This paper overlaps chapter ten of my book, *Logical Form in Natural Language* (Bradford/MIT Press, Cambridge, 1984), an extended defense of truth-theoretic semantics. I am grateful to the Press for their kind permission to reprint the relevant sections.

[1] He explicitly restricts himself to the latter claim in 'Belief and the Basis of Meaning', *Synthese*, 27 (1974): p. 309; cf. 'Reply to Foster', in *Truth and Meaning*, eds G. Evans and J. MacDowell (Oxford University Press, Oxford, 1976).

[2] Thus David Lewis:

In order to say what a meaning *is*, we may first ask what a meaning *does*, and then find something that does that.

A meaning for a sentence is something that determines the conditions under which the sentence is true or false. It determines the truth-value of the sentence in various possible states of affairs. ... ('General Semantics', in *Semantics of Natural Language*, ed. D. Davidson and G. Harman (D. Reidel, Dordrecht, 1972), p. 22)

A similar and somewhat deeper version of this argument is offered by Robert Stalnaker on p. 273 of 'Pragmatics', in Davidson and Harman, *Semantics of Natural Language*.

[3] E.g., Herbert Heidelberger, 'Understanding and Truth Conditions', *Midwest Studies in Philosophy*, 5 (1980), pp. 401–10, and 'What Is It to Understand a Sentence that Contains an Indexical?', *Philosophy and Phenomenological Research*, 43 (1982), pp. 21–34; Michael Devitt, *Designation* (Columbia University Press, New York, 1981), ch. four; and even Lycan, 'Semantic Competence and Funny Functors', *Monist*, 62 (1979), pp. 209–22, and 'Semantic Competence and Truth-Conditions'.

consider one important sort of objection, which I think underlies much current dissatisfaction with Davidsonian semantics.

I *Methodological solipsism*

Davidson thinks of a truth theory for someone's language as part of an interpretation of that person's behavior; and though Davidson himself is not a granite-jawed realist regarding such interpretation,[4] others who have wedded truth-theoretic semantics to linguistic theory have tended to think of the result as being a contribution to psychology: a combined grammar and truth theory is thought somehow to serve in the explanation of subjects' behavior. Yet Hilary Putnam, Jerry Fodor and others have raised an issue that may seem to refute this suggestion outright.[5]

The issue turns on the key distinction between what is 'in the head' and what is not. For example, the 'content' or propositional object of a propositional attitude is not in the head, surprising as that may seem. Two subjects can be molecule-for-molecule alike inside their heads and still have intuitively different beliefs. My belief that water is wet is about H_2O, while my Twin Earth doppelgänger's belief 'that water is wet' is about XYZ, and their truth-conditions are accordingly different; my belief that I am lucky clearly differs in truth-condition from Twin Bill's belief that he is lucky. Such examples are now commonplace, and what they show is that the 'contents' of beliefs in the propositional or truth-conditional sense do not *per se* figure in the explanation of behavior, so long as 'behavior' is understood as brute physical motion of bodily parts, since people who are molecule-for-molecule alike will behave alike regardless of their belief contents, and people who believe the same proposition (people whose beliefs have the same truth-condition) may behave entirely differently depending on how that proposition is represented inside their heads.

Now, if not even the propositional content of a belief figures in the explanation of behavior, whyever should we think that knowledge of truth-conditions does? For that matter, why should anyone suppose that English sentences' having the truth-conditions that they do is a key element of any behavioral explanation? If the reference of a physical or mental symbol is not in its user's head, then neither is the truth-condition of any sentence or other

---

[4] See 'On the Very Idea of a Conceptual Scheme', *Proceedings and Addresses of the American Philosophical Association*, 47 (1973) pp. 5–20; 'Radical Interpretation', *Dialectica*, 27 (1973), pp. 313–28; 'Belief and the Basis of Meaning', p. 309; and 'Thought and Talk', in *Mind and Language*, ed. S. Guttenplan (Oxford University Press, Oxford, 1975).

[5] See Putnam, 'The Meaning of "Meaning"', *Minnesota Studies in the Philosophy of Science, VII: Language, Mind, and Knowledge*, ed K. Gunderson (University of Minnesota Press, Minneapolis, 1975); Fodor, 'Methodological Solipsism Considered as a Research Strategy in Cognitive Psychology', *Behavioral and Brain Sciences*, 3 (1980), pp. 63–72; S. Stich, 'Autonomous Psychology and the Belief-Desire Thesis', *Monist*, 61 (1978), pp. 573–91; T. Burge, 'Individualism and the Mental', *Midwest Studies in Philosophy*, 4 (1979), pp. 73–121; and Lycan, 'Toward a Homuncular Theory of Believing', *Cognition and Brain Theory*, 4 (1981), pp. 139–59. Also, S. Schiffer, 'Truth and the Theory of Content', in *Meaning and Understanding*, eds H. Parret and J. Bouveresse (Walter de Gruyter, Berlin, 1981), and Colin McGinn, 'The Structure of Content', in *Thought and Object*, ed A. Woodfield (Oxford University Press, Oxford, 1982).

representation containing that symbol, and what is not in the head cannot affect behavior.

This worry seems to be part of what bothers Putnam and Michael Dummett[6] regarding truth-theoretic semantics, and figures as an important sub-issue in the current debate between 'realists' and 'anti-realists' as Putnam and Dummett use those unhappy terms. It is also what has motivated some recent work in 'conceptual role' semantics, a purported competitor of Davidson's program. Let us consider whether 'methodological solipsism' – reliance in explaining behavior only on what is 'in the head' – embarrasses that program.

It must be conceded at once that if we continue to take a relentlessly narrow view of our explanandum, knowledge of truth-conditions will not figure *per se* in our explanans – for just the usual Fodorean reasons.[7] Neither a sentence's having a particular truth-condition nor typically even just the speaker's *believing* that the sentence has that truth-condition, is (entirely) in the speaker's head, and what is not in the head does not *in propria persona* produce behavior conceived as physical motion of the body. My belief that 'Snow is white' is true iff snow (as opposed to Twin snow, i.e., frosty crystalline XYZ) is white is indistinguishable in causal role from Twin Bill's belief that 'Snow is white' is true iff Twin snow is white; the difference in propositional content between our beliefs about truth-conditions is irrelevant to our matching behavior, and so plays no direct role in explaining it.[8] If semantics helps to 'explain behavior,' then 'behavior' must be understood more broadly than in the sense of particular physical motions of individual bodies.

I believe the answer lies in the fact that what a linguist studies is the structure of a *public* language, the language of some speech community. Suppose our target language is English. Then we would expect our explananda to be, not individual verbal act-tokens, but rather sociologically interesting regularities obtaining among these, as well as other facts about the community of English speakers. Linguistics is the study of what the members of a speech community have in common.[9]

---

6 Putnam, 'Realism and Reason' and 'Reference and Understanding,' both reprinted in *Meaning and the Moral Sciences* (Routledge and Kegan Paul, London, 1978); Dummett, 'The Philosophical Basis of Intuitionistic Logic' and other essays collected in *Truth and Other Enigmas* (Harvard University Press, Cambridge, Massachusetts, 1978), *Frege: Philosophy of Language* (Duckworth, London, 1973), 'What is a Theory of Meaning?' in Guttenplan, *Mind and Language*, and 'What is a Theory of Meaning, II' in Evans and MacDowell, *Truth and Meaning*. (Colin McGinn 'The Structure of Content' also assimilates Dummett's qualms to methodological solipsism.) On Dummett's arguments against Davidson, see my *Logical Form in Natural Language*, chapter 10, section 2.

7 This point is also made by Scott Soames in 'Semantics and Psychology', in *The Philosophy of Linguistics*, ed J. Katz (Oxford University Press, Oxford, forthcoming); and cf. McGinn in 'The Structure of Content'.

8 I have argued in 'Toward a Homuncular Theory of Believing' and in 'The Paradox of Naming' (in *Analytical Philosophy in Comparative Perspective*, ed J. Shaw (D. Reidel, Dordrecht, 1985)) that belief ascriptions are pragmatically ambiguous and do have solipsistic readings as well as their more easily perceived semantical-content readings. However, (i) the ambiguity claim is controversial, and (ii) it is non-solipsistic truth-conditions that concern us for the present discussion in any case.

9 This is my own suggestion, not Davidson's. Indeed, his recent paper 'A Nice Derangement of Epitaphs' (forthcoming in a *Festschrift* for H. P. Grice, ed by R. Grandy and R. Warner) indicates that he would reject it.

II *'Conceptual role' semantics*

I propose to bring out the explanatory need for truth theory in this regard by considering its rival, 'conceptual role' semantics (CRS), which is often solipsistically motivated.[10] According to CRS, the meaning of a sentence is a matter, not of its truth-condition, but of its conventional association with the belief or other propositional attitude that it would normally be used to express. Sentence meaning thus derives from attitude content. Attitude content is determined in turn by conceptual role, i.e., by the attitude's place in a system of states internal to its owner, which states are inferentially related to each other and also bear various functional relations to perceptual input and to action or motor output. Thus to specify the meaning of a sentence would be to specify its actual or potential role in such a conceptual scheme.

Gilbert Harman gives a fairly persuasive *ad hominem* argument for this view at the expense of Davidson's own:[11] Davidsonians would have it that speakers understand English in virtue of knowing the truth-conditions of English sentences. Thus Dudley understands 'Snow is white' in virtue of knowing *via* his finite truth theory that that sentence is true iff snow is white. In order to accomplish the latter epistemic achievement, Dudley must have (somehow) represented to himself *that* 'Snow is white' is true iff snow is white. But this requires an internal system of representation, say a 'language of thought,' capable of expressing the proposition that snow is white; and so the problem of meaning has only been put off. To suggest that a truth-theoretic semantics now be provided for the Mentalese language launches an obviously vicious regress, cognate with what D. C. Dennett has called "Hume's Problem" of self-understanding representations.[12]

---

[10] CRS goes back at least as far as Wilfrid Sellars' 'Some Reflections on Language Games' (in *Science, Perception, and Reality* (Routledge and Kegan Paul, London, 1963)). Its most vigorous defender at present is Gilbert Harman ('Meaning and Semantics', in *Semantics and Philosophy*, ed M. Munitz and P. Unger (New York University Press, New York, 1974); 'Language, Thought, and Communication,' in Gunderson, Minnesota Studies VII: 'Conceptual Role Semantics', *Notre Dame Journal of Formal Logic*, 23 (1982), pp. 242–56; and most recently '(Nonsolipsistic) Conceptual Role Semantics,' (xerox, 1984). It has close affinities with what AI researchers call 'procedural semantics'.

In *Logical Form in Natural Language* I incorrectly diagnosed Harman's CRS as being motivated, like others', by methodological solipsism, since Harman had seemed to be a straightforward functionalist regarding the representational character of thought (see *Thought* Princeton University Press, Princeton, 1973, chapter four) and considers linguistic expressions meaningful only insofar as they express thoughts. But he has made it clear, particularly in '(Nonsolipsistic) Conceptual Role Semantics,' that his functionalism is a species of 'wide' or nonsolipsistic functionalism and that his 'conceptual roles' are wide accordingly; moreover, he argues that a genuinely narrow conceptual role semantics would be hopelessly inadequate (hence the parentheses in his title). Naturally I concur in this last conclusion. My criticisms of 'CRS' in this paper are thus aimed not at Harman but at those who do appeal to methodological solipsism in attacking Davidsonian semantics – let 'CRS' now abbreviate 'conceptual role solipsism.'

[11] Harman, 'Language, Thought, and Communication,' p. 286.

[12] Davidson would already object to this first half of the argument, seeing no reason to grant Harman's representationalism. His own view of the propositional attitudes, as presented in 'Mental Events' (in *Experience and Theory*, ed L. Foster and J. W. Swanson (University of Massachusetts

The solution is to think of the 'language of thought' as hard-wired, as a language that we are simply *built* to use correctly. (Think of an output cell that is built to fire just in case each of two input cells fire; this is a hard-wired 'and'-gate.) I do not "understand' my own language of thought in the same sense as that in which I understand a natural language. To understand a natural language is (Harman says) to be able to translate it into one's language of thought, while to 'understand' one's language of thought – so far as this locution makes sense at all – is simply to use it correctly, where correctness is determined not by a convention or practice of any sort but by one's own functional design. Neither sort of understanding requires explication in terms of truth theory, though (Harman adds) a truth theory figures peripherally as exhibiting the respective conceptual roles of the logical connectives.

We must agree that subjects do not 'understand' their own languages of thought in virtue of representing to themselves truth theories directed upon those languages of thought. But it does not follow that a truth definition has no role to play. For we must ask, if a machine or a human hearer understands by translating, how does the translating proceed? Presumably a recursion is required, for all the familiar Chomskyan and Davidsonian reasons. And what property is the translation required to preserve? *Truth together with its syntactic determination* is the obvious candidate. Thus, even if one understands in virtue of translating, one translates in virtue of constructing a recursive truth theory for the target language.[13]

Perhaps it is question-begging to insist that the translation preserve truth. The CRSist (appropriately) may want to demand only that the translation preserve conceptual role. This suggestion requires that we make sense of the idea of a *public sentence's* having a 'conceptual role.' But as Wilfrid Sellars has emphasized, the network of inferential relations holding between sentences of a public language comes close to mirroring the inner network of functional relations holding between thoughts, and vice versa;[14] we might simply extend our use of the term 'conceptual role' to cover what corresponding nodes of the two networks have in common.

The idea that the translation involved in natural-language understanding need not preserve truth is an odd one. To see this, note again the lesson of methodological solipsism, that functionalism roles and truth-conditions are not correlated one–one. 'I am lucky' plays the same functional role in Twin Bill as it plays in me, but one may be true and the other false; similarly for 'Water is H_2O.' Conversely, my utterance of 'Twin Bill is lucky' and Twin Bill's utterance of 'I am lucky' have the same truth-condition and necessarily the

---

Press, Amherst, 1970)), seems incompatible with any very robust 'language of thought' hypothesis. It also seems incompatible with any very robust conceptual role semantics, since Davidson denies the possibility of any genuinely lawlike regularities holding between attitudes.

[13] In an unpublished paper called 'Why Semantic Theories of Natural Languages are not Psychological Theories of Understanding,' Scott Soames offers a competing picture of translation between English and the language of thought. I criticize it in fn 5 to chapter ten of *Logical Form in Natural Language*.

[14] Sellars, 'Some Reflections'; cf. Harman's *Thought* and Brian Loar, *Mind and Meaning* (Cambridge University Press, Cambridge, 1981). Stephen Schiffer has argued to me (in conversation) that this notion is far harder to spell out satisfactorily than is generally supposed.

same truth-value but entirely different respective conceptual roles. Thus, the requirement that the translation involved in understanding preserve just conceptual role seems both too weak and too strong. If my wife tokens 'Water is H_2O' and I translate this into the Mentalese sentence 'Water is H_2O,' I have preserved conceptual role but I have done nothing to distinguish the meaning of my wife's utterance from that of the corresponding one made by Twin Mary – yet the two still differ in truth-value. If Mary tokens 'I am lucky' and I translate this into the sentence that plays the same functional role in *my* inner system of representation, I will take her to have said that I am lucky rather than that she is. Sameness of conceptual role alone does not adequately anchor communication.

Let us reconsider the idea that the meaning of a sentence is a matter of its conventional association with the belief or other attitude that it would normally be used to express, in light of the fact that propositional attitudes themselves can be individuated either 'narrowly,' according to their causal roles, or 'widely,' according to their truth-conditions. Whether a particular sentence is normally used to express the thought *that P* depends on which scheme of individuation we have in mind. It is entirely natural to think that sentences simply express attitude content, so long as attitude content is itself widely individuated. But the CRSist's aims are solipsistic; the 'thoughts' he traffics in are behavior-explanatory items, and so must be individuated narrowly. The thesis that sentences simply express attitude content *narrowly individuated*, once we have made Fodor's distinction, is as peculiar as the idea that the translation involved in natural-language translation need not preserve truth, and for just the same reasons as those I have set out in the previous paragraph.

I conclude that Harman's argument fails.[15] But the onus is still on me to show in more detail why the notion of truth is needed in linguistics. As the foregoing remarks imply, I believe that the leading explanatory advantages of truth-theoretic semantics for public languages stem from the fact that while an

---

[15] Harman is well aware of Twin-Earth cases and the like, and makes an attempt to accommodate them ('Conceptual Role Semantics,' sec. 3.2). He proposes to relativize the functional role of a concept to a 'normal context', the 'content' of the concept now being determined by role together with context rather than by role alone. Our 'context' is Earth, while Twin Bill's is Twin Earth. (Of a spontaneously created person who comes into being in outer space with ostensible memories and beliefs about an Earthlike environment, Harman says it is 'quite arbitrary what we say' about the content of that person's concepts – we could take that person's 'normal context' to be either Earth or Twin Earth, whichever we liked. This seems quite wrong to me. I would say that the fortuitous person's concepts simply do not refer; on my view it is a fact that the person's thoughts are about neither Earth nor Twin Earth. After all, the person is the moral equivalent of an Evil Demon victim.) We might add here, following Stephen White in 'Partial Character and the Language of Thought' (*Pacific Philosophical Quarterly*, 63 (1982), pp. 347–65), that although functional role fails to determine reference, it does determine functions from 'normal contexts' (or as White treats them, from contexts of acquisition) to referents.

But I do not see that Harman's modification would halt the non-solipsistic drive of my earlier arguments (supposing falsely that he were concerned to do so). Even though functions from 'normal contexts' to things in the world may correspond to items that are securely lodged within speakers' heads, they play no behavior-explanatory role themselves, *in propria persona*. As Brian Loar puts it, ('Conceptual Role and Truth-Conditions', *Notre Dame Journal of Formal Logic*, 23 (1982), p. 280), they are not themselves constituents of functional roles. They seem to add nothing to the picture already provided by functionalist psychology, and have no point unless it is toward a different sort of semantic description and explanation.

internal language is employed in thinking, a public language is a vehicle of communication.

III *Uses of truth*

(i) As has been observed by Hartry Field and many others,[16] we seem to mobilize T-sentences in forming beliefs on the basis of authority; we often gain knowledge of the world by taking another person's word for something and having taken it, disquoting it. Ernest LePore and Barry Loewer offer this example:

> Arabella, Barbarella, and Esa are in a room with Arabella looking out the window. Arabella and Barbarella understand German but Esa does not. Arabella turns from the window to Barbarella and Esa and utters the words 'Es schneit.' On the basis of this utterance Barbarella comes to believe that it's snowing … while Esa comes to believe only that Arabella said something which is probably true.[17]

What would Esa need to have known in order to have gleaned the same information Barbarella did? The obvious candidate, as Loewer says, is the T-sentence ' "Es schneit" is true iff it is snowing'. The assignment of truth-conditions to sentences allows us to exploit the general reliability of other speakers' beliefs. Nor is this practice casual or only occasionally handy; most of what we know we know by authority. Moreover, the truth-condition of 'Es schneit' in the example is not a feature which that sentence just fortunately happens to have in addition to its actual meaning. Intuitively, Esa fails to learn from Arabella's utterance precisely because he does not know what it means.

Informing as well as learning makes use of T-sentences, as Michael Devitt points out.[18] Ubiquitously we pursue our own purposes by implanting beliefs in others (whether sincerely or mendaciously). We implant beliefs in others by uttering sentences having the corresponding truth-conditions; our hearers disquote them and form beliefs as Barbarella did.

More generally, the assignment of full-fledged truth-conditions to sentences of a natural language helps to explain why a population's having that language

---

[16] Field, 'Tarski's Theory of Truth', *Journal of Philosophy*, 69 (1972), pp. 347–75, and 'Logic, Meaning, and Conceptual Role', *Journal of Philosophy*, 74 (1977), pp. 379–409; Ernest LePore, 'Truth and Inference', *Erkenntnis*, 17 (1982); pp. 379–95; Barry Loewer, 'The Role of "Conceptual Role" Semantics', *Notre Dame Journal of Formal Logic*, 23 (1982), pp. 305–15; Loar's *Mind and Meaning*; McGinn, 'The Structure of Content'; S. Schiffer, 'Truth and the Theory of Content'; and Michael Devitt, *Realism and Truth* (Princeton University Press, Princeton, 1984). Schiffer is skeptical of the uniqueness of a reliability-maximizing assignment of truth-conditions to the formulae of someone's language of thought; I assume he is equally skeptical in the case of a person's public language. But for reasons which will emerge I believe the two languages should be treated very differently, as regards motivating their respective semantics.

[17] Loewer, 'The Role of "Conceptual Role" Semantics,' p. 306, Cf. LePore and Loewer, 'Translational Semantics', *Synthese*, 48 (1981), pp. 121–33, and 'Three Trivial Truth Theories', *Canadian Journal of Philosophy*, 13 (1983), pp. 433–47; LePore, 'Truth and Inference', and 'What Model-Theoretic Semantics Cannot Do', *Synthese*, 54 (1983), pp. 167–87.

[18] Michael Devitt stresses this in sec. 6.8 of *Realism and Truth*.

confers a selectional advantage over otherwise comparable populations which have none.[19] The ability to token and respond appropriately to such noteworthy sentences as 'There is a good water source behind those rocks', 'There is a freshly killed antelope over here,' and 'There is a sabre-toothed cat just behind you' just when those sentences' respective truth-conditions obtain is obviously of some assistance to individuals who were by chance genetically disposed to acquire that ability. A solipsistic semantics – a semantics designed precisely to establish no connection between a speaker's mind and the external world – makes no such explanatory contribution, though it might display selectional advantages of some other kind.

CRS has a possible competing explanation of learning and informing: When Barbarella hears Arabella's utterance, she has a good enough grasp of Arabella's functional organization to recognize the tokening of 'Es schneit' as the typical effect of an inner state of Arabella which is itself typically caused by perceptual registration of nearby snowfall. Since Barbarella has no reason to suspect abnormal circumstances, she infers the best causal explanation of Arabella's tokening, according to which explanation it is indeed snowing. Truth has nothing to do with it.

The trouble with this account of Barbarella's reasoning is that it does not readily generalize.[20] Suppose we try to state a general principle that licenses the inference:

(P) (S)(t) (If t is a token of S, then t is the typical effect of an inner state of t's utterer which is itself normally caused by perceptual registration of its being the case that S).

(Let us restrict our discussion to observation sentences.) But (P) as stated is ill-formed, since 'S' appears both as a variable ranging over sentences and as a schematic letter having sentences as substituends. Is there a way of repairing this use/mention flaw? The obvious suggestion is to understand (P)'s first quantifier substitutionally. This would make (P) effectively equivalent to the infinite conjunction of all its instances. How could Barbarella have learned such a conjunction? Only if S's substituends were composed of elements over which a recursion was defined. The CRSist must maintain that these elements are atomic conceptual roles rather naming relations and satisfaction-conditions. And here again we seem to get the wrong predictions about what hearers would learn from typical utterances involving Twin-Earth designators and/or indexicals. In LePore and Loewer's example, if Barbarella reasons by way of a recursion on atomic conceptual roles rather than by way of a T-sentence, she will not learn that it is snowing as opposed to XYZing, for the inner state of Arabella's that has been caused by perceptual registration of snow would just as easily (and just as normally) have been caused by registration of crystalline *XYZ*. Similarly, had Arabella said (pointing to Esa) 'He drank a Malaga cooler this

---

[19] This point is due to David Dowty, *Word Meaning and Montague Grammar* (D. Reidel, Dordrecht, 1979), pp. 379–80).

[20] I owe this point to Kim Sterelny; see his unpublished ms., 'The Language of Thought Revisited'.

morning,' Barbarella would not have learned that Esa as opposed to Twin Esa had drunk the Malaga cooler, for the relevant inner state of Arabella would be the same whether it had been produced by a glimpse of the still shuddering Esa or a similar glimpse of Twin Esa. What is needed to distinguish the two is the fact that it really was Esa rather than Twin Esa who figured appropriately in the etiology of Arabella's inner state. And that is as near as matters to saying that the truth-condition rather than the 'narrow' conceptual role is the vehicle of learning.

Notice, incidentally, that the schema (P) is not fully solipsistic as stated. What replaces the phrase 'its being the case that S' will normally describe a state of affairs in the utterer's external environment, not something in the utterer's head. If Barbarella were to give a *genuinely* 'narrow' explanation of Arabella's tokening, she would have to specify the input condition for Arabella's inner state in terms of surface receptors, not in terms of an extrinsic state of affairs. And this, I think, destroys the plausibility of the suggestion that Barbarella learns that it is snowing by constructing a 'narrow' causal explanation of Arabella's tokening, for in order to construct such an explanation she would have to have fairly detailed knowledge of the structure of Arabella's retina (in order to cite a retinal event as the typical cause of the relevant inner state), as well as the knowledge that the occurrence of that retinal event is best explained by the local presence of snow. Surely no such thing is needed for learning by authority.

(ii) Speakers' *reporting* of the sayings and beliefs of other speakers presupposes that utterance-meaning is tied to truth-condition rather than to conceptual role.[21] If Arabella says 'I am hungry,' we report her as having said *that she was* hungry; in constructing our own complement clause we modify the person of Arabella's pronoun and the tense of her verb in order to preserve truth-condition. (If we wanted to preserve conceptual role, we could simply use her own words, which would result in a wildly inaccurate report, such as 'Arabella said that I am hungry.') Note too that we often make *de re* reports of sayings, using our own rather than the original speaker's mode of referring to our common subject-matter. When I hear the police sergeant say, 'The criminal must have dropped the anchovies as she ran,' I can report to my daughter (who did the deed), 'They said you must have dropped the anchovies as you ran,' or to my wife, 'They said our little genius must have dropped the anchovies as she ran.' If utterance-meaning were determined by the contents of the utterer's head, such *de re* reports would either make no sense or be strikingly false; the *res de* which an utterer has said something is extracalvarian. To put the point in terms of Twin Earth: Twin Bill and I both utter 'Arabella is hungry,' but we do not thereby make the same assertion, for one of us may have spoken truly and the other falsely, and it would be false for me to state here on Earth that Twin Bill asserted *that Arabella* is hungry; Twin Bill has never heard of her.

(iii) Public linguistic meaning is what is shared by all or most speakers of a given language. But conceptual role is notoriously not widely shared; it varies

[21] Cf. Mark Platts' Introduction to *Reference, Truth and Reality* (Routledge and Kegan Paul, London, 1980), and J. McDowell, 'Anti-Realism and the Epistemology of Understanding', in Parret and Bouveresse, *Meaning and Understanding*, pp. 229–30.

idiosyncratically from speaker to speaker. If we think of sentence's conceptual role as represented by the various subjective conditional probabilities assigned by a speaker to that sentence, then it plainly will vary across speakers, since subjective probabilities do. Even on a nonprobabilistic (perhaps more purely functional) account such as Harman's, names and other designators whose reference is constant in the public language have different 'narrow' conceptual roles for different speakers. This is what gives rise to Fregean puzzles about coreferring but otherwise independent names such as 'Hesperus' and 'Phosphorus,' or so I have argued elsewhere:[22] whatever the details of one's way of handling such puzzles, one thing that is indisputable is that 'Hesperus' and 'Phosphorus' play different roles in the victim's behavioral economy. (A more obvious example is that of 'Clark Kent' and 'Superman.') Natural-kind terms provide another example, if Putnam is right about the 'division of linguistic labor' and the determination of such terms' extensions by appeal to the relevant experts: 'elm,' 'beech,' 'gold,' 'molybdenum' *et al.* are unambiguous (so far as I am aware) in English, yet different speakers associate different 'stereotypes' with them and draw different inferences from sentences containing them. Conceptual roles, then, are commonly not shared by speakers of the same language. What do the speakers share? Reference and truth-conditions. And a good thing, too; otherwise we would be forever doomed to talk past each other.

IV *Three further arguments*

In this section I shall offer three further arguments (only the third of which is original) for denying that any solipsistic proposal can capture key aspects of locutionary meaning. The first[23] is that meaning *determines* truth-conditions while conceptual role notoriously does not. If a person knows the meaning of a sentence and is omniscient regarding fact, then that person knows whether or not the sentence is true. Twin-Earth cases show that conceptual role does not satisfy this same conditional: I can know the conceptual role that is common to tokens of 'This is water' and also know just what things are H_2O and which are *XYZ*, without thereby knowing whether 'This is water' is true (in English) at a given spot, because the conceptual role does nothing to distinguish water from *XYZ*; similarly, as Putnam says, my stereotype for 'elm' does not distinguish genuine elms from trees of countless other species. What does determine truth-value given a totality of facts, is precisely, a truth-condition.

Robert Brandom[24] has pointed out a second reason why CRS alone cannot tell the whole story about locutionary meaning, at least if a sentence's 'conceptual role' is to be expressed in the form of an assertibility condition. In a language containing common sorts of sentential embedding devices, such as conditional antecedent places, the assertibility-values of compound sentences are not determined by the assertibility-values of those sentences' components. Brandom considers the first-person future-tensed sentence, 'I will marry Jane.'

---

[22] Cf. Field, 'Logic Meaning, and Conceptual Role', and Lycan, 'The Paradox of Naming'.

[23] Cf. Field, 'Logic, Meaning, and Conceptual Role', p. 379.

[24] Brandom, 'Truth and Assertibility', *Journal of Philosophy*, 73 (1976), pp. 137–49; Brandom follows Dummett's *Frege: Philosophy of Language*, p. 451.

For most people,[25] 'I will marry Jane' is assertible just when 'I foresee that I will marry Jane' is, yet those two sentences are not intersubstitutable *salva assertibility* in the context, 'If ——— , then I will no longer be a bachelor'. Similarly, a disjunction may be assertible to such-and-such a degree even though neither of its disjuncts is assertible at all. Thus, truth-conditions, or something that plays the role of truth-conditions,[26] are needed even by a theorist whose main concern is assertibility, for the job of projecting assertibility conditions through operations of sentential compounding.

I think similar considerations would apply to varieties of CRS that allude just to causal/functional roles rather than assigning assertibility-*values* to sentences. Truth-conditions will be needed for the task of projecting the functional roles of compound sentences from those of their parts, even if for purposes of dealing with individual behavior one cares about the truth-conditions. Indeed, it seems reasonable to say the same about theories of *understanding* generally:[27] A hearer understands a compound sentence only by decomposing it and exploiting his more basic understanding of the sentence's parts; so he will require the services of a recursion on truth or some truth-like notion for accomplishing the projection.

It may be replied (as it was recently by Michael Devitt in a moment of devil's advocacy) that while all this is so and while the arguments of this paper have rather easily succeeded in showing that CRS and other solipsistic conceptions are inadequate to capture the meanings of the sentences of public natural languages, I have done nothing to show that *the whole package deal* comprised of truth, meaning, propositional attitudes, communication, assertion, and the rest is worth its weight in quarks and gluons. It is currently fashionable (and, I grant, true) to observe that these notions are part of a large and inchoate folk theory which should be accepted by philosophers only if its explanatory utility can satisfactorily be demonstrated.

I have no such demonstration to offer, though I have taken some steps toward one elsewhere.[28] Fortunately, none is required for my more modest project here. For present purposes (and on the basis of previous defenses)[29] I am

---

[25] We must here disregard people whose foreseeings are logically guaranteed, and people whose malfunctioning introspectors keep 'I foresee that I will marry Jane' from being assertible even when the people do so foresee.

[26] Brandom himself expresses diffidence about the centrality and about the robustness of the truth-like notion that is needed to subserve a theory of assertibility: 'From the point of view of the technical project of generating assertibility conditions, the notions of truth and of truth conditions are theoretical auxiliaries, to be cut and pasted in whatever ways give us the nicest account of assertibility conditions' (p. 148). I take this to mean at least that Brandom would be happy with any notion answering to Convention T, and with a 'merely disquotational' as opposed to 'causal-explanatory' notion of truth, as current jargon has it. On the latter question I have no firm opinion, particularly since I have seen no clear and complete explanation of the alleged 'merely disquotational' sense of 'true', though I daresay the prosentential theory due to Grover, Camp and Belnap ('A Prosentential Theory of Truth', *Philosophical Studies*, 28 (1975),pp. 73–125) qualifies as the most promising explication of it to date.

[27] Cf. Dowty, *Word Meaning*, p. 383.

[28] See my 'Thoughts About Things', *The Representation of Knowledge and Belief, Vol. 1*, ed M. Brand and M. Harnish (University of Arizona Press, Tucson).

[29] Chiefly 'Toward a Homuncular Theory of Believing,' and 'Psychological Laws', *Philosophical Topics*, 12 (1981), pp. 9–38.

presupposing the integrity of the propositional attitudes and the truth of the
common-sense view that human subjects of such attitudes communicate with
each other. I would also appeal to the sorts of data that are traditionally
addressed by theories of meaning, and argue[30] that truth-theoretic semantics is
the best such theory. My main contention here is only that if we drop the
notions of truth and reference, we drop that of linguistic meaning as well;
whether the most recently proposed sentencing and execution of meaning is a
good idea, I leave for others to judge.

Thus I would insist that the issue of the probity of referential semantics for
natural languages is quite separate from that of the probity of referential
semantics for propositional attitudes. Elsewhere[31] I have defended what
LePore and Loewer call a 'dual aspect' semantics for belief, alternately
recognizing both 'wide' semantical features and 'narrow' or solipsistic causal/
computational features of belief states, but unlike some theorists[32] I do not
extend this duple treatment to public natural languages, precisely because they
are public. I suppose I am willing to concede a solipsistic notion of meaning,
'meaning-for-S-at-t' perhaps, which might be identified with 'conceptual role'
or some solipsistic property, but such a notion would be found within individual
psychology rather than making any significant contribution to linguistics.

I now turn to my third argument, a *reductio*. Let us try to *construct* a language
from which reference and truth-conditions are absent – a purely formal
calculus the use of which is governed by purely syntactic 'assertion' conditions.
('Assertions' of sign-designs belonging to the calculus are just acts of tokening;
imagine that the 'speakers' – or better, the players – hold up placards with the
sign-designs printed on them.) We may make the set of 'assertion' conditions
fairly large and have its members interlock in various complex ways. Now we
can shepherd a group of speakers or players into a room and have them begin
following the 'assertion' rules. Some of their tokenings will be triggered by the
appearance of external objects at the door or windows, others will be tokened in
response to previous tokenings by other players or of one's own; some tokenings
will themselves trigger various nonlinguistic acts.[33] After the players have had
some practice, the game can be played at tournament speed and everyone will
have a good time. The placards might be painted in different colors, in such a
way as to form pretty patterns that will make the game pleasing for spectators to
watch.

I have attempted to describe a paradigmatic 'conceptual role language.' Each
placard has a role in the players' respective behavioral economies, and what
determines tokening at any point is something directly accessible to the players.
Nothing is presumed about external things or events not directly visible at doors
or windows, and nothing is known to the players about the ultimate external
effects of the non-linguistic acts that are prompted by 'command' tokenings.
The players' 'verbal' behavior is simply determined by the directly visible events

[30] For a global defense, see *Logical Form in Natural Language*.

[31] 'Toward a Homuncular Theory of Believing', and 'The Paradox of Naming'.

[32] E.g., Field, 'Logic, Meaning, and Conceptual Role', and McGinn, 'The Structure of
Content'.

[33] Cf. Sellars, 'Some Reflections'.

and the machine program constituted by the (made-up) rules of the game. If CRS is correct (and perhaps if our game is complex enough), then our players are speakers of a language – it might even be, unbeknownst to them, a notational variant of some fragment of English under some disguising transformation.

My question is, in what sense if any *is* the game a language? In particular, have we succeeded in excluding reference and truth? Not obviously so; it may be that reference and truth have crept in unannounced. For we have sign-designs that are (by rule) tokened only in response to certain sorts of appearances at windows or door, and which lead in turn to other sorts of tokening and ultimately to action which may include behaving discriminatively toward the objects so appearing. If so, is it not natural to speak of the sign-designs as *referring* to individuals and to kinds? And if there is reference and predication, there is truth; there is also assertion in the full-blooded sense.[34]

On this construal we may see the players as constituting a speech community, united by their mutual use of the common formal calculus. Their use of it is public. But insofar as their terms have reference, the language is no longer solipsistic, because the assertion rules key on features of objects that are external to the individual speakers. A player would not succeed in obeying a rule that said, 'If a red cylinder appears at the south window, hold up the placard that says "SQUIGGLE"', unless what was in fact a red cylinder had appeared at what was in fact the south window, however scrupulously he may have tried to obey the rule from his own end. This makes the rule in effect into a truth-condition.

Suppose we tried more carefully to couch our input rules in solipsistic terms: 'If you are appeared to red-cylindrically in the south-windowish sector of your visual field, ...' Then, assuming a story similar to the foregoing one of how reference and truth might creep in unannounced, the players' sign-designs would now refer to internal appearings of various qualitative sorts and to phenomenal properties; they would still have truth-conditions, but these new truth-conditions would be solipsistic in the older sense of that term. Each speaker would be able to talk only about his or her own mental life. So long as it is coherent to suppose that what looks to spectators like a group of people speaking a communal and unambiguous public language is actually a collocation of individuals each of whom speaks his own solipsistic language and thereby talks past all his fellows, the meanings of an individual speaker's tokenings will still be given by a truth-definition idiosyncratically tailored to that speaker's private referents. (Given an incorrigibility assumption of the sort that naturally attends the idea of a solipsistic language, the truth-condition of a sentence of the language would coincide with its assertion or verification condition.)

---

[34] Readers who are fond of group organisms will see another way of looking at our present setup: The game-room together with its occupants is itself an input-output system, provided from outside with sense-data and eventually issuing responses. The players inside the room are merely the homunculi who corporately constitute the game-room's speech center, and the formal calculus functions as the game-room's language of thought. The game-room thus construed as a single organism speaks a private and solipsistic language if any; its terms refer only to the objects that the

However, suppose we ruthlessly refuse to let reference and truth creep as we have suspected back into our 'conceptual role language', either in its public or in its genuinely solipsistic and private form. That is, suppose the sign-designs' significance, in a broader use of that term, is exhausted by their conceptual roles *exclusive* of reference and truth, as is the intent of CRS. (I have dwelt on reference-infiltrated versions of our game only to distinguish a genuinely solipsistic version from them; I suspect that some people find CRS attractive only because they *are* tacitly infusing reference of some sort.)[35] Then, it seems to me, there is nothing to mark the speakers' activity as *linguistic* activity *per se*. For all we know about it on the present construal is that it is rule-governed, and not every rule-governed activity is linguistic in any full-blooded sense. Consider chess, or musical performance, or improvisation within a severely constrained musical form. We sometimes use linguistic metaphors in describing instances of these activities, as when chess gambits are said to be 'declined,' or a musical 'phrase' is said to take the form of 'question and answer,' but these cases contrast with ones in which chess moves or musical phrases *might literally be used as code symbols*, say as conveying secret messages between spies. Chess moves and musical phrases have no intrinsic locutionary meanings; they are not assertions *that* anything. Nor, I suggest, has a merely syntactically defined 'move' in a 'conceptual-role' game an intrinsic meaning (unless it is connected, however indirectly, to an input rule of the sort that would serve to establish either external or solipsistic reference). A move in a 'conceptual-role' game is not an assertion *that* anything either. What is missing? Reference and truth[36]

V *A final objection*

I shall close by considering an objection that applies at once to all the arguments I have made. It is that I have failed to distinguish two questions: (i) Why need we advert to any 'wide' semantical notion rather than sticking entirely to narrow or solipsistic features of human speakers, and (ii) why do we fasten on *reference*

---

player-homunculi can see, window-appearances being the functional equivalent of retinal hits. (This is because the assertion rules key only on properties of objects that are directly detectable by the players. For the same reason, Twin-Earth difficulties cannot arise.)

[35] This is the case with Harman's *wide* conceptual role theory (see fn 10 above), though Harman stops short of allowing that the extracalvarian functional relations he invokes are specifically *referential* relations in the full-blooded sense. Jerry Fodor has tried to salvage thought contents somewhat differently, by constructing an 'observation language' of appearings, in which contents can be expressed entirely in solipsistic terms (see 'Observation Reconsidered', *Philosophy of Science*, 51 (1984)).

[36] The reader may be reminded, pleasantly or unpleasantly, of John Searle's 'Chinese Room' argument against machine intentionality ('Minds, Brains, and Programs', *Behavioral and Brain Sciences*, 3 (1980), pp. 417–24). Since I have urged elsewhere that Searle's argument is a non-starter ('The Functionalist Reply (Ohio State)', *Behavioural and Brain Sciences*, 3 (1980), pp. 434–35), I must distinguish it from my own present complaint against CRS. Searle infers, from the single premise that *internally* a machine is only a formal manipulator of uninterpreted symbols, the conclusion that the machine's inner states must lack intentional content; this I take to be a glaring *non sequitur*, since 'content' in the semantical sense is an 'external' or wide property of states of organisms in any case. My own argument is rather that if our 'conceptual' role consists only in the formal manipulation of symbols *and if* by hypothesis no wide semantical properties are generated thereby (with the environment's collusion), then the game does not constitute a language, nor its players' competence at it understanding of one.

and *truth* in particular as against some other wide notions? John Wallace, Hartry Field and Stephen Leeds[37] have pointed out that besides the standard valuation function that assigns the intuitively correct extensions to our singular terms and predicates, there are countless other functions from expressions to items in the world that would preserve the same distribution of truth-values over sentences. The intuitively correct extensions can be systematically permuted. For example, let V be a function that maps each physical object onto the space-time chunk that lies exactly one mile in such-and-such a direction from the object itself, and let a predicate be 'V-satisfied' by an object x just in case it is satisfied by $V(x)$. Then in our truth theory for English we can replace the denotata of all the singular terms by their images under V and compensate by mobilizing V-satisfaction instead of 'real' satisfaction. Nothing else in the truth theory will be affected. Now, why are what we think of as 'genuine' reference and satisfaction to be thus distinguished from among all the other 'schemes of reference' we could devise in this arbitrary way? Not for any reason depending solely on Davidson's program. A truth theory for Native will not care whether 'gavagai' genuinely refers to rabbits or to rabbit-shaped space-time chunks over in the next county, so long as a compensating pseudo-satisfaction relation makes the truth-values of sentences come out right.

Davidsonian semantics is in no immediate trouble. Logical form is invariant under all the different reference schemes; from the viewpoint of the truth theory, they are notational variants of each other. And it is still a determinate fact (so far as has been shown) that the truth-condition of a Native sentence containing 'gavagai' is something involving rabbits, even if it is also a fact that the 'V-truth'-condition of the same sentence is something about oddly distributed rabbit-shaped space-time chunks. But this does not help to show why reference and truth themselves *as opposed to* 'V-reference' and 'V-truth' are of interest and importance to linguistics, which question incorporates (ii) above as well as (i).

The imposter notions generated by Field's permutations of extension are public and common to speakers of the same natural language. If 'elm' is satisfied for all English speakers just by genuine elms, then it is V-satisfied for all English speakers by elm-shaped chunks of space located one mile in direction so-and-so from genuine elms. Thus, my general run of objections to pure methodological solipsism does not distinguish satisfaction from V-satisfaction, and so does not show why the latter is only an 'imposter'. This omission alone would be no great crime, since (as I have noted) the compensatory shift from reference to V-reference would leave the theorems of our truth definition untouched. But why fasten upon a *truth* definition rather than on a V-*truth* definition?[38] Even though the class of true sentences and that

---

[37] Wallace, 'Only in the Context of a Sentence Do Words Have Any Meaning', in *Contemporary Perspectives in the Philosophy of Language*, ed P. A. French, T. E. Uehling and H. Wettstein (University of Minnesota Press, Minneapolis, 1979); Field, 'Conventionalism and Instrumentalism in Semantics', *Nous* 9 (1975), pp. 375–405; Leeds, 'Theories of Reference and Truth', *Erkenntnis*, 13 (1978), pp. 111–29. (And cf. Davidson's 'Reality without Reference', *Dialectica*, 31 (1977), pp. 247–58.) I believe the argument is originally due to Wallace.

[38] Fa is V-true iff *a* V-satisfies F. A V-truth-definition results when the move to V-satisfaction is not compensated by a corresponding move to V-reference.

of *V*-true sentences overlap hardly at all, *V*-truth is as public as truth and is 'shared' as widely in any linguistic community, so my objections to CRS do not apply.

Two cases must be distinguished: (a) Field's permutations range freely; any that affords a suitable recursion is allowed. (b) The permutations are restricted to what we might call 'individuative resections' of normal extensions. Let us begin with (a), the more drastic. Why is it more interesting or important to linguistics that 'Mose Allison is white' is true iff Mose Allison is white, than that 'Mose Allison is white' is *V*-true iff Mose Allison is a chunk of space located one mile west of a similarly shaped white object?

A first answer is that the argument from learning and informing still has some force here. The story of Arabella and her listeners gives epistemic and thereby linguistic significance to the fact that 'Es schneit' is true iff it is snowing, but I cannot think of a similar story that would give comparable significance to the fact that 'Es schneit' is *V*-true iff we are one mile west of a region in which it is snowing. Barbarella normally would have no reason to think that Arabella's beliefs (of the relevant kind) were almost invariably *V*-true. *V*-truth *could* figure in an argument from authority, I suppose, in a world whose inhabitants were *V*-reliable rather than reliable, but such a world would be an uncanny world, magical, causally very different from ours. In our own world a *V*-reliable person would be a freak, a weirdo, and as reproductively fit as a lighter-than-air python.

Such practical matters aside, a legitimate metaphysical concern also favors truth over *V*-truth. If causality, and in particular nondeviant causal chains, serve as our benchmark of reality, then whatever 'truthlike' notion best reflects a unified assembly of causal relations in nature will rightly be awarded pre-eminent ontological status as well as epistemic significance. The connection between 'Snow is white' and snow's being white is causally tight, due to the undoubted respective connections between utterances of 'snow' and snow, and utterances of 'white' and whiteness-instances. But there is no even faintly non-deviant connection between utterances of 'snow' and items' being one mile to the west of quantities of snow, nor between utterances of 'white' and chunks of space located one mile to the west of similarly shaped white objects. This seems sufficient to condemn *V*-truth to a very low ontological caste, at least in our current incarnation.[39]

---

[39] Wallace notes (*op. cit.*) that his skeptical conclusion is incompatible with causal theories of reference, but in arguing that such theories do not help their proponents establish determinacy he only addresses the case of demonstrative perceptual identification and reminds us *á la* Wittgenstein that demonstrative ostension is itself indeterminate and so cannot help restore determinacy to reference generally. This is true, but does not entail that perceptual identification is not in fact what grounds our intuitions about reference in particular cases. I would maintain that adequacy to such intuitions is a further constraint against which 'schemes of reference' may be tested, and that the intuitions do support a causal theory of some sort – at least, the wilder Wallacean permutations may fairly be ruled out by appeal to a causal *necessary* condition. (Thus I flatly disagree with those who hold that 'refer', 'designate', 'denote' and the like are purely philosophers' terms of art, regarding which neither ordinary people's nor philosophers' own intuitions are reliable or even relevant. Ordinary people do have a robust notion of linguistic aboutness, and causal theories do a fair job of capturing that notion. I would insist it is a fact that Esa's term 'Arabella' refers in the ordinary sense to Arabella rather than to Twin Arabella (for Esa is completely unaffected by Twin Arabella), and it

The more conservative case (b) eludes both these arguments. W. V. Quine's famous permutations of our standard reference scheme do not shift extensions into the next country, but merely change the standard referents' ontological categories. Where there is a rabbit, there are also collections of undetached rabbit-parts, rabbity time-slices, and the like, all of which could equally to be involved in the etiologies of utterances of 'gavagai', and causal notions do not discriminate as between these various individuative resections.[40] For an individuative resection of a state of affairs leaves that state of affairs' causal properties unchanged. Let V_c be a Field-style permutation that works by individuative resection alone. Then any speaker who is reliable is also V_c-reliable, and vice versa, the two notions being at least nomologically equivalent; and V_c-truth is causally as top-drawer as truth.

Here I believe we should grant some arbitrariness, pending the isolation of a truly basic unit of causality. That 'Lo, a rabbit' is true iff the speaker ostends a rabbit has no more intrinsic linguistic significance than that 'Lo, a rabbit' is V_c-true iff the speaker ostends a rabbit-stage. Here our choice of a 'scheme of reference' is only a matter of convenience, naturalness and so on. And why not? As Brian Loar has observed in regard to Quine's indeterminacy doctrine,[41] the 'arbitrariness' of our causal ascriptions as between individuative resections holds throughout our theory of nature, precisely because causality does not discriminate as between resections. To use Loar's example, where there is a heart pumping blood, there are also collections of undetached heart parts, cardiac time-slices, Hearthood instances and so on; insofar as it is 'indeterminate' or relative to an interpretive scheme which of these things is really doing the pumping, the indeterminacy is of little interest in general and of no interest in particular to the semanticist. Semantics is not singled out for embarrassment. Once the truly vicious imposters have been ruled out (case (a)), only convenience and naturalness are needed either to explain or to justify our appeal to truth rather than to V_c-truth in linguistics.[42]

---

is a fact that my term 'Mose Allison' refers to Mose Allison and not to any Allison-shaped chunk of space 5280 feet away. The question of *why we have* this concept of reference rather than that of V-reference or another imposter is a further, I suppose anthropological question, albeit an interesting one.)

[40] There is a chance of restoring determinacy even here, if whatever turns out to be the correct theory of causality itself tells us what ontological categories figure directly in causal relations (my own preference is for *events* rather than individuals or states or properties); if a theory of causality thus distinguishes an ontological category, then a causal theory of reference will after all distinguish a particular mode of rabbit individuation. As Field points out (pp. 383–84), this strategy merely shifts the skeptical question to that of why the authors of the relevant theory of reference chose to invoke causality proper rather than 'slice'-causality or 'state'-causality or some other easily definable variant; an answer to this would presumably fall out of the argument for the correctness of our chosen theory of causality. On the other hand, it may well be that 'events', 'processes', 'stages', and even 'properties' and 'individuals' are all mere abstractions from the more basic notion of a fact or state of affairs. If the sectioning of states of affairs is itself metaphysically indeterminate in this way, then the *ensuing* indeterminacy of reference as between resections is no further surprise.

[41] *Mind and Meaning*, pp. 234–37.

[42] I am grateful to Bernard Linsky for his excellent comments at the Davidson Conference, and to Ernie Lepore for lengthy and very helpful correspondence on the topic of this paper.

14

Information and the Mental

HILARY PUTNAM

When a linguist attempts to learn a language from native informants without relying on previous information about the language in the form of dictionaries or grammars, one problem he faces is that the meaning he assigns to any word or morpheme may have to be changed if it turns out that interpreting the word or morpheme in that particular way does not fit new utterances and new contexts of use. Interpretation is a matter of trade-offs, and it is difficult to imagine reducing it to a precise rule or algorithm. Philosophers who would like to 'naturalize' the notions of meaning and reference are faced with a hard choice. They can either try to account for the phenomena that we pre-analytically describe by saying that sentences *have meanings* on the basis of the use of just the individual sentences (including the causes and effects of such use) without taking into account the fact that each sentence has words in common with infinitely many other sentences, or they can try to construct a theory which describes languages as wholes consisting of interdependent parts. The latter approach sounds more realistic in principle, but threatens to be insuperably difficult in practice; for this reason, some philosophers (for example, Jerry Fodor)[1] have recently expressed an interest in reviving and rehabilitating the former, less holistic, approach. An ambitious start in this direction was made by Fred Dretske in his *Knowledge and the Flow of Information*.

In a precis of his book written for a well-known journal of cognitive psychology,[2] Dretske described his purpose as being 'to deepen our understanding of the baffling place of mind, the chief consumer of information, in the natural order of things'. The way in which Dretske hoped to do this was to employ an information-theoretic notion of sentence meaning. Information theory, in all its versions and spin-offs, starts with the notion of *probability*; thus

---

[1] In a paper read at the Chapel Hill Colloquium in Philosophy, 15 October 1983, titled 'Observation Reconsidered', Fodor argued that, while belief fixation is holistic, the identity conditions for denotations may *not* be. 'Suffice it to repeat the lesson that causal semantic theories have recently been teaching us,' he writes (p. 12), 'viz., that holism may not be true. Specifically it may not be true that (all) the semantical properties of sentences (/beliefs) are determined by the theoretical networks in which they are embedded.' In response to a question, Fodor identified Dretske's as the 'causal semantic theory' he had in mind.

[2] *The Brain and Behavior Sciences*, 6 (1983), pp. 55–63.

Dretske's idea is that it is probability relations between certain events (uses of signs) and certain other events (the events the signs represent) that will enable us to define the 'information' conveyed by a sign. Specifically, Dretske asserts that an event E gives the *information* that some other event X has taken place if the conditional probability of X relative to E is 1, while the prior (or 'absolute') probability of X in the situation(s) is less than 1. For example, let S be a type of situation in which the probability of there being a cat on a mat is less than 1, and let us suppose that when someone utters the sentence 'A cat is on a mat', the probability that there is a cat on a mat rises to 1. Then, on Dretske's definition, saying 'A cat is on a mat' in a situation of kind S conveys the information that there is a cat on a mat.

One problem with this definition is evident from the outset: the notion of a 'situation' is notoriously vague. If one wishes to give a materialist account of the notion of information, as Dretske does, then the use of notions of 'event' and 'situation', which are problematic from the point of view of one's own metaphysics, leaves the entire enterprise somewhat floating in the air. I assume that, on Dretske's account, the 'event' of seeing an eclipse is supposed objectively to convey the information that the reappearance of the sun will take place in a few minutes. But does it?

If the 'situation' is one in which the relative frequency of sun-reappearances on the condition that someone saw an eclipse is 1, then one of Dretske's requirements if fulfilled: the conditional probability is $1 - P$ (the sun will reappear in a few minutes/someone saw an eclipse) $= 1$ – but to show that Dretske's other requirement is also fulfilled, we need to know that the prior probability that the sun will reappear in a few minutes is less than 1. If we take the *astronomer's* description to be the *relevant description* of the 'situation', then, relative to *that* specification of the situation, the probability that the sun will reappear in a few minutes is 1 *whether anyone sees an eclipse or not*. The prior probability – P (the sun will reappear in a few minutes) – is not less than 1, and the eclipse-seeing does not give the information that the sun will reappear; it fails to give the information, on Dretske's definition, just because the reappearance was *predictable* whether one actually perceived the eclipse or not. But if the relevant description of the situation S is that someone looks at the sky, then relative to *that* reference class of situations, the probability that the sun will reappear in a few minutes (after an eclipse or a period of darkness) is, indeed, much less than 1. But this dependence of the probability – and hence the *information* – on what one takes to be the reference class is nowhere allowed for by Dretske.

In addition to explicating, or attempting to explicate, the notion of *information*, Dretske also sketches a way in which his approach might be extended to give a theory of *reference*. But this is simply a mistake: it is possible to show that no account of the kind Dretske gives, that is, no account consisting of clauses which refer to probabilities, can be a correct account of what it is for an event E (say, the uttering of 'A cat is on a mat') to refer to something (say, cats).

I shall give a simple 'impossibility proof'. The proof turns on the fact that probability obeys the following *L-Equivalence Rule*:

(To state the Rule, I write $p \equiv q$ for p is *logically equivalent to q*)

(1) $P(A,B) = P(A',B')$ whenever $A \equiv A'$ and $B \equiv B'$

(The rule is also assumed as a basic rule of inference in the standard mathematical theory of probability.)

From (1) we immediately derive:

(2) $P(A,B) = P(A,B')$ whenever $B \equiv B'$
(3) $P(A,B) = P(A',B)$ whenever $A \equiv A'$.

What (1), (2) and (3) say is that probabilities cannot distinguish between logically equivalent states of affairs.

In my recent book *Reason, Truth and History* (*RT&H*), I showed that there are properties which I called 'cat*' and 'mat*' such that (see *RT&H*, chapter II):

(i)   The things which possess the property of being cats* in the actual world are *cherries*.
(ii) The things which possess the property of being mats* in the actual world are *trees*.
(iii) *A cat being on a mat* and *a cat* being on a mat** are logically equivalent states of affairs. (See the appendix to *RT&H* for a generalization of this result.) In *RT&H* the purpose of this somewhat bizarre construction of properties was to argue that the materialist metaphysician lacks the resources to explain why the word 'cat' doesn't refer to cats* (doesn't have the set of *cherries* as its extension in the actual world). Can Dretske meet the challenge?

In a word, the problem is that 'A cat is on a mat' refers to cats and mats, while 'A cat* is on a mat*' refers to cats* (which happen to be cherries, in the actual world) and to mats* (which happen to be trees, in the actual world). Yet *a cat being on mat* and *a cat* being on a mat** are the same state of affairs, up to logical equivalence. Knowing what state of affairs, up to logical equivalence, a sentence corresponds to does not tell one what its words refer to. But *probability relations* only connect words (or rather the event of someone's uttering those words) to states of affairs ('events' in the jargon of probability theory) not to things. Even if we can determine that the event of someone's saying 'A cat is on a mat' gives the information that some cat is on some mat by using probability relations, that cannot tell us that those words referred to cats and mats and not to cherries and trees. The reason is clear: up to logical equivalence, that a cat is on a mat is the same information as the information that a cat* is on a mat*, and no notion that obeys the L-Equivalence Rule can fix states of affairs more finely than logical equivalence. If you 'pack in' a notion that does not individuate states of affairs more finely than logical equivalence, you cannot 'pack out' a notion that individuates things more finely than logical equivalence. The reference of the words in a sentence depends on *more* than the 'information' given by the uttering of the sentence, in Dretske's sense of 'information'. The approach Dretske takes cannot solve the problem that has come to be known as Brentano's,[3] the problem of giving a naturalistic account of reference.

---

[3] The scholastic word 'intentional' was revived by Brentano in connection with this problem. Brentano's thesis was that there is no breaking out of the intentional vocabulary by reducing intentional idioms to non-intentional ones. Cf. Chisholm's development of this thesis in *Perceiving*, ch. 11, and Quine's remarks in *Word and Object*, pp. 219–22.

Probability and counterfactuals

The notion of probability that Dretske has in mind seems to be the notion that we use in such statements as:

> If someone eats arsenic, the probability that he or she will die is greater than 0.9.

which have a 'dispositional' or 'causal' component. The above statement does not just say that the relative frequency of deaths in the population of all people who actually eat or have eaten arsenic is greater than nine-tenths. It means that eating arsenic would *cause* death in a certain proportion of cases. On the 'possible worlds' semantics for counterfactuals and for causal statements proposed by David Lewis,[4] the above statement asserts such things as that:

In all worlds sufficiently similar to the actual world in which people take arsenic the frequency of deaths soon after taking the arsenic is greater than 0.9

or

In any world W sufficiently similar to the actual world, (1) the frequency of deaths soon after taking the arsenic among the population of people in W who eat arsenic is greater than 0.9; and (2) if a person in W eats arsenic and dies within a short time, then (almost always) in any world W' sufficiently similar to the world W in which that person does not eat the arsenic, he or she does not die at that time or near it.

or

In any world W sufficiently similar to the actual world, (1) there is a subset S of the people who eat arsenic whose frequency relative to the whole population of those who eat arsenic in W is greater than 0.9, and such that all the members of S die soon after taking the arsenic, and such that (2) if any world sufficiently similar to W in which a member of S does not eat the arsenic, he or she does not die at that time or near it

or

something still more hideously complicated.

However, counterfactuals also obey the (analogue of) the L-Equivalence Rule under any fixed similarity metric: logically equivalent statements can be substituted for one another in a counterfactual *salva veritate*.

The bearing of this on projects similar to Dretske's is immediate. We have already seen that reference cannot be defined in terms of any notion that obeys

---

[4] Cf. Lewis's *Counterfactuals*.

the L-Equivalence Rule. Since counterfactuals obey the L-Equivalence Rule, counterfactual connection is a notion in terms of which reference cannot be defined. (Combining our two results, we can say that reference cannot be defined in terms of probabilities, or in terms of counterfactuals alone, or in terms of probabilities *and* counterfactuals.)

Someone might propose to abandon the Lewis-Stalnaker 'possible worlds semantics' for counterfactuals. But then what account, even of an informal kind, can we give of counterfactuals, causal statements, and dispositional statements?

A 'stab' at an account of the truth conditions for counterfactuals was made by Nelson Goodman in his celebrated *Fact, Fiction, and Forecast*. In this approach, we think of a counterfactual as typically asserting a kind of nomic dependence between events: an event at a certain time t_0 (one which is only a 'hypothetical event', i.e., which did not actually take place), is said to be such that *if* it had taken place, then, as a matter of *law*, another event E would have taken place at, say, t_1:

If C had happened at t_0, then E would have happened at t_1.

This is the sort of statement Goodman wishes to explicate. Of course, the explication will have to assume the existence of a definite set L of (known and unknown) true natural laws. The problem is that, when we say that

If John had eaten arsenic at t_0, then John would have been dead at t_1,

we do not mean that there are laws which imply that anyone who eats arsenic dies at a not-too-distant later time. We know that to be not the case: it is possible to eat arsenic and not die (if, for example, one has developed a tolerance for the substance). What we mean is that (1) there is a set of 'relevant conditions' (such as not having developed a tolerance for arsenic), such that there is a (perhaps very complicated) law to the effect that if those conditions obtain and one eats arsenic, then one dies; and (2) *those* conditions actually obtained (in John's case) at t_0.

What is a 'relevant condition'? We cannot take the 'relevant conditions' to be all the statements of a certain form (say, initial and boundary conditions on a suitable 'system' including John's body) that were in fact true of John at t_0, since some of these would have necessarily had to be different if John had eaten the arsenic, or, indeed, done *anything* other than what he did. (This is why Lewis considers possible worlds 'sufficiently similar' to the actual world, rather than the actual world.) Call a statement S (of the right form to be a 'relevant condition' at t_0) 'cotenable' with counterfactuals whose antecedent is 'John ate arsenic at t_0' just in case S is a statement which is (1) true in the actual world; and (2) would have remained true even if John had eaten the arsenic at t_0. Then Goodman's proposal is that the counterfactual is true just in case its consequent ('John is dead at t_1') follows *deductively* from the following set of statements: the set consisting of the set L of all natural laws together with all the statements which are 'cotenable' with the antecedent and the antecedent itself. In symbols, using T for the set of cotenable statements, the above counterfactual is true just in case

'John is dead at t_1' follows deductively from $L \cup T \cup$
$\cup$ {'John ate arsenic at t_0'}

Even if Goodman's proposal had been successful (and it seems reasonable), the difficulty from the point of view of Dretske's project would be the same as before. It is evident from the form of the truth-condition given above that the truth or falsity of the counterfactual would not be affected by substituting any logically equivalent statement for its antecedent or any logically equivalent statement for its consequent. In short, under Goodman's proposal, counterfactuals obey the L-Equivalence Rule (as, intuitively, they should). The impossibility of using counterfactuals to arrive at a notion of probability which does *not* obey the L-Equivalence Rule stems from the very meaning of the counterfactual itself: how can 'If A' had been the case ...' amount to a different supposition than 'If A had been the case ...' if A and A' are *logically equivalent*? How could it be the case that *if A had been the case, B would have happened*, and not the case that *if A had been the case, B' would have happened* if B and B' are *logically equivalent*?

We should try to keep two different sorts of questions in mind (without confusing them, but also without neglecting either). The first sort of question, to which the point about the L-Equivalence Rule speaks, is whether one or another program of 'reducing' reference to something else (whether the 'something else' be a probability-based notion of 'information', or the notion of 'functional organization', or the notion of causation, or any other notion whose place in 'the natural order' is thought to be clearer than that of reference itself) can really be carried out. The second sort of question is whether completing the program would really make the place of reference in 'the natural order' any clearer from the point of view of the deep philosophical worries that give rise to these various reduction programs in the first place. For example, we have just seen that reference cannot be reduced to counterfactual connection. Would it have made the place of reference in the 'natural order' clearer if a definition of reference in terms of counterfactual connection (as analysed by David Lewis or by Nelson Goodman) *had* been successfully given?

Goodman, moreover, advances his proposal only to point out a difficulty. 'Cotenability' itself was *explained using a counterfactual*. The purpose of Goodman's account of counterfactuals is not to 'solve' the problem of giving truth conditions for counterfactuals, but to illustrate the enormous difficulty of doing this in a non-circular way. Replacing the notion of 'cotenability' by the notion of 'similarity' does not avoid the circularity. For, as Jonathan Bennett has pointed out,[5] what Lewis calls 'similarity' of possible worlds is *not* over-all similarity or 'closeness' in any intuitive sense. Rather than speak of a 'similarity metric', Lewis should have spoken of a *cotenability* metric: his 'sufficiently similar' worlds are worlds that are highly 'cotenable' with the actual world, that is,

[5] Cf. 'Counterfactuals and Possible Worlds', *The Canadian Journal of Philosophy*, 4, (Dec. 1974), pp. 381–402.

worlds in which Goodman's 'relevant conditions' are more-or-less as they would (or anyway *might*) have been had the antecedent of some counterfactual been true. (This explains why, when we apply the Lewis theory to actual cases, we find that we often have to *change the similarity metric*[6] when we change the counterfactual under discussion; 'cotenability' depends on which counterfactual we have in mind.) If anyone giving truth conditions for counterfactuals has to take as primitive such notions as 'similarity' or 'cotenability', notions which reflect exactly what a rational scientist (in a state of what amounts to omniscience) would take to be 'relevant conditions', what he would take as 'other things being equal', what he would take as an 'important' respect of similarity between a hypothetical situation and the actual, then such truth conditions can hardly be regarded as contributing to our metaphysical understanding. For how can one regard such notions as 'built into' nature? One might as well say *reference* is built into nature and be done with it!

Elizabeth Anscombe has argued,[7] correctly in my opinion, that the notion of causation is not definable in terms of the counterfactual conditional. 'A caused B' cannot be analysed, *pace* David Lewis, as 'If A had not been the case, B would not have been the case either.' Taking account of this point complicates the discussion somewhat (which is why, in the last few pages, I wrote as if the problems of analysing causation and of analysing counterfactual connection were one and the same; not that I think this is the case, but that it makes for an easier exposition of the difficulties to write as if it were the case). Returning to our typical ordinary language probability statement

> If someone eats arsenic, the probability that he or she will die
> is greater than 0.9

with this complication in mind, we observe two things. The statement means,[8] as we said, that eating arsenic would cause death in a certain proportion of the cases (even if the people who ate it were not the same people as the ones who ate it in the actual world, provided that they were not specially selected for resistance to arsenic poisoning, and provided the situation were 'normal'). But this assertion is a counterfactual assertion which itself involves a causal claim.

---

[6] For an example see my *Realism and Reason*, p. 61.

[7] Consider her remark on the attempt of Max Born to explicate causation in terms of dependence of the effect on the cause: 'It is not quite clear what "dependence" is supposed to be, but at least it seems to imply that you could not get the effect without the cause. The trouble is that you might – from some other cause. That this effect was produced by this cause does not show that it could not, or would not, have been produced by something else in the absence of this cause' (p. 145). This occurs in her fundamental paper 'Causality and Determinism' (*Metaphysics and the Philosophy of Mind*, pp. 133–47).

[8] I do not mean that *all* probability statements can be interpreted as counterfactual relative frequency claims, but that this is the most plausible interpretation of ordinary language statements like the one used as an example here. In 'Probability and the Mental' (in 'Human Meanings and Existence', *Jadavpur Studies in Philosophy*, 5, ed. D. P. Chattopadhyaya, pp. 161–75, Macmillan India), I consider two fundamental scientific notions of probability and argue that neither is suitable for Dretske's purposes. Of course, those who like such things as 'probability metrics on possible worlds' can come up with much fancier interpretations of even the ordinary language probability statement than mine. The present paper borrows heavily from this earlier paper.

In short, the ordinary language probability statement makes a causal claim *and* is 'counterfactual supporting'.

We have already said something about the problem of counterfactuals, as it involves both the L-Equivalence Rule and as it bears on the metaphysical significance that Dretske attributes to his project of explaining how reference fits into 'the natural order of things'. What about the problem of analysing the notion of causation? The question, whether statements of the form *A caused B* obey an analogue of the L-Equivalence Rule is, perhaps, controversial. I am inclined to think that they *do*. 'A cat is on a mat' and 'A cat* is on a mat*' do not, in my view, describe different events; rather, they 'parse' the same event into objects, properties and relations in different ways. This can happen even in natural languages: a Hopi says 'Fork-pattern-brought-about-in-bush-by-hand-action-mine', or morphemes to that effect, where we say 'I pull a branch of the bush aside': we are not describing two different events, even though he mentions an abstract entity, 'fork pattern', which I fail to mention, but analysing the same event in different – different, but equivalent – ways. If this is right, then, as already pointed out, *causality* is not a notion that will (by itself, or in conjunction with the notions of probability and counterfactual connection) enable us to define *reference*.

Let us assume, however, that I am wrong, and that causality individuates 'events' more finely than this; that, in other words, 'A cat being on a mat' and 'A cat* being on a mat*' are different 'events' (and, perhaps, a forked pattern being made in the bush by hand action and a branch of the bush being pulled aside are different events), and that in each such case one of the two 'events' may 'bring about' a third event X even though the other – logically equivalent – event is not what 'brings it about'.

In this case, no simple 'knock down' argument, like the argument depending on the fact that certain notions obey the L-Equivalence Rule, will suffice to show that a 'causal theory of reference' cannot be given: we will just have to survey all the major types of efforts that have been made.

Another notion, related to the notions of counterfactual connection and causal connection, which has been used by a number of authors is the notion of 'nomic' (lawlike) connection. Dretske himself explains probability as *nomic relative frequency*. Only if a relative frequency obtains as a matter of 'law' (or is 'counterfactual supporting') should we take the relative frequency to be a probability.

The notion of 'nomic connection' is not explicated by Dretske. However, the suggestion that we simply take 'lawlike connection' as *primitive* has recently been advanced by Ted Honderich.[9]

But *would this solve any philosophical problems at all?* Given Dretske's aim, at least (I am not sure what Honderich's aim actually is), viz., to show that probability was 'there' (in the natural order) before 'mind', the answer is 'no'. *For we understand no better how this sort of 'lawlike connection' could be there independently of minds than we understand how intentional properties are possible on the world picture of metaphysical materialism.*

---

[9] Cf. 'Causes and *If p, even if x, still q*', *Philosophy*, 57 (1982), pp. 291–317.

The problem is this: granted that there is *a* notion of 'physical necessity' and 'physical possibility' that one might arguably take as primitive in a fundamental physical theory, that notion cannot be the one that Dretske and Honderich want. What is 'physically necessary' in such a theory is that one whole state of the universe (or of a 'closed system') will be followed or preceded by another whole state, or that certain properties (e.g., mass-energy) will be conserved in a transition, or certain symmetries maintained. But it is *not* 'physically necessary' in this sense that a person who eats arsenic will die; that depends on what we specify to be the exact circumstances under which he eats the arsenic, the condition of his body, etc. If one speaks of a 'lawlike connection' between 'eating arsenic' and 'dying' *so described*, one is talking of an emergent relation (in fact, the relation of *explanation*). One is not saying that it is *physically impossible* that a human being eat arsenic and not die (that has happened).

Let me elaborate on this point. Consider an example Honderich himself uses, the conditional 'if the door had not been shut, the room would not have gotten warmer.' (This is what it means to say 'shutting the door caused the room to get warmer' in a situation in which there is no 'overdetermination', according to Honderich.) When we make such an assertion, then, according to Honderich, there is an unstated categorical premise: that 'certain conditions exist' (Honderich, p. 302). 'We may say that the windows were not all wide open, and so on, perhaps actually using the words and so on.' This does not mean the speaker could actually *supply* a list of conditions which, together with the door's not being shut, would have made it impossible that the room get warmer. Honderich is explicit about this, and, in any case, it is clear that few speakers who utter such a statement are ever in a position to supply such a list. This is, indeed, just the problem of *cotenability*.

Honderich uses two notions: the notion that a description ('the windows were not all wide open, and so on') *excludes* a state of affairs even if it does not entail (alone or in conjunction with the laws of mechanics) that that 'excluded' state of affairs does not obtain (thus 'the windows were not all wide open and so on' excludes a 'catastrophic' event which heats up the room) and the notion of a 'simple' relation of lawlike connection.[10]

The first ('exclusion') makes no sense to me in the case where the speaker (or his community) *couldn't*, in fact, supply the list of conditions. What the conditions would have been if the door had remained open is a counterfactual question (Goodman's point). To use an unexplained notion of 'exclusion' is, in effect, to 'solve' Goodman's problem by just *taking cotenability as primitive*.

To say that there exists a 'simple' relation of lawlike connection between *partially specified* events – a door's remaining open and a particular room's not getting warmer – is to say that nature itself knows that a certain *part* of a total state of affairs – the door's being *open* – is an instigator or a *bringer-about*, as opposed to a 'background condition', and knows also what a cotenable set of

---

[10] The *grounds* for asserting a subjunctive conditional are complex in Honderich's view, and he spends much time describing these. (Even these-the grounds-need subjunctive conditionals and the notion of 'causal sequence' to explain.) But the truth conditions are just that what the conditional says would happen would in fact happen, Honderich says. The *meaning* of this is what he calls a 'simple' idea (even a 'clever monkey' has it, he thinks).

possible-but-not-actual conditions (a filling out of the 'and so on') should have looked like. I see absolutely no difference between this and simply postulating a primitive relation of explanation in the 'natural order' – a relation between events, independent of our minds, which picks out 'bringers-about', 'relevant conditions', and the rest. Perhaps Honderich himself does not have a metaphysical materialist (or any) world-picture into which all this is supposed to fit; but if a physicalist tried to take this line, I would have to say this is more a return to Scholasticism (to the twelfth-century idea of 'Substantial Forms') than a successful defense of materialism.

Now, I cannot presume to saddle Dretske with Honderich's views. Dretske himself does not speak of 'nomic connection' as holding between single events but between types of events. (Although he doesn't see that this makes 'probability' relative to a reference class, just as much as the frequency theory does.) But the problem is the same: if the classes of events 'shutting doors' and 'rooms getting warm' are 'nomologically connected' (in certain buildings), if the relation is 'counterfactual supporting', then (on Dretske's view) there is a relation in the 'natural order' which picks *the door being shut* out of the total state of the physical system in each case. How this could be so is even more puzzling than how reference is possible or how counterfactuals could have a truth value. We have been handed dark sayings about certain frequency relations being 'lawlike' and this being a fact about the 'natural order', and not clarity. In fact, talk about 'nomic connections' being in 'the natural order', like talk about 'lawlike connection' being 'simple' is … just talk.

References

Anscombe, G. E. M., *Metaphysics and the Philosophy of Mind*, University of Minnesota, 1981.

Chattopadhyaya, P. (ed.), *Human Meanings and Existences*, Macmillan India Ltd, New Delhi, 1983.

Dretske, Fred, *Knowledge and the Flow of Information*, MIT Press, 1982.

Goodman, Nelson, *Fact, Fiction and Forecast*, 4th edition, Harvard, 1983.

Lewis, David, *Counterfactuals*, Harvard, 1973.

Putnam, Hilary, *Realism and Reason*, Cambridge, 1983.

15

Davidson and Social Science

MICHAEL ROOT

Much has been written in philosophy about the problem of other minds. Each of us, it is allowed, can know the contents of her own mind; what is questioned is whether we can know the contents of any other. In this paper, I want to consider a related problem, the problem of radically other minds. Here it is allowed that each of us can know the contents of her own mind and the contents of the minds of close cohorts; what is questioned is whether we can know the contents of the minds of people whose lives are, in a significant respect, unlike our own. While interest in the first problem has been primarily the interest of philosophers, interest in the second, until recently, has been primarily the interest of social scientists.

Donald Davidson has changed this. In a number of recent papers, Davidson has challenged the idea of a mind radically different from our own. The point of this paper is, first, to show how Davidson's views on interpretation oppose the idea of radically other minds and, second, to show what bearing his views have on the social sciences. In section I, I survey the place of the idea of other-mindedness in anthropology and sociology. In sections II–V, I present Davidson's theory of interpretation. In sections VI and VII, I focus on one consequence of that theory, viz., that there is a limit to how different one mind can be from another. In sections VIII–X, I offer a Kantian interpretation of Davidson's theory. This interpretation shows, more clearly than most accounts of Davidson's view, what, if any, tension there is between Davidson's philosophy of interpretation and his realism. In section XI and XII, I consider the extent to which Davidson's view opposes ideas of other-mindedness in the social sciences.

I

There is an idea common to a great deal of writing in the social sciences and especially anthropology that there are or have been people who are radically different from one another in their thoughts or in their feelings. According to this idea, there are cultures or classes of people who are so different in taste and temperament or in imagination and intellect, that, in some interesting sense, they inhabit different and, in some important respect, incomparable worlds. This was the idea of the anthropologist Lucien Levy-Bruhl. He maintained that, due to differences in nature and nurture, people in 'primitive' societies have a mentality that is radically different from our own. He writes: 'The reality in which primitives move is itself mystical. There is not a being, not an object, not a natural phenomenon that appears in their collective representation in the way that it appears to us.'[1]

Other anthropologists have maintained that there are people whose view of the world is radically different from our own view, due not to birth or to training but to the material conditions of their lives. In his book about a tribe in Northern Uganda called the 'Ik', Colin Turnbull, for example, maintains that the Ik, as a result of extreme famine, have become a culture in which affection is shown much as we show disaffection in our own culture. According to Turnbull, the Ik do not have our concepts of moral right and moral wrong or our concepts of sympathy or affection. He writes:

> Men would watch a child with eager anticipation as it crawled toward the fire, then burst into gay and happy laughter as it plunged a skinny hand into the coals. Such times were the few times when parental affection showed itself; a mother would glow with pleasure to hear such joy occasioned by her offspring, and pull it tenderly out of the fire.[2]

The most famous chronicler of differences in cultures was Sir James Frazer. His twelve-volume work of fact and fancy called *The Golden Bough* is an encyclopedia of exotic religious beliefs and practices. Frazer tells us of people who believe what, from our point of view, seems impossible; he tells us of people who believe that the winds can be made to blow, the rain to fall, the sun to rise, animals to die or to be born by changing or handling stones, fire, foreskins or footprints or by bathing, dancing, drinking, singing, touching, jumping or eating. He presents us with people whose concept of cause and effect seems so different from our own that we hesitate to attribute this concept to them at all. He writes:

> To put an end to drought and bring down rain, women and girls of the village of Ploska are wont to go naked by night to the boundaries of the village and there pour water on the ground.[3]

> Amongst the Omaha Indians of North America, when the corn is withering for want of rain, the members of the sacred Buffalo Society fill a large vessel with water and dance four times round it. One of them drinks some of the water and spurts it into the air, making a fine mist of drizzling rain. Then he upsets the vessel, spilling the water on the ground; whereupon the dancers fall down and drink up the water getting mud all over their faces. Lastly, they squirt the water into the air, making a fine mist. This saves the corn.[4]

---

[1] Quoted in Steven Lukes, 'Relativism in Its Place', in *Rationality and Relativism*, eds Martin Hollis and Steven Lukes, (Cambridge 1982), p. 268.
[2] Colin Turnbull, *The Mountain People*, (New York, 1972) p. 112.
[3] Sir James Frazer, *The Golden Bough*, vol.1, 3rd edition, (New York, 1935), p. 248.
[4] Ibid., p. 249.

The idea that there are others whose minds are radically different from our own or different from the minds of everyone in our class, in our culture or of everyone who shares with us a certain achieved or ascribed status, is usually accompanied by the idea that our ability to understand other persons and other cultures is, in principle, limited. No amount of social science, no mode of explanation or interpretation, the idea goes, will enable us to understand a person who is radically other-minded. There is no point of comparison, it is said, between my thoughts and those of the Omaha Indians in virtue of which we can be said to agree or disagree with each other about the causes of rain or about the farming of corn; there is no common core of concepts in terms of which our actions or attitudes and those of the Omaha might be placed in correspondence.

The theme of the radical other is not limited to distant times or distant places. In centuries of writing about women one also finds the theme of alterity. The idea is that, due to birth or upbringing, a woman's experience of the world is so different from a man's, even the experience of men who are members of the same race, the same economic class or the same family, that most men are bound to find a woman's actions and attitudes very difficult, if not impossible, to understand.

The idea that female minds and male minds are radically different can be found in the writings of both misogynists and feminists. Philosophers like Aristotle, Kant, Rousseau and Schopenhauer, who maintain that women should be denied male privilege, defend their view by arguing that women have a distinctive character of mind that does not suit them for the economic, political or social lives that men are allowed or encouraged to lead. Rousseau writes in *Emile*, for example: 'The search for abstract and speculative truths, for principles and axioms in science, for all that tends to wide generalization, is beyond a woman's grasp.'[5]

On the other hand, there are feminists who maintain that to be a woman is to have thoughts and sentiments that are seldom, if ever, found in men; women, according to this view, have ways of seeing the world and ways of organizing what they see that are radically different from the ways that are common to men. In a paper entitled 'Maternal Thinking', Sara Ruddick, for example, suggests that there is an aspect of woman's thought that grows out of maternal practice and sets the way women think about and act towards their children apart from the way men do.[6] According to Ruddick, in the love or care of children, the attitudes of men and women are so different that men are not able to see, let alone understand, the attention and concern that women as mothers offer to their children. The parenting strategies of men and women are very different, Ruddick maintains, and different because the attitudes that lie behind these strategies are, in some important respects, not comparable.[7]

The idea of a radical other is an idea that has played a prominent role in social theory, but it has played a no less prominent role in social practice.

---

[5] Jean-Jacques Rousseau, *Emile*. (London, 1911), pp. 321–22.

[6] Sara Ruddick, (Summer 1980): 'Maternal Thinking', *Feminist Studies*, 6 (2), pp. 342–67.

[7] Ruddick believes that men can come to think maternally. Her view is not that the minds of men and women are different by nature. Rather, it is that men cannot understand maternal thinking until they engage in those practices that instill and sustain it.

Levy-Bruhl's treatise on the pre-logical mentality of people in primitive societies was cited in support of colonial policy, and treatises on the distinctiveness of black thought or women's thought are cited in support of proposals for political, educational or social separatism. Sara Ruddick cites differences in minds of men and women to argue for a change in the present social division of labor, and, through that, for an elimination of the differences in mind that support this division of labor. In short, the history of interest in the idea of a radical other is not merely a history of academic interest. The interest is not merely an interest in what to say about certain other people; it is also an interest in how to treat them. Because of the prominent role that the idea of radically other minds has played in social theory and practice, it seems to me, that the idea deserves the philosophical attention that Davidson has recently accorded it.

Davidson is interested in claims, such as Levy-Bruhl's and Frazer's, to know the mind of another that is radically other. However, Davidson is also interested in the very idea of a radical other; the first matter, Frazer's claim, is a matter of epistemology. Can we know of another mind that is it is radically other than our own? Is such knowledge possible? What would the evidence be that a person had such a mind? The second is a matter of metaphysics. Could there be a radically other mind? Is such a mind possible? For a realist at least, issues of epistemology and issues of metaphysics are separate issues. That is, for a realist, the question of whether there are radically other minds and the question of whether anyone could ever be in a position to know of any given mind that it was radically other are independent questions. In section VIII of this paper, I shall discuss the sense in which, on matters of mind, Davidson is a realist.

Davidson's papers on the interpretation of attitudes and actions, as I understand them, are meant to show that the idea of a radical other is a defective idea. That is, as Davidson sees it, there is no good sense to the idea that there are people who are so other-minded that we cannot hope to understand them. To understand why Davidson opposes the idea of a radical other is to understand his views on interpretation. The point of this next section and the two that follow it is to explain how Davidson's philosophy of interpretation supports his conclusions about other minds.

II

There is an interesting parallel between Davidson's remarks on the nature of our understanding of other minds and Kant's remarks on the nature of our understanding of physical objects. First, Davidson asks a Kantian question: how is knowledge of another person's attitudes or actions possible? Second, he offers a Kantian answer: it is only possible on the assumption that her attitudes or actions are substantially like one's own. Third, Davidson defends his answer with a Kantian argument: he argues from the conditions of interpretation, from what is necessary to interpret the thought or talk of others, to the conclusion that the thought and talk of others can not be radically different from our own.

In his paper 'On the Very Idea of a Conceptual Scheme', Davidson writes: 'Given the underlying methodology of interpretation, we could not be in a position to judge that others had concepts or beliefs radically different from our own'.[8] His argument for this thesis proceeds from three premises; each makes a point about understanding the minds of others. According to the first premise, interpretation is holistic. According to the second, interpretation is critical or normative, and, according to the third, the norms employed in interpretation are the norms of rationality.

The premise that interpretation is holistic means three things for Davidson. First, it means that the interpretation of one part of a person's thought is always relative to the interpretation of some other. Second, it means that the interpretation of one part of a person's speech is always relative to the interpretation of some other. And, finally, it means that the interpretation of any part of a person's speech is always relative to the interpretation of some part of her thought.

Davidson makes all three of these points in his paper 'Psychology as Philosophy'.[9] He tells us there that in semantics and psychology, the parts, the meaning of a person's words and the content of her attitudes, cannot be considered one by one but only together. It is only in the context of an entire theory of a person's thought, talk and action that an interpreter can speak about the meaning of her words or the contents of her attitudes at all.

The second premise in Davidson's argument to the limits of conceptual contrast is the premise that interpretation is critical. What does Davidson mean when he says that interpretation is critical? He means two things. Interpretation, on Davidson's view, is critical in two respects. One serves to distinguish it from physical theory, the other does not. One depends on the nature of the norms employed in interpretation, on the fact that they are the norms of rationality, the other does not. It will be helpful to have names for these. The critical feature that interpretation shares with physical theory I will call 'constitutiveness.' The critical feature that distinguishes them I will call 'reflexivity.'

The key here is the idea of a norm. It is important to distinguish between an interpretation of a person's speech or thought and the norms or principles that guide the interpretation. An interpretation of a person's speech is a statement of what she said: it is an indirect report of her speech. The interpreter paraphrases in her own words the words spoken by the speaker, the interpreted. In interpreting a person's speech, an interpreter says what the speaker's words mean or what the speaker means by using these words on a particular occasion.

An interpretation of a person's action is a rational explanation of the action; it is a description of the beliefs and desires that were her reason for what she did. In interpreting a person's action, an interpreter says what the speaker intended by what she did. The description of the beliefs and desires that were her reason for so acting is a description of these intentions.

An interpretation of a person's thought is an indirect report of those attitudes of mind that are propositional in their content. The interpreter describes in her

---

[8] Donald Davidson, 'On the Very Idea of A Conceptual Scheme', in *Inquiries into Truth and Interpretation* (New York, 1984), pp. 183–98.

[9] Donald Davidson, 'Psychology as Philosophy', in *Essays on Actions and Events*. (New York, 1980), pp. 229–39.

own words the contents of these attitudes. An interpretation of a person's action is also an interpretation of her thought, because the reasons that the interpreter cites to explain why she performed the action are propositional attitudes: they are beliefs and desires that, on the view of the interpreter, make it reasonable for the agent to have performed the action.

The norms or principles that guide interpretation are the norms of rationality. The thoughts that the interpreter attributes to the agent to explain her actions must rationalize them. They must be thoughts that make the action a reasonable one for the agent to have performed. Moreover, the beliefs that the interpreter attributes to the agent must be beliefs that are reasonable for her to hold. The sense of reasonableness here is the interpreter's sense. The standard of reasonableness she employs is supplied by the norms that guide her interpretation.

The standard of reasonableness that guides the interpretation of action, on Davidson's view, includes the norms or principles of decision theory. The norms or principles of decision theory guide interpretation in the following way. An interpreter seeks to interpret an agent's actions. This requires that she attribute thoughts to the agent. The thoughts she attributes must make the action out to be one that, according to the standard offered by the theory, is a reasonable action for the agent to perform. If, for example, the expected utility standard is judged by the interpreter to be the applicable standard, then in interpreting the action she must attribute beliefs and desires to the agent in virtue of which the action maximizes the agent's expected utility.

The principles of decision theory are descriptive so far as they describe the actions that people perform in the situation in which the principles offer a standard of action. The expected utility standard describes as person's actions if she acts to maximize expected utility whenever, according to the standard, so acting is the reasonable thing to do. However, because the principles of decision theory function as norms on the basis of which the interpreter decides what an agent is thinking, that these principles describe a person's actions is due as much to the activities of the interpreter as it is to the activity of the interpreted. The normative use of decision theory in interpretation contributes to the theory's success as a description of a person's thought and action.

It is now possible to explain the point that interpretation is a critical theory in the sense of being a constitutive theory. The norms that guide interpretation include standards on the basis of which the objects of interpretation are identified or constituted. Decision theory describes the behavior of rational agents, but whether a person is a rational agent is determined by whether the theory describes her behavior. When a person acts to maximize expected utility, decision theory describes her action if, according to the theory, the rational action in her situation is the action which maximizes expected utility, but what a person's expectations and desires are understood to be is itself due to the theory so far as the theory's norms are the norms that guide interpretation. So far as the norms of interpretation include the norms of decision theory or any similar theory of rational action or rational belief, the norms of interpretation constitute the objects of which the interpretation offers a description.

It is interesting to compare this view of decision theory with the view of mathematical truth made popular by the logical positivists. According to the positivists, the axioms of a mathematical theory are implicit definitions. They define the objects that the theory purports to describe. On this view, straight lines, for example, are whatever satisfy the axioms of Euclidean Geometry. The fact that these axioms function as norms on the basis of which something is identified as a straight line assures the theory's descriptive success. On the positivist view of Euclidean Geometry, if 'straight line' describes anything at all, what it describes is Euclidean. The axioms of the theory are not descriptions of physical objects like geodesics in space or surveyors' strings but norms on the basis of which an object is identified as a straight line.

The positivists' view of mathematical theories is based on a philosophy of language that Davidson rejects. It is based on the idea of truth by definition: the idea that there are statements whose truth is due to the meanings of words alone. According to the positivists, the truth of mathematical theories is analytic, while the truth of physical theories is synthetic. Davidson, like Quine, rejects the distinction between the analytic and the synthetic and the distinction between mathematical theories and physical theories that go with it. However, the analytic/synthetic distinction enabled the positivists to give an account of *a priori* knowledge within the framework of empiricism. They explained our confidence in the truth of Euclidean Geometry without agreeing with Kant that *a priori* knowledge of nature is possible. In maintaining that decision theory is a constitutive theory and, at the same time, rejecting the notion of analytic truth, Davidson returns to Kant. That is, on Davidson's view, the principles we employ in understanding a person's mind enable us to understand it, because minds are what we understand when we interpret a person's behavior, and the principles of decision theory, as norms of rationality, are the principles that guide our interpretations of behavior. Minds are, for the most part, rational because we cannot but understand them as so.

The premise that interpretation is holistic, on Davidson's view, does not distinguish interpretation from physical theory or our understanding of the mental from our understanding of the physical, for Davidson, like Quine, subscribes to Duhem's idea that one scientific hypothesis cannot be tested independently of others. In physics, we can't test the parts of a theory one by one any more than we can in semantics, for it is only in the context of the entire theory that the parts have the significance that they do.

The premise that interpretation is critical does not separate interpretation from physical theory either. Davidson admits that there are concepts in the physical sciences that are critical concepts and that physical theory like decision theory is not merely a descriptive theory but is a critical one as well. What Davidson means, I believe, is that there are some physical theories that like decision theory are constitutive of their objects. In 'Psychology as Philosophy,' for example, he says that fundamental measurement in physics includes norms that are constitutive of concepts like length, temperature and mass.[10] The conditions for measuring length or mass, he says, are constitutive of the range of application of these concepts just as the norms of rationality are constitutive of the range of application of such concepts as belief and desire.

---

[10] Ibid., p. 236–7.

It is not easy to describe in convincing detail an experiment that would persuade us that the transitivity of the relation of heavier than had failed. Though the case is not as extreme, I do not think we can clearly say what should convince us that a man at a given time (without change of mind) preferred a to b, b to c, and c to a. The reason for our difficulty is that we cannot make good sense of an attribution of preference except against a background of coherent attitudes.[11]

The axioms of measurement theory guide the application of concepts in physics just as the axioms of decision theory guide the application of concepts interpretation. In this respect, both interpretation and physical theory are critical theories. In interpretation, we may reject an attribution of belief to an agent, because it makes many of her actions appear to be irrational; similarly, in physics we may reject a measurement of a body's length, because it makes the body appear to be both longer and shorter than another. According to interpretation, a mind is such that, for the most part, it must be reasonable. According to physical theory, a body is such that, for the most part, it must be measurable. Bodies by their nature must conform to the norms of the theory of measurement, while minds by their nature must conform to the norms of the theory of rational decision.

Despite this, despite the fact that, on Davidson's view, theories of mind and body are alike in being constitutive theories, it is his view that theories of mind and body are in a significant respect different. How can this be? It is here that the third premise in Davidson's argument to the limits of conceptual contrast becomes important. Though norms guide us both in our description of nature and in our description of mind, the norms that guide us in these two activities are very different. The norms that guide our description of mind are the norms of rationality. Because the norms are the norms of rationality, interpretive theory is a critical theory in a way that physical theory is not. Because the norms of interpretation are the norms of rationality, interpretative theory is not only a constitutive theory it is a reflexive theory as well. This feature of interpretive theory is, I believe, at the center of Davidson's philosophy of mind.

What is it to say of interpretive theory that it is reflexive? It is to say that the norms of interpretation are norms that guide the interpreter and that they are norms that guide the interpreted as well. They guide the interpreter when she decides what interpretation to give of an agent's thought and action, but they also guide the agent in her thoughts and in her actions.

Consider decison theory again. It has two sides, a descriptive side and a prescriptive side. The theory can be taken to describe what people decide to do in those cases in which there is a choice of what to do, or it can be taken to prescribe what to do in these cases. Looked at from the descriptive side, the theory says that when faced with independent decision under risk, people maximize expected utility. Looked at from the prescriptive side, the theory tells people to maximize expected utility in such a situation.

The theory has a prescriptive in addition to a descriptive side because the individuals whose behavior it describes are agents. That is, they are individuals who can form intentions and who can conform their behavior to their

---

11 Ibid., p. 237.

intentions. The theory describes the behavior of individuals whose behavior happens to maximize a particular magnitude, viz, expected utility. The theory has a prescriptive side if the standards of decision that it offers are standards on the basis of which an agent makes her decisions or if they are standards to which the agent holds her decisions accountable. If decision theory is a norm on the basis of which agents choose their actions, then, as a theory of these choices or actions, it will describe what the agents do.

Decision theory describes the decisions or actions of an agent whenever she has beliefs and desires that, in terms of the principles of decision supplied by the theory, rationalize those decisions or actions. However, it is the task of interpretation to determine what the beliefs and desires of an agent are, and, in this task, the interpreter is guided by the principles of decision supplied by the theory. The interpreter assumes that these principles are norms to which the agent, as a rule, conforms her behavior and, as a result, that the agent's beliefs and desires are beliefs and desires that, as a rule, rationalize her behavior. If decision theory describes what an agent does, it does so because the interpreter, in interpreting the agent's thought and talk, attributes to her beliefs and desires that rationalize her behavior.

On Davidson's view, belief and desire are only attributable to rational agents, and rational agents are individuals whose beliefs and desires rationalize their behavior and whose beliefs and desires rationalize their behavior because the individuals conform their thoughts and their behavior to the norms of rationality. A rational agent is someone who if aware that her thoughts and actions do not conform to these norms, will regard that as a reason to change her thoughts or change her actions. An individual who is unmoved by the realization that her beliefs are inconsistent or that her actions are not rationalized by her beliefs and desires is not a rational agent. Moreover, an individual who is not a rational agent is not someone to whom beliefs and desires can be attributed and, as a result, is not someone whose behavior decision theory describes.

Decision theory is a theory of intentional behavior and a theory of rational agents. However, in the social sciences, the theory is sometimes used to describe behavior that is not intentional and is applied to individuals who are not rational agents. Two notable examples are the theory of the firm in economics and the theory of sociobiology in behavioral biology. According to these theories, it is enough if the individuals whose behavior the theory purports to describe act as if they were intending to maximize some magnitude. That is, it is not necessary that their behavior be intentional behavior or that the causes of their behavior be reasons for them to engage in it. It is enough that the behavior maximize an objective magnitude.

In the case of the theory of the firm, the magnitude that is maximized is profit. The theory does not require that the firm intend that its behavior should maximize this magnitude or that maximizing profit should be a reason for the firm's behavior. It is enough if the firm behaves as if profit maximization were its aim and as if the firm were acting with the intention of maximizing profit.[12]

---

[12] See Herbert Simon, 'From Substantive to Procedural Rationality', in *Philosophy and Economic Theory*, eds Frank Hahn and Martin Hollis, (New York, 1979), pp. 65–86.

Decision theory has been employed in a similar way in behavioral biology. Sociobiologists maintain that, so far as an animal's behavior is the expression of genotype, the behavior maximizes the animal's fitness. Fitness, is not a psychological magnitude but a biological one; it is the measure of an animal's ability to reproduce itself and to secure a place for its genes in future generations. This theory has one side, a descriptive side. That is, it may be, as sociobiologists maintain, that an animal like a fish behaves so as to maximize its reproductive fitness. In that case, the theory that fish maximize fitness describes the behavior of the fish. However, so far as fish form no intentions, the theory, with respect to the fish at least, does not have a prescriptive side; the theory offers no norm to the fish on the basis of which it may choose what to do. Fish don't choose to do anything; they are not agents. If the theory applies to the behavior of the fish, it is not because any fish intends that its behavior should maximize fitness. It is enough if the fish acts as if maximizing fitness were its aim and as if it were acting with the intention of increasing the representation of its genes in future generations.

Firms and fish can be behave as if they were intending to maximize profit or fitness, because these magnitudes are not the product of states of mind like beliefs and desires. Profits and fitness are not states of mind, and firms and fish do not have to have minds in order to maximize them. Expected utility is different. It is the product of two psychological attitudes, viz., belief and desire. Beliefs and desires are only attributable to individuals whose behavior is intentional. An individual is the bearer of a belief or desire only if beliefs and desires are reasons for her behavior. As a result, behavior has an expected utility for an individual only if its having an expected utility would be for her a reason for the behavior.

Unlike profit or fitness, expected utility is not a magnitude that can be maximized by an individual who cannot intend that her thoughts and actions conform to the norms of the theory, i.e., the norms of rationality. Properly speaking, decision theory only describes the behavior of agents. Expected utility, unlike fitness or profit, is an intentional concept and, as such, the norms of rationality are constitutive of the range of application of the concept. Though fish do not behave intentionally at all, they can behave as if they were behaving with the intention of maximizing their biological fitness. However, because their behavior is not intentional, they cannot behave as if they were behaving with the intention of maximizing their expected utility.

III

The norms of rationality are norms to which two forms of activity are accountable: the activity of the interpreter and the activity that the interpreter is interpreting. The interpreter holds her attributions of thought to a rational agent accountable to these norms and the rational agent holds her thoughts and choice of actions accountable to them as well. The objects that an interpretive theory describes are objects that are held accountable to the very norms to which the theory's descriptions are held accountable. That this is so is no accident. It follows from the fact that interpretive theory is a constitutive theory and the fact the norms of interpretation are the norms of rationality.

Because the norms of interpretation are the norms of rationality, they play an explanatory role in our understanding of mind that the norms of physical theory do not play in our understanding of body. That is, the explanation of why bodies conform to the norms of physical theory is different from the explanation of why minds conform to the norms of interpretation. Minds are intentional systems; they display agency. In interpretation, thoughts are attributed to agents in accordance with norms, because part of what it is to be an agent with these or any other thoughts is to be someone who conforms her thoughts to the norms of interpretation. That is, to be a mind or an agent, and, therefore, a proper subject for interpretation, is to be someone who intends that her thoughts and actions be rational and someone whose intentions explain why her actions and thoughts are rational, i.e., conform to the norms of rationality. On the other hand, this is no part of what it is to be a body. Bodies do not conform to the norms of physical theory, because they intend that they should conform. While the norms of interpretation must be viewed as norms for both the interpreter and her subject, as norms that guide both the interpretation of an action and the action itself, the norms of physical theory are norms for the theorist alone. No body is both longer and shorter than another, but this is not because bodies regulate their size to conform to the norms of measurement theory.

There is something old and something new here. The idea that bodies are purposeless, that they move but do not act, is the contribution to our understanding of nature of Galileo and Descartes. It is to them that we owe our view that the bodies of the non-human world are bodies without souls; nature, they taught us, is a grand machine. Bodies, they showed us, are not guided by purpose or intention.

As Descartes understood the principles of the motions of bodies, these principles are not norms to which bodies, by intention, conform their state. If these principles describe the states of bodies it is not because the bodies intend that they should; as Descartes interpreted nature, it is not the intentions of matter that matter. Matter, on Descartes' view, is inert and unable to move itself or bring itself to rest.

However, though physical theory does not prescribe to matter how it ought to behave, on Davidson's view, physical theory is, nevertheless, a critical theory. Though it does not serve as a norm to which bodies conform their behavior (nor as a norm to which God conforms his actions and the changes he produces in the world of body, as Descartes seems to have thought), it does serve as a norm to which natural scientists conform their descriptions of nature. According to Davidson, part of the reason why the theory of nature describes the behavior of bodies is that the theorist of nature intends that it should. Because some of the concepts employed in the theory are, on Davidson's view, critical concepts, there is a sense in which the intentions of the natural scientist have taken up the responsibility that, on Descartes' view, fell to the intentions of God, viz., to secure for us a nature that, in some respects at least, is a reasonable nature and a nature that we are able to understand.

It is the idea that the norms of interpretation are norms for the interpreted, for the object of the theory, that sets interpretation apart from physical theory. This is what I mean when I say that interpretive theory is a reflexive theory. The norms that guide an interpreter in describing an agent's actions reflect the norms that guide the agent in performing the actions. Both the interpreter and the interpreted are guided by the norms of a theory of rational decision and choice and both are guided by a theory of rational or reasonable belief. Moreover, the interpreter's reason for conforming her interpretation to these norms is her belief that these are the norms on the basis of which her subject guides her own thoughts and her own actions.

The interpreter's belief that her subject conforms her thoughts and actions to the norms of rationality, however, rest on the interpreter's interpretation of her subject's behavior. Whatever reason she has for believing that her subject conforms her thought to these norms are reasons she has as a result of her interpretations of her subject's behavior. As a result, the only principles of rationality she can understand her subject to be guided by are the norms that guide her in interpreting her subject's behavior. In short, because the norms of interpretation are the norms of rationality, interpretive theory is critical in two respects: it is a constitutive theory, and it is a reflective theory. Physical theory, on Davidson's view, is, at most, critical in one.

IV

A central issue in the philosophy of the social sciences is the issue of the unity of the natural and social sciences. Hume and the philosophers of the French Enlightenment maintained that advancement in the social or moral sciences depends on adopting the methods of the natural sciences, of adopting what Hume called 'the method of experimental reasoning'. Davidson's view of the social sciences is in an important respect opposed to Hume's. It is Davidson's view that there is a mode of explanation or understanding that applies only to 'psychological' subjects and that distinguishes these subjects from the subjects of natural science. His reason for this is that psychological subjects are rational agents and that as such they conform their behavior to the norms of rationality. As a result, the best explanation of why a rational agent did what she did is (1) that what she did was the rational thing for her to do in the circumstances and, given that she is a rational agent, (2) that she intended to do what was the rational thing for her to do.

Georg von Wright, in his book *Explanation and Understanding*, maintains that the history of scientific ideas has been marked by two traditions, one due to Galileo and other to Aristotle.[13] According to the first tradition, the world is to be understood through efficient causes; we understand an event when we discover its cause. According to the second tradition, the world is to be understood in terms of purpose; we understand an event when we discover its purpose. In his paper 'Action, Reasons and Causes', Davidson embraces both traditions.[14] It is his idea that the way to explain an action is to say what the agent's reasons were for performing it. This is what makes interpretation different from physical theory. However, it is also his idea that a reason for acting explains the action only if it causes the action. A belief and desire may

---

[13] Georg von Wright, *Explanation and Understanding*, (Ithaca 1971), pp. 1–4.
[14] Donald Davidson, 'Actions, Reasons and Causes,' in *Essays on Actions and Events*, pp. 3–19.

give a person a reason to perform an action but not cause her to act. An interpreter explains a person's actions by citing her attitudes only if her attitudes are the causes of her actions. In this respect interpretation is like physical theory: an event is explained by the cause.

John Stuart Mill, like Davidson, maintains that the way to explain a person's action is to cite a reason that is both her reason for acting and the cause of her action.[15] However, Mill parts with Davidson in maintaining that interpreters can cite a reason as a cause of an action only if they can subsume the action under a psychological law. It is Davidson's view that a person's belief and desire may have caused her to act even though there is no psychological law under which the action can be subsumed, i.e., even though there is no true statement that describes a lawlike relation between the belief and desire and the action. It is Davidson's idea that when interpreters say that a person's reasons for acting caused her to act, what they say may be true even though there are no psychological laws that warrant their asserting that.

It is a tenet of Davidson's philosophy of mind that mind is anomolous. According to Davidson, mental events do not fall under laws. 'There are not strict deterministic laws,' he writes, 'on the basis of which mental events can be predicted and explained.'[16] Davidson means two things by this; he means that there are no strict psychophysical laws, i.e., laws connecting the mental and the physical, and he means that there are no strict psychological laws, i.e., laws connecting the mental. It is the idea that there are no laws connecting the mental that is of interest here.

Psychological laws, as the notion might be applied to decision theory, are statements of law-like connection between an agent's thoughts and her actions. On Davidson's view, one of the assumptions on the basis of which an interpreter attributes thoughts to an agent is that the agent's thoughts rationalize her actions. It cannot turn out, then, that an agent, as a rule, acts in ways that are not rationalized by the thoughts that the interpreter attributes to her. As a result, the relation between an agent's thoughts and her actions is not a law-like relation but an analytical one. That is, there may be true general statements relating a rational agent's thoughts and actions, statements that have the logical form of a law, but these statements are not law-like. According to Davidson, law-like statements are general statements that support counterfactual and subjunctive claims and are supported by their instances.[17] While statements relating a rational agent's thoughts and actions support subjunctive claims, they are not supported by their instances and are not infirmed by their counter-instances. The relation of support goes the other way; it is the statements that support the instances. Support for these statements comes not from their instances but from their role as norms of interpretation. It is the fact that they are employed in the interpretation of instances that gives the statements their support. Our reason for believing the statement of decision theory that rational agents act so as to maximize expected utility is not that we

---

[15] John Stuart Mill, *On the Logic of the Moral Sciences*, Indianapolis, 1965, pp. 24–36.
[16] Donald Davidson, 'Mental Events,' in *Essays on Actions and Events*, p. 208.
[17] Ibid., p. 216.

know independently of the theory that rational agents act this way but that this statement is a norm on the basis of which we interpret the thoughts and actions of those agents, and, in so interpreting them, that it is a norm on the basis of which the agents decide how to act or, at least, to which the agents hold their actions accountable.

The three factors that distinguish an interpretive theory are, in Davidson's view connected; the holism, the norms and the fact that the norms are the norms of rationality. First, there is the holism: each interpretation should support and be supported by the other interpretations we offer of the person's thought and action. Next, there is the role of rationality as a norm: an interpretation of some of a person's thoughts supports the interpretation of others if the attitudes attributed to her in one offer reasons to her for holding the attitudes attributed to her in the other. The less our interpretations of a person's thoughts support one another, the more reason we have to think that the interpretations are in error and that we have misidentified her thoughts. This is Davidson's point in 'Thought and Talk' when he says that it is only against a background of attributions of rational actions and thoughts that we can identify a person's thoughts or a person's actions at all,[18] and this is his point in 'Psychology as Philosophy' when he says that the satisfaction of conditions of rationality are constitutive of the range of concepts like belief, desire, intention and action.[19]

V

Norms of rationality guide both the interpretation of thought and the interpretation of action. In the case of action, the norms are provided by the theory of rational decision or choice. In the case of thought, the norms are provided by a theory of rational or reasonable belief. Davidson's principle of charity is a norm that the interpreter employs in the interpretation of thought. It draws together two ideas. First, there is the idea that each of the thoughts we attribute to a person in interpretation must make the other thoughts we attribute to her reasonable. This is Davidson's holism. Second, there is the idea that the thoughts that the interpreter attributes to her must be reasonable relative to the interpreter's own thoughts. According to Davidson, a weighted majority of the beliefs that the interpreter attributes to her subject must be beliefs that, on the interpreter's own view, are true. There is, for this reason, a limit to the quantity and quality of the false beliefs, i.e., false according to the interpreter's lights, which the interpreter can attribute to her subject. The more false beliefs the interpreter attributes to a subject, the more reason she has to doubt that she has correctly identified the content of her subject's beliefs or understood what those beliefs are about.

An example will help here. There is man who lives in Vienna, and I am trying to interpret his thought on the basis of his speech. In this case, his words, I want to imagine, are written words, German words. One of my interpretative

---

[18] Donald Davidson, 'Thought and Talk', in *Inquiries into Truth and Interpretation*, pp. 168–9.
[19] Donald Davidson, 'Psychology as Philosophy', pp. 237–9.

hypotheses is that this man believes that infants have sexual desires. However, I can have no confidence in this hypothesis without taking more of his beliefs into account. I have to credit him with enough true beliefs about sexual desire to be in a position to conclude that it is sexual desire that he is attributing to infants. If I credit him with the false belief (on my view) that sexual desires are desires that are characteristically satisfied by eating and drinking, I may begin to doubt that it is sexual desire that he attributes to infants and begin to wonder whether his words express the belief that infants have sexual desires or the belief that infants are often hungry.

This example displays both the idea that interpretation is holistic and the idea that interpretation is critical. I interpret the writer's word 'geschlechtstrieb' to mean sexual desire if the word appears elsewhere in his text and is associated with persons whose desires I have reason to believe are sexual desires. I have reason to doubt this interpretation if I have reason to believe that the desire in each case is not sexual but hunger.

The three ideas that interpretation is holistic, that interpretation is critical and that the norms of interpretation are the norms of rationality lead Davidson to the conclusion that there is a limit to the number of beliefs that we can attribute to others that are contrary to our own. The reasoning, as I understand it, goes like this:

(1) If we identify the beliefs of others as beliefs contrary to our own, then, in the absence of a rational explanation of why they should have beliefs contrary to our own, we must conclude that these beliefs of theirs are unreasonable.
(2) If we conclude that the beliefs are unreasonable, then we lose an important reason for believing that we have correctly identified these beliefs.
(3) It is only if we have good reasons to believe that we have correctly identified the beliefs of others that we have good reason to believe that their beliefs are contrary to our own.

Davidson's argument for (2) is that the two principal reasons interpreters have for attributing a particular belief to a person are the person's speech and the other beliefs the interpreters have attributed to her. In both cases, according to Davidson, the reason depends on the reasonableness of the belief. When interpreters attribute a belief to a person on the basis of the other beliefs they have attributed to her, the interpreters assume that these other beliefs make the belief reasonable. When interpreters attribute a belief to a person on the basis of her speech, they assume that what she says is something that is reasonable to hold true.

VI

Davidson's principle of charity does not recommend that in interpreting the thoughts of others we simply maximize agreement between ourselves and others. The principle is more subtle. It is primarily a norm that the interpreter employs in the initial stages of interpretation; it helps her to get a foot in the door. The principle counsels her to assume that a speaker's sentence is true when the speaker holds it true. If the interpreter assumes that the sentence is an expression of what the speaker believes, this leads her to attribute beliefs to the speaker that agree with her own. However, Davidson allows that as the interpretation proceeds, the interpreter may have good interpretive or theoretical reasons to revise some of her initial hypotheses that equate true and holding true and to maintain that some of what the speaker said was in error, and, correlatively, that some of the speaker's beliefs are unreasonable or false.

Davidson's principle of charity does not preclude disagreement; what it precludes is inexplicable disagreement. That is, the interpreter is to interpret her subject's thought and talk as her own, unless she can explain why they should be different. Davidson writes in 'Belief and the Basis of Meaning':

> The general policy, however, is to choose truth conditions that do as well as possible in making speakers hold sentences true when (according to the theory and the theory builder's view of the facts) those sentences are true. That is the general policy to be modified in a host of obvious ways. Speakers can be allowed to differ more radically with respect to some sentences than others, and there is no reason not to take into account the observed or inferred individual differences that may be thought to have caused anomalies (as seen by the theory).[20]

> The aim is not the absurd one of making disagreement and error disappear. The point is rather that widespread agreement is the only possible background against which disputes and mistakes can be interpreted. Making sense of the utterances and behavior of others, even the aberrant behavior, requires us to find a great deal of reason and truth to them.[21]

To go back to the example in the preceding section and to Freud's belief that infants have sexual desires, even if that meant attributing to Freud many (on my view) false beliefs about sexual desire, I could interpret Freud's word 'geschlechtstrieb' as sexual desire if I could explain how Freud should have come to falsely believe these things.

If I do not myself believe what Freud believes about sexual desires then, I can sustain my interpretation of Freud's 'geschlechtstrieb' as sexual desire, if I can explain that given Freud's other beliefs or lack of information on matters over which I take myself to be informed, it is reasonable for him to have false beliefs about sexual desire.

To require that explanation of disagreement and error be explained but to deny that there are any psychological laws under which to explain them is to oppose the idea at the center of the sociology of knowledge. This idea is advanced by Robert K. Merton in his paper 'The Perspective of Insiders and Outsiders'.[22] According to Merton, if the view that one individual or group has of the thoughts of another, makes those thoughts out to be markedly different from the individual's own, then the question is no longer a question of whether

---

[20] Donald Davidson, 'Belief and the Basis of Meaning', in *Inquiries into Truth and Interpretation*, p. 152.

[21] Ibid., p. 153.

[22] Robert K. Merton, 'The Perspective of Insiders and Outsiders', in *The Sociology of Science* (Chicago, 1973), pp. 99–136.

the thoughts of the other are true or reasonable but, instead, is a causal question, viz., what was the non-rational cause of the thoughts.In this case, the 'alien' thoughts are to be explained by subsuming them under a covering law. This has the following connection to the principle of charity. According to Davidson, in identifying the beliefs of others, in order to identify their beliefs as beliefs that are contrary to our own, we have to explain how it is that they believe so. One way to explain it is to give the reasons these others have for believing so. Another way, Merton's way, is to give a covering-law explanation or a functional explanation of why they hold these beliefs. Merton suggests that when the beliefs that we attribute to others are significantly different from our own, we may not be able to offer a rational explanation of why they hold those beliefs and that a non-rational, covering-law explanation may be all that we can offer. The principle of charity places limits on conceptual contrast, but the limits depend on how we interpret that requirement that the interpreter make disagreements and errors explicable.

Consider again the example of interpreting Freud. I can attribute to Freud a number of false beliefs about sexual desire if I can explain why he has them. However, if to explain why he has them, I have to show that he has good reasons to think them true, i.e., if I have to justify what he believes in light of beliefs over which he and I are in agreement or in the light of information that (as I see it) is available to me but not to him, then I will be more limited in the false beliefs I can attribute to Freud than I would be were I only required to offer some explanation of those beliefs. That is, I may be able to explain why Freud should believe that infants have sexual desires by finding a cause of his believing this in his efforts to win Fleiss's approval and admiration or in a lesion on his brain. To cite these causes may be to offer an explanation of Freud's belief, but it is not to offer an explanation that makes the belief reasonable.

The anthropologist A. R. Radcliffe-Brown rejects the rational explanations of the ritual practices and exotic behavior that Sir James Frazer chronicles in *The Golden Bough*.[23] His reasons for rejecting these explanations is that in order to give the natives a reason for performing the action, Frazer attributes false beliefs to them about the effects of these practices. According to Frazer, the natives believed that their practices directed and controlled the course of nature. Radcliffe-Brown objects that this is to trade one mystery for another, for now the anthropologist has to explain why the natives have these false beliefs about cause and effect. If the anthropologist has to show that it was reasonable for the native to believe that a certain ceremony causes the wind to blow or the rain to fall or causes death to an enemy, on Radcliffe-Brown's view, she will not be able to explain why the native believes this about the ceremony. Frazer himself tries to offer rational explanations of these apparently irrational beliefs, when he writes:

> The reader may well be tempted to ask, How was it that intelligent men did not sooner detect the fallacy of magic? How could they continue to cherish

---

[23] A. R. Radcliffe-Brown, 'Taboo', in *Structure and Function in Primitive Society* (New York, 1965), pp. 133–52.

expectations that were invariably doomed to disappoint? With what heart persist in playing venerable antics that led to nothing, and mumbling solemn balderdash that remained without effect? Why cling to beliefs which were so flatly contradicted by experience. How dare to repeat experiments that had failed so often? The answer seems to be that the fallacy was far from easy to detect, the failure by no means obvious, since in many, perhaps in most cases, the desired event did actually follow, at a longer or shorter interval, the performance of the rite which was designed to bring it about; and a mind of more than common acuteness was needed to perceive that, even in these cases, the rite was not necessarily the cause of the event. A ceremony intended to make the wind blow or the rain fall, or to work the death of an enemy, will always be followed, sooner or later, by the occurrence it is meant to bring to pass; and primitive man may be excused for regarding the occurrence as a direct result of the ceremony, and the best possible proof of its efficacy.[24]

But Frazer's rational explanation, as Radcliffe-Brown sees it, is not a very good one; on occasions natives make very sophisticated judgments of cause and effect and display remarkable ability to distinguish spurious from real causes. That is, there is reason to think that the natives have a mind of more than common acuteness and are able to evaluate causal hypotheses as well as the next person. This leads Radcliffe-Brown to conclude that in trying to offer a rational explanation of these practices, Frazer was barking up the wrong tree. What Radcliffe-Brown offers instead is a functional explanation of the ceremonies and of the natives' beliefs about their effect on nature. He explains why the natives engage in these rites by citing the salutary effects they have on social life. We understand these practices, according to Radcliffe-Brown, once we see that by performing them the natives are helping to maintain the social relations that give the society its structure.

Now on Davidson's view, the explanations of apparently irrational actions or beliefs that Radcliffe-Brown or Robert Merton propose are not good explanations. Neither explanation is good, because both depend on strict psychophysical laws and, on Davidson's view, there can be no such laws. Merton proposes to explain the holding of beliefs that, from our view, are irrational, by citing laws that link the holding of the beliefs to the social or material conditions of the agents' world. That is, what Merton proposes is a covering-law explanation of individual or group's beliefs, and the laws under which Merton proposes to subsume the beliefs or the holding of the beliefs are laws that connect an event described in an intentional vocabulary to events or states described in the vocabulary of the physical sciences or in the vocabulary of functionalism. Were there such laws, they would be psychophysical laws, for the vocabulary of structural-functionalism and the vocabulary of the physical sciences are not either of them intentional.

Radcliffe-Brown, on the other hand, proposes to explain the performance of certain actions, e.g., rain dances, by citing the effects that these actions have on social structure. This, as I understand it, is also to propose a covering-law explanation of a mental event. Because the behavior to be explained is

---

[24] Sir James Frazer, *The Golden Bough*, pp. 242–3.

intentional behavior, the behavior, for Davidson, is a mental event, but the effects that are supposed to explain the behavior are not mental events; they are not mental events, because these effects are not intended; the events that Radcliffe-Brown cites in his explanations of ritual actions are not intended by any of the participants whose actions bring them about. Consequently, if the actions are to be explained by subsuming them under a law as Radcliffe-Brown proposes, it must be a 'heteronomous' law, a law that draws from more than one conceptual domain.

Davidson argues that there are no strict laws that connect events described in the vocabulary of the intentional with events described in a physicalistic or non-intentional vocabulary. His position, as I understand it, is an elaboration of Brentano's thesis that there is no breaking out of the intentional vocabulary by explaining its members in other terms.[25] If Davidson is right, then it is not possible to present, as Merton and Radcliffe-Brown propose to do, covering-law explanations of apparently irrational thoughts or actions.

Davidson's argument against psychophysical laws is presented in his papers 'Mental Events'[26] and 'The Material Mind'.[27] The claim that there are no psychophysical laws, no heteronomic laws of the mental, is one side of his claim that mental events are anomalous. Psychophysical laws describe law-like relations between mental and physical events. What Davidson argues in 'Mental Events' is that there are no law-like relations between the mental and the physical or, to be more precise, he argues that there is a categorical difference between mental and physical descriptions of events in virtue of which, there is no strong correlation between events to which some mental description applies and events to which some physical description applies.

Davidson's reason for thinking that this is so is that mental descriptions are applied to events on the basis of the norms of rationality, i.e., on the basis of whether they make the agent out to be rational, while physical descriptions are not. If Davidson is right about this, then, as I have been arguing, there is a feature of interpretation, viz., that it is guided by the norms of rationality, that opposes the sociology of knowledge and other attempts to provide covering-law explanations of the thoughts of an individual or group.

VII

According to the principle of charity, we are to interpret a person's words in such a way that the speaker agrees with us or explicably disagrees with us most of the time. In Davidson's examples, the agreement is over the world common and external to both interpreters and speakers. The beliefs that interpreters attribute to speakers are beliefs about nature rather than beliefs about the speaker's beliefs about nature. However, speakers on occasion talk about their own mind and attitudes. When interpreters interpret a person's speech to be

---

[25] W. V. O. Quine, *Word and Object* (Cambridge, 1960), p. 220.
[26] Donald Davidson, 'Mental Events', p. 222.
[27] Donald Davidson, 'The Material Mind', in *Essays on Actions and Events*, pp. 253–5.

about her own thoughts, if charity applies here too, then the interpreters must assume that the speaker's thoughts about her own mind are not very different from their own thoughts about her mind.

So, for example, when interpreters explain a person's actions, they will attribute beliefs to her that give her a reason for acting, and when they interpret the participant's own explanations of her actions, charity will require that the beliefs that the interpreters have her attributing to herself in her own explanations, for the most part, be the same beliefs that the interpreters cite in their explanations of her actions. As a result, the critical principles that guide interpretation will limit the differences between the participant's account, (the insider's account), and the interpreter's account, (the outsider's account), of an action. The greater the difference between the two, the more reason interpreters have for thinking that their interpretation of the participant's account is mistaken, unless, of course, they can explain how it should be that the participant is in error about the reasons for her own actions.

There are social scientists, Freud and Marx are notable examples, who maintain that participants are often mistaken about the reasons for their actions. Participants, according to this view, are frequently self-deceived. They suffer illusion or false consciousness. Their social or psychological situation is such that they do not themselves correctly understand what they believe or desire or why they act the way they do. However, Freud and Marx do not merely discount the participants' account of their own thoughts or their own actions, they go on to explain the cause of the participants' errors.

As I read them, Freud's explanations of these errors are rational explanations. Freud explains why the participant misunderstands her own desires by attributing to her unconscious reasons for doing so. Marx's explanations of the participant's misunderstanding, on the other hand, are not rational explanations. They are functional explanations.[28] According to Marx, in class-divided societies, much of what people believe about their own psychological attitudes they believe because believing it has certain unrecognized and unintended effects; their having these beliefs causes the forces of production to increase. Marx's explanation in terms of effects relies on psychophysical laws.[29] If Davidson is correct, there are no laws here for Marx to rely on, and, as a result, if Davidson is correct, Marx's explanations of widespread self-deception must fail.

Charity tells against the idea that there may be a great difference between the perspective of the insider and the perspective of the outsider. Charity counsels the outsider to attribute a perspective to the insider that is very close to her own. Departures from her own perspective have to be explained and the explanations have to show that the departures are reasonable. The interpreter must show that the insider has a good reason to be mistaken in her thoughts about her own attitudes. However, the more mistakes that need to be explained this way, the more reason the interpreter has for believing that it is she who is mistaken. That is, the more reason she has for believing that she is mistaken about either (a) the

---

[28] This is controversial. See G. A. Cohen, *Mark's Theory of History: A Defense*, (Princeton, 1978).

[29] Here I am following Cohen who argues that functional explanations are a distinctive form of covering-law explanations (in which the covering-laws are what Cohen calls 'consequence laws').

beliefs and desires she attributes to the insider or (b) the belief she attributes to the insider about those beliefs and desires. Freud says that my beliefs about my own desires are mistaken and tries to show that though mistaken, given the circumstances, these beliefs of mine are reasonable. However, Freud's evidence for this view of my mind supports a different view equally well; namely that Freud is mistaken either in his interpretation of my desires or Freud is mistaken in his interpretation of my beliefs about my desires. In either case, it is Freud and not me who has misunderstood the state of my mind.

VIII

Davidson, as I have argued in the previous sections of this paper, argues that there are no cultures whose view of the world is radically different from our own. He argues this on the basis of the three features that, in his view, mark the practice of interpretation. These are the holistic and the critical nature of interpretation and the character of the norms of interpretation. Davidson's argument, I suggested, resembles Kant's argument for those regulative principles that, according to Kant, relate the categories of thought to the possibility of objective experience. It resembles, for example, Kant's argument for the principle of causality, i.e., for the principle that all alterations in nature occur in accordance with the law of the connection of cause and effect.

Kant's argument for his regulative principles is a transcendental argument. He tries to prove that we must accept these principles, if we are to believe that we make any objective perceptual judgments at all. That is, Kant argues that all objective empirical judgments involve the application of the categories and, as a result, if we accept any of these judgments, then we must accept the regulative principles that make them possible.

Davidson's argument to the limits of conceptual contrast, like Kant's argument, is directed towards a necessary condition for a certain type of knowledge. For Kant it was knowledge of nature. For Davidson it is knowledge of other minds. To push the analogy with Kant further, Davidson's norms of interpretation, e.g., his principle of charity, are regulative principles. If we believe that we make objective judgments about the thoughts or actions of others, then we must accept these norms. It is the norms that make these judgments possible. The applicability of the norms of interpretation are a necessary condition of understanding the thought or talk of other person's or other cultures in so far as they are understandable. As a result, any judgement about other persons or other minds that does not conform to these norms must be rejected, and since judgments that others are radical others do not conform to these norms, we must reject them.

As most readers interpret Kant's argument, it has two parts. The first part, the 'subjective deduction', is supposed to show that the world must appear to us in a certain way, viz., in a way that conforms to the regulative principles of thought if it is to appear to us at all. However, this part of the argument, even if it is correct, does not prove that the world is as it appears to us to be. That is, the sceptic can grant that we can't but perceive the world as we do and, at the same time, deny that we have good reason to believe that the world is as we perceive it. There is a gap, the sceptic can argue, between how we must judge something to be and how it truly is.

The sceptic can make a similar point, it would seem, against Davidson's argument. Even if Davidson's argument shows that we must understand the minds of others as being a certain way, their minds may not be as they appear to us to be. Even if we are compelled to think of a person's thought or a person's talk as being like our own, it does not follow, the sceptic can argue, that her thought or talk is like our own.

The second part of Kant's argument, 'the objective deduction', is meant to address this scepticism; it is meant to show that the subjective conditions of thought have objective reality. It is meant to bridge the gap between the way we behold the world and the nature of the world beheld. What Kant offers is an argument that is meant to show that the world, and not just our understanding of it, is in conformity with the regulative principles of thought. Kant's argument is dense, and most commentators do not believe that it adequately meets the objections of the sceptic. However, what is of interest here is not whether Kant's answer to the sceptic is a good one, but whether Davidson or the Davidson of my Kantian interpretation has any answer at all. Whatever we might make of Kant's efforts to defuse the sceptic, my concern is with the sceptical objection to the argument I attribute to Davidson. How can Davidson show that the subjective conditions of the understanding of other minds have objective reality? Davidson, it would appear, needs to bridge the gap between the way we behold other minds and the nature of other minds beheld. It is to this problem that I turn in the next section.

IX

How much more can I squeeze out of my analogy between Kant and Davidson? Kant maintains that we have knowledge of nature that is both synthetic and *a priori*. Davidson, I have argued, maintains that we have knowledge of other minds that is both synthetic and *a priori*. Kant defends his claim with an argument that is intended to show that nature must be the way we perceive it to be. Is there a similar argument in Davidson, i.e., an argument that is intended to show that other minds must be the way we understand them to be?

Kant offers an argument, the objective deduction, to bridge the gap between the world and our understanding of it; Davidson offers no similar argument. He offers no argument to bridge the gap between other minds and our understanding of them, and, if I understand his views on interpretation correctly, he offers no argument to bridge this gap, because, given his views on interpretation, there is no gap to bridge. That is, as I understand Davidson's theory of interpretation, the subjective conditions of thought about other minds is the objective reality of other minds, and this, as I see it, is, on Davidson's view, the fundamental difference between mind and body.

For Davidson, I want to suggest, bodies are real in a way that minds are not, and this is so even though, for Davidson, minds are bodies. That is, minds are given their shape by our efforts to understand them in a way that bodies are not. Bodies are independent of physical theory in a way that minds are not independent of interpretation. Davidson's two points that interpretation is a critical theory and that the norms of interpretation are the norms of rationality are crucial here.

In offering an interpretation of other minds, the interpreter, as I suggested in earlier sections of this paper, does not subsume the thoughts or actions under laws but fashions a description of the thoughts and actions in accordance with a set of norms. The interpreter does not attribute attitudes to others and test his principles against these attributions but, instead, tests the attributions of attitudes against the interpretative norms. However, the norms to which the interpreter conforms her descriptions of other minds are also norms to which other minds are understood to conform their thoughts and actions. As a result, it is more appropriate to say that other minds are the products of interpretation than it is to say that they are the objects of interpretation. Other minds, on Davidson's view, are what we get when we interpret the behavior of others. Bodies are what we have before we interpret their behavior.

It is here that Davidson's views are close to Quine's. For both Quine and Davidson, we owe our idea of the mental to our interest in explaining the behavior of others, and, for both, our idea of the mental is constituted by the way that we pursue that interest: we offer a rational explanation of the behavior. Our explanations are based on the assumption that these others are agents. That is, in giving an explanation of the behavior, we assume that the persons chose or decided what to do and that their choice was based on a conception of their situation and on the disposition to do what was rational in light of this conception. Minds, according to Davidson and Quine, are what we attribute to a person when we give a rational explanation of her behavior. Minds have no more reality than that. This point becomes clear when we consider some particular psychological attitudes. Belief, Davidson tells us, is what the interpreter posits when, in the course of interpretation, she decides that her subject has misspoken.[30] Interpreters attribute beliefs to their subject in order to explain how it is that a sentence she holds true is nonetheless false. If the speaker only spoke the truth, the interpreter could explain why she holds a sentence true by merely noting that the sentence is true. Interpreters could explain the fact that the speaker holds it true without allowing that she has her own way of seeing and thinking about the world. The situation is similar when we attempt to explain a person's nonverbal behavior. If we assume, as some economists assume, that the person has perfect knowledge of her immediate world, we could explain her behavior without attributing any beliefs to her at all. We could explain her behavior without distinguishing between the way the world is and the way the world looks to her. In this case, it is the utility of her choices that count and not her expectation of it.

The interpreter attributes beliefs to a speaker in order to explain her errors, but that she has made an error is not itself a matter of fact but a matter of interpretation. That is, the interpreter can always wipe the error away by retranslating the speaker's words. Similarly, the interpreter attributes beliefs to a speaker in order to explain her actions, but that she is performing an action and what action she is performing are not themselves facts but matters of

---

[30] Donald Davidson, 'Belief as the Basis of Meaning', p. 153.

interpretation. The interpreter can wipe the action like the error away by an act of reinterpretation.

On Davidson's view, there is no gap between other minds and other minds as we understand them, because the satisfaction of the norms of interpretation are constitutive of our very idea of belief, desire, intention and action. Physical concepts have a constitutive element too, but the norms whose satisfaction is constitutive of these concepts are different in an important way from the norms of interpretation. The norms of interpretation are the norms of rationality, and what this means is that when we attribute attitudes to an agent in a way that conforms to these norms, we posit an agent who herself intends that her attitudes conform to the norms. That is, in applying a norm of rationality to behavior, we must view the behavior as intentional, and we must assume that the intentions of the agent include the intention that her thoughts and her actions be rational and that her standard of rationality is the standard offered by our norm.

It is the agent's view of the world that we try to capture in interpretation, and so the norms we employ in interpreting the agent's actions must be the norms that the agent herself employs in deciding what actions to perform. However, that the individual whose life we interpret is an agent, is someone who acts and is someone whose actions are chosen on the basis of norms of rationality, is a fact that is itself constituted by the act of interpretation. That is, the norms that we operate within in attempting to understand the agent's actions are the agent's own norms, but that the norms are the agent's norms is a fact that is itself constituted by our interpretation of her actions.

The idea that the norms we follow in trying to understand an agent's actions are the agent's own norms is what sets interpretation off from physical theory. As Davidson writes:

> When we attribute a belief, a desire, a goal, an intention or a meaning to an agent, we necessarily operate within a system of concepts in part determined by the structure of beliefs and desires of the agent himself. Short of changing the subject, we cannot escape this feature of the psychological; but this feature has no counterpart in the world of physics.[31]

However, because our understanding that a norm is the agent's norm is itself based on our interpretation of the agent's actions, the agent's norms and our norms, i.e. the norms that guide our interpretation of her actions, are the same. In this way, the mind of an agent reflects and is reflected in the norms of interpretation. There is no counterpart to this in physical theory. It is part of our concept of mind that a mind is something that conforms itself to the norms to which its interpreters conform their interpretations. This is no part of our concept of body.

It is because we adjust psychological concepts to one set of norms and physical concepts to another that the distinction between the world of body and our understanding of that world makes sense while the distinction between the world of mind and our understanding of that world does not. The sceptic

---

[31] Donald Davidson, 'Psychology as Philosophy', p. 230.

cannot make the point against Davidson that the mental might not be as it appears to be. There is no gap between the way we behold the minds of others and the minds beheld, and no content to the idea that, in case of other minds, the world might not be in conformity with the regulative principles of thought.

X

Kant tried to refute idealism; he did not try to embrace it. One objection that might be raised to the response to the sceptic that I have here attributed to Davidson is that it does not refute idealism but embraces it. It might be objected that, as I have made out Davidson's view, Davidson is not a realist about other minds but an idealist about them. This does not fit, the objection might proceed, with Davidson's overall realism in matters of semantics and epistemology.

There is, I think, truth in this objection. The view of mind that I have attributed to Davidson not only sets minds off from bodies it sets the language of mind off from the language of body. It is possible to understand the language of the body without knowing how to go about determining whether the sentences in that language are true, but not so for the language of mind.

Realism, as I understand it here, is a doctrine that Davidson supports and Michael Dummett opposes;[32] it is the doctrine that a speaker may understand the meaning of a sentence of her language and, at the same time, lack the capacity to determine whether or not the sentence is true.[33] Anti-realism, as I understand it here, is the denial of this. That is, it is the doctrine that if a speaker lacks the capacity to determine whether a sentence is true, then she cannot understand the meaning of the sentence. When applied to sentences about minds, anti-realism comes to this: a person who lacks the capacity to interpret a mind cannot understand the meaning of a sentence about the contents of that mind. According to anti-realism, if we cannot interpret the mind of the Ik, then we are unable to understand sentences that attribute thoughts to the Ik.

Now, it would seem, at first glance, that the view that I have attributed to Davidson, the interpretative view of mind, is not anti-realist in this sense. The question of how we could learn the truth conditions of a sentence whose truth value we are not able to determine is a question of language learning, and the interpretative view, so far as I have made it out, is silent on this question. It says nothing about how a person learns to understand psychological discourse. Consequently, it seems that there is nothing in the view that I have attributed to Davidson that opposes realism about other minds.

However, according to Davidson, to understand the meaning of a sentence is to understand the truth conditions of the sentence. Moreover, if a sentence has truth conditions, then the sentence is either true or it is false. Consequently, if a

---

[32] Michael Dummett, 'What is a Theory of Meaning? (I)', in *Mind and Language*, ed Samuel Guttenplan (New York, 1975), pp. 97–138.

[33] See John McDowell, 'Truth-conditions, Bivalence and Verificationism', in *Truth and Meaning: Essays in Semantics*, eds Gareth Evans and John McDowell (New York, 1976), p. 48.

person understands the meaning of a sentence, in Davidson's view, then that sentence is true or it is false. Now, according to the doctrine of realism, the meaning of a sentence may be understood by the speakers of the language, even though no speaker of the language has the capacity to determine whether or not it is true. Thus, the sentence may be true or false, even though no speaker is able to discover the truth value of the sentence. Applied to sentences about minds, realism, so understood, comes to this: a sentence about the content of a mind may be true or false, even though no speaker has the capacity to interpret that mind, and, as a result, no capacity to discover whether the sentence is true or whether it is false. Now it seems to me that the view of mind that I have attributed to Davidson opposes this, for if this doctrine were true, then the thesis that there are radical others would make sense even if we lacked the capacity to know of any other that she was a radical other. That is, it would be possible that there are radically other minds, though no one has the capacity to interpret any of them. However, it is this very possibility that, as I understand it, Davidson's attack on the idea of a radical other is meant to rule out.

The view I have attributed to Davidson comes to his. The very idea of a radical other is a bad idea. It is bad because there is no mind that is not interpretable. Every mind is interpretable, because mind is the understanding we have of body and the movements of body when we interpret them. This being so, a description cannot be true or false of a mind if no one can interpret it. Thus, Davidson's realism, on my interpretation of his philosophy of mind, is at best a mitigated realism. Its object are our theories of nature and not our theories of mind.

There is another objection I want to consider to the Kantian view of mind which, in the last sections of this paper, I have attributed to Davidson. It is that the view I have described is too rooted in the third person. That is, as I have made things out, the concept of mind arises in the context of interpreting the behavior of others. Beliefs and desires are simply what we attribute to others when we view them as agents. Minds are what we attribute to them in the course of seeing them as acting with intentions. The formal and empirical constraints on interpretation, on my account of Davidson, are what gives our ideas of belief and desire whatever significance they have.

This view, according to the present objection, takes no account of the first-person perspective. That is, it overlooks the fact that a person understands the contents of her own mind directly and without interpretation. Even if we attribute beliefs to others when we interpret their behavior and, in particular, their speech, we attribute beliefs to ourselves on a quite different basis. Each person knows her own mind, this objection continues, not through interpretation but through introspection. According to Davidson, or at least according to the Davidson of my essay, interpretation is privileged; it is the only access we have to the understanding of mind. It is this doctrine of 'privileged access' that the present objection opposes.

How is this objection to be answered? There are, so far as I can see, two answers that might be offered on behalf of the interpretive view of mind. The first answer is an old one; it is to maintain that there are two concepts of mind, a first-person concept and a third-person concept. Introspection, it might be said, is what gives the first-person concept its meaning, while interpretation is what gives meaning to the third-person concept.

There is, however, a decisive objection to this line of reply. If there were these two concepts of mind, then no first-person attribution of belief could have the same meaning as any third-person attribution. In speaking about my mind, you and I could never contradict one another. In fact, if there were two concepts of mind, there would be no one mind of mine that both of us could speak about at all. This is absurd. You do not change the subject each time you respond to a statement of mine about the state of my own mind.

The second answer is less old but no less bold; it is to maintain that there is only one concept of mind, and that it is the concept of the third person. According to this reply, my understanding of my own mind is no different from my understanding of the mind of another; both are based on interpretation. When I attribute a belief to myself, the aptness of my attribution is judged by the same norms that I use to judge the aptness of my attributions of belief to others. That is, a first-person ascription of a psychological attitude is subject to the same norms of interpretation as are third-person ascriptions. I cannot intelligibly attribute beliefs piecemeal to myself any more than I can to others. What grasp I have of the content of one of my beliefs, I have in virtue of what I take to be the content of other beliefs of mine. If it comes to my attention that a body of my beliefs is not coherent, I have to give something up. I could give up the beliefs, but I have another alternative: I can give up my understanding of them. That is, the fact that my beliefs, as I understand them, are inconsistent, is a reason to change the beliefs, but it is equally a reason to change the way I understand them. In short, charity must guide me when I try to understand others, but it must guide me when I try to understand myself as well. Charity does not begin with other minds: it begins at home.

It might be objected at this point that in the first person case the recognition of irrationality gives a person a reason to change her beliefs, while in the third person case, the recognition of irrationality gives her, the interpreter, a reason to believe that she incorrectly identified or interpreted, the beliefs of the other. In one case, the first person case, what we change is the mind, while in the other, the third person case, what we change is our interpretation of the mind. This, it might be said, displays an important difference in the two cases, and it supports the idea that, in attributing beliefs to ourselves, we do not engage in interpretation.

This objection, however, begs the question; whether there is a difference between a change of mind and a change in the interpretation of mind is just what is at issue. According to the interpretive view of mind, the distinction between changing one's mind and reinterpreting one's mind is not a real distinction. The fact of the matter is that where once we attribute some belief to ourselves or to another, we no longer do so.

For example, suppose that I attribute a belief in a proposition to myself, and it is pointed out to me that, according to other testimony of mine, I also believe the denial of that proposition. Now I could respond in two ways to this. I could say that though I have believed both propositions, I now see that I must have been mistaken in believing one of them or I could say that I must have been mistaken in attributing a belief in one of these propositions to myself. The present point is that I may have no more reason to say the one thing than I have to say the other.

There are parallels between our understanding of our own thoughts and our understanding of the thoughts of others, because what we understand ourselves to be thinking we understand ourselves to be thinking at some time. Moreover, our understanding of our present thoughts is based, at least in part, on our understanding of what we have thought in the past. That is, when I attempt to understand what I am thinking now, I proceed from what I have taken myself to have been thinking up to now. Charity guides me here much as it guides me when I interpret the thoughts of others. I attempt to maximize agreement. That is, I assume that my present self and my past self are thinking the same thoughts, unless it is reasonable that what they are thinking be different.

Interpretation of oneself like the interpretation of others depends upon a background of common thought. I cannot understand another person unless I assume that, for the most part, she thinks like me, and I cannot understand myself now, unless I assume that I think now much as I understand that I thought before. There is only so much difference I can allow between myself and others and still understand them, and similarly, there is only so much difference I can allow in my own thoughts over time and still understand myself. In both cases, to understand the mind is to minimize inexplicable difference. In both cases, understanding places limits on conceptual contrast.

When I interpret my mind now as being different in some respect from what I have taken it to have been before, I see myself as having changed my mind. Charity in the interpretation of one's own mind counsels against attributing to oneself wholesale changes in mind; Whatever changes in mind I attribute to myself should be changes for which I can offer some explanation. In the absence of an explanation of why my mind should have changed, I have reason to doubt that it has changed and reason to believe that I have merely misunderstood what it is that I am thinking now or what it was that I was thinking before. What I can find in my own mind is no different from what I can find in the mind of another. In both cases the mind I find must be a reasonable mind. According to the interpretive theory of mind, the differences between understanding oneself and understanding others are more apparent than real.

XI

It is a consequence of Davidson's philosophy of language and mind, or at least of my account of it, that there are no radical others: no persons whose minds are so different from our own that it is, in principle, impossible for us to understand them. What, then, are we to make of those authors who maintain that there are others whose minds are radically other than our own? What are we to make of the views I described in the first section of this paper?

The first thing to note is that often these and other accounts of remarkable conceptual differences and contrasts are overstated or rhetorically extravagant. There is hyperbole in much that is written about exotic people. The differences that are actually cited are not as great as they are made out to be, and the fact that they are not so great is shown by the authors' own easy descriptions of them. This seems to me to be the case with Colin Turnbull's account of the Ik. That the mind of the Ik is not radically different from our own is suggested by all that Turnbull has to say about them. That they call things good that we call bad is a difference but a difference that can only be understood and identified in light of what is common between us. To show that the alleged difference in moral outlook is a real difference and not a misinterpretation of their thought and talk, Turnbull has to show that it is reasonable for them to disagree with us about good and bad in light of what else they think and do and in light of how and where they lead their lives. And this is precisely what he attempts to do in his book. Turnbull attempts to show that the judgements of the Ik are reasonable in light of the desperate conditions under which they attempt to maintain life and limb.

The same might be said of the differences in attitude of which Levy-Bruhl and James Frazer made so much. Once we look closely at the practices or at the speech on the basis of which Levy-Bruhl or Frazer made a group of people out to be radically other, we see that there is no good reason to think that the attitudes of these people are very different from our own or to think that the differences that there are between us are beyond explanation.

Moreover, to describe that about a person's mind in virtue of which she is radically other is to offer reasons for thinking that she isn't so other after all. One cannot show that a mind is indescribable by proceeding to describe it, and yet it seems that this is what Levy-Bruhl and Frazer want to do. If we can interpret a mind, then we cannot interpret it to be radically other than our own if what it means for a mind to be radically other is for it to be uninterpretable by us. But to allow this is not to shake the earth or to oppose the idea that there are some people whose thoughts and actions are particularly difficult for us to understand.

A theme common to a good deal of contemporary philosophy is that where once we thought in terms of sharp dichotomies, e.g., the analytic and synthetic, the like and unlike in meaning, the theoretical and observational and the voluntary and involuntary, we see now that it is better to think in terms of graded notions and degrees. Understanding, to carry this theme forward, is not an all-or-nothing affair. We may more or less understand some thought or talk, and there are some people whose thoughts or talk may be more difficult to understand than others.

There are a number of ways to grade the notion of understanding or, more to our purpose, to grade difficulties in understanding. We might look at the words we use to report, in our own language, i.e., in indirect discourse, the thoughts of another and introduce some measure on those words that reflects, or so we have reason to think, the closeness of fit between their thoughts and our own. We might introduce a measure of the quality or quantity of the disagreements that, in the course of our interpretation of their thoughts, we allege there to be between them and us. We might look at the explanations we offer of the differences in our thoughts and find in the explanations a reason for saying that some differences in thought are deeper than others. That is, we might view others as more different from us the more difficult it is, on some measure of difficulty, to interpret what they say or do in a way that makes their words and deeds, according to our lights, rational.

To proceed in any of these ways, however, is not to allow that there are conceptual differences between ourselves and others that, in principle, prevent us from interpreting their thoughts or that support the thesis that their minds are in no way like our own. The idea here is that though there are no radical others, some minds may be less like our own than others.

What the interpretive view of mind tells us about talk of otherness in the social sciences is that our interpretation of the minds of others depends as much on what we, as interpreters, believe and desire as it does on what these others say or do. According to the interpretive view, the minds of others are, in large measure, a reflection of our own minds. If our minds were different, if we were to change what we believe about some matter or to change what we desire, if we were to change our thoughts about what is good and what is evil, about the causes of rain or of rich harvests or our thoughts about children and child rearing, then so too would our understanding of the thoughts of others on these same matters change. That is, on the interpretive view of mind, we cannot understand others without, to a great extent, agreeing with them; there is a limit to how many beliefs we can attribute to others that we do not share with them, and so as our minds change, our understanding of their minds must change too.

If there is a limit to the difference between my mind, as I understand it, and the minds of others, as I understand them, there are two ways to stay within this limit of difference and to allow a change of mind; one is for me to change my understanding of the minds of the others and the other is for me to change my understanding of my own mind; The emphasis, in this discussion, has been primarily on the former. Davidson explains how charity may require us, as interpreters, to change our understanding of another's mind. However, there is another way to be charitable; we can change our understanding of our own mind. To reduce the difference between our minds and the minds of others, we have to move something, but the something can be their minds or our own. To understand others, we have to stand with them in more or less the same shoes, but the size of our own feet are not fixed in advance.

If Sara Ruddick is correct and there are substantial differences between the way men and women think about rearing children, differences that make it difficult for a man to understand a woman's thoughts, then a man can understand a woman better by narrowing these differences. He can do this by attributing his own thoughts to her, but he can also do this by attributing her thoughts to himself. This last supports the idea, offered by some feminists, that men will only share a woman's thoughts about children and child rearing when they share with them their practices of caring for and attending to children.

There is another point that can be drawn from the interpretive view of mind and applied to social scientific discussions of otherness. On the interpretive view, given the role that charity plays in interpretation, two individuals may each be able to understand the mind of some other but only if they understand her differently. I may be able to understand your mind and you and I the mind of some third person, but I may not be able to understand her mind as you do. Let me explain how this might be so.

Assume that you and I, as I understand your mind and mine, have somewhat different thoughts. Though some of our thoughts are different, these differences are not great enough to put my interpretation of your mind or my own in doubt. Assume now that I interpret the mind of a third person. The interpretation that I offer of her mind allows that she thinks somewhat differently on some matters than I do, but these differences are not so great that they place my interpretation in doubt. However, when I compare your mind, as I have interpreted it, with hers, I realize that I could not think as I understand you to and interpret her mind as I do. That is, if I saw things as I understand you to, then the thoughts that I attribute to her would look so unreasonable that I would have reason to doubt my interpretation of her mind. If I thought as I understand you to, it would seem unreasonable to me that she should think as I understand her to. On the other hand, the interpretation that I would offer of her mind if I thought as I interpret you to would be an interpretation that, given my own thoughts, I could not myself reasonably offer. Thoughts that you can attribute to another within the limits of difference allowed by the principle of charity might overrun those limits were I to attribute those thoughts to her. Thus, though each of us is able to interpret the mind of this other, the interpretations that we are able to offer are different.

This supports the ideas in sociology that individuals with the same ascribed or achieved status may understand one another differently than outsiders do. Thus, for example, a woman may be able to offer an interpretation of a mind of another woman that a man is not able to offer even though the man is able to interpret the mind of both women. However, this by itself does not support the insider's doctrine that persons of the same ascribed or achieved status are able to understand one another better than persons of a different status are able to. This doctrine requires not only that persons of a different status understand one another differently than persons of the same, it requires that the understanding in one case be in some sense better than it is in the other. According to this insider's doctrine, not only do insider's know differently; they know better.

XII

Though I think that Davidson's view of mind offers a perspective from which the idea of otherness, as it is presented in the social sciences, can be appreciated and appraised, it does leave something important out of the picture. Davidson's notion of understanding is intellectualist. That is, on his view of mind, to understand a person's thoughts or actions is to attribute to her attitudes towards propositions. Thus, to consider why a person acts as she does or what she is thinking, on Davidson's view, is to understand her to be thinking that something is the case. To interpret her action is to understand what the intention was with which she performed it and to understand this is to attribute to her psychological attitudes.

However, there is more to understanding others than intellectualism allows. There are actions which we misunderstand when we try to interpret them. Some words or deeds are misunderstood when they are rationalized. Davidson's account of understanding, as any other purely intellectualist account, overlooks the ritualistic and symbolic nature of some of our actions.

This is the point that Wittgenstein, in his *Remarks on Frazer's* Golden Bough,[34] and A. R. Radcliffe-Brown, in his paper 'Taboo',[35] raised against Sir James Frazer's notion of understanding. According to Wittgenstein and Radcliffe-Brown, Frazer's effort to understand the magical and religious practices described in *The Golden Bough* overlooks the fact that they are magical and religious practices. Frazer proposed rational explanations of these practices. He attributed to the participants the belief that by engaging in the practices nature would be made bountiful. According to Wittgenstein and Radcliffe-Brown, this is to misunderstand the nature of these practices. Frazer mistakenly thinks that magic and religion are bad science. Wittgenstein writes: 'it is nonsense if we go on to say that the characteristic feature of *these* actions is that they spring from wrong ideas about the physics of things. (This is what Frazer does when he says magic is really false physics, or as the case may be, false medicine, technology, etc.)'[36]

However, on Wittgenstein's view, Radcliffe-Brown also has it wrong. Though he does not offer a rational explanation of the practices, he offers a functional explanation and tries to understand the practices by drawing them under laws. Radcliffe-Brown does not try to understand the natives by seeing them as doing science, but he does try to understand them by trying to make the art of seeing them into a science. The way to understand the practices, according to Wittgenstein, is not through science. To understand the practice all we need to do is to see it as similar to practices that we ourselves engage in. An understanding of a primitive religion, according to Wittgenstein, is not won by constructing or reconstructing the reasons that led the natives to engage in the religious activities or by discovering the effects that the activities have on the structure of the natives' social life; it is won by seeing the activities in a certain way: by seeing them as similar to activities that we partake in and in which we invest importance. To understand the practices we, the outsiders, must bring them into connection with own feelings and thoughts.[37]

There are people who bring food to the graves of their dead for weeks following the burial. How are we to understand this practice? Frazer proposes a rational explanation. We undersand, on Frazer's view, why they place food on the grave when we learn what they believe the benefits of this to be. What Frazer offers is an interpretation of the action in the sense that Davidson talks about. What he cites are the beliefs and desires that, as he sees it, led to the placing of the food. On Wittgenstein's view, this is to mistake religion for food science. It is to view the practice as aiming at something, as based on the belief that the placing of the food will have an effect on the dead, but it does not aim at anything; it is an expression or evocation of a feeling or sentiment. Consequently, to understand the action is not to discover what it aims at but to see it in a

[34] Ludwig Wittgenstein, *Remarks on Frazer's* Golden Bough, ed Rush Rhees (Nottinghamshire, 1979).

[35] A. R. Radcliffe-Brown, 'Taboo', pp. 133–52.

[36] Ludwig Wittgenstein, *Remarks on Frazer's* Golden Bough, p. 7e.

[37] Ibid., p. 13e.

perspicuous way; to understand it, we need to see how the action resembles a ritual that we ourselves engage in. When we see it so, the action will evoke in us certain feelings and sentiments. To have these feelings and to have these sentiments is to understand the action.

Frazer looked at the magical and religious practices of other people and concluded that their beliefs about nature must be radically different from his own. This is a mistake, on Wittgenstein's view, not because charity prevents us from attributing so many irrational beliefs about nature to other people, but because these practices are not based on any beliefs about nature at all. According to Wittgenstein, Frazer was not able to understand the practices not because those who engaged in them had thoughts about the natural world that were radically unlike his own, but because of the narrowness of his own spiritual life.

> What narrowness of spiritual life we find in Frazer! And as a result: how impossible for him to understand a different way of life from the English one of his time!
>
> Frazer cannot imagine a priest who is not basically an English parson of our times with all his stupidity and feebleness.[38]

> Frazer is much more savage than most of his savages, for these savages will not be so far from any understanding of spiritual matters as an Englishman of the twentieth century. His explanations of the primitive observances are much cruder than the sense of the observances themselves.[39]

What is important in Wittgenstein's rebuke of Frazer is this. The intellectualist shows us how the norms of rationality limit the difference between our minds and the minds of others, but the intellectualist overlooks the fact that not all of a person's actions are technical actions. There are people who are engaged in ritual actions that are so different from our own actions that we may not be able to understand them, but this does not show that they have beliefs or desires that are to us inscrutable. It shows nothing so exciting or dramatic. According to Wittgenstein, it shows nothing more than that we cannot see these actions as resembling any of our own. It shows that, while the actions move the participants, they leave us cold. And so, despite his differences with the intellectualist, Wittgenstein too discounts the idea of the radical other. Once the nature of mind is correctly understood, we can see that there is little to the idea that there are minds that must to us always remain inscrutable.

---

[38] Ibid., p. 5e.
[39] Ibid., p. 8e.

Special thanks are due to Ernest LePore, Brian McLaughlin, Naomi Scheman, and students in a seminar in the philosophy of language, spring 1983.

Part V
Language and Reality

16

A Coherence Theory of Truth and Knowledge*

Donald Davidson

[handwritten marginalia: as it will be if it also pretends as a criterion of truth]

In this paper I defend what may as well be called a coherence theory of truth and knowledge. The theory I defend is not in competition with a correspondence theory, but depends for its defense on an argument that purports to show that coherence yields correspondence.

The importance of the theme is obvious. If coherence is a test of truth, there is a direct connection with epistemology, for we have reason to believe many of our beliefs cohere with many others, and in that case we have reason to believe many of our beliefs are true. When the beliefs are true, then the primary conditions for knowledge would seem to be satisfied.

Someone might try to defend a coherence theory of truth without defending a coherence theory of knowledge, perhaps on the ground that the holder of a coherent set of beliefs might lack a reason to believe his beliefs coherent. This is not likely, but it may be that someone, though he has true beliefs, and good reasons for holding them, does not appreciate the relevance of reason to belief. Such a one may best be viewed as having knowledge he does not know he has: he thinks he is a skeptic. In a word, he is a philosopher.

Setting aside aberrant cases, what brings truth and knowledge together is meaning. If meanings are given by objective truth conditions there is a question how we can know that the conditions are satisfied, for this would appear to require a confrontation between what we believe and reality; and the idea of such a confrontation is absurd. But if coherence is a test of truth, then coherence is a test for judging that objective truth conditions are satisfied, and we no longer need to explain meaning on the basis of possible confrontation. My slogan is: correspondence without confrontation. Given a correct epistemology, we can be realists in all departments. We can accept objective truth conditions as the key to meaning, a realist view of truth, and we can insist that knowledge is of an objective world independent of our thought or language.

Since there is not, as far as I know, a theory that deserves to be called 'the' coherence theory, let me characterize the sort of view I want to defend. It is obvious that not every consistent set of interpreted sentences contains only true sentences, since one such set might contain just the consistent sentence *S* and another just the negation of *S*. And adding more sentences, while maintaining consistency, will not help. We can imagine endless state-descriptions – maximal consistent descriptions – which do not describe our world.

My coherence theory concerns beliefs, or sentences held true by someone who understands them. I do not want to say, at this point, that every possible coherent set of beliefs is true (or contains mostly true beliefs). I shy away from this because it is so unclear what is possible. At one extreme, it might be held that the range of possible maximal sets of beliefs is as wide as the range of possible maximal sets of sentences, and then there would be no point to insisting that a defensible coherence theory concerns beliefs and not propositions or sentences. But there are other ways of conceiving what it is possible to believe which would justify saying not only that all actual coherent belief systems are largely correct but that all possible ones are also. The difference between the two notions of what it is possible to believe depends on what we suppose about the nature of belief, its interpretation, its causes, its holders, and its patterns. Beliefs for me are states of people with intentions, desires, sense organs; they are states that are caused by, and cause, events inside and outside the bodies of their entertainers. But even given all these constraints, there are many things people do believe, and many more that they could. For all such cases, the coherence theory applies.

Of course some beliefs are false. Much of the point of the concept of belief is the potential gap it introduces between what is held to be true and what is true. So mere coherence, no matter how strongly coherence is plausibly defined, can not guarantee that what is believed is so. All that a coherence theory can maintain is that most of the beliefs in a coherent total set of beliefs are true.

This way of stating the position can at best be taken as a hint, since there is probably no useful way to count beliefs, and so no clear meaning to the idea that most of a person's beliefs are true. A somewhat better way to put the point is to say there is a presumption in favor of the truth of a belief that coheres with a significant mass of belief. Every belief in a coherent total set of beliefs is justified in the light of this presumption, much as every intentional action taken by a rational agent (one whose choices, beliefs and desires cohere in the sense of Bayesian decision theory) is justified. So to repeat, if knowledge is justified true belief, then it would seem that all the true beliefs of a consistent believer constitute knowledge. This conclusion, though too vague and hasty to be right, contains an important core of truth, as I shall argue. Meanwhile I merely note the many problems asking for treatment: what exactly does coherence demand? How much of inductive practice should be included, how much of the true theory (if there is one) of evidential support must be in there? Since no person has a completely consistent body of convictions, coherence with *which* beliefs creates a presumption of truth? Some of these problems will be put in better perspective as I go along.

It should be clear that I do not hope to define truth in terms of coherence and belief. Truth is beautifully transparent compared to belief and coherence, and I take it as primitive. Truth, as applied to utterances of sentences, shows the disquotational feature enshrined in Tarski's Convention T, and that is enough to fix its domain of application. Relative to a language or a speaker, of course, so there is more to truth then Convention T; there is whatever carries over from language to language or speaker to speaker. What Convention T, and the trite sentences it declares true, like '"Grass is green" spoken by an English speaker, is true if and only if grass is green,' reveal is that the truth of an utterance depends on just two things: what the words as spoken mean, and how the world is arranged. There is no further relativism to a conceptual scheme, a way of viewing things, a perspective. Two interpreters, as unlike in culture, language and point of view as you please, can disagree over whether an utterance is true, but only if they differ on how things are in the world they share, or what the utterance means.

I think we can draw two conclusions from these simple reflections. First, truth is correspondence with the way things are. (There is no straightforward and non-misleading way to state this; to get things right, a detour is necessary through the concept of satisfaction in terms of which truth is characterized.[1] So if a coherence theory of truth is acceptable, it must be consistent with a correspondence theory. Second, a theory of knowledge that allows that we can know the truth must be a non-relativized, non-internal form of realism. So if a coherence theory of knowledge is acceptable, it must be consistent with such a form of realism. My form of realism seems to be neither Hilary Putnam's internal realism nor his metaphysical realism.[2] It is not internal realism because internal realism makes truth relative to a scheme, and this is an idea I do not think is intelligible.[3] A major reason, in fact, for accepting a coherence theory is the unintelligibility of the dualism of a conceptual scheme and a 'world' waiting to be coped with. But my realism is certainly not Putnam's metaphysical realism, for *it* is characterized by being 'radically non-epistemic', which implies that all our best researched and established thoughts and theories may be false. I think the independence of belief and truth requires only that *each* of our beliefs may be false. But of course a coherence theory cannot allow that all of them can be wrong.

But why not? Perhaps it is obvious that the coherence of a belief with a substantial body of belief enhances its chance of being true, provided there is reason to suppose the body of belief is true, or largely so. But how can coherence alone supply grounds for belief? Mayhap the best we can do to justify one belief is to appeal to other beliefs. But then the outcome would seem to be that we must accept philosophical skepticism, no matter how unshaken in practice our beliefs remain.

This is skepticism in one of its traditional garbs. It asks: Why couldn't all my beliefs hang together and yet be comprehensively false about the actual world? Mere recognition of the fact that it is absurd or worse to try to *confront* our beliefs, one by one, or as a whole, with what they are about does not answer the question nor show the question unintelligible. In short, even a mild coherence theory like mine must provide a skeptic with a reason for supposing coherent

---

[1] See my 'True to the Facts', *The Journal of Philosophy* (1960), pp. 216–34.

[2] Hilary Putnam, *Meaning and the Moral Sciences* (Routledge and Kegan Paul, London, 1978), p. 125.

[3] See my 'On the Very Idea of a Conceptual Scheme', in *Proceedings and Addresses of the American Philosophical Association* (1974), pp. 5–20.

beliefs are true. The partisan of a coherence theory can't allow assurance to come from outside the system of belief, while nothing inside can produce support except as it can be shown to rest, finally or at once, on something independently trustworthy.

It is natural to distinguish coherence theories from others by reference to the question whether or not justification can or must come to an end. But this does not define the positions, it merely suggests a form the argument may take. For there are coherence theorists who hold that some beliefs can serve as the basis for the rest, while it would be possible to maintain that coherence is not enough, although giving reasons never comes to an end. What distinguishes a coherence theory is simply the claim that nothing can count as a reason for holding a belief except another belief. Its partisan rejects as unintelligible the request for a ground or source of justification of another ilk. As Rorty has put it, 'nothing counts as justification unless by reference to what we already accept, and there is no way to get outside our beliefs and our language so as to find some test other than coherence.'[4] About this I am, as you see, in agreement with Rorty. Where we differ, if we do, is on whether there remains a question how, given that we cannot 'get outside our beliefs and our language so as to find some test other than coherence', we nevertheless can have knowledge of, and talk about, an objective public world which is not of our own making. I think this question does remain, while I suspect that Rorty doesn't think so. If this is his view, then he must think I am making a mistake in trying to answer the question. Nevertheless, here goes.

It will promote matters at this point to review very hastily some of the reasons for abandoning the search for a basis for knowledge outside the scope of our beliefs. By 'basis' here I mean specifically an epistemological basis, a source of justification.

The attempts worth taking seriously attempt to ground belief in one way or another on the testimony of the senses: sensation, perception, the given, experience, sense data, the passing show. All such theories must explain at least these two things: what, exactly, is the relation between sensation and belief that allows the first to justify the second? and, why should we believe our sensations are reliable, that is, why should we trust our senses?

The simplest idea is to identify certain beliefs with sensations. Thus Hume seems not to have distinguished between perceiving a green spot and perceiving that a spot is green. (An ambiguity in the word 'idea' was a great help here.) Other philosophers noted Hume's confusion, but tried to attain the same results by reducing the gap between perception and judgement to zero by attempting to formulate judgements that do not go beyond stating that the perception or sensation or presentation exists (whatever that may mean). Such theories do not justify beliefs on the basis of sensations, but try to justify certain beliefs by claiming that they have exactly the same epistemic content as a sensation. There are two difficulties with such a view: first, if the basic beliefs do not exceed in content the corresponding sensation they cannot support any inference to an objective world; and second, there are no such beliefs.

---

[4] Richard Rorty, *Philosophy and the Mirror of Nature* (Princeton University Press, Princeton, (1979), p. 178.

A more plausible line is to claim that we cannot be wrong about how things appear to us to be. If we believe we have a sensation, we do; this is held to be an analytic truth, or a fact about how language is used.

It is difficult to explain this supposed connection between sensations and some beliefs in a way that does not invite skepticism about other minds, and in the absence of an adequate explanation, there should be a doubt about the implications of the connection for justification. But in any case, it is unclear how, on this line, sensations justify the belief in those sensations. The point is rather that such beliefs require no justification, for the existence of the belief entails the existence of the sensation, and so the existence of the belief entails its own truth. Unless something further is added, we are back to another form of coherence theory.

Emphasis on sensation or perception in matters epistemological springs from the obvious thought: sensations are what connect the world and our beliefs, and they are candidates for justifiers because we often are aware of them. The trouble we have been running into is that the justification seems to depend on the awareness, which is just another belief.

Let us try a bolder tack. Suppose we say that sensations themselves, verbalized or not, justify certain beliefs that go beyond what is given in sensation. So, under certain conditions, having the sensation of seeing a green light flashing may justify the belief that a green light is flashing. The problem is to see how the sensation justifies the belief. Of course if someone has the sensation of seeing a green light flashing, it is likely, under certain circumstances, that a green light is flashing. *We* can say this, since we know of his sensation, but *he* can't say it, since we are supposing he is justified without having to depend on believing he has the sensation. Suppose he believed he didn't have the sensation. Would the sensation still justify him in the belief in an objective flashing green light?

The relation between a sensation and a belief cannot be logical, since sensations are not beliefs or other propositional attitudes. What then is the relation? The answer is, I think, obvious: the relation is causal. Sensations cause some beliefs and in *this* sense are the basis or ground of those beliefs. But a causal explanation of a belief does not show how or why the belief is justified.

The difficulty of transmuting a cause into a reason plagues the anti-coherentist again if he tries to answer our second question: What justifies the belief that our senses do not systematically deceive us? For even if sensations justify belief in sensation, we do not yet see how they justify belief in external events and objects.

Quine tells us that science tells us that 'our only source of information about the external world is through the impact of light rays and molecules upon our sensory surfaces.'[5] What worries me is how to read the words 'source' and 'information'. Certainly it is true that events and objects in the external world cause us to believe things about the external world, and much, if not all, of the causality takes a route through the sense organs. The notion of information, however, applies in a non-metaphorical way only to the engendered beliefs. So

---

[5] W. V. Quine, 'The Nature of Natural Knowledge', in *Mind and Language*, ed. S. Guttenplan, (Clarendon Press, Oxford, 1975), p. 68.

'source' has to be read simply as 'cause' and 'information' as 'true belief' or 'knowledge'. Justification of beliefs caused by our senses is not yet in sight.[6]

The approach to the problem of justification we have been tracing must be wrong. We have been trying to see it this way: a person has all his beliefs about the world – that is, all his beliefs. How can he tell if they are true, or apt to be true? Only, we have been assuming, by connecting his beliefs to the world, confronting certain of his beliefs with the deliverances of the senses one by one, or perhaps confronting the totality of his beliefs with the tribunal of experience. No such confrontation makes sense, for of course we can't get outside our skins to find out what is causing the internal happenings of which we are aware. Introducing intermediate steps or entities into the causal chain, like sensations or observations, serves only to make the epistemological problem more obvious. For if the intermediaries are merely causes, they don't justify the beliefs they cause, while if they deliver information, they may be lying. The moral is obvious. Since we can't swear intermediaries to truthfulness, we should allow no intermediaries between our beliefs and their objects in the world. Of course there are causal intermediaries. What we must guard against are epistemic intermediaries.

There are common views of language that encourage bad epistemology. This is no accident, of course, since theories of meaning are connected with epistemology through attempts to answer the question how one determines that a sentence is true. If knowing the meaning of a sentence (knowing how to give a correct interpretation of it) involves, or is, knowing how it could be recognized to be true, then the theory of meaning raises the same question we have been struggling with, for giving the meaning of a sentence will demand that we specify what would justify asserting it. Here the coherentist will hold that there is no use looking for a source of justification outside of other sentences held true, while the foundationalist will seek to anchor at least some words or sentences to non-verbal rocks. This view is held, I think, both by Quine and by Michael Dummett.

Dummett and Quine differ, to be sure. In particular, they disagree about holism, the claim that the truth of our sentences must be tested together rather than one by one. And they disagree also, and consequently, about whether there is a useful distinction between analytic and synthetic sentences, and about

---

[6] Many other passages in Quine suggest that Quine hopes to assimilate sensory causes to evidence. In *Word and Object* (MIT Press, Massachusetts, 1960), p. 22 he writes that 'surface irritations ... exhaust our clues to an external world.' In *Ontological Relativity* (Columbia University Press, New York, 1969), p. 75, we find that 'The stimulation of his sensory receptors is all the evidence anybody has had to go on, ultimately, in arriving at his picture of the world.' On the same page: 'Two cardinal tenets of empiricism remain unassailable. ... One is that whatever evidence there *is* for science *is* sensory evidence. The other ... is that all inculcation of meanings of words, must rest ultimately on sensory evidence.' In *The Roots of Reference* (Open Court Publishing Company, Illinois, 1974), pp. 37–8, Quine says 'observations' are basic 'both in the support of theory and in the learning of language', and then goes on, 'What are observations? They are visual, auditory, tactual, olfactory. They are sensory, evidently, and thus subjective. ... Should we say then that the observation is not the sensation. ...? No ...' Quine goes on to abandon talk of observations for talk of observation sentences. But of course observation sentences, unlike observations, cannot play the role of evidence unless we have reason to believe they are true.

whether a satisfactory theory of meaning can allow the sort of indeterminacy Quine argues for. (On all these points, I am Quine's faithful student.)

But what concerns me here is that Quine and Dummett agree on a basic principle, which is that whatever there is to meaning must be traced back somehow to experience, the given, or patterns of sensory stimulation, something intermediate between belief and the usual objects our beliefs are about. Once we take this step, we open the door to skepticism, for we must then allow that a very great many – perhaps most – of the sentences we hold to be true may in fact be false. It is ironical. Trying to make meaning accessible has made truth inaccessible. When meaning goes epistemological in this way, truth and meaning are necessarily divorced. One can, of course, arrange a shotgun wedding by redefining truth as what we are justified in asserting. But this does not marry the original mates.

[margin note: notice this is not an issue about realism]

Take Quine's proposal that whatever there is to the meaning (information value) of an observation sentence is determined by the patterns of sensory stimulation that would cause a speaker to assent to or dissent from the sentence. This is a marvellously ingenious way of capturing what is appealing about verificationist theories without having to talk of meanings, sense-data, or sensations; for the first time it made plausible the idea that one could, and should, do what I call the theory of meaning without need of what Quine calls meanings. But Quine's proposal, like other forms of verificationism, makes for skepticism. For clearly a person's sensory stimulations could be just as they are and yet the world outside very different. (Remember the brain in the vat.)

Quine's way of doing without meanings is subtle and complicated. He ties the meanings of some sentences directly to patterns of stimulation (which also constitute the evidence, Quine thinks, for assenting to the sentence), but the meanings of further sentences are determined by how they are conditioned to the original, or observation sentences. The facts of such conditioning do not permit a sharp division between sentences held true by virtue of meaning and sentences held true on the basis of observation. Quine made this point by showing that if one way of interpreting a speaker's utterances was satisfactory, so were many others. This doctrine of the indeterminacy of translation, as Quine called it, should be viewed as neither mysterious nor threatening. It is no more mysterious than the fact that temperature can be measured in Centigrade or Fahrenheit (or any linear transformation of those numbers). And it is not threatening because the very procedure that demonstrates the degree of indeterminacy at the same time demonstrates that what is determinate is all we need.

In my view, erasing the line between the analytic and synthetic saved philosophy of language as a serious subject by showing how it could be pursued without what there cannot be: determinate meanings. I now suggest also giving up the distinction between observation sentences and the rest. For the distinction between sentences belief in whose truth is justified by sensations and sentences belief in whose truth is justified only by appeal to other sentences held true is as anathema to the conherentist as the distinction between beliefs justified by sensations and beliefs justified only by appeal to further beliefs. Accordingly, I suggest we give up the idea that meaning or knowledge is grounded on something that counts as an ultimate source of evidence. No doubt meaning and knowledge depend on experience, and experience ultimately on sensation. But this is the 'depend' of causality, not of evidence or justification.

I have now stated my problem as well as I can. The search for an empirical foundation for meaning or knowledge leads to skepticism, while a coherence theory seems at a loss to provide any reason for a believer to believe that his beliefs, if coherent, are true. We are caught between a false answer to the skeptic, and no answer.

The dilemma is not a true one. What is needed to answer the skeptic is to show that someone with a (more or less) coherent set of beliefs has a reason to suppose his beliefs are not mistaken in the main. What we have shown is that it is absurd to look for a justifying ground for the totality of beliefs, something outside this totality which we can use to test or compare with our beliefs. The answer to our problem must then be to find a *reason* for supposing most of our beliefs are true that is not a form of *evidence*.

My argument has two parts. First I urge that a correct understanding of the speech, beliefs, desires, intentions and other propositional attitudes of a person leads to the conclusion that most of a person's beliefs must be true, and so there is a legitimate presumption that any one of them, if it coheres with most of the rest, is true. Then I go on to claim that anyone with thoughts, and so in particular anyone who wonders whether he has any reason to suppose he is generally right about the nature of his environment, must know what a belief is, and how in general beliefs are to be detected and interpreted. These being perfectly general facts we cannot fail to use when we communicate with others, or when we try to communicate with others, or even when we merely think we are communicating with others, there is a pretty strong sense in which we can be said to know that there is a presumption in favor of the overall truthfulness of anyone's beliefs, including our own. So it is bootless for someone to ask for some *further* reassurance; that can only add to his stock of beliefs. All that is needed is that he recognize that belief is in its nature veridical.

Belief can be seen to be veridical by considering what determines the existence and contents of a belief. Belief, like the other so-called propositional attitudes, is supervenient on facts of various sorts, behavioral, neurophysiological, biological and physical. The reason for pointing this out is not to encourage definitional or nomological reduction of psychological phenomena to something more basic, and certainly not to suggest epistemological priorities. The point is rather understanding. We gain one kind of insight into the nature of the propositional attitudes when we relate them systematically to one another and to phenomena on other levels. Since the propositional attitudes are deeply interlocked, we cannot learn the nature of one by first winning understanding of another. As interpreters, we work our way into the whole system, depending much on the pattern of interrelationships.

Take for example the interdependence of belief and meaning. What a sentence means depends partly on the external circumstances that cause it to win some degree of conviction; and partly on the relations, grammatical, logical or less, that the sentence has to other sentences held true with varying degrees of conviction. Since these relations are themselves translated directly into beliefs, it is easy to see how meaning depends on belief. Belief, however, depends equally on meaning, for the only access to the fine structure and individuation of beliefs is through the sentences speakers and interpreters of speakers use to express and describe beliefs. If we want to illuminate the nature of meaning and belief, therefore, we need to start with something that assumes neither. Quine's suggestion, which I shall essentially follow, is to take *prompted assent* as basic, the causal relation between assenting to a sentence and the cause of such assent. This is a fair place to start the project of identifying beliefs and meanings, since a speaker's assent to a sentence depends both on what he means by the sentence and on what he believes about the world. Yet it is possible to know that a speaker assents to a sentence without knowing either what the sentence, as spoken by him, means, or what belief is expressed by it. Equally obvious is the fact that once an interpretation has been given for a sentence assented to, a belief has been attributed. If correct theories of interpretation are not unique (do not lead to uniquely correct interpretations), the same will go for attributions of belief, of course, as tied to acquiescence in particular sentences.

A speaker who wishes his words to be understood cannot systematically deceive his would-be interpreters about when he assents to sentences – that is, holds them true. As a matter of principle, then, meaning, and by its connection with meaning, belief also, are open to public determination. I shall take advantage of this fact in what follows and adopt the stance of a radical interpreter when asking about the nature of belief. What a fully informed interpreter could learn about what a speaker means is all there is to learn; the same goes for what the speaker believes.[7]

The interpreter's problem is that what he is assumed to know – the causes of assents to sentences of a speaker – is, as we have seen, the product of two things he is assumed not to know, meaning and belief. If he knew the meanings he would know the beliefs, and if he knew the beliefs expressed by sentences assented to, he would know the meanings. But how can he learn both at once, since each depends on the other?

The general lines of the solution, like the problem itself, are owed to Quine. I will, however, introduce some changes into Quine's solution, as I have into the statement of the problem. The changes are directly relevant to the issue of epistemological skepticism.

I see the aim of radical interpretation (which is much, but not entirely, like Quine's radical translation) as being to produce a Tarski-style characterization of truth for the speaker's language, and a theory of his beliefs. (The second follows from the first plus the presupposed knowledge of sentences held true.) This adds little to Quine's program of translation, since translation of the speaker's language into one's own plus a theory of truth for one's own language add up to a theory of truth for the speaker. But the shift to the semantic notion of truth from the syntactic notion of translation puts the formal restrictions of a theory of truth in the foreground, and emphasizes one aspect of the close relation between truth and meaning.

---

[7] I now think it is essential, in doing radical interpretation, to include the desires of the speaker from the start, so that the springs of action and intention, namely both belief and desire, are related to meaning. But in the present talk it is not necessary to introduce this further factor.

The principle of charity plays a crucial role in Quine's method, and an even more crucial role in my variant. In either case, the principle directs the interpreter to translate or interpret so as to read some of his own standards of truth into the pattern of sentences held true by the speaker. The point of the principle is to make the speaker intelligible, since too great deviations from consistency and correctness leave no common ground on which to judge either conformity or difference. From a formal point of view, the principle of charity helps solve the problem of the interaction of meaning and belief by restraining the degrees of freedom allowed belief while determining how to interpret words.

We have no choice, Quine has urged, but to read our own logic into the thoughts of a speaker; Quine says this for the sentential calculus, and I would add the same for first-order quantification theory. This leads directly to the identification of the logical constants, as well as to assigning a logical form to all sentences.

Something like charity operates in the interpretation of those sentences whose causes of assent come and go with time and place: when the interpreter finds a sentence of the speaker the speaker assents to regularly under conditions he recognizes, he takes those conditions to be the truth conditions of the speaker's sentence. This is only roughly right, as we shall see in a moment. Sentences and predicates less directly geared to easily detected goings-on can, in Quine's cannon, be interpreted at will, given only the constraints of interconnections with sentences conditioned directly to the world. Here I would extend the principle of charity to favor interpretations that as far as possible preserve truth: I think it makes for mutual understanding, and hence for better interpretation, to interpret what the speaker accepts as true when we can. In this matter, I have less choice than Quine, because I do not see how to draw the line between observation sentences and theoretical sentences at the start. There are several reasons for this, but the one most relevant to the present topic is that this distinction is ultimately based on an epistemological consideration of a sort I have renounced: observation sentences are directly based on something like sensation – patterns of sensory stimulation – and this is an idea I have been urging leads to skepticism. Without the direct tie to sensation or stimulation, the distinction between observation sentences and others can't be drawn on epistemologically significant grounds. The distinction between sentences whose causes to assent come and go with observable circumstances and those a speaker clings to through change remains however, and offers the possibility of interpreting the words and sentences beyond the logical.

The details are not here to the point. What should be clear is that if the account I have given of how belief and meaning are related and understood by an interpreter, then most of the sentences a speaker holds to be true – especially the ones he holds to most stubbornly, the ones most central to the system of his beliefs – most of these sentences *are* true, at least in the opinion of the interpreter. For the only, and therefore unimpeachable, method available to the interpreter automatically puts the speaker's beliefs in accord with the standards of logic of the interpreter, and hence credits the speaker with plain truths of logic. Needless to say there are degrees of logical and other consistency, and perfect consistency is not to be expected. What needs emphasis is only the methodological necessity for finding consistency enough.

Nor, from the interpreter's point of view, is there any way he can discover the speaker to be largely wrong about the world. For he interprets sentences held true (which is not to be distinguished from attributing beliefs) according to the events and objects in the outside world that cause the sentence to be held true.

What I take to be the important aspect of this approach is apt to be missed because the approach reverses our natural way of thinking of communication derived from situations in which understanding has already been secured. Once understanding has been secured we are able, often, to learn what a person believes quite independently of what caused him to believe it. This may lead us to the crucial, indeed fatal, conclusion that we can in general fix what someone means independently of what he believes and independently of what caused the belief. But if I am right, we can't in general first identify beliefs and meanings and then ask what caused them. The causality plays an indispensable role in determining the content of what we say and believe. This is a fact we can be led to recognize by taking up, as we have, the interpreter's point of view.

It is an artifact of the interpreter's correct interpretation of a person's speech and attitudes that there is a large degree of truth and consistency in the thought and speech of an agent. But this is truth and consistency by the interpreter's standards. Why couldn't it happen that speaker and interpreter understand one another on the basis of shared but erroneous beliefs? This can, and no doubt often does, happen. But it cannot be the rule. For imagine for a moment an interpreter who is omniscient about the world, and about what does and would cause a speaker to assent to any sentence in his (potentially unlimited) repertoire. The omniscient interpreter, using the same method as the fallible interpreter, finds the fallible speaker largely consistent and correct. By his own standards, of course, but since these are objectively correct, the fallible speaker is seen to be largely correct and consistent by objective standards. We may also, if we want, let the omniscient interpreter turn his attention to the fallible interpreter of the fallible speaker. It turns out that the fallible interpreter can be wrong about some things, but not in general; and so he cannot share universal error with the agent he is interpreting. Once we agree to the general method of interpretation I have sketched, it becomes impossible correctly to hold that anyone could be mostly wrong about how things are.

There is, as I noted above, a key difference between the method of radical interpretation I am now recommending, and Quine's method of radical translation. The difference lies in the nature of the choice of causes that govern interpretation. Quine makes interpretation depend on patterns of sensory stimulation, while I make it depend on the external events and objects the sentence is interpreted as being about. Thus Quine's notion of meaning is tied to sensory criteria, something he thinks that can be treated also as evidence. This leads Quine to give epistemic significance to the distinction between observation sentences and others, since observation sentences are supposed, by their direct conditioning to the senses, to have a kind of extra-linguistic justification. This is the view against which I argued in the first part of my paper, urging that sensory stimulations are indeed part of the causal chain that leads to belief, but cannot, without confusion, be considered to be evidence, or a source of justification, for the stimulated beliefs.

What stands in the way of global skepticism of the senses is, in my view, the fact that we must, in the plainest and methodologically most basic cases, take

✳ the objects of a belief to be the causes of that belief. And what we, as interpreters, must take them to be is what they in fact are. Communication begins where causes converge: your utterance means what mine does if belief in its truth is systematically caused by the same events and objects.[8]

The difficulties in the way of this view are obvious, but I think they can be overcome. The method applies directly, at best, only to occasion sentences – the sentences' assent to which is caused systematically by common changes in the world. Further sentences are interpreted by their conditioning to occasion sentences, and the appearance in them of words that appear also in occasion sentences. Among occasion sentences, some will vary in the credence they command not only in the face of environmental change, but also in the face of change of credence awarded related sentences. Criteria can be developed on this basis to distinguish degrees of observationality on internal grounds, without appeal to the concept of a basis for belief outside the circle of beliefs.

Related to these problems, and easier still to grasp, is the problem of error. For even in the simplest cases it is clear that the same cause (a rabbit scampers by) may engender different beliefs in speaker and observer, and so encourage assent to sentences which cannot bear the same interpretation. It is no doubt this fact that made Quine turn from rabbits to patterns of stimulation as the key to interpretation. Just as a matter of statistics, I'm not sure how much better one approach is than the other. Is the relative frequency with which identical patterns of stimulation will touch off assent to 'Gavagai' and 'Rabbit' greater than the relative frequency with which a rabbit touches off the same two responses in speaker and interpreter? Not an easy question to test in a convincing way. But let the imagined results speak for Quine's method. Then I must say, what I must say in any case, the problem of error cannot be met sentence by sentence, even at the simplest level. The best we can do is cope with error holistically, that is, we interpret so as to make an agent as intelligible as possible, given his actions, his utterances and his place in the world. About some things we will find him wrong, as the necessary cost of finding him elsewhere right. As a rough approximation, finding him right means identifying the causes with the objects of his beliefs, giving special weight to the simplest cases, and countenancing error where it can be best explained.

Suppose I am right that an interpreter must so interpret as to make a speaker or agent largely correct about the world. How does this help the person himself who wonders what reason he has to think his beliefs are mostly true? How can he learn about the causal relations between the real world and his beliefs that lead the interpreter to interpret him as being on the right track?

The answer is contained in the question. In order to doubt or wonder about the provenance of his beliefs an agent must know what belief is. This brings with it the concept of objective truth, for the notion of a belief is the notion of a state that may or may not jibe with reality. But beliefs are also identified, directly and indirectly, by their causes. What an omniscient interpreter knows a

---

[8] It is clear that the causal theory of meaning has little in common with the causal theories of reference of Kripke and Putnam. Those theories look to causal relations between names and objects of which speakers may well be ignorant. The chance of systematic error is thus increased. My causal theory does the reverse by connecting the cause of a belief with its object.

fallible interpreter gets right enough if he understands a speaker, and this is just the complicated causal truth that makes us the believers we are, and fixes the contents of our beliefs. The agent has only to reflect on what a belief is to appreciate that most of his basic beliefs are true, and among his beliefs, those most securely held and that cohere with the main body of his beliefs are the most apt to be true. The question, how do I know my beliefs are generally true? thus answers itself, simply because beliefs are by nature generally true. Rephrased or expanded, the question becomes, how can I tell whether my beliefs, which are by their nature generally true, are generally true?

All beliefs are justified in this sense: they are supported by numerous other beliefs (otherwise they wouldn't be the beliefs they are), and have a presumption in favor of their truth. The presumption increases the larger and more significant the body of beliefs with which a belief coheres, and there being no such thing as an isolated belief, there is no belief without a presumption in its favor. In this respect, interpreter and interpreted differ. From the interpreter's point of view, methodology enforces a general presumption of truth for the body of beliefs as a whole, but the interpreter does not need to presume each particular belief of someone else is true. The general presumption applied to others does not make them globally right, as I have emphasized, but provides the background against which to accuse them of error. But from each person's own vantage point, there must be a graded presumption in favor of each of his own beliefs.

We cannot, alas, draw the picturesque and pleasant conclusion that all true beliefs constitute knowledge. For though all of a believer's beliefs are to some extent justified to him, some may not be justified enough, or in the right way, to constitute knowledge. The general presumption in favor of the truth of belief serves to rescue us from a standard form of skepticism by showing why it is impossible for all our beliefs to be false together. This leaves almost untouched the task of specifying the conditions of knowledge. I have not been concerned with the canons of evidential support (if such there be), but to show that all that counts as evidence or justification for a belief must come from the same totality of belief to which it belongs.

17
Empirical Content*

DONALD DAVIDSON

The dispute between Schlick and Neurath over the foundations of empirical knowledge illustrates the difficulties in trying to draw epistemological conclusions from a verificationist theory of meaning. It also shows how assuming the general correctness of science does not automatically avoid, or provide an easy answer to, skepticism. But while neither Schlick nor Neurath arrived at a satisfactory account of empirical knowledge, there are promising hints of a better theory in their writings. Following up these hints, and drawing on further ideas in Hempel, Carnap and particularly Quine, I suggest the direction I think a naturalistic epistemology should take.

The logical positivists agreed that the empirical content of an interpreted sentence derives from its relations to a subset of sentences that report, or are based on, observation or experience. Two main sources of difficulty and dispute immediately became evident. One was the question how to characterize the relations between protocol sentences and other sentences. The history of the developments and changes in the views of the logical positivists and their followers on this problem has been masterfully recorded, as well as much contributed to, by Carl Hempel.[1] This is not my present subject.

The second question was how protocol sentences should be formulated, and what their relation to experience or observation is. This is the issue I wish to discuss, and on which Schlick and Neurath disagreed, Schlick endorsing a foundationalist epistemology and Neurath a coherence theory. The difference was expressed in fairly strong terms. Neurath described the foundationalist position as 'related to the belief in *immediate experiences* which is current in traditional academic philosophy', and remarked that 'methodological solipsism' (Carnap's term for a view like Schlick's) does 'not become more serviceable because of the addition of the word "methodological".'[2] Schlick in turn called

---

*©Donald Davidson

[1] See 'Empiricist Criteria of Cognitive Significance: Problems and Changes', in *Aspects of Scientific Explanation*, (The Free Press, New York, 1965).

[2] Otto Neurath, 'Protocol Sentences' *Erkenntnis*, 3 (1932/3). Here and elsewhere I quote from the translation in *Logical Positivism*, ed. A. J. Ayer, (The Free Press, New York, 1959), pp. 204 and 206.

Neurath's version of the coherence theory an 'astounding error'.[3]

Astounding error or not, Carnap and Hempel at one time seemed to agree with Neurath. In 1935 Hempel wrote, 'I think that there is no essential difference left between protocol statements and other statements', and he concurred with Carnap in holding that once the question which sentences were basic was put in the 'formal mode', the answer became a matter for convention to decide. 'This insight', he concluded, echoing Carnap's words, 'eliminates from the Logical Positivist's theory of verification and truth a remainder of absolutism which is due to metaphysical tendencies.'[4] Schlick jeered at such conventionalism, saying it made truth as relative as 'all the measuring rods of physics'. In an ironic vein he added, 'and it is this view with its consequences that has been commended as banishing the last remnant of "absolutism" from philosophy.'[5]

It is not entirely clear, however, just where matters stood. Fifteen years later, in a quasi-historical article, Hempel asserted that 'The fundamental tenet of modern empiricism is the view that all non-analytic knowledge is based on experience.' He went on to explain what it means for knowledge to be based on experience: non-analytic knowledge can be expressed by sentences that are confirmed (in a specified way) by observation sentences, which in turn are 'ascertained' to be true by direct observation.[6] This sounds more like Schlick, and indeed like the 'fatal confrontation of statements and facts' which Hempel had previously rejected.[7]

In a note added in 1959 to a reprinting of 'Studies in the Logic of Confirmation' Hempel suggests a way of partially reconciling the apparently opposed points in view. Truth, he and Carnap had come to realize in the light of Tarski's work, is a legitimate semantic notion, and should not be treated as a matter of coherence. Confirmation, on the other hand, was of two sorts, *relative* and *absolute*. The logical study of confirmation was the study of the extent to which an arbitrary set of sentences confirmed a hypothesis. In this context, one could only say that relative to a set of sentences (whatever its provenance), a hypothesis was confirmed or disconfirmed. Absolute confirmation, on the other hand, depended on a 'pragmatic' decision to treat certain sentences as true. Neurath and Carnap, Hempel suggests, were thinking of relative confirmation, which invites a coherence theory. Schlick (and Hempel in 1950) were thinking of absolute confirmation.

This important distinction of Hempel's is revealing, since it does seem at times that early discussions of protocol sentences vacillated between treating such sentences as any sentences with a specified syntax, and treating them as sentences that were accepted, perhaps on the basis of observation or experience. But the distinction cannot reconcile all the differences. The differences that remained were these: Schlick held, while Neurath denied, that protocol

---

[3] Moritz Schlick, 'The Foundation of Knowledge', *Erkenntnis*, 4 (1934). Here and elsewhere I quote from the translation in *Logical Positivism*. Page 215.

[4] Carl Hempel, 'On the Logical Positivist's Theory of Truth', *Analysis*, 2 (1935), pp. 58,59.

[5] 'The Foundation of Knowledge', p. 213.

[6] 'The Empiricist Criterion of Meaning', *Revue International de Philosophie*, 4 (1950). The quotations are from pages 108–110 of the reprinted article in *Logical Positivism*.

[7] 'On the Logical Positivist's Theory of Truth', p. 51.

sentences may be established as true once and for all; Schlick claimed, while Neurath denied, that a sentence could intelligibly be said to be compared to reality. There were also differences over the question of the proper subject matter of protocols, and the question whether they reported something private or something public. Obviously, these various points are closely related to one another.

One way to approach our central problem is to ask what the nature of *evidence* is: does it consist of objects, events, facts, experiences, sensations, beliefs, propositions, or sentences? Almost every one of these possible answers can be found in the writings of the Vienna Circle.

> I observe two pieces of green paper [writes Schlick] and determine that they have the same color. The proposition which asserts the sameness of color is verified, among other ways, by the fact that at the same time I have two experiences of the same color. The proposition: 'there are two spots of the same color before me now' cannot be reduced to others; it is verified by the fact that it describes the given.[8]

What exactly does the verifying? Schlick says it is the fact that he has certain experiences which are veridical. But if the same experiences were not veridical, would they still verify the same proposition? The fact that I see a piece of paper implies that there is a piece of paper, but here we do not move from evidence to hypothesis in an interesting way; we merely deduce an entailed proposition. Elsewhere, Schlick insists that we must start with statements that 'have their origin' in observation sentences; and he elaborates this as: 'they derive, as one may confidently say in the traditional way of speaking, "from the experience".'[9] In the same essay, he declares that

> It is clear, and is so far as I know disputed by no one, that knowledge in life and science in *some* sense *begins* with confirmation of facts, and that the 'protocol statements' in which this occurs stand in the same sense at the *beginning* of science.[10]

In another passage he says that everything goes back to what is 'immediately observed'.[11] As Ayer put it, some propositions can be 'directly confronted with the facts'.

Let me try to bring out in one further way the apparently puzzling question of the ontological status of evidence. We say that laws are confirmed by their positive instances; so the positive instances are, presumably, evidence for the laws they confirm. Suppose, for the sake of clarity in one direction, we identify laws with universally quantified conditional sentences – sentences which are, needless to say, interpreted. What is a positive instance? Let the law be the sentence '$(x)(Fx \to Gx)$.' Then, suggests Hempel, it is reasonable to suppose

---

[8] 'Positivism and Realism', *Erkenntnis*, 3 (1932/3). The quotation is from the translation in *Logical Positivism*, pp. 92–3.
[9] 'The Foundation of Knowledge', p. 215.
[10] Ibid., p. 210.
[11] Ibid., p. 220.

that an *object* that is F and G confirms the law.[12] (Goodman often talks this way in *Fact, Fiction, and Forecast*.) Hempel then explains that instead of viewing confirmation as a 'relation between an object or an ordered set of objects, representing the evidence, and a sentence, representing the hypothesis' he will take it to be a relation between a sentence that describes the evidence, and the hypothesis. Thus,

> The evidence adduced in support or criticism of a scientific hypothesis is always expressed in sentences, which frequently have the character of observation reports ... The evidence ... consists, in the last analysis, in data accessible to what is loosely called direct observation and such data are expressible in the form of 'observation reports'.[13]

What are accessible to observation are objects and events. These are not the same things as facts, nor, of course, as sentences. Sentences can, in some loose sense, express facts (i.e. true propositions), and describe objects. None of what I say is meant remotely as criticism of Hempel's exemplary work on confirmation as a relation between sentences; I am using the distinction among various ways of describing positive instances of laws (or lawlike sentences) in order to emphasize the very different ways in which it is natural to talk of evidence.

Perhaps it is not strange to call a black raven – some actual bird – an *instance* of a law, but it does seem odd to say the bird is *evidence* for the law. At best this seems to be shorthand for saying it is the *fact* that this bird is a black raven that constitutes the evidence; or we could speak of the truth of the proposition, or of some appropriate sentence. So far however, we have not touched on the epistemological issue, the question what it means for *someone* to have a reason to accept the law, to *possess* evidence. Neither the existence of the black raven nor the truth of the proposition or sentence that says there is a black raven in itself gives anyone a reason to believe there is a black raven, much less a reason to believe all ravens are black. For someone to have a reason to believe all ravens are black, it is necessary for him to *believe*, for example, that here is a black raven.

We are off on a well worn track. Surely it is not enough simply to believe that here is a black raven; not enough, either, that the belief should also be true. For both of these conditions together do not add up to evidence unless the person has an adequate reason for holding the belief. If the reason must be another belief, we are faced by an infinite regress or a circle. A regress would make knowledge impossible, while a circle would lead to the difficulties of a pure coherence theory of knowledge. I'll come back to the latter in a moment.

Here we come to the standard attempts – standard at least from Hume onward – to find states of mind that bridge or eliminate the gap between sensation, where no question of truth can arise, and judgement, which is plausibly a source of evidence. Quasi-sentences like 'Black here now' are supposed to express such states of mind. And perhaps we will be persuaded that there are such states of mind if we overlook the fact that the verb has been omitted (since putting it in would push things too far in the direction of

---

[12] Hempel, 'Studies in the Logic of Confirmation', in *Aspects of Scientific Explanation*, p. 14.
[13] Ibid., pp. 21–2.

judgement) and that words like 'here' and 'now' cannot be understood except as involving a reference to an agent. In any case, the attempt to base science on such states of mind is doomed, since no one has ever succeeded in showing how to base knowledge of an objective, common world on such 'evidence'. Even Schlick, who somehow hoped to back protocol sentences of the form 'A experiences black at time t' by whatever it is that is expressed by 'Black here now' as said or thought by A at t, did not believe in a construction of science or a public world, with the construction based on 'immediate experiences'.

It should be clear that no appeal to perception can clear up the question what constitutes a person's ultimate source of evidence. For if we take perception to consist in a sensation caused by an event in the world (or in the body of the perceiver), the fact of causality cannot be given apart from the sensation, and the sensation cannot serve as evidence unless it causes a belief. But how does one know that the belief was caused by a sensation? Only further beliefs can help. If perception is expressed by locutions like 'A perceives that there is a black raven,' then this can certainly serve as evidence. But the problem has not been solved, but rather transferred to the concept of perception, since to perceive that there is a black raven is to be caused by a raven, and *in the right way*, to believe that there is a black raven.

One is struck, in reading early writings of the members of the Vienna Circle, at the embarrassed way in which they refer to experience, what is immediately given, what is directly observed. Thus Schlick says that all meaning goes back to ostensive situations, 'and this means, in an obvious sense, reference to "experience" or "possibility of verification".'[14] In 'The Turning Point in Philosophy' he says 'The act of verification in which the path to the solution finally ends is always of the same sort: it is the occurrence of a definite fact that is confirmed by observation, by means of immediate experience,'[15] but in 'Positivism and Realism' he expresses grave doubts about terms like 'the given' ('das Gegebene'), and worries that if we use the word 'experience' we will 'presuppose a distinction between what experiences and what is experienced'.[16]

There is, then, very good reason to conclude that there is no clear meaning to the idea of comparing our beliefs with reality or confronting our hypotheses with observations. This is not, of course, to deny that there is an ordinary sense in which we perform experiments and note the results, or discover in our everyday pursuits that some of our beliefs are true and others false. What should be denied is that these mundane events are to be analysed as involving evidence which is not propositional in character – evidence which is not some sort of belief. No wonder Neurath and Carnap were attracted to the idea of a coherence theory!

Not that a coherence theory of knowledge is without difficulties, and these, as we have seen, Schlick was quick to point out. Let me pause here for a moment to make the obvious distinction between a coherence theory of knowledge and a

---

[14] 'Meaning and Verification', *The Philosophical Review*, 4 (1936), p. 148.
[15] 'The Turning Point in Philosophy', *Erkenntnis*, 1 (1930/1). The quotation is from the translation in *Logical Positivism*, p. 56.
[16] 'Positivism and Realism', p. 84.

coherence theory of truth. In his 1935 paper 'On the Logical Positivist's Theory of Truth' Hempel had barely distinguished between the two; understandably, since he was not then aware of Tarski's method for defining truth semantically. He therefore was at the time inclined to think the only sense we can make of the phrase 'Sentence S is true' is 'S is highly confirmed by accepted observation reports.'[17] But the concept of being highly confirmed by accepted observation reports belongs rather in the domain of epistemology; and when coupled with the idea that protocol statements 'may only be characterized by the historical fact' that they are accepted (i.e. believed true), leads directly to a coherence theory of knowledge. This is the theory to which Schlick strongly objected.

Schlick agreed with Neurath that protocols belong, in a general way, to the hypotheses of science. They are objective, and therefore intersubjectively understood and testable. They are *about* observations or experiences, but they don't attempt to *express* them. They take the form, roughly at least, of sentences like 'A saw a black raven at time *t*.' It is clear that one cannot be certain of the truth of such sentences – not even A at time *t* can be certain he is seeing a black raven; or, leaving the question of certainty aside, it is clear that anyone who judges such a sentence to be true may be wrong. Further evidence is always relevant, and may come to outweigh the evidence of the moment. Where Schlick disagreed with Neurath is on the question whether there are indisputable grounds on the basis of which we judge protocols to be true.[18]

The objection to Neurath's coherence theory was the standard objection to all such theories: consistency is not enough, since it leaves no basis on which to choose between various and conflicting consistent theories. Perhaps a theory of this kind banishes the last remnant of absolutism from philosophy, as Schlick said of Neurath's claims, but it leaves us with no basis for judging truth. Schlick insisted that we must have, and do have, indubitable grounds for choosing some sentences as the true ones rather than others. There are statements, which are *not* protocol statements, which 'express facts of one's own "perception"' ('or whatever you like to call it,' he adds).[19] Schlick then admits that 'in spite of the fact that statements of this sort seem so simple and clear, philosophers have found themselves in a hopeless labyrinth the moment they actually attempted to use them as the foundation of all knowledge.' But he thinks we can steer clear of the familiar difficulties if we remember that 'one's *own* statements in the end play the only decisive role'.[20]

One must admit that Schlick's attempt to explain his view ends in obscurity. The observation 'sentences' which constitute the 'ultimate criterion' of all knowledge are not really sentences, being always of the form 'Here now so and so',[21] such sentences cannot be written down (since they lose their certainty in a moment)[22]; they express a feeling of *'fulfillment*, a quite characteristic satisfaction: we are *satisfied'*.[23] 'One cannot build any logically tenable structure upon

---

[17] 'Studies in the Logic of Confirmation', p. 42.
[18] 'The Foundation of Knowledge', p. 213.
[19] Ibid., p. 218.
[20] Ibid., p. 219.
[21] Ibid., p. 225.
[22] Ibid., p. 222.
[23] Ibid.

such confirmations, for they are gone the moment one begins to construct.'[24] Finally, 'the occasion of understanding [observation statements] is at the same time that of verifying them: I grasp their meaning at the same time I grasp their truth.'[25] One can sympathize with Neurath for rejecting this last step. But then one is left with a coherence theory.

Hempel calls the Neurath-Carnap position a 'restrained' coherence theory;[26] the reason is that Neurath and Carnap do provide us with a criterion for picking out one scientific theory from among the consistent ones. The criterion is that it is the consistent theory that maximizes agreement with the statements historically held true by 'mankind especially the scientists of our culture circle'.[27] In the end, protocol sentences have no pride of place; like any others they may be abandoned if they conflict with too much else we hold true.

Thus it turns out, rather surprisingly, that both Schlick and Neurath held views that could be called 'restrained' coherence theories. They agreed that everything in the corpus of science, including protocol sentences, must be viewed as only tentatively established at any stage in the progress of science, and all sentences remain open to revision in the light of new evidence. They likewise agreed that when revision was called for, there were no strict rules for deciding where the revision should be made; it was a matter for 'decision'. Their sole important difference concerned the question how the whole pattern of sentences accepted in the going phase of science was to be related to experience, observation, or the real world. And on this score their answers were, I have suggested, less than clear or satisfactory.

Schlick's answer was unsatisfactory because it ended with something so private that even its meaning could only be given at a moment for an individual. How such a basis could warrant belief in a public objective world was simply not explained. Neurath rejected the idea of a confrontation between a belief about the world and the world itself as well as the idea of an incorrigible subjective basis for scientific knowledge. But his suggestion as to how to 'restrain' a coherence theory is unappealing. He suggests that we start with protocols of the form 'A sees a black raven at *t*', and he dismisses the idea that such protocols are anymore the basis of A's knowledge than of B's. This guarantees the intersubjective aspect of the language of science right down to the protocols (since, as Neurath said, '*every* language *as such* is inter-subjective'[28] – clearly a crack at Schlick and his observation statements whose meaning is revealed to only one person, and then only for a moment). Neurath imagines all protocols being thrown into one great machine; a bell rings if a contradiction arises; something must then be thrown out, either one or more protocols, or perhaps a law or other theoretical statement; but '*who* rebuilds the machine, or *whose* protocol sentences are thrown into the machine is of no consequence whatsoever.'[29]

---

24 Ibid.
25 Ibid., p. 225.
26 'The Logical Positivist's Theory of Truth', p. 49, p. 57n.
27 Ibid., p. 57.
28 'Protocol Sentences', p. 205.
29 Ibid., p. 207.

There is an obvious difficulty here. If protocol sentences are known only by their form, throwing them *all* in the machine will mean each sentence *and* its negation will be thrown in, as well as 'A sees a black raven at spot *s* at *t*' and 'B sees a non-black raven at spot *s* at *t*'. No basis for science can emerge from this, just endless consistent systems. If, on the other hand, the protocols are limited to the sentences that express *beliefs*, it *will* matter who mends the machine and whose protocols are thrown in. For each person will weigh the sentences he accepts (whether protocols or not) in accord with the strength of his beliefs – that's what it means to say they are *his* beliefs. He will give weight to other people's protocols to the extent that he believes they are true, just as Schlick maintained.

I would not dwell at such length on the familiar epistemological problems that beset Schlick and Neurath and their followers (and here I have picked out Carnap and particularly Hempel – Hempel partly because of the importance of his contributions, and partly because to the delight of all of us he is here to speak for himself) – I would not dwell on these problems if I thought philosophy has now rejected them or solved them. On the contrary, I think the members of the Vienna Circle and their friends emphasized in a particularly useful way, even if partly in spite of themselves, a central unsettled problem in epistemology. And I think we can find a number of ideas and intuitions in the writings I have been discussing that point in the direction of a new view of the old problem.

The central problem may be stated as a dilemma in the theory of knowledge. Each person has a complex network of beliefs and attitudes. Knowledge requires at least two things: that some of these beliefs are true of the public objective world, and that each person has adequate reasons for holding these beliefs. I am willing to assume that the first condition is satisfied; the hard problem concerns the second issue, the way in which the system of beliefs is related to the world not merely semantically, but epistemologically. The dilemma arises because if we take as the connecting link something self-certifying (like Schlick's observation statements or events), it is so private as to lack connection with the sentences of the public language which alone are capable of expressing scientific, or even objective, claims. But if we start with sentences or beliefs already belonging to the public language (or what can be expressed in it), we find no intelligible way to base it on something self-certifying (Neurath's problem). In short, the foundations of knowledge must be subjective and objective at once, certain and yet open to question.

The problems I am rehearsing belong, we all know, to the foundations of epistemology, and in one form or another the problems are ancient. The logical positivists, one senses at once in their writings, were impatient with such problems, which they felt verged on the meaningless, or were to be solved by mere 'conventions' or 'decisions'. This attitude now seems to us, rereading these bold classics, cavalier almost to the point of irresponsibility. But the giddy conviction that a clear and correct line would somehow open up in the face of all that enthusiasm and intellectual power did, I am convinced, produce some profoundly novel and valuable hints. What on the surface now may seem naive and failed attempts contained deeply suggestive intuitions of radical new ideas.

Given the positivist's tendency to remain within the vocabulary of inter-subjective ideas and hypotheses, the flirtations of Neurath and Schlick, as also Hempel and Carnap, with some form of epistemological coherence theory is not surprising. But coherence theories have always been bedeviled by failure to distinguish between coherence theories of truth and coherence theories of knowledge. This is natural enough, since if knowledge, which is of the true, demands nothing but coherence of belief, how can truth require anything more than a set of coherent propositions? Thus we are invited – not quite reasonably – to dismiss the difference between coherence of beliefs and coherence of sentences (or statements or propositions) as tests of knowledge and truth. But while we find this confusion in the writings of Schlick and Neurath, we also find moments when the distinction is clearly made. Neurath, we remember, hoped to destroy any aura of subjectivity in protocol statements by insisting that though it may be an 'historical accident' that A is more inclined to accept his own protocols than those of B, in fact both are to be accepted on the same level.[30] This leads him to the picture of the impersonal 'sorting-machine' into which protocol sentences are thrown. In this fairly lengthy passage, there is no hint that it is only sentences *believed true* by someone that are to count. It is this fact that occasioned Schlick's outburst: 'The astounding error of the "coherence theory" can be explained only by the fact that its defenders and expositors were thinking only of such statements as actually occur in science.'[31] And here Schlick means, of course, such as occur *as assertions*. Yet in spite of much that we find in Neurath's article on protocol sentences, can he really be accused of having forgotten the difference between coherence with an arbitrary set of sentences and coherence with a set of sentences held true? The famous metaphor of the ship which must be rebuilt at sea piece by piece proves he was aware that it is beliefs that are at stake, not mere sentences.[32] For if we were dealing with an arbitrary set of sentences, nothing would stop us from putting them all in drydock at once! And Hempel, as I have mentioned before, makes the distinction clear.

Since standard objections to coherence theories of knowledge parallel standard objections to coherence theories of truth, it is not immediately apparent why it is so important to distinguish between them. But of course beliefs are not historically or causally arbitrary; even if our *reasons* for our beliefs are always other beliefs, the *causes* sometimes lie elsewhere. Some appreciation of the importance of this point must, as we will see, be credited to the logical positivists.

The logical positivists preferred to talk of sentences or 'statements' rather than beliefs, and we can easily enough make this switch as long as we remember that the sentences that correspond to beliefs are (1) sentences held true by someone, and (2) sentences that have an interpretation. Someone else can know what I believe if he knows what sentences I hold true, and what those sentences mean. Let me review some of the logical positivist views in the light of these simple considerations.

---

[30] Ibid., p. 206.
[31] 'The Foundation of Knowledge', p. 215.
[32] 'Protocol Sentences', p. 201.

There is Schlick's idea that observation sentences are understood in the act of grasping their truth. This may well seem extreme or obscure; but it is related to the correct doctrine that an interpreter is constrained to take first-person present-tense attributions of attitude as presumptively true. Such sentences (of English) as 'I believe I now see a black raven' if held true by a speaker, require of an interpreter that he assign a high a priori probability to their truth. This means: so interpret such sentences as to make them true when possible.

Hempel comments on the fact that the protocol statements 'produced' by different men might not admit the construction of a unique system of scientific statements. He goes on:

> but fortunately this possibility is not realized: in fact, by far the greater part of scientists will sooner or later come to an agreement, and so, as an empirical fact, a perpetually increasing and expanding system of coherent statements and theories results from their protocol statements.[33]

Again, we must assume that protocol statements are not any sentences written down, or uttered; they must be sentences their speakers believe to be true, or at least that a hearer believes the speaker to have held true. But it is surely odd to consider it merely 'fortunate' that there is a large degree of consensus: and *why* should we expect agreement to increase over time?

Schlick has an even more surprising discussion of the possibility that someone might discover that all his own observations in no way substantiate the assertions made about the world by other men. He says that under these circumstances one would not, as Neurath's protocol-machine would, simply sacrifice one's own protocol statements. Instead, one would cling to a

> system of knowledge into which one's own observations fitted unmutilated. And I can always construct such a system. I need only view the others as dreaming fools, in whose madness lies a remarkable method, or – to express it more objectively – I would say that the others live in a different world from mine. ... In any case no matter what world picture I construct, I would test its truth always in terms of my own experience.[34]

This is a remarkable admission from someone who has objected that a coherence theory leaves us with an unacceptable relativism.

Elsewhere in Schlick, however, we find a rather different way of viewing the possibility of massive disagreement. He notes a basic contrast between a disagreement over whether two pieces of paper are the same color, and a disagreement over what color both pieces are. With respect to the first he says that 'by virtue of linguistic usage the proposition expresses just that experience' – i.e., the experience of sameness. But in the case of color, there is no objective way – that is, no way – to tell if you and I experience the same color. Even if all your judgements (Schlick writes) about color agree entirely with mine I cannot infer from this that you experience this same quality. It would ... forever be

---

[33] 'On the Logical Positivist's Theory of Truth', p. 57.
[34] 'The Foundation of Knowledge', p. 219.

impossible to discover these differences between your experience and mine. We should always understand one another perfectly, and could never be of different opinions regarding our environment if ... the inner *order* of your experiences agrees with that of mine. The quality doesn't matter, only the question of being arranged into similar patterns.[35]

Schlick seems in the end to reject the view that the experiences may be undetectably different. 'The statement that different individuals have the same experience has its sole verifiable meaning in the fact that all their assertions ... exhibit certain agreements ... the statement *means* nothing but this.'[36] It is not easy to tell from this passage whether Schlick thinks the experiences might be qualitatively different while we could not in principle discern this, or meaning-fully claim it; or whether he thinks no such situation could arise. The radical suggestion, which it is not impossible to read into Schlick's attack on the coherence theory, is that interpersonal agreement, and hence objectivity, are built into the way in which we determine the meanings of other people's utterances, and hence the contents of their beliefs.

I mentioned above Hempel's remark that 'fortunately' the protocol statements of different people allow the construction of a unique system of science. He adds that Carnap has 'perhaps provided us a possibility of explaining this fortunate fact'.[37] The possible explanation lies in the fact that 'young scientists are conditioned' to produce 'true' protocol statements, and he adds, 'Perhaps the fact of the general and rather congruous conditioning of scientists may explain to a certain degree the fact of a unique system of science.'[38]

It would be mysterious if people were first taught what various sentences mean, and *then* were conditioned to 'produce' the true ones; this would amount to teaching them on the one hand how to be better observers, and on the other hand to be honest. But the situation may be seen rather as a matter of conditioning people, as we surely do, to hold certain sentences true under publicly observable conditions, and fixing on the interpretation of the sentences in accord with the success of the conditioning. This would explain interpersonal agreement on the main features of the environment in a natural way.

Carnap at one point seems clearly to take this line. In 'Psychology in Physical Language' (written in 1932) Carnap flatly rejects Neurath's idea that I must or can treat your protocol sentences on a par with my own.

> Generally speaking [he writes], a psychologist's spoken, written, or printed protocol sentences, when they are based on so-called introspection, are to be interpreted by the reader, and so figure in inter-subjective science, *not chiefly as scientific sentences, but as scientific facts*. The epistemological confusion of contemporary psychology stems, to a large extent, from this confusion of facts in the form of sentences with the sentences themselves considered as parts of science.[39]

---

[35] The second half of this paragraph quotes from pages 92–3 of 'Positivism and Realism' with omissions and slight changes.

[36] Ibid., p. 93.

[37] 'On the Logical Positivist's Theory of Truth', p. 57.

[38] Ibid., p. 58.

[39] 'Psychology in Physical Language', *Erkenntnis*, 3 (1932/3). The quotation is from the translation in *Logical Positivism*, p. 195.

The inferences we are permitted to draw from the fact that someone else utters a sentence are not the deductive consequences that flow from that sentence as interpreted, but rather the sort of inference we can draw from observing the movements of a volt-meter, or the movements of a raindrop. The point is not that others do not mean anything by the sentences they utter but that we cannot take for granted that we know in advance *what* they mean; and interpretation is explicitly called for or implicitly assumed.

I think that by following out this line, along with several other suggestions drawn from passages I have been quoting, we can discover the outline of a correct view of the foundations of empirical knowledge, a view that reconciles Neurath's coherentist theory with Schlick's insistence on a basic tie to experience and observation.

From here on, although I shall be drawing in many and obvious ways on ideas of Schlick, Neurath, Hempel and Carnap, I am stating my own position. This is a position deeply influenced by Quine, though it is not his position.

Neurath was right in rejecting the intelligibility of comparing sentences or beliefs with reality. We experiment and observe, but this is not 'comparing' in any but a metaphorical sense, for our experimentation bears no epistemological fruit except as it *causes* us to add to, cling to, or abandon our beliefs. This causal relation cannot be a relation of *confirmation or disconfirmation*, since the cause is not a proposition or belief, but just an event in the world or in our sensory apparatus. Nor can such events be considered in themselves to be evidence, unless, of course, they cause us to believe something. And then it is the belief that is properly called the evidence, not the event.

Neurath was also right in saying that given this situation, we may as well admit that protocols, like any other propositions of science or common sense, can be wrong; we stand ready to tinker where tinkering does the most good. As Hempel observed, no epistemological priority is left to protocols – they are like the rest. All this is, of course, the line Quine was later to exploit so successfully in arguing against the analytic-synthetic distinction.

We are left, then, as Neurath insisted, in a situation where our only evidence for a belief is other beliefs; this is not merely the *logical* situation, but also the pragmatic situation. And since no belief is self-certifying, none can supply a certain basis for the rest. How then can we escape Schlick's objection that this makes 'arbitrary fairy stories to be as true as a historical report ...'? He concludes: 'Thus the coherence theory is shown to be logically impossible ... for by means of it I can arrive at any number of consistent systems of statements which are incompatible with one another.'[40] It's not clear what it means to say I could 'arrive' at various systems, since I do not invent my beliefs; most of them are not voluntary. Still, the point of the criticism would seem to remain in the form of a challenge to say what reason I have to consider the bulk of my beliefs true.

The key to the answer lies, I think, in generalizing Carnap's two suggestions that we are conditioned to produce (hold true) specific sentences under particular conditions, and that we cannot use other people's statements as evidence until we have interpreted them. Carnap said this only about protocol sentences, but the same should be said about all language.

---

[40] 'The Foundation of Knowledge', p. 216.

Language is in its nature, as Neurath insisted, intersubjective; what someone else's words mean on occasion is always something that we can in principle learn from public clues. Consider how we discover what some simple sentence means, say 'There's a table,' or 'Here's a green piece of paper.' Our basic evidence is that the speaker is caused to assent (not just on this occasion, but generally) to these sentences by the presence of tables or pieces of green paper, while the absence of these objects causes him (generally) to dissent from the same sentence. I do not think of assent and dissent as overt speech acts, but as attitudes towards sentences sometimes revealed in speech and sometimes in other ways. My main point is that our basic methodology for interpreting the words of others necessarily makes it the case that most of the time the simplest sentences which speakers hold true *are* true. It is not the *speaker* who must perform the impossible feat of comparing his belief with reality; it is the *interpreter* who must take into account the causal interaction between world and speaker in order to find out what the speaker means, and hence what he believes. Each speaker can do no better than make his system of beliefs coherent, adjusting the system as rationally as he can as new beliefs are thrust on him. But there is no need to fear that these beliefs might be just a fairy tale. For the sentences that express the beliefs, and the beliefs themselves, are correctly understood to be about the public things and events that cause them, and so must be mainly veridical. Each individual knows this, since he knows the nature of speech and belief. This does not, of course, tell him *which* of his beliefs and sentences are true, but it does assure him that his overall picture of the world around him is like the picture other people have, and is in its large features correct.

Neurath, Carnap and Hempel were right, I believe, in abandoning the search for a basic sort of evidence on which our knowledge of the world could rest. None is available, and none is needed. What they perhaps failed to appreciate is *why* it is not needed. It is not needed because the causal relations between our beliefs and speech and the world also supply the interpretation of our language and of our beliefs. In this rather special sense, 'experience' is the source of all knowledge. But this is a sense that does not encourage us to find a mental or inferential bridge between external events and ordinary beliefs. The bridge is there all right – a causal bridge that involves the sense organs. The error lies as Neurath saw in trying to turn this causal bridge into an epistemological one, with sense data, uninterpreted givens, or unwritable sentences constituting its impossible spans.

There are of course some beliefs that carry a very high degree of certitude, and in some cases their content creates a presumption in favor of their truth. These are beliefs about our own present propositional attitudes. But the relative certitude of these beliefs does not suit them to be the foundation of empirical knowledge. It springs, rather, from the nature of interpretation. As interpreters we have to treat self-ascriptions of belief, doubt, desire and the like as privileged; this is an essential step in interpreting the rest of what the person says and thinks. The foundations of interpretation are not the foundations of knowledge, though an appreciation of the nature of interpretation can lead to an appreciation of the essentially veridical nature of belief.

18

Pragmatism, Davidson and Truth

RICHARD RORTY

I Less is more

Davidson has said that his theory of truth 'provides no entities with which to compare sentences', and thus is a 'correspondence' theory only in 'an unassuming sense'.[1] His paper 'A Coherence Theory of Truth and Knowledge' takes as its slogan 'correspondence without confrontation'.[2] This slogan chimes with his repudiation of what he calls the 'dualism of scheme and content' – the idea that something like 'mind' or 'language' can bear some relation such as 'fitting' or 'organizing' to the world. Such doctrines are reminiscent of pragmatism, a movement which has specialized in debunking dualisms and in dissolving traditional problems created by those dualisms. The close affiliations of Davidson's work to Quine's and of Quine's to Dewey's make it tempting to see Davidson as belonging to the American pragmatist tradition.

Davidson, however, has explicitly denied that his break with the empiricist tradition makes him a pragmatist.[3] He thinks of pragmatism as an identification of truth with assertibility, or with assertibility under ideal conditions. If such an identification is essential to pragmatism, then indeed Davidson is as anti-pragmatist as he is anti-empiricist. For such an identification would merely be an emphasis on the 'scheme' side of an unacceptable dualism, replacing the emphasis on the 'content' side represented by traditional empiricism. Davidson does not want to see truth identified with anything. He also does not want to view sentences as 'made true' by anything – neither knowers or speakers on the one hand nor 'the world' on the other. For him, any 'theory of truth' which analyses a relation between bits of language and bits of non-language is already on the wrong track.

On this last, negative, point, Davidson agrees with William James. James thought that no traditional theory of truth had come close to explaining 'the particular go'[4] of such a special relation, and that it was a hopeless quest. On his

---

[1] Donald Davidson, *Inquiries into Truth and Interpretation* (Oxford University Press, Oxford, 1984), p. xviii.

[2] This article appears in *Kant oder Hegel?*, ed. Dieter Henrich (Klett-Cotta, Stuttgart, 1983). It is reprinted in the present volume. The quoted slogan is on p. 423 of the original publication.

[3] *Inquiries*, p. xviii.

[4] William James, *Pragmatism* (Hackett, Indianapolis, 1981), p. 92.

view, there was no point in trying to give sense to a notion of 'correspondence' which was neutral between, e.g., perceptual, theoretical, moral and mathematical truths. He suggested that we settle for 'the true' as being 'only the expedient in our way of thinking'.[5] When his critics chorused that 'truths aren't true because they work; they work because they are true', James thought they had missed his point, viz., that 'true' was a term of praise used for endorsing, rather than one referring to a state of affairs the existence of which explained e.g., the success of those who held true beliefs. He thought that the moral of philosophers' failures to discover, as it were, the micro-structure of the correspondence relation was that there was nothing there to find, that one could not use truth as an *explanatory* notion.

James, unfortunately, did not confine himself to making this negative point. He also had moments in which he inferred from the false premise that

> If we have the notion of 'justified', we don't need that of 'truth'

to

> 'True' must mean something like 'justifiable'.

This was a form of the idealist error of inferring from

> We can make no sense of the notion of truth as correspondence

to

> Truth must consist in ideal coherence.

The error is to assume that 'true' needs a definition, and then to infer from the fact that it cannot be defined in terms of a relation between beliefs and non-beliefs to the view that it must be defined in terms of a relation among beliefs. But, as Hilary Putnam has pointed out in his 'naturalistic fallacy' argument, 'it might be true but not X' is always sensible, no matter what one substitutes for X (the same point G. E. Moore made about 'good').[6]

Suppose that we prescind from the moments in which James fell into this error, as well as from Peirce's unfortunate attempt (of which more later) to define truth in terms of 'the end of inquiry'. Suppose that we follow up James's negative point – his polemic against the notion of 'correspondence' – and forget his occasional attempts to say something constructive about truth. We can then, I think, isolate a sense for the term 'pragmatism' which will consist *simply* in the dissolution of the traditional problematic about truth, as opposed to a constructive 'pragmatist theory of truth'. This dissolution would start from the claim that 'true' has no explanatory use, but merely the following uses:

(a) an endorsing use
(b) a cautionary use, in such remarks as 'Your belief that S is perfectly justified, but perhaps not true' – reminding ourselves that justification is relative to, and no better than, the beliefs cited as grounds for S, and that such

---

[5] Ibid., p. 100.
[6] Hilary Putnam, *Meaning and the Moral Sciences* (Cambridge University Press, Cambridge, 1978), p. 108.

justification is no guarantee that things will go well if we take S as a 'rule for action' (Peirce's definition of belief)
(c) A disquotational use: to say metalinguistic things of the form 'S' is true iff
———.[7]

The cautionary use of the term was neglected by James, as was the disquotational use. The neglect of the former led to the association of pragmatism with relativism. The misleading association of the latter (by Tarski) with the notion of 'correspondence' has led people to think that there must have been more to this notion than James realized. Davidson, on my view, has given us an account of truth which has a place for each of these uses while eschewing the idea that the expediency of a belief can be explained by its truth.

In the sense of 'pragmatism' in which Davidson and James are both pragmatists, the term signifies adherence to the following theses:

(1) 'True' has no explanatory uses.
(2) We understand all there is to know about the relation of beliefs to the world when we understand their causal relations with the world; our knowledge of how to apply terms such as 'about' and 'true of' is fallout from a 'naturalistic' account of linguistic behavior.[8]
(3) There are no relations of 'being made true' which hold between beliefs and the world.
(4) There is no point to debates between realism and anti-realism, for such debates presuppose the empty and misleading idea of beliefs 'being made true'.[9]

Notice that, so defined, pragmatism offers no 'theory of truth'. All it gives us is an explanation of why, in this area, less is more – of why therapy is better than system-building.

---

[7] There is much to be said about the relations between these three uses, but I shall not try to say it here. The best attempt to do so which I have seen is found in an unpublished paper by Robert Brandom called 'Truth Talk'. Brandom shows how the 'primitive pragmatism' which tries to define truth as assertibility is defeated by the use of 'true' in such contexts as the antecedents of conditionals. But he then suggests a way of developing a sophisticated pragmatism which, invoking Frege and the Grover-Camp-Belnap prosentential theory of truth, saves Dewey's intentions. Brandom not only shows how 'anaphoric or prosentential theories' can, as he says 'retain the fundamental anti-descriptive thrust of the pragmatist position, while broadening it to account also for the embedded uses on which primitive pragmatism founders', but suggests ways of reconciling these theories with Davidsonian disquotationalism.

[8] This thesis does not, of course, entail that you can define intentional terms in non-intentional terms, nor that a semantical metalanguage can somehow be 'reduced' to Behaviorese. It is one thing to say 'You learn which sentences using the term "X" are true by finding out which sentences using the term "Y" are true' and another to say 'You can explain the meaning of "X" in terms of "Y"' or 'You can reduce "X"s to "Y"s'. Our intentional concepts are not fall-out from our observation of causal relationships, but our knowledge of how to apply them is. See Section IV below for a discussion of Davidson's non-reductive brand of physicalism.

[9] Jamesian pragmatists heartily agree with Dummett's claim that lots and lots of the traditional 'problems of philosophy' (including the problems which Peirce thought to solve with his "Scotistic realism") are best seen as issues between realists and anti-realists over whether there are "matters of fact" in, e.g., physics, ethics, or logic. But whereas Dummett sees himself as having rehabilitated these fine old problems by semanticizing them, the pragmatist sees him as having conveniently bagged them for disposal.

Both James and Davidson would urge that the only reason philosophers thought they needed an 'explanation of what truth consists in' was that they were held captive by a certain picture – the picture which Davidson calls 'the dualism of scheme and content' and which Dewey thought of as 'the dualism of Subject and Object'. Both pictures are of disparate ontological realms, one containing beliefs and the other non-beliefs. The picture of two such realms permits us to imagine truth as a relation between particular beliefs and particular non-beliefs which (a) is non-causal in nature, and (b) must be 'correctly analyzed' before one can rebut (or concede victory to) the epistemological skeptic. To adopt (1)–(4) above is to erase this picture, and thereby to erase most of the traditional philosophical dualisms which Dewey thought ought to be erased. It is also to drop the picture which the epistemological skeptic needs to make his skepticism interesting and arguable – to make it more than the philosopher's pursuit of *Unheimlichkeit* of a sense of the strangeness of the world.

II Peirce's half-way measure

Before turning to the question of whether Davidson in fact adheres to (1)–(4), it may be helpful to say something about Peirce's 'end of inquiry' pragmatism. This is the version of the so-called 'pragmatist theory of truth' (a misleading textbook label for a farrago of inconsistent doctrines) which has received most attention in recent years. It represents, on my view, a half-way house between idealist and physicalist theories of truth on the one hand, and (1)–(4) on the other.

Idealism and physicalism have in common the hope that

   (A)   'There are rocks' is true

is true if and only if

   (B)   At the ideal end of inquiry, we shall be justified in asserting that there are rocks

This suggestion requires them, however, to say that

   (C)   There are rocks

is implied by (B) as well as by (A). This seems paradoxical, since they also wish to assert

   (D)   'There are rocks' is linked by a relation of correspondence – accurate representation – to the way the world is

and there seems no obvious reason why the progress of the language-game we are playing should have anything in particular to do with the way the rest of the world is.

Idealism and physicalism are attempts to supply such a reason. The idealists suggest that

   (E)   The world consists of representations arranged in an ideally coherent system

thus permitting them to analyse (C) as

   (F)   'There are rocks' is a member of the ideally coherent system of representations.

Idealists support this move by saying that the correspondence relation of (D) cannot be a relation whose existence could be established by confronting an assertion with an object to see if a relation called 'corresponding' holds. Nobody knows what such a confrontation would look like. (The relation of 'customary response to' which holds between tables and assertions of the presence of tables is clearly not what is wanted.) Since the only criterion of truth is coherence among representations, they say, the only way of saving (D) while avoiding skepticism is (E).

The physicalists, on the other hand, analyse (A) as (D) and then argue that playing the language-games we play will eventually lead us to correspond with reality. It will do so because, so to speak, the world takes a hand in the game. This is the view of philosophers like Friedrich Engels, Jerry Fodor, Michael Devitt, Jay Rosenberg and Hartry Field. They reject the possibility of a priori discovery of the nature of reality, illustrated by the idealists' (E), but they think that one or another empirical science (or the 'unified' ensemble of them all) will provide an answer to the skeptic. These philosophers think that, although there are no entailments, there are deeply buried connections between the conditions of the truth of (B) and of (C). These connections will not be discovered by an analysis of meanings but by empirical scientific work which will pry out the causal connections between, e.g., rocks and representations of rocks.

Peirce, in his earlier period, wanted to avoid both the revisionary metaphysics of idealism and the promissory notes of physicalism. He tried for a quick fix by analysing (D) as (B). He shared with the idealist and the physicalist the motive of refuting the skeptic, but he thought it enough to say that 'reality' means something like 'whatever we shall still be asserting the existence of at the end of inquiry'. This definition of reality bridges the gap the skeptic sees between coherence and correspondence. It reduces coherence to correspondence without the necessity either for metaphysical system-building or for further empirical inquiry. A simple reanalysis of the term 'reality' does the trick.

I do not think (though I once did)[10] that Peircian pragmatism is defensible, but before transcending it I want to remark that Peirce was moving in the right direction. The Peircian pragmatist is right in thinking that the idealist and the physicalist share a common fallacy – namely that 'correspondence' is the name of a relation between pieces of thought (or language) and pieces of the world, a relation such that the relata must be ontologically homogenous. The idealist generalizes Berkeley's point by saying: nothing can correspond to a representation except a representation. So he saves us from skepticism by redescribing reality as consisting of representations. The physicalist thinks that nothing can correspond to a bit of spatio-temporal reality except by being another bit linked

---

[10] As, for instance, when I said, falsely, that 'we can make no sense of the notion that the view which can survive all objections might be false' (*Consequences of Pragmatism* (University of Minnesota Press, Minneapolis, 1982), p. 165 – passage written in 1979). I started retracting this Peircianism in the Introduction to that book (e.g., p. xlv, written in 1981) and am still at it. I was persuaded of the untenability of Peircian view by Michael Williams' 'Coherence, Justification and Truth' (*Review of Metaphysics* XXXIV (1980) pp. 243–72) in particular by his claim (p. 269) that 'we have no idea that it would be for a theory to be ideally complete and comprehensive... or of what it would be good for inquiry to have an end'. Cf. his suggestion that we drop the attempt to think of truth as 'in some sense an epistemic notion' (p. 269). Davidson spells out what happens when the attempt is dropped.

to the first by appropriate causal relationships. So he saves us from skepticism by offering a physicalistic account of the nature of our representations – one which shows that, as Fodor once said, the correspondence theory of truth corresponds to reality. The Peircian rises above this debate by saying that the 'about' and 'true of' relations can link utterly disparate relata, and that problems of ontological homogeneity need not arise.[11] All that is necessary is to redefine 'reality' as what the winners of the game talk about, thus insuring that the conditions laid down by (B) and (D) coincide.

The Peircian redefinition, however, uses a term – 'ideal' – which is just as fishy as 'corresponds'. To make it less fishy Peirce would have to answer the question 'How would we know that we were at the end of inquiry, as opposed to merely having gotten tired or unimaginative?' This is as awkward as 'How do we know we are corresponding to reality, rather than merely making conventionally correct responses to stimuli?' Peirce's idea of 'the end of inquiry' might make sense if we could detect an asymptotic convergence in inquiry, but such convergence seems a local and short-term phenomenon.[12] Without such a clarification of 'ideal' or 'end', the Peircian is merely telling that the conditions laid down by (B) and (D) coincide without giving us any reason for thinking they do. Nor is it clear what such a reason could consist in.

Peirce went half-way towards destroying the epistemological problematic which motivated the metaphysical quarrels between idealists and physicalists. He did so by leaving out 'mind' and sticking to 'signs'. But he went *only* half-way because he still thought that (D) was an intuition which any philosophy had to assimilate. James went the rest of the way by saying that not only was 'true of' not a relation between ontologically homogenous relata, but was not an analyzable relation at all, not a relation which could be clarified by a scientific or metaphysical description of the relation between beliefs and non-beliefs. Deciding that no reason could be given for saying that the constraints laid down by (B) and (D) would coincide, he simply dropped (D), and with it the problematic of epistemological skepticism. He thereby set the stage for Dewey's argument that it is only the attempt to supplement a naturalist account of our interaction with our environment with a non-naturalist account (involving some third thing, intermediate between the organism and its environment – such as 'mind' or 'language') which makes that problematic seem interesting.

---

[11] Peircian pragmatism is often criticized on the ground that, like idealism, it raises problems about ontological homogeneity and heterogeneity through a counter-intuitive claim Kantian claim that 'objects in the world owe their fundamental structure – and, if they couldn't exist without displaying that structure, their existence – to our creative activity' (Alvin Plantinga, 'How To Be An Anti-Realist', *Proceedings of the American Philosophical Association*, 56 (1982), p. 52). But this confuses a criterial claim with a causal one: the Peircian claim that 'If there are rocks, they will display their structure at the end of inquiry' and the idealist claim that 'If there were no inquiry, there would be no rocks.'

[12] See Mary Hesse's distinction between 'instrumental progress' – increase in predictive ability – and 'convergence of concepts' (*Revolutions and Reconstructions in the Philosophy of Science* (Indiana University Press, Bloomington, 1980), pp. x–xi). The possibility of scientific revolutions endangers conceptual convergence, which is the only sort of convergence which will do the Peircian any good. To insure against the indefinite proliferation of such revolutions in the future one would need something like Peirce's 'metaphysics of evolutionary love', or Putnam's attempt to certify contemporary physics as 'mature'.

III   Davidson and the field linguist

What justification is there for attributing (1)–(4) to Davidson? He has asserted (3) on various occasions. But it may seem odd to attribute (4) to him, since he has often been treated as a prototypical 'realist'. (2) may also sound unDavidsonian, since he has had no truck with recent 'causal theories' in semantics. Further, his association with Tarski, and Tarski's with the notion of 'correspondence', may seem to make him an unlikely recruit for the pragmatist ranks – for pragmatism, as I have defined it, consists very largely in the claim that only if we drop the whole idea of 'correspondence with reality' can we avoid pseudo-problems.

Nevertheless, I propose to argue that all four pragmatist theses should be ascribed to Davidson. To defend this claim, I shall begin by offering an account of what I shall call 'the philosophy of language of the field linguist'. I shall claim that this is all the philosophy of language (and, in particular, all the doctrine about truth) which Davidson has, and all that he thinks anybody needs.

Davidson, like the traditional philosopher who wants an answer to the epistemological skeptic, wants us to step out of our language-game and look at it from a distance. But his outside standpoint is not the metaphysical standpoint of the idealist, looking for an unsuspected ontological homogeneity between beliefs and non-beliefs invisible to science, nor the hopeful standpoint of the physicalist, looking to future science to discover such an homogeneity. Rather, it is the mundane standpoint of the field linguist trying to make sense of our linguistic behavior. Whereas traditional theories of truth asked 'what feature of the world is referred to by "true"?', Davidson asks 'how is "true" used by the outside observer of the language-game?'

Davidson is surely right that Quine 'saved philosophy of language as a serious subject' by getting rid of the analytic-synthetic distinction.[13] Quine's best argument for doing so was that the distinction is of no use to the field linguist. Davidson follows upon this argument by pointing out that, *pace* Dummett and Quine himself,[14] the distinction between the physical objects the natives react to and their neural stimulations is of no use either. The linguist cannot start with knowledge of native meanings acquired prior to knowledge of native beliefs, nor with translations of native observation sentences which have been certified by matching them with stimulations. He must be purely coherentist in his approach, going round and round the hermeneutic circle until he begins to feel at home.

All the linguist has to go on is his observation of the way in which linguistic is aligned with non-linguistic behavior in the course of the native's interaction with his environment, an interaction which he takes to be guided by rules for action (Peirce's definition of 'belief'). He approaches this data armed with the

---

[13] 'A Coherence Theory ...', p. 431.

[14] See 'A Coherence Theory ...', p. 430: 'Quine and Dummett agree on a basic principle, which is that whatever there is to meaning must be traced back somehow to experience, the given, or patterns of sensory stimulation, something intermediate between belief and the usual objects our beliefs are about. Once we take this step, we open the door to skepticism ... When meaning goes epistemological in this way, truth and meaning are necessarily divorced.'

regulative principle that most of the native's rules are the same as ours, which is to say that most of them are true. The latter formulation of the principle is an extension of Quine's remark that any anthropologist who claims to have translated a native utterance as '*p* and not-*p*' just shows that she has not yet put together a good translation manual. Davidson generalizes this: any translations which portrays the natives as denying most of the evident facts about their environment is automatically a bad one.

The most vivid example of this point is Davidson's claim that the best way to translate the discourse of a brain which has always lived in a vat will be as referring to the vat-cum-computer environment the brain is actually in.[15] This will be the analogue of construing most native remarks as about, e.g., rocks and diseases rather than about trolls and demons. In Davidson's words:

> What stands in the way of global skepticism of the senses is, in my view, the fact that we must, in the plainest and methodologically most basic cases, take the objects of a belief to be the causes of that belief. And what we, as interpreters, must take them to be is what they in fact are. Communication begins where causes converge: your utterance means what mine does if belief in its truth is systematically caused by the same events and objects.[16]

In this passage, Davidson weds the Kripkean claim that causation must have *something* to do with reference to the Strawsonian claim that you figure out what somebody is talking about by figuring out what object most of his beliefs are true of. The wedding is accomplished by saying that Strawson is right if construed holistically – if one prefaces his claim with Aristotle's phrase 'on the whole and for the most part'. You cannot, however, use Strawson's criterion for individual cases and be sure of being right. But if *most* of the results of your translation-scheme, and consequent assignment of reference, do not conform to Strawson's criterion, then that scheme must have something terribly wrong with it. The mediating element between Strawson and Kripke is the Quinean insight that knowledge *both* of causation *and* of reference is (equally) a matter of coherence with the field linguist's own beliefs.

Thesis (2) above can be construed in either a Kripkean or a Davidsonian way. On the former, building-block, approach to reference, we want to trace causal pathways from objects to individual speech-acts. This approach leaves open the possibility that speakers may get these pathways all wrong (e.g., by being largely wrong about what there is) and thus that they may never know to what they are referring. This allows the possibility of a wholesale divorce between referents and intentional objects – just the kind of scheme-content gap which Davidson warns us against. By contrast, Davidson is suggesting that we maximize coherence and truth first, and then let reference fall out as it may.

This guarantees that the intentional objects of lots of beliefs – what Davidson calls 'the plainest cases' – will be their causes. Kripkean slippage (e.g., the Goedel-Schmidt case) must be the exception. For if we try to imagine that a

---

[15] As far as I know, Davidson has not used this example in print. I am drawing upon unpublished remarks at a colloquium with Quine and Putnam, Heidelberg, 1981.

[16] 'A Coherence Theory ...', p. 436. This line of argument – together with Davidson's account of reference as fallout from translation (as at *Inquiries*, pp. 219ff., 236ff.) – is my chief textual evidence for imputing (2) to Davidson.

split between entities referred to and intentional objects is the rule we shall have drained the notion of 'reference' of any content. That is: we shall have made it, like 'analytic', a notion which the field linguist has no use for. The linguist can communicate with the natives if he knows most of their intentional objects (i.e., which objects most of their rules for action are good for dealing with, which objects most of their beliefs are true of). But he can make as little sense of the skeptical claim that this is not 'really' communication (but just accidentally felicitous cross-talk) as of the suggestion that the 'intended interpretation' of some platitudinous native utterance is 'There are no rocks.'

Davidson's application of this view of the job of the field linguist to epistemological skepticism is as follows. Unless one is willing to postulate some intermediary between the organism and its environment (e.g., 'determinate meanings', 'intended interpretations', 'what is before the speaker's mind', etc.) then radical interpretation begins at home. So, like all other natives, we turn out to have mostly true beliefs. The argument is neat, but does it *answer* the skeptic, as the idealist and the physicalist want to do? Or does it simply tell the skeptic that his question, 'Do we ever represent reality as it is in itself?' was a bad one, as the Jamesian pragmatist does?

A skeptic is likely to reply to Davidson that it would take a lot more than an account of the needs of the field linguist to show that belief is, as Davidson says, 'in its nature veridical'.[17] He will think that Davidson has shown no more than that the field linguist must assume that the natives believe mostly what we do, and that the question of whether most of *our* beliefs are true is still wide open. Davidson can only reply, once again, that radical interpretation begins at home – that if we want an outside view of our own language-game, the only one available is that of the field linguist. But that is just what the skeptic will not grant. He thinks that Davidson has missed the philosophical point. He thinks that Davidson's outside standpoint is not, so to speak, far enough outside to count as philosophical.

As far as I can see, the only rejoinder readily available to Davidson at this point is to remark on the intuitive appeal of (2): the naturalistic thesis, which he shares with Kripke, that there is nothing more to be known about the relation between beliefs and the rest of reality than what we learn from an empirical study of causal transactions between organisms and their environment. The relevant result of this study is the field linguist's translation-manual-cum-ethnographic-report.[18] Since we already have (in dictionaries) a translation manual for ourselves, as well as (in encyclopedias) an auto-ethnography, there is nothing more for us to know *about our relation to reality* than we already know. There is no further job for philosophy to do. This is just what the pragmatist has been telling the skeptic all the time. Both the pragmatist and Davidson are saying that if 'correspondence' denotes a relation between beliefs and the world which can vary though nothing else varies – even if all the causal relations remain the same – then 'corresponds' cannot be an explanatory term. So if truth is to be thought of as 'correspondence', then 'true' cannot be an explanatory term. Pressing (2) to the limit, and freeing it from the atomistic presuppositions

---

[17] 'A Coherence Theory ...', p. 432.

[18] That such a manual cannot be separated from such a report is entailed by the Quine–Davidson argument that you cannot figure out beliefs and meanings independently of one another.

which Kripkean 'building-block' theories of reference add to it, results in (1).

Thus Davidson's strategy with the skeptic would seem to give him reason to subscribe to (1) as well as to (2). Whereas the physicalist invokes (2) with an eye to finding something for 'correspondence' to refer to, Davidson takes the absence of such a thing in the field linguist's results as a reason for thinking that there is nothing to look for. Like Dewey's (and unlike Skinner's) his is a *non-reductive* naturalism, one which does not assume that every important semantical term must describe a physical relationship.[19] He thinks that there will be lots of terms used by theorists who study causal relations (e.g., field linguists, particle physicists) which do not themselves denote causal relations.

On my interpretation, then, Davidson joins the pragmatist in saying that 'true' has no explanatory use.[20] His contribution to pragmatism consists in pointing out that it has a disquotational use in addition to the normative uses seized upon by James. The traditional philosophical attempt to conflate these two kinds of use, and to view them both as explained by the use of 'true' to denote a non-causal relation called 'correspondence', is, on this account, a confused attempt to be inside and outside the language-game at the same time.

My interpretation, however, must deal with the fact that Davidson, unlike the pragmatist, does not present himself as repudiating the skeptic's question, but as answering it. He says that 'even a mild coherence theory like mine must provide a skeptic with a reason for supposing coherent beliefs are true.'[21] Again, he says 'the theory I defend is not in competition with a correspondence theory, but depends for its defense on an argument that purports to show that coherence yields correspondence.'[22] This sounds as if Davidson were not only adopting something like (D) above, but claiming to deduce (D) from (B), in the manner of idealism and Peircean pragmatism. In wanting 'correspondence without confrontation', he shows that he shares with these latter 'isms' the view that we cannot compare a belief with a non-belief to see if they match. But what does Davidson suppose is left of correspondence after confrontation is taken away? What is it that he thinks the skeptic wants? What is it that he proposes to give the skeptic by making coherence yield it?

Davidson says that the skeptical question he wishes to answer is: 'how, given that we "cannot get outside our beliefs and our language so as to find some test other than coherence" we nevertheless can have knowledge and talk about an objective public world which is not of our making?'[23] But this does not help us much. Only if one held some view which made it mysterious that there could be

---

[19] Davidson's 'Mental Events' illustrates his strategy of combining identity-with-the-physical with irreducibility-to-the-physical.

[20] One might object, as Alan Donagan has suggested to me, that the fact that both the linguist's and the native's beliefs are mostly true is an explanation of the fact that they are able to communicate with one another. But this sort of explanation does not invoke a causally efficacious property. It is like explaining the fact of communication by saying that the two inhabit the same space-time continuum. We do not know what it would be like for them not to, any more than we know what it would be like for one or the other to have mostly false beliefs. The only candidates for causally efficacious properties are properties which we can imagine away.

[21] 'A Coherence Theory ...', p. 426.

[22] 'A Coherence Theory ...', p. 423.

[23] 'A Coherence Theory ...', pp. 426–7. Davidson correctly says, in this passage, that I do not think this is a good question. I am here trying to explain what is wrong with it, and why I think Davidson too should regard it as a bad question.

such knowledge and such talk (e.g., one which required ontological homogenei-ty between beliefs and non-beliefs, or one which thought that there was an intermediary 'scheme' which 'shaped' the non-beliefs before they became talkable-about), would this be a challenging question. If there is to be a problem here, it must be because the skeptic has been allowed to construe 'objective' in such a way that the connection between coherence and objectivity has become unperspicuous.[24] What sense of 'correspondence' will both preserve this lack of perspicuity and yet be such that Davidson can argue that coherence will yield it?

To make a start, we can note that Davidson thinks 'correspondence' is not, as correspondence-to-*fact* theorists believe, a relation between a sentence and a chunk of reality which is somehow isomorphic to that sentence. In 'True to the Facts', he agrees with Strawson that facts – sentence-shaped chunks of the world – are *ad hoc* contrivances which do not answer to the skeptic's needs. What does, he thinks, is the more complex notion of correspondence made intelligible by Tarski's notion of satisfaction. Rather than thinking of the correspondence of language to reality as symbolized by the relation between two sides of a T-sentence, Davidson says, we should attend to word–world rather than sentence–world mappings, and in particular to the constraints on such mappings required for 'the elaboration of a nontrivial theory capable of meeting the test of entailing all those neutral snowbound trivialities' (viz., the T-sentences).[25]

These constraints are what guide the field linguist who tries to guess the causes of the native's behavior, and then goes around the hermeneutic circle long enough to come up with T-sentences which maximize the truth of the native's beliefs. The eventual theory will link native words with bits of the world by the satisfaction-relation, but these links will not be the basis for the translations. Rather, they will be fallout from the translations. Going around this circle means not attempting (in the manner of building-block theories of reference) to start with some 'secure' links, but rather going back and forth between guesses at translations of occasion-sentences and of standing sent-ences until something like Rawlsian 'reflective equilibrium' emerges.

The correspondence between words and objects provided by the satisfac-tion-relations incorporated in a T-theory are thus irrelevant to the sort of correspondence which was supposed to be described by 'true of', and which is supposed to be revealed by 'philosophical analysis', culminating in a 'theory of truth'. So whatever the skeptic's desired correspondence may be, it is not something which is captured in Tarski's account of satisfaction. For 'true' does not offer material for analysis. As Davidson says

> Truth is beautifully transparent compared to belief and coherence and I take it as primitive. Truth, as applied to utterances of sentences, shows the disquotational feature enshrined in Tarski's Convention T, and that is enough to fix its domain of application.[26]

---

[24] I think that Davidson may be worrying, in this passage, about the sort of identification of criterial and causal relations for which I criticized Plantinga in note 11 above. This is the sort of identification which is characteristic of idealism, and which generates fear that coherence theories will result in human beings having 'constituted the world'. On my interpretation, he has already disposed of that identification, and thus of the need for worry.

[25] *Inquiries*, p. 51.

[26] 'A Coherence Theory ...', p. 425.

So we cannot define 'true' in terms of satisfaction, nor of anything else. We can only explain our sense that, as Davidson says, 'the truth of an utterance depends on just two things, what the words mean and how the world is arranged' by explaining how we go about finding out these two things, and by pointing out that these two inquiries cannot be conducted independently.

I think Davidson should be interpreted as saying that the plausibility of the thesis just cited – that there is no third thing relevant to truth besides meanings of words and the way the world is – is the best explanation we are going to get of the intuitive force of (D): the idea that 'truth is correspondence with reality.' This thesis is all there is to the 'realistic' intuition which idealists, physicalists, and Peirceans have been so concerned to preserve. But, so construed, (D) makes the merely *negative* point that we need not worry about such *tertia* as, in Davidson's words, 'a conceptual scheme, a way of viewing things, a perspective' (or a transcendental constitution of consciousness, or a language, or a cultural tradition). So I think that Davidson is telling us, once again, that less is more: we should not ask for more detail about the correspondence relation, but rather realize that the *tertia* which have made us have skeptical doubts about whether most of our beliefs are true are just not there.

To say that they are not there is to say, once again, that the field linguist does not need them – and that therefore philosophy does not need them either. Once we understand how radical interpretation works, and that the interpreter can make no good use of notions like 'determinate meaning', 'intended interpretation', 'constitutive act of the transcendental imagination', 'conceptual scheme', and the like, then we can take the notion of 'correspondence to reality' as trivial, and not in need of analysis. For this term has now been reduced to a stylistic variant of 'true'.

If this is indeed what Davidson is saying, then his answer to the skeptic comes down to: you are only a skeptic because you have these intentionalistic notions floating around in your head, inserting imaginary barriers between you and the world. Once you purify yourself of the 'idea idea' in all its various forms, skepticism will never cross your enlightened mind. If this *is* his response to the skeptic, then I think he is making exactly the right move, the same move which James and Dewey were trying, somewhat more awkwardly, to make. But I also think Davidson was a bit misleading in suggesting that he was going to show us how coherence yields correspondence. It would have been better to have said that he was going to offer the skeptic a way of speaking which would prevent him from asking his question, than to say that he was going to answer that question. It would have been better to tell him that when confrontation goes, so does representation, and thus the picture which made possible both the fears of the skeptic and the hopes of the physicalist, the idealist and the Peircean.

Davidson's favorite characterization of the picture which the skeptic should abjure is 'the dualism of scheme and content'. A common feature of all the forms of this dualism which Davidson lists is that the relations between the two sides of the dualism are non-causal. Such *tertia* as a 'conceptual framework' or an 'intended interpretation' are non-causally related to the things which they organize or intend. They vary independently of the rest of the universe, just as do the skeptic's relations of 'correspondence' or 'representation'. The moral is that if we have no such *tertia*, then we have no suitable items to serve as representations, and thus no need to ask whether our beliefs represent the world accurately. We still have beliefs, but they will be seen from the outside as the field linguist sees them (as causal interactions with the environment) or from the inside as the pre-epistemological native sees them (as rules for action). To abjure *tertia* is to abjure the possibility of a third way of seeing them – one which somehow combines the outside view and the inside view, the descriptive and the normative attitudes. To see language in the same way as we see beliefs – not as a 'conceptual framework' but as the causal interaction with the environment described by the field linguist, makes it impossible to think of language as something which may or may not (how could we ever tell?) 'fit the world'. So once we give up *tertia*, we give up (or trivialize) the notions of representation and correspondence, and thereby give up the possibility of formulating epistemological skepticism.

If my understanding of Davidson is right, then – apart from his appeal to physicalistic unified science, the appeal formulated in the pragmatist's (2) – his only arguments for the claim that the philosophy of language of the field linguist is all we need will be the arguments offered in 'On the Very Idea of a Conceptual Scheme' to the effect that various 'confrontationalist' metaphors are more trouble than they are worth. All that we might add would be further arguments to the same point drawn from the history of philosophy – illustrations of the impasses into which the attempts to develop those metaphors drew various great dead philosophers. It will not be an empirical or a metaphysical discovery that there is no *tertium quid* relevant to the truth of assertions, nor a result of 'analysis of the meaning' of 'true' or 'belief' or any other term. So, like James (though unlike Peirce) Davidson is not giving us a new 'theory of truth'. Rather, he is giving us reasons for thinking that we can safely get along with less philosophizing about truth than we had thought we needed. On my interpretation, his argument that 'coherence yields correspondence' comes down to

> From the field linguist's point of view, none of the notions which might suggest that there was more to truth than the meaning of words and the way the world is are needed. So if you are willing to assume this point of view you will have no more skeptical doubts about the intrinsic veridicality of belief.

IV *Davidson as non-reductive physicalist*

Before turning to a well-known set of objections to the claim that the philosophy of the field linguist is all the philosophy of language we need – those of Michael Dummett – it will be useful to compare Davidson with a philosopher to whom he is, beneath a few superficial differences in rhetoric, very close: Hilary Putnam. Putnam is a proponent of many familiar pragmatist doctrines. He makes fun, as James and Dewey did, of the attempt to get an outside view – a 'God's-eye-view' of the sort which the traditional epistemologist, and the skeptic, have tried for. But when he confronts disquotationalist theories of truth he is troubled. They smell reductionist to him, and he sees them as symptoms of a lingering positivism, a 'transcendental Skinnerianism'. Putnam says:

> If a philosopher says that *truth* is different from *electricity* in precisely this way: that there is room for a theory of electricity but *no room* for a theory of truth, that

knowing the assertibility conditions is *all there is to know* about truth, then, in so far as I understand him at all, he is denying that there is a *property* of truth (or a property of rightness or correctness), not just in the realist sense, but in *any* sense. But this is to deny that our thoughts and assertions are *thoughts* and *assertions*.[27]

Putnam is here assuming that the only reason why one might disclaim the need for a theory of the nature of X is that one has discovered that Xs are 'nothing but' Ys, in good reductivist fashion. So he thinks that Davidson's abjuration of 'an account of what it is for an assertion to be correct and what it is for it to be incorrect' must be made on the basis of a reduction of true assertions to conventionally accepted noises.[28] On this view, to assume the point of view of the field linguist is to reduce actions to movements. But Davidson is not saying that assertions are nothing but noises. Rather he is saying that truth, unlike electricity, is not an explanation of anything.

The idea that the property of truth can serve as an explanation is a product of the misleading picture which engenders the idea that its presence requires an explanation. To see this, notice that it would be a mistake to think of 'true' as having an explanatory use on the basis of such examples as 'He found the correct house because his belief about its location was true' and 'Priestley failed to understand the nature of oxygen because his beliefs about the nature of combustion were false.' The quoted sentences are not explanations but promissory notes for explanations. To get them cashed, to get real explanations, we need to say things like 'He found the correct house because he believed that it was located at …' or 'Priestley failed because he thought that phlogiston …'. The explanation of success and failure is given by the details about what was true or what was false, not by the truth or falsity itself – just as the explanation of the praiseworthiness of an action is not 'it was the right thing to do' but the details of the circumstances in which it was done.[29]

If truth *itself* is to be an explanation of something, that explanandum must be of something which can be caused by truth, but not caused by the content of true beliefs. The function of the *tertia* which Davidson wishes to banish was precisely to provide a mechanism outside the causal order of the physical world, a mechanism which could have or lack a quasi-causal property with which one might identify truth. Thus to say that our conceptual scheme is 'adequate to the world', is to suggest that some cogs and gears are meshing nicely – cogs and gears which are either non-physical or which, though physical, are not mentioned in the rest of our causal story. To suggest, with the skeptic, that our language-game may have nothing to do with the way the world is, is to call up a picture of a gear-wheel so out of touch with the rest of the mechanism as to be spinning idly.[30]

---

[27] Hilary Putnam, *Realism and Reason* (Cambridge University Press, Cambridge, 1983), p. xv.

[28] Ibid., p. xiv.

[29] The line of argument I have been employing in this paragraph may also be found in Michael Levin, 'What Kind of Explanation is Truth?' (in *Scientific Realism*, ed Jarrett Leplin (Berkeley, University of California Press, 1984) pp. 124–39) and in Michael Williams, 'Do We Need a Theory of Truth for Epistemological Purposes?', forthcoming in an issue of *Philosophical Topics* devoted to epistemology.

[30] Davidson's position as Alan Donagan has pointed out to me, is the same as Wittgenstein's: no gears are necessary, for the sentences in which our beliefs are expressed touch the world directly. See *Tractatus Logico-Philosophicus.* 2. 1511–2.1515.

Given his distaste for intentionalist notions, Putnam should have no relish for such pictures, and thus no inclination to regard truth as an explanatory notion. But because he still retains the idea that one should give an 'account of what it is for an assertion to be correct', he demands more than Davidson is in a position to give. He retains this idea, I think, because he is afraid that the inside point of view on our language-game, the point of view where we use 'true' as a term of praise, will somehow be weakened if it receives no support from 'a philosophical account'. Consider the following passage:

> If the cause-effect-description [of our linguistic behavior qua production of noises] is complete from a philosophical as well as from a behavioral-scientific point of view; if all there is to say about language is that it consists in the production of noises (and subvocalizations) according to a certain causal pattern; *if the causal story is not to be and need not be supplemented by a normative story* ... then there is no way in which the noises we utter ... are more than mere 'expressions of our subjectivity'...[31]

The line I have italicized suggests that disquotationalist theorists of truth think that there is only one story to be told about people: a behavioristic one. But why on earth should such theorists not allow for, and indeed insist upon, supplementing such stories with 'a normative story'? Why should we take the existence of the outside point of view of the field linguist as a recommendation never to assume the inside point of view of the earnest seeker after truth? Putnam, I think, still takes a 'philosophical account of X' to be a synoptic vision which will somehow synthesize every other possible view, will somehow bring the outside and the inside points of view together.

It seems to me precisely the virtue of James and of Dewey to insist that we cannot have such a synoptic vision – that we cannot back up our norms by 'grounding' them in a metaphysical or scientific account of the world. Pragmatism, especially in the form developed by Dewey, urges that we not repeat Plato's mistake of taking terms of praise as the names of esoteric things – of assuming, e.g., we would do a better job of being good if we could get more theoretical knowledge of The Good. Dewey was constantly criticized, from the Platonist right, for being reductionistic and scientistic, inattentive to our needs for 'objective values'. This is the kind of criticism Davidson is currently getting from Putnam. He was also constantly criticized, from the positivist left, for a light-minded relativistic instrumentalism which paid too little attention to 'hard facts', and for trivializing the notion of 'truth' by this neglect.[32] This is the kind of criticism Davidson gets from physicalists such as Field.

Attack from both sides is the usual reward of philosophers who, like Dewey and Davidson, try to stop the pendulum of philosophical fashion from swinging endlessly back and forth between a tough-minded reductionism and a high-minded anti-reductionism. Such philosophers do so by patiently explaining that norms are one thing and descriptions another. In Davidson's case, this comes down to saying that the understanding you get of how the word 'true' works by contemplating the possibility of a Tarskian truth-theory for your language is

---

[31] Hilary Putnam, 'On Truth', in *How Many Questions*, ed. Leigh S. Caulman et al. (Indianapolis, Hackett, 1983), p. 44.

[32] So, simultaneously, was Neurath – who is beginning to get a better press these days.

utterly irrelevant to the satisfaction you get by saying that you know more truths today than you did yesterday, or that truth is great, and will prevail. Putnam's insistence that there is more to truth than disquotationalism can offer is not based on having looked at 'true', or at the language-games we play, and having seen more than Davidson saw. Rather, it is based on a hope that there is more to the notion of a 'philosophical account' than Dewey or Davidson think there can be.

This parallel between Dewey and Davidson seems to me reinforced by Stephen Leeds' formulation of what he calls 'Naturalistic Instrumentalism': the Quine-like combination of the view that 'the only goal relative to which our methods of theory construction and revision fall into place as a rational procedure is the goal of predicting observations'[33] with the claim that the world is, really and truly *is*, made up of the entities of current science. As Leeds says, this new 'ism' may sound like an oxymoron (as a similar 'ism' did to Dewey's critics.) But it only sounds that way if, as Leeds says, one thinks that 'a theory of truth is needed to explain why our theories work'[34] – if one thinks, that 'truth' can be an explanatory notion. Leeds and Arthur Fine[35] have pointed out the circularity of attempts to use semantics to explain our predictive successes. Such circularity is the natural consequence of trying to be both outside our inquiries and inside them at the same time – to describe them both as motions and as actions. As Davidson has reiterated in his writings on the theory of action, there is no need to choose between these two descriptions: there is only a need to keep them distinct, so that one does not try to use both at once.

V *Davidson and Dummett*

The question of whether 'truth' is an explanatory property encapsulates the question of whether the philosophy of the field linguist is philosophy of language enough or whether (as Michael Dummett thinks) we need a philosophy of language which links up with epistemology, and with traditional metaphysical issues. Dummett says that a theory of meaning should tell us how:

> an implicit grasp of the theory of meaning, which is attributed to a speaker, issues in his employment of the language and hence ... in the content of the theory. Holism in respect of how one might, starting from scratch, arrive at a theory of meaning for a language, on the other hand, has no such implications, and is, as far as I can see, unobjectionable and almost banal. It is certain that Davidson intends his holism as a doctrine with more bite than this.[36]

Dummett thinks that what you get out of Davidsonian radical interpretation does not include 'the content' of a theory of meaning – 'the specific senses

---

[33] Stephen Leeds, 'Theories of Reference and Truth', *Erkenntnis*, 13 (1978), p. 117.

[34] Dewey would not have restricted theory construction and revision to the sciences which aim at prediction and control, but this difference between Dewey and Leeds is not relevant to the point at hand.

[35] In his 'The Natural Ontological Attitude', in *Essays on Scientific Realism*, ed. J. Leplin.

[36] Michael Dummett, 'What Is a Theory of Meaning?' in *Mind and Language*, ed. Samuel Guttenplan (Oxford University Press, Oxford, 1975), p. 127.

speakers attach to the words of the language'. But on the interpretation of Davidson I have been offering, what Dummett calls a 'sense' is just the sort of *tertium quid* which Davidson wants us to forget about. So the bite of Davidson's theory is not the sort Dummett wants. Dummett wants a theory that bites down on the problems which he thinks can only be formulated when one has a theory of 'sense' – e.g., epistemological and metaphysical issues. Davidson wants a theory of meaning which will serve the field linguists' purposes and to which such problems are irrelevant.

Dummett's argument that more is needed than Davidson gives us is that somebody could know the ensemble of truth-conditions produced by a Davidsonian interpreter without knowing the content of the right-hand, metalinguistic, portions of the T-sentences. He thinks that 'a T-sentence for which the metalanguage contains the object-language is obviously unexplanatory' and that if this is so then 'a T-sentence for an object-language disjoint from the metalanguage is equally unexplanatory.'[37] Davidson will reply that no single T-sentence – no single 'neutral snowbound triviality' – will tell you what it is to understand any of the words occurring on the left-hand sides, but that the whole body of such sentences tells you *all* there is to know about this. Dummett regards that reply as an admission of defeat. He says:

> On such an account, there can be no answer to the question what constitutes a speaker's understanding of any one word or sentence: one can say only that the knowledge of the entire theory of truth issues in an ability to speak the language, and, in particular, in a propensity to recognize sentences of it as true under conditions corresponding, by and large, to the T-sentences.[38]

And again:

> no way is provided, even in principle, of segmenting his ability to use the language as a whole into distinct component abilities.[39]

Now it is of the essence of Davidson's position, as of the positions of Wittgenstein and Sellars, that there are no such distinct component abilities.[40] For when you get rid of such *tertia* as 'determinate meanings', 'intended interpretations', 'responses to stimuli', and the like, you are left with nothing to split up the overall know-how into component bits – nothing to reply to 'How do you know that that's called "red"?' save Wittgenstein's: 'I know English.' Davidson has to insist that the individual T-sentences do not replicate any inner structures, and that any attempt to provide such structures will pay the price of reintroducing *tertia*, entities which will get between our words and the world.

---

[37] Ibid., p. 108. Dummett actually says 'M-sentence' (i.e., a sentence of the form '"——" means ——') rather than 'T-sentence'. I have changed the quotation for the sake of perspicuity. As Dummett rightly says, for Davidson's purposes the two sorts of sentence are interchangeable.

[38] Ibid., p. 115.

[39] Ibid., p. 116.

[40] A similar position is adopted by Ernst Tugendhat in his *Traditional and Analytical Philosophy* (Cambridge University Press, Cambridge, 1983). Tugendhat thinks of this position as the only alternative to the 'objectualist' account of the understanding of language which has dominated the philosophical tradition up through Husserl and Russell.

Dummett notes that Davidson tries 'to make a virtue of necessity', but insists that doing so 'is an abnegation of what we are entitled to expect from a theory of meaning'.[41] For Dummett thinks that we are entitled to a theory of meaning which will preserve the traditional notions of empiricist epistemology. He thinks that any such theory must grant that 'an ability to use a given sentence in order to give a report of observation may reasonably be taken, as a knowledge of what has to be the case for that sentence to be true.'[42]

Dummett's paradigm case of grasping the content of an expression is what you do when you observe that something is red. He thinks that the contrast between 'That's red!' and cases like 'Caesar crossed the Rubicon', 'Love is better than hate', and 'There are transfinite cardinals' is something which any adequate philosophy of language must preserve. But for Davidson's and Wittgenstein's holism there simply is no contrast. On their view, to grasp the content is, in *all* these cases, to grasp the inferential relationships between these sentences and the other sentences of the language.[43]

The same point can be made in reference to Dummett's presentation of the issue about realism and anti-realism in terms of bivalence. Dummett seems to think that the question of bivalence, of whether statements are 'determinately true or false, independently of our knowledge or our means of knowing'[44] arises only for statements made by means of sentences 'belonging to the less primitive strata of our language'.[45] He has no doubt that for the 'lower storeys' – e.g., for statements like 'That's red!' – bivalence obtains. Our inarticulable knowledge of what it is for such a statement to be true, presumably, is enough to make us realists about redness. For these types of statements we can have a strong sense of 'correspondence to reality' – 'strong' in that we are confident that what makes the statement true is 'reality' rather than merely ourselves. Here we have the empiricist picture, shared by Quine and Dummett, according to which language stands as a veil between us and reality, with reality punching its way through (or being known to punch its way through) only at the tips of a few sensory receptors. The farther into the upper storeys we get, on the other hand, the more doubt there is that we are in touch with the world, and the more

---

[41] Ibid., p. 117. Some of the complaints about Davidson I have been citing from Dummett are modified in the appendix to 'What is a Theory of Meaning?' (ibid., pp. 123ff.). But the insistence on the point that Davidson 'can make no sense of knowing part of the language' (p. 138) and the unargued-for presumption that philosophy of language must preserve an unQuinean language-fact distinction (p. 137) remain.

[42] Dummett, 'What Is a Theory of Meaning? (II)' in Gareth Evans and John McDowell (eds), *Truth and Meaning* (Oxford University Press, Oxford, 1976), p. 95.

[43] Dummett thinks that Wittgenstein's view that 'acceptance of any principle of inference contributes to determining the meaning of words' – a view which Davidson shares – is unacceptably holistic. (See 'What Is A Theory of Meaning? (II)', p. 105). Elsewhere Dummett has said that this sort of holism leads to the view that 'a systematic theory of meaning for a language is an impossibility' and thus to the view that philosophy 'seeks to remove, not ignorance or false beliefs, but conceptual confusion, and therefore has nothing positive to set in place of what it removes' (*Truth and Other Enigmas* (Harvard University Press, Cambridge, Massachusetts, 1978), p. 453). By 'a systematic theory of meaning for a language' Dummett means one which gives him 'what we are entitled to expect', viz., a handle on traditional philosophical problems. But he begs the question against Davidson when he rebuts the holism shared by Davidson and Wittgenstein on the ground that it leads to the therapeutic approach to traditional problems shared by Dewey and Wittgenstein.

[44] 'What Is a Theory of Meaning?' (II), p. 101.

[45] Ibid., p. 100.

temptation to be an 'anti-realist' in regard to certain entities – that is, to adopt a theory of meaning which explains the truth of such statements 'in terms of our capacity to recognize statements as true, and not in terms of a condition which transcends human capacities'.[46]

By contrast, if one follows Davidson, one will not know what to make of the issue between realist and anti-realist. For one will feel in touch with reality *all the time*. Our language – conceived as the web of inferential relationships between our uses of vocables – is not, on this view, something 'merely human' which may hide something which 'transcends human capacities'. Nor can it deceive us into thinking ourselves in correspondence with something like that when we really are not. On the contrary, using those vocables is as direct as contact with reality can get (as direct as kicking rocks, e.g.). The fallacy comes in thinking that the relationship between vocable and reality has to be piecemeal (like the relation between individual kicks and individual rocks), a matter of discrete component capacities to get in touch with discrete hunks of reality.

If one thinks that, one will, for example, agree with Plato and Dummett that there is an important philosophical question about whether there really are moral values 'out there'. For Davidson, on the other hand, there is goodness out there in exactly the same trivial sense in which there is redness out there. The relevant sense is explicated by saying that the field linguist will come up with a T-sentence whose right-hand side is 'that's morally right' in just the same manner as he comes up with one whose right-hand side is 'that's red'. He will assume that insofar as the natives fail to find the same things red, or morally right, as we do, our disagreements with them will be explicable by various differences in our respective environments (or the environments of our respective ancestors).

I conclude that for Dummett no philosophy of language is adequate which does not permit the perspicuous reformulation of the epistemological and metaphysical issues discussed by the philosophical tradition. For Davidson this ability is not a desideratum. For James and Dewey, the *in*ability to formulate such issues was a desideratum. I should like to attribute this latter, stronger, view to Davidson, but I have no good evidence for doing so. I commend it to him, because I think that his only recourse in arguing with those who think they have a right to expect more philosophy of language than he offers is to adopt this therapeutic stance. More specifically, all he can do is point out that Dummett's expectations stem from the habit of construing correspondence as confrontation, and then exhibit the unhappy history of this construal, a history which stretches from Plato through Locke to Quine. In the end, the issue is going to be decided on a high metaphilosophical plane – one from which we look down upon the philosophical tradition and judge its worth.

VI *Davidson, realism and anti-realism*

If the argument of the preceding section is right, then Davidson has been put in a false position by Dummett's attempts to place him on the 'realist' side of a distinction between realism and anti-realism. That distinction, stated in terms

---

[46] What Is a Theory of Meaning? (II), p. 116.

of a distinction between truth-conditions and assertibility-conditions, will seem a plausible way of classifying philosophical doctrines only if one accepts what Michael Devitt has called Dummett's 'propositional assumption': the assumption that 'an L–speaker's understanding of a sentence of L consists in his knowing that the sentence is true-in-L in such and such circumstances.'[47] Davidson, however, thinks it hopeless to isolate such circumstances. His holism makes him reject the idea of such knowledge. Yet Dummett gives an account of Davidsonian 'truth-conditions' which is radically non-holistic. As Devitt rightly says, Dummett tries to infer from 'X knows the meaning of S' and 'The meaning of S = the truth-conditions of X' to 'S knows that the truth-conditions of X are TC', an inference which only goes through if we construe 'S knows the meaning of S' as 'there exists an entity which is the meaning of S and X is acquainted with it.'[48] The latter construal will be made only by someone who accepts the propositional assumption.

Davidson would not accept it,[49] and therefore cannot be seen as a theorist of 'truth-conditions' in Dummett's sense. Davidson thinks that one great advantage of his view is that it gives you a theory of meaning without countenancing such things as 'meanings'. Since he agrees with Quine that a theory of meaning for a language is what comes out of empirical research into linguistic behavior, Davidson would be the first to agree with Devitt, against Dummett, that 'any propositional knowledge of a language that a person has is something over and above his competence, something gained from theorizing about the language.'[50] If we bear Davidson's holism and behaviorism in mind, he will seem the last philosopher to believe that users of S are typically able to envisage acquaintance with sets of circumstances which would conclusively verify S.

Dummett misconstrues Davidson because he himself believes that (in Devitt's words), 'The only sort of behavior that could manifest the speaker's understanding of S is that behavior which brings him into the position in which, if the condition obtains that conclusively justifies the assertion of S, he recognizes it as so doing.'[51] As Devitt says, this expresses Dummett's commitment to 'anti-holist epistemology'.[52] Dummett thinks that there are some familiar cases (e.g., so-called 'observation sentences') where there are indeed such conditions, and such acts of recognition. But for Davidson there are never any of either. So the contrast which Dummett draws between, e.g.,

---

[47] Michael Devitt, 'Dummett's Anti-Realism', *Journal of Philosophy*, 80 (1983), p. 84.
[48] Ibid., p. 86.
[49] Devitt disagrees. He says 'Davidson is open to [Dummett's] argument because he accepts the propositional assumption' (ibid., p. 90). This willingness to accept Dummett's description of Davidson seems to me a blemish in Devitt's incisive criticism of Dummett's attempt to semanticize metaphysics. (Though, as I say below, I also disagree with Devitt's claim that desemanticizing metaphysics restores the purity of that discipline. I think that doing so merely exposes its barrenness.) I suspect the reason why Devitt thinks of Davidson as accepting the propositional assumption is that Davidson, in his earlier articles, identified a theory of meaning for L with what a speaker of L understands, an identification which suggests that the speaker *does* have 'distinct component abilities' corresponding to the various T-sentences. But this identification is, as far as I can see, either incompatible with the holism I have described in the previous section or as misleading a metaphor as that billiard balls have 'internalized' the laws of mechanics.
[50] Ibid., pp. 89–90.
[51] Ibid., p. 91.
[52] Ibid., p. 92.

realism about tables and anti-realism about values makes no sense for Davidson. For holists, so to speak, truth is *always* evidence-transcendent. But that is to say that *X*'s understanding of *S* is *never* manifested in the kind of recognitional abilities which Dummett envisages.[53]

Dummett takes the upshot of Frege's linguistification of philosophy to be that the only way to make sense of a metaphysical disagreement is by semantic ascent – jacking up the old metaphysical issue into a new semantical issue. Davidson, on my interpretation, thinks that the benefit of going linguistic is that getting rid of the Cartesian mind is a first step toward eliminating the *tertia* which, by seeming to intrude between us and the world, created the old metaphysical issues in the first place. We can take the final step, and dissolve those issues for good, by not letting philosophy of language recreate the factitious contrasts in terms of which those issues were formulated, e.g., the contrast between 'objective realities' and 'useful fictions', or that between the 'ontological status' of the objects of, respectively, physics, ethics and logic. For Davidson, Quine's idea of 'ontological commitment' and Dummett's idea of 'matter of fact' are both unfortunate relics of metaphysical thought; they are among the ideas which metaphysics wove together to form the scheme-content dualism.

These ideas form such a large, mutually reinforcing, network that it is hard to pick one out as crucial. But the best candidate for being at the center of this network may be the idea repudiated in the pragmatists' thesis (3): the idea that sentences can be 'made true'. Davidson says that 'all the evidence there is is just what it takes to make our sentences or theories true. Nothing, however, no thing, makes sentences or theories true: not experience, not surface irritations, not the world, can make a sentence true.'[54] I interpret this passage as saying that the inferential relations between our belief that *S* and our other beliefs have nothing in particular to do with the aboutness relation which ties *S* to its objects. The lines of evidential force, so to speak, do not parallel the lines of referential direction. This lack of parallelism is the burden of epistemological holism. To know about the former lines is to know the language in which the beliefs are expressed. To know about the latter is to have an empirical theory about what the people who use that language mean by what they say – which is also the story about the causal roles played by their linguistic behavior in their interaction with their environment.

The urge to coalesce the justificatory story and the causal story is the old metaphysical urge which Wittgenstein helped us overcome when he told us to beware of entities called 'meanings' – or, more generally, of items relevant to

---

[53] See Paul Horwich, 'Three Forms of Realism', *Synthese*, 51 (1982), p. 199: '[Dummett's] inference from not being able to establish when *p* is true to not being able to manifest knowledge of its truth-conditions is not at all compelling. All it takes to know *p*'s truth-conditions is to understand it; and all it takes to understand *p* is the ability to use it in accordance with community norms, implicit in linguistic practice, for judging in various circumstances, the degree of confidence it should be given.' Horwich's own suggestion that we combine what he calls 'semantic realism' (the claim that truth may extend beyond our capacity to recognize it) with a 'use theory of meaning and a redundancy account of truth' (p. 186) seems to me a succinct description of Davidson's strategy. (For an earlier statement of Horwich's anti-Dummett point, see P. F. Strawson's criticism of Crispin Wright: 'Scruton and Wright on Anti-Realism', *Proceedings of the Aristotelian Society*, 1977, p. 16.)

[54] *Inquiries*, p. 194.

the fixation of belief which are, in Davidson's words, 'intermediate between belief and the usual objects which beliefs are about'.[55] For such entities are supposed to be *both* causes *and* justifications: entities (like sense-data or surface irritations or clear and distinct ideas) which belong both to the story which justifies me in believing that S and to the story which the observer of my linguistic behavior tells us about the causes of my belief that S. Devitt succumbs to this pre-Wittgensteinian urge when he follows Field in suggesting that we can explicate the 'intuitive idea of correspondence to a "world out there"' by making truth dependent on 'genuine reference relations between words and objective reality'.[56] Dummett succumbs to it when he thinks of a given state of the world as capable of 'conclusively verifying' a belief. The latter notion embodies just the idea of bits of the world making a belief true which Davidson rejects.

Devitt is, I think, right in saying that, once we drop Dummett's anti-holism, the issue about 'realism' is de-semanticized. But it is also trivialized. For there is now nothing for 'realism' to name save the banal anti-idealist thesis which Devitt formulates as 'Common-sense physical entities objectively exist independently of the mental.'[57] Devitt thinks this an interesting and controversial thesis. It is an embarrassment for my interpretation of Davidson as a pragmatist that he apparently does too: witness his pledge of allegiance, cited above, to the idea of 'an objective public world which is not of our making'.[58] This formula strikes me as no more than out-dated rhetoric. For on my view the futile metaphysical struggle between idealism and physicalism was superseded, in the early years of this century, by a metaphilosophical struggle between the pragmatists (who wanted to dissolve the old metaphysical questions) and the anti-pragmatists (who still thought there was something first-order to fight about).[59] The latter struggle is *beyond* realism and anti-realism.[60]

---

[55] 'A Coherence Theory …', p. 430.

[56] Devitt, p. 77.

[57] Devitt, p. 76.

[58] See also *Inquiries into Truth and Interpretation*, p. 198: 'In giving up the dualism of scheme and world, we do not give up the world, but re-establish unmediated touch with the familiar objects whose antics make our sentences and opinions true or false.' Yet surely these familiar objects are simply not the world which anti-idealist philosophers have tried to underwrite. The idealists had these objects too. The world which their opponents were concerned about was one which could vary independently of the antics of the familiar objects; it was something rather like the thing-in-itself. (I developed this distinction between two senses of 'world', the familiar objects on the one hand and the contrived philosophical counterpart of 'scheme' on the other, in an earlier (1972), and rather awkward, attempt to latch on to Davidson's arguments; see 'The World Well Lost', reprinted in *Consequences of Pragmatism*.)

[59] I should try to account for this change by reference to (a) Hegel's demonstration that idealism eventually eats its itself up (like the Worm Ourouboros) by deconstructing the mind-matter distinction which it started out with and (b) the disenchantment with that distinction brought about by the theory of evolution. Dewey's importance, I think, lies in having brought Hegel and Darwin together. But this is a long and controversial story.

[60] Current debates about Heidegger's 'destruction of the Western metaphysical tradition' and Derrida's 'deconstruction of the metaphysics of presence' form another wing of the same struggle. For some connections between Davidson and Derrida, see the essay by Samuel Wheeler in the present volume, and also his 'The Extension of Deconstruction,' forthcoming in *The Monist*. For parallels between Heidegger's attempt to get beyond both Plato and Nietzsche and Fine's and Davidson's attempts to get beyond realism and anti-realism see my 'Beyond Realism and

So, despite his occasional pledges of realist faith, is Davidson.[61] On my version of the history of twentieth-century philosophy, logical empiricism was a reactionary development, one which took one step forward and two steps back. Davidson, by subverting the scheme-content dualism which logical empiricism took for granted, has, so to speak, kept the logic and dropped the empiricism (or better, kept the attention to language and dropped the epistemology). He has thus enabled us to use Frege's insights to confirm the holistic and pragmatist doctrines of Dewey. His work makes possible the kind of synthesis of pragmatism and positivism which Morton White foresaw as a possible 'reunion in philosophy'.[62] From the point of view of such a synthesis, the Peirce-Frege turn from consciousness to language (and from transcendental to formal logic) was a stage in the dissolution of such traditional problems as 'realism vs. anti-realism', rather than a step towards a clearer formulation of those problems.[63]

Anti-Realism', forthcoming in the first volume ('Wo steht die sprachanalytische Philosophie heute?') of *Weiner Riehe: Themen der Philosophie*, ed. Herta Nagl-Docekal, Richard Heinrich, Ludwig Nagl and Helmet Vetter.

[61] Arthur Fine has offered the best recent account of why we ought to get beyond this struggle. See the anti-realist polemic of his 'The Natural Ontological Attitude' (cited in note 35 above) and the anti-anti-realist polemic of 'And Not Anti-Realism Either', *Nous*, 18 (1984), pp. 51–65. The latter paper (p. 54) makes the point that 'The anti-realism expressed in the idea of truth-as-acceptance is just as metaphysical and idle as the realism expressed by a correspondence theory.' On my interpretation of Davidson, his position pretty well coincides with Fine's 'Natural Ontological Attitude'.

Frederick Stoutland ('Realism and Anti-Realism in Davidson's Philosophy of Language', Part I in *Critica* XIV (August, 1982) and Part II in *Critica* XIV (December, 1982)) has given excellent reasons for resisting attempts (by, e.g., John McDowell and Mark Platts) to construe Davidson as a realist. However, I think that he is wrong in construing him as an anti-realist who holds that 'sentences are not true in virtue of their extra-linguistic objects: they are true in virtue of their role in human practise' (Part I, p. 21). To repeat, Davidson thinks that we should drop the question 'In virtue of what are sentences true?' Therefore, as I said earlier, he does not wish to be associated with pragmatism, for too many people calling themselves 'pragmatists' (including myself) have said things like 'a sentence is true in virtue of its helping people achieve goals and realize intentions' (Stoutland, Part II, p. 36). Despite my disagreement with Stoutland, however, I am much indebted to his discussion. In particular, his remark (Part II, p. 22) that Davidson opposes the idea that it is the 'intentionality of *thoughts* – their being directed to objects, independently of whether they are true or false – which accounts for the relation of language to reality' seems to me an admirably clear and succinct expression of the difference between Davidson's holism and the 'building-block' approach common to Russell, Husserl, Kripke and Searle.

[62] See Morton White, *Toward Reunion in Philosophy* (Harvard University Press, Cambridge, Massachusetts, 1956).

[63] I am very grateful to Robert Brandom, Alan Donagan and Arthur Fine for comments on the penultimate version of this paper. I made substantial changes as a result of their comments, but have not tried to acknowledge my indebtedness in every case.

19

Radical Interpretation and Epistemology

COLIN MCGINN

How do we set about establishing what beliefs a person has? How does a person form his beliefs? These two questions cannot be quite independent of each other. For a method of discovering someone's beliefs can be expected to incorporate some conception of the processes that lead to belief-formation; the method will in some way reflect or recapitulate how beliefs are acquired. Beliefs are discovered by tracing the route by which they were acquired. Thus it is that radical interpretation meshes with epistemology. Recognition of this connexion has long been explicit in Quine: in translating the native's language we proceed from information about the very sensory stimulations which cause the subject to believe what he does.[1] Thus in Quine's method our evidence for what the subject believes is the subject's evidence for believing what he does. The connexion has not, however, been prominent in Davidson's writings on radical interpretation; not, that is, until 'A Coherence Theory of Truth and Knowledge'.[2] In that paper Davidson links his account of how we attribute beliefs and meanings to another with a theory of justification and belief-formation. In particular, he spells out the epistemological implications of his use of the principle of charity in interpretation. My purpose in the present paper is to criticize Davidson's account of radical interpretation, specifically his adherence to charity, from an epistemological standpoint; and to erect on its ruins an account of interpretation which gets the epistemology right. Needless to say, I am indebted to Davidson for the foundations.

This paper is based upon three talks I gave at Rutgers University in the Spring of 1984. I am very grateful for the invitation to give the talks, for the comments I received on them, and for the hospitality shown to me during my stay – especially by Peter Klein, Ernie LePore and Brian McLaughlin.

[1] See Quine's *Word and Object* (MIT Press, Cambridge, Massachusetts, 1960), chapter 2.

[2] In *Kant oder Hegel*, ed. Dieter Henrich (Klett-Cotta, 1983), pp. 423–38. See also Davidson's 'Empirical Content', *Grazer Philosophische Studien*, ed. Rudolf Haller, 16/17 (1982), pp. 471–89.

I

To specify a method of radical interpretation is to specify an ordered sequence of inferential steps which take us from evidence available in advance of interpretation to a total set of psychological and semantic ascriptions to the subject of interpretation. The steps are not, of course, deductive; the aim is to articulate principles which, in conjunction with the evidence, make it *reasonable* to interpret the subject in a certain way. Davidson's fundamental idea is to use evidence about the external causes of assent simultaneously to ascribe beliefs and meanings to the subject: the truth conditions of the subject's beliefs and sentences are given by the external states of affairs that prompt him to hold sentences true. For example, suppose the subject assents to (holds-true) a sentence *S* as a causal result of a rabbit running by: Davidson's method tells us to attribute to the subject the belief that a rabbit is running by. This method is charitable in an obvious way: we take the subject to believe precisely what we observe to be objectively the case about his surroundings. Charity may be tempered in the later stages of interpretation, as Davidson often remarks, but to begin with and generally it must be adhered to if interpretation is to be possible. Thus he says:

> Since charity is not an option, but a condition of having a workable theory, it is meaningless to suggest that we might fall into massive error by endorsing it. Until we have successfully established a systematic correlation of sentences held true with sentences held true, there are no mistakes to make. Charity is forced on us; – whether we like it or not, if we want to understand others, we must count them right in most matters.[3]

Nor is charity merely an unavoidable assumption of the process of interpretation; it is of the very nature of belief to be veridical. We do not know what it would *be* to interpret and communicate with a person whose beliefs were not mainly true. So the charitable method rests upon a thesis about the conditions of interpretability which in turn is justified by a thesis about the essence of belief. Or rather: since the charitable method is the only *possible* method, it is idle to speculate that it might on occasion yield incorrect results; for nothing could ever *show* that charity was misguided. It is a conceptual truth about belief that beliefs can be ascribed only if they are, in the main, true.

In 'Charity, Interpretation and Belief'[4] I made a criticism of Davidson's defence of charity which questioned his account of what determines the objects of belief. Davidson had claimed that for two people to have beliefs about the same object it is necessary that they agree (in the main) about the properties of that object: if you and I are both to have beliefs about (say) the earth or the stars then we must have the same *conception* of these entities. Thus if I am to ascribe to you a *false* belief about the earth or the stars, I must, as a presupposition of

---

[3] 'On the Very Idea of a Conceptual Scheme', reprinted in *Inquiries into Truth and Interpretation* (Clarendon Press, Oxford, 1984), p. 197.

[4] *Journal of Philosophy*, 74 (1977), pp. 521–35.

this, also ascribe to you a whole range of *true* beliefs about them.[5] We can disagree about something only if we agree about *what* it is that we disagree about. My earlier objection to this claim about the conditions of genuine disagreement was that the claim is false of *relational* beliefs. For it seems that I can say of you that you believe *of* the earth that it is stationary without attributing to you any particular conception of the earth, let alone the conception I myself entertain: you can believe something *of* the earth without knowing that it is the *earth* that you have a belief about. And isn't it just straightforwardly true that the ancients had wildly erroneous ideas about the nature of celestial objects? The reason for this feature of relational beliefs, I conjectured, is their tie with perception: seeing an object can suffice for a relational attribution, and seeing something does not require the perceiver to have preponderantly true beliefs about what he is seeing. So it seems that people can disagree *about* some object without necessarily agreeing (in other respects) about it.

Now I still think this objection is right as far as it goes, but it no longer seems to me to go far enough. For it leaves the following retort open to Davidson: charity may not be required for the ascription of relational beliefs, but it is required for the ascription of *notional* beliefs, i.e., it is required for the ascription of shared *concepts*. Thus if I am to ascribe to you the concept *earth* or *star* (or any other concept) I must presume that you agree with me about (most of) the properties of the things falling under these concepts. And since every relational ascription implies the existence of a true notional ascription, charity will be required as globally as Davidson suggests: it will be required whenever the interpreter ascribes a concept to his subject. More formally, for any concept C, if the interpreter is to ascribe C to his subject, he must assume that most of his subject's beliefs of the form ... C ... are true. I want to argue in what follows that this thesis too is mistaken: concept-attribution is not essentially charitable in this way.

II

The line of objection I want to pursue may be put (baldly and unsympathetically) as follows: if Davidson were right about the inherently charitable nature of interpretation, then we could dismiss certain kinds of traditional scepticism; but it is absurd to suppose that scepticism could be dismissed in this oblique and roundabout way. For, if it is a condition of having beliefs about (say) the external world or other minds that these beliefs be mainly true; and if it is a condition of having an interpretable language that most of what the speaker says is true: then we know, just by knowing that we believe and speak, that most of what we think and say is true – and so the sceptical claim that we might be globally mistaken about the external world or other minds can be dismissed as inconceivable. There is then no need to provide any demonstration that our particular modes of belief formation in these areas are in fact reliable; we can reject the suggestion that they are not, simply by considering the nature of

---

[5] See, in particular, Davidson's 'Thought and Talk', reprinted in *Inquiries into Truth and Interpretation*, p. 168.

radical interpretation. But this seems, to put it mildly, a surprising result, one that should persuade us to question the premises: for how *could* scepticism be dismissed in this way? How *could* epistemologists have been so wrong about what is necessary to defeat the sceptic? These rhetorical questions do not, of course, constitute an argument; they merely record the sense that something is going wrong in Davidson's adherence to charity. They do not indicate exactly what it is that is going wrong. And they cannot be regarded as disturbing to Davidson for the simple reason that he *explicitly* draws the conclusion from his account of interpretation that scepticism of this kind has been thereby refuted.[6] So we need, if we are to press the objection, to examine his reasoning.

Davidson sets up the sceptical problem as follows. He first claims that justification is always a matter of the coherence of beliefs: nothing can count as a reason for belief except another belief. This means that there is no such thing as confronting a belief with 'reality' or with some non-doxastic representative of reality (sense-data, stimulations, etc.).[7] But then the question arises of whether a coherent set of beliefs is a *true* set: how can we move from coherence to correspondence? Well, not by seeking further justification – *that* just enlarges the set of coherent beliefs. Rather, 'the answer must be to find a *reason* for supposing most of our beliefs are true that is not a form of *evidence*.'[8] And here is where the methodology of interpretation comes in, specifically the principle of charity: when we look at how beliefs must be ascribed we see that we could not assign a consistent set of beliefs to a person without assigning a largely true set of beliefs to him. And if this goes for another whom we interpret, then it also goes for *us* as potential *subjects* of interpretation. Thus Davidson concludes: 'What stands in the way of global scepticism of the senses is, in my view, the fact that we must, in the plainest and methodologically most basic cases, take the object of a belief to be the cause of that belief. And what we, as interpreters, must take them to be is what they in fact are.'[9] Belief is essentially (largely) veridical because we assign content to beliefs on the basis of the facts in the world that prompt belief. So to answer the sceptic *we* need do nothing save ensure coherence; it can be left to the nature of belief itself, as seen through interpretation, to guarantee that our beliefs are mainly true.

Clearly the crucial question about Davidson's argument is whether he is right to suppose that belief content can be read off the world in the way he suggests. Let us first note a contrast with Quine, concerning the role Quine assigns to sensory stimulations in his account. It is these stimulations which, for Quine, determine content and provide the primary evidence for interpretation. Such stimulations function as what Davidson calls 'epistemic intermediaries' between the subject and the world, between beliefs and facts. Now Davidson points out,

---

[6] In fact, I had the idea of using the anti-sceptical consequences of the principle of charity as a *reductio* before I learned that Davidson regarded this as a *virtue* of his account of interpretation.

[7] Thus Davidson says: 'No such confrontation makes sense, for of course we can't get outside our skins to find out what is causing the internal happening of which we are aware' ('A Coherence Theory of Truth and Knowledge', p. 429). I am, in fact, very suspicious of this whole way of thinking, with its suggestion that we are somehow not directly aware, through perception, of what lies outside us in the external world; but I won't pause to criticize Davidson on this point.

[8] Ibid., p. 431.

[9] Ibid., p. 436.

quite correctly, that Quine's conception of interpretation leaves open the possibility of global error and thus leads to scepticism, since the stimulations could conceivably stay constant while the facts are varied: we would then ascribe the same beliefs to our subject though the world failed to match those beliefs. Imagine hooking a person up to a stimulation machine that caused the same irritations of nerve-endings as are commonly caused by tables and mountains and rabbits; this person would, on Quine's conception, believe and mean what we believe and mean – and he would accordingly be very wrong in his beliefs. By contrast, Davidson cuts out the content-determining epistemic intermediary and lets the external facts provide the evidence for interpretation; so if the facts are varied, then so too is the interpretation. Thus Davidson sees a link between his view of justification and his view of the data of interpretation.

It seems to me that Quine is basically in the right in this dispute, but I want to propose a revision in his conception of the nature of the intermediaries. Let us consider, not peripheral sensory stimulations, but conscious perceptual experiences: having a visual experience as of a brown rabbit-like creature and the like.[10] Now I take it as uncontroversial that experiences are not always veridical; there are such things as illusions and hallucinations. When a person's experience is non-veridical in these ways it is rational (other things equal) for him to form a belief in accordance with the content of his experience. We have here, in the possibility of non-veridical experience, a potent source of false belief, of a kind made familiar to us by generations of sceptics about our knowledge of the external world. Whether this source of error can lead to the possibility of *global* mistake depends upon whether it is necessarily local: so could *most* of our experiences be non-veridical? Sceptics have argued that this could be so: it might be, for example, that a super-scientist is causing us to have systematic hallucinations by stimulating our brains appropriately with implanted electrodes. If this is a coherent possibility, as it certainly *seems* to be, then global error in our beliefs *is* possible, and an interpreter of our beliefs must acknowledge such global error. So, clearly, Davidson must dispute the coherence of this kind of case if he is to preserve his anti-sceptical argument and his general account of interpretation.

It is not difficult to predict Davidson's reply to this objection.[11] He would say that we *could* not, given the basic methodology of interpretation, interpret someone in such a way as to make most of his perceptual experiences non-veridical. For the content of an experience, as of a belief, is determined by its causes, and in the alleged counterexample to general veridicality, content and cause systematically don't match. In the case of the stimulation machine, or the (different) case of the brain in a vat, the causes of belief are electrode stimulations or scientists' actions or afferent nerve impulses, not tables and mountains and rabbits; and so we must interpret accordingly – i.e., let the

---

[10] A main reason for this modification is that I do not think that stimulations of a person's nerve-endings can function as the sensory evidence upon which his beliefs are based, on account of their inaccessibility to the person's belief-system; whereas experiences are ideally suited to this role. I discuss this point in my review of Quine's *Theories and Things* (Harvard University Press, Cambridge, Massachusetts, 1981) which appeared in the *Journal of Philosophy*, 80 (1983).

[11] Davidson does not, so far as I know, make this reply in print, but it seems to be suggested by what he has written, and he is reported to have made the reply (or something like it) in discussion.

content of the subject's beliefs be determined by those non-standard causes. We are misled, Davidson would say, by what we can allow once we have got interpretation going, viz., exceptional mismatches of cause and content; but when we look at the matter more radically we see that the policy of matching cause and content must be adhered to in the main. So when the sceptic tells his story of globally non-veridical experience he forgets that he is arranging for types of causes of experience and belief which will recommend different ascriptions of content by the interpreter; he is thus, in effect, spinning an incoherent story.

The question then is whether this hard-line response to the sceptical possibility is defensible. Before I argue that it is not, let me make a remark about supervenience. On this development of Davidson's view, there is a rather extreme failure of the supervenience of the mental on the cerebral, because my brain and the brain on the stimulation machine or in the vat could be physically indiscernible and yet we would, on the Davidsonian view, experience and believe totally different things. I believe that there is a brown rabbit running by and I have a visual experience as of a brown rabbit-like creature running by; they believe (say) that an electrode is sending n volts into their occipital lobe and they have an experience with just this content. But there is no difference in what is going on in our brains. Content is thus right out of the head. This is not a result calculated to please neuro-physiologists, who believe that they are investigating (say) the physical basis of shape and colour perception; but it is not inconsistent with the letter of Davidson's own position on the supervenience of the mental on the physical, since the physical extends beyond the confines of the brain.[12] Still, it is, I think, a result that ought to give us pause: can the intrinsic physical constitution of the brain be *quite* so irrelevant to what a person experiences and believes?

I want to focus my misgivings about the hard-line reply by considering the rationalization of action in relation to these non-standard assignments of content. Suppose your brain and that of the person on the stimulation machine are sending out impulses causing your respective legs to move in a running motion (your brains, remember, are physically identical). Suppose also that you (but not he) are seeing a tiger running at you with ferocious intent and you believe that this is what you are seeing; you also desire to keep your life. Then we can say that you are intentionally moving your legs in this way because you believe there's a dangerous animal around and you want to escape from it (or some such). But what can we say of your cerebral twin? We cannot say of him what we said of you because he does not *have* experiences and beliefs and desires with these contents. Nor can we rationalize his action by saying that he believes he is being stimulated by an electrode, etc. – for *that* belief would not rationalize his intentionally moving his legs (unless it was, *per impossibile*, connected with beliefs about tigers, etc.). It doesn't help matters to redescribe the action as intentional *qua* the sending out of efferent nerve impulses; for, again, how is *that* action rationalized by the experiences, desires and beliefs we

---

[12] See his 'Mental Events', reprinted in *Essays on Actions and Events* (Clarendon Press, Oxford, 1980), p. 214. There is no hint here, however, that the supervenience base needs to extend beyond the head (nor that it need not).

have, following Davidson's policy, attributed to him? The problem here is a general one: we just don't get a coherent, rational, sensible psychology by following Davidson's policy; but we do if we allow the intrinsic properties of the brain a larger role in determining content – in particular, if we attribute the same *experiences* to you and your cerebral twin. So what we have given here is in effect an argument for the mentalistic version of an essentially Quinean position on interpretation.

Does the argument I just gave commit me to the idea that content is in the head, contrary to much recent thought? Yes and No. Yes, in that I am suggesting that the (phenomenological) content of experience is fixed by the intrinsic condition of the brain. No, in that this does not commit me to the quite general thesis that the content of propositional attitudes (and sentences) is so fixed; for it may be that there are types of belief content which are not fixed by the content of experience. The position I wish to occupy is the following: experiential content is a proper subset of belief content, and beliefs whose content goes beyond the experiential are not in the head. Thus, in particular, beliefs about concrete individuals and natural kinds are not in the head: they are determined by causal relations to the environment, in the way sketched by causal theorists of belief content. But beliefs which involve concepts that also characterize the content of experience – observational concepts, if you like – *can* be possessed independently of such extrinsic relations. Thus suppose someone (you or an envatted brain) has an experience as of a round, red object, as a result of some event in his brain; this person may, on the basis of this experience, then form beliefs involving the concepts *round* and *red* – *even though he may never have had causal contact with (specifically perceived) round or red objects.* On the other hand, a person cannot have beliefs involving the concepts *water* or *tiger* without the appropriate causal contact with water and tigers. The reason for the difference, I suggest, is that experience can ground concept possession if it can represent the property denoted by the concept in question but it cannot do so if the property is not *capable* of being represented in experience (i.e., if it is not a property relating to the *appearance* of things). So I am advocating a mixed position on concept possession and the location of content: concepts partition into two sets, and one set is in the head while the other is not, depending upon their capacity for entering into the content of experience.[13]

Is this mixed position plausible? Admittedly it seems *ad hoc* at first; but consider the alternatives. There are three that I can see, none of them attractive. First, we might try denying that the envatted brain can experience what a normal person can, so that there is simply no *basis* for concept possession independently of causal contact with the environment in this case. This alternative cuts experience off from the brain too radically, as I argued above. Second, we might try maintaining that, though the envatted brain does have experiences as of (say) a round, red object, this does not enable it to form the corresponding concepts (have beliefs with such a content) – causal contact with round, red objects is needed for that. While not easily refuted, this alternative

---

[13] This mixed position is consistent with the conception of content-determination suggested in my 'Realist Semantics and Content-Ascription', *Synthese*, 52 (1982) and applied to the envatted brain; but the position is not to be found explicitly in that paper.

seems deeply implausible: surely if it can *seem* to me that I am seeing something red and round (have an experience qualitatively indistinguishable from the experience I have when I actually *see* a round, red object) then it is possible for me to *think* that that is indeed what I am seeing. Who needs causal contact if the property is directly represented in experience? Third, we might try abandoning the idea that *any* concepts require causal contact for their possession, thus embracing a unitary theory which puts *all* concepts in the head. But this would be to unlearn all that we have learned in recent years about reference and content-determination – and we cannot unlearn what is true. What we need to do, I suggest, is to accept the lessons of Twin Earth and related considerations but not overgeneralize them: *some* concepts just don't work like that, viz., those that characterize the appearances of things (you can't get a Twin-Earth case for 'red' or 'round'). Moreover, my mixed position does not seem intrinsically unmotivated, just a desperate attempt to avoid unpalatable alternatives: for there is a genuine division of observational and non-observational concepts, and their different relation to experience sets up the expectation that they may require different sorts of basis for their possession.[14] But let me not pursue this topic further now; I am supposed to be discussing Davidson's views on radical interpretation.

The upshot of this consideration of the sources of possible error in belief may be summarily stated as follows: we can make sense of the possibility of global error by reflecting on the character of perceptual experience. Whether or not experiences can function as epistemic as well as causal intermediaries is not here to the point: if we imagine someone's experience to be globally non-veridical, as I have argued we can, then we have imagined a case in which globally false belief is possible, indeed inevitable. But then belief is not essentially veridical and scepticism has not been refuted. It remains to enquire how radical interpretation should proceed in the light of all this: what method can mesh properly with the facts about belief-formation? If interpretation cannot depend upon charity, what can it depend on?

III

We need to describe a method of radical interpretation which leaves open the possibilities of error upon which the skeptic trades. As we have seen, such a method will accord an important role to the ascription of *experience* to the subject, a type of ascription usually neglected in discussions of radical interpretation.[15] The method I have in mind is, like Quine's, a two-stage method, in contrast to Davidson's one-stage method: that is to say, the causal link from the environment to the subject's belief-system will pass through an

---

[14] We might see the classical empiricists as wishing to construct natural kind concepts (meanings) out of concepts derivable from the content of experience because of a commitment to a unitary theory of concept possession. Indeed, this may be part of what prompts 'description theories' of such concepts (meanings).

[15] David Lewis, for one, makes no mention of the ascription of perceptual experience to the subject in his 'Radical Interpretation', *Synthese*, 23 (1974).

epistemic intermediary – stimulations for Quine, experiences for me. I will assume, with both Quine and Davidson, that we have access to information about assent or holding-true, and that we know what physical forces are impinging on the subject's body and from what distal sources. The ultimate aim is to assemble sufficient evidence for an ascription of propositional attitudes and semantic properties in explanation of the subject's behaviour. The overall plan of the two-stage method I envisage is as follows: first, settle on an assignment of perceptual experiences to the subject, on the basis of the observable physical facts about his environment and his relation to it; second, go from what has been established at the first stage to an ascription of beliefs and meanings. The question then is by what principles these two moves can be justified. Remember that the inferential moves are not intended to be deductive; the aim is only to assemble evidence which makes a certain interpretation reasonable – we do not want our method to aspire to an apodicticity that our actual interpretations of each other do not possess. What is important is that each stage should be in principle completeable in advance of the next: in particular, we do not want our assignment of experiences to depend essentially upon a prior knowledge of what the subject believes and means. If we could not achieve this interpretative ordering we could not claim that assignments of experience can function as evidence for ascriptions of belief and meaning; and it would then become questionable whether we really had described something deserving to be called a *method*. So let us consider each of the two stages I have identified in turn.

Stage One. The general method at this stage is easily described: having identified the subject's sense-organs and their receptive condition, we then make a suitable ascription of experience. Thus if, for example, the subject's eyes are open and a running rabbit is in his line of vision, then we suppose that he has an experience as of a running rabbit. This stage needs to exploit some criteria for perceptual illusion and to make ascriptions of experience accordingly. I am here assuming that the identification of the subject's sense-organs is a matter of physical inspection, not requiring detailed psychological knowledge of the subject. This assumption is, of course, legitimate in the usual human case, but it is a question what should be said of a more radical case of radical interpretation – the case in which the subject is an alien life-form with a quite different anatomy and physiology from the human. What if its eyes are physically quite unlike the eyes with which we are familiar? What if its sense-modalities are disjoint from those of the interpreter? These possibilities introduce a new element of difficulty into the problem, which I do not propose to explore here; in common with other writers on 'radical' interpretation I shall assume that we are dealing with subjects with a sufficient degree of similarity to the interpreter. But it is worth making this assumption explicit and indicating the scope and limits of the account I am proposing. (It *may* indeed be that without the assumption of such a shared 'form of life' between interpreter and interpreted interpretation is not possible.)[16]

---

[16] This appears to be a thesis of Wittgenstein's about the conditions of communication: see sections 241–2 of *Philosophical Investigations* (Basil Blackwell, Oxford, 1958). It is doubtful, however, that his notion of a 'form of life' exactly coincides with that alluded to in the text: he would

Am I entitled to suppose that, once the sense-organs have been identified, it is legitimate to make an ascription of experience to the subject? It seems to me that I am, at least prima facie: the disposition of a person's sense-organs is prima facie good evidence for how he is perceiving the world, even though an initial ascription may be corrected in the light of further knowledge of the subject's psychology. Furthermore, I am not alone in supposing this: both Quine and Davidson make the same assumption, though less explicitly. There is much talk in Quine of the 'conspicuous presence' (p. 29) of rabbits, of 'glimpses' (p. 37) of rabbits, of the native assenting to 'gavagai' in 'plain sight' (p. 39) of a rabbit, of being prompted by 'the sight of a face' (p. 42), of a child hearing the word 'Mama' while 'sensing the mother in the periphery of his visual field' (p. 81).[17] In fact it is clear that it is precisely because of the presence of suitable perceptual experiences that the native assents at all: he assents to 'gavagai' when a rabbit goes by because he *sees* a rabbit. And we similarly find Davidson suggesting that a particular ascription of belief be made to the subject on the strength of the fact that his 'vision is good and his line of sight favourable:[18] again, this serves as evidence for belief precisely because Davidson is assuming that the subject *sees* a certain state of affairs; without this assumption the suggested belief ascription would be unjustified. So it seems to me that ascriptions of experience are possible, tacitly assumed by other writers on interpretation, and anyhow inescapable in the ascription of belief.

What would be objectionable would be a dependence upon knowledge of belief and meaning in the ascription of experience, for then such ascriptions could not function as a *basis* for the interpreter's knowledge of the subject's propositional attitudes and language. However, it seems to me that I am in the clear on this point: for the perceptual system is (as we might say) *autonomous* with respect to the belief system.[19] That is to say, what a person perceives is in general independent of what he believes: you need not believe what you see or see what you believe. This means that even a total assignment of experiences to a person does not *entail* that he has any particular set of beliefs. We can thus often know what someone sees without knowing what he believes. In this respect I think my account is better off than Davidson's: for ascriptions of holding-true *are* ascriptions of (one kind of) belief – the belief that a sentence is true – and so they link up with ascriptions of other beliefs in a way that threatens their prior availability. But experiences are not beliefs and so they belong to a separate department of the subject's psychology.

---

certainly want to include more under this heading than the kinds of biological facts I am speaking of.

[17] These quotations are all from *Word and Object*, chapter 2. No doubt Quine does not *intend* the quoted phrases to be taken mentalistically, but it is revealing how natural and unavoidable it is to invoke such perceptual locutions in describing what is going on in radical interpretation.

[18] 'On the Very Idea of a Conceptual Scheme', p. 196. Davidson is here suggesting that we can use facts about perception to correct attributions of belief invited by the subject's words. Oddly enough, he goes on to say, inconsistently as it seems, that 'knowledge of beliefs comes *only* with the ability to interpret words' (my italics).

[19] Here I am adopting the kind of view of the relation between belief and perception put forward by Jerry Fodor in *The Modularity of Mind* (MIT Press, Cambridge, Massachusetts, 1983). I am suggesting that the modularity shows up in radical interpretation.

It therefore seems to me reasonable to suppose that Stage One can be undertaken in advance of Stage Two, and that Stage One can itself be got off the ground on the basis of evidence that does not just assume that we know how our subject experiences the world. We can solve for experience on the basis of the physical facts without assuming that we have already solved for belief and meaning.

Stage Two. Our problem now is to see how to get from knowledge of experience to knowledge of belief, and thence to knowledge of meaning. This step is, I think, more problematic than it initially appears – more problematic, indeed, than Stage One. There is one small difficulty and two large ones. The small difficulty is that we need a test for the attitude of belief that is more general than that of assent to a sentence. The reason we need this is that we (I) want to make room for the interpretation of creatures without language; and also a realistic reconstruction of our interpretation of creatures *with* language needs to reckon with more than just sentential assent as evidence of belief. So we cannot say simply that our test for whether the subject believes there's a rabbit running by is that he assents to a certain sentence just when he has an experience as of a rabbit running by. But let us, in order not to multiply our difficulties, take it that we have devised such a non-linguistic test, so that we have a criterion for when an experience gives rise to a belief. Then we still have two larger difficulties.

The first is familiar, though it presents itself in a slightly new form under our present way of conceiving the matter: this is the problem of indeterminacy (construed here epistemologically not metaphysically). Even if we know that the subject has formed a belief as a result of seeing a rabbit and that this belief gets its content from the content of the experience, we do not yet know what the *content* of the belief is and hence what the meaning of the held-true sentence is: does he believe and mean that a rabbit has run by or an undetached rabbit-part or a rabbit stage etc.? The point is that an experience as of a rabbit is *also* an experience as of an undetached rabbit-part etc. Perceptual experiences represent a great many features of the world simultaneously, whereas beliefs and sentences select out their content from this multiplicity. In other words, experiences underdetermine the content of the belief expressed in much the same way that Quine's stimulations do; they thus leave open too many choices of belief and meaning. This problem, like the first smaller one, is not, however, peculiar to my own account, though its form is, and I have nothing to add to the very extensive literature which addresses itself to the indeterminacy problem; so I shall not pursue the issue further, being content to have raised the question.

The second large problem *is* (I think) peculiar to the account I am proposing; it arises from the fact, remarked earlier, that a person is not constrained to believe what he sees (hears, etc.). It is this that prevents us directly inferring from someone's experience what it is that he believes: for he might distrust his senses. What if he believes that he is the victim of a hallucination experiment? Matters are pretty straightforward when the subject can be assumed to form his beliefs in accordance with his experience (waiving our first two difficulties): we can then ascribe to him the belief that the world is as it seems to him, thus using the content of his experience to determine the content of his belief. But this will not work when the subject's beliefs are not formed in this simple way. What then should we say of this possibility?

The problem, clearly, is that our usual and best mode of access to a person's beliefs has been abrogated in the case under consideration. Can we somehow make up for this lack? We could if we had interpreted his language, of course, but that is part of what we are supposed to be establishing. We might alternatively try relying upon behavioural data. So far we have (like Quine and Davidson) been trying to figure out a person's beliefs from knowledge of their *causes*; perhaps we could get somewhere by turning to their *effects*. The trouble with this suggestion is that, unlike perceptual input, behaviour is not itself contentful and so threatens to be inadequate as evidence for belief content: it underdetermines ascriptions of belief and meaning too severely. This idea also appears to give up on the ambition of supplying a *method* of interpretation: all it says is that we should so ascribe beliefs and meanings as to make best sense of the subject's behaviour; it does not prescribe a series of steps which will achieve this goal. The attraction of going from perception to belief was precisely that it offered a method of interpretation which proceeds from a firm foundation; we do not get the mirror-image of this firmness by moving to the behavioural effects of belief.

I think that reflection upon the case of the subject who distrusts his senses encourages the following response: it is a *condition of interpretability* that the subject by and large believes what he perceives. That is, if a person systematically and globally refuses to let his beliefs be shaped by his experience, then he just cannot be interpreted. It is only the illicit assumption that we know his language that makes us think that we can ascertain such a person's beliefs; when this assumption is abandoned it becomes virtually impossible to see how we could have any confidence in our ascriptions of belief to such a person. (This is not to say such a person is *impossible*; it is just that he is not *interpretable*.) We just have no decent way of finding out what he believes and hence what his words mean. If this is right, then it is not a defect in my account that it does not work for someone who does not form his beliefs on the basis of his experience in the usual way; for such a believer just *is* not interpretable. There would be a defect only if someone who is interpretable were not interpretable by following my method. We can, *pace* Davidson, interpret someone with preponderantly false beliefs, because we can have reason to attribute globally non-veridical experiences; but I think it is doubtful that we could ever interpret someone whose beliefs were radically cut off from his experience. Fortunately there are few such eccentric souls around asking to be interpreted, possibly because distrusting one's senses in this radical way is a sure way to perish (even madmen trust their senses *some* of the time). My method will work well enough for ordinary people who rely on their senses; it is only sceptics who are uninterpretable.[20]

---

[20] I have said nothing in this paper about the attribution of desires, but my position on this is similar to my position on belief. In 'Mental Events', Davidson says of the subject of interpretation: 'In our need to make him make sense, we will try for a theory that finds him consistent, a believer of truths, and a lover of the good (all by our own lights, it goes without saying)' (p. 222). Finding him 'a lover of the good' is finding that he shares our values and desires; and so we know that *our* values and desires will agree with those of any interpreter, including the omniscient one. But then we know that what we value is what we *ought* to value, and hence that moral scepticism (or scepticism about what is prudent) can be ruled out. Again, this result makes me suspicious of the method, so I should like to propose a different method. The method I would propose would again be two-stage: first,

Despite these difficulties, which seem to me to be inherent in the problem rather than artifacts of the particular method I have recommended, I think that the two-stage procedure I have sketched is a plausible reconstruction or idealization of the way we set about interpreting others. The underlying idea of the method is extremely simple and I think highly intuitive: if you want to find out what a complete stranger believes you first notice how the world appears to him – how he experiences it – and then you take it that he believes by and large what he has perceived. In principle, the world could appear to him otherwise than it is, and then your ascriptions of belief will, in finding him rational, credit him with error – but you would believe the same if you had had his misleading perceptual evidence.[21] The intermediate stage of experience does not, in the normal run of things, command our attention – assuming that his experience is veridical, we move straight to an ascription of (true) belief – but it is present nonetheless and will enter explicitly when it does not represent the world correctly. It is neglect of the role of experience in belief-formation that leads Davidson to advocate his charitable method; when experience is given its due epistemologically and interpretatively, charity goes by the board as a universally applicable precept. Scepticism is not therefore ruled out by the very nature of interpretation; rather, interpretation must respect the premises on which scepticism rests. There is thus no way of avoiding the hard work of showing (or showing that we need not show) that our particular methods of forming beliefs are reliable – that what we habitually *take* as good evidence for belief *is* good evidence for belief. Scepticism must be defeated in some other way than through consideration of the nature of radical intepretation.

---

discover what gives the subject pleasure and pain; second, take it that by and large he values what gives him pleasure and disvalues what gives him pain. On this method, there is no reason why he should necessarily turn out to value and desire what we the interpreters value and desire. Clearly this sketch of a method is rough and unqualified, but it may serve to give some idea of how one might forsake charity in the attribution of desires.

[21] Thus I *am* supposing that charity about *rationality* is a requirement of interpretation, i.e., I am endorsing a 'principle of humanity'. And I would also agree with Davidson about the limits to the amount of plain *inconsistency* we can intelligibly impute to people. Note, however, that these kinds of 'charity' do not sustain the conclusions Davidson wishes to derive from the nature of interpretation: they do not undermine scepticism, and they (therefore) do not deliver the sorts of metaphysical results that Davidson hopes for (see 'The Method of Truth in Metaphysics', reprinted in *Inquiries into Truth and Interpretation*).

20

Radical Interpretation and Global Skepticism

Peter D. Klein

Introduction

The purpose of this paper is to examine whether Davidson's account of radical interpretation can be employed, as he believes it can, to undermine global skepticism.[1] I hope to show that even if one grants that Davidson has produced a sound argument with the conclusion that the thesis of global skepticism is false, that form skepticism is not significantly endangered. The reason is simply that the argument presupposes that we have some of the very knowledge which the skeptic denies we possess. In order to demonstrate that, I will explore several ways of construing Davidson's argument before presenting what I think is its strongest form. Along the way, I hope to shed a little light on skepticism *per se* and what would be required in order to show that the relevant form of global skepticism is untenable.

The paper naturally divides into three steps: (I) I would like to clarify what I think the global skeptic – or at least the relevant variety of global skeptic – is arguing for; (II) I would like to exhibit what I take to be Davidson's argument against the possibility of global skepticism; (III) finally, I would like to show how the global skeptic's position is not significantly endangered by the Davidsonian account of belief.

An earlier draft of this paper was read at the Davidson Conference at Rutgers University, April 1984. Richard Foley was the commentator and, as a result of his comments, I have made many changes in the structure of the argument of this paper. I am not confident that I have successfully answered his objections to the earlier draft, but I am certain that without modifying it as I have, it would surely have been unsuccessful. Needless to say, I want to thank him for his comments. In addition, I would like to thank Brian McLaughlin, Martha Bolton, Ernie LePore and Colin McGinn for their criticisms of earlier drafts of this paper.

[1] His attack on global skepticism occurs most explicitly in two very recent papers, but it is a consequence of his views as developed in the papers appearing in *Truth and Interpretation*, especially those in the section entitled 'Radical Interpretation'. The two recent papers are: 'A Coherence Theory of Truth and Knowledge' (*CT*), which was delivered to the Stuttgart Hegel Congress, 1981, and published in *Kant oder Hegel?*, ed. Dieter Henrich, Klett-Cotta Buchhandlung, Stuttgart, 423–38, reprinted in this volume (pp. 307–19); 'Empirical Content' (*EC*), *Grazer Philosophische Studien*, 16/17 (1982), 471–89, reprinted in this volume (pp. 320–32). All page references to those articles refer to the appropriate pages in this volume.

I *Global skepticism*

The function of this section is to clarify the relevant form of skepticism. That task is not quite as easy as it might first appear because 'skepticism' has so many guises. But I think Davidson gives us sufficient information to determine the relevant form. In *CT* it is described in the following ways (pp. 309–10):

It is a view that doubts that we have any knowledge 'about the actual world'.

It concedes that all of 'my beliefs [about the world] hang together'.

It questions whether there is any (good) 'reason for supposing coherent beliefs are true'.

Davidson's characterization of global skepticism has both a Pyrrhonian and Cartesian ancestry. But it does not fit precisely within either historical tradition.

Let us consider the Pyrrhonians first. Their skepticism was certainly global concerning the possibility of obtaining knowledge about the real nature of the objects in the world beyond what was immediately evident. As Sextus says:

> When we question whether the underlying object is such as it appears, we grant the fact that it appears, and our doubt does not concern the appearance itself but the account given of that appearance ... For example, honey appears to us to be sweet ... but whether it is also sweet in its essence is for us a matter of doubt, since this is not an appearance but a judgement regarding the appearance.[2]

The doubt, and hence the Pyrrhonian suspension of judgement about the non-evident nature of the objects in the world, is based upon such considerations as the variations in the sense organs of humans and other animals, the variability of sensations from one human to another and the differences between the sensations of one person in different circumstances. The argument concludes that we are not justified in believing that the objects in the world really have any of the properties which they appear to have because we are unable to provide a criterion for adjudicating between the varied appearances.

Thus, there is a similarity between the Pyrrhonian view and that of Davidson's global skeptic. Both believe that we have no knowledge of the real nature of the objects in the world.

There is, however, a significant difference. Given that Davidson's global skeptic would be willing to accept an argument which shows that his skepticism is untenable, this global skeptic does not share the Pyrrhonian doubts concerning the reality of 'proofs'. The Pyrrhonians not only oppose 'appearances to appearances' but 'judgements to judgements' as well (*OP*, I, 9). They would question our ability to produce a proof of any non-evident proposition, including the proposition that we have knowledge of the real nature of the world about us (*OP*, II, esp. chapters XII and XIII).

The Pyrrhonian, as opposed to the Academic skeptic, would grant that there could be apparently good reasons for denying global skepticism. But he would

---

[2] Sextus Empiricus, *Outlines of Pyrrhonism* (*OP*), trans. R. G. Bury (Harvard University Press, Cambridge, Massachusetts, 1976), I, 19–20.

believe that there would be equally, apparently good reasons for affirming global skepticism. The Pyrrhonian doubts that there is any argument form in which to place one's confidence. Consequently, Pyrrhonian skepticism would not be endangered if there were discovered an apparently good argument for thinking that coherent beliefs were true. Davidson, of course, is assuming throughout that we do have the ability to produce arguments which could dispose of the global skeptic.

The Cartesian ancestry of Davidson's global skeptic is clearly evident.[3] The examples which Davidson uses are reminiscent of Descartes' own examples of what is doubtful, namely, beliefs about tables, pieces of paper and other 'external objects' whose existence is normally held to be detectable by the senses. These are the beliefs which Davidson called methodologically basic, i.e., the ones whose truth conditions must be determined in the early stages of interpreting the speech of others.

Now, before discussing one significant difference between Davidson's global skeptic and the Cartesian skeptic, let us pause for a moment on the area of agreement between the varieties of skepticism considered so far, namely, the universal doubt concerning the certification as knowledge of any belief about the objects in the world. The universality of the skeptic's claim distinguishes this form of skepticism from others which have been advocated from time to time. But what is more important for our purposes, its universality establishes an important constraint on any possible reply to global skepticism.

Let us contrast this universal skepticism with one less robust. Russell, for example, thought the possibility that during our sleep everything had doubled in size provided grounds for a significant form of skepticism.[4] This is not a form of global skepticism. Too much knowledge of the world remains intact. The reason is identical to the one which Descartes employed in order to distinguish the type of skepticism which would result from supposing that, at the moment, he was dreaming from genuine global skepticism. As Descartes says, the 'things that appear in sleep are like painted representations, which cannot have been formed except in the likeness of real objects' (*D*, 63).[5] Thus, too many of our beliefs about the world would remain knowledge if they had been knowledge prior to our somnambulant experiences.

Similarly, in Russell's fantasy, although everything might have doubled in size, many of our beliefs 'gotten by means of the senses' would remain knowledge. We would still know that object A is twice as large as object B; that object A was to the right of object B; and more importantly, we would still know that there are corporeal objects and that there is a causal order. As Descartes puts it, we would still have knowledge of 'corporeal nature in general, and its extension; the shape of extended objects; quantity ... the number of the objects; place for them to exist in and time for them to endure through; and so on' (*D*, 63). In other words, our beliefs about the world of corporeal objects would remain knowledge in the main.

---

[3] It should be obvious that by 'Cartesian skepticism' I am not referring to Descartes' considered view, but rather that view with which the reader is left at the end of the 'First Meditation'.

[4] Bertrand Russell, *Human Knowledge* (Simon and Schuster, New York, 1967), p. 178.

[5] All references to Descartes' writings will be to the Anscombe and Geach edition: *Descartes' Philosophical Writings* (*D*) (Bobbs Merril, New York, 1971).

The situation is similar if we consider one interpretation of a version of the brain-in-the-vat hypothesis. Consider a person, we can call 'Biv' – short for *Brain in the Vat*. Suppose that, without Biv's knowledge, her brain were transplanted into a vat and hooked up to a computer which is programmed to give her a set of sensations which are indistinguishable (by her) from a set which she might have had were she not to have been transplanted. She would, no doubt, have some false beliefs. But many others would remain knowledge *if they once were knowledge*. She would still know that leaves turn green in the spring, that there are corporeal objects and, what is most important for our purposes, she would still know that there is a causal order – if she ever did.

No doubt, at the beginning, some of Biv's beliefs would be false, e.g., that I (Biv) am presently seeing a leaf, or that my (Biv's) body is similar to what it was two days ago. But, as we shall see later when we consider Davidson's attack on skepticism, it would become increasingly difficult to say which, if any, of Biv's beliefs were false as her tenure in the vat increased. In fact, if I understand Davidson's view correctly, the version of the brain-in-the-vat hypothesis which I have just given, is not one which is consistent with his account of belief. I will return to this example later in order to make the necessary adjustments. The point of employing it here is to underscore the universality of the skepticism about our knowledge of the world.

Because this form of skepticism is universal, there is an important constraint on any argument employed against it: *an argument against global skepticism cannot employ any premise whose plausibility depends upon knowledge of the actual world*. To do so would clearly presuppose that we have some of the knowledge which the skeptic questions. That is a crucial point and one to which I will return when we evaluate the success of Davidson's argument against global skepticism.

To sum up what we have said thus far about Davidson's global skeptic: the global skeptic doubts that we are able to gain any knowledge about the world but does not doubt the efficacy of arguments. In addition and what is most crucial for our purposes, since the skepticism is global, an argument against it cannot contain any premise which depends for its support upon knowledge of the objects in our environment.

Descartes' argument against skepticism appears to satisfy that constraint because it depends upon showing that there is an epistemically benevolent creator whose creation (our mental equipment) is reliable if we exercise the appropriate restraint on our will. The premises which Descartes employs to demonstrate that there is such a benefactor are either 'revealed by the light of nature' or self-evident claims about the introspectively available contents of our beliefs. From the Cartesian viewpoint, neither premise depends upon any knowledge about the 'external' world. Of course, that could be challenged. But this is not the place.

As we shall see, Davidson's argument also appears to satisfy that constraint. For it depends upon recognizing that the nature of belief is such that coherent beliefs are true in the main. That recognition does not appear to depend upon any information about the actual world.

There is one important difference, however, between Davidson's global skeptic and the Cartesian variety. The Cartesian skeptic requires that in order for a proposition to be known, it must be 'plainly certain and indubitable' (*D*, 61). It must be free from all 'legitimate' doubt (*D*, 64). He grants that many propositions based upon the senses are 'highly probable and far more reasonably believed than denied' (*D*, 65). But since they are 'doubtful in a way', they fall short of the being knowledge.

Certainty is a rigorous standard. It was not required by all skeptics. For example, the Pyrrhonian skeptics merely required that there be a criterion by which we could generally distinguish true beliefs about what is non-evident from the false ones. Tipping the balance in the direction of one of a set of many contraries would have been sufficient for assent. And, of course, many non-skeptics have rejected Cartesian skepticism by arguing that beliefs about the world need not meet the rigorous standard of certainty in order to be certifiable as knowledge.[6] Davidson does not attack global skepticism on those grounds because it is clear that his skeptic is a much less demanding one. His skeptic does not demand that a belief be certain in order to be known. Instead, as we shall see, his skeptic will be satisfied if it can be shown that there is a strong presumption in favor of the truth of each belief which is among a vast set of coherent beliefs.

Thus, Davidson's argument, if successful, will not be effective against those historically important forms of Cartesian skepticism which required that beliefs be certain in order to be knowledge. In addition, it would not be effective against the historically important forms of Pyrrhonism which were unwilling to grant the efficacy of arguments. Nevertheless, all forms of global skepticism share one important feature, namely, they all claim that *all* of my beliefs about the actual world, though coherent, fail to be knowledge. And it is that basic claim which Davidson's argument is apparently designed to show is incompatible with a correct understanding of the nature of belief.

I said 'apparently' in the previous sentence because this way of characterizing the basic claim of the global skeptic tends to obscure what may seem to be a central area of disagreement between Davidson and the global skeptic. Davidson thinks that the central point of disagreement turns on whether there is a good reason for thinking that coherent beliefs are *true*. The task, from his point of view, is to provide such a reason.

To the contrary, I should think that the task is to show that there is some good reason for thinking that coherent beliefs arising from sense experiences constitute *knowledge*. In other words, I take it that skepticism is a thesis concerning whether beliefs of a particular type are knowledge rather than a thesis concerning whether beliefs of a certain type are true. For the skeptic, it is far from clear that 'when beliefs are true, then the primary conditions for knowledge would seem to be satisfied' (*CT*, p. 307).

Put another way: if we suppose that knowledge entails at least true, justified, belief, it is the justification condition rather than the truth or belief condition which the skeptic has challenged. Davidson seems to believe that if our

---

[6] I believe that such a requirement is both legitimate and satisfiable. See my *Certainty: A Refutation of Scepticism* (University of Minnesota Press, Minneapolis, 1981).

coherent beliefs based upon the senses can be shown to be in the main true, then a reason for rejecting global skepticism has been provided. For if such beliefs are true and we know that they are, then, I take it that he believes that the justification condition is, so to speak, satisfied automatically on a particular occasion if there is no contravening evidence. I will return to a consideration of the justification condition shortly.

I think that the thesis of the relevant form of global skepticism should be put as follows:

> Global skepticism   None of the beliefs about the external world, though coherent with other such beliefs, is knowledge.

The alternative way of putting the thesis of global skepticism would be to say that the global skeptic holds that it is possible that none of the beliefs about the world, though coherent, is true. But this way of putting the thesis must be rejected if we are to be able to raise the question which I wish to ask, namely: can we argue successfully against the global skeptic that because we know that beliefs about the world are coherent and true that we have any reason to believe that we have knowledge about the world?

Since we will be referring to *co*herent *b*eliefs *a*bout the *w*orld so often, some shorthand will be useful. Let us call one member of a set of coherent beliefs about the world a 'cobaw'. Now, I take it that the skeptical arguments for the claim that no cobaw is knowledge are not designed to show merely that *as a matter of fact* no cobaw is known; rather, they are designed to show that it is not possible that a cobaw is knowledge. In other words, the conclusion of the arguments are not generalizations based upon having shown that some cobaw, say c_1, fails to be knowledge because it lacks some feature, say F, and that some other cobaw, say c_2, fails to be knowledge because it lacks F, and so forth for many cobaws. Rather the argument is designed to show that there is some perfectly general reason which shows that no cobaw could be knowledge because no cobaw could have F.

The arguments designed to show that cobaws lack one of the necessary conditions of knowledge are legion. As mentioned above, the Pyrrhonians argued that since there is no criterion by which we can distinguish the true cobaws from those which are false, we are not justified in assenting to any cobaw. Descartes claimed that no cobaw was knowledge because there was a 'reason for doubt' which could be raised against them all. And there are many, many variations of those arguments.

Now, given the number of the arguments which have been advanced for global skepticism, Davidson's strategy for confronting the skeptic seems to be the one of choice. It is to find a sound argument none of whose premises depends for its evidential support on knowledge of the world and which has the conclusion that some of our cobaws are knowledge. If such an argument were available, we would know that any argument for global skepticism was unsound. There would be no need to slug it out in the epistemological trenches by confronting the arguments for global skepticism one by one. The upshot of my argument in this paper is that such trench warfare is necessary.

II *Davidson's argument against global skepticism*

The sought-after, general argument described at the end of the last section depends upon Davidson's account of the methodology for interpreting the words of others and its consequences for the correct understanding of the nature of belief. The account of radical interpretation is so well known that there is no point in repeating it here. However, what is necessary, is to make clear what Davidson takes to be the consequences of that methodology for global skepticism.

The argument against skepticism is a consequence of his proposal that 'we take the fact that speakers of a language hold a sentence true ... as prima-facie evidence that the sentence is true.'[7] The gist of his argument is that 'what stands in the way of global skepticism of the senses is ... the fact that we must, in the plainest and methodologically most basic cases, take the objects of belief to be the causes of those beliefs' (*CT*, pp. 317–18). That is, since in those cases the objects of belief are (generally) the causes of beliefs, the beliefs must, in general, be true. As he puts it, 'the general presumption in favor of the truth of belief serves to rescue us from a standard form of traditional skepticism [what I have called 'global skepticism'] by showing why it is impossible for all of our beliefs to be false together' (*CT*, p. 319).

In 'Empirical Content', he develops the connection between radical interpretation and global skepticism in the following passage:

> My main point is that our basic methodology for interpreting the words of others necessarily makes it the case that most of the time the simplest sentences which speakers hold true *are* true. It is not the *speaker* who must perform the impossible feat of comparing his belief with reality; it is the *interpreter* who must take into account the causal interaction between world and speaker in order to find out what the speaker means, and hence what he believes. Each speaker can do no better than make his system of beliefs coherent, adjusting the system as rationally as he can as new beliefs are thrust upon him. But there is no need to fear that these beliefs might just be a fairy tale. For the sentences that express the beliefs, and the beliefs themselves, are correctly understood to be about the public things and events that cause them, and so must be mainly veridical. Each individual knows this, since he knows the nature of speech and belief. This does not, of course, tell him *which* of his beliefs are true, but it does assure him that his overall picture of the world around him is like the picture other people have, and is in its large features correct (*EC*, p. 322).

Although we will consider other reconstructions of Davidson's argument later, it seems initially plausible to construe it in the following way:

P1. If cobaws are interpretable, then they are true in the main.
P2. Cobaws are interpretable.
P3. (Therefore,) cobaws are true in the main.

---

[7] Donald Davidson, *Truth and Interpretation*, p. 152.

C1. (Therefore,) global skepticism is false.

And what's more, since we can know the 'nature of speech and belief,' (C2) each individual has a (good) reason for believing that his/her cobaws are true.

The apparent, main conclusion, C1, contains the denial of global skepticism and follows, supposedly, from P3. Davidson appears to draw the auxiliary conclusion, namely C2, from the fact that we can know that C1 is true. This auxiliary conclusion is important for, if true, it would show that an important form of skepticism besides global skepticism is untenable. It is that form which I have elsewhere called 'iterative skepticism' and it is the view that one cannot know that he/she knows.[8] But, in so far as the argument against iterative skepticism depends upon the argument against global skepticism, we can kill two anti-skeptical birds with one stone which blocks the inference to C1 from P3. On the other hand, in a construction of the argument to be considered later, C2 will play a significantly different role, and, consequently, in that version of the argument, it cannot be rejected because it is parasitic on C1. But to mix metaphors, that is a bridge to be crossed only after we have burned this one.

III *Examination of Davidson's argument*

The purpose of this section is to evaluate the success of Davidson's argument against the global skeptic. My strategy will be to work through a series of criticisms of the argument, strengthening it as much as possible and granting as much as possible on behalf of the global skeptic. Then I want to determine whether the revised argument endangers the global skeptic's thesis. My conclusion is that the argument, even strengthened as much as possible, should not prove troublesome to the global skeptic.

I think that the first objection which the global skeptic may have to the argument is that it would not follow from the claim that a set of beliefs is true or even known to be true by the person possessing the beliefs, that the beliefs constitute knowledge.

P3 asserts that our cobaws are true in the main. Now, even if that were granted, it does not follow that the other conditions of knowledge are satisfied. In particular, it does not follow that any of the beliefs are adequately justified. It is the lack of justification for our beliefs, rather than their falsehood, which the skeptic believes prevents our beliefs from being certified as knowledge.

Now what is apt to be misleading is the way in which the skeptic sometimes chooses to put his thesis. Sometimes the skeptic will say something like this: 'For all I know, it is possible that all of my cobaws are false.' The reason I say that this is a misleading way to put the issue is that often the possibility mentioned above is cashed out this way: for every cobaw it is logically possible both that I believe it and that it is false.

---

[8] See my *Certainty*, esp. pp. 5–11.

The skeptic does (should) not mean something like that misleading way of putting his claim for reasons not at all connected with the extent of our knowledge about the actual world.[9] For the misleading way of cashing out the claim leads to an absurdity. Consider any pair of mutually exclusive propositions, one of which is necessarily true and one necessarily false. If one had no proof of either, or for that matter, no idea of how to begin proving either of them, it might seem perfectly all right to say of each that for all I know, it is possible both that I believe it and that it is false. But since one of them must be true, it is not logically possible with regard to each both that I believe it and that it is false. For one of them is necessarily true. Hence, the 'epistemic possibility' envisioned by the skeptic in the expression 'For all I know, it is possible that x' cannot be construed to mean that it is *logically* possible both that I believe that x and that not-x.

Roughly, I take it that the skeptic means (or should mean) that x is epistemically possible [for S] *iff* there is no justification (adequate to produce knowledge) that not-x [for S]. Giving a full account of epistemic possibility is a difficult task. But, luckily, it is not necessary for the purpose of this paper. For we have taken the global skeptic to mean nothing more than that none of the beliefs about the world, though coherent with other beliefs, is knowledge.

Nevertheless, there is an apparent connection between P3 and C1 and C2. It is this: if I know that most of my cobaws are true, it would seem that, at the very least, I have a reason for believing any particular cobaw unless I had some evidence against it. That is, if Davidson has established the truth that P3 and if I know that P3 is true, then the argument for C1 could be put this way. Since (C2) I know that my cobaws are true in the main, I have a good reason for believing that 'there is no need to fear that these beliefs might just be a fairy tale.' In other words, since I can recognize that the meta-belief about my cobaws has been demonstrated, I can know that global skepticism is false. Hence, global skepticism is false.

In this reconstruction of the argument, C2 is far from being an 'auxiliary conclusion'. It is the glue between a slightly revised version of P3 and the old C1. The structure of the argument against the global skeptic can now be put as follows:

P1*. If I know that cobaws are interpretable, then I know that cobaws are true in the main.

P2*. I know that (P2) cobaws are interpretable.

P3*. (Therefore,) I know that (P3) cobaws are true in the main.

C2. (Therefore,) I know that (C1) global skepticism is false.

C1. (Therefore,) global skepticism is false.

---

[9] Keith Lehrer makes a similar point in 'Why Not Scepticism?', *Philosophical Forum*, 11 (1971), p. 287.

Now, does this version of the argument fare any better than the one considered earlier? Once again, let us grant on behalf of the global skeptic that P1* and P2* are true, and, hence, that P3* is true. In addition, C1 does follow from C2, since for any x, if x is known, x is true. But does P3* entail C2?

Well, not for the same reason that accounts for the fact that (P1* and P2*) entails P3*. That is merely an instantiation of *modus ponens*. But the inference from P3* to C2 is not an instance of a valid inference in either propositional or quantificational logic.

Nevertheless, it might be thought the inference from P3* to C2 is an instance of a general principle of the transmissibility of epistemic predicates through entailment. The relevant form of that principle would be: *If y is entailed by x, and I know that x, then I know that y.* Presumably, it is a principle of that sort which warrants P1*.

There is significant disagreement over the status of transmissibility principles. It may seem to some that only a more moderate version of it is correct. That version may either add more conjuncts to the antecedent or weaken the consequent.[10] For example, some might argue that the antecedent should include a conjunct such as 'I know that y is entailed by x.' Or, some might think that the consequent should be replaced with 'I can know that y' because we don't always believe what we are entitled to believe.

Nevertheless, whether any version of that principle is valid is irrelevant. For P3* is equivalent to this: I know that P3. And, C2 is equivalent to this: I know that C1. But since it has already been shown that P3 does not entail C1, the antecedent of the principle is not fulfilled. In other words, since a set of beliefs can be true without being known, it is possible for any S, that S's beliefs are true and not known by S.

There is, however, a general principle to which Davidson might be appealing, which could be put like this: If I know that a set of beliefs of a certain sort, say the cobaws, contains only true beliefs, then I have some knowledge of the 'objects' of my beliefs. Or more generally, for any proposition, x, and any person, S, if S knows that x is true, then S knows that x. For example, if I know that my belief that the table is round is true, then I know that the table is round. Thus, it may seem comforting to anyone to discover that his cobaws are true.

I say 'seem' in the previous sentence, because the supposed comfort here is, alas, illusory. For I can know that a belief is true without knowing the truth expressed by the belief. I could, for example, know that most of Biv's cobaws are true without knowing the truth of any of those beliefs. And what's more, Biv could know that her beliefs of a certain sort, say the methodologically basic ones, are true without knowing the truths of any of the propositions.

Beliefs or sets of beliefs can be identified in various ways. For example, I could identify a belief as the first one which I held on Tuesday or the first belief which Biv held on Tuesday. It should be clear, I think, that one can know that those beliefs so characterized are true without knowing, thereby, any truth about the world. However, if the beliefs were identified as the beliefs that there is a table in front of me and the belief that Biv's computer is in state s_c, then knowing that those beliefs so decribed are true is sufficient to know something

---

[10] See my discussion of the so-called 'transmissibility principles' in *Certainty*, esp. pp. 26–81.

about the world. In general, the inference from '*S* knows that *x* is true', to '*S* knows that *x*', is valid only if '*x*' is replaced by a clause which expresses what would be the case were the belief true. The content of the belief, i.e., its truth condition, is used to identify it.

I believe that Davidson is making a similar point when he says:

> We can know that a speaker holds a sentence to be true without knowing what he means by it or what belief it expresses for him. But if we know he holds the sentence true *and* we know how to interpret it, then we can make a correct attribution of belief.[11]

For a Cartesian, knowing a belief's truth condition is simply a matter of introspection. As Descartes says:

> Now ideas considered in themselves, and not referred to something else, cannot strictly be false; whether I imagine a she-goat or a chimera, it is not less true that I imagine one than the other. ... the chief and commonest error that is to be found in this field consists in my taking ideas within myself to have similarity or conformity to some external object; for if I were to consider them as mere modes of my own consciousness, and did not refer them to anything else, they could give me hardly any occasion of error. (*D*, 78).

Thus, for the Cartesian, what one's beliefs are about is a matter of their 'internal' features which are available by introspection. But, of course, it is a cornerstone of Davidson's account of methodologically basic beliefs that what they are about is a matter of the causal interaction of the world with the speaker. There is no 'internal' content of a belief which determines its meaning. Rather its meaning is fixed by the principle of maximizing truth (and other principles such as simplicity) and by a causal relation between my assenting utterances and objects in the world. As he says: 'if I am right, we can't in general first identify beliefs and meanings and then ask what caused them. The causality plays an indispensable role in determining the content of what we say and believe' (*CT*, p. 317). Thus, Davidson's view avoids the possibility of the mismatch between the content of beliefs and the objects of beliefs which provides the basis of Cartesian skepticism.

As mentioned above, the Cartesians hold that the content of the belief is available through introspection. So, no knowledge of the world is presupposed by the Cartesian who specifies the content of beliefs. On the other hand, since the content of cobaws is what typically causes them (according to Davidson), in order to specify the content in the way which permits the inference from '*S* knows that *x* is true' to '*S* knows that *x*', we must presuppose that '*x*' contains an expression which designates the typical cause of the belief. And that, of course, presupposes that *S* and we who are identifying the belief by its typical cause have the very knowledge of the world which the skeptic asserts is beyond our ken.

Thus, the move from P3* to C2 is acceptable only if I also know what my beliefs are about. And, no doubt, Davidson holds that we do know what our

---

[11] Donald Davidson, *Truth and Interpretation*, p. 162.

beliefs are about. But the question is whether that knowledge can be appealed to in this argument against the global skeptic. I think the answer is clearly that it cannot. It would violate the general constraint on any successful argument against global skepticism; namely, that no premise in the argument can depend upon our knowledge of the objects which we sense.

Let us consider an example. Suppose, *first*, that I knew that my beliefs of certain sort, say those I held on Tuesdays, were true. As I argued previously, it would not follow from that supposition alone that any of my beliefs held on Tuesdays were knowledge or that I knew that 'global' skepticism about Tuesdays' beliefs is false. For all of those beliefs could fail to be justified. But suppose, *second*, that I also knew that my Tuesday beliefs were that my cat, Victoria, was on the mat and that leaves are green in the springtime and that my office is located in Davison Hall, etc. From those two suppositions, I could infer that I know that my cat is named Victoria and that I know that leaves are green in the springtime and that I know that my office is in Davidson Hall. The information about the content of the belief, i.e., what the belief is about, coupled with the knowledge that the belief is true, permits the inference to the claim that I have the knowledge of the object of the belief.

Return to cobaws: if I knew what my cobaws are about (tables, pieces of paper, cats, mats, etc.), then I could infer from that and from the knowledge that cobaws are true in the main, that at least some of the cobaws are knowledge. In other words, I could infer that I knew that global skepticism about cobaws is false. But to appeal to knowledge about the contents of my cobaws is ruled out by the general constraint on any successful argument against global skepticism with regard to cobaws.

In sum, the global skeptic can grant P1 and P1*, P2 and P2*, and, consequently, P3 and P3*. But nothing which the skeptic thereby grants entails that we have any knowledge about the world unless the skeptic also grants that we know what our methodologically basic beliefs are about. And, of course, that is just the issue at hand.

Thus, the argument as it stands will not provide any reason for rejecting global skepticism. The primary reason is that in order to conclude that we have knowledge our argument must establish that at least some of our cobaws fulfill *all* of the conditions of knowledge. Showing that the truth condition is fulfilled is not sufficient.

But I think that the argument can be strengthened in a way which avoids these objections. For Davidson, the justification condition is satisfied if our beliefs are coherent. As he says: 'the point is to say there is a presumption in favor of the truth of a belief that coheres with a significant mass of belief. Every belief in a coherent total set of beliefs is justified in the light of this presumption' (*CT*, p. 308). In addition, in the long quotation cited earlier (see page 375) Davidson said that although the speaker cannot perform the impossible task of comparing his/her beliefs to their causes, the speaker is able to make them coherent. One may wonder how that is possible if their content is not introspectively available. But that kind of worry is not appropriate here. For we are granting the general account of belief which Davidson proposes.

Thus, P3 and P3* can be strengthened. Since each member of a coherent set of beliefs is justified, we can say that cobaws are justified as well as true in the main. In fact, if one thought that the correct analysis of knowledge is some variety of the so-called causal accounts, then Davidson would have produced an argument which contains a premise to the effect that all of the necessary conditions of knowledge are satisfied and that we know them to be satisfied. For Davidson would have shown that most of our beliefs about a certain set of objects are true, justified and appropriately caused. The 'causal' condition is satisfied because in order to interpret the beliefs, the appropriate causal conditions must be fulfilled, i.e., those conditions which are such that we reliably obtain true beliefs about the objects when those conditions obtain.

The defeasibility theorists may not be so easily satisfied with this argument. For they would require that in order for an argument to demonstrate that all of the conditions of knowledge are satisfied, it would have to be shown that there are no defeaters of the justified, true and appropriatley caused beliefs. However, this objection can, I think, be rejected by Davidson.

Recall that Davidson's global skeptic does not require what the Cartesian skeptic does; namely, that beliefs be indubitable or certain in order for them to be knowledge. We have granted that the person possessing beliefs can make them coherent. That is, we have granted that the justification condition of knowledge is fulfilled. To further require, as the defeasibility theorists would, that there is no true proposition which would defeat the justification, is suspiciously like requiring that in order for a belief to be certifiable as knowledge not only must it be justified, but it must also be free from all grounds for doubt. That is, one might reasonably suppose that the Cartesian require-ment of indubitability is nothing more (or less) than the defeasibility theorist's requirement that there be no true proposition which would undercut the justification.[12] Hence, since Davidson's global skeptic does not require that a belief be certain in order to be knowledge, Davidson's argument against the skeptic need not show that there are no defeaters of our justified, true, appropriately caused beliefs.

Let me restate the argument in what I take to be its *best* form:

BP1. If cobaws are interpretable, then they are true in the main, justified and appropriately caused.
BP2. Cobaws are interpretable.
BP3. (Therefore,) cobaws are true in the main, justified and appropriately caused.
BP4. (Therefore,) A set of sufficient conditions of knowledge is satisfied for cobaws.

C1. (Therefore,) global skepticism is false.

The issue now becomes this: does this strengthened argument provide good grounds for rejecting the type of global skepticism which is Davidson's apparent

---

[12] I have argued for that very thesis in *Certainty*. The argument there had the twist that since many of our beliefs are in fact such that there are no defeaters, the Cartesian requirement of indubitability is, in fact, satisfied.

target? Unlike the earlier versions of the argument which we considered, I believe that this strengthened argument is valid and has true premises. Nevertheless, I think that there are some questions which can be raised that show that the argument is not as effective against the global skeptic as it might seem.

Let us return to Biv. Suppose that Biv had always been envatted. I take it that under those conditions Biv's words, and, hence beliefs, would be about various states of the computer. For example, if whenever we heard Biv say 'There's a cat on the mat' all we could detect was uniform correlation between that utterance and certain states of the computer to which Biv is connected, Biv's utterances, and, hence beliefs, would be about those computer states.[13] For example, by 'cat,' Biv would mean a certain type of computer state, say s_c. Exactly how we would come to know that is not the issue here. For example, the question here is not why Biv's utterances would be taken to refer to the states of the computer rather than, for example, the electrical impulses in the wires connecting Biv to the computer or to Biv's own brain states. At this point, we are granting on behalf of the global skeptic that there is a correct way of maximizing the truth of Biv's methodologically basic utterances.

Recall the version of the brain-in-the-vat hypothesis considered earlier. In that scenario, Biv had once been in a human body and then was transferred to the vat. Presumably, given the requirement of maximizing the truth of Biv's methodologically basic beliefs, had we followed Biv from her original human container to her new vat, we would arrive at a more complex interpretation than the one envisioned in our previous discussion. We had assumed that Biv retained much of her previous knowledge about the world. In particular, we had supposed that she still knew that leaves turn green in the springtime. We had presupposed that her beliefs remained roughly the same after she had been envatted. But, given the requirement of maximizing the truth of her methodologically basic utterances, such a presumption is not warranted.

In fact, there seem to be two strategies for maximizing the truth of those utterances: (1) We might think that Biv's language had evolved. At one time, Biv was referring to a furry animal when she uttered 'cat'; at a later time she meant s_c when she said 'cat'. (2) On the other hand, we might adopt an interpretation somewhat reminiscent of the grue cases. That is, we might think that 'cat' meant something like 'domesticated member of the genus *felis* prior to t_v' and 'computer state s_c after t_v' where the time v is the time Biv was envatted. In fact, we could always maximize the truth of any speaker's methodologically basic utterances by constructing a sufficiently long disjunction such that each disjunct was satisfied on at least one occasion when the speaker uttered the sounds whose meaning we are trying to interpret. Given this strategy, it is somewhat difficult to imagine how such beliefs could ever be false. But that is not our question because we are granting on behalf of the skeptic that Davidson's account of belief is correct.

Thus which interpretation we should make in such situations and how we should balance constraints other than the maximizing truth, e.g., simplicity, is not important for our consideration of Davidson's argument against the global

---

[13] We are extending the science-fiction example to include hooking up a voice box to the brain.

skeptic. All that is needed is that there is some method of interpretation with the result required by BP3, namely, that cobaws are in the main true, justified and appropriately caused. And we have already granted that on behalf of the global skeptic.

But in order to begin to evaluate the success of this strengthened argument, let us multiply the scenarios in which Biv's beliefs are correlated with various 'objects'. Suppose Biv is moved from her vat back to a human body but is immediately hypnotized so that what corresponds to her belief that there is cat on the mat are certain states of the hypnotist. That is, whenever she utters 'There's a cat on the mat' all we could detect was a rather uniform connection between those utterances and certain activities of the hypnotist.

In fact, one could re-introduce Descartes' evil genius here. For suppose that states of the evil genius are correlated with Biv's utterances, and hence, the beliefs which Biv has.

In this four-stage sequence, our choices for making Biv's methodologically basic beliefs true in the main are variations on the two strategies discussed earlier. First, we could suppose that her language has gone through four successive stages. In the first stage, 'cat' designates a furry animal; in the second, it designates states of the computer; in the third it designates actions of the hypnotist; and in the fourth, it designates evil genius states. Second, we could say that the expression 'cat' designates the disjunction: member of the genus *felis* or computer state s_c or hypnotist's action h_c or evil genius state e_c. Finally, we could choose some combination of the two methods just discussed. That is, we could assume that at one time 'cat' designated either a furry animal or s_c; and at a later time it designated either h_c or e_c. For the sake of simplicity, I will discuss only the first two choices. The comments about them can easily be transferred to the combination methods of interpretation.

On the first way of making Biv's beliefs true, Biv's beliefs change radically. But Biv is, *of necessity*, ignorant of one very important fact, namely, that the content of her beliefs has changed. Biv would never be able to think, 'I am now experiencing a computer state, whereas earlier I was looking at a furry animal.' This thought is beyond her capacities because at no time does she have words for *both* the computer state and the furry animal. Biv's methodologically basic beliefs are true in the main. But because Biv's language has evolved over time she must remain blissfully ignorant of the fact that the world outside of her body has changed radically. Could anything be much more pleasing to the skeptic?

The second way of satisfying the truth requirement seems preferable, but, when looked at carefully, would be equally pleasing to the skeptic. Biv's methodologically basic beliefs are true, since at least one of the disjuncts is true every time Biv utters 'There's a cat.' In addition, Biv could know that her methodologically basic beliefs have not changed their objects, since the 'object' of the beliefs over time is the compound disjunctive set of four objects. But there would surely be something quite satisfying to the skeptic about this manner of fulfilling the truth requirement. For in this case, the content of Biv's beliefs becomes less and less specific – in fact, truth is gained by sacrificing an informative picture of the world. Cats, computer states, the hypnotist's actions and those of the evil genius all become the same type of object. Biv could not distinguish between those four objects. She lacks the language to do so. She can no longer believe that there is a cat, *simpliciter*, before her. That should please the skeptic sufficiently.

Now, it might be objected that Biv could not have evolved a language under these circumstances or that no belief system like Biv's is possible. In reply, it is first worth noting that in this four-stage scenario we have fulfilled the primary constraint on belief which Davidson suggests. For the beliefs are correlated with certain events outside the body of the belief-holder. But the more important issue here concerns the nature of any additional constraint which can be placed upon the possibility of various coherent belief systems. That constraint cannot be derived from our knowledge of the actual evolution of beliefs or the manner in which we are causally affected by events outside of our bodies. Such a constraint would clearly be improper to introduce into an argument against global skepticism. For it would presuppose the existence of the knowledge which the skeptic is questioning.

It must be noted that Davidson explicitly shies away from a discussion of the constraints on a possible belief system. He says:

> I do not want to say, at this point, that every possible coherent set of beliefs is true (or contains mostly true beliefs). I shy away from this because it is so unclear what is possible. At one extreme, it might be held that the range of possible maximal sets of beliefs is as wide as the range of possible maximal sets of sentences, and then there would be no point in insisting that a defensible coherence theory concerns beliefs and not propositions or sentences. But there are other ways of conceiving what it is possible to believe which would justify saying not only that all actual coherent beliefs systems are largely correct but that all possible ones are also. The difference between the two notions of what is possible to believe depends on what we suppose about the nature of belief, its interpretation, its causes, its holders, and its patterns. (*CT*, p. 308).

No doubt Davidson's point here is correct. What it is actually (causally) possible to believe depends upon how the states of people are 'caused by, and cause, events inside and outside the bodies of their entertainers'. (*CT*, p. 308). But in order to show that in the four-stage scenario described above it is not possible for Biv to maintain a coherent belief system, one would need to produce evidence showing that the stimulations on Biv's 'bodies' could not be such that they are the causal intermediaries in sequences which result in Biv's beliefs. But such evidence would be inappropriate to introduce in an argument against the global skeptic because it is part and parcel of the coherent picture of the world which the skeptic is challenging. In short, such a claim would beg the very question at issue, namely: is there a reason to suppose that my coherent beliefs are, in the main, knowledge?

Thus, we have seen that we can grant the premise (BP2) that beliefs are interpretable, and still maintain a good deal of what the skeptic wished. But I think what we have already said about the strengthened argument and, in particular, the reply to the objection just considered, hint at a deeper problem with this way of confronting the global skeptic. Thus far we have granted, without any significant protest, that beliefs are interpretable. It is the status of that premise which I wish now to investigate. I think that, in the end, the argument employing such a premise must either remain inconclusive or presuppose that we have knowledge of the actual world. (Similar comments could be made about P2 and P2*, but for brevity's sake, I won't make them.)

Recall that at the outset I pointed out that an effective argument against global skepticism cannot employ any premise which depends upon the knowledge which the global skeptic denies. In general, we said that no premise of the argument could rest upon any particular knowledge of the world.

Now, in light of that, I wish to ask this: how are we to understand the claim that methodologically basic beliefs are interpretable? It could be a generalization built up from many attempts to interpret the belief system of others. That is, we could have discovered that beliefs are, in fact, interpretable by noting that various assentings of others are typically caused by relatively similar events. In that event, the interpreter's hope would have been fulfilled. For there would be a coherent set of true beliefs which can be attributed to those belief-holders whose language we had hitherto not understood. But, surely, such evidence cannot provide a reason for accepting BP2 which is put forth in an argument which has as its conclusion that we have knowledge about the world! For that premise would, itself, depend upon such knowledge for its acceptance.

No, the claim that 'beliefs are interpretable' cannot depend upon evidence about the world. Rather, it depends upon the claim that with regard to methodologically basic beliefs, at least, what a belief is about is what typically causes it. It is the equation of the content and the typical cause of beliefs which guarantees that the basic beliefs are true in the main.

Now the skeptic is surely going to point out that among the propositions which he thinks are beyond our ken is the proposition that there is a causal order which is such that events of a given type (utterances like 'This is a cat', for example) are typically correlated with events of another type (the presence of cats, for example). That is, the skeptic will deny that we can know that events of a certain type typically bring about events of another type. To know that would require having an extremely important bit of knowledge about the objects of our beliefs.

Thus, if the global skeptic grants that beliefs are interpretable, he must not be taken to be granting that there is a causal order. Rather, he is granting an *a priori* proposition. Thus, methodologically basic beliefs are taken to be just those kinds of events which are correlated with events outside of the belief-holder's body. But just as when one grants that red is a color, one is not thereby granting that there is anything red or that there are colors, granting that beliefs are interpretable does not commit one to granting that either there are beliefs or there is a causal order. What the skeptic would grant is this: *if* I have beliefs, *then* they are interpretable. The issue, then, becomes this: do I have any beliefs? For the Cartesian, the answer is self-evident. But this is because the Cartesian takes beliefs and their contents to be knowable by introspection. On the other hand, for Davidson, whether there are beliefs depends upon whether there are 'states of people ... that are caused by, and cause, events inside and outside the bodies of their entertainers' (*CT*, p. 308).

It may, indeed, seem odd to those of us who share the Cartesian view about the availability of beliefs to introspection to question whether there are any beliefs. It is obvious that there are. Whether there is a she-goat, it is obviously true that I, on occasion, believe that there is one. But, given the Davidsonian account of belief, whether there are such beliefs depends upon whether some of my states do have a causal history which correlates them with states outside of my body. To suppose that there are such events – events with such a causal history – is to suppose that we have some of the very knowledge which the skeptic denies that we have. For it presupposes that we already know that the world is such that events of one type are typically caused by events of another type. And that is just one of the claims about the world which the skeptic believes is not certifiable as knowledge.

I think that the point at issue here can be made most clearly by considering Davidson's gloss of his own argument. He says:

> My argument has two parts. First I urge that a correct understanding of … belief … leads to the conclusion that most of a person's beliefs must be true … Then I go on to claim that anyone with thoughts, and so in particular anyone who wonders whether he has any reason to suppose he is generally right about the nature of his environment, must know what a belief is, and how in general beliefs are to be detected and intepreted (*CT*, p. 314).

If I am right about the structure of Davidson's argument and the concept of belief inherent in it, then, we could know *a priori* that *if* there are beliefs, then they are true in the main. But in order to know that there are any beliefs, we would have to know at least one very important truth about our environment, namely, that there are events outside of our bodies which are (causally) correlated with states of ourselves. Any argument employing a single premiss entailing the claim that there are such correlations would be ineffective against the global skeptic. For it would presuppose that we have some of the very knowledge whose existence is to be established by the argument.

In sum, I think the global skeptic's point could be put this way: Either the premiss, BP2, in the strengthened argument is put forth as a general truth about the world or it is not. If the former, then it presupposes the denial of global skepticism, i.e, the view that we do not know any truth about the world. If the latter, then the argument cannot establish that we do, in fact, have knowledge since BP2 would have to be construed as nothing more (or less) than a hypothetical claim about beliefs. The most that such an argument could show is that if we have beliefs, then we have knowledge. But what is then called for is an argument which provides a good reason for the claim that we have beliefs. That argument, in turn, must not presuppose that we have any knowledge of states outside of our bodies if it is to be employed against the global skeptic.

21

'Circular' Coherence and 'Absurd' Foundations

ERNEST SOSA

A *Prolegomena*

Epistemology has two branches: one practical and one theoretical. *Practical epistemology* is like engineering or like the lore of carpentry. Such learning or lore is directed at certain special ends or goals (other than that of knowing more in general), and a body of such learning is a set of specified means/ends relationships. To be real (useful) practical learning, however, such a body of learning must not rest with means/ends relationships totally detached from human goals and needs and from materials and skills accessible to human beings. (It seems best therefore to think of practical learning as a relative notion: what is practical learning for one group, time, or place may not be practical learning for another.) *Theoretical learning*, by contrast, simply specifies facts, independently of whether they help attain any special goals. Theoretical epistemology, in particular, aims to develop a body of truths. It is hence in that respect to be classed with geometry, psychology, and American History. Practical learning is easily drawn from some bodies of theoretical learning: from some bodies of theoretical learning specifying cause/effect relationships, for example. Not any such body of theoretical learning will yield real practical learning, however, since it must be theoretical learning connected in known ways with human needs or goals, and with skills and materials accessible to human beings.

Each chapter of practical epistemology is an organon directed at the attainment of some specific sort of knowledge. Such an organon is constituted by rules to further one's aim of attaining knowledge of that sort.

Theoretical epistemology, by contrast, specifies facts about the nature, conditions, or extent of knowledge independently of whether such facts could yield any manual for the attainment of that whose nature, conditions, or extent they specify.

Descartes seeks epistemological learning of both sorts. The *Rules for the Direction of the Mind* is mainly about practical epistemology, as its title would suggest, and gives rules (strategies, heuristics) for attaining truth and avoiding error. But it does say something about the nature of knowledge: 'Science in its entirety is true and evident cognition,' as Haldane and Ross translate the first sentence under Rule II. And it also specifies conditions of knowledge: either intuition or deduction from the intuitive is required for real knowledge (see the comments under Rule III). Their placement in that manual, however, and even their wording suggest that Descartes conceived even these general reflections on the nature and conditions of knowledge as part of the practical learning suitable for the would-be knower. Thus he concludes his discussion of intuition and deduction as the conditions of true knowledge by saying: 'These two *methods* are the most certain *routes* to knowledge, and the mind should admit no others' [my italics].

The first two *Meditations*, by contrast, are meant mainly to determine the true extent of our supposed knowledge, a project of theoretical epistemology. But in later meditations Descartes takes up yet a third project of epistemology, distinct both from developing a manual or organon and also from developing an account of the nature, conditions and extent of knowledge. Having shown in the early meditations the narrow extent of true knowledge by comparison with the much greater width of supposed knowledge, Descartes tries in later meditations to regain territory lost to the skeptic. Since by then he takes himself to have shown that true knowledge requires intuition or deduction, it is clear what he must do. He must next intuit or deduce the bodies of commonsense belief to which he is so strongly drawn; or at least, more realistically, he must show how one could really do so with sufficient ingenuity and diligence.

Philosophers often waver in their conception of epistemology between the practical and the theoretical. A good example is the 'Introduction' by Ernest Nagel and Richard Brandt to their excellent anthology, *Meaning and Knowledge*, whose second paragraph reads as follows:

> As we read the history of theories of knowledge in Western philosophy, most of them were developed as **generalized critiques of currently held notions of what constitutes knowledge** [1], and can be interpreted as so many proposals of **policies for obtaining reliable if not completely certain beliefs** [2]. Such critiques were undertaken in some cases to locate and eliminate specific sources of error in perceptual and other judgments, in some cases to supply a comprehensive foundation for adjusting traditional beliefs to scientific and social innovations, and in many cases simply to satisfy theoretical curiosity concerning the power of human reason. But whatever the specific purposes of historic theories of knowledge may have been, we share the conception to which their authors in the main subscribed: the central task of epistemology is to provide **a generalized critique of the grounds on which claims to knowledge are supported** [3], by constructing **a systematic account of the principles by which the truth of statements may be properly assessed** [4], as well as of the rationale of these principles. A theory of knowledge so understood is indistinguishable from **a theory of logic that is general enough to deal not only with the formal validity of arguments, but with the basis on which cognitive claims of any sort can be judged to be warranted, either as cases of knowledge or as instances of probable or reasonable belief** [5].

That gives five distinct characterizations of epistemology, two of which seem practical, two theoretical, and one ambiguous.

A connection is made between practical and theoretical epistemology by the following explication (the 'organon' explication):

A belief is justified (warranted, reasonable, ...) iff it is obtained by appropriate use of an adequate organon (O).

(According to my dictionary, an 'organon' is 'an instrument for acquiring knowledge; specif.: a body of principles of scientific or philosophic investigation.')

What would the principles (policies, rules) in an organon look like? There could be principles of at least two general sorts: (a) *indirect rules*: those helpful in seeking knowledge or true belief, though they do not say exactly what to believe in given circumstances; (b) *direct rules*: those that do say what to believe (or at least what is permissible) in given circumstances. Thus an example of an indirect rule might be: Stay sober! And an example of a direct rule might be: If P is clear and distinct, then (one may) accept P! (Most of Descartes' rules in his *Rules for the Direction of the Mind* are indirect.) Surely an adequate organon, one that can possibly serve for the explication of justification as in O above, will have not only indirect rules, but also direct rules. And surely the 'appropriateness' required for justification demands that the rules in the organon used be followed with *acceptance*. (One could hardly gain true knowledge merely by *conforming* to such rules just to spite someone or just as a joke.) Moreover, to be 'appropriate', to give knowledge, one's following such rules must not be wildly arbitrary or irrational, but must reflect justified acceptance of them.

The most general form of a rule would seem to be:

In conditions C, one is to X.   (R)

And conditions for following such a rule with justified acceptance on an occasion t would seem to include:

(a) Accepting R with relevant justification
(b) Knowing onself to be in conditions C
(c) X'ing
(d) X'ing because of (a) and (b).
(All, of course, on occasion *t*.)

But now the organon explication of justification (O above) seems viciously regressive or circular; and this for two reasons. *First*, whence derives the justification for accepting the rules used? *Second*, knowing oneself to be in conditions C requires justified belief that one is in conditions C. And where would one get *that* justification?

One could perhaps apply certain rules to themselves. Thus perhaps the *practical rule* that one is to accept what is self-evidently right is itself self-evidently right and hence acceptable. Consider, by contrast, the *theoretical principle* that one is justified in accepting whatever is clear and distinct (obvious, intuitive). Might that not be clear and distinct, so that the principle would itself explain why its own acceptance is justified?

But in either case surely it is not *just* the fact that the rule or principle applies to itself that provides justification for it. For there are many rules or principles that apply to themselves with no semblance of justification. Thus consider:

> If a rule or principle contains the proposition that the earth is flat, then it is acceptable, as is the proposition that the earth is flat (E).

Rule or principle E is of course wrong, and that makes it a counterexample to the notion that *just* by applying to itself a rule or principle could justify itself. That, however, does not preclude a rule or principle which does apply to itself and which does justify itself. It precludes only that such a rule or principle justify itself **merely** by applying to itself. And if so, then possibly Descartes' principle that the intuitive is always acceptable is itself an acceptable principle for the reason that it is intuitive (i.e., by applying to itself though not *merely* by applying to itself).

If it is not just by applying to itself that a rule could derive justification, however, then suspicion remains about the organon explication (O). How could it avoid both vicious regress and circularity?

Not that otherwise all suspicion would have been removed; for in applying the rules one needs justified belief that conditions are appropriate for such application, that the antecedents of the rules are justified. And could *all* such justification in turn derive from further applications of rules in the organon? According to the organon explication (O) the only way one could acquire such justification is through a further appropriate application of an adequate organon. But that application in turn requires the appropriate following of rules, which in turn requires one's knowing oneself to be in the conditions required for the application of *these* rules. And so on.

So much for preliminaries, meant to prepare the way for the two sections that remain, one on foundationalism and one on coherentism.

B *The 'absurdity' of foundations*

Foundationalism has drawn fire repeatedly of late and stands multiply accused of itself resting on no better foundation than a 'myth of the given', and of requiring the evident absurdity of a 'test' that compares our beliefs with reality itself in the absence of any intermediary concepts or beliefs. Since the latest salvo is by Donald Davidson in an important paper, let us take this occasion to examine the damage.

Davidson's 'Coherence Theory of Truth and Knowledge'[1] argues both against foundations and in favor of coherence. It attacks foundationalism for requiring a confrontation intrinsically absurd; and objects to specific foundational 'sources of justification' outside the scope of our beliefs. That is on the negative. On the affirmative, it presents and defends a coherentist alternative.

---

[1] *Kant oder Hegel?* ed. by Dieter Henrich (Klett-Cotta, Stuttgart, 1983) 423–38. Parenthetical page references in our text will be to this paper. Compare also 'Empirical Content', *Grazer Philosophische Studien*, 17/17 (1982) 471–89, where Davidson traces in detail some historical background of his theory of knowledge.

An allegedly foundationalist idea, that of 'confrontation between what we believe and reality' is first argued to be 'absurd', thus opening the way for coherentism, subsequently offered as the alternative.

> What distinguishes a coherence theory is simply the claim that nothing can count as a reason for holding a belief except another belief. Its partisan rejects as unintelligible the request for a ground or source of justification of another ilk. (426)

In explanation and support we are referred to Rorty, who claims that 'nothing counts as justification unless by reference to what we already accept, and there is no way to get outside our beliefs and our language so as to find some test other than coherence.'[2]

Confrontational foundationalism, according to Davidson,

> must be wrong. We have been trying to see it this way: a person has all his beliefs about the world – that is, all his beliefs. How can he tell if they are true, or apt to be true? Only, we have been assuming, by connecting his beliefs to the world, confronting certain of his beliefs with the deliverances of the senses one by one, or perhaps confronting the totality of his beliefs with the tribunal of experience. No such confrontation makes sense, for of course we can't get outside our skins to find out what is causing the internal happening of which we are aware. (429)

> What we have shown is that it is absurd to look for a justifying ground for the totality of beliefs, something outside this totality which we can use to test or compare with our beliefs. (431)

Suppose:

(a) that for a belief to be justified is for the subject to justify it or to have justified it;
(b) that for one to justify a belief (really, successfully) is for one correctly and seriously to use considerations, reasons in its favor; and
(c) that seriously and correctly to use considerations or reasons in favor of a belief is to use (i) other things one believes with justification and (ii) their (justifiedly believed) appropriate connection with the belief targeted for justification.

These are apparently involved in Davidson's view of epistemic justification as inevitably *argumentative*. They are at least one way to make sense of his remarks, and no better way comes to mind, nor even any as good. Compare now the organon conception of justification (O). Clearly all organon justification must be argumentative justification. Perhaps the view that all epistemic justification is argumentative justification derives its currency, or some of it, from the attraction of the organon conception. In any case, it is worth noting the connection between the two, and two things bear emphasis in that connection: first, that the organon conception of justification stands indicted of vicious

---

[2] Richard Rorty, *Philosophy and the Mirror of Nature* (Princeton University Press, Princeton, 1979), p. 178.

circularity or regress; and second, that theoretical epistemology *need not* be tied to practical epistemology in the way required by the organon conception. For these facts may lead us to question the view of epistemic justification as inevitably argumentative.

Suppose, again, that to justify a belief is to reason or argue in favor of its object from premises believed with justification; and that the only way a belief can come to be justified is by the justifying of it through such argumentation or reasoning. Then it is beyond doubt that no full source of such justification for a belief can fail to include other beliefs. And if confrontation is the attempt to give such argumentative justification to a belief while leaning on no other beliefs, then confrontation is necessarily futile and indeed absurd. Certainly such argumentative justification must always be acquired coherentially if this means only that its acquisition requires appeal to other beliefs used as premises or reasons.

A crucial question yet remains open to doubt, however, and is not settled by *that* argument: the question, namely, whether *such* justification is always required for knowledge, whether it is argumentative justification that figures among the 'primary conditions for knowledge' (423). For if some sort of epistemic authority can come to a belief independently of any *justifying* of it by argument from premises, and if such epistemic authority can help to make a belief knowledge even in the absence of any justifying of that belief by any argument from premises, then we might after all have a source of epistemic authority that is *neither* 'confrontational' nor 'coherential' (as these terms are here defined). Again: if there is a sort of epistemic justification that may accrue to a belief independently of any *justifying* of it by any reasoning on given grounds, and if such epistemic justification can help to make a belief knowledge even absent any justifying of that belief by any reasoning on given grounds, then we might after all have a foundational source of epistemic justification.

Note the caution. It would not follow that in fact there *is* such a non-confrontational but foundational source. It *would* follow, however, that such a source of justification or authority has not yet been *ruled out* by the argument advanced.

But in what *sense* could there possibly be an epistemic 'source' of justification which was not somehow a process of arguing or reasoning on the basis of already justified beliefs? My answer is based on the supervenience of the epistemically evaluative. Suppose S and Twin-S live lives indistinguishable physically or psychologically, indistinguishable both intrinsically and contextually, on Earth and Twin-Earth respectively. Surely there can then be no belief of S epistemically justified without a matching belief held by Twin-S with equal epistemic justification. Epistemic justification must accordingly supervene upon or derive from physical or psychological properties of the subject of belief, properties either intrinsic or contextual.

All epistemic justification, authority, warrant, or any other epistemic status of belief hence derive from what is not epistemically evaluative. Any epistemically justified belief must have non-epistemic properties which make it thus justified, so that any other belief sharing all such properties would be equally epistemically justified. Would it not be proper and natural to speak of such properties as 'sources' of justification? Not just causal sources, either, not just causes of the belief, but providers or sustainers of its epistemic status as justified. The important point now is that *argument or reasoning from something already believed with justification* could not possibly serve as *such* a source of epistemic justification. For the property of a belief of its *having been supported by argument from something already believed with justification* is not a non-epistemic property, since it talks of *justification*, epistemic justification, already attained.

It may still be argued that the epistemic justification of any belief must anyhow derive from its coherence-inducing relations (of logic, say, and probability and explanation) to *other beliefs* already in place. Nothing said here so far rules this out. But now the argument in its favor cannot be the simple and apparently conclusive platitude that the argumentative justification of a belief requires appeal to other beliefs already in place. For such justification by the already justified cannot serve as a source of justification in our present sense. Since it is a justification-including source, it cannot serve as a non-epistemic source of justification. And if freed of such epistemic content, if conceived simply as argument from premises (justified or not) or reasoning from grounds (justified or not) then, far from being the *only* source of justification, it is not even clearly a sufficient source of justification at all.

The first of Davidson's arguments against foundationalism is hence inconclusive. Yes, confrontation is of course absurd if it means arguing seriously and correctly in favor of something so as to justify belief in it, *without appeal to anything already accepted or believed with justification*. What is not so obvious, however, and may in fact be false, and has yet to be given adequate support, is the assumption crucial to the attack on foundationalism: the assumption, namely, that beside justification by argument or reasoning from other beliefs, there is no alternative source of epistemic justification (or authority, warrant, etc.); that beside such *argumentative justification* there is only the absurd confrontational source of testing our target belief by comparing it with reality *neat*, unfiltered by any belief; of arguing for it without appeal to any believed premises; of reasoning to it with no reliance on any believed grounds. No argument we have yet seen rules out the possibility of a source of justification or authority *not* constituted by any reasoning or arguing *at all*, or by any testing properly so-called.

There is a second prong to Davidson's anti-foundations argument, the attack on specific foundationalist proposals. This attack is inconclusive, nor do we find here any claim to the contrary, since it is said only 'to review very hastily some of the reasons for abandoning the search for a basis for knowledge outside the scope of our beliefs' (427). Even if it conclusively refutes its specific foundationalist targets, moreover, that still falls short of refuting foundationalism itself.

Let us turn accordingly to the positive part of Davidson's contribution, his defense of coherentism.

C *The 'circularity' of coherence*

We have found both a trivial version of coherentism and the suggestion of a more interesting version. The trivial version requires for the truth of coherentism only that 'confrontation' be absurd, only that the justifying of a belief by arguing or reasoning inevitably involve the use of believed propositions as premises or reasons. Coherentism is then trivially undeniable. But in that case the interesting question becomes whether it is *such* justification that figures as one of the primary conditions for knowledge. Put another way, the question to face is then what can possibly serve as a non-epistemic source of epistemic justification. What can no longer serve as *such* a source is the feature of a belief of its having been epistemically justified by appeal to justified premises or reasons. For that is obviously epistemic.

We now have reason to believe that there must be some 'source' of epistemic justification other than the property of a belief of its having been justified by epistemically good reasoning or argument. What now might possibly count as such a source? No longer will it do to urge that there is no answer but the internal coherence of our body of beliefs since 'confrontation' is absurd. That is now insufficient, since the absurdity of 'confrontation' does not rule out any source of epistemic justification that is foundational without being absurdly 'confrontational'. Suppose a proposed source of justification for a belief which is not just the property of its having been supported on the basis of already justified beliefs nor just the property of its cohering with a comprehensive and coherent enough body of one's own beliefs; perhaps some such source as its deriving from perception, introspection, or memory, or deriving from a reliable faculty of one's own. No reason has yet been provided to show that there can be *no* such foundational source of epistemic justification. But let us anyhow put aside the possibility of such foundationalism, and let us turn instead to coherence among one's beliefs as basic 'source' of justification. Why opt for such coherence?

'What distinguishes a coherence theory,' according to Davidson, recall, is 'simply the claim that nothing can count as a reason for holding a belief except another belief. Its partisan rejects as unintelligible the request for a ground or source of justification of another ilk' (426). Davidson joins Rorty's attack on foundationalism as involving a disastrous confusion between causation and justification. How, now, is such a charge to be supported? One might simply conceive of justification as by definition always argumentative. But such support is too insubstantial, and insufficient to the task.

Not that it's outrageous, or even unacceptable, to conceive of justification thus as necessarily the outcome of a justificatory process of providing reasons or arguments. But argument will often have premises that are 'ultimate', not having been supported by argument or buttressed by reasons. No ultimate premise is *argumentatively justified*, therefore, and yet some way must be found to distinguish those that in a given context can be used by a given thinker to help justify other things from those that are there then useless for that purpose. I can argue for quite some time in favor of the proposition that at least n Fs occupy location L (for any n, F, and L you please) by simply alleging the presence there of at least $n + 1$, in support of which in turn I allege the presence of at least $n + 2$, and so on. But any such argument by any of us must eventually end, if we are all finite, and anyhow must eventually reach ultimate premises. Such ultimate premises will of course fail to be argumentatively justified. Can it be their being unbuttressed by argument that makes ineffectual any argument that hangs from them? Not obviously, since *all* ultimate premises must be equally unbuttressed and ultimate premises there must likely be for *any* complete argument that avoids vicious circularity and regress.

An argument seems viciously regressive if it requires a sequence of premises, and premises for these premises, and premises for these in turn, and so on *ad infinitum*. No human mind seems spacious enough to hold such an argument. (And even could such an argument be grasped and endorsed, that would not make one justified in holding the conclusion, as is shown by the case of the *n* Fs at location L.)

One incurs circularity relative to a stretch of time if within it one both relies essentially on P as a premise in arguing for Q and relies essentially on Q in arguing for P. Is such circularity vicious?

There is really no evident vice in accepting P on the basis of support that includes *in part* one's acceptance of Q while yet one accepts Q on the basis of support that includes *in part* one's acceptance of P. The appearance of vice derives more from the metaphor of 'support', which may just be inapt at this point, than from any intrinsic absurdity in such mutual epistemic support. Indeed, there had better be no vice or absurdity in such mutuality of support: sooner or later we find it unavoidable anyhow.

If there is no evident vice in mutuality of support, neither is it evident that such mutuality or coherence is an epistemic source of justification (much less a basic source, and least of all *the* basic source). We have seen moreover that *such* coherence does *not* have absurd 'confrontation' as its only rival for being an epistemic source of justification. No longer does an argument by elimination of alternatives seem obvious, therefore, and we need some other reason to find virtue in coherence as source of justification.

According to Davidson, what we need in favor of coherence is some reason to think that any belief coherent with a total body of beliefs is likely to be true. And he has the credit of facing that need squarely and arguing ingeniously and imaginatively to fill it. His argument has two main threads, though exactly how they intertwine is not really obvious.

One thread has the leading idea that the content of a belief is determined by its causal role in such a way that given the identities and contents of our beliefs, they could not possibly be globally false, for if they were generally caused in some way other than the way they are in fact generally caused, then they would have different contents and identities, they would not be the beliefs they are, they would be about something else.

The other main thread has as its leading idea a principle of charity which requires that, to know the mind of another, one interpret him as importantly and widely in agreement with oneself. For suppose our world changed only just enough to accommodate the presence of a superinterpreter who knows all there is to know about one's physical being including one's behavioral dispositions, linguistic or not, and who is omniscient about logic, mathematics, physical science, history, geography, cosmology, etc. If one's mind would be knowable to such an interpreter but only through his charitable attribution of wide and important agreement to the two of us, then it is hard to see how one's present body of beliefs could possibly fail to be widely and importantly right.

Many questions arise about these intriguing ideas. Here I will mention only some that seem either especially salient or especially pertinent to their proposed use in epistemology.

First, even if both threads prove sound, how do they uphold the importance of coherence in epistemology? Coherence seems epistemically superfluous. A set of totally independent beliefs would seem to enjoy an equal presumption of truth. It is not enough to answer that there could not be any total set of largely independent beliefs. Surely that beliefs must cohere and that a total set of beliefs must be widely and importantly true does not show it to be the coherence of the beliefs that makes them justified. For there are many other properties that a total set of beliefs must also have: it must be plural, the members must be caused, the members must have effects, etc. – all this in accordance with the assumptions used by Davidson for the very argument under study. And then nothing would permit a choice between coherence and these other properties equally essential to beliefs, so as to distinguish coherence as especially pertinent to epistemology.

Second, the very double-threaded argument used to uphold the epistemic importance of coherence serves equally to uphold foundational reliability. For it shows equally that beliefs by their very nature must be reliably caused so as to be mostly true. Hence, if what it shows about coherence displays the importance of coherence to epistemology, then what it shows about reliability would seem to display the equal importance of reliability to epistemology.

Third, and finally, the form of Davidson's argument seems in fact to give a certain priority to reliability, since the way it tries to sustain coherence is by showing it to be an intellectual virtue, a reliable source of truth. By its very form the argument therefore at least suggests reliability as epistemologically most basic, inasmuch as even coherence is to be validated by reference to it.[3]

D *Conclusion*

Having first distinguished two branches of epistemology, the practical and the theoretical, we then connected the two by considering the organon explication of justification: that a belief becomes justified only through the justifying of it by use of an organon. Next we took note of the *intellectualist* view of justification shared by Rorty and Davidson, according to which a belief acquires justification only by the support of argument or reasoning, a view that for some may derive from the organon conception of justification. We examined Davidson's attack on foundationalism, an attack we found based on intellectualism. And we turned finally to Davidson's defense of coherentism by a double-threaded argument that intertwines assumptions about (a) the nature of belief and its content, and (b) the charity required for interpretative knowledge of other minds. What is the relevance of that double-threaded argument to holding up

---

[3] This even if by arguing thus one secures the *coherence* within one's world view of the claim that coherence is reliable.

coherence as against its rivals, especially reliability? In conclusion that seemed surprisingly occult.[4]

---

[4] I do not deny the truth of Davidson's main positive conclusions nor the suggestiveness and value of his main arguments. I agree on the importance of coherence for epistemology, and I agree especially on the necessity to argue that coherence is bound to be reliable and an intellectual virtue. Indeed I have myself argued elsewhere for these same conclusions: cf. 'The Coherence of Virtue and the Virtue of Coherence', in the forthcoming proceedings of the naturalized epistemology conference held by the History and Philosophy of Science Department of the University of Pittsburgh in the spring of 1981, edited by Peter Machamer, *Synthese* (1985).

My thanks to Gerald Barnes for his commentary at the Davidson Conference, and to the Rutger's philosophical community for helpful discussion at my pre-Conference seminar on Davidson's epistemology based on an earlier version of this paper.

22

The Third Dogma

ROBERT KRAUT

Kant tried to articulate the basic features essential to any possible object of empirical knowledge. Such a project might have been wrong-headed, deriving from an illegitimate model of the mind and its activity, and from an equally illegitimate faith in the presence of a priori constraints, invariant across discourses, governing the concept of an object. A theory of Categories – a theory, that is, which delineates the general concepts under which the mind necessarily subsumes its objects – is surely doomed from the start. For once we endow the experiencing mind with a categorial structure – a hierarchy of general predicates necessarily applicable to any object of any cognitive attitude – we embrace the spectre of a priori knowledge (grounded in the categorial structure of the mind), and of Cartesian certainty about the output of the mind's synthesizing activity. Such epistemic consequences surely constitute a formidable *reductio* to any possible theory of Categories.

One is inclined to say, with Richard Rorty, that Kant should have talked about sentences rather than inner representations; that Kant confused predication with synthesis; that the Kantian distinction between sensory intuitions and a priori concepts makes sense only within an implausible explanatory theory.[1] And, with Rorty, we may condemn Kant's view that diversity is *found* in experience, whereas unity is imposed on experience; for such a view is simply a vestige of Locke's blundering. All these criticisms and puzzles lead one to suspect that, *pace* Kant, objects of cognition are not constructed (synthesized, constituted, etc.) out of more basic items (whether simple representations, intuitions, or whatever). Thus any attempt to isolate the basic rules of construction is bound to fail.

Some of the ideas discussed in this paper were first introduced in a seminar on Objects and Attitudes which I taught at the University of Pittsburgh in winter 1983; I am grateful to the participants in that seminar for valuable discussion. My greatest debt is to Charles David McCarty, with whom I discussed these issues in considerable depth, and whose comments and criticisms were invaluable.

[1] Richard Rorty, *Philosophy and the Mirror of Nature* (Princeton University Press, Princeton, 1979), ch. 3.

Well, that's one way to look at things. But there is an opposing sentiment, one which finds attractiveness in the idea that people somehow 'constitute' the objects of which they speak. For example: Ian Hacking, echoing Foucault, suggests that 'attempting to understand how objects constitute themselves in discourse must be a central topic of the theory of knowledge.'[2] Gabbay and Moravcsik, concerned with individuation and identity, claim that 'the objects of science and everyday experience are *constructions*, and these constructions require the understanding of the general terms under which the objects are subsumed ... particulars do not come "ready-made" as parts of the domain of discourse.'[3] Later they say

> These elements [out of which objects are constructed] are not objects of scientific or everyday experience. Rather, they are infinitesimal 'parts' that underlie whatever construction determines a range of objects acknowledged in science or by common sense. In this way, this domain on the first level resembles Aristotle's prime matter.[4]

In a similar spirit, Jaakko Hintikka, the neo-Kantian of semantic theory, provides an elegant semantic account of the epistemic modalities, according to which objects of knowledge (and other attitudes) are treated as 'constructions' out of more basic individuals. The principles of construction are embodied in 'individuating functions', in terms of which we cross-identify and unify members of different 'possible worlds'.[5]

Thus we have here a major dilemma. On the one hand, there are compelling indictments against certain traditional distinctions, viz., spontaneity vs. receptivity, the given vs. the fabricated in experience, the active vs. the passive faculties of mind, questions of meaning vs. questions of fact. Rorty goes so far as to say that 'without the notions of "the given" and of "the a priori" there can be no notion of "the constitution of experience."'[6] But, on the other hand, there is all the exciting talk about objects as constructions. Are objects of experience, or objects of discourse, or objects *simpliciter*, somehow constituted by the knowing mind, or by the community, or by the discourse? What reason might there be for thinking so? What sorts of phenomena are best understood and explained in terms of the constructionist picture?

Wherever there's talk about the constitution of objects, or about the construction of objects out of ontologically more basic entities (whether sense-data, properties, molecule moments or space-time points), there's bound to be talk of conceptual schemes. Such schemes embody the rules or principles of construction in terms of which the more simple elements – whatever they may be – are unified or synthesized into the kinds of objects we ordinarily

---

[2] Ian Hacking, 'Michel Foucault's Immature Science', *Nous*, 13 (March 1979), p. 51.

[3] D. Gabbay and J. M. Moravcsik, 'Sameness and Individuation', *Journal of Philosophy*, 70 (September 1973), pp. 513–26.

[4] Ibid., p. 523.

[5] See, e.g., Jaakko Hintikka, *Models For Modalities* (D. Reidel, Dordrecht, Holland, 1969); Jaakko Hintikka, *Intentions of Intentionality and Other New Models For Modalities* (D. Reidel, Dordrecht, Holland, 1975).

[6] Richard Rorty, 'The World Well Lost', reprinted in his *Consequences of Pragmatism* (University of Minnesota Press, Minneapolis, 1982), p. 5.

experience and discourse about. Thus any attack on the idea of a conceptual
scheme is likely to be an attack on the correlative notion of construction.

Donald Davidson has questioned the utility, and the very intelligibility, of the
idea of a conceptual scheme. Doubting that we can make good sense of the idea
that there are (or could be) seriously divergent total conceptual schemes, he
says

> I want to urge that this second dualism of scheme and content, of organizing
> system and something waiting to be organized, cannot be made intelligible and
> defensible. It is itself a dogma of empiricism, the third dogma.[7]

Much depends on how we take the phrase 'something waiting to be organized'.
In one obvious sense, the *world* is waiting to be organized, and sentient beings,
armed with interests and taxonomies, carve up the environment into nomologically viable classes. Thus construed, the scheme-content dualism is simply the
dualism of world (which consists of items in principle representable via beliefs,
desires, and perceptions) vs. the representational apparatus itself (whether
linguistic, psychological, or artistic). Content is what is represented; scheme is
how it is represented. This dualism, between representational acts and their
immanent objects ('represent*ings*') vs. the items toward which such acts are
intentionally directed ('represent*eds*') is surely indispensable to all, save an
occasional idealist or textualist.

On another reading, the 'something waiting to be organized' corresponds to a
domain of simple representations, Kantian intuitions, which fall somehow
between the world and our full-blown representations of it. On this construal,
what waits to be organized is the common observational given, upon which all
theories of the world ultimately depend – both causally and for their epistemic
justification ('grounding'). On this latter reading, rejection of the scheme-
content dualism is simply rejection of what Sellars has dubbed the 'Myth of the
Given'.

There are perhaps other construals of 'something waiting to be organized', in
which case there are further interpretations of Davidson's indictments. It is
obviously important to get clear about precisely who the enemy is, and to see
whether the Constructionist Ontologist, some of whose sentiments were voiced
at the outset, need despair. Perhaps some variants of the scheme-content
distinction can be sustained, despite Davidson's arguments.

I

Davidson's rejection of the conceptual-scheme idea involves subtle connections
among the concepts of interpretation, translation, truth, reference, and observationality. Here is a schematic overview of his arguments:

---

[7] Donald Davidson, 'On the Very Idea of a Conceptual Scheme', reprinted in Meiland and
Krausz (eds), *Relativism: Cognitive and Moral* (University of Notre Dame Press, Indiana, 1982),
p. 72.

Objection 1. Suppose we associate having a language with having a conceptual scheme; conceptual schemes might then be viewed as sets of intertranslatable languages. Different conceptual schemes, then, would correspond to languages between which translation is not possible. But it is hard to make sense of a total failure of translatability between languages: 'nothing, it may be said, could count as evidence that some form of activity could not be interpreted in our language that was not at the same time evidence that that form of activity was not speech behavior ... [this amounts to] making translatability into a familiar tongue a criterion of languagehood.'[8] Thus, Davidson's objection to the notion of an untranslatable language grounds this portion of his indictment against conceptual schemes.

Objection 2. The scheme-content dichotomy is intimately related to the dichotomy between analytic and synthetic truths; sentences guaranteed true by the structure of the scheme are true purely on the basis of meaning, rather than on the basis of empirical fact. But this is an untenable dualism, and thus any other dualism which embraces it is thereby tainted.

Objection 3. The dualism of scheme and content presupposes a 'common something', a scheme-independent stuff, which alternative schemes somehow organize (or confront, or cope with, or systematize, etc.): 'It is essential to this idea that there be something neutral and common that lies outside all schemes.'[9] Quite apart from the implausibility of such a *ding an sich*, which can't possibly play a useful explanatory role, there is another problem: 'This common something cannot, of course, be the *subject matter* of contrasting languages, or translation would be possible.'[10] So: either translation succeeds or it fails. If it succeeds, we conclude that the one language is a notational variant of the other, using unfamiliar words to express the same concepts. If translation fails, then by (1) above, there's no inclination to impute any conceptual scheme at all (for we don't seem to be dealing with linguistic behavior at all). Here is how Davidson expresses the dilemma:

> if translation succeeds, we have shown there is no need to speak of two conceptual schemes, while if translation fails, there is no ground for speaking of two. If I am right then, there never can be a situation in which we can intelligibly compare or contrast divergent schemes, and in that case we do better not to say that there is one scheme, as if we understood what it would be like for there to be more.[11]

Objection 4. Those in the clutches of the scheme idea (call such people 'schemers') are in the throes of either of two images or metaphors to which they frequently resort. But we cannot provide rigorous cash for these metaphors while retaining the excitement of the scheme idea.

---

[8] Ibid., p. 68.
[9] Ibid., p. 72.
[10] Ibid.
[11] Donald Davidson, 'Reply to Solomon', in *Essays on Actions and Events* (Clarendon Press, Oxford, 1980), p. 243.

(a)   First metaphor:

		uninterpreted content
	organize	the stream of experience
conceptual schemes	systematize	the given
	divide up	surface irritations
		the world

Objection: you can't organize a single object unless it's already partitioned into other objects. 'We cannot attach a clear meaning to the notion of organizing a single object (the world, nature, etc.) unless that object is understood to contain or consist in other objects. Someone who sets out to organize a closet arranges [not the closet itself but] the things in it.'[12] But any two languages which organize the same items must, Davidson thinks, have at least some common ontological core. So if they organize the same entities they must at least talk about the same entities, but this in turn allows for intertranslatability, thus undermining the ascription of alternative schemes. Though the predicates of one language might not line up straightforwardly with those of the other, there must be 'an ontology common to the two languages, with concepts that individuate the same objects'.[13] Any translational breakdowns must be merely local, since without a background of generally successful translation such failures would make no sense.

Upshot: the metaphor of language organizing the closet of nature can't be coherently conjoined with any criterion of language-hood that fails to entail translatability.

(b)   Second metaphor:

language	fits	
(the conceptual scheme)	faces	experience
	copes with	the world
	predicts	nerve hits
		etc.

Objection: this transition from the metaphor of organization to that of fitting or coping with, moves us from considerations about referential apparatus to whole sentences. It is sentences, rather than terms, which predict, deal with things, get disconfirmed by evidence, face the tribunal of experience as a corporate body, and so on. But to say that the sentences of some theory T fit all the possible sensory evidence (actual, possible, present and future) seems to say little more than that T is true. If this is right, then the claim that T1 and T2 both fit the evidence but in different ways amounts to the claim that T1 and T2 are both largely true; and if they embrace different schemes, then presumably translation fails (if only locally). The 'fitting' metaphor tries to get by with truth and without translation; but we cannot divorce the notion of truth from that of translation. So this metaphor either sacrifices intelligibility, by severing truth from translation, or it sacrifices excitement, since it says no more than that theories couched in different languages can be true.

---

12 'On the Very Idea of a Conceptual Scheme', p. 74.
13 Ibid., p. 74.

The general upshot of all this is that, given the methodology of interpretation, 'we could not be in a position to judge that others had concepts or beliefs radically different from our own.'[14] There is, however, more to be said on both sides of the issue.

II

In a discussion of Davidson's argument, Nicholas Rescher objects that Davidson leans too heavily upon the claim that translatability into our own language is a criterion for something's being a language, and thus for the presence of a conceptual scheme.[15] We should, he urges, insist only upon *interpretability*, a weaker requirement. But Rescher ignores the fact that for Davidson, this claim is *not* an a priori constraint on languagehood; rather, it emerges as the conclusion of an argument. The problem with untranslatable languages is that they threaten the connection between the notion of translation and the notion of truth. We cannot, as noted above, understand truth independent of translation; and we cannot understand the imputation of a theory to someone without at the same time accepting that most of the sentences which constitute the theory are true. Thus, for Davidson, the notion of a true but largely untranslatable theory strains at our very idea of truth.

At one point, Davidson offers us

> a formula for generating distinct conceptual schemes. We get a new out of an old scheme when the speakers of a language come to accept as true an important range of sentences they previously took to be false (and, of course, vice versa.)[16]

Rescher objects to this 'formula'. Different conceptual schemes don't, he says, simply redistribute truth values over the class of sentences held true-or-false; 'differentiation of conceptual schemes does not lie in different allocations of the determinate truth-values T and F.'[17] Rather, speakers in one scheme embrace sentences to which the others would assign no truth value at all. The key to scheme differentiation, Rescher urges, lies in the 'non-overlap of theses' – the fact that what can be said by one is simply outside the range of the other. Rescher reminds us that Caesar neither held true nor held false the translational counterparts of sentences which we accept about the half-life of Californium, or about the electrical conductivity of carbon. Rescher worries about Davidson's very characterization of what a divergence of conceptual scheme would look like.

How is the notion of conceptual scheme supposed to play a useful explanatory role here? We may grant that Caesar neither held true nor held false the sentence 'Swords contain carbon, and they conduct electricity,' or any translational counterpart. One might try to explain this important difference

---

14 Ibid., p. 79.
15 Nicholas Rescher, 'Conceptual Schemes', in French, Uehling and Wettstein (eds), *Midwest Studies in Philosophy Volume V* (*Studies in Epistemology*) (University of Minnesota Press, Minneapolis, 1980), pp. 323–45.
16 'On the Very Idea of a Conceptual Scheme', p. 70.
17 Rescher, 'Conceptual Schemes', p. 332.

between Caesar and ourselves, by claiming that his conceptual scheme is interestingly divergent from our own – that's why he can't formulate, much less assent to, such sentences. But in saying that his conceptual scheme is distinct from ours, what do we thereby *add* to the bare behavioristic claim that he fails to hold true (or false) any such sentences? We may grant that Caesar lacks the concept of molecular structure, of electricity, of voltage potential. But this is only to say that there is a range of sentences toward which he is disposed to offer neither acceptance nor rejection. Analogy: Quine argues that the appeal to convention cannot account for knowledge of logic or mathematics. The thesis of conventionalism adds nothing to the behavioristic claim that certain statements are firmly accepted. Just so, the appeal to divergent schemes cannot account for Caesar's acceptance, rejection, or impotence with respect to any class of sentences. It is incumbent upon Rescher to show that the scheme idea can turn any explanatory wheels in connection with Davidson's data base: i.e., the class of sentences held true by a person. Of course, to say that Caesar has a different conceptual scheme might simply be to say that there is a noteworthy disparity between the class of sentences we hold true, and the class of sentences (suitably interpreted) he holds true. But this, as Davidson notes, doesn't retain the excitement in the scheme idea. The schemer wants something more than mere disparity between classes of sentences held true.

There is another way to make the same point. Traditionally, to have a concept is to have an ability – an ability to think of a quality, relation, or kind. We may say, in more modern dress, that concept possession is an ability to use a piece of language properly. Caesar couldn't properly use the word 'electricity', or any functional equivalent. But – and here we encounter the relevant Fregean thesis – only in the context of a sentence does a word have any meaning. Caesar learns to use the word by learning to make true assertions which contain the word. *Ex hypothesi*, Caesar lacks the relevant sentential skills. Thus he lacks the appropriate concepts. The appeal to an alternative scheme does not usefully explain this sentential impotence on his part. Don't say: he doesn't have attitudes toward such sentences because he lacks the relevant concepts. That's true, in a way, but not useful; for his lacking the concept amounts to his lacking the disposition to have attitudes toward such sentences. The imputation of an alternative conceptual scheme to Caesar *presupposes*, rather than explains, Caesar's impoverished sentential attitudes.

Rescher is right to insist that sentences formulable in one discourse might not be formulable in another, and that conceptual-scheme variation might demand more than a person's holding true a sentence that another holds false. But, I urge, it must be shown how considerations of this kind bear upon a language's referential apparatus (singular terms, quantifiers, the identity predicate) if we are to appreciate what the schemer is trying to capture.

III

In 'Ontological Relativity', Quine entertains a possibility which smacks of scheming. Quine's discussion may enable us to learn more, both about Davidson's qualms, and about the sorts of considerations which lead one to scheme.

We cannot know what something is without knowing how it is marked off from other things. Identity is thus of a piece with ontology. Accordingly it is involved in the same relativity [i.e. relativity to a background theory, and relativity to a choice of translation manual] as may be readily illustrated. Imagine a fragment of economic theory. Suppose its universe comprises persons, but its predicates are incapable of distinguishing between persons whose incomes are equal. The interpersonal relation of equality of income enjoys, within the theory, the substitutivity property of the identity relation itself; the two relations are indistinguishable. It is only relative to a background theory, in which more can be said of personal identity than equality of income, that we are able even to appreciate the above account of the fragment of economic theory, hinging as the account does on a contrast between persons and incomes.[18]

This suggestion calls for several comments.

It is not clear, given the expressive resources attributed to this economic theory, that we ought to regard its 'universe' as consisting of persons. *Ex hypothesi*, there is no open sentence constructible in the theory which is satisfied by one person but fails to be satisfied by any other person with the same income. What sense can be made, then, of the claim that the theory is properly treated as being about *persons*? Better to treat the theory as being about income groups – equivalence classes of persons *modulo* income. To treat the theory as being about persons is to endow it with more descriptive and discriminative capability than it has. Quine insists that knowing what something is requires a knowledge of 'how it is marked off from other things.' My suggestion is similar: a theory is not plausibly treated as containing singular terms which refer to Øs unless that theory offers the descriptive apparatus for discriminating among distinct Øs. This is a constraint upon interpretation: the referential apparatus of a language should not introduce a realm of items which are indiscernible relative to the expressive resources of that language. In Quine's envisaged fragment of economic theory (call it ET) we could not construct any open sentence satisfied by Jones and not by Smith, if indeed Smith and Jones have the same yearly income. Nor, for that matter, can we construct any open sentence in two free variables satisfied by Smith and Jones in one order but not in the other (this would render them discriminable, even if not uniquely specifiable, relative to ET's resources).[19] If the identity predicate is defined in terms of the familiar Leibniz-Russell schema, and the predicate variables are restricted to those properties expressible in the language (so that identity becomes a matter of indiscernibility relative to the theory), then sentences like 'Smith = Jones' will be true in ET; the theory will have no way of discriminating them. What sense could we make of the claim, then, that some sentence of ET is about Smith rather than Jones? And if we cannot make sense of such claims, importing Smith into the interpretive domain for ET would at best be gratuitous; it would also be misleading.

[18] W. V. Quine, 'Ontological Relativity', in his *Ontological Relativity and Other Essays* (Columbia University Press, New York, 1969), p. 55.

[19] There are, Quine has noted, several non-equivalent ways of characterizing the notion of discriminability relative to a language. Items may, for example, be 'moderately discriminable' in L if L contains a sentence in two variables which they satisfy in one order but not in the other; yet the items may fail to be 'strongly discriminable' if there is no sentence in one variable which is satisfied by the one item but not by the other. For illustrations and further discussion, see Quine's 'Grades of Discriminability', *Journal of Philosophy*, 73 (1976), pp. 113–16.

Quine saw this in earlier writings. In 'Identity, Ostension, and Hypostasis', where the example was first introduced, he says 'Our discourse is simplified, then, by shifting its subject matter from person stages to income groups. Distinctions immaterial to the discourse at hand are thus extruded from the subject matter.'[20] Here we see at work what Quine calls the maxim of the *identification of indiscernibles*:

> Objects indistinguishable from one another within the terms of a given discourse should be construed as identical for that discourse. More accurately: the references to the original objects should be reconstrued for purposes of the discourse as referring to other and fewer objects, in such a way that indistinguishable originals give way each to the same new object.[21]

This has enormous ontological significance; for, in designating the interpretive domain (the subject matter) of a given theory, we must pay attention to the store of predicates – the expressive and discriminative resources – of the theory.

A natural metaphor forces itself upon us. We begin with a domain of persons. We find that persons with the same yearly income are indiscernible relative to a certain theory. We may say that our own partitioning of the universe is somehow not respected by the theory – it is, after all, a rather impoverished theory. Perhaps such a theory could not constitute the entirety of a living organism's stock of sentences held true; Quine does, after all, describe it as a *fragment* of an economic theory. But the scheme-content way of talking is useful here. The content is contributed by our own scheme: a domain of persons, some of whom fall into the same income group. But the envisaged economic theory looks at the world through spectacles of lesser resolving power, unable to see where Jones ends and his equal-incomed counterpart begins. There is no appeal here to a neutral, scheme independent given. There is, rather, appeal to the way we talk about the world, and, against that backdrop, to the way another theory talks about it.

Is ET about the same world that we usually talk about? Of course it is. But there is a difference here which makes a difference. The objects of which ET speaks – the values of its variables, the *denotata* of its singular terms – are not those of which our background theory speaks. For ET lacks the resolving power, the expressive structure, required to make such references.

This example suggests an intimate connection between ontology, the subject matter of a discourse, and ideology, the store of predicables available in that discourse. Quine urges that we do not learn first what to talk about and then what to say about it.[22] I agree; and I urge that radical interpretation recapitulates phylogeny: we do not learn first what someone is talking about and then what he is saying about it. Those who lack certain descriptive resources – those for whom certain sentences are not formulable – are incapable of making references to certain kinds of things.

---

[20] W. V. Quine, 'Identity, Ostension, and Hypostasis', in *From A Logical Point of View* (Harper and Row, New York, 1961), p. 71.

[21] Ibid.

[22] See W. V. Quine, *Word and Object* (MIT Press, Cambridge, Massachusetts, 1960), p. 16.

We could use here, if so inclined, at least one sort of metaphor which Davidson dismisses. A conceptual scheme organizes items that are waiting to be organized. In the present case, the items in question are persons. To say that ET imposes some systematization, or division, or organization, over this class, is to say that the expressions of ET gerrymander the class, and take no single member of it as denotation. ET 'looks out' at a class of discriminable objects – discriminable to us. Because of a paucity of descriptive resources in the language defined by ET, structure is somehow lost, and this emerges in connection with the schemes of reference which may plausibly be defined over the language. Quine speaks as though the principle of identification of indiscernibles is a useful maxim of interpretation; I am claiming that it is a necessity. The ascription of ontology to a discourse must take account of the expressive power of the discourse, since reference demands at least rudimentary discriminability.

It might be urged that whatever version of the scheme-content distinction is at work here is *not* the one with which Davidson is concerned. For he says 'It is essential to this idea that there be something neutral and common that lies outside all schemes.' The class of persons, which we construed as constituting the content which gets 'organized' by ET (in the sense that it is the initial interpretive domain in terms of which we try to understand ET) is in *no* sense common stuff which lies outside all schemes. It is, rather, the ontology dictated by our mother tongue. I know of no other way to begin. Had I been a crass physicalist, wedded to the explanatory adequacy of microparticles. I might have begun with an ontology of mass points. In that case, a parallel interpretive problem would have emerged, since precious few discourses are likely to demand an ontology of mass points, given their descriptive and discriminative resources.

So: either I've changed the subject, by switching to a scheme-content model which demands no scheme-neutral invariants across all discourses, or else Davidson has placed an unreasonably strong demand on the scheme idea. The point so far is a modest one: one can do something that looks suspiciously like scheming, while remaining opposed to a scheme-transcendent *urstoff* into which all languages *must* be interpreted.

I have not mobilized here any concept of reference with which Davidson would find fault. We begin with those sentences constructible in the language of ET. We then need an interpretive theory; this can take the form of a recursive account of the truth conditions of the sentences. These conditions are explicated in terms of the semantical features of subsentential components. A way to achieve this end is to define a scheme of reference for the language, which specifies denotations for singular terms and extensions for predicate expressions. This 'relation' of reference can be treated as a theoretical or auxiliary relation, legitimized solely by its capacity to provide a holistically adequate account of truth conditions for all the sentences in the language. The primary object of our concern was the sentential capacities of the language of ET; but these impoverished capacities placed constraints on the class of plausible reference schemes. There are, of course, rival schemes, schemes which treat singular terms as referring to persons and '=' as expressing some equivalence relation other than 'genuine identity'. But at least some of these rival schemes violate the maxim of identification of indiscernibles, to which we are here committed. No commitment to semantical holism, which urges that truth is the prior notion in terms of which radical interpretation proceeds, rules out anything said thus far. Only in the context of certain expressive and discriminative resources can a word have a certain reference. No singular term in our envisaged language of ET can plausibly be construed as referring to a person. Certain reference schemes, then, which depend for their plausibility upon the availability of certain expressive power, should not be imposed upon certain languages – else we should be guilty of having decided what a language talks about prior to having decided what it is capable of saying about it. The envisaged case is not one of radical incommensurability; we've obviously managed to line up a substantial number of predicate expressions from one language to the other. The disparity in question is thus local, presupposing no radical failure of translation. We may insist with Davidson that local break-downs require a background of generally successful translation. At least initially, we were willing to treat the language of ET as sharing an ontology with us (witness Quine's initial claim that the universe of ET 'comprises persons'). It was when we discovered that 'x makes the same amount of money as y' was a congruence relation in the language of ET – an equivalence relation which confers substitutivity – that we changed our minds about the ontology of ET. Our final decision, to shift from persons to 'income groups', involved a theoretical verdict of some moment.

Whatever version of the scheme-content distinction we've got here is itself theory-relative; for the content with which we began our interpretive enterprise was dictated by our own preferred way of talking about things. The content is in no way 'uninterpreted' *simpliciter*; it is, however, uninterpreted relative to the ideology of ET, in the sense that no item distinguishable from its same-incomed counterparts is treated as the referent of any singular term in that discourse.

Thus we have some vindication of the 'scheme organizing the world' metaphor, since we found it useful in the context of a legitimate semantical inquiry, found that it commits us to no untenable dogmas, and even located a reasonably exciting connection between ontology and the expressive power of a discourse.

Michael Dummett makes a quite similar point in some of his earlier work. In 'Nominalism' he says

> If someone says, 'This is red,' but his language is too poor for him to understand the question 'This what?' it is senseless to ask whether 'red' was a name or a predicate. If he can answer the question, if he says, e.g., 'This flower,' 'red' was a predicate, but if he says, 'This color,' it was a name. The use of general nouns like 'flower' and 'color' (as opposed to adjectives) involves the use of 'same' (in the context of 'same flower' or 'same color'). The use of a proper name, like 'red' as the name of a color, presupposes an understanding of a general noun such as 'color'. The use of 'red' as a predicate presupposes the use of some noun like 'flower'. What is used as a criterion for *identity* of color is used as a criterion for the obtaining of the relation of being like-colored between, e.g., flowers.[23]

---

[23] Michael Dummett, 'Nominalism', *The Philosophical Review*, 65 (1956); reprinted in E. D. Klemke (ed.), *Essays on Frege* (Illinois Press, Illinois, 1968), p. 330.

The ontological punchline for all this emerges in an extremely insightful (though fairly murky) passage:

> By a 'particular' I understand an object of a kind such that we do not speak of objects of any kind such that the criterion for the obtaining of some equivalence relation between objects of this latter kind coincides with the criterion of identity for objects of the former kind. Whether or not objects of a given kind are particulars is relative to the language in question: I hold that there is no kind of objects such that they must be particulars relative to every possible language.[24]

This provides a non-trivial, and fairly exciting, respect in which particulars may be said to be 'constituted by a discourse': no entity without identity, no identity without the resources for expressing the criteria of identity. The distinction between scheme and content corresponds to the distinction between someone's individuative/discriminative resources and those resources we employ – at least initially – in providing an account of their language. Here, then, is a methodological moral: the scheme-content distinction need not be thought of as the implementation of an outmoded and misguided epistemological theory. In fact, it need not be the implementation of an epistemological theory at all. The matter at hand is ontology, as dictated by a plausible semantical theory. Our metaphysical method is the method of truth. Davidson reminds us that

> what appear to be singular terms sometimes melt into something less ontic in implication when their logical relations with other sentences are studied, while the requirements of theory may suggest that a sentence plays a role which can be explained only by treating it as having a quantificational structure not apparent on the surface.[25]

Part of my point is that this wisdom cuts both ways. Scheming is the natural manifestation of a willingness to acknowledge alternative ontologies, as spawned by alternative expressive resources.

There are at least two kinds of criticism, intimately related, which might be offered by the anti-schemer at this point:

(1) Dummett's poor devil, too stupid and ill equipped to distinguish among like-colored items, and Quine's envisaged economic theorist who cannot discriminate among persons with the same yearly income, are unrealistic idealizations. Neither ET nor the theory of colors can constitute the entirety of any agent's linguistic resources – for, in each case, we've left out something which is needed to make sense of the rest. The concept of a person is essential to making sense of ET; the concept of a colored item (a flower or a pool of liquid) is essential to making sense of Dummett's flower-blind color freak.

---

[24] Ibid., p. 336. Thus we might say that the very concept of an *object* is itself relative to a discourse. One consequence of this approach, which derives some inspiration from Geach's views on 'relative identity', is that the notion of *rigid designation* might best be understood not in terms of identity, but rather in terms of indiscernibility relative to a particular discourse. For a detailed examination of this approach and its consequences, see Robert Kraut, 'Indiscernibility and Ontology', *Synthese*, 44 (1980), pp. 113–35.

[25] Donald Davidson, 'The Method of Truth in Metaphysics', in French, Uehling and Wettstein (eds) *Contemporary Perspectives in the Philosophy of Language* (University of Minnesota Press, Minneapolis, 1981), p. 301.

Such an objection is suggested by Davidson's own reply to the obvious criticism that he himself is committed to alternative conceptual frameworks, viz., commonsense psychology and mathematical physics. For the predicates of the one framework are nomologically irreducible to those of the other, yet in some cases they characterize the very same events (hence anomalous monism). But mathematical physics, according to Davidson, could not constitute the entirety of someone's language: 'We cannot conceive a language without psychological terms or expressions – there would be no way to translate it into our own language.'[26] Our own examples perhaps make the mistake of leaving concepts out which are 'needed to make sense of the rest'.

But needed by *whom* to make sense of the rest? The interpreter, or the envisaged speaker? Can't we make sense of an outlaw community of Rortyian eliminative materialists, who have systematically purged their language of mental predicates? Can't we grasp Sellars' myth about a community of Rylean behaviorists who lack the concept of an inner private mental episode, but who possess instead semantical concepts relating to the functional roles played by bits of language? Against this latter backdrop, according to Sellars' story, the genius Jones introduced the theoretical notion of an inner episode, a *thought*, modelled on overt verbal behavior.[27] In time (the story goes), psychological discourse comes to play a reporting as well as an explanatory role.

The point is this: as controversial as Sellars' account of the relation between psychological and semantical discourse might be, it is nonetheless intelligible. Perhaps, on closer scrutiny, it isn't clear that we really can envisage such non-standard and attenuated conceptual repertoires; but neither is it clear that we can't. Translation would take us from their language to a proper sub-part of our own. It thus remains to be shown that the envisaged languages cannot endure as autonomous wholes.

(2) The second possible objection is intimately related to the first, but easier to get a grip on: we are envisaging schemes of reference which embody an ontology other than our own. The kinds of schemes advocated here, in which people 'slice the pie of reality' one way rather than another, will, of course, affect the intepretation of the predicates. For what touches the extensions of singular terms touches everything; we can no longer, after applying the identification of indiscernibles, treat any predicate in ET as having a certain set of persons as its extension – for we have, in effect, purged the interpretive domain of persons, substituting income groups. What, then, can ET's predicates have in common with our own? And, if nothing, how can we so smugly claim to have been able to interpret ET's discriminative resources? Our earlier interpretation, following the introduction of the revised reference scheme, seems to have fallen apart in our hands. We've been, in effect, advocating the motto 'No ontology without adequate ideology.' But our critic reminds us that the reverse is equally true. You can't get a grip on the aliens' predicates unless their extensions have something in common with the extensions of your predicates.

---

[26] Davidson, 'Reply to Solomon', p. 244.
[27] See Wilfrid Sellars, 'Empiricism and the Philosophy of Mind', reprinted in his *Science, Perception, and Reality* (Routledge and Kegan Paul, London, 1963), sect. VI.

The reply to this simply shifts the onus: we motivated each of our envisaged cases of expressive weakness by invoking equivalence classes *modulo* those properties expressible in the languages. The originally imputed ontology – whether persons or flowers – worked well enough to get radical interpretation off the ground, until we felt qualms, in light of inferential data, about having imported unwarranted descriptive structure into the language. At this point, we revised the ontology. Whether the subsequent mandated revision in the extensions of predicates brings unintelligibility in its wake remains to be shown.

IV

I turn now to another metaphor, that of languages or theories 'carving up' the environment. What sense can be made of it? In what contexts is it useful to talk this way?

To see that the scheme-content idea naturally arises, quite independent of any commitment to phenomenalism, pure observationality, or the distinction between matters of fact and matters of language, consider a recent discussion of Davidson's anomalous monism. In 'Weak Supervenience', John Haugeland argues that one can preserve intuitions about the 'primacy of the physical' – in the sense that fixing the physical truths fixes all the others, including those of psychology – without embracing any token–token identity thesis concerning physical events and mental events.[28] The claim is that psychological theory may *supervene* upon mathematical physics, without thereby generating identities between mental and physical events. I am not concerned here with Haugeland's reasons for rejecting Davidson's version of token identity; I am rather concerned with the notion of supervenience advocated, and the way it naturally leads to the scheme idea.

Let us say that a theory T2 (e.g., psychology) supervenes upon a theory T1 (e.g., mathematical physics) if and only if the following condition is met:

Any two worlds which are indiscernible relative to T1 are indiscernible relative to T2.

What we actually have in mind here is indiscernibility relative to the language in which the respective theories are formulated – the language of mental-state ascriptions and the language of mathematical physics, in this case. For brevity I speak simply of 'T1 indiscernibility'; two possible worlds are *T1 indiscernible* iff there is no sentence formulable in T1 vocabulary which is true in one world but false in the other. We might also describe the supervenience relation thus: T2 supervenes on T1 iff the world cannot alter in some T2 respect without altering in some T1 respect also.

Haugeland argues that one can consistently claim that T2 supervenes upon T1 without holding that the entities of which T2 speaks are the very same entities as those of which T1 speaks. As he puts it, 'weak supervenience is

---

[28] John Haugeland, 'Weak Supervenience', *American Philosophical Quarterly*, volume 19, no. 1 (January 1982) pp. 93–103.

compatible with the denial of the token-identity thesis.'[29] If this is right, then we can capture our intuition that physics has 'primacy' over psychology, without holding that mental events are identical with physical events.

I do not want to argue about the joint tenability of these positions, or about whether the token-identity thesis ought to be rejected on independent grounds. I want only to call attention to certain 'metaphysical' intuitions which, Haugeland thinks, ought to be captured by any account of the relation between certain theories:

> Just as objectors to so-called type identity theories urge that physics need not capture how the mental is 'carved up' into kinds, I urge that it need not capture how the mental is 'carved up' into individuals. The essential constraint is on sets of *truths*, without regard to how (or even whether) those truths are decomposed into properties of individuals.[30]

His conclusion, which is very similar in spirit to one I advocated earlier, is this:

> the individuals, or 'tokens,' of which our sentences are true are just as 'relative' to the level of description as are the kinds or 'types' into which those sentences sort them. The world does not come metaphysically individuated, any more than it comes metaphysically categorized, prior to and independent of any specific description resources ... the individuals we can discuss in one way of talking need not be identified with the individuals we can discuss in another way of talking, even if the latter way of talking is somehow 'basic and comprehensive.'[31]

This is fine, so far as it goes; but an important part of the story has been left out. For there is the requirement that T1 and T2 be interpretable at the worlds in question, i.e., that the truth conditions of T1 sentences and T2 sentences be recursively specifiable.

The intuitive picture we get is that there is some kind of neutral material ('the world') which serves as a model of both T1 and T2. The sentences of both theories *must* be interpretable over the same worlds; the subsentential components might, however, gerrymander their way around in the world differently, both on the level of 'kinds' (general terms) and on the level of 'tokens' (individual singular terms). But what is the stuff of which the models (of both the physical and the psychological truths) are made? What is the composition of the worlds which are such that

> any two worlds (of some set W of possible worlds) discernible with T2 are discernible with T1?

This is required for the account of 'supervenience' which Haugeland advocates. What else can the possible worlds in question be, but sets of individuals with relations defined over them? The interpretability of T1 and T2 demands a recursive specification of 'truth relative to a world w'. At this point we need a

---

[29] Ibid., p. 97.
[30] Ibid.
[31] Ibid., p. 101.

scheme of reference, as well as all the other apparatus needed to make the recursions go. What sorts of events should we populate our worlds with? We do not want to populate each world with two disjoint domains – a domain of mental events and a domain of physical events – for this would undermine Haugeland's intuition (which I share) that it is somehow the same world which is getting 'carved up' differently by the two theories or languages. Disjoint classes of events, in addition to making the metaphor of 'carving' totally inappropriate, would leave it mysterious *why* the relation of supervenience holds between T2 and T1. We are thus driven to populate our worlds with some kind of 'ur-events', in terms of which both theories can be interpreted; then we can talk about T1 and T2 'carving up reality into different kinds and different individuals'. Once we've introduced enough ontology to interpret the theories at each relevant world, we find ourselves talking about *content* – though hardly a theory-independent content – which can be individuated in distinct ways: the mental way (episodes of intending and believing), and the physical way (episodes of variation in the values of physical magnitudes at a region).

Haugeland conducts his discussion on the level of *sentences* ('The essential constraint is on sets of *truths* ...'). But the next step in the inquiry consists in recursively characterizing the notion of truth in terms of theoretical relations like reference. It is when we take this step, from the truth of whole sentences to the referential apparatus in terms of which truth conditions are explained, that we find ourselves talking about 'carving up reality in one way rather than another', 'slicing the world into discriminable and reidentifiable particulars', and the like. These are all metaphors which Davidson finds questionable and of dubious utility. Yet they naturally arise in contexts which seem not to presuppose any of the traditional distinctions to which Davidson objects. What do they mean? At the very least, they express a certain comparison: between the referential resources of one language (e.g. psychology or economic theory) and the referential resources of another (e.g., the commonsense theory of persons, or mathematical physics). If we decided to interpret both T1 and T2 into some more basic domain – e.g. the cumulative hierarchy associated with ZF set theory – then the standard models of ZF would serve as our 'content', in terms of which we would at least try to understand the referential apparatus of T1 and T2. What counts as content, and what counts as scheme, is determined by the standpoint of the interpreter. But this does not invalidate the scheme idea; rather, it *relativizes* it, in much the way that the notion of *observationality* ('the given') is relativized to the linguistic practices of a community.

In his comments on an earlier version of this paper, Lowell Kleiman offers the schemer the following dilemma:

> Either 'content' is independent of 'scheme,' or it is not. If it is, then the world lies outside of all schemes, which is absurd, as Davidson has argued. If not, then there is no need to speak of a scheme at all, as if there were truly more than one. Hence, either the scheme-content way of talking is unintelligible or misleading.[32]

---

[32] Lowell Kleiman, 'Response to Robert Kraut', presented at the Conference in honor of Donald Davidson: New Brunswick, April 1984.

'Independence' is a misleading notion here – 'transcendence' might do better; and the solution to the dilemma is obvious. For what transcends one scheme need not transcend all schemes; items which are, according to some interpretation of an agent's linguistic behavior, out in the world waiting to be represented, are, on some other interpretation, merely artifacts of the representational apparatus itself. (Think of Carnap's systematic denunciation of various ontological claims as merely 'quasi-syntactic claims misleadingly formulated in the material mode of speech' – i.e., as *really* about the linguistic framework by means of which the world gets represented.) If I'm right, the scheme–content distinction is not unlike the 'inside–outside' distinction: it's a genuine distinction, hard to get along without; but it hardly commits us to the existence of a region necessarily excluded from everyone's living space.

V

One sometimes gets the impression that Davidson's objections to the scheme idea – or to one particular variant of it – rest on refusals to take seriously certain ways of thinking about reference. Some pictures of language suggest that the roles of singular terms can be understood in terms of the conditions governing their proper application and reapplication to the environment. We may think of the singular term 'Cayster' as somehow carving out a segregable hunk of the environment; a speaker's grasping the idea of the Cayster is, Quine says, 'an induction: from our grouping the sample momentary objects *a*, *b*, *d*, *g*, and others under the head of Cayster, he projects a correct general hypothesis as to what further momentary objects we would also be content to include.'[33] Here we seem to be speaking, not about the truth conditions of entire sentences, but rather about the reference (application conditions) of a singular term in isolation from other pieces of language. One might be made nervous by this; singular terms are not cookie cutters, used to slice the amorphous dough of reality into discriminable objects of discourse. Surely this way of thinking about the reference of singular terms borders on incoherence. What exactly is the relation? And what are the entities related? And, above all, can this metaphor be construed in terms of a semantical theory which Davidson himself would find congenial?

The picture Quine offers is blatantly constructivist. We begin with an ontology of 'momentary objects': molecule moments, point-events, hunks of matter-time. Time-consuming objects – like rivers, ships, and persons – are to be construed as constructions out of these more basic entities. One knows what a river is, and thus how to properly use the name of a river, if one knows how to tie the basic items together into riverish summations. Had the language been different, we might have tied the momentary objects together into quite different summations, those which we presently regard as unnatural and as not corresponding to a 'well-defined persisting object'. Why might one be led to embrace such a picture?

---

[33] W. V. Quine, 'Identity, Ostension, and Hypostasis', p. 68.

One motivation might be epistemological; we might hold that a person's knowledge of continuants is somehow mediated by, or inferred on the basis of, knowledge of momentary objects. But this is dubious; our observation reports concern rivers, not time-slices of rivers. Moreover, 'grasping the idea of the Cayster' is surely not a mere discriminative recognitional capacity, a matter of being able to volunteer 'Cayster' under the appropriate stimulatory conditions. It's rather a matter of being able to use the expression in true sentences, and to engage in the activity of providing reasons and justifications for sentences in which the expression occurs. Yet even in the face of this kind of sophisticated holism concerning concept possession, there's still something to be said for knowing where the Cayster begins, where it ends, and where it's vague and indeterminate: for we want to know the truth conditions of sentences like 'I've been swimming for three hours, and I'm still in the river Cayster.' So our question remains: we here have a dualism of *scheme* (the principles of application associated with singular terms; the standards of similarity or 'counterpart relations' on the basis of which certain momentary objects are integrated into genidentical strings) and *content* (the basic manifold of point events, in terms of which Quine discusses the conditions of appropriate application for singular terms.) What do we gain by scheming? It seems terribly unnatural.

The basic entities with which Quine begins – the elements in the 'manifold of content' – are in no respect theory-neutral or scheme-independent. They are dictated as the ontology of a theory which Quine finds useful (mathematical physics) and in terms of which he wants to understand the stimulatory conditions for certain kinds of verbal behavior. Our speaker 'constructs the Cayster out of momentary objects' in this sense: we radical interpreters, attempting to understand why our speaker holds true certain sentences, are able to define an adequate scheme of reference for his language against the backdrop of a domain of momentary objects. The scheme idea, with its inevitable images of slicing, organizing, and carving up, need not be regarded as the implementation of a misguided epistemological theory. In the cases we've considered, the 'content' corresponds to the favored ontology embraced by the interpreter. The possibility of alternative schemes corresponds to the possibility of non-trivial expressive and discriminative disparities between theories. Such disparities need not entail global translational breakdowns; but they nonetheless have fairly interesting ontological consequences, consequences of the sort that schemers everywhere are trying to capture with their metaphors.

The evidential base in radical interpretation, the data which Davidson wants to explain, involves the attitudes which people have toward sentences. The stock of sentences toward which a person has attitudes determines a stock of expressive and discriminative resources. I have suggested an intimate relationship between the expressive resources of a discourse and the referential apparatus plausibly defined over the discourse. This in turn provides a connection between a speaker's ontology and the speaker's capacity to make discriminations. If this is right, then we have a way of maintaining that 'objects constitute themselves in discourse' without embracing any outmoded dogmas or flirting with totally untranslatable languages. The basic tenets of Davidson's views about interpretation, truth, and reference have not been violated. Yet we have managed to improve on the intelligibility of the scheme idea, while retaining at least some of the excitement.

23

The Metaphysics of Interpretation

CAROL ROVANE

The term 'category' means different things to different philosophers. For Aristotelians, it suggests a system of ontological distinctions largely based on a study of 'grammatical' categories. For those of a Kantian persuasion, the term 'category' vaguely suggests a rule of thought, but more typically, it refers to any one of a bundle of interrelated concepts that together yield some general notion of 'objectivity'. My use of the term in this paper will be loosely Kantian, though I shall not be concerned with anything so systematic as Kant's categorial principles. Rather, I shall be concerned with those elusive things Donald Davidson calls 'broad features of reality' – things he thinks may be discovered through his 'Method of Truth in Metaphysics', as he argues in a paper with that title.[1] For my purposes, then, what I call categorial issues are issues about what, in the most general sense, the world is, or perhaps must be, like, i.e., what categories of thing there must be in the world. I will focus on Davidson's claim that the conditions on interpretation or communication provide a basis on which we can settle at least some such categorial issues.

For Davidson, the conditions on intepretation amount to the general constraints (both formal and empirical) on any theory of meaning, where a theory of meaning for a language is a theory of truth which is modelled on a Tarski-style (inductive) definition of truth. The 'method of truth' directs us to isolate those common features of such truth-conditional theories of meaning that follow from the general constraints on them, and to examine the features for metaphysical significance. The presumption is that the large and constant features of language that would emerge in any theory of meaning either correspond to, or reflect, or in some way gauge, certain large features of reality. Of course, Davidson doesn't really base his metaphysics on mere presumption. Attributions of belief play a central role in meaning-theory, and the principle which governs such attributions – the principle of charity – ultimately supplies the rationale for the 'method of truth'. In Davidson's words, it ensures that 'Successful communication proves the existence of a shared, and largely true,

---

[1] D. Davidson, 'The Method of Truth in Metaphysics' in *Inquiries into Truth and Interpretation* (Oxford University Press, Oxford, 1984).

view of the world,' and 'the common view shapes the shared language. This is why it is plausible to hold that by studying the most general aspects of language we will be studying the most general features of reality.'[2]

Although I won't go so far as to defend Davidson's method of truth *per se*, I will argue that the underlying point of view which motivates it is sound. Davidson's basic premise is that language, meaning and belief can't be understood apart from their respective and related roles in communication. And what I hold in common with him is the view that a study of the conditions on interpretation or communication can yield metaphysical, i.e., categorial, insights. But while I find great merit in the general point of view that gives rise to Davidson's 'method of truth', part of the burden of this paper will be that the method itself, at least as Davidson presents it, yields little by way of firm categorial conclusions, My reservations about the method are not founded on objections to Davidson's truth-conditional analysis of meaning, or to his account of the general constraints on meaning-theory, both of which have done more than any other recent work to make the subject of linguistic meaning a tractable area of philosophical study. My worry is over how to move *from* the latter *to* metaphysical conclusions. Davidson seems to think that the move is relatively straightforward. He says:

> What we must attend to in language, if we want to bring into relief general features of the world, is what it is in general for a sentence in the language to be true. The suggestion is that if the truth-conditions of sentences are placed in the context of a comprehensive theory, the linguistic structure that emerges will reflect large features of reality.[3]

Before I give my reasons for saying why the 'method of truth' does not point towards metaphysical conclusions. I first want to show why the underlying point of view that serves to support it has great plausibility. Having done that, I shall move on to my criticisms of Davidson, i.e., to the limitations of his way of proceeding from this point of view. Finally, I shall in the briefest and broadest terms outline an alternative approach and indicate what it might yield, if worked out with greater care than I have the space to do here. The key difference is this: while Davidson locates the metaphysical significance of his interpretive perspective in the structural details of meaning-theory itself, I suggest that we examine the conditions which surround and make possible meaning-theory and which may not be reflected at all in its structure. For example, it may be that certain categories – those of substance, event, cause and person – must already be in the picture *prior* to the construction of theories of meaning. Why prior? Because they may figure in certain (necessary) *presuppositions* of a speaker–interpreter situation as such. And if so as I will argue later, they may not be any part of the theories themselves. The point is that if we did not already establish them as such presuppositions in advance of devising the meaning-theories, we would lose our hold over the object of these theories, i.e., communication between speakers and their interpreters. So here we might have an important

---

[2] Ibid., p. 201.
[3] Ibid., p. 201.

source of categorial insight which is intimately connected with (but not, by any means, identical with) Davidson's outlook, focusing as it does on the conditions on communication and interpretation.

But why should the conditions on interpretation tell us anything about the world at large? Davidson's approach to metaphysics is at bottom, i.e., in its very general features, a Kantian stance in metaphysics, the aim of which is to expose the metaphysical significance of the conditions on the possibility of judgement or belief (or of what come to the same thing, the 'presuppositions' of the *concept* of judgement or belief). The difference, on this score, between Kant and someone like Davidson, lies only in where the concept of judgement or belief is situated: while Kant supposes it has application only in the context of a possible experience, Davidson maintains that it must be located in the context of communication. Though I don't mean to de-emphasize this very important difference between Kant's and Davidson's positions, I do here also want to stress their common perspective. For according to both, the concept of belief (or judgement) must be our point of departure in metaphysics. Prima facie, I think there is very good reason to agree with them that what is presupposed by this concept has metaphysical import, because the concept of belief is inextricably bound up with the concept of truth. And this is what binds them: since a belief is essentially capable of being true or false, it follows that the concept of belief involves a distinction between what is believed true and what is true. Where this distinction is lacking, the concept of belief can have no application. And everything which goes into the making of this distinction is a condition on the very possibility of belief.[4]

This intimate connection between the concept of belief and the concept of truth, I have said, provides a prima facie rationale for the Kantian stance. But a bit of reflection shows that this stance is more deeply motivated by the connection between both these concepts and skepticism. It is only those who have beliefs and who understand that what they believe true may not be true who can even begin to entertain skepticism. But even the skeptic cannot coherently deny that the conditions on the possibility of belief obtain, for if they do not, there are no beliefs and hence no perspective from which a skeptical hypothesis is even visible. The crucial Kantian insight, then, is that skepticism cannot be formulated without appeal to the concept of belief or to what it presupposes. And so, in turn, the presuppositions of the concept of belief must be immune from skeptical attack. Insofar as we are skeptics, we are believers, and insofar as we are believers, the world must be such that the conditions whose obtaining is presupposed by the concept of belief actually do obtain, i.e., we cannot be skeptical about those conditions.

---

[4] My free use of the term 'truth' might surprise some, since I have not taken the trouble to address Dummett-style objections to a realist conception of truth. So at this point I should qualify my position, and say that the concept of belief is bound up with *some* concept of truth – that is, it must be contrasted with a notion of what is 'objective' in some suitable sense. For example, the idea that a linguistic community should count a given sentence as verified and yet fail to be *true*, is an idea that harbors perfectly adequately one such suitable sense. It will be clear from the rest of the paper, however, that my main theses do not depend on any particular further account of truth (for instance, they do not rely on any causal-physicalist underpinning of the concept of truth as in Hartry Field's suggestion).

   Thus it is that the Kantian approach to metaphysics is essentially anti-skeptical, and because of this, it must respect the distinction between how things are judged to be and how they are: between belief and truth. The next step is to effect this distinction between the subjective and the objective without driving a permanent wedge between the two. On the contrary, the Kantian will insist that there is a definite and symmetrical relation between them. First, she insists, as we've already seen, that the notion of the subjective makes sense only in contrast with the objective, and this contrast is what makes for skeptical possibilities. But also, truth, or what is objective, must, in a Kantian framework, be understood as something that judgements and beliefs are in principle fit to capture. For if beliefs couldn't be true, it would make no sense to say that they were false – that is, there would be no genuine skeptical possibilities.

   Notice that it is a hallmark of the Kantian perspective that subjects are essentially self-conscious. By this I mean that they understand that what they take to be the case may not be the case in fact. So subjects (in this self-conscious sense) and subjects alone can be skeptics. There is another notion of subjectivity which some would apply to creatures that lack this understanding, this self-consciousness – to dogs, for instance. I myself don't want to quarrel over whether it makes sense to ascribe thoughts or mentality to unselfconscious creatures. Whether they have thoughts or not, they don't count as subjects in the Kantian sense. There will be no room in such creatures' so-called 'thoughts' for notions like appearance, judgement or belief on the one hand, and reality or truth on the other. Let me say as an aside here that something like the same point will apply also to those philosophers who think that beliefs or propositional attitudes in general can be given a functionalist reduction. This cannot be in line with the Kantian concept of belief or judgement, for since such a reductionist account has no place for a referential semantics, it cannot bring in the distinction between believing true and being true that Kant thought constitutive of belief. For reasons I cannot spell out here, a purely disquotational conception of truth appended to such a functionalist account will not be sufficient to yield belief in my sense either. So to repeat, whatever does count as a subject of beliefs in the Kantian sense must have the conceptual resources to make the distinction between the subjective and the objective. And the distinction once made, skeptical possibilities loom. But on the other hand, these possibilities are constrained – they cannot be actualized in a way that undermines this distinction which forms the very basis for skepticism. To formulate my point now without reference to skepticism, the Kantian metaphysician seeks to establish what metaphysical or categorial notions a subject must suppose have application in order that the distinction between belief and truth be intelligible to her, i.e., in order that she can be a self-conscious believer.

   A familiar objection to this sort of Kantian maneuver charges that it can't really make a contribution to *metaphysics*. For it tells us *not* about the world but about what subjects must find themselves *supposing* about the world (or 'presupposing' as the case may be). Now this objection should deter the Kantian only if there is some reason to think that the quite special epistemic commitments in question might be in error. The problem is that the objection draws upon the very distinction (that between what we suppose or take to be the case and what is the case) which the Kantian claims is unintelligible apart from the prior epistemic commitments which are under dispute. So it seems fair to say that the Kantian project does not founder on this familiar objection, and the presuppositions of the concept of belief can be allowed their full metaphysical force. Thus if the Kantian project is in the end unworkable, it will be rather because we cannot find such presuppositions, and not because they are without metaphysical significance.

So far I have sketched the general Kantian strategy, which when described at this level of generality, is a strategy that I also see in Davidson. But, as I said, this general method is situated in quite different specific contexts for the two of them. For Kant the context is that of the skeptical challenge that may emerge as a consequence of empiricist epistemology. The primary challenge of skepticism in this context would be to call into question the very distinction between the subjective and the objective that I claimed is that starting point for a Kantian metaphysics. Now rather than *assume* the distinction, Kant actually provides a positive argument (in the 'Transcendental Deduction') for the claim that the distinction is required in any self-conscious experience. Kant's aim there is to show that a self-conscious understanding of one's subjective experiential states qua subjective states isn't possible unless those states provide a ground for the existence of something permanent which is distinct from, or independent of, those subjective states. And further, his claim is that *this* isn't possible unless those states are taken to be experiences *of* an objective order in which various categorial notions have application. The categories must have application because they are constitutive of that very order.

My objection to Kant is not directed against the general strategy as I described it earlier, but against this particular context in which he wields it. For in the end, I claim, he never allows himself a way out of the empiricism that gives rise to the skepticism that is his target. Though he, more than any other philosopher of the modern period, gives the notion of judgement its full due as the fundamental epistemic unit, he nevertheless never escapes the empiricist framework, insofar as he gives the notion of a sensory given a central role in the critical philosophy. By this I mean of course Kant's division of the conditions on experience into two sorts – those on sensibility and those on understanding. This raises for him the following well-known difficulties. First, since our understanding can work only with what is given in sensation, the notion of objectivity provided by the understanding must be restricted to the realm of appearance. That realm can be defined only in contrast with the supra-objective realm of noumena – the unknowable reality independent of sensibility. As Kant restricts our potential knowledge to appearances and at the same time locates objective reality within the realm of appearance, he takes on the aspect of a somewhat rarified (in the sense of being once-removed) phenomenalist. Worse yet, he allows that a self-conscious subject can 'think' other forms of sensibility. This means that we can conceive that there are other kinds of experience, and because our notion of the objective is tied to *our* experience, it follows that to conceive other kinds of experience is also to conceive other kinds of objectivity. In other words, Kant's view allows the conceptual possibility of relativism.[5]

---

[5] I have deliberately overstated Kant's position: strictly, he does not allow that we can 'conceive' other kinds of experience. He holds that we can't imagine what they would be *like*, or what notions of 'objectivity' they would involve. Nevertheless, Kant is clearly agnostic about the possibility of

In addition to these problems, there's also a certain lack of categorial comprehensiveness in Kant's positive account of the objective. Some categories we might think of as basic to our ontology are simply not covered in his conclusions. He makes no provision for objectivity with respect to minds, selves, persons, etc. For his categories define the objective in terms of space, time, Newton's laws and various quasi-logical principles. All of these notions combined provide no clue to the difference between those objects which do, and those which don't, exhibit intentional behavior or evidence of thought.[6] And, moreover, I am no better off with respect to knowledge of myself than I am with respect to knowledge of others within Kant's framework. The 'self-consciousness' which is made possible by the 'unity of apperception' is not exactly consciousness of any particular self. Kant is very clear that the 'I' of the 'I think' which expresses self-consciousness and the unity of apperception does not refer to a self in the usual sense, and has absolutely nothing to do with the *identity* of anything. All Kant seems to mean by 'self-consciousness' is consciousness of self-*hood* (as opposed to consciousness of oneself). That's why in Kant's framework the unity of apperception can no more provide for knowledge of a subject than the categories can.

Davidson's Kantian approach improves on Kant's own in one crucial respect – that it is not situated in an empiricist problematic. In his important paper 'On the Very Idea of a Conceptual Scheme'[7] Davidson does as much as anyone has to undermine the empiricist distinction between concepts and intuitions (scheme and content), what he calls the 'third dogma of empiricism'. What is retained is the overall spirit of Kant's strategy which is to preserve the transcendental maneuver of arguing for metaphysical conclusions by placing constraints on the concepts of judgement, belief and subjecthood. Davidson's own alternative is to situate this strategy in the quite different context of communication. He has often said that one can be a self-conscious believer (or a believer at all) only if one is a communicator. The best statement of his reasons for taking this view is to be found in the concluding paragraphs of his paper 'Rational Animals'. There he offers the following analogy with triangulation:

> If I were bolted to the earth, I would have no way of determining the distance from me of many objects. I would only know they were on some line down from me toward them. I might interact successfully with objects, but I could have no way of

other kinds of experience, despite his view that our conceptions of them are merely 'negative' and hence empty.

[6] Part of the problem here is that Kant's interest in persons is *practical* and not theoretical. Indeed, the features of personhood which engage him (freedom and duty) seem to ensure that *knowledge* of persons is beside the point. Thus it might seem that my call for an account of 'objectivity' with respect to persons is not in keeping with the Kantian spirit, and actually represents a departure from it. I agree, but only up to a point; Nothing bars us from both (1) concentrating on Kant's treatment of the relations between belief, self-consciousness, objectivity and certain categorial concepts, and (2) including 'selves' in the epistemological story. A chief advantage of adopting the stance I advocate in the paper (departing from Kant in adding the communicative element) is precisely that it allows us to include it.

[7] D. Davidson, 'On the Very Idea of a Conceptual Scheme', in *Inquiries into Truth and Interpretation*.

giving content to the question where they were. Not being bolted down, I am free to triangulate. Our sense of objectivity is the consequence of another sort of triangulation, one that requires two creatures. Each interacts with an object, but what gives each the concept of the way things are objectively is the base line formed between the creatures by language. The fact that they share a concept of truth alone makes sense of the claim that they have beliefs, that they are able to assign objects a place in the public world.

The conclusion of these considerations is that rationality is a social trait. Only communicators have it.[8]

The basic idea is that one cannot recognize that one's beliefs constitute a subjective point of view on something objective, or independent of one's beliefs, except insofar as one also recognizes other subjective points of view. Hence self-conscious believers must also be self-conscious communicators, i.e., interpreters of others. If these conceptual connections traced by Davidson are allowed to stand, then one's consciousness of other points of view must be on equal footing with consciousness of one's own point of view.

This thesis is rather subtler and deeper than another one Davidson vigorously defends.[9] And that is, that the only things to which we can justifiably ascribe beliefs are speakers and interpreters of language. His argument for this latter claim turns on holism: Given that any belief is thoroughgoingly interconnected with other beliefs, we cannot ascribe one where we cannot ascribe the connecting beliefs. And the only behavior which is fine-grained enough to warrant the ascription of a whole set of holistically interconnected beliefs is linguistic behavior. So we can have no evidence that something is the subject of propositional attitudes where we cannot interpret, i.e., provide a theory of meaning by which we can make sense of its behavior as speech behavior. The upshot is that there is no basis on which we can say that creatures without language think.

Superficially these two theses (the deep and the not so deep) which I want to distinguish might seem to come down to the same thing: namely, only speakers of language – communicators – can properly be called subjects of belief. But there is a vital difference. The argument for the second assumes a third-person perspective on subjecthood. That is, it has to do with the ascription of beliefs (and hence subjecthood) to others. The first thesis goes deeper because it makes no initial commitment to the third-person perspective. It concerns the conditions on self-consciousness, or first-personal ascriptions of subjecthood. The contention is that one can be a self-conscious believer only if one can ascribe beliefs to others too. Thus, Davidson means to establish by the triangulation analogy that first-personal ascriptions of subjectivity are not possible without third-personal ascriptions. Viewed in this way, Davidson's position looks very Kantian indeed. Interpretation emerges as a condition on the possibility of self-conscious belief in much the same way as the application of categorial concepts emerges, in Kant's account, as a condition on the possibility of self-conscious experience.

---

[8] D. Davidson, 'Rational Animals', *Dialectica*, 36 (4) (1982), p. 327.
[9] See D. Davidson, 'Thought and Talk', in *Inquiries into Truth and Interpretation*.

Davidson does not claim to have produced an air-tight argument for his view, but only an analogy, the triangulation analogy. Nevertheless, it is one that I find very persuasive. It's important to keep in mind that Davidson's maneuver is quite unlike the following ploy of Strawson's.[10] Strawson argues that if I have a conception of *my*self, I must have the general concept of *a* self, a concept which I can apply to others. Davidson's maneuver is different because he pays attention to the properties peculiar to subjectivity. In contrast Strawson's point would apply to any concept whatsoever, for it only amounts to the claim that any concept must be general – it must have more than one application.

What peculiar property of subjectivity does Davidson appeal to in his triangulation analogy? The very property I've been harping on all along – its interplay with the notion of objectivity. The dilemma this analogy addresses is this: as a self-conscious subject I must understand the potential gap between what I take to be the case and what is the case. Yet all I ever have at my disposal is what I take to be the case. I can't escape my own subjective point of view to a neutral standpoint from which the difference between my point of view and how things objectively are may be surveyed. So how can I come to see that there may be a difference? What Kant has taught us is that this question should not be treated in a Cartesian fashion – we do not have a clear and distinct grasp of our own selves as constituted by our subjective states which is prior to or independent of our grasp on what is objective. In the 'Refutation of Idealism' Kant sums up his particular account of the interdependence of the subjective and the objective within his empiricist epistemology. The message of the triangulation analogy is that this interdependence owes to the connection between self-consciousness and the sort of *inter*-subjectivity afforded by communication.

There is, admittedly, more than one way to make the case for this position, and I won't every try and make the case myself. Rather, I shall just point to the work of Wittgenstein, and also the American pragmatists, and mark the path these philosophers have opened up; one which Davidson's triangulation analogy is clearly following. The issue, remember, is how self-consciousness in the Kantian sense – a consciousness of one's subjectivity as contrasted with the objective – is possible. One distinctive feature of subjectivity is fallibility, and the contention is that awareness of one's fallibility depends on the publicness of one's thoughts, and on the discovery of disagreement with others through interpretation. If we think of interpretation in Gricean terms for a moment, we can readily see that it involves the simultaneous ascription of subjective states (in particular, intentions) to oneself and to another, both when one is the speaker and when one is the interpreter. What needs arguing is that nothing short of this complex social context provides a place for the thought of one's subjective point of view – for self-consciousness. Further, the communicative context must be shown to be rich enough – given the possibility of comparing and criticizing thoughts once they are public – to give substance to the subjective/objective contrast. Finally, we must insist, as Davidson does, on the difference between the capacity for coping, adjusting, changing one's habits and

---

[10] See P. F. Strawson, 'Self, Mind and Body,' *Freedom and Resentment and Other Essays* (Methuen, London, 1973).

dispositions on the one hand, and the self-consciousness possessed by social, communicative beings on the other. I admit once again that what allows me to insist upon all this is not an argument but a striking and compelling analogy.

A while back, I spelled out some of the reasons why Davidson thinks that language is required in the discovery of other subjects or subjective points of view. Owing to the holistic nature of belief, we can ascribe one belief only where there is evidence of many, many more interlocking beliefs. Davidson maintains, therefore, that only linguistic behavior is rich enough to warrant ascriptions of belief. And according to him the only mark of linguistic behavior is our ability to interpret it via a theory of meaning of the kind he advocates. At this point it should be clear that all of the steps which lead to situating the Kantian project within a communicative context have been assembled. As I said before, I don't claim any more than Davidson does to have produced an air-tight argument that only communicators can be self-conscious subjects. But insofar as we are persuaded by the triangulation analogy, and accept a holistic view of belief, then we ought to pursue his meaning-theoretic approach to metaphysics. What is the step from talk of the concept of communication theory to meaning-theory? I think Davidson intends that it is this: once we have granted this much, we must count the conditions on communication as conditions on self-conscious belief.And since meaning-theory is supposed to describe explicitly what goes on implicitly in communication, it only makes sense to regard the general constraints on meaning-theory as conditions on communication. Our question then is, how are these constraints metaphysically significant? What can they tell us about the world?

Let me sum up our progress so far. Discarding Kant's particular empiricist framework, we may still retain his overall strategy, sketched at the beginning of the paper, of getting metaphysical conclusions by looking at the presuppositions of the concept of belief. Davidson's triangulation idea helps us to tie belief, not to the concept of experience, as Kant does, but to the concept of communication. And his idea is that since a theory of meaning describes our implicit communicative practices, constraints on such a theory will provide the relevant category-yielding constraints on the concept of belief (in this context of communication). Let me now quickly expound and criticize Davidson's way of developing his thought. My criticism will be directed not at the idea that belief must be situated in the context of communication, but at the idea that the metaphysically relevant constraints on belief will be constraints that attach to theories of meaning. Rather, I think the constraints that are important to metaphysics move from the *concept* of communication; not from the theory of meaning that purports to describe our communicative practice.

Because I am only interested in those of Davidson's constraints on meaning-theory which might contribute metaphysical results, I will be very selective in my discussion of them. I mentioned at the outset that a Davidsonian theory of meaning for a language is a theory of truth; hence the slogan 'the method of truth in metaphysics'. The aim of such a theory is to specify the truth-condition of each sentence of a language on the basis of the meanings of its parts. The primary evidence for meaning is the circumstances in which speakers assent to sentences, or hold them true. That we construct theories of meaning on the basis of such evidence has a well-known consequence: we can assign meanings to speakers' utterances or to the sentences they utter only insofar as we ascribe beliefs to them. Moreover, which meanings we assign will depend on which beliefs we ascribe. This leads to a constraint on meaning-theory which seems to offer the best hope of metaphysical progress, viz., the principle of charity. Since beliefs are holistically connected, what makes one belief the belief it is, is the network of surrounding beliefs that go with it. Davidson holds that as interpreters we cannot find that a speaker has a belief which is false by our lights except insofar as the speaker has other and related beliefs that are true by our lights. He concludes that since intelligible disagreement requires a background of agreement, disagreement between subjects can never outrun agreement. The principle of charity directs us to maximize agreement between our beliefs and the beliefs of the speaker (of course accounting for all disagreement that is tied to differing states of incoming information). I'm not going to question Davidson's idea that the constraint of charity on theories of meaning or interpretation rules out the possibility of the idea of massive disagreement, or even the doctrine of conceptual relativism, when that doctrine is founded on that idea. It seems to me reasonable that it does. The idea is simple. We cannot attribute a belief, say, in ghosts (false by our lights) unless we attribute beliefs, say, in persons and death (true by our lights). Without some such latter beliefs that *are* shared, we would put into doubt that the initial belief attributed was one about *ghosts*. That is why disagreement requires a back-ground of agreement.[11]

So far I have only talked of truth and falsity by an interpreter's lights, i.e., agreement and disagreement. How does one make the transition from agree-ment to truth, disagreement to error? Given the Kantian premise connecting belief and the concept of truth sketched at the beginning of the paper, and given the Davidsonian premise connecting belief with the concept of communication, and finally now, given this plausibility of the idea that charity constrains theories of meaning that capture our communicative practices by ruling out massive disagreement, we can see how the transition is inevitable. But having said that it is successful as a weapon against relativism and the possibility of global error. I think it is instructive to see how little the principle of charity can yield for the metaphysical issues at hand.

Here is the problem: charity tells us we are all in agreement and what we agree on is the fact the truth (more or less). But it does not tell us *what it is* that we are all in agreement about. It depends, obviously, on the nature of the agreement charity requires. But by itself the constraint of charity doesn't seem to require agreement about anything in particular. To see this imagine the following scenario: suppose that I interpret a subject so that she has mostly true beliefs only about her sensory states. If I suppose that she is acquainted with more sensory states than I am with objective circumstances, then since she is mostly right about her sensory states, I could say that she and I agree more than we disagree, thereby satisfying the charity constraint. And yet I would have interpreted my subject to be, in essence, an idealist. Now if charity guarantees

---

[11] My example has been carelessly phrased because it talks of 'beliefs in'. But unless one is committed to an implausibly strong analytic-synthetic distinction, one should not be tempted to distinguish between 'belief in' as being not quite 'belief' but rather as 'having a concept'.

that our beliefs are true, but then allows idealism to be intelligible and coherent, the result is disappointing, given Davidson's avowedly Kantian goal of anti-skeptical metaphysical results.

My point is that the way I have set up the Davidsonian position so far, there is nothing in the position to rule out this scenario. We could of course point out that we don't ordinarily have beliefs about our sensory states, or more weakly, that we could not have true beliefs about them, without also having some true beliefs about the organs of sense and the external causes of sensation. And to do so would be to turn our backs on idealism and skepticism. But my complaint is that whatever arguments we have for doing so are not to be found in the general constraint of *charity*. They will necessarily be *additional* arguments and not meaning-theoretic arguments in the sense that Davidson's argument appealing to charity *is* a meaning-theoretic argument. What his meaning-theoretic argument *does* accomplish is the refutation of global error and conceptual relativism. But these latter skepticisms are so general and underdescribed that it is not at all clear what in particular we have secured in refuting them. One way of showing why these skepticisms are underdescribed is precisely by showing why a successful attack on them yields no categorial metaphysical results, as a successful attack on more interesting skepticisms about the external world, other minds and causality would yield. Unlike these latter skepticisms, a skepticism which simply says 'All our beliefs could be false' may be refuted without furnishing us with the slightest idea of what the world may be like, and what sorts of thing there must be.

If I am right, then Davidson has not given us reason to think that certain categories of thing must exist. Does this mean that the move from Kant's version of the Kantian approach to the question (what I have called the empiricist approach) to a Davidsonian version (what we may call the interpretive approach) is of no real help after all? I think not, for my criticism has not been directed against that general move but against Davidson's specific method and argument once the move has been made. The criticism attaches not to the general idea of spelling out the preconditions on belief in communication, but to the specific idea that that be done by identifying constraints on theories of meaning that aim to describe and explain our communicative practices. In the next few paragraphs I want to make a few and alas necessarily brief and unsatisfactory remarks about why cleaving to the more general idea – that of seeing the presuppositions of the *concept* of belief in communication – may prove to be a more promising 'method in metaphysics'.

Kant asked our categorial question by asking the question, 'What are the conditions on the possibility of having beliefs or making judgments in the sense of having experience?' and we are asking the question, 'What are the conditions on the possibility of having beliefs or making judgements in the sense of understanding or make sense of others?' What is common in these questions is what's worth retaining in the Kantian approach. What makes the second different from the first, however, yields some very real advantages in both sectors (mentioned earlier) where Kant failed. First in that we escape the relativism and phenomenalism inevitable given his empiricist setting. The relativism, as we have seen, has been effectively repudiated by Davidson's 'method of truth'. The phenomenalist skepticism, as we just saw, is not repudiated by Davidson's specific method; but if my remarks that follow about how his general strategy may be exploited are convincing, that result should emerge by way of increasing the range and comprehensiveness missing in Kant's own categorial conclusions.

Notice that by situating beliefs in the communicative context, we immediately have the concept of subject, self or mind added to the Kantian picture. We might even say that Davidson's triangulation analogy should do for the concept of other minds what Kant's 'Transcendental Deduction' does for the concept of an object, namely, guarantee that any subject can legitimately apply it, and in fact must be able to apply it in order to be self-conscious in the Kantian sense. If this is so, then Davidson's maneuver supplies us with a new ground for ruling out the sort of sense-datum idealism we considered before. So long as we must view the subjects we interpret as self-conscious, we cannot intelligibly suppose that they have beliefs only about sense-data. For without beliefs about other subjects, they would not have a ground in their beliefs for the distinction between belief and truth, and hence they could not be self-conscious. This might seem like a rehash of familiar Wittgensteinian material. We all know that communication requires a plurality of subjects who inhabit a common, intersubjective world. So if self-conscious belief requires communication (i.e., if there is no private language) then it requires all that communication entails. However: the story doesn't end here. For we have not yet considered carefully enough just what *is* entailed in communication.

All we've actually established is that communication requires a plurality of subjects, and perhaps also that something can be counted as a subject only if its beliefs can be discovered via a method of interpretation like Davidson's. Now I want to pose what may at first seem an odd question: if a subject is something that can interpret and be interpreted, what *sort* of thing must it be in order that it *can* engage in interpretation? That is, what properties must subjects have in order that they can individuate one another for the purposes of interpretation, and what categorial concepts must have application in order that communication can take place among them? In a way, what I'm after is this: according to the triangulation analogy *any* self-conscious subject must be an interpreter of others and hence committed to the existence of other subjects. But it may well be that we cannot *apply* the concept of a subject of interpretation without applying other categorial concepts at the same time. Thus a commitment to the existence of other subjects may entail further, unanticipated, categorial commitments. And so the distinctive and perhaps unique metaphysical, or anti-skeptical, contribution of Davidson's perspective may be precisely the discovery of these interrelated categorial commitments.

When we reflect on what usually goes on during communication between two subjects, we find that several categorial notions typically have simultaneous application. We identify subjects by their bodies, for the most part. That is, we identify them as enduring spatio-temporal particulars – we might say as *substances* – quite independently of identifying them as bona fide subjects of propositional attitudes. These substances are regarded *as* subjects insofar as they may be interpreted, and they are then also regarded as *persons*. When persons communicate they undergo non-mental changes in the form of linguistic utterances, and these *events* result in communication only if they have effects on other persons, which must therefore bring *causality* into the picture. These categorial notions – substance, event, cause and person – seem to constitute the metaphysical underpinnings of human communication, and moreover, communicators must actually *employ* these categories as they interpret.

One worthwhile project would be to determine just how these categories are in general understood by people when they communicate. Another, more ambitious project would be rather more abstract. It would seek to determine whether any or all of these categories *must* have application in order that the mere possibility of communication be intelligible. And this latter is the project I envisage in connection with the perspective that underlies Davidson's 'method of truth'. Rather than look to the method and constraints (such as charity) involved in the devising of theories of meaning, which is Davidson's own favored procedure and which, as we saw, paid no metaphysical dividends, I've been suggesting that the task should be one of drawing out the presuppositions of what a theory of meaning is a theory *of* – i.e., communication. Such a project is one which may justly be thought of as being in a very general sense at once Kantian and Davidsonian.

Part VI
Limits of the Literal

24

A Nice Derangement of Epitaphs*

DONALD DAVIDSON

Goodman Ace wrote radio sitcoms. According to Mark Singer, Ace often talked the way he wrote:

> Rather than take for granite that Ace talks straight, a listener must be on guard for an occasional entre nous and me ... or a long face no see. In a roustabout way, he will maneuver until he selects the ideal phrase for the situation, hitting the nail right on the thumb. The careful conversationalist might try to mix it up with him in a baffle of wits. In quest of this pinochle of success, I have often wrecked my brain for a clowning achievement, but Ace's chickens always come home to roast. From time to time, Ace will, in a jerksome way, monotonize the conversation with witticisms too humorous to mention. It's high noon someone beat him at his own game, but I have never done it: cross my eyes and hope to die, he always wins thumbs down.[1]

I quote at length because philosophers have tended to neglect or play down the sort of language-use this passage illustrates. For example, Jonathan Bennett writes,

> I doubt if I have ever been present when a speaker did something like shouting 'Water!' as a warning of fire, knowing what 'Water!' means and knowing that his hearers also knew, but thinking that they would expect him to give to 'Water!' the normal meaning of 'Fire!'[2]

Bennett adds that, 'Although such things could happen, they seldom do.' I think such things happen all the time; in fact, if the conditions are generalized in a natural way, the phenomenon is ubiquitous.

Singer's examples are special in several ways. A malapropism does not have to be amusing or surprising. It does not have to be based on a cliché, and of course it does not have to be intentional. There need be no play on words, no

*©Donald Davidson
[1] *The New Yorker*, 4 April 1977, p. 56. Reprinted by permission, © 1977, The New Yorker Magazine, Inc.
[2] Jonathan Bennett, *Linguistic Behavior* (Cambridge 1976), p. 186.

hint of deliberate pun. We may smile at someone who says 'Lead the way and we'll precede', or, with Archie Bunker, 'We need a few laughs to break up the monogamy', because he has said something that, given the usual meanings of the words, is ridiculous or fun. But the humour is adventitious.

Ace's malaprops generally make some sort of sense when the words are taken in the standard way, as in 'Familiarity breeds attempt', or 'We're all cremated equal', but this is not essential ('the pinochle of success'). What is interesting is the fact that in all these cases the hearer has no trouble understanding the speaker in the way the speaker intends.

It is easy enough to explain this feat on the hearer's part: the hearer realizes that the 'standard' interpretation cannot be the intended interpretation; through ignorance, inadvertence, or design the speaker has used a word similar in sound to the word that would have 'correctly' expressed his meaning. The absurdity or inappropriateness of what the speaker would have meant had his words been taken in the 'standard' way alerts the hearer to trickery or error; the similarity in sound tips him off to the right interpretation. Of course there are many other ways the hearer might catch on; similarity of sound is not essential to the malaprop. Nor for that matter does the general case require that the speaker use a real word: most of 'The Jabberwock' is intelligble on first hearing.

It seems unimportant, so far as understanding is concerned, who makes a mistake, or whether there is one. When I first read Singer's piece on Goodman Ace, I thought that the word 'malaprop', though the name of Sheridan's character, was not a common noun that could be used in place of 'malapropism'. It turned out to be my mistake. Not that it mattered: I knew what Singer meant, even though I was in error about the word; I would have taken his meaning in the same way if he had been in error instead of me. We could both have been wrong and things would have gone as smoothly.

This talk of error or mistake is not mysterious nor open to philosophical suspicions. I was wrong about what a good dictionary would say, or what would be found by polling a pod of experts whose taste or training I trust. But error or mistake of this kind, with its associated notion of correct usage, is not philosophically interesting. We want a deeper notion of what words, when spoken in context, mean; and like the shallow notion of correct usage, we want the deep concept to distinguish between what a speaker, on a given occasion, means, and what his words mean. The widespread existence of malapropisms and their kin threatens the distinction, since here the intended meaning seems to take over from the standard meaning.

I take for granted, however, that nothing should be allowed to obliterate or even blur the distinction between speaker's meaning and literal meaning. In order to preserve the distinction we must, I shall argue, modify certain commonly accepted views about what it is to 'know a language', or about what a natural language is. In particular, we must pry apart what is literal in language from what is conventional or established.

Here is a preliminary stab at characterizing what I have been calling literal meaning. The term is too incrusted with philosophical and other extras to do much work, so let me call what I am interested in *first meaning*. The concept applies to words and sentences as uttered by a particular speaker on a particular occasion. But if the occasion, the speaker, and the audience are 'normal' or 'standard' (in a sense not to be further explained here), then the first meaning of an utterance will be what should be found by consulting a dictionary based on actual usage (such as Webster's Third). Roughly speaking, first meaning comes first in the order of interpretation. We have no chance of explaining the image in the following lines, for example, unless we know what 'foison' meant in Shakespeare's day:

> Speak of the spring and foison of the year,
> The one doth shadow of of your beauty show,
> The other as your bounty doth appear ... [3]

Little here is to be taken literally, but unless we know the literal, or first, meaning of the words we do not grasp and cannot explain the image.

But 'the order of interpretation' is not at all clear. For there are cases where we may first guess at the image and so puzzle out the first meaning. This might happen with the word 'tires' in the same sonnet:

> On Helen's cheek all art of beauty set,
> And you in Grecian tires are painted new.

And of course it often happens that we can descry the literal meaning of a word or phrase by first appreciating what the speaker was getting at.

A better way to distinguish first meaning is through the intentions of the speaker. The intentions with which an act is performed are usually unambiguously ordered by the relation of means to ends (where this relation may or may not be causal). Thus the poet wants (let us say) to praise the beauty and generosity of his patron. He does this by using images that say the person addressed takes on every good aspect to be found in nature or in man or woman. This he does in turn by using the word 'tire' to mean 'attire' and the word 'foison' to mean 'harvest'. The order established here by 'by' can be reversed by using the phrase 'in order to'. In the 'in order to' sequence, first meaning is the first meaning referred to. ('With the intention of' with 'ing' added to the verb does as well.)

Suppose Diogenes utters the words 'I would have you stand from between me and the sun' (or their Greek equivalent) with the intention of uttering words that will be interpreted by Alexander as true if and only if Diogenes would have him stand from between Diogenes and the sun, and this with the intention of asking Alexander to move from between him and the sun, and this with the intention of getting Alexander to move from between him and the sun, and this with the intention of leaving a good anecdote to posterity. Of course these are not the only intentions involved; there will also be the Gricean intentions to achieve certain of these ends through Alexander's recognition of some of the intentions involved. Diogenes' intention to be interpreted in a certain way requires such a self-referring intention, as does his intention to ask Alexander to move. In general, the first intention in the sequence to require this feature specifies the first meaning.

---

[3] Shakespeare, Sonnet 53.

Because a speaker necessarily intends first meaning to be grasped by his audience, and it is grasped if communication succeeds, we lose nothing in the investigation of first meaning if we concentrate on the knowledge or ability a hearer must have if he is to interpret a speaker. What the speaker knows must correspond to something the interpreter knows if the speaker is to be understood, since if the speaker is understood he has been interpreted as he intended to be interpreted. The abilities of the speaker that go beyond what is required of an interpreter – invention and motor control – do not concern me here.

Nothing said so far limits first meaning to language; what has been characterized is (roughly) Grice's non-natural meaning, which applies to any sign or signal with an intended interpretation. What should be added if we want to restrict first meaning to linguistic meaning? The usual answer would, I think, be that in the case of language the hearer shares a complex system or theory with the speaker, a system which makes possible the articulation of logical relations between utterances, and explains the ability to interpret novel utterances in an organized way.

This answer has been suggested, in one form or another, by many philosophers and linguists, and I assume it must in some sense be right. The difficulty lies in getting clear about what this sense is. The particular difficulty with which I am concerned in this paper (for there are plenty of others) can be brought out by stating three plausible principles concerning first meaning in language: we may label them by saying they require that first meaning be systematic, shared, and prepared.

(1) *First meaning is systematic.* A competent speaker or interpreter is able to interpret utterances, his own or those of others, on the basis of the semantic properties of the parts, or words, in the utterance, and the structure of the utterance. For this to be possible, there must be systematic relations between the meanings of utterances.

(2) *First meanings are shared.* For speaker and interpreter to communicate successfully and regularly, they must share a method of interpretation of the sort described in (1).

(3) *First meanings are governed by learned conventions or regularities.* The systematic knowledge or competence of the speaker or interpreter is learned in advance of occasions of interpretation and is conventional in character.

Probably no one doubts that there are difficulties with these conditions. Ambiguity is an example: often the 'same' word has more than one semantic role, and so the interpretation of utterances in which it occurs is not uniquely fixed by the features of the interpreter's competence so far mentioned. Yet, though the verbal and other features of the context of utterance often determine a correct interpretation, it is not easy or perhaps even possible to specify clear rules for disambiguation. There are many more questions about what is required of the competent interpreter. It does not seem plausible that there is a strict rule fixing the occasions on which we should attach significance to the order in which conjoined sentences appear in a conjunction: the difference between 'They got married and had a child' and 'They had a child and got married.' Interpreters certainly can make these distinctions. But part of the burden of this paper is that much that they can do ought not to count as part of their basic *linguistic* competence. The contrast in what is meant or implied by the use of 'but' instead of 'and' seems to me another matter, since no amount of common sense unaccompanied by linguistic lore would enable an interpreter to figure it out.

Paul Grice has done more than anyone else to bring these problems to our attention and to help sort them out. In particular, he has shown why it is essential to distinguish between the literal meaning (perhaps what I am calling first meaning) of words and what is often implied (or implicated) by someone who uses those words. He has explored the general principles behind our ability to figure out such implicatures, and these principles must, of course, be known to speakers who expect to be taken up on them. Whether knowledge of these principles ought to be included in the description of linguistic competence may not have to be settled: on the one hand they are things a clever person could often figure out without previous training or exposure and they are things we could get along without. On the other hand they represent a kind of skill we expect of an interpreter and without which communication would be greatly impoverished.

I dip into these matters only to distinguish them from the problem raised by malapropisms and the like. The problems touched on in the last two paragraphs all concern the ability to interpret words and constructions of the kind covered by our conditions (1)–(3); the questions have been what is required for such interpretation, and to what extent various competencies should be considered linguistic. Malapropisms introduce expressions not covered by prior learning, or familiar expressions which cannot be interpreted by any of the abilities so far discussed. Malapropisms fall into a different category, one that may include such things as our ability to perceive a well-formed sentence when the actual utterance was incomplete or grammatically garbled, our ability to interpret words we have never heard before, to correct slips of the tongue, or to cope with new idiolects. These phenomena threaten standard descriptions of linguistic competence (including descriptions for which I am responsible).

How should we understand or modify (1)–(3) to accommodate malapropisms? Principle (1) requires a competent interpreter to be prepared to intepret utterances of sentences he or she has never heard uttered before. This is possible because the interpreter can learn the semantic role of each of a finite number of words or phrases and can learn the semantic consequences of a finite number of modes of composition. This is enough to account for the ability to interpret utterances of novel sentences. And since the modes of composition can be iterated, there is no clear upper limit to the number of sentences utterances of which can be interpreted. The interpreter thus has a system for interpreting what he hears or says. You might think of this system as a machine which, when fed an arbitrary utterance (and certain parameters provided by the circumstances of the utterance), produces an interpretation. One model for such a machine is a theory of truth, more or less along the lines of a Tarski truth definition. It provides a recursive characterization of the truth conditions of all possible utterances of the speaker, and it does this through an analysis of utterances in terms of sentences made up from the finite vocabulary and the finite stock of modes of composition. I have frequently argued that command of such a theory would suffice for intepretation.[4] Here however there is no reason to be concerned with the details of the theory that can adequately model the ability of an interpreter. All that matters in the present discussion is that the theory has a finite base and is recursive, and these are features on which most philosophers and linguists agree.

To say that an explicit theory for interpreting a speaker is a model of the interpreter's linguistic competence is not to suggest that the interpreter knows any such theory. It is possible, of course, that most interpreters could be brought to acknowledge that they know some of the axioms of a theory of truth; for example, that a conjunction is true if and only if each of the conjuncts is true. And perhaps they also know theorems of the form 'An utterance of the sentence "There is life on Mars" is true if and only if there is life on Mars at the time of the utterance.' On the other hand, no one now has explicit knowledge of a fully satisfactory theory for interpreting the speakers of any natural language.

In any case, claims about what would constitute a satisfactory theory are not, as I said, claims about the propositional knowledge of an interpreter, nor are they claims about the details of the inner workings of some part of the brain. They are rather claims about what must be said to give a satisfactory description of the competence of the interpreter. *We* cannot describe what an interpreter can do except by appeal to a recursive theory of a certain sort. It does not add anything to this thesis to say that if the theory does correctly describe the competence of an interpreter, some mechanism in the interpreter must correspond to the theory.

Principle (2) says that for communication to succeed, a systematic method of interpretation must be shared. (I shall henceforth assume there is no harm in calling such a method a theory, as if the interpreter were using the theory we use to describe his competence.) The sharing comes to this: the interpreter uses his theory to understand the speaker; the speaker uses the same (or an equivalent) theory to guide his speech. For the speaker, it is a theory about how the interpreter will interpret him. Obviously this principle does not demand that speaker and interpreter speak the same language. It is an enormous convenience that many people speak in similar ways, and therefore can be interpreted in more or less the same way. But in principle communication does not demand that any two people speak the same language. What must be shared is the interpreter's and the speaker's understanding of the speaker's words.

For reasons that will emerge, I do not think that principles (1) and (2) are incompatible with the existence of malapropisms; it is only when they are combined with principle (3) that there is trouble. Before discussing principle (3) directly, however, I want to introduce an apparent diversion.

The perplexing issue that I want to discuss can be separated off from some related matters by considering a distinction made by Keith Donnellan, and something he said in its defence. Donnellan famously distinguished between two uses of definite descriptions. The *referential* use is illustrated as follows: Jones says 'Smith's murderer is insane', meaning that a certain man, whom he

---

[4] See the essays on radical interpretation in my *Inquiries into Truth and Interpretation*, (Clarendon Press, Oxford, 1984).

(Jones) takes to have murdered Smith, is insane. Donnellan says that even if the man that Jones believes to have murdered Smith did not murder Smith, Jones has referred to the man he had in mind; and if that man is insane, Jones has said something true. The same sentence may be used *attributively* by someone who wants to assert that the murderer of Smith, whoever he may be, is insane. In this case, the speaker does not say something true if no one murdered Smith, nor has the speaker referred to anyone.

In reply, Alfred MacKay objected that Donnellan shared Humpty Dumpty's theory of meaning: "'When *I* use a word", Humpty Dumpty said, ... "it means just what I choose it to mean."' In the conversation that went before, he had used the word 'glory' to mean 'a nice knock-down argument'. Donnellan, in answer, explains that intentions are connected with expectations and that you cannot intend to accomplish something by a certain means unless you believe or expect that the means will, or at least could, lead to the desired outcome. A speaker cannot, therefore, intend to mean something by what he says unless he believes his audience will interpret his words as he intends (the Gricean circle). Donnellan says,

> If I were to end this reply to MacKay with the sentence 'There's glory for you' I would be guilty of arrogance and, no doubt, of overestimating the strength of what I have said, but given the background I do not think I could be accused of saying something unintelligible. I would be understood, and would I not have meant by 'glory' 'a nice knockdown argument'?[5]

I like this reply, and I accept Donnellan's original distinction between two uses of descriptions (there are many more than two). But apparently I disagree with *some* view of Donnellan's, because unlike him I see almost no connection between the answer to MacKay's objection and the remarks on reference. The reason is this. MacKay says you cannot change what words mean (and so their reference if that is relevant) merely by intending to; the answer is that this is true, but you can change the meaning provided you believe (and perhaps are justified in believing) that the interpreter has adequate clues for the new interpretation. You may deliberately provide those clues, as Donnellan did for his final 'There's glory for you.'

The trouble is that Donnellan's original distinction had nothing to do with words changing their meaning or reference. If, in the referential use, Jones refers to someone who did not murder Smith by using the description 'Smith's murderer', the reference is none the less achieved by way of the normal meanings of the words. The words therefore must have their usual reference. All that is needed, if we are to accept this way of describing the situation, is a firm sense of the difference between what *words* mean or refer to and what *speakers* mean or refer to. Jones may have referred to someone else by using words that referred to Smith's murderer; this is something he may have done in ignorance or deliberately. Similarly for Donnellan's claim that Jones has said

---

[5] Keith Donnellan, 'Putting Humpty Dumpty Together Again'. *The Philosophical Review*, 77 (1968), p. 213. Alfred MacKay's article, 'Mr Donnellan and Humpty Dumpty on Referring' appeared in the same issue of *The Philosophical Review*, pp. 197–202.

something true when he says 'Smith's murderer is insane', provided the man he believes (erroneously) to have murdered Smith is insane. Jones has said something true by using a sentence that is false. This is done intentionally all the time, for example in irony or metaphor. A coherent theory could not allow that under the circumstances Jones' sentence was true; nor would Jones think so if he knew the facts. Jones' belief about who murdered Smith cannot change the truth of the sentence he uses (and for the same reason cannot change the reference of the words in the sentence).

Humpty Dumpty is out of it. He cannot mean what he says he means because he knows that 'There's glory for you' cannot be interpreted by Alice as meaning 'There's a nice knockdown argument for you.' We know he knows this because Alice says 'I don't know what you mean by "glory"', and Humpty Dumpty retorts, 'Of course you don't – til I tell you.' It is Mrs Malaprop and Donnellan who interest me; Mrs Malaprop because she gets away with it without even trying or knowing, and Donnellan because he gets away with it on purpose.

Here is what I mean by 'getting away with it': the interpreter comes to the occasion of utterance armed with a theory that tells him (or so he believes) what an arbitrary utterance of the speaker means. The speaker then says something with the intention that it will be interpreted in a certain way, and the expectation that it will be so interpreted. In fact this way is not provided for by the interpreter's theory. But the speaker is nevertheless understood; the interpreter adjusts his theory so that it yields the speaker's intended interpretation. The speaker has 'gotten away with it'. The speaker may or may not (Donnellan, Mrs Malaprop) know that he has got away with anything; the interpreter may or may not know that the speaker intended to get away with anything. What is common to the cases is that the speaker expects to be, and is, interpreted as the speaker intended although the interpreter did not have a correct theory in advance.

We do not need bizarre anecdotes or wonderlands to make the point. We all get away with it all the time; understanding the speech of others depends on it. Take proper names. In small, isolated groups everyone may know the names everyone else knows, and so have ready in advance of a speech encounter a theory that will, without correction, cope with the names to be employed. But even this semantic paradise will be destroyed by each new nickname, visitor, or birth. If a taboo bans a name, a speaker's theory is wrong until he learns of this fact; similarly if an outrigger canoe is christened.

There is not, so far as I can see, any theory of names that gets around the problem. If some definite description gives the meaning of a name, an interpreter still must somehow add to his theory the fact that the name new to him is to be matched with the appropriate description. If understanding a name is to give some weight to an adequate number of descriptions true of the object named, it is even more evident that adding a name to one's way of interpreting a speaker depends on no rule clearly stated in advance. The various theories that discover an essential demonstrative element in names do provide at least a partial rule for adding new names. But the addition is still an addition to the method of interpretation – what we may think of as the interpreter's view of the current language of the speaker. Finding a demonstrative element in names, or for that matter in mass nouns or words for natural kinds, does not reduce these words to pure demonstratives; that is why a new word in any of these categories requires a change in the interpreter's theory, and therefore a change in our description of his understanding of the speaker.

Mrs Malaprop and Donnellan make the case general. There is no word or construction that cannot be converted to a new use by an ingenious or ignorant speaker. And such conversion, while easier to explain because it involves mere substitution, is not the only kind. Sheer invention is equally possible, and we can be as good at intepreting it (say in Joyce or Lewis Carroll) as we are at interpreting the errors or twists of substitution. From the point of view of an ultimate explanation of how new concepts are acquired, learning to interpret a word that expresses a concept we do not already have is a far deeper and more interesting phenomenon than explaining the ability to use a word new to us for an old concept. But both require a change in one's way of interpreting the speech of another, or in speaking to someone who has the use of the word.

The contrast between acquiring a new concept or meaning along with a new word and merely acquiring a new word for an old concept would be salient if I were concerned with the infinitely difficult problem of how a first language is learned. By comparison, my problem is simple. I want to know how people who already have a language (whatever exactly that means) manage to apply their skill or knowledge to actual cases of interpretation. All the things I assume an interpreter knows or can do depend on his having a mature set of concepts, and being at home with the business of linguistic communication. My problem is to describe what is involved in the idea of 'having a language' or of being at home with the business of linguistic communication.

Here is a highly simplified and idealized proposal about what goes on. An interpreter has, at any moment of a speech transaction, what I persist in calling a theory. (I call it a theory, as remarked before, only because a description of the interpreter's competence requires a recursive account.) I assume that the interpreter's theory has been adjusted to the evidence so far available to him: knowledge of the character, dress, role, sex, of the speaker, and whatever else has been gained by observing the speaker's behaviour, linguistic or otherwise. As the speaker speaks his piece the interpreter alters his theory, entering hypotheses about new names, altering the interpretation of familiar predicates, and revising past interpretations of particular utterances in the light of new evidence.

Some of what goes on may be described as improving the method of intepretation as the evidential base enlarges. But much is not like that. When Donnellan ends his reply to MacKay by saying 'There's glory for you' not only he, but his words, are correctly interpreted as meaning 'There's a nice knockdown argument for you.' That's how he intends us to interpret his words, and we know this, since we have, and he knows we have, and we know he knows we have (etc.), the background needed to provide the interpretation. But up to a certain point (before MacKay came on the scene) this interpretation of an earlier utterance by Donnellan of the same words would have been wrong. To put this differently: the theory we actually use to interpret an utterance is geared to the occasion. We may decide later we could have done better by the occasion, but this does not mean (necessarily) that we now have a better theory for the next occasion. The reason for this is, as we have seen, perfectly obvious: a speaker may provide us with information relevant to interpreting an utterance in the course of making the utterance.

Let us look at the process from the speaker's side. The speaker wants to be understood, so he utters words he believes can and will be interpreted in a certain way. In order to judge how he will be interpreted, he forms, or uses, a picture of the interpreter's readiness to interpret along certain lines. Central to this picture is what the speaker believes is the starting theory of interpretation the interpreter has for him. The speaker does not necessarily speak in such a way as to prompt the interpreter to apply this prior theory; he may deliberately dispose the interpreter to modify his prior theory. But the speaker's view of the interpreter's prior theory is not irrelevant to what he says, nor to what he means by his words; it is an important part of what he has to go on if he wants to be understood.

I have distinguished what I have been calling the *prior theory* from what I shall henceforth call the *passing theory*. For the hearer, the prior theory expresses how he is prepared in advance to interpret an utterance of the speaker, while the passing theory is how he *does* interpret the utterance. For the speaker, the prior theory is what he *believes* the interpreter's prior theory to be, while his passing theory is the theory he *intends* the interpreter to use.

I am now in a position to state a problem that arises if we accept the distinction between the prior and the passing theory and also accept the account of linguistic competence given by principles (1)–(2). According to that account, each interpreter (and this includes speakers, since speakers must be interpreters) comes to a successful linguistic exchange prepared with a 'theory' which constitutes his basic linguistic competence, and which he shares with those with whom he communicates. Because each party has such a shared theory and knows that others share his theory, and knows that others know he knows (etc.), some would say that the knowledge or abilities that constitute the theory may be called conventions.

I think that the distinction between the prior and the passing theory, if taken seriously, undermines this commonly accepted account of linguistic competence and communication. Here is why. What must be shared for communication to succeed is the passing theory. For the passing theory is the one the interpreter actually uses to interpret an utterance, and it is the theory the speaker intends the interpreter to use. Only if these coincide is understanding complete. (Of course, there are degrees of success in communication; much may be right although something is wrong. This matter of degree is irrelevant to my argument.)

The passing theory is where, accident aside, agreement is greatest. As speaker and interpreter talk, their prior theories become more alike; so do their passing theories. The asymptote of agreement and understanding is reached when passing theories coincide. But the passing theory cannot in general correspond to an interpreter's linguistic competence. Not only does it have its changing list of proper names and gerrymandered vocabulary, but it includes every successful – i.e. correctly interpreted – use of any other word or phrase, no matter how far out of the ordinary. Every deviation from ordinary usage, as long as it is agreed on for the moment (knowingly deviant, or not, on one, or both, sides), is in the passing theory as a feature of what the words mean on that occasion. Such meanings, transient though they may be, are literal; they are what I have called first meanings. A passing theory is not a theory of what anyone (except perhaps a philosopher) would call an actual natural language. 'Mastery' of such a language would be useless, since knowing a passing theory is only knowing how to interpret a particular utterance on a particular occasion. Nor could such a language, if we want to call it that, be said to have been learned, or to be governed by conventions. Of course things previously learned were essential to arriving at the passing theory, but what was learned could not have been the passing theory.

Why should a passing theory be called a theory at all? For the sort of theory we have in mind is, in its formal structure, suited to be the theory for an entire language, even though its expected field of application is vanishingly small. The answer is that when a word or phrase temporarily or locally takes over the role of some other word or phrase (as treated in a prior theory, perhaps), the entire burden of that role, with all its implications for logical relations to other words, phrases, and sentences, must be carried along by the passing theory. Someone who grasps the fact that Mrs Malaprop means 'epithet' when she says 'epitaph' must give 'epithet' all the powers 'epitaph' has for many other people. Only a full recursive theory can do justice to these powers. These remarks do not depend on supposing Mrs Malaprop will always make this 'mistake'; once is enough to summon up a passing theory assigning a new role to 'epitaph'.

An interpreter's prior theory has a better chance of describing what we might think of as a natural language, particularly a prior theory brought to a first conversation. The less we know about the speaker, assuming we know he belongs to our language community, the more nearly our prior theory will simply be the theory we expect someone who hears our unguarded speech to use. If we ask for a cup of coffee, direct a taxi driver, or order a crate of lemons, we may know so little about our intended interpreter that we can do no better than to assume that he will interpret our speech along what we take to be standard lines. But all this is relative. In fact we always have the interpreter in mind; there is no such thing as how we expect, in the abstract, to be interpreted. We inhibit our higher vocabulary, or encourage it, depending on the most general considerations, and we cannot fail to have premonitions as to which of the proper names we know are apt to be correctly understood.

In any case, my point is this: most of the time prior theories will not be shared, and there is no reason why they should be. Certainly it is not a condition of successful communication that prior theories be shared: consider the malaprop from ignorance. Mrs Malaprop's theory, prior and passing, is that 'A nice derangement of epitaphs' means a nice arrangement of epithets. An interpreter who, as we say, knows English, but does not know the verbal habits of Mrs Malaprop, has a prior theory according to which 'A nice derangement of epitaphs' means a nice derangement of epitaphs; but his passing theory agrees with that of Mrs Malaprop if he understands her words.

It is quite clear that in general the prior theory is neither shared by speaker and interpreter nor is it what we would normally call a language. For the prior theory has in it all the features special to the idiolect of the speaker that the interpreter is in a position to take into account before the utterance begins. One way to appreciate the difference between the prior theory and our ordinary idea of a person's language is to reflect on the fact that an interpreter must be expected to have quite different prior theories for different speakers – not as different, usually, as his passing theories; but these are matters that depend on how well the interpreter knows his speaker.

Neither the prior theory nor the passing theory describes what we would call the language a person knows, and neither theory characterizes a speaker's or interpreter's linguistic competence. Is there any theory that would do better?

Perhaps it will be said that what is essential to the mastery of a language is not knowledge of any particular vocabulary, or even detailed grammar, much less knowledge of what any speaker is apt to succeed in making his words and sentences mean. What is essential is a basic framework of categories and rules, a sense of the way English (or any) grammars may be constructed, plus a skeleton list of interpreted words for fitting into the basic framework. If I put all this vaguely, it is only because I want to consider a large number of actual or possible proposals in one fell swoop; for I think they all fail to resolve our problem. They fail for the same reasons the more complete and specific prior theories fail: none of them satisfies the demand for a description of an ability that speaker and interpreter share and that is adequate to interpretation.

First, any general framework, whether conceived as a grammar for English, or a rule for accepting grammars, or a basic grammar plus rules for modifying or extending it – any such general framework, by virtue of the features that make it general, will by itself be insufficient for interpreting particular utterances. The general framework or theory, whatever it is, may be a key ingredient in what is needed for interpretation, but it can't be all that is needed since it fails to provide the interpretation of particular words and sentences as uttered by a particular speaker. In this respect it is like a prior theory, only worse because it is less complete.

Second, the framework theory must be expected to be different for different speakers. The more general and abstract it is, the more difference there can be without it mattering to communication. The theoretical possibility of such divergence is obvious; but once one tries to imagine a framework rich enough to serve its purpose, it is clear that such differences must also be actual. It is impossible to give examples, of course, until it is decided what to count in the framework: a sufficiently explicit framework could be discredited by a single malapropism. There is some evidence of a more impressive sort that internal grammars do differ among speakers of 'the same language'. James McCawley reports that recent work by Haber shows

> that there is appreciable variation as to what rules of plural formation different speakers have, the variation being manifested in such things as the handling of novel words that an investigator has presented his subjects with, in the context of a task that will force them to use the word in the plural ... Haber suggests that her subjects, rather than having a uniformly applicable process of plural formation, each have a 'core' system, which covers a wide range of cases, but not necessarily everything, plus strategies ... for handling cases that are not covered by the 'core' system ... Haber's data suggest that speakers of what are to the minutest details 'the same dialect' often have acquired grammars that differ in far more respects than their speech differs in.[6]

---

[6] James McCawley, 'Some Ideas Not to Live By', *Die Neuen Sprachen*, 75 (1976), p. 157. These results are disputed by those who believe the relevant underlying rules and structures are prewired. My point obviously does not depend on the example, or the level at which deviations are empirically possible.

I have been trying to throw doubt on how clear the idea of 'speaking the same dialect' is, but here we may assume that it at least implies the frequent sharing of passing theories.

Bringing in grammars, theories, or frameworks more general than, and prior to, prior theories just emphasizes the problem I originally presented in terms of the contrast between prior theories and passing theories. Stated more broadly now, the problem is this: what interpreter and speaker share, to the extent that communication succeeds, is not learned and so is not a language governed by rules or conventions known to speaker and interpreter in advance; but what the speaker and interpreter know in advance is not (necessarily) shared, and so is not a language governed by shared rules or conventions. What is shared is, as before, the passing theory; what is given in advance is the prior theory, or anything on which it may in turn be based.

What I have been leaving out of account up to now is what Haber calls a 'strategy', which is a nice word for the mysterious process by which a speaker or hearer uses what he knows in advance plus present data to produce a passing theory. What two people need, if they are to understand one another through speech, is the ability to converge on passing theories from utterance to utterance. Their starting points, however far back we want to take them, will usually be very different – as different as the ways in which they acquired their linguistic skills. So also, then, will the strategies and stratagems that bring about convergence differ.

Perhaps we can give content to the idea of two people 'having the same language' by saying that they tend to converge on passing theories, degree or relative frequency of convergence would then be a measure of similarity of language. What use can we find, however, for the concept of a language? We could hold that any theory on which a speaker and interpreter converge is a language; but then there would be a new language for every unexpected turn in the conversation, and languages could not be learned and no one would want to master most of them.

We just made a sort of sense of the idea of two people 'having the same language', though we could not explain what a language is. It is easy to see that the idea of 'knowing' a language will be in the same trouble, as will the project of characterizing the abilities or capacities a person must have if he commands a language. But we might try to say in what a person's ability to interpret or speak to another person consists: it is the ability that permits him to construct a correct, that is, convergent, passing theory for speech transactions with that person. Again, the concept allows of degrees of application.

This characterization of linguistic ability is so nearly circular that it cannot be wrong: it comes to saying that the ability to communicate by speech consists in the ability to make oneself understood, and to understand. It is only when we look at the structure of this ability that we realize how far we have drifted from standard ideas of language mastery. For we have discovered no learnable common core of consistent behaviour, no shared grammar or rules, no portable interpreting machine set to grind out the meaning of an arbitrary utterance. We may say that linguistic ability is the ability to converge on a passing theory from time to time – this is what I have suggested, and I have no better proposal. But if we do say this, then we should realize that we have abandoned not only the ordinary notion of a language, but we have erased the boundary between knowing a language and knowing our way around in the world generally. For there are no rules for arriving at passing theories, no rules in any strict sense, as opposed to rough maxims and methodological generalities. A passing theory really is like a theory at least in this, that it is derived by wit, luck, and wisdom from a private vocabulary and grammar, knowledge of the ways people get their point across, and rules of thumb for figuring out what deviations from the dictionary are most likely. There is no more chance of regularizing, or teaching, this process than there is of regularizing or teaching the process of creating new theories to cope with new data in any field – for that is what this process involves.

The problem we have been grappling with depends on the assumption that communication by speech requires that speaker and interpreter have learned or somehow acquired a common method or theory of interpretation – as being able to operate on the basis of shared conventions, rules, or regularities. The problem arose when we realized that no method or theory fills this bill. The solution to the problem is clear. In linguistic communication nothing corresponds to a linguistic competence as often described: that is, as summarized by principles (1)-(3). The solution is to give up the principles. Principles (1) and (2) survive when understood in rather unusual ways, but principle (3) cannot stand, and it is unclear what can take its place. I conclude that there is no such thing as a language, not if a language is anything like what many philosophers and linguists have supposed. There is therefore no such thing to be learned, mastered, or born with. We must give up the idea of a clearly defined shared structure which language-users acquire and then apply to cases. And we should try again to say how convention in any important sense is involved in language; or, as I think, we should give up the attempt to illuminate how we communicate by appeal to conventions.

25

The Parody of Conversation

IAN HACKING

'A Nice Derangement of Epitaphs': that is the remarkable title of one of Donald Davidson's most recent essays.[1] I doubt if any philosopher has hitherto written at length about malaprops. Yet if the topic is unusual, the conclusion is downright astonishing:

> I conclude that there is no such thing as a language, not if a language is anything like what many philosophers and linguists have supposed. There is therefore no such thing to be learned, mastered, or born with. ['Derangement', 446]

What does this iconoclasm do to Davidson's philosophy of language? Is there no longer language for there to be philosophy of? When we turn to Davidson's second volume of collected papers, the longest pair of entries in the index is, inevitably, 'Tarski' and 'Tarski-style Theories of Truth'. When we look for items not built around the name of a person, our longest pair is 'Convention T' and 'T-sentences'. 'True-in-L' is at the heart of Davidson's philosophy. What is left, is there is no such thing as an L?

We do not expect Davidson's philosophy to be the only one challenged by his conclusions. For example, Michael Dummett's linguistic approach to what he calls 'realism' led him to ask what it is to know, and to acquire mastery of, a language. That, he urges, has become the central question for philosophy of language, heir to the extinct – as Dummett would have it – science of epistemology. Were Davidson correct, Dummett's question is a non-starter. There is no such thing as a language, of which one may acquire mastery.

I shall leave to others the difficult question, how well does Davidson reason to his conclusion. I shall, for once, take Davidson's oft-stated advice, and proceed holistically. I shall ask, what does Davidson's new conclusion do to other philosophical propositions that he has long urged with great consistency?

---

[1] Davidson, Donald, 'A Nice Derangement of Epitaphs', this volume pp. 433–46. Henceforth referred to as 'Derangement'.

The target

Davidson is not intending philosophical suicide, but there is an element of retraction in his paper. He thinks that our ability to understand malaprops, slips of the tongue, incomplete sentences (and also, not unconnected, proper names) threatens 'standard descriptions of linguistic competence (including descriptions for which I am responsible)' ['Derangement', p. 437]. However, a very substantial part of the Davidson programme has not budged; I think that taking his conclusions seriously means that more of it ought to change. On one central issue Davidson is quite unmoved. We find in the malaprop paper paragraphs that might have been written by an able student trying to summarize Davidson's philosophy. He requires

> a competent interpreter to be prepared to interpret utterances of sentences he or she has never heard uttered before. This is possible because the interpreter can learn the semantic role of each of a finite number of words or phrases and can learn the semantic consequences of a finite number of modes of composition. This is enough to account for the ability to interpret utterances of novel sentences. And since the modes of composition can be iterated, there is no clear upper limit to the number of sentences, of which utterances can be interpreted. The interpreter thus has a system for interpreting what he hears or says. You might think of this system as a machine which when fed an arbitrary utterance (and certain parameters provided by the circumstances of the utterance) produces an interpretation. One model for such a machine is a theory of truth, more or less along the lines of the Tarski truth definition. It provides a recursive characteriza-tion of the truth conditions of all possible utterances of the speaker, and it does this through an analysis of utterances in terms of sentences made up from the finite vocabulary and the finite stock of modes of composition. ... All that matters in the present discussion is that the theory has a finite base and is recursive, and these are features on which most philosophers and linguists would agree. ['Derangement', pp. 437–38].

How does this fit with the idea that there is no such thing as a language? Very simply. The paragraph is entirely one-sided: interpreter-sided. So is *most* of Davidson's lifetime discussion of interpretation. But the malaprop paper is about communication, conversation, interaction between speaker and hearer. Although there is little mention of nested intentions, the problems – but not the conclusions – of this paper fit well into a book of essays for Paul Grice.

How is a two-sided account different from a one-sided, interpreter-sided account? We might well expect Davidson to favour the following story. When J and K talk to each other in common English, they share a Tarski-style theory of truth about that language (or may be modelled as sharing such a theory). J uses it to interpret K that way, and K interprets J that way. That is also the theory they bring to conversation with friends and colleagues. They use it for following TV newscasters, and newscasters expect them to do so.

There is, in short, a shared language which people of a community bring to each other, and which makes possible extended conversation. Possession of this ability – plus what Davidson once called 'psychological trappings' – suffices for communication. The trappings may be more than 'psychological' – social sense, shared interests. The essential idea is, however, that there is a shared language. Moreover, there is an important sense, doubtless in need of clarification, in which this shared language is governed by regularities that are features of the language, not of the individuals. Davidson's own summary of this idea is that the literal meanings of our words and utterances 'are governed by learned conventions or regularities. The systematic knowledge or competence of the speaker or interpreter is learned in advance of occasions of interpretation and is conventional in character' ['Derangement', p. 436]. *That* is what Davidson rejects. The concluding paper of *Inquiries*[2] is titled 'Communication and Convention'. Its thesis is *communication without convention*. The thesis of the malaprop paper is a substantial generalization of that. It is *communication without a language* (if a language is anything like what philosophers and linguists have taken it to be).

It is important to notice here something that Davidson has reiterated. He thinks that we have pretty adequate generality, in a study of communication, when we consider just two people, speaker and hearer. We get some way to Davidson's position if we think as follows: each pair of conversationalists evolves its own language. There is no such thing as a linguistic framework that they bring to each other and which makes their conversation possible.

Malaprops and interpretation

Malaprops have played no previous role in philosophy, I think – except once, in 1974. In his famous APA address, 'On the very Idea of a conceptual Scheme', Davidson said that, 'As philosophers, we are peculiarly tolerant of systematic malapropism, and practised at interpreting the result' (*Inquiries*, p. 196). This sentence immediately follows an example of ketches and yawls (craft that differ as to whether the mizzen is stepped fore or aft the rudder). Someone speaks of a yawl when only a ketch is in the offing. We might conclude that he has mistaken a ketch for a yawl (or, more likely, that he does not know or cannot tell the difference). But we may also conclude that he does not use the word 'yawl' quite as we do. 'We do this sort of off the cuff interpretation all the time, deciding in favour of reinterpretation of words in order to preserve a reasonable theory of belief' (ibid.). The chief development of this idea since 1974 is one of emphasis: we do this sort of off the cuff interpretation *all the time*. Even when you say, 'there's a ketch', and there is a ketch, and I take you to be saying so, I am engaged in interpretation – radical interpretation, albeit 'homophonic'.

Although the yawl/ketch example immediately precedes the sentence about malapropism, Davidson cannot intend it as an example of a malaprop. My first dictionary (the old Concise Oxford) defines a malaprop as 'a ludicrous use of a word, esp. in mistake for one resembling it (e.g., *a nice derangement of epitaphs* ...)'. The yawl/ketch is neither ludicrous nor, more importantly, a matter of

---

[2] Davidson, Donald, *Inquiries into Truth and Interpretation*, (Clarendon Press, Oxford, 1984); henceforth referred to as *Inquiries*.

confusing words of similar sounds. The 1974 paper mentions malaprops but gives no actual examples. We should not think that the yawl/ketch is altogether like a malaprop. The chief resemblance is that both are *mistakes*: mistakes of different kinds. Someone who has things back to front, and thinks that a ketch has a mizzen that is stepped abaft the rudder, is wrong about things (or how they are called). Someone who commits a malaprop is first of all confusing sounds. Of course a mistake can be of several kinds at once. Thus I once wrote a letter supporting an entirely self-taught student, calling him an autodictat, instead of an autodidact. That was a malaprop. The resonance 'dictat' almost certainly arose, unwittingly, because the man always wore jackboots and other semblance of SS garb, so my mistake was also a Freudian slip. But undoubtedly autodidact is the right word, and ketch the right word in Davidson's example. Is it not because there are facts about our language, against which the malaprop and the yawl/ketch are mistakes?

Well, there is a question about 'the' language. In the 1973 'Radical Interpretation' paper, Davidson begins by saying that, 'The problem of interpretation is domestic as well as foreign: it surfaces for speakers of the same language in the form of the question, how can it be determined that the language is the same?' (*Inquiries*, p. 125).

Oddly, this is a question that seems never to surface for me, even though I live in a polyglot neighbourhood that boasts newspapers in forty-seven different languages. Or rather, it arose once, with an elderly newcomer who simply could not get her tongue around her phonemes; it took me some time to be sure that she was speaking English at all. How did we determine we were speaking the same language? Chiefly by patient listening and encouragement. That is a real case of wondering whether the other is speaking the same language as I am. When I wonder whether you are using the words 'yawl' and 'ketch' correctly, I may bluster because I fear that I am confused, not you. But I am not worrying whether we are speaking the same language. On reading my letter, you may suppose that I regularly use the word 'autodictat'. That is a quirk about me, you may guess, but not a sign that we are speaking different languages.

Undoubtedly, Davidson holds that there is a problem about whether we are speaking the same language, because of his views on the nature of interpretation. I shall presently explain this, but first a comment on Davidson's use of the word 'interpretation' itself.

To interpret, says my old dictionary, is to 'expound the meaning of (abstruse words, writings &c.)'. Other dictionaries also give 'clarify', 'elucidate', 'explain' and the like. My dictionary continues with other senses of our word: 'to make out the meaning of; bring out the meaning of, render by artistic representation or performance; explain, understand in a specified manner, as *this we interpret as a threat*; act as interpreter.' An interpreter is a simultaneous translator, i.e. 'one whose office is to translate orally, in their presence, the words of persons speaking different languages.'

Now when you say 'look at the handsome ketch' in a normal, chatty sort of way, and there is a ketch and only a ketch there, I am not interpreting you in any of the above senses. I hesitate to say, of someone who understands my sentence, 'This man is an autodictat,' that he is interpreting me, but at least he can be said to 'make out my meaning', and so this fits the definition. If, after the handsome-ketch remark, I say to my daughter, 'But the crewmen are strictly off limits,' no one interprets me in the dictionary sense. All listeners understand full well what I mean. On the other hand, suppose I responded with, 'Oh, my dear, the Taj Mahal.' That might need interpretation. At a first level, I am comparing this ornate, exuberantly decorated tax-write-off ketch to the Taj Mahal, and thereby panning the claim that this craft is handsome. The philosophically learned will add that I am copying an example of John Wisdom's, in connection with a lady's bonnet. Maybe that is interpretation. Who knows – it may even be hermeneutical. The vast majority of things we say to our peers in ordinary conversation are not interpreted at all.

Quine wrote of radical translation. What he had in mind was commerce between two mutually alien peoples. He proposed that linguists on at least one side would construct translation manuals, to understand the other. It has been remarked that a translation manual, of itself, merely says that two words, in different languages, mean the same. It does not tell what the alien word means. This point was hammered home to me in my first philosophy lessons, by my own teacher, Casimir Lewy, so it seems to me to be rather pedantic. That is how we treat wisdom learned at parents' knees: we are astonished that anyone could want to make much out of a matter so trivial. But Davidson (and John MacDowell reporting Davidson) do a service by repeating the banal point.

In dropping Quine's 'translation', however, Davidson also does something not at all banal, something that could even be downright suspicious. He writes not of radical translation but of radical interpretation. That is the first shift, but a second one follows swiftly. He holds that radical interpretation is needed for domestic commerce as well as foreign.

Davidson says that this surfaces in the question of how we know that we are speaking the same language. It is as if every time that I enter into conversation with another, I have to hold before me the possibility that he is an alien. But even in successive versions of the horror movie *The Body Snatchers*, the problem is not whether other seeming-humans are speaking English. The problem about the aliens is that they are speaking English and acting small-town American. The problem is precisely that we do *not* need to interpret them. Our fear is that despite this, they are aliens.

These negative remarks contrast Davidson's use of the word 'interpretation', and what I take to be more common ways of expressing ourselves. Note, however, that something more plausibly called interpreting comes into play when we turn to malaprops and other mistakes or tropes. A philosophy of language couched in terms of domestic interpretation needs and feeds on things like malaprops.

The malaprop argument

I wish only to give the flavour of the argument, not its full substance. An important part of Davidson's paper is about proper names, and the ways in which speaker and hearer figure out which proper names refer to whom (which Bill is the man just called 'Bill'?)

The paper begins with some marvellous malaprops. It notes that we follow a farcical paragraph full of them with glee, not confusion. Typically we are at once able to understand a speaker who uses a malaprop. Here is a recent example. In a seminar on crucial experiments, a nervous arts undergraduate referred to 'the parody of conversation'. Those were, at any rate, the sounds I heard. Out of context you might not know what he meant, but around that table, everyone knew. The sounds he wanted to utter may have been 'the parity of conservation'. He in fact referred to the famous crucial physics experiment refuting the conservation of parity.

It is fair to say that I understood the sentence in which these words occurred, as well as anything else my student said that day. Malaprops, slips of the tongue, incomplete sentences and the like, are so readily understood that they 'threaten standard descriptions of linguistic competence (including descriptions for which I am responsible)' ['Derangement', p. 437].

Davidson lists three standard ingredients of such descriptions. He couches them in terms of the literal meaning or what he now prefers to call 'first meaning' of our words.

(1) *First meaning is systematic* ....
(2) *First meanings are shared* ....
(3) *First meanings are governed by learned conventions or regularities* .... ['Derangement', p. 436].

The first two are, he thinks, salvageable, but not the third. Here is his present picture of communication. When I begin to speak with someone, I have a *prior theory* of how to do it. But this is not only a theory about the English language. It is a theory about my respondent. I speak English differently in different settings. I have different prior theories about different people, largely according to stereotypes. Davidson's own examples are these: 'We ask for a cup of coffee, direct a taxi driver, or order a crate of lemons.'

> We may know so little about our intended interpreter that we can do no better than to assume that he will interpret our speech along what we take to be standard lines. But all this is relative. In fact we always have the interpreter in mind; there is no such thing, as how we expect, in the abstract, to be interpreted. We inhibit our higher vocabulary, or encourage it, depending on the most general considerations .... ['Derangement', p. 443]

Our conversation may start on standard lines with prior theory, but if we engage each other at all, we quickly pass from prior assumptions to what Davidson calls a *passing theory*.

> For the speaker, the prior theory is what he *believes* the interpreter's prior theory to be, while his passing theory is the theory he *intends* the interpreter to use. ['Derangement', p. 442].

> As speaker and interpreter talk, their prior theories become more alike; so do their passing theories. The same asymptote of agreement and understanding is when passing theories coincide. But the passing theory cannot in general correspond to an interpreter's linguistic competence. Not only does it have its changing list of

proper names and gerrymandered vocabulary, but it includes every successful – i.e. correctly interpreted – use of any other word or phrase, no matter how far out of the ordinary. Every deviation from ordinary usage, as long as it is agreed on for the moment (knowingly deviant, or not, on one, or both, sides) is in the passing theory as a feature of what the words mean on that occasion. Such meanings, transient though they may be, are literal .... ['Derangement', pp. 442–3]

There is, then, no such thing as a language that speakers bring to their conversations. People have all sorts of expectations about each other. These may include prior or standard theory but that is not necessary. Whether we are speaking with a neighbour or an alien, what makes the conversation possible is the steadily evolving passing theory.

No language, some L

We can now see what happens to true-in-L in the no-language story. Once again let us return to an earlier paper, this time 'The Inscrutability of Reference' of 1979. This is one of numerous pieces asserting that the language a person speaks is less a natural property of the person, than a theoretical construct attributed to a person in the light of evidence. Several kinds of underdetermination invite the idea that numerous different languages might be attributed to a person.

Even if we consider truth invariant, we can suit the evidence by various ways of matching words and objects. *The best way of announcing the way we have chosen is by naming the language*; but then we must characterise the language as one for which reference, satisfaction, and truth have been assigned specific roles. An empirical question remains, to be sure: is this language one that the evidence allows us to attribute to the speaker? (*Inquiries*, p. 240, my italics)

Recall my longest quotation above, which I called the interpreter-sided part of Davidson's philosophy, and which is entirely preserved in the malaprop paper. The interpreter can be modelled as interacting with his speaker by a Tarski-style theory, or so we were told. But we now have the picture of the interpreter going through a whole series of constantly modified Ls very quickly. Interestingly, Davidson has from the start always had a slight tendency to elide the L in T-sentences. In the 1970 'Semantics for Natural Languages', for example, we read:

A theory of truth entails, for each sentence s, a statement of the form, 's is true if and only if p.' (*Inquiries*, p. 60)

I am inclined to say that the Ls (often so happily elided) are not languages at all, in any common sense of the world, and one could still keep the Ls even if one said that there is no such thing as a language.

This may be connected with a change acknowledged by Davidson in the introduction to *Inquiries*, and in his 'Reply to Foster' of 1976. He came to see that Tarski was interested in defining truth for a formal language, and could take the concept of translation for granted. Davidson had reversed the role of Convention T; Tarski 'could take the concept of translation for granted. But in *radical* interpretation, this is just what cannot be assumed' (*Inquiries*, p. 172).

> To accept this change in perspective is not to give up convention *T* but to read it in a new way. Like Tarski I want a theory that satisfies Convention *T*, but where he assumes the notion of translation in order to throw light on that of truth, I want to illumine the concept of translation by assuming a partial understanding of the concept of truth. (*Inquiries*, p. 173)

The malaprop paper may bring an additional change in perspective. Perhaps in the 'Reply to Foster' Davidson still supposed there was such a thing as a language, something in some contrast to the formal *L*s of the historical Tarski's work. But now that there is no such thing as a language, the *L*s in Davidson's theory in certain ways revert to merely formal constructs.

This further change of perspective is in some ways satisfying. For example, I once objected as follows.[3] Davidson admits some indeterminacy of translation. He should not. For indeterminacy implies there are two acceptable systems of interpretation J and K, such that for some utterance s made by X speaking language L, J implies that s is true in L if and only if p, while K implies the contrary. How then can both be acceptable, not just in the light of some passing evidence, but in the light of all conceivable evidence? Davidson replied to me in 'Inscrutability' that this is no

> contradiction if the theories are relativized to a language, as all theories of truth are. Our mistake was to suppose there is a unique language to which a given utterance belongs. But we can without paradox take that utterance to belong to one or another language. (*Inquiries*, p. 239)

Without paradox? Without contradiction, yes, but it is highly paradoxical to suppose that I can in one utterance be speaking two or indeed indefinitely many languages. Tom Stoppard manages to keep that up for ten minutes in *Cahoots MacBeth. That*, I would say, is having my utterances occur in two different languages simultaneously, and only the greatest philosophical spoofster of our times can do it. But the air of paradox disappears when it turns out that my s is not being spoken in different languages simultaneously. It is merely two different formal constructions that are applied to my s, two different *L*s. *Those Ls are not languages*, for indeed there is no such thing as a language. I do wish Davidson were not so well disposed to the indeterminacy of translation (albeit in weaker forms than Quine's) but my argument against him is satisfactorily quashed – at the price of giving up my language for this or that non-language L.

Theories and recursion

My longest quotation from the malaprop paper ended with the words: 'All that matters in the present discussion is that the theory has a finite base and is recursive, and these are features on which most philosophers and linguists

---

[3] Hacking, Ian, 'Why Does Language Matter to Philosophy?' (Cambridge University Press, Cambridge, 1975), p. 154.

agree' ['Derangement', p. 438]. I am in the minority. I have never seen that linguistic ability should be recursive, or should be modelled realistically by a recursive theory (not if we use 'recursive' in the strict logician's sense of the word).

Davidson does not retract his enthusiasm for recursion for one moment, but I detect a certain tension. Here is a passage in which I emphasize two phrases:

> An interpreter has, at any moment of a speech transaction, what I *persist in calling a theory*. (I call it a theory, as remarked before, *only* because a description of the interpreter's competence requires a recursive account). ['Derangement', p. 441, my italics]

Turning to the end of the paper we read that,

> A passing theory *really is like a theory at least in this*, that it is derived by wit, luck, and wisdom from a private vocabulary and grammar, knowledge of the ways people get their point across, and rules of thumb for figuring out what deviations from the dictionary are most likely. There is no more chance of regularizing or teaching this process than there is of regularizing or teaching the process of creating new theories to cope with new data in any field – for that is what this process involves. ['Derangement', p. 446, my italics]

The tenor of these two passages seems very different. There seems to be a dangerous equivocation about the word 'theory'. In both quotations, we are concerned with what the speaker or hearer brings to conversation and communication. In the first, Davidson 'persists' in calling that a theory 'only' because it is recursive. In the second it 'really' is like a theory because of the give-and-take, groping and exploration way in which it hooks up with experience of another person. The second seems to me to have nothing to do with whether the theory itself is recursive, or asserts that a recursive structure L can be used to model a person's speech. Hence: two ideas of theory must be in play.

I speculate: once the passing theory is made essential, recursivity, as a demand, is doomed.

It happens that my long quotation, about recursion, is Davidson's explication of a shorter statement. He calls it the first requirement on an account of literal meaning, that literal meaning is *systematic*:

> A competent speaker or interpreter is able to interpret utterances, his own or those of others, on the basis of the semantic properties of the parts, or words, in the utterance, and the structure of the utterance. For this to be possible, there must be systematic relations between the meanings of the terms. ['Derangement', p. 436]

With that we agree. But it does not imply that there must be one all-embracing (recursive or otherwise) system. There can be lots of systematic relations which listener must bring to hearer, but there is no necessity for one monolithic whole.

One of the arguments for recursion was our ability to perceive logical connections between sentences. Now it is a constraint on an axiomatized formal theory that, whether or not a given string is a proof, it is itself a recursive property. Likewise theoremhood is a recursively enumerable property. Such formal, timeless, facts have nothing to do with passing theories of another person's speech. In conversation outside the tea room of the math department we make only the shortest of deductive inferences, and even inside they make precious few. As well as uttering the ungrammatical sentences noticed by Davidson, we contradict ourselves all the time. One of the more preposterous features of the principle of charity, especially if applied to causal conversation with another, is the demand that we interpret the other as being consistent. Any modified family of principles, including what Richard Grandy[4] called the principle of humanity, would make us expect other people to be inconsistent. It is not charitable, but rather inhumane, to pretend that I am talking to a god. Now of course the fact that I think I detect inconsistencies in what you are saying, shows that I am somewhat systematic. But it does not show that I bring one whole recursive system that goes on forever spinning unintelligible deductions. It shows rather that I have a whole bunch of tricks for seeing what connects with what. It is good that students of formal logic can to some extent regiment these into one or a few formal systems, but what the 'interpreter' brings to conversation is a whole bunch of little, not too closely connected moves.

Davidson rightly remarks that as passing theories pass on, a single shift gets incorporated into lots of sentences. If I use 'autodictat' for autodidact, so be it; you will understand quite a lot of sentences I might utter. Not many that I *do* utter, for I use the word at most once a year. Today I'm mentioning it far more than I have ever used it in my entire life. There's system here all right, but nothing more than a little grammar. I shall not seriously challenge that grammars are recursive, although there are now plenty of linguists who doubt that they are, or doubt that recursiveness is relevant to grammar. Davidson has always wanted to separate semantics from syntax. He has urged that the imperialism of grammarians, who seek to conquer semantics, is founded upon confusion. Let us agree, for the nonce. Even if I allow myself a recursive grammar in an account of how sentences with funny words get manipulated, I have no need for one uniform recursive system for generating meanings.

I have said that you can have your L and swallow, or at any rate dismiss, your language. That is, there could be no such thing as a language, although we still wade in to communication with true-in-L. But now it seems to me we do not want L at all, for its chief force was to be part of a recursive system. This cheers me. Casimir Lewy assured me from our first meeting that there was no such thing as true-in-L in life beyond logic. There is just truth. So I mischievously suggest that Davidson's oft eliding L, noted above, was a step in the right direction.

Holism

Holism and atomism are what Gerald Holton calls themata that have guided thinkers from time immemorial. Jung made them deep polar features of the human psyche. You can be a holist or an atomist for any number of reasons, and

    [4] Grandy, Richard, 'Reference, Meaning and Belief', *The Journal of Philosophy*, 70 (1973), p. 443.

probably most of us are one or the other for no reason at all. It would be impossible to refute holistic attitudes in general. But we may now chip away at some of Davidson's base for his holism. When passing theory rules the day, why do we have to be holistic about language? Why have one big whole, rather than lots of lesser wholes? Davidson was succinctly described the 'holistic method' approach to language, in particular to reference. It 'starts with the complex (sentences, at any rate) and abstracts out the parts' (*Inquiries*, p. 221). This contrasts with the atomistic approach, which Davidson here calls the 'building-block method, which starts with the simple and builds up.' In this intricate discussion (in 'Reality without Reference') Davidson uses his standard approach to resolve certain questions in an ingenious way. Here I am more simplistic. Full-blown holism is not the only contrary of the building-block method. Let us be good Fregeans, and commence our understanding with the sentences. That does not imply that we have to commence our analysis with all the sentences taken as a whole.

My next-door neighbour, as it happens, has political views founded on compassion, from which I have much to learn. He is also far gone into not only homeopathic medicine (good holistic stuff) but also such pastimes as automatic writing. These are three among the many facets of life about which we converse, literally over the garden fence. There are also more mundane matters like fixing the gutters and baby-sitting. Davidson writes of my interpretation of the other being founded upon 'the total theory of the person'. Why should I have a total theory of my neighbour? He and I agree not to talk much about automatic writing or his choice in horrible teas. We do agree to talk about subsidized housing in the area. I have a number of only loosely connected views about my neighbour, and he about me. One person can have many voices. So be it. If I were a neo-Davidsonian interpreter, I would come in with one passing theory about his discourse on automatic writing, and another about his discourse on local politics. Of course it is true that there is a good deal of shared core, that shared core of fixing gutters and baby-sitting. But there is a very great looseness of fit between that shared core, and the different aspects of our different lives. To be able to converse coherently with my neighbour about automatic writing, I would have to engage in a Pascalian abetisement, and mingle with the local (large) population of automatic writers who believe their writings say deep things about the soul.

It is this looseness of fit between the interesting things we do (as opposed to dull things like gutter-fixing and time for baby-sitting) that seems to me to be ignored in Davidson's paper 'On the Very Idea of a Conceptual Scheme'. I think he would be more willing to countenance alternatives if he were less keen on totalizing theories of people, who are non-total. The more one thinks of conversation as evolving passing theories, the more open one may be to a lot of different passing theories about different aspects of a person's life. These 'theories' are clumps of expectations about the beliefs, desires and ways of talking of the other. No one has emphasized more than Davidson how recognizing and guessing at belief and desire are ingredients to understanding others. I am calling in question only his idea that we construct a 'total' theory of the other. To suppose that in interacting with another person, we construct such a total theory as we construct a passing systematic theory of truth for him is to force upon ourselves a parody of conversation.

Language games

A disunified picture of language could lead on to the first real use, in many a year, of Wittgenstein's idea of a multitude of loosely interlocking language games. But a moment's reflection on Wittgenstein's ideas would also lead us to query another aspect of Davidson's stance. The issue of a private language has mattered little to Davidson, who is concerned with communication. (But I did, above , quote the phrase 'private vocabulary' which is perhaps not so innocent, even in context). It takes two for there to be interpretation, interpreter and speaker. For Davidson, only two. If we think there have to be criteria of correctness, will two people suffice?

I said above that malaprops and the ketch/yawl error were two different kinds of error. It is a larger background of English that makes them so. Davidson's passing theories suddenly seem too permissive. He seems to admit only differences in practice between two people, as opposed to error posed in a larger linguistic community.

By a community I do not mean some communion of all of the speakers of 'English', nor an elitist group of standard speakers. My divide-and-communicate strategy rejects any such fantasies. It assumes only the truism that my neighbour and I have some communities in common, and others that do not overlap much, although we can join up if so moved. The notion of correctness arguably arises within those communities.

Such communities must, I think, have numerous members. Lovers, of course, evolve their own ways of talking to each other. They are no counterexample. Love is precisely the relationship in which error and correctness fade away. Notoriously each lover usually knows what the other is thinking before it is said.

I think that Davidson's present philosophy has something in common with solipsism. The solipsist thinks that a private language is not only possible, but the only one. Davidson is infinitely far away from that limit point, but he has passed only from one to two. We might call him a duetist. The possibility of error implies that there have to be more than duets.

We can readily accommodate this possibility within Davidson's observations, but only if we become less attached to holism than he has been. Let us conclude not that 'there is no such thing as a language' that we bring to interaction with others. Say rather that there is no such thing as the one total language that we bring. We bring numerous only loosely connected languages from the loosely connected communities that we inhabit.

26

A Nice Derangement of Epitaphs: Some Comments on Davidson and Hacking

Michael Dummett

First, two points concerning which Hacking has, I believe, misunderstood Davidson. Hacking cast doubt on Davidson's idea that 'linguistic ability should be modelled ... by a recursive theory'; but I suspect that this apparent disagreement turns on no more than divergent interpretations of the word 'recursive'. It is an interesting question whether a syntactic property such as that of being a well-formed or grammatical sentence of some natural language, or a semantic relation such as that of being synonymous in that language, can be considered, at least to a second approximation, to be recursive in the sense of 'effectively decidable'. I do not believe, however, that Davidson has ever intended to raise, let alone to insist on a particular answer to, this question. I think, rather, that he uses the term 'recursive' to mean 'specified inductively'.

More relevant to our present purpose is Hacking's understanding of Davidson's terminology of 'prior theory' and 'passing theory'. Davidson treats of communication in terms of a conversation between two participants, the speaker and the hearer, whom, to avoid pronoun trouble, I shall designate S and H. On Davidson's account, both S and H have a prior theory and a passing theory; let us, for the moment, confine our attention to H. H's theories are about how to understand S when S is addressing H. The use of the adjective 'prior' is, however, misleading, and has misled Hacking about the distinction between the two theories, prior and passing, that H has, and the two that S has. Hacking takes the prior theory of each participant to be that which he brings to the conversation at the outset, and his passing theory to be that into which it evolves in the course of the conversation. On this account, H begins with a prior theory, which comprises his initial propensities to understand in particular ways whatever S may say to him. In the course of the conversation, he revises this theory, the theory that thus evolves being his passing theory. This is not Davidson's picture, however; for he speaks of H's prior theory itself as undergoing modification. Rather, H has, at every stage, both a prior theory and a passing theory, both being subject to continual revision.

What, then, distinguishes H's prior theory from his passing theory? If I have understood correctly, his prior theory is a theory about how, in general, to understand S when S addresses H; and this theory may obviously change in response to what S says in the course of the particular conversation. His passing theory, on the other hand, is a theory about how to understand specific utterances of S made during that conversation. H may guess, for example, that in a particular sentence S is deliberately using some word in a non-standard way, without any intention of so using it in future, and hence with no wish that H be prepared for such a future use of it by S. H's ascription to S of a non-standard use of that sentence then becomes part of his passing theory, which concerns how to understand that particular utterance; but, construing S's intentions as he does, H will refrain from incorporating this non-standard use into his evolving 'prior' theory of how, in general, to understand S when he talks to H.

The terms 'prior' and 'passing' are in large part responsible for Hacking's misunderstanding, and are better replaced by 'long-range' and 'short-range'. If my understanding of the distinction between H's prior theory and his passing theory is correct, there is, however, some confusion in the way Davidson draws the distinction between S's two theories, which has contributed to Hacking's misinterpretation. S's prior theory, Davidson says, is what he believes H's prior theory to be. In my terminology, then, S's initial long-range theory comprises his expectations concerning how, in general, H is disposed to understand S when S addresses H. Davidson remarks, however, that S may deliberately speak in such a way as to prompt H to modify his prior theory; in view of this, he explains S's passing theory as that which S intends H to use. Basing the distinction between S's prior and passing theories on this contrast between his expectations and his intentions has the effect of drawing that distinction in a different way from that between H's prior and passing theories. The same principle of distinction ought to be used in both cases; and that applied to H seems the more illuminating. At any stage before the conversation ends, S will be making certain suppositions about what, at that moment, are H's long-term dispositions to understand in particular ways what S says to him. He will also have expectations about what these dispositions on H's part will become as soon as H has heard what S intends immediately to say to him. It seems a matter of indifference whether we identify the long-range theory held by S at that moment with the former or the latter; but symmetry should inhibit us from describing the latter as S's passing theory, since it is concerned with long-term dispositions, that is, with what S intends and expects H to incorporate into his long-range theory. We should take S's passing or short-range theory to relate to how he intends, and expects, H to understand particular utterances he makes during the conversation, when he does not intend, or expect, H to incorporate his interpretations of those utterances into his long-range theory.

Davidson evidently regards the distinction between prior and passing theories as important: if it is important, it is worth while to draw it with precision.

It would be natural to think that Davidson is concerned with the well-known distinction between what a speaker means and what his words mean; but this would be an oversimplification. In an early passage, Davidson refers to the notion of incorrect usage, saying that it is not mysterious or open to philosophical suspicions, but that it is philosophically uninteresting. The contrast here is between what a word means in the common language and what the speaker wrongly takes it to mean in the common language; but Davidson attaches little philosophical importance to the notion of the common language. In place of the shallow conception, yielded by this notion, of what words mean, 'we want,' he says, 'a deeper notion of what words, when spoken in a context, mean.' This deeper notion will yield a different, and deeper, distinction 'between what a speaker, on occasion, means, and what his words mean'. If I understand him aright, this deeper distinction, which has nothing to do with that between correct and incorrect uses of words, relates to the divergence, when there is one, between the speaker's long-range theory and his short-range theory: between how he wants the hearer usually to understand certain words that he has uttered, and how he wants him to understand that particular utterance of them. We have not only to draw this distinction, Davidson says, but to safeguard it, since it is threatened by the generalized phenomenon of malapropism; to do so, 'we must revise our ideas of what it is to know a language.'

He raises the topic again by alluding to Donnellan's distinction between referential and attributive uses of descriptions, which he endorses, saying that we need 'a firm sense of the difference between what words mean or refer to and what speakers mean or refer to'. I think, however, that we need to understand the occurrences of the word 'mean' in this particular sentence differently from all other occurrences of it in Davidson's paper, namely as no more than a synonym of 'refer to'. What he is here endorsing is Donnellan's distinction between two uses of descriptions; but, he observes, that distinction has 'nothing to do with words changing their meaning or reference'. He argues that if Jones employs the description 'Smith's murderer' in its referential use, thus referring to someone who did not murder Smith, 'the reference is nonetheless achieved by way of the normal meanings of the words', which 'therefore, must have their usual reference.' He thus allows a distinction between what the phrase refers to, in virtue of its meaning and of the circumstances, namely the person who in fact murdered Smith, and what Jones was referring to, in virtue of his beliefs and his having made a referential use of the phrase, namely the person he falsely supposed to have murdered Smith. But I take him to be denying that Jones means anything unusual by the words 'Smith's murderer', in the more normal sense of attaching any unusual meaning to them: in this more normal sense of 'mean', there will therefore be no room for any distinction between what the words mean and what Jones means by them. Donnellan's distinction thus proves to be a distraction: it does not exemplify either the shallow or the deep distinction of speaker's meaning from word-meaning treated in the earlier passage.

Davidson is concerned with a phenomenon distinct from that of referential use, namely a hearer's understanding of a word or phrase in a sense unfamiliar to him. A speaker cannot attach a meaning to an expression, Davidson says, unless he intends his hearer to understand him as doing so, and he cannot intend him to understand him thus unless he has a reasonable expectation that he will. The phenomenon occurs in three kinds of case: that in which, unknown to the speaker, the hearer is unfamiliar with the expression; that in which the speaker inadvertently makes a deviant use of a word (the malapropism); and that in which his deviant use is deliberate. In the third case, he will drop clues prompting the hearer either to modify his long-range theory, or to adopt the correct short-range theory, as the case requires, and may therefore well succeed in conveying his meaning. In the first two cases, he has a false long-range theory concerning the hearer, that is, a false idea of the hearer's long-range theory, but the hearer may still succeed in understanding him as he intended.

Deviant uses of language illustrate what Davidson has dismissed as the shallow distinction between what a speaker means and what his words mean. I entirely sympathize with Hacking's recoil from Davidson's dismissive treatment of the notion of the common language, which underlies his characterization of this way of drawing the distinction as shallow. As Hacking emphasizes, Davidson's paper drives towards the conclusion that 'there is no such thing as a language;' but, in the earlier stages of the paper, he deploys the notion of a language. The notion of a language that he deploys is not, however, that according to which English is one language and Farsi another, but one according to which 'no two speakers need speak the same language.' It is, rather, that which identifies a language with an idiolect, indeed the language spoken by a particular individual at a particular time; Davidson speaks of 'my language next year'. He is thus in the tradition of Frege, for whom, if two people attach different senses to a name, they do not speak the same language. This approach does not entail repudiating that notion of a language according to which English and Dutch are languages; but it involves taking the notion of an idiolect as fundamental to an account of what language is, and explaining a common language as a range of largely overlapping idiolects.

Hacking applauds Davidson for adopting, in this paper, a two-sided account concerned with 'interaction between speaker and hearer', as opposed to the one-sided account, exclusively from the viewpoint of the interpreter, adopted in other papers. Davidson is indeed here crucially concerned with the use of language for communication; and he pays as much attention to the theories of the speaker as to those of the hearer. It is, however, an exaggeration to describe him as concerned with interaction. In his picture, there is no interaction, no exchange of the roles of speaker and hearer: the hearer remains mute throughout the conversation, or, rather, monologue. The hearer can therefore seek from the speaker no elucidation of what he has said: and it is this artificial restriction that deprives the notion of incorrect use of its interest for Davidson. Figures of speech and other deliberately non-standard uses apart, a speaker holds himself responsible to the accepted meanings of words and expressions in the language or dialect he purports to be speaking; his willingness to withdraw or correct what he has said when made aware of a mistake about the meaning of a word in the common language therefore distinguishes erroneous uses from intentionally deviant ones. He cannot become aware of any mistake if the only other party to the dialogue is constrained to silence, and for this reason Davidson takes no note of this feature of his linguistic behaviour. For the same reason, Davidson can take no account of the phenomenon called by Putnam 'the division of linguistic labour,' or of the closely related and pervasive exploitation by speakers of the possession by some word of an accepted meaning in the common language, even though they themselves have only a partial knowledge of it.

A valuable but modest project would be to investigate the means by which a hearer comes to understand non-standard uses of expressions and uses of expressions unfamiliar to him, taking for granted as a background an extensive knowledge of the language on his part. From his denial that he is 'concerned with the infinitely difficult problem of how a first language is learned' it might appear that this was Davidson's project in 'A Nice Derangement of Epitaphs'. 'By comparison', he says, 'my problem is simple. I want to know how people who already have a language ... manage to apply their skill or knowledge to actual cases of interpretation. All the things I assume an interpreter knows or can do depend on his having a mature set of concepts, and being at home with the business of communication.'

If Davidson were engaged on this modest project, Hacking would be quite right to dismiss as 'pedantic' his insistence that a translation only tells you that two expressions of different languages mean the same, not *what* either means. He would be wrong, however, to criticize Davidson's continual use, in this paper, of the term 'interpretation'; for interpretation is just what a hearer has to engage in when the speaker uses some expression unfamiliar to him or in a way unfamiliar to him. As Hacking complains, Davidson in fact gives 'interpretation' a far more extended application, to any case in which a hearer understands what a speaker is saying, even when he is making a straightforward use of a language the hearer knows. This is one of many things that show Davidson's project to be a more ambitious one. Another is the final conclusion: the modest project could not possibly arrive at the result that there is no such thing as a language. A third is what Davidson immediately goes on to say after the passage quoted above about the business of communication: 'the problem is to describe what is involved in the idea of "having a language" or being at home with the business of communication.' He is not taking for granted the hearer's prior understanding of standard uses of expressions of the language, and seeking to explain in terms of it how he comes to understand non-standard uses. Rather, he is aiming, by extending the results of a study of the understanding of non-standard uses, to arrive at an account of the understanding of language in general.

Such an account must explain what communicative abilities are possessed by someone who has acquired his first language; all that Davidson can have meant to forswear, as an infinitely difficult problem, was a claim to explain the process of acquiring it. Even this is rendered dubious by his characterization of his task, in an early passage of the paper, as being to 'describe what an interpreter knows that allows him to understand a speaker, and show how he could come to know this on the basis of evidence plausibly available before interpretation has begun.' If the project were the modest one, 'before interpretation has begun' could mean 'before the particular utterance has been made.' Since the project is the ambitious one, what the interpreter knows must include what he learned when he acquired his first language, which cannot rank, in this project, as assumed background knowledge; and so 'before interpretation has begun' may be taken to mean 'before he has learned to talk.' Admittedly, in this early passage, Davidson is describing the intention of earlier papers, and is recanting some of the solutions proposed in them; but the recantation surely is not meant to cover the statement of the problem.

Since the project is ambitious, Hacking cannot reasonably object to David-son's contrast between a translation manual and a theory of meaning. A philosopher of language is not interested in a theory of meaning as enabling him to master another language, a purpose better served by a translation manual: he is interested in the *idea* of a theory of meaning as throwing light on what meaning is. An actual theory of meaning would specify the meaning of every expression of the language directly, rather than in terms of the meanings of other expressions, taken as given; the form to be taken by such a theory will therefore show what it is for an expression to have a meaning. Since a translation manual does something quite different, enquiring what form it should take cannot lead to an answer to the question what meaning is.

Hacking is justified, on the other hand, in cavilling at Davidson's extended use of the term 'interpretation'. Where I have spoken of the speaker and the hearer, Davidson speaks throughout of the speaker and the interpreter; where I spoke of the hearer as understanding the speaker's words in a particular way, Davidson speaks of his adopting a particular interpretation of them. A crucial observation made by Wittgenstein in his discussion of following rules is that 'there is a way of grasping a rule which is *not* an *interpretation*' (*Investigations*, 201). Similarly, there is a way of understanding a sentence or an utterance that does not consist in putting an interpretation on it. Whatever the full content of Wittgenstein's distinction between an *Auffassung* (way of grasping) and a *Deutung* (intepretation) may be, it at least means that one who grasps a rule or understands a sentence need not be able to *say* how he understands it. He does not have to be able to say it even to himself: we must not make the mistake Wittgenstein attributes to St Augustine, of describing a child's learning his mother-tongue 'as if he already had a language, only not this one' (*Investigations*, 32).

It is just this that Hacking objects to in Davidson's use of the word 'interpretation'. He allows, grudgingly, that the word may be used in any case in which the hearer needs to guess at or search for the speaker's meaning. In such cases the hearer may say to himself, 'A ketch must be a two-masted boat in which the mizzen is stepped forward of the rudder', or, 'He must mean "autodidact"', or, 'He means that it is showy and over-ornate.' But when the hearer does not have to search for the speaker's meaning, but takes for granted that he is using words in just the way with which he is familiar, there is, as Hacking says, no process of interpretation going on; to assimilate this case to the other by describing it as an instance of 'homophonic' interpretation disguises the radical difference between them.

Homophonic interpretation is not impossible. Listening to Mrs Malaprop, I might say to myself with surprise, 'By "incorrigible" she really does mean "incorrigible"', or, 'She means by "incorrigible" what is normally meant by it.' In normal cases, I should have no such thought; even in this case, though my having it explains my attaching that meaning rather than some other to Mrs Malaprop's utterance of the word, it makes no contribution at all to explaining in what my attaching that meaning to it consists. The reason is obvious: my having that thought will not result in my attaching the standard meaning to her utterance unless I know what that standard meaning is; and the thought, as formulated, does not embody the content of that knowledge.

Just because interpretation depends upon having a language in which the interpretation is stated, the difference between a translation and a proposition of a theory of meaning is not significant when the term 'interpretation' is truly in place. It makes no difference whether the hearer says to himself, ' "Ketch" must mean "a two-masted boat in which ..." ', or, 'A ketch must be a two-masted boat in which ... ', or, 'It must be that "is a ketch" is true of a thing if and only if that thing is a two-masted boat in which ... '. It would indeed be pedantic to insist that he might have the first of these three thoughts without understanding the definition that he had formulated: what is common to all three is that his adoption of the interpretation explains his understanding of what the speaker says only because we assume that he grasps the sense of the phrase in which the interpretation is stated. Davidson claims that ordinary speakers may plausibly be said to 'know certain theorems of a theory of truth' for their language, 'such as "An utterance of 'The cat is on the mat' is true if and only if the cat is on the mat".' Here Frege's pedantic use of distinct terms for the sentence stating a theorem and the thought expressed by that sentence would stand us in good stead. A speaker's knowledge of the truth of the sentence stating the theorem in no way guarantees his understanding of the sentence 'The cat is on the mat.' His knowing that an utterance of the latter sentence is true just in case the cat is on the mat may possibly do so; but, from this thesis, unsupplemented by an account of what his having that knowledge consists in, we gain little insight into the character of his understanding.

The occurrence of the phenomena that interest Davidson is incontrovertible: but how can an investigation of them lead to the conclusion that there is no such thing as a language? Oppressive governments, such as those of Franco and Mussolini, attempt to suppress minority languages; under such regimes teachers punish children for speaking those languages in the playground. In India, crowds demonstrate against the proposal to make Hindi the sole official language. Bretons, Catalans, Basques and Kurds each declare that their language is the soul of their culture. The option does not seem to be open to us to declare that such governments and such peoples are under an illusion that there is anything they are suppressing or cherishing. I know that there are people who know Swahili, Burmese and Slovene, and that I know none of these languages; moreover, I know just what I have to do to acquire such knowledge. In what does the fact that I know no Yoruba consist? Not, surely, in the fact that I have no tendency to form the same short-range (passing) theory of the utterances of a Yoruba speaker on a particular occasion as he has. Malay is a language whose speakers cultivate allusiveness, and so, with 'Malay' substituted for 'Yoruba', that might be quite a good description of someone who knew only what is called bazaar Malay: but my ignorance of Yoruba is more fundamental than that. It consists, in Davidson's terms, in my lacking any long-range theory whatever for Yoruba speakers; or, rather, since a great many Yoruba speakers also know English, in my lacking any such theory for them when they are speaking Yoruba. It thus appears that there is no way to characterize this piece of ignorance on my part without appeal to the concept of a language. It is true that Davidson tags to his conclusion that 'there is no such thing as a language' the proviso 'if a language is anything like what philosophers ... have supposed': but he offers no alternative account of what a language is. Whatever force his arguments may have, they cannot sustain the bald conclusion, but cry out for some account of an indispensable concept.

Davidson's argument is this. The apparatus of prior and passing theories, or, as I have called them, long-range and short-range theories, is required to explain the phenomena, of malapropisms and of deviant and unfamiliar uses, that interest him. It is also sufficient to explain linguistic communication in general. But neither the short-range nor the long-range theory has the right form to be described as a theory of a language. Hence the notion of a language is not needed for the philosophy of language, but only that of language.

As applied to a short-range (passing) theory, this argument is cogent. A short-range theory is a theory of how specific utterances are to be understood. Davidson appears to conceive of it as massively reduplicating the long-range theory ('Mrs Malaprop's theory, prior and passing, is that ...'), but there seems no good reason for this: if we think of the two theories as used in conjunction, the short-range theory may be taken as bearing only on those utterances for which the long-range one does not yield the correct interpretation. The short-range theory, so viewed, will not be a structured theory, but only a collection of disconnected propositions. A theory of meaning for a language, by contrast, relates to words and expressions as types, and must be structured in the manner on which Davidson insists when he demands that it be recursive. A long-range theory, on the other hand, will resemble a theory of meaning for a language in both these respects.

At this stage we may well wonder just *which* notion of a language it is that Davidson is repudiating. If it is our ordinary notion of a language, according to which one person may be said to speak six languages and another to know none but his own, then the breast-beating is out of place ('I must revise *my* ideas', 'the trouble I am in'). For Davidson's résumé of the enterprise of his earlier papers sets aside this ordinary notion as shallow, and treats as fundamental the quite different one of an idiolect; and, though the long-range theories of 'A Nice Derangement of Epitaphs' cannot be equated to idiolects, they do not differ from them so sharply as to warrant cries of 'mea culpa'.

In this talk of theories, we need to take care what we consider each theory to be a theory of. According to Davidson, the speaker's long-range theory is a theory of what the hearer's long-range theory is; we may call any theory about what another theory is a second-order theory. There is certainly a place for second-order theories, since eavesdroppers, as well as speakers and hearers, need to engage in interpretation. In order to form a true picture of what is going on, the eavesdropper needs to decide what the speaker intends to convey to the hearer; he also needs to decide what the hearer takes the speaker to mean. He must therefore, in Davidson's terms, frame a theory of what the speaker's (long-range and short-range) theories are, and he must also frame a theory of what the hearer's theories are; the two theories he frames are both second-order theories. A literary critic is an eavesdropper on a monologue by the author addressed to those of his contemporaries, or those members of his posterity, whom he conceived as his readers; his criticism consists in presenting a second-order theory and giving reasons for it. The literary historian presents second-order theories about the interpretation of literary works by their contemporary readers. We must beware, however, of representing all theories as of second order. We cannot say both that the speaker's theory is a theory about what the hearer's theory is, and that the hearer's theory is a theory about what the speaker's theory is, without falling into an infinite regress: there must be some first-order theory. A first-order theory is simply a theory of meaning: it is irrelevant for present purposes whether, as Davidson believes, it takes the form of a truth theory, or some other.

What does matter is its scope. We must distinguish between three things: a language; a theory of meaning for that language; and a second-order theory. A language is an existing pattern of communicative speech: it is not a theory, but a phenomenon. A theory of meaning for that language, as conceived by Davidson, is a theory of the content of expressions belonging to it – what that content is and how it is determined by the composition of the expressions. It does not itself employ the notion of meaning, but can be recognized as an adequate representation of the meanings of words and expressions of the language. It serves to explain how the language functions, that is, to explain the phenomenon of speech in that language; but it does so only indirectly. This is so because the theory itself contains no reference to speakers or to their beliefs, intentions or behaviour, linguistic or non-linguistic. Instead it uses theoretical terms such as 'true' applying to certain expressions of the language. In order, therefore, to assess a theory of meaning for a language as correct or incorrect, we must have some principles, implicit or explicit, that make the connection between the theoretical notions and what the speakers of the language say and do. These principles are not regarded by Davidson as part of the theory of meaning itself: they are presumably constant over all theories of meaning and all languages. We may call them the linking principles. Save in their presence, it will make no sense to speak of believing or disbelieving a theory of meaning, since they alone provide a criterion for its being correct.

A second-order theory is of a quite different character. If it is a long-range theory, it consists of a set of beliefs about what expressions of some language mean, or about what certain individuals intend or take them to mean; if it is a short-range theory, then about what certain specific utterances were intended or taken to mean.

Two unresolved questions leave it uncertain whether we ought to restrict second-order theories to those constituting interpretations in the strict sense. One arises from our having left the linking principles tacit: we do not know whether or not they connect the theory of meaning to the linguistic practice by imputing theories to the speakers, or, if so, whether these are first- or second-order theories. We get no help here from Davidson, who does not distinguish between second-order theories and theories of meaning, nor between interpretations in the strict sense and ways of understanding something in general (between a *Deutung* and an *Auffassung*). He says, for instance, that 'Mrs Malaprop's theory … is that "a nice derangement of epitaphs" means a nice arrangement of epithets.' It is plainly Davidson's (correct) theory about Mrs Malaprop that by 'a nice derangement of epitaphs' she means 'a nice arrangement of epithets'. This is a second-order theory, or part of one, and constitutes an interpretation in the strict sense: there is therefore nothing problematic in attributing this theory to Davidson, or in describing him as believing it. It is less clear that Mrs Malaprop herself may be said to have a second-order theory. It is indeed highly natural to say that Mrs Malaprop believes that 'a nice derangement of epitaphs' means 'a nice arrangement of epithets'; but there is then a problem about how she represents this belief to herself, since she certainly does not represent it in those words. We are here talking, not of an interpretation in the strict sense, but of how Mrs Malaprop understands the words, or of what she means by them. It is unclear whether this is a matter of her holding some belief, properly so called, at all, or, if so, whether the belief is of second or of first order: whether, that is, it is part of some second-order theory which she holds, or should be schematically represented by attributing to her some theory of meaning.

Only the linking principles, when made explicit, will reveal whether a theory of meaning for a language is genuinely an object of knowledge, in some mode of knowledge, on the part of everyone who knows that language. Independently of whether it is or not, however, someone's knowledge of the language may be schematically represented by attributing such a theory to him. In knowing the language, he thereby attaches to expressions belonging to it the meanings they have in that language. The theory of meaning purports to provide the only possible analysis of what it is for those expressions to have those meanings. The speaker himself may be ignorant of that analysis: but, by attributing to him the corresponding theory of meaning, we simultaneously represent him as attaching those meanings to the expressions and supply an analysis of their having those meanings. In the same way, a second-order theory is not literally to the effect that such-and-such a theory of meaning is correct, or is the theory held by a certain individual. Its literal content is that certain expressions have certain meanings, or that some individual intends them to have or takes them as having those meanings. Since a theory of meaning makes explicit what it is or would be for them to have those meanings, however, the second-order theory can be represented as a theory about that theory of meaning.

The second unresolved question is in what manner we should, in the first instance, identify the languages to which the apparatus of theories of meaning and second-order theories is to apply. We must make such a choice, because the application of the entire apparatus waits upon a selection of the languages to which the theories of meaning relate. Whatever our choice, we shall have to leave a place for broader or narrower ways of using the term 'languages'. We must, however, take one way of using it as fundamental for our account. It will be theories of meaning for languages in this fundamental sense that we shall need to consider; we shall not need to take account of theories of meaning for languages in a broader or narrower sense, which we shall be able to explain in terms of languages in our fundamental sense and their associated theories of meaning.

One natural choice for the fundamental notion of a language is that of a common language as spoken at a given time – either a language properly so called, such as English or Russian, or a dialect of such a language. If we make this choice, we shall have to acknowledge the partial, and partly erroneous, grasp of the language that every individual speaker has. The theory of meaning for the language will give the meanings that its words and expressions in fact have. Davidson, as we saw, does not consider this notion open to philosophical suspicion, just uninteresting. Actually, it is neither so uninteresting nor so unproblematic as he supposes; but let us take it, for present purposes, as given. In any account of actual linguistic practice, we must recognize that no speaker knows every word of the language or uses correctly every word he does know: in other words, the linking principles for a theory of meaning for a language in this sense of 'language' must employ the notion of an idiolect. The obvious way for it to do so is by treating an idiolect as a second-order theory: a partial, and partly incorrect, theory about what the meanings of the expressions are in the common language, that may be represented as a partial theory of what the correct theory of meaning for the language is. Such a second-order theory is *not* an interpretation in the strict sense; given this choice of the fundamental notion of a language, then, we cannot restrict second-order theories to those constituting such interpretations. To be quite accurate, the second-order theory in question will not give a perfect representation of a speaker's idiolect, since, strictly speaking, his idiolect comprises only his own speech habits, and all speakers of, say, English both understand certain expressions that they would never use and recognize them as correct English. But this is an unimportant detail: on the present view, a common language is related to an idiolect essentially as the rules of a game are related to a player's beliefs about what they are.

Davidson's original choice for the fundamental notion of a language was quite different, namely to take the language as constituted by the linguistic habits of an individual at a given time. Here the idiolect becomes fundamental, and hence no longer explicable as a second-order theory: it is, rather, that to which a (first-order) theory of meaning relates. 'A Nice Derangement of Epitaphs' insists that this choice of fundamental notion is defective. The ground offered for this is that we all adapt our mode of speech to our audience. The observation is just: once we have rejected the common language as the fundamental notion, we cannot stop at the idiolect, but must make a finer discrimination. We must take a language in the fundamental sense to consist, not of the general speech habits of an individual at a particular time, but, rather, his habits of speech when addressing a particular hearer at that time.

None of this justifies the claim that we must jettison the notion of a language altogether. We cannot dispense with it, for, if we do, our theories of meaning have no subject-matter. Davidson has not shown how to do without it: he has merely made a proposal for a new way of picking out a language, in the fundamental sense, those languages, namely, of which we are to take the theories of meaning as treating. Given this new principle for circumscribing the language, all goes ahead as before. Granted, Davidson has introduced some new features into the apparatus. The short-range theories, which relate to non-standard interpretations of particular utterances – interpretations deviant by the standard of the long-range theories – are one such novel ingredient. If the distinction between first- and second-order theories be accepted, the second-order theories are another. But the first-order long-range theories are simply theories of meaning for languages identified by means of a finer grid than before.

It might be objected that I have missed the point. I explained a language as a pattern of communicative speech. Davidson is not concerned to deny either that communicative speech occurs, or that there are patterns discernible in it: he is therefore not denying that there are languages, if this is what is meant by 'languages'. Rather, he is equating a language with a theory of meaning; and what he is saying is that neither a long-range nor a short-range theory is anything like a theory of meaning, as he formerly conceived of it. That a short-range theory does not resemble a theory of meaning is clear: but what else can a long-range theory be, if it is of first order?

Since it seems that there can be no retort to this question, this defence of Davidson must claim that all long-range theories are of second order. This claim makes no sense, however. Since a theory of higher order is a theory about what some other theory is, to say that no theory is of first order is to say that every theory is of infinite order; but there can be no theories of infinite order. It is not inconceivable that the theories we need to pay most attention to are of order much higher than the second: for instance, a speaker's theory of what his hearer's theory of what the speaker's theory of what the hearer's theory of what the speaker's theory is. It is in principle impossible that there should be any theories a statement of the subject-matter of which would require a phrase like the foregoing, but one that could never be completed; let alone that all theories should be of this kind. If someone holds a theory of finite order, then the theory last referred to in the phrase stating its subject-matter must be a theory of first order: and this will be a theory of meaning. Davidson refers to the Gricean circle: he cannot give a coherent account if he converts it into an exitless loop.

Davidson's tendency, in 'A Nice Derangement of Epitaphs', to suppose that every theory must be of higher order is due to his adoption of a quasi-Gricean account of what it is to mean something by an expression. There are two natural pictures of meaning. One depicts words as carrying meanings independently of speakers. It was to this conception that Alice was appealing when she objected to Humpty Dumpty, 'But "glory" doesn't mean a "nice knock-down argument".' According to Alice, Humpty Dumpty could not mean that by the word, because the word itself did not have it in it to bear that meaning. The opposite picture is that which Humpty Dumpty was using. On this conception, it is the speaker who attaches the meaning to the word by some inner mental operation; so anyone can mean by 'glory' whatever he chooses. Each picture is crude; each is easily ridiculed by a philosopher or a linguist. But each theorist of language tends to offer a more sophisticated version of one picture or the other. Davidson's is a version of the second picture. His reason for denying that, by 'glory', Humpty Dumpty could, in speaking to Alice, mean 'a nice knock-down argument' is quite different from Alice's: it is that Humpty Dumpty knew that Alice would not understand him as meaning that. If he had expected her so to understand him, and had intended her to do so, then his intention, or, perhaps, his expectation, would have conferred that meaning on the word as uttered by him. Given this picture of what meaning is, it appears to follow that the relevant theories are all of higher order, being theories about the theories held by other participants in the dialogue.

Language is both an instrument of communication and a vehicle of thought; it is an important question of orientation in the philosophy of language which role we take as primary. I welcome Davidson's attention to the communicative function of language, since I am disposed to take that as its primary role: language is a vehicle of thought because it is an instrument of communication, and not conversely. And yet it is an error to concentrate too exclusively on communication. Wittgenstein is well known to have taken language primarily as a social activity; and yet his challenge to say one thing and mean something else thereby has to do with language in its role as a vehicle of thought. The difficulty of saying, 'It's cold here', and meaning, 'It's warm here' (*Investigations*, 510), or of saying, 'The sky is clouding over', and meaning, 'There is no odd perfect number', does not lie in the presence of an audience, but is just as great if you are saying it to yourself, as in the experiment Wittgenstein surely intends. Davidson's mode of explanation is impotent here: the difficulty is not that I have no reason to expect myself to know what I mean. Alice was more nearly right: the difficulty lies in the fact that 'The sky is clouding over' does not mean 'There is no odd perfect number.'

The choice of idiolects, or, rather, of linguistic practices yet more narrowly circumscribed, as languages in the fundamental sense, makes the matter easier to understand in the first instance, but in the end, I think, renders it incomprehensible. It makes it easier at the outset because such a choice of the fundamental notion of a language leaves us free to treat all higher-order theories as interpretations in the strict sense, that is, as principles for construing the speech of others that the subject can state to himself: such a principle, for example, as that when one whose mother-tongue is German says, 'I mean that ... ', he is likely to mean, 'I think that ... ', or that when he says, 'If I would do ... ', he probably means, 'If I were to do ... '. Now a speaker who suspects his hearers' knowledge of the language to be imperfect, or his use of it in some other way to diverge from his own, will be careful to avoid expressions liable to be misunderstood, but will very rarely misuse any expression in order to accord with his hearer's faulty understanding of it, or even employ an expression which he (the speaker) finds unnatural. Hence the speaker's knowledge of the linguistic abilities and habits of the hearer will, for the most part, have only an inhibiting effect, prompting him to avoid certain forms of expression. His theory about the hearer's linguistic propensities – his second-order theory – will thus not be that in virtue of which what he does say has the meaning that it does; that, rather, if it is to be called a theory at all, will be his first-order theory – his theory of meaning for the language he is using to address that hearer. The hearer, on the other hand, may well appeal to principles of interpretation in order to hit on the speaker's meaning. In describing the speaker as employing a long-range theory of what the hearer's theory is, Davidson has therefore put the matter the wrong way round. It is the speaker's first-order theory that determines the meanings of his remarks; the hearer may advert to his own theory of what the speaker's first-order theory is in order to interpret him.

All this, however, is a detail. The essential point is that interpretation, in the strict sense, is of necessity an exceptional occurrence; and, by the same token, the appeal to a second-order theory is of necessity the exception. In the normal case, the speaker simply says what he means. By this I do not mean that he first has the thought and then puts it into words, but that, knowing the language, he simply speaks. In the normal case, likewise, the hearer simply understands. That is, knowing the language, he hears and thereby understands; given that he knows the language, there is nothing that his understanding the words consists in save his hearing them. There are, of course, many exceptional cases. They occur, for the speaker, whenever he uses a word with which he suspects the hearer may be unfamiliar, whenever he very deliberately uses a subtle or humorous figure of speech, when he is conscious of knowing the language imperfectly or believes his hearer to do so. They occur, for the hearer, when the speaker misuses an expression, or uses an unfamiliar one, or employs a difficult figure of speech, or, again, when one or other is speaking in a language he is not fully at home in. These are just the cases that aroused Davidson's interest. They are, however, in the nature of things, atypical cases: if taken as prototypes for linguistic communication, they prompt the formulation of an incoherent theory.

How can there be cases of the kind I have labelled 'normal'? In such a case, speaker and hearer treat the words as having the meanings that they do in the language. Their so treating them does not consist in their having any beliefs about the other person, but, rather, in their engaging in the way they do in the conversation, reacting as they do to what the other says, and, perhaps, acting accordingly after it is over. They may be compared to players of a game. A game with two or more players is a social activity; but the players' grasp of the rules does not consist in any theories they have about the knowledge of the rules on the part of the other players. It is manifested by their playing the game in accordance with the rules (or cheating by surreptitiously breaking them), that is, in their acting in a manner that makes sense only in the light of the rules. There is a greater problem in the linguistic case. The players of the game can probably state the rules, perhaps only haltingly, if challenged to do so, even though they seldom actually advert to those rules when playing. Speakers of a language know the meanings of the words belonging to it, but are frequently unable to state them; it is in principle impossible for their knowledge of the language, if it be their mother-tongue, to consist in its entirety in knowledge that they could state. We may represent their knowledge as a grasp of a theory of meaning for the language; but we face a great difficulty in explaining the character of this representation. This, however, is a problem which, though central to the philosophy of language, is not to be solved by replacing the theory of meaning by a second-order theory about the theories held by other speakers.

What, in the normal case, both speaker and hearer are going on are their beliefs (if they can be called beliefs) about what the words mean, not about what the other takes or intends them to mean; these second-order beliefs are operative only in the exceptional cases. To say that they go on these beliefs is to say that they are engaging in a practice that they have learned, just as the games-players do: they speak and act in accordance with the meanings of the words in the language, as the players act in accordance with the rules of the game. But is it possible to mean something by an expression without intending one's hearer to understand it? If the hearer is a mere eavesdropper, it certainly is, for instance when soliloquizing aloud or speaking in an aside; if Galileo really said, 'Eppur, si muove', that would be a case. It is even possible when the hearer is the person addressed. In *Top Hat*, the character played by Eric Blore addresses a string of insults in English to an Italian policeman, and is dismayed to find that he has been understood. Naturally, one cannot fail to intend someone to understand what one is attempting to convey to him. That, however, is a trivial tautology, not a deep truth about meaning; and, even so, the speaker need have no reasonable expectation of being understood, as anyone who has observed the behaviour of tourists can testify. Second-order theories may be brought into play when the speaker wants to communicate and is conscious of obstacles to understanding: in the normal case, he takes for granted that his hearer speaks his language, just as a chess-player takes for granted that his opponent knows the moves of the pieces.

A language is a practice in which people engage. There can be solitary practices, in the sense of those in which one engages on one's own; but a practice is essentially social, in the different sense that it is learned from others and is constituted by rules which it is part of social custom to follow. The conception of a practice in which only one person ever engages is thus very questionably coherent. We might reinterpret Davidson as taking, as his fundamental notion of a language, the language spoken between any pair of individuals who converse with one another, so that each language constitutes a practice in which just two people engage. This is plainly contrary to Davidson's intentions, according to which the roles of speaker and hearer are not interchanged; and it does not tally with the idea that the speaker is operating only with a second-order theory, or, under our proposed emendation, that this is true of the hearer. The natural choice for the fundamental notion of a language, from the viewpoint that sees a language as a practice, is a language in the ordinary sense in which English is a language, or, perhaps, a dialect of such a language.

The view that I am urging against Davidson is an adaptation of Alice's picture, according to which words have meanings in themselves, independently of speakers. Of course, they do not have them intrinsically, and hence independently of anything human beings do. They have them in virtue of belonging to the language, and hence in virtue of the existence of a social practice. But they have them independently of any particular speakers. No speaker needs to form any express intention, or to hold any particular theory about his audience, or, indeed, about the language, in order to mean by a word what it means in the language: he has only to know the language and to utter the word in an appropriate context, such as that of a sentence. In particular cases, he may have some interpretation in mind; but he could not have an interpretation in mind in every case. This is to say that we cannot grasp senses without any vehicle for them, and associate those senses to the words as semaphore associates flag positions to letters: to invest a word with a sense is just to grasp the pattern of its use.

All this raises interesting questions about how a language changes, which must here be set aside. These questions have much to do with the phenomena that interest Davidson. They are not, however, to be answered in such a way as to make expression of meaning depend wholly upon the intentions of the speaker, and thus to liberate speakers from all responsibility to the language as a social institution. The crude version of such an answer is the picture of language favoured by Humpty Dumpty. Davidson's is a refinement, which still commits the same essential error. Davidson's refinement consists in insisting that the speaker must have regard to the hearer's discernment of his intention. Without the background of the common practice of speaking the language, it remains mysterious how the hearer can discern it; with that background, it becomes easy to explain how he can do so in the exceptional cases in which discernment is necessary. That I am not caricaturing Davidson is shown by his concluding remarks, directed against the role of convention in language. Conventions, whether they be expressly taught or picked up piecemeal, are what constitute a social practice; to repudiate the role of convention is to deny that a language is in this sense a practice. In the exceptional cases – those in which it is in place to speak of interpreting what someone says – there are indeed no rules to follow: that is what makes such cases exceptional. In such cases, the hearer has to apprehend the speaker's intention much as he has to apprehend the intentions behind non-linguistic actions (the part played by convention in which it is easy to overlook). This feature is always present in discourse, since, besides grasping what someone means, in the sense of what he is saying, we must make out why he says it – what relevance he takes it to have, what point he is driving at, and so on. Davidson would like to believe that our whole understanding of another's speech is effected without our having to know anything: 'there is no such thing' as a language, he says, 'to be learned or mastered', and the implication is that there is nothing to be learned or mastered. He claims to 'have erased the boundary between knowing a language and knowing our way around in the world generally': we understand someone's speech by divining his intentions, as we divine those informing his actions. But the distinction is that ordinary actions make a difference to the world independently of any conventional significance they may have, whereas utterances seldom make any noticeable difference independently of their meanings: without a knowledge of the language, we therefore do not have the same clues to the intentions behind utterances, because, without understanding, we do not know what the speaker has done by uttering those sounds. Since the meaning is all, or almost all, that matters, it would make no difference what sounds were made, as long as the intention behind them remained constant, if things were truly as Davidson supposes, and there were no language to which they belonged. But, to quote Euclid, this is absurd.

The need for the notion of a language is apparent if we ask what long-range theory someone brings to a first linguistic encounter with another. Davidson answers this question by saying, 'We may know so little about our intended interpreter that we can do no better than to assume that he will interpret our speech along what we take to be standard lines.' This assumption is dreadfully familiar: it is that which used to made by many British tourists, often expressed in the words, 'They will understand you perfectly well as long as you speak loud enough.' This, it may naturally be said, is unfair: Davidson was not thinking of an encounter with a randomly selected human being, but of one with a fellow-countryman. The word 'fellow-countryman' represents an evasion, however. It would be quite inappropriate in Belgium, Switzerland, the Soviet Union, India or most African countries: even the United States is not as monoglot as it pretends. What is really meant is an encounter with someone presumed to speak the same language. It would, after all, be ridiculous to speak of the standard manner of interpreting the speech of human beings in general; there is no such thing. All this, indeed, is expressly acknowledged by Davidson in this very passage, for he inserts the proviso 'assuming we know he belongs to our language community'. What, then, is a language community? It obviously cannot be defined geographically: it cannot be defined without using the concept of a language. But with what possible right can Davidson make essential appeal to this concept in the course of an argument purporting to show it to lack application?

Taking a language in the fundamental sense to be such a thing as Japanese or Bengali involves allowing that a second-order theory need not be an intepretation. We shall need to distinguish between the theory of meaning for a language and an individual's imperfect grasp of that theory. The latter is of second order in so far as that individual purports to be speaking the given language, and hence is disposed to modify what he says if he becomes aware of a linguistic error. Since it is not an interpretation, however, it operates as we have been considering a first-order theory to do: it is not the content of a piece of theoretical knowledge which the speaker has and to which he can advert. The linking principles for a theory of meaning for a language of this kind will be very complex, since they have to describe an immensely complex social practice: they will treat, among other things, of the division of linguistic labour, of the usually ill-defined sources of linguistic authority, of the different modes of speech and the relations between the parent language and various dialects and slangs. But this is no objection to such a choice of the fundamental notion of a language; no other choice can find any place for phenomena of this sort, which are genuine features of the human use of language.

The attribution to a speaker of a theory of meaning, or of an imperfect and partial grasp of one, is only schematic: he in no sense literally knows such a theory. What he has done is to master a practice; and the notion of a practice is one requiring rather careful philosophical characterization. To the question whether mastery of a practice is theoretical or practical knowledge we can only reply that the categorization is too crude: it falls between. A character in Wodehouse is asked whether she can speak Spanish, and replies, 'I don't know: I've never tried.' Suppose she had been asked whether she could swim, and had given the same answer. The answer would still have been absurd, but it would have been absurd for an empirical reason only, namely that we know from experience that human beings are unable to swim unless they have been taught, something that is not true of dogs. This fact – that, if you are to swim, you must *learn* to do so – appears to be the only reason for our speaking of *knowing* how to swim; and this is so for all pure cases of practical knowledge. It is not the same for knowing Spanish. Even if you have not been taught to swim, you can *try* to swim, though you will surely fail. You can try because you know what swimming is; you can tell, for sure, whether someone else is swimming or not. If you do not know Spanish, on the other hand, you cannot so much as *try* to speak Spanish, and you cannot tell, for sure, whether someone else is speaking Spanish or not. You cannot do so because you do not know what it *is* to speak Spanish. This is what characterizes mastery of a practice: you cannot know what the practice is – though you may be aware that it resembles certain others in statable respects – until you have mastered it. But, although this makes it a genuine case of knowledge, unlike practical knowledge, which is knowledge only by courtesy, it does not make it theoretical knowledge.

Why, then, is it so compelling to *represent* mastery of a language as if it were theoretical knowledge? Although there is no one who knows what it is to speak

Spanish other than those who speak Spanish, it is not strictly true that there is no other way to come to know what speaking Spanish is. Theoretical knowledge, the content of which was a fully explicit description of a practice, would also amount to knowing what the practice was. In the case of a language, such a description would be a theory of meaning for that language, complete with all the linking principles. To give such a description is exceedingly difficult. To attain one would be the realization of the philosopher's hopes of analysing the complex activity of using a language, which is the chief vehicle of our mental life and the chief medium of our interactions with one another. We shall go astray, however, if we make a literal equation of the mastery of a practice with the possession of theoretical knowledge of what that practice is: even so far astray as to conclude that there is no such thing as a language.

27

Indeterminacy of French Interpretation: Derrida and Davidson

SAMUEL C. WHEELER III

I *Who and Davidson?*

My conclusions in this paper will be scarcely news to those who are already familiar with both Davidson's and Derrida's work. Since there are relatively few of those people, however, there is some point to stating the obvious. I hope to persuade a few of you, who are already presumably familiar with Davidson's work, that Derrida supplies important, if dangerous, supplementary arguments and considerations on one of the topics on which Davidson has done exciting work.

I show how a line of thought of the French philosopher Jacques Derrida is a version of the thesis of indeterminacy of radical interpretation as purified by Davidson. I claim that the basic conception of language and its relation to thought and to what passes for reality is much the same for Derrida and for Davidson. More importantly, I maintain that some of the basic ideas and (perhaps) insights that move their respective arguments are the same for the two thinkers.

This similarity in where they have arrived is partly obscured by the fact that these thinkers come from rather different traditions. By a 'tradition' I mean a family of theories and a complex of shared metaphors, shared formulations of problems, shared texts, shared shorthands, and shared styles which more or less shape the way philosophy is done. Just as our mention of 'canonical notation' alludes to a familiar but complex part of our canon, so a continental's use of 'primordial' animates a reader's prior absorption of texts from that tradition.

II *Frege and Husserl and the presence of meaning*

I begin with some simple-minded reminders and questions about Frege's remarks on sense. For Frege, a given term on a given occasion of use designates

This paper has profited from the comments of John Vickers on the paper as a whole and from discussions with John Searle and John Troyer about Derrida's central arguments.

its referent and expresses a sense. How, according to Frege, does one know what sense it is that one's utterance is expressing? There are two phenomena here, the connection of expression to sense and the identification and re-identification of the sense. So, first, when an utterance expresses a sense, the speaker seems to bring about a connection between the word and the sense, or to endorse a connection that is already there.[1] Second, the speaker is able to know which sense his utterance is expressing and to know a number of things about that sense. When I say 'elephant', expressing its ordinary sense, for example, I know that the sense my term expresses determines no plants.

On Frege's picture, some senses must be present in themselves,[2] directly apprehended in their own nature. Senses, though sign-like insofar as they determine objects, differ from ordinary signs in that somehow there is no possibility of misinterpreting them. A sense is, as it were, a sign that forces us to take it in exactly one way, and which means itself. Frege's theory seems to require, then, a kind of direct and unmediated presence of sense. At least this object is directly present to a thinker and speaker and can be connected (presumably by *intending* that this sense be connected) with this utterance of this word.

While having many similarities to Frege in examples, concerns, and even terminology,[3] Husserl tries to deal especially with what propositional contents are, our access to them, and their connection to human acts of language-production. Husserl spends much effort trying to describe how it is that a person attaches a sense to a sign and exactly what senses are.[4]

Both Frege and Husserl are anti-reductionists. They both take the defense of mathematical and logical consequence from psychologism to be of central concern. Part of this effort for both thinkers is the requirement that thought and language be ultimately grounded on a kind of non-linguistic or pre-linguistic meaning which is present to us without the mediation of a sign. 'Presence', for the moment, is the unmediated, transparent access we are alleged to have to entities such as senses and to the pre-linguistic 'directedness' by which we can allegedly associate our acts with such entities.

---

[1] A connection could be already there in the sense that others have used tokens of this kind in the appropriate connected way with that sense. It is then still up to the current speaker to endorse that connection or not. This decision about endorsement, really, is the decision whether to speak German, for instance.

[2] If a sense is given by description (i.e., 'the sense that Fred was discussing yesterday'), access to that sense must be by direct and unmediated access to some other senses. In this case, those other senses are of 'sense', 'that', 'Fred', etc.

[3] See, for instance, Edmund Husserl's *Logical Investigations, Volume I* (Routledge and Kegan Paul, London, 1970; translated by J. N. Findlay), p. 287, where Husserl makes many of the same observations we find in Frege.

[4] See, for instance, Husserl, ibid., Investigation I, Section 7, p. 276ff. The first few sections of Investigation I deal with the topics of expression and indication and how signs are invested with meaning.

Some of Derrida's arguments for the indeterminacy of interpretation consist of detailed analysis of Husserl's particular attempt to construct senses out of intentions, to make inner signs specially connected with contents, and to explain how natural languages get their meaning determined (or enmeshed) in the history of these pure intentions. See Jacques Derrida, *Speech and Phenomena*, translated by David Allison (Northwestern University Press, Evanston, 1973).

The 'presence' model common to both Husserl and Frege is shared by many theories which are, on the surface, hard-headed and anti-metaphysical. Any theory which has a domain of objects or acts to which we are alleged to have direct epistemological access is a 'presence' theory.[5]

III *Derrida and Davidson and the absence of meanings*

Frege and Husserl thus can be taken as very similar starting points for Davidson and Derrida, respectively, even given that Davidson's tradition and interests are otherwise very different from Derrida's. That is, though Quine and Davidson only rarely discuss Freudian analyses of *The Purloined Letter* and Derrida seems not to concern himself with first-order languages or physics, both Davidson and Derrida are in a position to question the same fundamental commitment to 'presence' and non-linguistic foundations in analyses of language, meaning and necessity. I will show this by presenting some of Derrida's thinking as a supplement to such Davidson articles as 'Radical Interpretation',[6] 'On the Very Idea of a Conceptual Scheme',[7] and others.

The indeterminacy of radical interpretation Derrida proposes can be presented as consequences of the rejection of 'present' unmediated semantic items. The rejection of presence itself turns on some very fundamental reflections on the way signs must function in order to be signs.

Derrida's analysis starts with a framework from Saussure. He accepts Saussure's point that signs are arbitrary. This truism means that there are no intrinsic characters of linguistic signs that determine what they mean. A linguistic sign, then, cannot by itself force an interpretation or be self-interpreting.

More importantly, he accepts part of Saussure's view that both phonetic and conceptual systems are systems of differences. That is, for instance, what defines an '*a*' as an *a* is its difference from other phonemes within the system, rather than intrinsic characters of the sound. Analogous remarks apply to

---

[5] Empiricist theories used sense contents as 'present'. 'Senses' were analysed in terms of sensual contents of something rather than as Platonic objects, but still in terms of something present to intuition. For another kind of instance, Chisholmian theories of knowledge require some kind of entity to which we have epistemological and therefore semantic direct access. Chisholm is brilliantly explicit about this in *Person and Object* (George Allen and Unwin, London, 1976), chapter 1 and appendix D.

Empiricism with the dogmas also held that the contents of certain *acts* are present to unmediated inspection. We know how we meant something on a given occasion, for instance. Quine and Derrida reject these ideas. The notion of 'definition' required for 'true by definition', as Quine pointed out in 'Necessary Truth', in *Ways of Paradox*, (Random House, New York, 1966), p. 55, seems to require the idea that a determination about how we will speak can stay attached to a term or sentence. Quine's dismissal of the force of such a promise agrees with Derrida's insistence in 'Signature, Event, Context', in *Margins of Philosophy* (University of Chicago Press, Chicago, 1982), translated by Alan Bass, *passim*. The point is developed at great length in 'Limited Inc.', *Glyph*, 2, pp. 162–254) on the detachability of utterances from their originating contexts and intentions.

[6] Donald Davidson, 'Radical Interpretation', *Dialectica*, 3–4 (1973), pp. 313–28.

[7] Donald Davidson, 'On the Very Idea of A Conceptual Scheme', *Proceedings of the American Philosophical Association*, 47 (1973–4), pp. 5–20.

conceptual schemes (whose Very Idea is not questioned by Saussure). A concept is defined by its differences from other concepts.[8] A conceptual scheme is a system of differences.

This Saussurean idea that conceptual schemes are systems of differences is like Quine's Web of Belief.[9] While the Saussurean model deals with terms rather than with sentences, and its concentration on difference gives it a logically impoverished account of the structure of a theory, the central idea is very like that of the interanimation of sentences.[10] Just as the meaning of a sentence for Quine is (more or less) a function of its connections with other sentences with their various strengths and connections, so the meaning of a term for Saussure is a function of the differences of its associated concept from other concepts. Both models for the most part make the meanings depend on relations rather than on intrinsic features of concepts or sentences. Quine's departure from the single-experience-packet theory of sentence meaning is in many ways parallel with Saussure's departure from the pre-existing concept theory of term-meaning.

Now, in Saussure there seems to be imagined a kind of conceptual field which various languages divide up in various ways. The concepts signified in a language then are various partitions of this conceptual field. The field itself seems to be the sort of thing that is present to thought, so that there is a fact of the matter whether two cultures have what conceptual overlaps.

For reasons dealt with below, Derrida rejects the comprehensibility of this kind of 'conceptual field' and the possibilities it allows. He is left with differences without anchors to any intrinsic contents. The same difference also divides Quine from Saussure. While stimulus meaning does retain the idea of a given field that is divided up among sentences, it is not a *conceptual* field. Thus Quine's theory is substantially purified of the notion that there is something isolable and *semantic* behind language for interpretation to link up to.

Let us now see how Derrida transforms a Saussurean theory: Derrida starts with Saussurean properties of words, and combines these with the more or less Husserlian idea that semantical properties must somehow be understood in terms of a relation to utterances. That is, what words mean is derived from how people have meant them. In some sense, meaning is use. This is really the same basic starting point, less behavioristically conceived, as Quine's in *Word and Object*. Meaning, to the extent that it is a real phenomenon, is a function of what people say when. We begin Derrida's argument with his characterizations of linguistic signs and other significant items:

(1) Linguistic signs are arbitrary, so they have no intrinsic properties to tie them to any particular referent or use. Senses, contents, and meanings, on the other hand, have intrinsic features which identify them in isolation. The sense of a term, for instance, must have enough content so that the reference can be a

---

[8] Ferdinand Saussure, *Course in General Linguistics*, translated by Wade Baskin (McGraw-Hill Book Company, New York, 1966), ch. IV, especially p. 111.

[9] W. V. Quine and Joseph Ullian, *The Web of Belief* (Random House, New York, 1970).

[10] 'Interanimation of sentences' is from W. V. Quine, *Word and Object*, (MIT Press, Cambridge, Massachusetts, 1960), chapter I, section 3.

function of it. Even in Saussure's conceptual field, the various areas of the field seem to have properties intrinsically, even though this conflicts[11] with the claim that a system of concepts is a system of differences only. Any significant items which are like linguistic signs in being arbitrary require interpretation or supplementation to supply their meaning, since they are not self-interpreting. Arbitary signs defer and differ from their significance.

(2) Signs are essential iterable. This is the fundamental principle on which, really, the whole of Derrida's argument depends. Very striking consequences are alleged to follow from this feature of significant items.[12]

A singular non-linguistic event can be attached to a particular circumstance, but as a causal or accidental accompaniment. Insofar as an event or item is significant in any way, as a linguistic sign or not, it must be a repeatable whose import is not tied to a particular event. 'The possibility of repeating, and therefore identifying, marks is implied in every code, making of it a communicable, transmittable, decipherable grid that is iterable ... for any possible user.'[13] It is some iterable aspect of the semantic item that carries the meaning. Whatever is semantic is so in virtue of and by means of what is taken as iterable in it.

This central concept of the argument deserves to be dwelt upon, especially in those respects which affect the arguments denying the possibility of fully present representations. Let us start with the apparently harmless type-token distinction:[14] surely the simplest kind of 'interpretation' of an utterance is saying what words were said, 'what the person said' in the most transparent sense.

Now, a token *qua* token is essentially an instance of a repeatable. What makes the entity meaningful is that it is a token of a given type. Of course, as far as its intrinsic features go, a linguistic item or event could be a token of any number of types. An utterance which sounds like 'bloo' could be token of several words, even in English. As a simplest and least problematic first place where interpretation could matter, correct interpretation could be taken to be a specification of what type a token is *really* a token of.

How is this 'really' to be understood? Tokens either really have significance in given situations or they have significance only relative to a given language-scheme (leading to familiar 'regresses to a background language'). It doesn't help essentially to connect a linguistic token to thought tokens, because the same question of selecting what universal a token is a token of applies there as well. In the case of a thought token, given that the thinker is really thinking of something, the language is, we might think, really built into the thinker. Ideas are tokens in the language of thought. In a mental tokening, it might seem the

---

[11] See Derrida's critique of this difficulty in his *Of Grammatology*, translated by G. Spivak, (Johns Hopkins University Press, Baltimore, 1974), chapter 2.

[12] These far-reaching claims are made in 'Limited Inc.' and other works.

[13] Derrida, 'Signature, Event, Context', p. 315.

[14] 'Type-token' is a contrast that is ultimately rejected by Derrida, but is useful here. The discussion of iterability and its consequences here was written in response to questioning from John Searle and John Troyer. Their comments made it clear that I had not really gotten Derrida's argument straight. That may still be true.

token can be correctly taken in only one way, since it really is a token of a given type, either by some kind of intention attached by the thinker, or by its very nature, or by some privileged relational properties. That is, what thought is being thought is the question of what the real interpretation of a token is.

If an item is really a token of a given type, then it is necessarily possible that it be repeatable. Its being of that type entails that other tokens of its type would function in other contexts in ways defined by the type. These other possibilities are built into *its* nature *as* a token of that type. Whether this necessity is conceived as part of the intrinsic nature of the token or as due to relational properties of the token, there is an appeal to an apparent objective necessity in the notion that a token is 'really' a token of precisely this one of the types of which it could be construed to be a token.

The real problem in getting an account of meaning which allows determinacy of meaning is to give an account of this necessity. How are we to understand the 'necessarily' in the above sentence, so that an entity can be 'really' a token of one type rather than another? The treatment of 'necessarily' in both Davidson and Derrida is really the point on which all the radical claims turn. Their radical claims are really consequences of rejecting realist conceptions of necessity and so objecthood.

There seem to be three kinds of account of the 'necessarily' which makes a token really a repeatable of a given type:

First, one could be the sort of essentialist that the case seems to require. Aristotle's idea would be that the token itself, at least in the case of thought, has a privileged, natural sameness to other tokens. There is a real universal explaining the sameness of thoughts of Animals, since each of these thoughts is really of the same species, without the matter. This is perhaps the model of the basic idea of the 'idea' idea, the notion that items of thought have an intrinsic nature that identifies ideas of the same kind and ideas with the same meaning.

This way of explaining the necessity (or identifying objects as really tokens of a given universal) amounts to essentialism about thought contents. As Nelson Goodman has pointed out,[15] objective sameness is a notion that goes together with objective necessity and non-system-relative objecthood. An explanation of the real grouping of entities of a given kind by appeal to their natures requires a realist ontology of natures. Since the token's nature is the universal which is its type, the relation between a token and its type has the same problems as that between an Aristotelian substance and its essence. (Analogous problems arise even if it is relations rather than intrinsic natures which constitute a token as a token of a given type.)

The second way to explain necessity and thus objecthood and objective sameness is by some version of linguistic convention or practice. I don't see how this strategy can work as an account of the objective sameness of tokens needed to account for the existence of language itself. At some level, these theories suppose real *natures* and so real objective necessities about linguistic and semantical items, which then constitute linguistic conventions and practices. Quine's savaging of the analytic/synthetic distinction can be taken as pointing

---

[15] Goodman's discussions of sameness, objecthood, and related topics occur throughout his works. See especially *Problems and Projects* (Bobbs-Merrill, New York, 1972).

out that 'conventionalist' accounts of necessity would have to be essentialist about linguistic items.

The third way to account for necessity and objective natures is the Kantian strategy of treating the objects as constructed and so having the features by which they are constructed necessarily. This seems to be the favored strategy for Husserl, and the one to which Derrida's remarks are addressed. On this account, objects are constituted by structuring some kind of raw material with concepts. The object then necessarily has properties by which it was constituted.

In the case at hand, the universal which is the type is constructed of the potentially infinite repetitions of the token, past and future. The universal is constructed out of the repeatability of the token. A token's being a token of a type, then, is defined in terms of future and past repetitions. Now, it is only on the Aristotelian picture that repetitions of 'the same thing' depend on an intrinsic sameness in the very nature of the items. On the Kantian view Derrida is supposing, the sameness is derivative from being posited *as* the same, from being constituted as the same. The sameness is constructed, not given. The *a priority* is synthetic, due to the constituting power of the subject. In Chisholm's terminology, then, the property of being a token of a given type is 'rooted outside times at which it is had.'[16]

From this point of view, the iterability of representations, their status as tokens of given types, is a feature which cannot be completely present. What a token really is, its status *as* a token, extends past what can be completely there at a moment. Thus a token, *qua* token, is essentially non-present. (This dependency on the non-present is rather like what occurs according to one reading of Goodman's account of 'grue' versus 'green'. That is, since whether *grue* or *green* is meant is a matter of what is said in future circumstances rather than depending on intrinsic properties of words, whether a token of 'green' is really a token of the concept 'green' or 'grue' is non-present.)

If universals must be construed as constructions out of past and future instances, then iterability might arguably have the exotic consequences Derrida ascribes to it. If being a token of a given type is problematic because it essentially involves what is not present, then even determining that a token is of a type is a matter of interpretation, rather than something which can provide a basis for interpretation.

The identification of items as instances of universals, even in the simplest case where the universals are word-types, already involves reference to rules of language, and so forth. All of these rules of language, social practices, etc., are themselves built on repeatable, iterable significant items which are themselves tokens of types. Thoughts, intentions, and so forth are significant only *qua* tokens of some kind of semantic universals. So all significant items are non-present in the way I have argued that tokens are.

So nothing significant can be totally present. Significant items are thus always sign-like in referring to something else and deferring their meaning. Displacements and non-standard uses of a token of a type are not accidental deviations but essential to what the thing is. Its nature as a significant item *is*

---

[16] Roderick Chisholm, *Person and Object*, p. 100.

this displacement from full presence. Thus, in any mark, 'no matter how fine this point may be, it is like the *stigma* of every mark, already split.'[17] All significant items, then, are sign-like in being thus incomplete. This is one reason,[18] why Derrida insists that 'marginal' speech acts cannot be set aside to be dealt with as special cases of the more general theory.

The core problem which drives the analyses of both Derrida and Davidson, it seems to me, is that allegedly non-Aristotelian and non-essentialist accounts of the world (e.g. Kantian and 'linguistic' ones) still seem to rest on essentialism about conceptual or linguistic items. That is, when we ascribe all necessity (and so objecthood, objective sameness, etc.) to the nature of linguistic or conceptual phenomena, there are still some natures and essences left, namely those of linguistic and conceptual phenomena. The radical break which both Davidson and Derrida make is to work out the consequences of denying essentialism and objective necessities across the board.

Iterability, according to Derrida, most clearly undermines the meaning of speech acts, the force with which they are to be taken. The undermining of reference and sense follows, given that reference and sense are constructed out of expressive speech acts. If, following Derrida, Davidson and Quine, we start with sentences as meant on occasions, in order to construct meanings of sentences and words, the force with which an utterance is made as well as the 'contents' attached to particular words must be gotten out of iterable utterances.

Why does iterability create a problem about understanding utterances? Because something beyond the linguistic item must be brought in to complete meaning, apparently. And this is part of the essence of what it is to be a linguistic item. That is, unless it were possible for this very sentence to be taken as, for instance, non-serious, it would not have significance. The meaning of the sentence itself, in virtue of the iterability described above, is not tied to the particular personal intention which produced it.

Davidson has made similar remarks in discussing Austin's theories of illocutions,[19] Frege's use of the assertion sign, and the general distinction between force and content. For Davidson, there is no way to put force into words or to guarantee by a linguistic form that an expression is to be taken in a certain way. Any such attempt at a performative form creates an item which itself can be used for an example, for instance. Anything which could not be misused would not be a linguistic item at all. It is necessarily possible for linguistic items to occur with difference forces and so to be interpreted in deviate ways. So what?

Now we can state Derrida's argument, starting from this Davidsonian observation and the principle that iterability is a mark of any sign. The

---

[17] Jacques Derrida, 'Limited Inc.', p. 185.

[18] Derrida glorifies the marginal, non-serious, etc., as part of his project of 'deconstructing Western metaphysics'. The point here, though, is that the marginal uses are not really deviations from an ideal, but are rather paradigmatic of the basic sign-relation.

[19] My source here is Davidson's 1968 class in philosophy of language. The parallel with Derrida shows up strikingly in this quotation from 'Limited Inc.', p. 208: 'no criterion that is simply *inherent* in the manifest utterance is capable of distinguishing an utterance when it is serious from the same utterance when it is not. ... Nothing can distinguish a serious or sincere promise from the same 'promise' that is non-serious or non-sincere except for the intention which informs and animates it.'

discussion of iterability makes it clear that words alone will not specify how a sentence is meant in any kind of complete and full way. Given that how a sentence is meant is the basis from which an account of linguistic meaning must start, any indeterminacy or lack of fullness in the meaning that comes in utterances will corrupt the whole theory. Derrida will argue that this lack of fullness of meaning in words themselves used on occasions is in principle unfillable. So to start: what must be added to words to yield a determinate speech act?

Derrida considers two alternatives: (a) There could be *present* meanings, thoughts, or intentions which would consist of some kind of representation which needed no interpretation. I avoid the Husserlian complications of analysing the intention with its object into the intending (which is present in its nature) and the object (likewise present in its nature). (b) If presence proves inadequate, then perhaps the context in which an utterance is made could suffice to fill out the residue, or totalize the meaning.

The problem with presence has been covered in the discussion of iterability: No significant item can be fully present in a way which makes it non-arbitrary or which removes it from the necessity of being interpreted. If iterability and detachability from context is required in order for an item to be significant, and iterability destroys full presence, then significant items of any kind, alone, cannot fill in what is missing to complete the specification of the meaning of a speech act.

It is important that this result holds, even if the notion of presence is not tied to oddities about the notion of a sign. Suppose there are significant *states* of an organism which are present to it in their totality but which are not, strictly, signs. In order to be meaningful, such states would have to be iterable, at least, in the sense that they are tokens of universals with semantic import.

If such a state were iterable as signs are, then it would require interpretation to say what it meant on this occasion in this mind. If it is a sign at all, and thus functioning semantically, then it is iterable and so usable on more than one occasion. If it is iterable, though, it can be taken and used more than one way. Iterability thus destroys the possibility of a non-arbitrary significant item, and makes all significant items like linguistic signs.

Such significant items, whether linguistic signs or thought events, cannot be fully present. In fact, no significant item, by the very nature of what it takes to be significant, can be fully present, according to Derrida's iterability argument.

'Representations', as thought tokens of some kind which are fully present in their own nature and so need no interpretation, are an illusion unless 'their own nature' is understood as Aristotle understands forms without matter, i.e. unless one is an essentialist about referential properties of an organism's states. Representations thus will not provide the kind of totalization needed to complete meaning, but will rather be just spiritual words in need of interpretation. States which are not iterable, i.e. which are not essentially tokens of types, do not really 'stand for', but are rather causal accompaniments.

If all significant items are essentially iterable, then they can be no better than signs. But signs, besides being incomplete in specifying the whole speech act on a given occasion, are essentially different and deferring from meanings and referents. Thus there can be no significant items which cannot be otherwise used or understood.

For these among other reasons,[20] Derrida rejects the idea that meanings or any other entities are present to us in the way that would fulfil meaning. He agrees with Sellars[21] that even experience itself is not given without mediation.[22] Any awareness is mediated by language or language-like phenomena. I will sketch some of the consequences he draws below.

If totally present significant items cannot exist and so cannot totalize meaning and fill out the residual remnant words leave out (point (b) above), perhaps context will suffice. It might be claimed that context, for instance, fixes such features as the references of words and whether an utterance is correctly to be taken seriously, and thus freezes the repeatable expression in precisely one of its possible ways of being taken. If this were the case, then the total theory of meaning would be a theory which would pair contexts, specified non-linguistically, and sentences to yield meanings. The difficulty then is that contexts are not exhaustively specifiable without reference to intentions, beliefs, and so forth, which are themselves subject to interpretation.

By an argument which is very like the Brentano-Chisholm-Quine[23] argument either that intentional entities are irreducible to anything else or that translation is indeterminate, Derrida points out that there is always a residue in the specification of a context which would fix the meaning of an utterance. 'For a context to be exhaustively determinable, in the sense demanded by Austin, it at least would be necessary for the conscious intention to be totally present and actually transparent for itself and others'.[24] Without the availability of intentions which need no interpretation, but carry meaning on their own, and without significant items which are purely present in themselves (as Putnam's intuitions of the Forms),[25] there is no locking an utterance event into one fully stable and determinate meaning. Without some level of unmediated, directly present thought, the wandering possibilities of individual utterances cannot be pinned down.

To see the consequences of denying presence and holding that there is nothing isolable and semantic behind language, consider what the thesis of indeterminacy of radical translation really means: one way to *mis*understand Quine and Davidson is to suppose that indeterminacy of translation or interpretation is a problem of figuring out which meaning a given sentence has when the evidence gives equal support to several. This model of indeterminacy

---

[20] The illusoriness of presence is argued on many other less rigorously formulable grounds. Perhaps most important is Derrida's reading of Freud as doing away with the illusion of the transparency and unambiguity of the self.

[21] Sellars rejects the 'myth of the given' in 'Empiricism and the Philosophy of Mind', in *Science, Perception, and Reality* (Routledge and Kegan Paul, London, 1963) pp. 127–96, among other places.

[22] Derrida, 'Signature, Event, Context', p. 318.

[23] W. V. Quine, *Word and Object*, p. 221.

[24] 'Signature, Event, Context', p. 327. See also 'Limited Inc.', especially p. 208ff. Derrida also seems to argue that just the structure of iterability alone is sufficient to guarantee that even context cannot make meaning fully present in a sign. If it were present, it would not be deferred by the sign.

[25] Hilary Putnam, 'Realism and Reason', in *Meaning and the Moral Sciences* (Routledge and Kegan Paul, London, 1978), p. 127. On rereading this paper, it is clear that there is a paper for a Putnam conference called 'Derrida and Putnam'. What is less clear is how intuition would help. How would direct access to a Form give one anything semantic? Why couldn't a Form be misapplied?

supposes that there are non- or pre-linguistic meanings, and that indeterminacy is a problem of linking a sentence to one of those meanings.

The picture required by the denial of presence, however, is that there are only the interpretee's dispositions as to what to say when (his theory) and our dispositions as to what to say when. A translation or interpretation is just a mapping based on these items. A question of what an utterance in one language *really* means in another language is like the question which football position is the shortstop. There are no unmediated meanings and no magical links between acts of utterance and these meanings.

The same kind of theory of meaning that is rejected by Quine and Davidson is implicit in the notion of polysemy as an account of what is the case when a text can be taken in several ways. That is, polysemy, multiple ambiguity, presupposes that there are meanings which words ambiguously express. Thus Derrida's rejection of polysemy agrees with Quine's and Davidson's accounts of the translation situation.

On a theory which denies presence (i.e. a theory without the myth of the given) there is no level of meaning which is not subject to indeterminacy problems. All the way down there is just more language. All significant items are sign-like, non-self-interpreting, and so defer something.

(3) Deferral is the third feature of signs Derrida draws attention to. Signs as signs defer or put off access to what they are signs of. The central idea is that, without presence, this deferral is a deferral which is never consummated. This deferral can only regress to an unending sequence of background languages, to use Quine's term.[26] Sign-like representation is never really fully present, but rather always involves a residue, a remainder that is left out. Sentences and terms are traces or tracks of some absent beast which is in principle inaccessible in itself.

This structure of deferral, combined with the consequences of iterability, makes the very terminology in which we describe semantic phenomena inappropriate to the case, much as the denial of the analytic synthetic distinction does for talk of 'meaning'. If we think of the concept of 'sign' as a token of a meaning or of an item separate from language, then the notion of *sign* supposes distinctions that 'cannot be made comprehensible'. In the same way, the notion of *deferral*, of putting off contact with what language 'communicates', namely a meaning, is inappropriate in a theory which holds that there is no interpretation into anything which is not another language.

The 'distance' alleged to obtain between language and what language expresses is not exactly a deferral or delay of some presence, since the presence is in principle always deferred. On the other hand, even though language is inseparable from what it is about (that is, even though the theory-content contrast cannot be made) the world is not just words. Language differs from what it is about and defers what it is about, but without the structure of two domains which both of these terms ('deferral' and 'differing') presuppose.

---

[26] W. V. Quine, 'Ontological Relativity', in *Ontological Relativity* (Columbia University Press, New York, 1969), p. 49, and *passim*.

The inappropriateness of these dualisms removes essential conditions for the application of 'sign', 'reference', and so forth. This is at least part of Derrida's thinking in his neologism 'differance'.[27] We are likewise cast adrift from familiar contrasts in thinking about language and the world by the abandonment of dualisms in Davidson's 'On the Very Idea of A Conceptual Scheme'. Davidson encourages us to be more relaxed about the destruction of the divide between our language and the world (what else could we reasonably expect?), but the abyss is still there.

If all interpretation is by regress to a background language, (or if, in the best of circumstances, truth-definitions relate language to language), then the problem that iterability produces is in part a kind of disposition of terms to drift.[28] Without the absolute efficacy of the anchors (or more accurately completions to *fullness*) of either context or of totally present representations, any privileged interpretation of a term or text is cut loose. There can be no privileged complete assignments of translations from one language to another. Drift is in principle built into interpretation; there is always a residue or a kind of 'slack' between an interpretation and the evidence for it. Derrida assigns this slack to iterability, but that is really to assign the slack to the essence of language itself. That is, just as for Quine and Davidson, the real reason for indeterminacy of translation is that there is nothing to language but items with language-like properties, so for Derrida drift is a feature built into what it is for any mark to function as a sign.

Derrida's rejection of polysemy as a model for interpretation problems has a similar basis. The term Derrida uses rather than the inappropriate 'polysemy' is 'dissemination', which basically describes the kind of fluidity 'correct' interpretations will have, given that there is nothing semantical beyond language and thus nothing capable of freezing interpretation between languages or among discourses within one language.

The phenomenon of dissemination is akin to the Davidsonian variety of indeterminacy[29] rather than to the kind of global, total sets of alternatives that Quine envisions in chapter Two of *Word and Object*.[30] I think that Quinean indeterminacy of translation still depends on a (perhaps correct but non-Davidsonian) dualism between observation and theory. Quine must somehow hold that there is a level of semantic content, the observation sentence, which is invulnerable to theoretical change, i.e. to change of scheme. Part of what transpires can be purified and separated from language. Only if the theoretical views of a theory are separable from observation or some directly present content can sense be made of the notion that there are alternatives available to our present system of organizing experience. Without some *present* experience which is separable from linguistic phenomena, the notion that there

---

[27] See Derrida's 'Differance', in *Margins of Philosophy*, pp. 1–27.

[28] See Derrida, 'Signature, Event, Context', p. 316: 'This essential drifting, due to writing as an iterative structure cut off from all absolute responsibility, from *consciousness* as the authority of the last analysis ...'

[29] One statement of Davidson's version of the indeterminacy of interpretation is in 'Belief and the Basis of Meaning', *Synthese*, 27, nos 3/4 (July/August 1974), pp. 309–23.

[30] W. V. Quine, *Word and Object*, p. 21.

is the organized as opposed to what organizes cannot be made sense of. This paraphrases Davidson's remark that, 'this second dualism of scheme and content, of organizing system and something waiting to be organized, cannot be made intelligible and defensible.'[31]

Davidson's apparently milder kind of indeterminacy is thus more radical and pure than Quine's, since Davidson denies there is any sub-basement of content which can be separated from the linguistic framework. Davidson absolutely abandons the dualism between 'scheme and content',[32] so that even the notion that experience is something organized by theory or that there are alternative schemes doesn't make sense. So Wilson's concept of 'charity'[33] applies to ontology as well.[34] There is only ontological relativity if there is something stable for ontology to be relative to. There are only alternatives for how a scheme fits content if there are separable phenomena. For Davidson, language and what language is about are inextricably bound. There is no 'presence' behind language, but rather, what is behind language is inseparable from further language.[35] Without the crutches of dualisms, this is the view to which he and Derrida are forced.

Davidsonian indeterminacy then, shows up at specific locations where there is some inhomogeneity between our speech and that of the other. In interpretation, there arise equally good alternatives of whether and where to assign falsehood (by our lights), re-interpret a predicate, or assign some unusual attitude or valuation in an area of another's discourse.

One apparently obvious difference between Derridian indeterminacy and Davidsonian is only apparent. I do not believe that Derrida's disparaging remarks about truth are really incompatible with Davidson's theories. Although Davidson sometimes gives the impression that his theory is concerned primarily with assertions, he is well aware that the claim that a native sentence is a serious and sincere attempt to inform us cannot be the opening of a theory but is rather already the result of a rather far-developed theory. Some readers have taken the fact that Davidson deals with truth-definitions to mean that his theory takes 'fact-reporting' discourse to be primary. But this confuses truth with assertion. For Davidson, interpretation starts with what people do in what situations, and

---

[31] This dualism is abandoned by Davidson as a 'third dogma of empiricism' in 'On the Very Idea of a Conceptual Scheme', p. 11.

[32] Donald Davidson, 'On the Very Idea of a Conceptual Scheme', p. 11.

[33] N. L. Wilson, 'Substances without Substrata', *Review of Metaphysics*, 12 (1959), pp. 521–39.

[34] Donald Davidson, 'Belief and the Basis of Meaning', p. 321.

[35] Actually, Davidson's text is not homogeneous on this matter. In a piece written before 'On the Very Idea of a Conceptual Scheme', he says, 'Indeterminacy of meaning or translation does not represent a failure to capture significant distinctions; ...If there is indeterminacy, it is because when all the evidence is in, alternative ways of stating the facts remain open' (Belief and the Basis of Meaning', p. 322). Are facts about what is believed and meant real? This passage, and 'On the Very Idea of a Conceptual Scheme', should be read together with 'Mental Events', (Foster and Swanson (eds), *Experience and Theory*, University of Massachusetts Press, Amherst, 1970), where the primacy of non-mental concepts seems to be claimed. There, the constraints on translation seem to constitute a scheme in which the physical facts are interpreted; and the constraints on physical theory constitute another and more inclusive scheme. It is difficult to read these texts as expressions of a single position.

parcels out the verbal part of this behaviour into speech acts. The determination of what speech act is being undertaken and what its content is, are holistically and simultaneously hypothesized about.

The eruptions of Davidsonian indeterminacy seem to occur only at margins, since interpretation itself depends on overall agreement. Thus there can be no global breakdown while interpretation is possible. It seems that, in the best of circumstances, there is stability for Davidson's theory. According to Derrida, on the other hand, since iterability itself brings about displacement of interpretation, indeterminacy obtains even in the best of circumstances. Even though not everything is overturned at once, there is no part of our theory which is safe from drift.

Even on Davidson's principles, though, there may well be the repressed germ of insidious Derridian piece by piece global indeterminacy which Davidson is trying to conceal from us by his calm reassurances. First, given the interanimation of sentences, indeterminacy may well seep into other areas from the original problem areas. Second, if we extend Davidson's ideas to cases of interpreting discourse from our own past and from our culture's past, indeterminacy of translation, especially about the cultural, social and moral topics on which much of our literature dwells, becomes much more creeping and pervasive. Third, and most importantly, if we do not make the simplifying assumption that a person's language or theory *at a time* is a unified whole, then areas of our own language are indeterminate relative to other areas of our own language. This kind of indeterminacy threatens to supplant the calm picture of indeterminacy as largely concerned with minor aspects of the psychology of the other with which Davidson often comforts us.

Derrida's indeterminacy of interpretation starts out Davidsonian, and rests on much the same kind of basic considerations. Since there is nothing to interpretation but interpretation into more essentially iterable and so unfixed language, that is, since the deferrals are to further deferrals, there are no anchors to fix interpretations even between languages or phases of the same language. In any relation of one discourse to another, there will be breaks, places where things don't fit. As we adjust interpretation for that case, another interpretation has to be adjusted. Exactly this kind of situation is sometimes used to illustrate indeterminacy in the construction of truth-definitions, given the interanimation of sentences. Once we have accommodated Jones's remark 'Dromedaries have two humps' by assigning him a desire to test our zoological knowledge, we have to re-examine his other zoological remarks, with other expanding consequences. A given indeterminacy thus affects evidence for other cases throughout the interpretation, especially in the cases of pervasive terms of social practice.[36]

Derrida illustrates this kind of plague-like displacement in interpreting particular texts. A given assertion doesn't fit with other parts of a text, somehow. The interpretation of that part of a discourse then proceeds to unhinge the prior interpretation of the rest of the discourse. This is not to say that the subsequent reading is now all finalized, any more than pointing out an

---

[36] If we have an indeterminacy about what 'right' means, for instance, since it is an important term in practical thought, lots of actions as well as sentences will be ambiguous.

alternative interpretation for Davidson shows that either reading was correct. If there is no presence behind language, then, as languages and relations between them shift, so do correct interpretations. Even at a given time, there are alternatives. The alternatives at a given time, furthermore, come back to re-infect and displace their point of origin. There is always a residue which cannot be finally filled in.

There are clearly many ways in which Davidson's analysis is superior to Derrida's: the notion of structure, the format of the truth-definition, the detailed analysis of individual locutions to show exactly what *one* interpretation would be, are all lacking in Derrida's work. On the other hand, there are some important things Derrida dwells on which Davidson does not emphasize. Two things strike me as especially important:

First, Derrida extends interpretation to texts explicitly in a way Davidson doesn't. Interpretation needn't be between languages or total theories as commonly understood, but may also be between fragments of languages or particular discourses.

Second, Derrida spends much more effort on interpretation of our own theory in terms of parts of it. It is of most interest to Derrida that theories *do not fit with themselves*, let alone with other languages and discourses. Unless we are divine, the closure of our beliefs under logical consequence (let alone weaker consequence relations), typically yields inconsistent views. Thus, even in understanding our own views, and in explicating what we ourselves mean, there will be indeterminacy of paraphrase, and incompatible defensible alternatives. The project of cleaning up our theories, as Quine has observed,[37] leaves us choices. Since Derrida observes that the possibility of alternative interpretation is essential to a sign qua sign, interpretation and indeterminacy of interpretation must be in principle unending. But exactly this residue, this unfilled remainder, is also implicit in Davidson's view that meaning is given by truth-definitions. Words are interpreted by mapping onto words, and what is meant cannot be exhaustively put into words. (Not that there is anything else to put it into.)

IV *Why writing?*

The true Davidsonian nature of Derridian indeterminacy of interpretation is illuminated by reflecting on one of Derrida's more famous hyperboles. Derrida claims that writing precedes speech and that all speech is really writing.[38]

---

[37] This second point is often made by Quine in his metaphors of holism (in *Word and Object*, *passim*.) If our web of belief connects all the sentences of our theory, and if the achievement of consistency by adjustment to changes in occasion sentences held-true requires adjustment throughout, then at any given time, our theory will not be consistent, and interpretation of one part in terms of another part will be in flux, since adjustments will require changes which themselves require changes in the spots where the original adjustments were made.

A typical Quinean example of holistic adjustment is the adjustment of theory to the stresses and inconsistencies imposed by the results of the Michelson-Morley experiment (an example from *The Web of Belief*, p. 47). When this is taken together with a Derridian deconstruction of Rousseau, in *On Grammatology*, we have an illustration of the ways these traditions are different.

[38] The most sober presentation of this thesis is in 'Signature, Event, Context', p. 316ff.

This can be understood in several ways: first, writing is the least deceptive form of language, in the sense that it is the form which is least likely to foster a certain illusion. Just as Heraclitus regards fire as the form of existence least likely to support the illusion of stability, so Derrida views writing as the form of language least likely to support the illusion of pure presence to the self and special semantic attachment to a producer. For those of us raised in the Quinean fold, much of Derrida's discussion will seem directed at mysterious foes. Who believes that speech is special? For Quineans, speech is just inscription with sound waves.

To see what Derrida is concerned with, we have to imagine thinking that speech is somehow more directly connected with full meaning than writing, that somehow speech directly puts meaning fully into sound. The idea gets strong intuitive support from the experience of thinking to oneself, the interior monologue that seems directly to put meaning into something which, if overt, would be speech. But what could this full meaning be?

The real issue here is the notion of an inner sign which directly expresses content, i.e., the representations, the signs which are immune to misinterpretation discussed above. Speech seems to be inner signs made manifest. How do transcripts of interior monologues differ from their contents? Husserl, whom Derrida takes to be the paradigm metaphysician, struggles to maintain a hybrid notion of 'expressive sign' which will be a *sign* endowed with but distinct from its content.[39] According to Derrida, the nature of the sign relation – basically the iterability, deferral, and difference of signs from what they are signs of, is a kind of force within Husserl's thought which threatens to loosen these interior signs and turn them into indications, things which can stray from the attached thought contents.[40]

For Quineans, of course, it is obvious already that speech and thought are brain-writing, some kind of tokenings which are as much subject to interpretation as any other. For our (analytic) tradition, speech is not overtly valorized. Still, there seems in non-Quinean circles to be a covert belief that somehow inner speech is directly expressive of thought. The intuitive primacy of speech may be part of the shocked reaction to Quine's claims in *Ontological Relativity*[41] that there is indeterminacy of translation even in our own case, of how we understand ourselves. This conclusion is a direct consequence of taking thought to be inscriptional and taking inscriptions to be writing-like. If inscriptions are writing-like, then all we have, even in our inner speech, is a text which can be taken in many ways. Without something besides texts in the brain, there is nothing to be made of the 'correct' interpretation or the one that conformed to the intentions of the author. (The author's intentions, after all, are just more writing in the brain.)

The notion that everything is a text is a metaphor widely used by hermeneuticists, structuralists, etc. When Derrida combines it with the radical drift of indeterminacy of interpretation, and replaces polysemy with dissemination, the

---

[39] Edmund Husserl, *Logical Investigations*, Investigation I, especially chapter 1, sections 1 through 11.

[40] Derrida, *Speech and Phenomena*. This seems to me the major topic of the book.

[41] W. V. Quine, *Ontological Relativity*, p. 46: 'radical translation begins at home'.

metaphor says something very different – the text/meaning distinction goes the way of the scheme/content distinction.

Derrida's claim that all language is really writing, then, is that all language is subject to interpretation in exactly the way writing is. So, first, the interpreting language is also subject to interpretation, without end, so that we have the 'regress to a background language'. Second, just as writing, because it is a token and iterable in virtue of being a linguistic sign, is meaningful in separation from the conditions of production from which it issues, and so has, so to speak, a life of its own, so all systems of representation are detachable from their speaker. (Of course, 'representation' misrepresents things, and should be replaced with the less misleading 'differance'). Third, the separation of representing tokens from their conditions of production is essential to their being representing tokens at all. If they were essentially tied to their context, they would not be representations. 'By all rights, it belongs to the sign to be legible, even if the moment of its production is irremediably lost, and even if I do not know what its alleged author-scriptor meant consciously and intentionally at the moment he wrote it, that is abandoned it to its essential drifting.'[42] If all representation is like that, then ontological relativity, in its purified and radicalized Davidsonian and Derridian form, indeed begins at home.

Thus, the claim that all language is really writing or that writing is prior to speech is the proposal of a model of thought whose consequences dislodge the illusion of anchoring provided by the alternative of presence. Only presence would provide a means of giving sense to the notion of *the* correct interpretation of an utterance.

For Derrida, like Davidson, but unlike Quine, all of our (?)access to the(?) world is impure and subject to drift and being cut off from its origin.

> This structural possibility of being severed from its referent or signified … seems to me to make of every mark, even if oral … the non-present *remaining* of a differential mark cut off from its alleged 'production' or origin. And I will extend this law even to all 'experience' in general, if it is granted that there is no experience of *pure* presence, but only chains of differential marks.[43]

The notion that writing is prior, then, requires that we take seriously the *language* part of 'the language of thought'. If the linguistic model is indeed the way thought is to be thought of, then it too is meaningful in the absence of the producer, and it too is subject to the kinds of drifts to which language is subject. More accurately, if all language is writing, then the contrast with something by which writing could be anchored to a determinate preferred interpretation is lost. Without a pure non-written present meaning opposed to writing, there could not be determinacy of interpretation of writing.

V *Conclusion*

Some brief disavowals and disclaimers will be required to show that this paper is serious as a whole, and not to be taken as an attempted demonstration that

---

[42] Derrida, 'Signature, Event, Context', p. 317.
[43] Derrida, 'Signature, Event, Context', p. 318.

Davidson can be read as anybody's co-believer: I do not pretend to have given thorough accounts of either Derrida's or Davidson's theories of interpretation, but have indicated some (to me) important interrelations. I have ignored a great deal that is important and interesting in Derrida's work, and would not claim that his main significance is as a fellow-traveler with Davidson's views of interpretation.

28
Metaphor, Dreamwork and Irrationality

Marcia Cavell

At its best, a metaphoric use of language is a case of saying something literally false which none the less inspires a revelation. Most theories attempt to account for this interesting fact by attributing two meanings to a metaphor – either to the metaphoric sentence itself or one to the sentence and the other to its use – so that it may be literally false yet metaphorically true. Davidson, however, is as insistent on the revelatory power of metaphor as he is in denying that we can put together some propositional contents that capture it. 'How many facts or propositions are conveyed by a photograph?' he rhetorically asks. 'Bad question. A picture is not worth a thousand words, or any other number. Words are the wrong currency to exchange for a picture' (*ITI*, p. 263).[1]

Metaphor functions to change not so much what we believe as what we see, causing us to see one thing as another by making a literal statement that prompts the insight. The metaphoric sentence expresses a proposition; but the *seeing as* response that it inspires is not a propositional attitude. If I show you Wittgenstein's duck-rabbit and you see it as a duck, and then I say 'It's a rabbit', you will suddenly see it as a rabbit, and you can say that's what you see. But no proposition expresses what Wittgenstein calls the 'dawning of an aspect'. Not only are we unable to provide an exhaustive description of what has been attended to when we are led to see something in a new light. 'The difficulty is more fundamental. What we notice or see is not, in general, propositional in character' (*ITI*, p. 263).

Not the least virtue of Davidson's account is that it links the verbal to the non-verbal arts, which are also surely often metaphorical. But more to my point is that it opens a path to exploring other kinds of non-propositional envisioning. One in particular, which Freud calls 'dreamwork', plays an important role in irrational mental processes and actions. Dreamwork envisioning is typically

---

[1] 'What Metaphors Mean', in *Inquiries into Truth and Interpretation* (Clarendon Press, Oxford, 1984). Further references to *ITI* are to this essay and volume.

accompanied, furthermore, by the mechanisms of 'condensation' and 'displace-ment', virtually other names for metaphor and metonymy. Davidson incidentally alludes to dreamwork in his opening metaphor: metaphor as the dreamwork of language. I propose to develop this comparison, as he does not, as a way of giving some detail to the scheme for understanding irrationality that he sketches in other essays.

In Section I, I say what I understand by 'dreamwork'. Since Freud's own remarks on the subject are often contradictory, any interpretation is bound to be controversial. My aim, however, is not primarily to interpret but to offer an account of my own – inspired by Freud – that makes the best sense of what I take to be the phenomena in question, and incidentally, also of Freud. These phenomena are not only dreams, but more importantly, a kind of waking mental process – instanced in phantasy, in works of art, in so-called 'symptomatic' behaviors – which 'dreamwork' names and describes. It is related to wishful thinking, though that phrase conjures up a process more intrinsically rational than the ones I have in mind. (Whether or not all dreams are wish-fulfilling in Freud's sense is not my concern.) By the same token, dreamwork wish-fulfillment, rooted as it typically is in anxiety, and anxiety of a primitive (i.e. infantile) sort, has little to do with wishing as we ordinarily understand it.

In Section II, I discuss dreamwork in relation to Davidson's model of irrationality.

At the end of the paper I comment briefly on some connections between irrationality and metaphor.

I *Dreamwork*

Freud distinguishes two separate functions in mental activity during the construction of a dream: the production of the dream thoughts and their transformation – wrought by dreamwork – into the manifest content.[2] Under-standing dreamwork yields the principles, such as they are, of dream intelligi-bility: condensation, displacement, considerations of representability, and secondary revision. I begin with the third, or with dreaming as a mode of thought (for lack of a better word) that in some sense is a visualizing, because it most clearly reveals both the kinship and the dissimilarity between the *seeing as* of dreamwork and of metaphor *per se*.

On Freud's theory, a dream is the representation, or the visualization, of a wish fulfilled. The representation – hence the wish – is not easily recognized for what it is by the dreamer awake, partly because the wish is infantile, or

---

[2] Freud's most extended discussion of dreamwork is of course in *The Interpretation of Dreams* (vols. IV and V in *The Standard Edition of the Complete Psychological Works of Sigmund Freud* (Hogarth Press, London, 1953–4), hereafter referred to as *SE*). Whether or not the dream is to be understood as a translation of ordinary thoughts into a strange, unrecognizable mode – presumably for purposes of disguises, repression, and intra-psychic defense – or as, in part, the way the mind naturally works in certain of its states, is a question I do not take up here. If we think of dreaming in the second way, then 'dreamwork' becomes all but interchangeable with what Freud calls 'primary process'. I define 'primary process' briefly in note 22, below. Freud discusses it at length in many places, but particularly in chapter VII of *The Interpretation of Dreams*.

connected by associations to one that is. As infantile, it is foreign to the wishes and desires of the normal, conscious adult, though it remains active in the dreamer's present mental life. Furthermore, the wish is surrounded by anxiety and is for that reason as well scarcely identifiable as a wish. The thought of having the wish provokes anxiety. (The granting of the child's longing for intimacy with his father would require the child to be castrated as he thinks his mother is.) Or the wish takes the particular form it does by answering an anxious thought, which is nevertheless still present in inchoate form. (The child imagines intercourse *per anum*, which does not require castration.)[3] And finally, the visual or fictive mode in which the representation takes place operates differently from language proper.

As such an envisioning, the dream is the prototype of what Freud sometimes calls 'hallucinatory wish-fulfillment' and sometimes unconscious 'phantasy'. Apropos of the adult, 'phantasy' refers to a quasi-articulate scenario which preserves in broad structure some anxiety-provoking situation from the past and which one is ready to enact, envision, or act out in the present in a way that (one imagines) sets things right. Dreaming provides Freud with the model for symptomatic acts of all kinds, acts that have explanations in terms of something like beliefs and desires, but that are not done *on purpose*, though the agent herself may think they are; and that are irrational in a special sense.

Consider the much-discussed case of the middle-aged woman, long separated from her husband, who obsessionally runs every day into the room next to her bedroom, takes up a particular position beside a table, rings the bell for the maid, and then runs back into her bedroom, behavior as distressing and unintelligible to the woman as it is at first to Freud. As her story unfolds, the symptom is linked to her husband's impotence on their wedding night years before. Many times he had come from his bedroom to hers to try again, but without success. The next morning he had said angrily that he would feel ashamed in front of the housemaid when she made the bed, and had taken up a bottle of red ink and poured it onto the sheet, but not on exactly the spot where a stain might have been appropriate.

As Freud and his patient reconstruct her 'reasoning', she is, by repeating the scene, (unconsciously) 'correcting' it and putting it right in two ways: She is 'correcting' the placement of the stain, for if she calls the maid in to observe it, it must be in the right place. And she is 'correcting' her husband's impotence as well. Freud writes: 'So the obsessional action was saying: "No, it's not true. He had no need to feel ashamed in front of the housemaid; he was not impotent." It represented this wish, in the manner of a dream, as fulfilled in the present-day action. ...'[4]

Does what she did (as described by Freud) count as an action, behavior to be explained in terms of a pattern of beliefs and desires that constitute the reasons why an agent acts as she does? If so, we apparently have to impute to the woman something like the particular desire to revise her wedding night and the particular belief that running to the table and so on is a way of having her desire,

---

[3] This example comes from the case history of 'the Wolf Man', in 'From the History of an Infantile Neurosis', *SE*, vol. XVII.

[4] S. Freud, *Introductory Lectures on Psychoanalysis*, *SE*, vol. XVI, p. 263.

and some general beliefs such as that the past can be redone, that one can redo it by acting as if it had been the way one wishes it had been, that objects which resemble each other in some ways (like table cloths and bedsheets) are – as it were – functionally equivalent.

The difficulty with Freud's account is that these beliefs and desires are so strange as scarcely to qualify as beliefs and desires in the first place. It is one thing to ascribe a mental attitude to someone of which she is not aware at the time, but which she would nevertheless find perfectly intelligible as a possible mental attitude. If I believe I have told you a hurtful truth out of concern for your welfare and someone suggests that I was retaliating for an injury I believe you have done me, I accept that as a motive someone might understandably have, whether or not I recognize it as mine in this instance. If you have in fact misled me and I believe you have done so intentionally, my belief may be unfounded and in that sense irrational, yet it is understandable to you as a belief. It is another thing, however, to ascribe to someone beliefs and desires so fundamentally odd, not only by our standards but also by hers, that neither we nor she would think they provided reason for doing anything whatever.[5]

The fact that explanations like the one above cannot be accommodated to some version of the practical syllogism might seem a good reason for rejecting them out of hand as explanations of action. In a way I think this is right: so-called symptomatic acts are not actions *per se*, though they resemble them. We might begin by thinking of the acting out of phantasy, not on the pattern of action but of imaginative or quasi-imaginative activity.[6] If *x* is an action, then I do it in the belief that it will bring about *y* which I desire. (Of course I must have all sorts of other beliefs and desires as well, beliefs, among others, about the nature of *x* and *y*.) Such an interrelationship between belief, desire and action is what the practical syllogism describes. But if I imagine doing *x*, or if I act *x* out, where the action I imagine would be likely to have *y* as a consequence, I do not imagine doing *x* in the belief that imagining it is a way, in fact, of achieving *y*.

In hallucinatory wish-fulfillment, there is an act of imagining caused by a wish. Here, too, one does not imagine in the belief that doing so is a way of performing the action and achieving its consequences in fact. Yet there is something like this belief, for unconscious phantasizing or wishing is a mental state governed by what Freud calls 'omnipotence of thought', an implicit theory of mind that credits wishing with the efficacy of doing.[7] Hallucinatory wish-fulillment – which of course is not truly a form of hallucination – cannot be accommodated, then, to the practical syllogism, but neither is it a species of ordinary imagining; for in imagining – as in using language metaphorically – one presumably knows the difference between belief and make-believe, also between thinking about doing or pretending to do *x*, on the one hand, and doing or trying to do *x* on the other, between wishing that something were so and its

---

[5] Such difficulties as these in typical psychoanalytic explanations are discussed by P. Alexander in 'Rational Behavior and Psychoanalytic Explanation', *Mind* (July 1962), pp. 326–41, and in T. Mischel's reply, *Mind* (January 1965), pp. 71–8.

[6] J. Hopkins makes this suggestion in his introduction to *Philosophical Essays on Freud*, eds R. Wollheim and J. Hopkins (Cambridge University Press, Cambridge, 1984).

[7] The notion of omnipotence of thought as a 'theory of mind' is R. Wollheim's in *The Thread of Life* (Cambridge University Press, Cambridge, 1984).

being the case that it is. Apropos of her phantasizing, these distinctions do not exist for the phantasizer. The wish – or the state of anxiety, lack, or need – causes an activity of imagining, an imagining tantamount to the belief that the anxiety-provoking state does not exist or has somehow been dealt with satisfactorily.[8] In phantasizing, one does not acknowledge such principles of rationality as those that describe practical reasoning.

Freud speaks of 'wish' rather than of 'desire' advisedly, for compared to desire, even conscious wishing operates in relative freedom from the constraints of time, space and reality generally. One can wish – but not desire – that the past had been different, that one were in two places at once, that things were in this very moment other than one knows them to be; and for the having of things one believes it is impossible to have. In these ways wishing – but not desiring – can be counter-factual. Conscious wishing – wishing one recognizes as such – is thus more complex than desire. But unconscious wishing is less complex in the sense that the wisher makes fewer differentiations. (Aristotle distinguishes wish from desire in ways similar to these in Book III of *The Nicomachean Ethics*. He is, of course, speaking about conscious wishes.)

One can consciously wish that the past had been different. One can unconsciously wish/believe that the past *is* different. Freud's patient known as the Rat-Man (who himself described his state of mind as crediting thought with omnipotence) compulsively acts out a phantasy in which his father is watching him masturbate in front of a mirror. Only at the end of the first session does Freud learn that, as the Rat-Man himself has known, the father has long been dead.[9] For reasons too complex to elaborate here, the man wishes – but cannot be said to desire – that his father were alive and that he were witness to the masturbatory act. His unconscious wishing produces a state of assertion expressed by 'My father is alive', though he does not consciously believe this to be so. Because of its relative indifference to reality, I would then call hallucinatory wish-fulfillment a pro-attitude that has not yet achieved the logical structure of desire. For the same reason – that the distinction between thinking *p* is true and wishing it were is blurred – the state of assertion in phantasy has not achieved the logical structure of belief.

Of course, the needs and desires that the wish expresses are not truly gratified, nor would it be accurate to say one believes they are. This is the respect in which the wishing of phantasy is appropriately called 'hallucinatory'. One does not hallucinate – as one believes – *that* something is the case; one hallucinates *the world* as being a certain sort of way. To take a very simple example, Freud's dream that he is drinking water after having gone to bed in a state of thirst: while dreaming he does not believe *p*, that his thirst is satisfied, since in dreaming one is in no position to judge that *p* is true or false. Phantasy is a waking state in which one's affirmations are equally invulnerable to evidence.

Consider again the Rat-Man, to whom the dreadful thought obsessively occurs that a terrible punishment, which he vividly imagines, is happening to his

---

[8] I have profited from R. Wollheim's discussion of hallucinatory wish-fulfillment in chapter 3 of *The Thread of Life*.

[9] S. Freud, 'Notes upon a Case of Obsessional Neurosis,' *SE*, vol. x.

father and his 'lady'. Over the course of the analysis this thought emerges as a conflicted, aggressive wish, presenting itself at first as 'just a thought' – a propositional attitude which he does not recognize as his and in which the identity of the attitude is obscure. His own response to the proposition, however, is fascination and anxious guilt, which suggests something both about the character of his attitude and about his mental state, namely that for him it is as if what he envisions were about to come true, though he does not believe that it is, and indeed knows, in some sense, that it is not. If we were to describe this discrepancy as a conflict between mental structures, then there is on the one hand a structure of beliefs and desires that are open to evidence and so subject to revision in the ordinary way, and on the other a structure of pro-attitudes and 'as-if' affirmations that are relatively closed to evidence. It is this second structure, hovering between 'would that the world were ...' and 'this is how the world is' that I have been calling unconscious phantasy.

And just here is one of Freud's most important insights: that in general, no firm line can be drawn between belief and desire. They are abstractions from a less tidy and more ambiguous process, as the systematic interdependency between belief and desire suggests, though they work well enough as categories when we are dealing with normal, adult thinking. Normally we can distinguish the kind of affirmation that asserts p from another kind that says 'yea for p' or 'would that p were so'. Obviously to affirm, state, or say 'yes' to a proposition is not the same thing as giving consent to an impulse, a wish, or a desire. But phantasy does not make this distinction. As an envisioning it is, of course, not a propositional attitude at all. But the envisioning caused by an attitude like desire, then causes an attitude like belief, one denied by the agent and discordant with other beliefs he acknowledges as his.

By its nature, phantasy must falsify reality in two ways: it misrepresents inner reality or the state of the agent, and it misrepresents outer reality or what he is doing in the world.[10] In Freud's thirst dream, for example, while thirsty, the dreamer portrays himself as gratified, and while suffering a desire he portrays himself as gratifying it. Intrinsic to the condition of phantasy is that it obscures what one is experiencing and doing, keeping both from awareness. The wish remains unrecognized, ungratified, and unmodified. And while it may disturb others of one's mental attitudes, it cannot qualify their content. Such conscious thoughts, for example, as the Rat-Man's 'I love and admire and wish to honor my father' do not take into account the angry wish to dishonor and defy him, and the latter is not qualified by the Rat-Man's genuine if exaggerated feelings of affection.

The condition of phantasy differs, then, from self-deception, since the latter description presupposes that one has first registered what one takes to be the truth. In phantasy an experience of anxiety or lack produces an envisioning that forestalls the belief 'I lack what I desire.' Instead of the thought 'x is desirable and I want it' – which requires acknowledging that one does not have it – a state of affairs is portrayed in which what there is, is what one desires. If called to one's attention, the desires are hard to recognize as such, furthermore, since they are archaic remnants from a period in which one was in the grip of

---

[10] I am indebted to J. Hopkins (*Philosophical Essays*) for this point.

erroneous beliefs about the world and of anxieties out of keeping with anything now regarded as a danger.

Even the more ordinary devices of phantasy are not those of self-deception but of wishful thinking: failure to make what one knows generally more specific, to question oneself about a contemplated action or an apparent desideratum, to gear desire to the details of observed reality.[11]

Phantasy is then a species of proto-desire, operating under a primitive theory of the mind, in a mode characterized by condensation, displacement and secondary revision, mechanisms well illustrated by the phantasy told to Freud by four different female patients, in which a child is being beaten. Is this a memory, a belief, merely a thought that is being entertained? The answer is unclear, except that in each case it is accompanied by intense sexual excitement, which suggests that the phantasy is related to desire. The terms of the phantasy are also unclear. Was the child being beaten the one producing the phantasy or another? Was it always the same child? Who was it who was beating the child? 'Nothing could be ascertained,' Freud writes, 'that threw any light upon all these questions – only the hesitant reply: I know nothing about it: a child is being beaten. ... Under these circumstances it was impossible at first even to decide whether the pleasure attaching to the beating-phantasy was to be described as sadistic or masochistic.'[12]

As the phantasy is slowly spelled out, it is revealed to reflect wishes and anxieties interacting with each other from different periods of the phantasizer's life, all of the wishes and anxieties preserved in the structure of the phantasy. It expresses, and condenses, a number of transformations: in the first instance, the child who is being beaten is a rival (brother or sister, if there is one) for the father's love, and the beating is a proof that the phantasizer is his preferred love object. Then under the influence of the guilt which the child came to feel – through omnipotence of thought – for her incestuous wishes, the child being beaten becomes the girl herself, and the motive for the transformation is punishment for the guilty wish. This does not mean, however, that the first motive is replaced. The phantasy expresses the jealous wish, and simultaneously the punishment for it, and something else as well, though Freud does not explicitly say so here: a symbolic representation of the act of intercourse as understood by a child and colored by her feelings of guilt.

By 'condensation' Freud means, then, the convergence of a number of different meanings on a single idea. With regard to dreams, it is the mechanism of dreamwork responsible for the highly laconic expression of the manifest dream in comparison with the dream interpreted, a brevity that might be accounted for as an act of omission; but dream interpretation reveals instead that images and thoughts in the manifest content of the dream are compressed allusions to many others.

'Condensation' is a misleading term, for it suggests that, like the maker of metaphor, the dreamer/phantasizer takes thoughts, ideas, images, which she considers to be distinct, and conflates them into a single idea. Instead, as in 'A

---

[11] J. Elster speaks of wishful thinking – distinguishing it from self-deception – in something like these ways in *Sour Grapes* (Cambridge University Press, Cambridge, 1983).

[12] S. Freud, 'A Child Is Being Beaten', *SE*, vol. XVII, p. 181.

Child Is Being Beaten', the thoughts have not been spelled out in the first place. They are inherently ambiguous. And this ambiguity accounts, in part, for the mechanism Freud calls 'displacement', since thoughts and thought-fragments that are not spelled out and discriminated facilitate a slippage of significance and weighting from one to the other.

Freud says that condensation serves the purpose of disguise, but that it is not necessarily motivated by that purpose. (Certainly one does not dream on purpose.) It is simply the way the mind works in certain of its states – in dreaming, in the creative process, and in phantasy.[13] He does not say of displacement that it, too, may serve the purpose of disguise but is not necessarily generated by it. But because of the kinship between displacement and condensation, both should be characterized in the same way.

Freud posits the fourth mechanism of dreamwork – secondary revision – to account for the fact that the dream can be told. It must then contain the conditions of its own narratability. Secondary revision would seem to be a kind of editing in the direction of rational discourse. A closer look at narrative reveals, however, that intrinsic to it are features facilitating condensation and displacement. Think again of 'A Child Is Being Beaten' and of its ambiguity with regard to crucial details like who is agent and who is victim, why the child is being beaten, and who is watching. Narrative itself allows for such ambiguities, both because it can shift its point of view, looking at the same events from the vantage of different agents, at the agents as they are seen from the outside, at the world as it appears to different agents; and because it must present events sequentially: what is given as mere temporal sequence leaves open the question of logical structure, whether the events occur in the order they do as cause to effect, plan to execution of plan, crime to punishment, and so on.[14] Both the narrative in which the dream seems to unfold, and the narrative in which one unfolds the dream in the later telling of it, allow it to express different (and even in some sense incompatible) thoughts simultaneously.

The dream is of course not identical with the waking narration that puts it into words. Yet the narratability of the dream provides an argument for thinking of dream activity as a species of the mental. Narration involves mental processes. And it would be odd if the dream were a disjunctive activity such that in its final but not its earlier stages mental causes are at work.[15] That a person who dreams is conscious of the contents of her dream, though typically, while dreaming, unaware of them as dream contents, or as thoughts (in some sense) which are about the world, rather than the face of the world, may preclude our describing the dream as expressing propositional attitudes. By definition, dreaming is a state in which one is not aware of one's mental attitudes as such, and so, I have argued, is phantasy – yet both dream and phantasy embody

---

[13] Many psychoanalysts would want to distinguish between unconscious processes in psychopathology, on the one hand, and in creativity, on the other. My final remarks on the relation between metaphor and irrationality are to this point.

[14] For his illuminating remarks about the relations between narrative and phantasy, I am indebted once again to R. Wollheim (*The Thread of Life*).

[15] This is a point that B. O'Shaughnessy makes in 'The Id and the Thinking Process', in *Philosophical Essays on Freud*, eds J. Hopkins and R. Wollheim.

attitudes towards the one familiar world, seen in a particular way, a way that is more rather than less articulable in language. Certainly it is expressible in painting, literature and the arts generally, and in other forms of play.

II *Irrationality*

Many of the things we might mean in calling a thought process or an action irrational do not involve paradox. The sort of irrationality that does, and that therefore makes conceptual difficulty for a theory of action (Davidson points out) is the failure of coherence within a single person in the pattern of her desires, beliefs, actions and so on. The paradox is engendered by the fact that desires, beliefs and the actions they explain, are distinguished and identified partly by their logical relations with each other, relations defining of 'rationality' in the broad sense. These logical relations are describable in terms of certain over-arching principles such as 'Believe that proposition for which there is the greatest amount of evidence', and 'Perform the action you think would be best, all things considered.' We must then ascribe such over-arching principles of rationality to anyone whose behavior we wish to describe and explain as *actions* in the first place. The problem is that weakness of the will and self-deception seem to be cases precisely of not believing or acting in accord with the over-arching principles of rationality or coherence. As Davidson puts it: 'The difficulty in explaining irrationality is in finding a mechanism that can be accepted as appropriate to mental events and yet does not rationalize what is to be explained.'[16]

One of Davidson's examples of irrationality is a variation on an incident from Freud's case-history of the Rat-Man. Here is the example as Davidson tells it:

> A man walking in a park stumbles on a branch in the path. Thinking the branch may endanger others, he picks it up and throws it in a hedge beside the path. On his way home it occurs to him that the branch may be projecting from the hedge and so still be a threat to unwary walkers. He gets off the tram he is on, returns to the park, and restores the branch to its original position. Here everything the agent does (except stumble on the branch) is done for a reason, a reason in the light of which the corresponding action was reasonable. Given that the man believed the stick was a danger if left on the path, and a desire to eliminate the danger, it is reasonable to remove the stick. Given that, on second thought, he believed the stick was a danger in the hedge, it was reasonable to extract the stick from the hedge and replace it on the path. Given that the man wanted to take the stick from the hedge, it was reasonable to dismount from the tram and return to the park. In each case the reasons for the action tell us what the agent saw in his action, they give the intention with which he acted, and they thereby give an explanation for the action. Such an explanation must exist if something a person does is to count as an action at all.[17]

---

[16] D. Davidson, 'Incoherence and Irrationality', in *Proceedings*, 1984 Entretiens, Institute International de Philosophie (forthcoming).

[17] D. Davidson, 'Paradoxes of Irrationality', in *Philosophical Essays on Freud*, eds J. Hopkins and R. Wollheim, p. 292.

What the man did was nevertheless irrational, Davidson continues, because though he had a motive (a reason) for removing the stick, and a motive for returning to the park to restore it, he had yet another motive for not returning, namely the time and trouble it would cost him. Presumably in his own judgement this last consideration was not just one reason among others, but the consideration that outweighed the rest. Yet he acted contrary to his own best judgement. 'What needs explaining is not why the agent acted as he did, but why he *didn't* act otherwise, given his judgement that all things considered it would be better.'[18]

On the model Davidson provides, the irrational step in the sequence leading to akrasia or self-deception is the drawing of the boundary that keeps inconsistent beliefs apart. In particular it is the requirement of total evidence, or the principle that tells us to act in accord with our best judgement, that must be walled off. 'What causes it to be thus temporarily exiled or isolated is, of course, the desire to avoid accepting what the requirement counsels. But this cannot be a *reason* for neglecting the requirement. Nothing can be viewed as a good reason for failing to reason according to one's best standards of rationality.'[19] Davidson draws a crucial distinction between a reason for ignoring the principle 'Do what you think best, all things considered', and a reason for thinking the principle no longer good or one by which we need to abide. There can be a reason for the former but not for the latter. The man has a motive or a desire – the sort of thing that might be a (good) reason for some actions in some circumstances – that is the cause of his behavior. So it is describable in the language of rationality in the broad sense. But he does not have a reason for going against his own over-arching principle of rationality.

Irrationality is then explained in terms of sub-sets of propositional attitudes perfectly coherent in themselves, but conjoined, or disjoined, so as to permit the irrationality.

Freud also thought that some kinds of irrationality are to be described as some such self-division. He called them 'splits in the ego'. In one of the many texts that could be cited here he writes:

> The study of hypnotic phenomena has accustomed us to a bewildering realization that in one and the same individual there can be several mental groupings, which can remain more or less independent of one another, which can 'know nothing' of one another and which can alternate with one another in their hold upon consciousness. ... If, where a splitting of the personality such as this has occurred, consciousness remains attached regularly to one of the states, we call it the *conscious* mental state and the other, which is detached from it, the *unconscious* one.[20]

This is the notion of the unconscious in what Pears calls a 'functional' sense, where the line between conscious and unconscious is drawn to reflect the interactions between a person's mental attitudes rather than his consciousness

---

[18] D. Davidson, 'Paradoxes of Irrationality', p. 296.

[19] D. Davidson, 'Deception and Division', in J. Elster, *The Divided Self* (Cambridge University Press, Cambridge, forthcoming).

[20] S. Freud, 'Five Lectures on Psychoanalysis', *SE*, vol. XI, p. 19.

of them *per se.*[21] Neither sense corresponds to 'the unconscious' as dreamwork (or primary process), and it is 'the unconscious' in this sense that Freud implicitly invokes to explain the Rat-Man's compulsive-obsessive behavior.[22]

Here is the incident of the man in the park as Freud tells it.

> One day, when he was out with her [his lady] in a boat and there was a stiff breeze blowing, he was obliged to make her put on his cap, because a command had been formulated in his mind that *nothing must happen to her*. This was a kind of *obsession for protecting*, and it bore other fruit besides this ... On the day of her departure he knocked his foot against a stone lying in the road, and was *obliged* to put it out of the way by the side of the road, because the idea struck him that her carriage would be driving along the same road in a few hours' time and might come to grief against this stone. But a few minutes later it occurred to him that this was absurd, and he was *obliged* to go back and replace the stone in its original position on the road.[23]

On Davidson's description, given the man's belief that the stone was a danger and his desire that the lady not be harmed, it was reasonable to remove the stone. Reading on in Freud's telling of the story we understand, however, that the man himself thought this belief absurd; that the stone – in his own eyes – could not realistically be perceived as a danger; and that it seemed one to him at first only because he was in the grip of a phantasy involving infantile rage at both his lady and his father, rage operating under the aegis of omnipotence of thought. He saw the stone as dangerous because of his wish that someone be harmed, a wish contrary to the one on which he believed he acted. The wish that someone – lady and father condensed into one – be harmed, caused the quasi-belief that someone would be harmed, which provided the reason for acting so as to prevent the wish from coming true.

In Freud's version, this is another case of hallucinatory wish-fulfillment in action – a bit of phantasy acted out. While I agree with Davidson that we might analyse the man's behavior in terms of conflicting sub-structures of mental attitudes, the structures are not on the same footing. And since one structure is relatively oblivious to evidence in the first place, I wouldn't describe the division

---

[21] D. Pears, *Motivated Irrationality* (Clarendon Press, Oxford, 1984).

[22] In addition to omnipotence of thought, there are other basic and equally odd beliefs about how the world works that seem to characterize not only schizophrenic but also neurotic mental processes; for example: that others can literally read one's mind as they can literally read a book, and that their actions can be directly caused by one's unexpressed thoughts. Because such beliefs confuse categories like 'thing' and 'thought of thing' that are presumed by ordinary propositional thinking, they suggest a grey area of mental process that we are not sure we ought to describe as 'thought'. Freud calls this grey area 'primary process'. It is characterized by such beliefs as the ones above, by hallucinatory wish-fulfillment with its accompanying confusion between wishing that something were so and asserting that it is, and by condensation and displacement. So far, then (Freud gave it other characteristics as well, among them the absence of negation), 'primary process' is more or less interchangeable with 'dreamwork'.

It would not be odd for a child to be subject to the confusions indicated by 'primary process', since accepting as well as discovering the limits of one's power, learning about the basic properties of physical objects in relation to space and time and about the otherness of other minds, cannot happen all at once. This is one of the reasons that Freud considers primary process to be the earliest form that thinking takes.

[23] S. Freud, 'Notes upon a Case of Obsessional Neurosis', *SE*, vol. x, pp. 189, 190.

in question as allowing the man to ignore the principle of total evidence; though if one thinks that this is what a model of irrationality calls for, the concept of phantasy may help elaborate how such an ignoring occurs. In any case, phantasy interferes with other structures not as counter-argument to argument, but as hallucinatory wish-fulfillment interferes with realistic assessment of reality and the desires and beliefs that are qualified by it.

Now I want to modify my earlier account of phantasy to include the notion, first, that the operative phantasies in a person's life are not occasional, sporadic, and thematically unconnected, but form a schema on which particular phantasies are variations. An example of such a schema is 'A Child Is Being Beaten'. (Freud does not construct the Rat-Man's various phantasies into a schematic form, but he suggests the elements.) Second, the themes and dominant emotions are interpersonal: envy, jealousy, conflicts between the desire for gratification and the fear of provoking another's anger or disapproval. That the themes are of such a primitive interpersonal sort tells us to look for a world-view in which events are seen to be related in a very particular causal way, as gratification to demand, punishment to guilt or 'badness', reward to 'goodness'. That the phantasies are connected guides us to look at a number of odd behaviors in the person's life as reflected in the light of each other. The Rat-Man's business with the stone should be juxtaposed with his ritual before the mirror, with his 'obsession for protecting', with the 'rat' punishment itself, behaviors that are of a piece in feeling alien to the agent and in having a stereotypical character suggesting a repetition of the past. They are to be explained by a common mental structure characterized by such beliefs as the omnipotence of thought, by infantile anxieties, by hallucinatory wish-fulfillment, and by the mechanisms of condensation and displacement.

Metaphor *per se* has nothing to do with irrationality. On the contrary, it is often a vehicle for bringing about just the kinds of self-recognition that may lead to greater integration of one's mental attitudes. For example, in the context of that continual redescribing and cross-sorting of autobiographical detail that any psychoanalytic therapy creates, many interpretations have a metaphoric value, which is one of the reasons that the changes in perspective they can effect over time are so resistant to paraphrase. 'Castration anxiety', for example, doesn't name an anxiety about literal castration as understood by a normal adult. It suggests that concerns about potency of one sort are to be seen as concerns about different sorts as well. And as the psychoanalytic dialogue evokes something like the interpersonal world of one's childhood, adult concerns about potency can also be seen as childhood anxieties about one's adequacy to satisfy another's needs, hence to keep her love, as linked to anxieties about bodily integrity. Such interpretations no more reduce one thing to another than do metaphors: to call Juliet the sun is not to say that she is some 93,000,000 miles from the earth.

As Davidson has said, a metaphoric use of language is parasitic on literal language, and so on ordinary rational thinking. Metaphor calls on mental processes, however – the abilities to envision and to see one thing under many descriptions – that can easily be used (not deliberately and consciously) to confuse and confound. In the envisioning of dreamwork, one stops short of forming a desire, hence stops short of forming the propositional attitudes that would allow one to act rationally. And the metaphoric devices of condensation and displacement – as they characterize unconscious phantasy – help account for the fact that one doesn't recognize the identity of the propositional attitudes one has implicitly formed.

If we think of rationality as that condition in which one acts in the light of all one's beliefs and desires, and in which one's mental attitudes are spontaneously revised in the light of all the rest, then phantasy is inimical to rationality. It is inimical to learning from the past (which is part of what Freud means in speaking of a 'repetition compulsion'), and also to the forming of intentions in the sense in which an imagined, future state, valued as desirable, serves as an end, a purpose, or an aim of one's present activity, since a condition for forming such an aim is precisely that one recognize the imagined future state as something to be striven for, something not present now. The aim is a program for the future and an appraisal of the present, by which it is normally itself refined.[24] The phantasizer, however, not recognizing the imagined scene or scenario as imaginary, is in no position to ask herself whether it would in fact be gratifying, nor of course to achieve it even if it would.

A metaphoric use of language rests on recognizing x under a certain description, and recognizing the description as such. In dreamwork, wishing causes one to describe the world in a certain way, and one's description is mistaken for the world.

---

[24] Cf. J. Dewey, who describes the process of forming aims as

beginning with a wish, an emotional reaction against a state of things and a hope for something different. Action fails to connect satisfactorily with surrounding conditions. Thrown back upon itself, it projects itself in an imagination of a scene which if it were present would afford satisfaction. This picture is often called an aim, more often an ideal. (*Human Nature and Conduct*, Allen and Unwin, London, 1922, p. 234)

Index